MODERN CONSTITUTIONAL LAW

Second Edition

by

Chester James Antieau

Emeritus Professor of Constitutional Law
Georgetown University

VOLUME 1

The Individual and the Government

1997

WEST GROUP

Bancroft-Whitney • Clark Boardman Callaghan
Lawyers Cooperative Publishing • WESTLAW® • West Publishing

is a trademark used herein under license.

The trademarks used throughout this publication are used herein under license.

WEST
GROUP

Library of Congress Catalog Card Number 97-76525

ISBN 0-7620-0194-1

PREFACE

American constitutional law has been concerned primarily with three tasks: (a) determining the extent to which individual liberty is consistent with the common weal; (b) demarcating the powers of the state and federal governments; and (c) delineating the powers and obligations of the three branches within the Federal Government. The function of defining individual freedom is not, of course, peculiar to the United States but exists in every *rechtstaat*—wherever the rule of law prevails. Jellinek, the great European jurist, wrote in 1901: "To reconcile the true boundaries between the individual and the community is the highest problem that thoughtful consideration of human society has to solve."[1] While in some societies this task has been the responsibility of legislative or executive organs, since the veritable beginning of the nation it has been that of the United States Supreme Court.

In this area the record of the Supreme Court has been reasonably adequate, although neither its results nor its methods can be said to be outstanding. It has condoned legislative and executive action in depriving literally thousands of citizens of their liberty when such interference with freedom of the person was by no means necessary for the security of the body politic. In the words of one Justice, the Court has succumbed to expediency in time of war.[2]

Admittedly, the adjustment between freedom and authority is no easy task. A Supreme Court Justice has aptly noted: "Perhaps the most delicate, difficult and shifting of all balances which the Court is expected to maintain is that between freedom and authority,"[3] but if this is to be a land where "the sanctity of the individual counts for more than that of authority,"[4] human freedom cannot so readily be sacrificed for unjustified fears.

In a federal society if the nation is to survive, some organ of that

---

1. Jellinek, *The Declaration of the Rights of Man and of Citizens* (1901) 98.

2. Jackson, *The Supreme Court in the American System of Government* (1955) 25.

3. Jackson, *The Supreme Court in the American System of Government* (1955) 75.

4. Sir Arthur Bryant, *The Medieval Foundation of England* (1967) ix.

nation must be able to say where the authority of the lesser political units ends. In the United States the obligation has been imperatively necessary since the very beginning of this nation. Towards the end of the eighteenth century Massachusetts threatened to disbar any lawyer who sued to enforce the federal fugitive slave laws and Georgia comparably threatened with death any federal marshal attempting to enforce a 1793 judgment of the United States Supreme Court.[5] The delineation of competencies in a federal society between lesser and larger political entities is a function challenging the statesmanship of jurists. Justice Frankfurter once wrote that it is "subtle business calling for great wariness."[6]

The United States Supreme Court has accomplished the responsibility of demarcating state power in a superior manner, although at times providing inadequate guidance as to the extent of state power to regulate and tax interstate commerce, and sometimes failing to hold the states to their constitutional responsibilities. The companion task of defining federal power has also been accomplished with general satisfaction by the Supreme Court. Except for an interregnum, when the Court's majority felt a rather constant compulsion to protect the country from the Congress, the Court has generally recognized the need for the federal government to possess adequate power to cope effectively with national and international problems.

Once the United States Constitution implicitly incorporated from Montesquieu the doctrine of separation of powers, it could be anticipated that some agency of the federal government would have to determine where federal powers were deposited and to decide interbranch disputes. Clashes between the three branches of government are unavoidable. Viscount Grey once aptly remarked that the American Constitution "not only makes possible, but, under certain conditions, renders inevitable conflict between the Executive and the Legislature,"[7] and the same can be said of conflict between both these branches and the judiciary. Since *Marbury v. Madison*[8] in 1803 it has been firmly established that the Supreme Court defines the constitutional competence not only of the judiciary, but of the

---

5. Freund, *Of Law and Justice* (1968) 36.

6. Palmer v. Com. of Mass., 308 U.S. 79, 60 S. Ct. 34, 84 L. Ed. 93 (1939).

7. Letter to The Times, January 31, 1920, quoted by Quincy Wright, *The Control of American Foreign Relations* (1922).

8. Marbury v. Madison, 5 U.S. 137, 2 L. Ed. 60 (1803).

legislature and executive, as well. The Court's record as umpire within the federal government has been generally satisfactory.

The Court has been horribly wrong in a number of very important cases, and in the most of these it erred in striking down congressional legislation, as in the *Dred Scott* case,[9] the original Legal Tender Case,[10] the Income Tax Case,[11] the Child Labor Law Case,[12] and other social legislation. Robert H. Jackson, soon to become a Justice of the Supreme Court, said in 1941 that the Court's "judgment was wrong on the most outstanding issues upon which it has chosen to challenge the popular branches."[13] Furthermore, in none of these cases has the Court ultimately prevailed in its error, being repudiated by judicial overruling, constitutional amendment, and tragically, civil war. The nation undoubtedly would survive if the Court did not have power to invalidate acts of the national legislature, as Justices have themselves acknowledged and as is the situation in another federal republic, Switzerland. Perhaps at least legislation passed by the Senate and the House and then approved by the President should be subject to invalidation by the Court only upon unanimous vote of the Justices.

The prevailing jurisprudence of the Supreme Court in its first century was undoubtedly that of natural rights, but the doctrine is today rather in desuetude, largely because judges imagined that some rather bizarre privileges were natural rights, because they wrongly treated certain of the natural rights as absolutes, and because the doctrine, though properly acknowledging the propriety and, indeed, the need for limiting such rights for the common weal, confessedly gave little concrete guidance as to permissible limitations in specific cases.

The prevailing school of jurisprudence in twentieth century American constitutional law is neither philosophical nor historical,

---

9. Dred Scott v. Sandford, 60 U.S. 393, 19 How. 393, 15 L. Ed. 691 (1856).

10. Hepburn v. Griswold, 75 U.S. 603, 89 Wall. 603, 19 L. Ed. 513 (1869) (overruled in part on other grounds by, Legal Tender Cases, 79 U.S. 457, 12 Wall. 457, 20 L. Ed. 287 (1870)).

11. Pollock v. Farmers' Loan & Trust Co., 157 U.S. 429, 15 S. Ct. 673, 39 L. Ed. 759 (1895) (overruled by, South Carolina v. Baker, 485 U.S. 505, 108 S. Ct. 1355, 99 L. Ed. 2d 592 (1988)).

12. Hammer v. Dagenhart, 247 U.S. 251, 38 S. Ct. 529, 62 L. Ed. 1101 (1918) (overruled in part on other grounds by, U.S. v. Darby, 312 U.S. 100, 312 U.S. 657, 61 S. Ct. 451, 85 L. Ed. 609 (1941)).

13. Jackson, *The Struggle for Judicial Supremacy* (1941) x.

but sociological. The *interessenjurisprudenz* of the great German jurist, Rudolf von Jhering (1818-1892),[14] became known in this country in the last quarter of the nineteenth century. In 1897 Holmes was saying: "I think that the judges themselves have failed adequately to recognize their duty of weighing social advantage. The duty is inevitable, and the result of the often proclaimed judicial aversion to deal with such considerations is simply to leave the very ground and foundations inarticulate, and often unconscious."[15] On another occasion Holmes wrote: "I think it most important to remember whenever a doubtful case arises, with certain analogies on one side and other analogies on the other, that what really is before us is a conflict between two social desires, each of which seeks to extend its dominion over the case, and which cannot both have their way. The social question is which desire is stronger at the point of conflict."[16]

About 1911 sociological jurisprudence was greatly advanced in this country by the writings of Roscoe Pound, who enthusiastically endorsed the jurisprudence of interests of von Jhering.[17] Ten years later Cardozo in his profound *Nature of the Judicial Process* was urging adoption in constitutional law of sociological jurisprudence and especially *interessenjurisprudenz*.

The clashes of societal interest that are most important in American constitutional law can be categorized as three-fold: (1) a clash of national versus state interests; (2) a clash of different interests, both important to the nation; and (3) a clash of interests between two or more states.

The principal clash of societal interests arising from the federal nature of our society is between various state interests, such as protecting local health and safety, and the national interest in the free flow of interstate commerce. All too often in times past, the task of resolving these disparate interests has been resolved by the Court indulging in "burden" terminology, and only rarely, as under

---

14. *Der Zweck im Recht* (1877), translated by Husik as *Law as a Means to an End* (1913).

15. Holmes, The Path of the Law, 10 Harv L Rev 457, 467 (1897).

16. *Collected Legal Papers* (1920) 239.

17. Pound, The Scope and Purpose of Sociological Jurisprudence, 24 Harv. L. Rev. 591 (1911), 25 Harv. L. Rev. 140 (1911).

the guidance of Chief Justice Stone,[18] has the Supreme Court openly identified the contrasted societal interests and explained why one must prevail over the other.

The clash of different national interests can be illustrated by the conflicts inevitably arising between the societal interest in freedom of expression and other societal interests, such as preserving the security of the state and safeguarding public morality. Occasionally the Court has confused its function by thinking it is weighing only an individual interest in communication against opposed societal interests, with results that can readily be imagined.[19] The Court's utilization of the clear and present danger criterion in this area implicitly necessitates a realization that there are clashing societal interests, with the further understanding that if the interest opposed to freedom of communication is not substantial or not surely and seriously endangered, freedom of expression must prevail. "We are of the opinion," said the Court in 1939, "that the purpose to keep the streets clean and of good appearance is insufficient to justify an ordinance which prohibits a person rightfully on a public street from handing literature to one willing to receive it."[20]

The clash of interests between states occasionally occurs in American constitutional law, as when (1) one state has an interest in stimulating its economy even at the cost of polluting the air and water and another state nearby has an interest in safeguarding the health of its people;[21] (2) one state has an interest in marketing its crops, products, livestock, etc., and another state has an interest in protecting the public health;[22] or (3) one state has an interest in encouraging industry and another state has an interest in conserving its natural resources.[23]

The scholarly community recognizes that the function of the

18. Southern Pac. Co. v. State of Ariz. ex rel. Sullivan, 325 U.S. 761, 65 S. Ct. 1515, 89 L. Ed. 1915 (1945).

19. Barenblatt v. U.S., 360 U.S. 109, 79 S. Ct. 1081, 3 L. Ed. 2d 1115 (1959).

20. Schneider v. State of New Jersey, Town of Irvington, 308 U.S. 147, 60 S. Ct. 146, 84 L. Ed. 155 (1939).

21. State of Missouri v. State of Illinois, 180 U.S. 208, 21 S. Ct. 331, 45 L. Ed. 497 (1901).

22. Turner v. State of Maryland, 107 U.S. 38, 2 S. Ct. 44, 27 L. Ed. 370 (1883).

23. Commonwealth of Pennsylvania v. State of West Virginia, 262 U.S. 553, 43 S. Ct. 658, 67 L. Ed. 1117, 1 Ohio L. Abs. 627 (1923), reh'g granted, 263 U.S. 671, 44 S. Ct. 4, 68 L. Ed. 499 (1923) and aff'd, 263 U.S. 350, 44 S. Ct. 123, 67 L. Ed. 1144, 2 Ohio L. Abs. 51 (1923).

Supreme Court is the identification, evaluation, and reconciliation of opposed societal values or interests. Professor Paul Freund has cogently remarked: "The great constitutional issues which come before the Court reflect not so much a clash of right and wrong as a conflict between right and right."[24] The Court is going to have to resolve these opposed societal interests either by an imposition of personal predilections masked in mystical and meaningless phrases or by a conscious cognition of the contrasted interests, followed by a process of weighing and adjustment which must be openly shared with the bar and the larger community.

Effective application of *interessenjurisprudenz* by the Supreme Court requires:

(1) *that the Court openly identify the opposed societal interests in each case.*

Notwithstanding its too frequent error in times past of thinking of freedom of communication as an "individual" rather than a societal interest, it is suggested that the Court has experience here, as in the Commerce Clause cases, and this should be accomplished quite readily. Mere identification of the opposed interests will often go a long way towards a resolution of the issues.

(2) *that the Court carefully weigh the opposed societal interests.*

Admittedly this is no easy task, but it is done regularly by legislators and it must be done by the Supreme Court. The bar may well have to be reoriented to fulfill its role of advocacy in this instance. The Court was doing just this when it explained that the interest in clean streets could not prevail over the interest in freedom of expression. Justice Cardozo, who saw the judicial function more clearly than any of his colleagues, once wrote: "If you ask how he [the judge] is to know when one interest outweighs another, I can only answer that he must get his knowledge just as the legislator gets it, from experience and study and reflection; in brief, from life itself."[25]

(3) *that the Court investigate whether one interest can be safeguarded satisfactorily while allowing by some alternative means free play for the other interest.*

This the Court has done on the rare occasion when it has ap-

---

24. Freund, *On Law and Justice* (1968) 36.
25. Cardozo, *The Nature of the Judicial Process* (1921) 113.

plied the "reasonable alternative" test in Commerce Clause controversies,[26] and its equivalent in First Amendment cases. Here the difficulty is not in the complexity of the function, but in simply holding constant before the Court the realization of its need.

(4) *that the Court inquire whether the interest allegedly involved is actually safeguarded or advanced by the governmental action called in question under the Constitution.*

This has been done openly at times, as under the guidance of Chief Justice Stone,[27] but furtively on many more occasions.

(5) *that the Court ascertain if conduct manifesting one interest, such as freedom of communication, constitutes a clear and present danger to another important interest of society.*

No important values or interests, especially those which we have deliberately enshrined in the Constitution, are to be negated unless their exercise surely and seriously endangers another very substantial interest of society. To deprive citizens of their liberty under any other circumstances is a gross abuse of political power.

Succeeding in these functions of *interessenjurisprudenz,* the Supreme Court can be assured that its decisions will more satisfactorily serve our society, that criticism of decisions will be upon a more meaningful and loftier level, and that the work of the Court—aboveboard, rational, and comprehensible—will be more readily accepted and appreciated by both the legal profession and the larger community.

Any constitutional society commits itself to certain values, and the United States by the original Constitution and the Bill of Rights is consciously dedicated to individual liberty, integrity, and equality, an open society, and the rule of law. Of these values the Supreme Court is the ultimate guardian and trustee. Justice Cardozo wrote so beautifully:

> The great ideals of liberty and equality are preserved against the assaults of opportunism, the expediency of the passing hour, the erosion of small encroachments, the scorn and derision of

---

26. Dean Milk Co. v. City of Madison, Wis., 340 U.S. 349, 71 S. Ct. 295, 95 L. Ed. 329 (1951).

27. Southern Pac. Co. v. State of Ariz. ex rel. Sullivan, 325 U.S. 761, 65 S. Ct. 1515, 89 L. Ed. 1915 (1945).

those who have no patience with general principles, by enshrining them in constitutions, and consecrating to the task of their protection a body of defenders.[28]

To insist that there be an "equality of values" in constitutional decision is to demand of the Justices the unfair, the unwise, and the impossible. When today's Justices, for instance, consider the value in freedom of communication to be larger than the value in property, they are capturing the value judgments of our permanent majority and honoring the philosophy of the American Founding Fathers, who treasured the property right, but as a means to a larger end— the integrity, dignity, and security of the individual.

Beyond the most general statements of basic principles, there is little room in constitutional law for "absolute" rules. Robert H. Jackson, then Attorney General and later Justice of the Supreme Court, wrote in 1941 that "constitutional law is not a fixed body of immutable doctrine."[29] Justice Cardozo adds that "the great generalities of the Constitution have a content and a significance that vary from age to age."[30]

In organic law intended for many generations there must be not only room at the joints for experimentation, but also for growth and maturation within the society, for differing resolutions between various values and interests, all properly cherished by the culture, and for variant responses in war and crisis. Chief Justice Vinson once remarked: "To those who would paralyze our government in the face of impending threat by encasing it in a semantic straitjacket, we must reply that all concepts are relative."[31] The demand that the Court respond today as it did in the eighteenth or nineteenth century is to chain the Justices and ourselves as well, in a manner that is the very negation of a constitutional society. One concerned with judging the work of the Supreme Court cares not especially how often opinions have been overruled, but how effectively the Court contributes to safeguarding our permanent values of human dignity and equality while contributing, directly or indirectly, to the solution of the economic, social, and political problems facing the nation.

---

28. *The Nature of the Judicial Process* (1921) 92-3.

29. Jackson, *The Struggle for Judicial Supremacy* (1941) xiv.

30. Cardozo, *The Nature of the Judicial Process* (1921) 17.

31. Dennis v. United States, 341 U.S. 494, 508, 71 S. Ct. 857, 95 L. Ed. 1137 (1951).

Growth in a constitutional society should be based in part at least upon amendments to the organic law emanating from the people. By such a criterion, American constitutional law has not been an outstanding success. Only on rare occasions has the amendment process been effective and on even rarer instances has the amendment contributed greatly to the growth of constitutional law. Consideration should be given to greater ease of amendment of the Constitution by the democratic process. Although Supreme Court Justices may be willing to reinterpret the Constitution in its broader norms, they are understandably reluctant to repudiate or rewrite the Constitution in its specifics, and the time inevitably comes when specific constitutional provisions, such as the twenty-dollar guarantee of civil jury trial, demand amendment. Again, since Justices are mortals they will err and sometimes impose upon our society gross and tragic errors, which must be eliminated by the amending process when the Court long delays repudiating its own aberrations.

To the Justices of the Supreme Court of the United States and to the judges of the other federal and state courts who have shown the High Court what the American Constitution means, our society owes a tremendous debt. From John Marshall to the present, the Supreme Court has, by interpreting the Constitution, given us a national economy that has provided the majority of our people with a material standard of living previously unknown. The Supreme Court, more than the legislature or executive, has kept constant the enduring values of our nation in human dignity and an open society where ideas can be freely exchanged in the marketplace of thought and individuals can fully explore their potentials. To the Court, too, the nation is indebted for profound improvements in the administration of criminal justice, as well as in related fields where persons are deprived of their liberty by the state.

When, as herein, the Court is subjected to constructive criticism, it understands thoroughly that suggested changes and improvement are not only for society but for the Court itself. A long time ago Chief Justice Taney said of the Court, "its opinion upon the construction of the Constitution is always open to discussion when it is supposed to have been founded in error,"[32] and this is equally true of today and tomorrow. A strong case can be made for restructuring the Court by obviating its concern for such things as statutory interpretations, patents and copyrights, admiralty, diversity

---

32. Smith v. Turner, 48 U.S. 283, 7 How. 283, 470, 12 L. Ed. 702 (1849).

appeals, divorce, etc., and devoting its energies solely to constitutional appeals. Like the Constitution, which is always subject to amendment to make the fundamental law more responsible to the needs and problems of our people, the Supreme Court, too, is an experiment and to the extent that it serves our society well it deserves perpetuation and high honor.

Chester James Antieau
Emeritus Professor of Constitutional Law
Georgetown University
December, 1997

CONSTITUTION OF THE UNITED STATES

PREAMBLE

WE THE PEOPLE of the United States, in Order to form a more perfect Union, establish Justice, insure domestic Tranquility, provide for the common defence, promote the general Welfare, and secure the Blessings of Liberty to ourselves and our Posterity, do ordain and establish this CONSTITUTION for the United States of America.

ARTICLE I—THE CONGRESS

Section 1. All legislative Powers herein granted shall be vested in a Congress of the United States, which shall consist of a Senate and House of Representatives.

Section 2. The House of Representatives shall be composed of Members chosen every second Year by the People of the several States, and the Electors in each State shall have the Qualifications requisite for Electors of the most numerous Branch of the State Legislature.

No Person shall be a Representative who shall not have attained to the Age of twenty five Years, and been seven Years a Citizen of the United States, and who shall not, when elected, be an Inhabitant of that State in which he shall be chosen.

Representatives and direct Taxes shall be apportioned among the several States which may be included within this Union, according to their respective Numbers, which shall be determined by adding to the whole Number of free Persons, including those bound to Service for a Term of Years, and excluding Indians not taxed, three fifths of all other Persons. The actual Enumeration shall be made within three Years after the first Meeting of the Congress of the United States, and within every subsequent Term of ten Years, in such Manner as they shall by Law direct. The Number of Representatives shall not exceed one for every thirty Thousand, but each State shall have at Least one Representative; and until such enumeration shall be made, the State of New Hampshire shall be entitled to chuse three, Massachusetts eight, Rhode-Island and Providence

Plantations one, Connecticut five, New-York six, New Jersey four, Pennsylvania eight, Delaware one, Maryland six, Virginia ten, North Carolina five, South Carolina five, and Georgia three.

When vacancies happen in the Representation from any State, the Executive Authority thereof shall issue Writs of Election to fill such Vacancies.

The House of Representatives shall chuse their Speaker and other Officers; and shall have the sole Power of Impeachment.

Section 3. The Senate of the United States shall be composed of two Senators from each State, chosen by the Legislature thereof, for six Years; and each Senator shall have one Vote.

Immediately after they shall be assembled in Consequence of the first Election, they shall be divided as equally as may be into three Classes. The Seats of the Senators of the first Class shall be vacated at the Expiration of the second Year, of the second Class at the Expiration of the fourth Year, and of the third Class at the Expiration of the sixth Year, so that one third may be chosen every second Year; [and if Vacancies happen by Resignation, or otherwise, during the Recess of the Legislature of any State, the Executive thereof may make temporary Appointments until the next Meeting of the Legislature, which shall then fill such Vacancies].

No Person shall be a Senator who shall not have attained to the Age of thirty Years, and been nine Years a Citizen of the United States, and who shall not, when elected, be an Inhabitant of that State for which he shall be chosen.

The Vice President of the United States shall be President of the Senate, but shall have no Vote, unless they be equally divided.

The Senate shall chuse their other Officers, and also a President pro tempore, in the Absence of the Vice President, or when he shall exercise the Office of President of the United States.

The Senate shall have the sole Power to try all Impeachments. When sitting for that Purpose, they shall be on Oath or Affirmation. When the President of the United States is tried, the Chief Justice shall preside: And no Person shall be convicted without the Concurrence of two thirds of the Members present.

Judgment in Cases of Impeachment shall not extend further than to removal from Office, and disqualification to hold and enjoy any Office of honor, Trust or Profit under the United States: but the Party convicted shall nevertheless be liable and subject to Indictment, Trial, Judgment and Punishment, according to Law.

Section 4. The Times, Places and Manner of holding Elections for

Senators and Representatives, shall be prescribed in each State by the Legislature thereof; but the Congress may at any time by Law make or alter such Regulations, except as to the Places of chusing Senators.

The Congress shall assemble at least once in every Year, and such Meeting shall be on the first Monday in December, unless they shall by Law appoint a different Day.

Section 5. Each House shall be the Judge of the Elections, Returns and Qualifications of its own Members, and a Majority of each shall constitute a Quorum to do Business; but a smaller Number may adjourn from day to day, and may be authorized to compel the Attendance of absent Members, in such Manner, and under such Penalties as each House may provide.

Each House may determine the Rules of its Proceedings, punish its Members for disorderly Behaviour, and, with the Concurrence of two thirds, expel a Member.

Each House shall keep a Journal of its Proceedings, and from time to time publish the same, excepting such Parts as may in their Judgment require Secrecy; and the Yeas and Nays of the Members of either House on any question shall, at the Desire of one fifth of those Present, be entered on the Journal.

Neither House, during the Session of Congress, shall, without the Consent of the other, adjourn for more than three days, nor to any other Place than that in which the two Houses shall be sitting.

Section 6. The Senators and Representatives shall receive a Compensation for their Services, to be ascertained by Law, and paid out of the Treasury of the United States. They shall in all Cases, except Treason, Felony and Breach of the Peace, be privileged from Arrest during their Attendance at the Session of their respective Houses, and in going to and returning from the same; and for any Speech or Debate in either House, they shall not be questioned in any other Place.

No Senator or Representative shall, during the Time for which he was elected, be appointed to any civil Office under the Authority of the United States, which shall have been created, or the Emoluments whereof shall have been encreased during such time; and no Person holding any Office under the United States, shall be a Member of either House during his Continuance in Office.

Section 7. All Bills for raising Revenue shall originate in the House of Representatives; but the Senate may propose or concur with Amendments as on other Bills.

Every Bill which shall have passed the House of Representatives and the Senate, shall, before it become a Law, be presented to the President of the United States; If he approve he shall sign it, but if not he shall return it, with his Objections to that House in which it shall have originated, who shall enter the Objections at large on their Journal, and proceed to reconsider it. If after such Reconsideration two thirds of that House shall agree to pass the Bill, it shall be sent, together with the Objections, to the other House, by which it shall likewise be reconsidered, and if approved by two thirds of that House, it shall become a Law. But in all such Cases the Votes of both Houses shall be determined by yeas and Nays, and the Names of the Persons voting for and against the Bill shall be entered on the Journal of each House respectively. If any Bill shall not be returned by the President within ten Days (Sundays excepted) after it shall have been presented to him, the Same shall be a Law, in like Manner as if he had signed it, unless the Congress by their Adjournment prevent its Return, in which Case it shall not be a Law.

Every Order, Resolution, or Vote to which the Concurrence of the Senate and House of Representatives may be necessary (except on a question of Adjournment) shall be presented to the President of the United States; and before the Same shall take Effect, shall be approved by him, or being disapproved by him, shall be repassed by two thirds of the Senate and House of Representatives, according to the Rules and Limitations prescribed in the Case of a Bill.

Section 8. The Congress shall have Power

To lay and collect Taxes, Duties, Imposts and Excises, to pay the Debts and provide for the common Defence and general Welfare of the United States; but all Duties, Imposts and Excises shall be uniform throughout the United States;

To borrow Money on the credit of the United States;

To regulate Commerce with foreign Nations, and among the several States, and with the Indian Tribes;

To establish an uniform Rule of Naturalization, and uniform Laws on the subject of Bankruptcies throughout the United States;

To coin Money, regulate the Value thereof, and of foreign Coin, and fix the Standard of Weights and Measures;

To provide for the Punishment of counterfeiting the Securities and current Coin of the United States;

To establish Post Offices and post Roads;

To promote the Progress of Science and useful Arts, by securing for limited Times to Authors and Inventors the exclusive Right to their respective Writings and Discoveries;

To constitute Tribunals inferior to the supreme Court;

To define and punish Piracies and Felonies committed on the high Seas, and Offences against the Law of Nations;

To declare War, grant Letters of Marque and Reprisal, and make Rules concerning Captures on Land and Water;

To raise and support Armies, but no Appropriation of Money to that Use shall be for a longer Term than two Years;

To provide and maintain a Navy;

To make Rules for the Government and Regulation of the land and naval Forces;

To provide for calling forth the Militia to execute the Laws of the Union, suppress Insurrections and repel Invasions;

To provide for organizing, arming, and disciplining, the Militia, and for governing such Part of them as may be employed in the Service of the United States, reserving to the States respectively, the Appointment of the Officers, and the Authority of training the Militia according to the discipline prescribed by Congress;

To exercise exclusive Legislation in all Cases whatsoever, over such District (not exceeding ten Miles square) as may, by Cession of particular States, and the Acceptance of Congress, become the Seat of the Government of the United States, and to exercise like Authority over all Places purchased by the Consent of the Legislature of the State in which the Same shall be, for the Erection of Forts, Magazines, Arsenals, dock-Yards, and other needful Buildings;— And

To make all Laws which shall be necessary and proper for carrying into Execution the foregoing Powers, and all other Powers vested by this Constitution in the Government of the United States, or in any Department or Officer thereof.

Section 9. The Migration or Importation of such Persons as any of the States now existing shall think proper to admit, shall not be prohibited by the Congress prior to the Year one thousand eight hundred and eight, but a Tax or duty may be imposed on such Importation, not exceeding ten dollars for each Person.

The Privilege of the Writ of Habeas Corpus shall not be suspended, unless when in Cases of Rebellion or Invasion the public Safety may require it.

No Bill of Attainder or ex post facto Law shall be passed.

No Capitation, or other direct, Tax shall be laid, unless in Proportion to the Census or Enumeration herein before directed to be taken.

No Tax or Duty shall be laid on Articles exported from any State.

No Preference shall be given by any Regulation of Commerce or Revenue to the Ports of one State over those of another: nor shall Vessels bound to, or from, one State, be obliged to enter, clear, or pay Duties in another.

No Money shall be drawn from the Treasury, but in Consequence of Appropriations made by Law; and a regular Statement and Account of the Receipts and Expenditures of all public Money shall be published from time to time.

No Title of Nobility shall be granted by the United States: And no Person holding any Office of Profit or Trust under them, shall, without the Consent of the Congress, accept of any present, Emolument, Office, or Title, of any kind whatever, from any King, Prince, or foreign State.

Section 10. No State shall enter into any Treaty, Alliance, or Confederation; grant Letters of Marque and Reprisal; coin Money; emit Bills of Credit; make any Thing but gold and silver Coin a Tender in Payment of Debts; pass any Bill of Attainder, ex post facto Law, or Law impairing the Obligation of Contracts, or grant any Title of Nobility

No State shall, without the Consent of the Congress, lay any Imposts or Duties on Imports or Exports, except what may be absolutely necessary for executing its inspection Laws: and the net Produce of all Duties and Imposts, laid by any State on Imports or Exports, shall be for the Use of the Treasury of the United States; and all such Laws shall be subject to the Revision and Controul of the Congress.

No State shall, without the Consent of Congress, lay any Duty of Tonnage, keep Troops, or Ships of War in time of Peace, enter into any Agreement or Compact with another State, or with a foreign Power, or engage in War, unless actually invaded, or in such imminent Danger as will not admit of delay.

ARTICLE II—THE PRESIDENT

Section 1. The executive Power shall be vested in a President of the United States of America. He shall hold his Office during the Term of four Years, and, together with the Vice President, chosen for the same Term, be elected, as follows:

Each State shall appoint, in such Manner as the Legislature thereof may direct, a Number of Electors, equal to the whole Number of Senators and Representatives to which the State may be entitled in the Congress: but no Senator or Representative, or Person holding an Office of Trust or Profit under the United States, shall be appointed an Elector.

The Congress may determine the Time of chusing the Electors, and the Day on which they shall give their Votes; which Day shall be the same throughout the United States.

No Person except a natural born Citizen, or a Citizen of the United States, at the time of the Adoption of this Constitution, shall be eligible to the Office of President; neither shall any Person be eligible to that Office who shall not have attained to the Age of thirty five Years, and been fourteen Years a Resident within the United States.

In Case of the Removal of the President from Office, or of his Death, Resignation, or Inability to discharge the Powers and Duties of the said Office, the Same shall devolve on the Vice President, and the Congress may by Law provide for the Case of Removal, Death, Resignation or Inability, both of the President and Vice President, declaring what Officer shall then act as President, and such Officer shall act accordingly, until the Disability be removed, or a President shall be elected.

The President shall, at stated Times, receive for his Services, a Compensation, which shall neither be encreased nor diminished during the Period for which he shall have been elected, and he shall not receive within that Period any other Emolument from the United States, or any of them.

Before he enter on the Execution of his Office, he shall take the following Oath or Affirmation:— "I do solemnly swear (or affirm) that I will faithfully execute the Office of President of the United States, and will to the best of my Ability, preserve, protect and defend the Constitution of the United States."

Section 2. The President shall be Commander in Chief of the Army and Navy of the United States, and of the Militia of the several States, when called into the actual Service of the United States; he may require the Opinion, in writing, of the principal Officer in each of the executive Departments, upon any Subject relating to the Duties of their respective Offices, and he shall have Power to grant Reprieves and Pardons for Offenses against the United States, except in Cases of Impeachment.

He shall have Power, by and with the Advice and Consent of the Senate, to make Treaties, provided two thirds of the Senators present concur; and he shall nominate, and by and with the Advice and Consent of the Senate, shall appoint Ambassadors, other public Ministers and Consuls, Judges of the supreme Court, and all other Officers of the United States, whose Appointments are not herein otherwise provided for, and which shall be established by Law: but the Congress may by Law vest the Appointment of such inferior Officers, as they think proper, in the President alone, in the Courts of Law, or in the Heads of Departments.

The President shall have Power to fill up all Vacancies that may happen during the Recess of the Senate, by granting Commissions which shall expire at the End of their next Session.

Section 3. He shall from time to time give to the Congress Information of the State of the Union, and recommend to their Consideration such Measures as he shall judge necessary and expedient; he may, on extraordinary Occasions, convene both Houses, or either of them, and in Case of Disagreement between them, with Respect to the Time of Adjournment, he may adjourn them to such Time as he shall think proper; he shall receive Ambassadors and other public Ministers; he shall take Care that the Laws be faithfully executed, and shall Commission all the Officers of the United States.

Section 4. The President, Vice President and all civil Officers of the United States, shall be removed from Office on Impeachment for, and Conviction of, Treason, Bribery, or other high Crimes and Misdemeanors.

ARTICLE III—THE JUDICIARY

Section 1. The judicial Power of the United States, shall be vested in one supreme Court, and in such inferior Courts as the Congress may from time to time ordain and establish. The Judges, both of the supreme and inferior Courts, shall hold their Offices during good Behaviour, and shall, at stated Times, receive for their Services, a Compensation, which shall not be diminished during their Continuance in Office.

Section 2. The judicial Power shall extend to all Cases, in Law and Equity, arising under this Constitution, the Laws of the United States, and Treaties made, or which shall be made, under their Authority;—to all Cases affecting Ambassadors, other public Ministers and Consuls;—to all Cases of admiralty and maritime Jurisdiction;—to Controversies to which the United States shall be a Party;—to Controversies between two or more States;—between a State and Citizens of another State;—between Citizens of different States;—between Citizens of the same State claiming Lands under Grants of different States, and between a State, or the Citizens thereof, and foreign States, Citizens or Subjects.

In all Cases affecting Ambassadors, other public Ministers and Consuls, and those in which a State shall be Party, the supreme

Court shall have original Jurisdiction. In all the other Cases before mentioned, the supreme Court shall have appellate Jurisdiction, both as to Law and Fact, with such Exceptions, and under such Regulations as the Congress shall make.

The Trial of all Crimes, except in Cases of Impeachment, shall be by Jury; and such Trial shall be held in the State where the said Crimes shall have been committed; but when not committed within any State, the Trial shall be at such Place or Places as the Congress may by Law have directed.

Section 3. Treason against the United States, shall consist only in levying War against them, or in adhering to their Enemies, giving them Aid and Comfort. No Person shall be convicted of Treason unless on the Testimony of two Witnesses to the same overt Act, or on Confession in open Court.

The Congress shall have Power to declare the Punishment of Treason, but no Attainder of Treason shall work Corruption of Blood, or Forfeiture except during the Life of the Person attainted.

ARTICLE IV—STATES—RECIPROCAL RELATION-SHIP BETWEEN STATES AND WITH UNITED STATES

Section 1. Full Faith and Credit shall be given in each State to the public Acts, Records, and judicial Proceedings of every other State. And the Congress may by general Laws prescribe the Manner in which such Acts, Records and Proceedings shall be proved, and the Effect thereof.

Section 2. The Citizens of each State shall be entitled to all Privileges and Immunities of Citizens in the several States.

A person charged in any State with Treason, Felony, or other Crime, who shall flee from Justice, and be found in another State, shall on Demand of the executive Authority of the State from which he fled, be delivered up, to be removed to the State having Jurisdiction of the Crime.

No Person held to Service or Labour in one State, under the Laws thereof, escaping into another, shall, in Consequence of any Law or Regulation therein, be discharged from such Service or Labour, but shall be delivered up on Claim of the Party to whom such Service or Labour may be due.

Section 3. New States may be admitted by the Congress into this Union; but no new State shall be formed or erected within the

Jurisdiction of any other State; nor any State be formed by the Junction of two or more States, or Parts of States, without the Consent of the Legislatures of the States concerned as well as of the Congress.

The Congress shall have Power to dispose of and make all needful Rules and Regulations respecting the Territory or other Property belonging to the United States; and nothing in this Constitution shall be so construed as to Prejudice any Claims of the United States, or of any particular State.

Section 4. The United States shall guarantee to every State in this Union a Republican Form of Government, and shall protect each of them against Invasion; and on Application of the Legislature, or of the Executive (when the Legislature cannot be convened) against domestic Violence.

ARTICLE V—AMENDMENTS

The Congress, whenever two thirds of both Houses shall deem it necessary, shall propose Amendments to this Constitution, or on the Application of the Legislatures of two thirds of the several States, shall call a Convention for proposing Amendments, which, in either Case, shall be valid to all Intents and Purposes, as Part of this Constitution, when ratified by the Legislatures of three fourths of the several States, or by Conventions in three fourths thereof, as the one or the other Mode of Ratification may be proposed by the Congress; Provided that no Amendment which may be made prior to the Year One thousand eight hundred and eight shall in any Manner affect the first and fourth Clauses in the Ninth Section of the first Article; and that no State, without its Consent, shall be deprived of its equal Suffrage in the Senate.

ARTICLE VI—DEBTS VALIDATED—SUPREME LAW OF LAND—OATH OF OFFICE

All Debts contracted and Engagements entered into, before the Adoption of this Constitution, shall be as valid against the United States under this Constitution, as under the Confederation.

This Constitution, and the Laws of the United States which shall be made in Pursuance thereof; and all Treaties made, or which shall be made, under the Authority of the United States, shall be the supreme Law of the Land; and the Judges in every State shall be bound thereby, any Thing in the Constitution or Laws of any State to the Contrary notwithstanding.

The Senators and Representatives before mentioned, and the Members of the several State Legislatures, and all executive and judicial Officers, both of the United States and of the several States, shall be bound by Oath or Affirmation, to support this Constitution; but no religious Test shall ever be required as a Qualification to any Office or public Trust under the United States.

ARTICLE VII—RATIFICATION OF ORIGINAL ARTICLES

The Ratification of the Conventions of nine States, shall be sufficient for the Establishment of this Constitution between the States so ratifying the Same.

DONE in Convention by the Unanimous Consent of the States present the Seventeenth Day of September in the Year of our Lord one thousand seven hundred and Eighty seven and of the Independence of the United States of America the Twelfth. IN WITNESS whereof We have hereunto subscribed our Names,

GO. WASHINGTON—*Presidt. and Deputy from Virginia*

Attest William Jackson *Secretary*

New Hampshire

JOHN LANGDON	NICHOLAS GILMAN

Massachusetts

NATHANIEL GORHAM	RUFUS KING

Connecticut

WM. SAML. JOHNSON	ROGER SHERMAN

New York

ALEXANDER HAMILTON

New Jersey

WIL: LIVINGSTON	WM. PATERSON.
DAVID BREARLEY.	JONA: DAYTON

Pennsylvania

B FRANKLIN	THOS. FITZSIMONS
THOMAS MIFFLIN	JARED INGERSOLL
ROBT. MORRIS	JAMES WILSON
GEO. CLYMER	GOUV MORRIS

Delaware

GEO: READ	RICHARD BASSETT
GUNNING BEDFORD JUN	JACO: BROOM
JOHN DICKINSON	

Maryland

JAMES MCHENRY	DANL CARROLL
DAN OF ST. THOS. JENIFER	

Virginia

JOHN BLAIR   JAMES MADISON JR.

North Carolina

WM. BLOUNT   HU WILLIAMSON
RICHD. DOBBS SPAIGHT

South Carolina

J. RUTLEDGE   CHARLES PINCKNEY
CHARLES COTESWORTH   PIERCE BUTLER
  PINCKNEY

Georgia

WILLIAM FEW   ABR BALDWIN

AMENDMENTS

Amendment I. Freedom of Religion, Speech and Press; Peaceful Assemblage; Petition of Grievances

Congress shall make no law respecting an establishment of religion, or prohibiting the free exercise thereof; or abridging the freedom of speech, or of the press; or the right of the people peaceably to assemble, and to petition the Government for a redress of grievances.

Amendment II. Right To Bear Arms

A well regulated Militia, being necessary to the security of a free State, the right of the people to keep and bear Arms, shall not be infringed.

Amendment III. Soldiers Denied Quarter in Homes

No Soldier shall, in time of peace be quartered in any house, without the consent of the Owner, nor in time of war, but in a manner to be prescribed by law.

Amendment IV. Search and Seizure

The right of the people to be secure in their persons, houses, papers, and effects, against unreasonable searches and seizures, shall not be violated, and no Warrants shall issue, but upon probable cause, supported by Oath or affirmation, and particularly describing the place to be searched, and the persons or things to be seized.

Amendment V. Grand Jury Indictment for Capital Crimes; Double Jeopardy; Self-Incrimination; Due Process of Law; Just Compensation for Property

No person shall be held to answer for a capital, or otherwise infamous crime, unless on a presentment or indictment of a Grand Jury, except in cases arising in the land or naval forces, or in the Militia, when in actual service in time of War or public danger; nor shall any person be subject for the same offence to be twice put in jeopardy of life or limb; nor shall be compelled in any criminal case to be a witness against himself, nor be deprived of life, liberty, or property, without due process of law; nor shall private property be taken for public use, without just compensation.

Amendment VI. Jury trials for crimes, and procedural rights

In all criminal prosecutions, the accused shall enjoy the right to a speedy and public trial, by an impartial jury of the State and district wherein the crime shall have been committed, which district shall have been previously ascertained by law, and to be informed of the nature and cause of the accusation; to be confronted with the witnesses against him; to have compulsory process for obtaining witnesses in his favor, and to have the Assistance of Counsel for his defence.

Amendment VII. Civil Trials

In Suits at common law, where the value in controversy shall exceed twenty dollars, the right of trial by jury shall be preserved, and no fact tried by a jury, shall be otherwise reexamined in any Court of the United States, than according to the rules of the common law.

Amendment VIII. Excessive Bail, Fines, Punishments

Excessive bail shall not be required, nor excessive fines imposed, nor cruel and unusual punishments inflicted.

Amendment IX. Construction of Enumerated Rights

The enumeration in the Constitution, of certain rights, shall not be construed to deny or disparage others retained by the people.

Amendment X. Reserved Powers to States

The powers not delegated to the United States by the Constitution, nor prohibited by it to the States, are reserved to the States respectively, or to the people.

Amendment XI. Suits Against States

The Judicial power of the United States shall not be construed to extend to any suit in law or equity, commenced or prosecuted against one of the United States by Citizens of another State, or by Citizens or Subjects of any Foreign State.

Amendment XII. Presidential Electors

The Electors shall meet in their respective states and vote by ballot for President and Vice-President, one of whom, at least, shall not be an inhabitant of the same state with themselves; they shall name in their ballots the person voted for as President, and in distinct ballots the person voted for as Vice-President, and they shall make distinct lists of all persons voted for as President, and of all persons voted for as Vice-President, and of the number of votes for each, which lists they shall sign and certify, and transmit sealed to the seat of the government of the United States, directed to the President of the Senate;—The President of the Senate shall, in the presence of the Senate and House of Representatives, open all the certificates and the votes shall then be counted;—The person having the greatest number of votes for President, shall be the President, if such number be a majority of the whole number of Electors appointed; and if no person have such majority, then from the persons having the highest numbers not exceeding three on the list of those voted for as President, the House of Representatives shall choose immediately, by ballot, the President. But in choosing the President, the votes shall be taken by states, the representation from each state having one vote; a quorum for this purpose shall consist of a member or members from two-thirds of the states, and a majority of all the states shall be necessary to a choice. And if the House of Representatives shall not choose a President whenever the right of choice shall devolve upon them, before the fourth day of March next following, then the Vice-President shall act as President, as in the case of the death or other constitutional disability of the President.—The person having the greatest number of votes as Vice-President, shall be the Vice-President, if such number be a majority of the whole number of Electors appointed, and if no person have a majority, then from the two highest numbers on the list, the Senate shall choose the Vice-President; a quorum for the purpose shall consist of two-thirds of the whole number of Senators, and a majority of the whole number shall be necessary to a choice. But no person constitutionally ineligible to the office of President shall be eligible to that of Vice-President of the United States.

Amendment XIII. Slavery Abolished; Enforcement

Section 1. Neither slavery nor involuntary servitude, except as a punishment for crime whereof the party shall have been duly convicted, shall exist within the United States, or any place subject to their jurisdiction.

Section 2. Congress shall have power to enforce this article by appropriate legislation.

Amendment XIV. Citizenship; Privileges And Immunities; Due Process; Equal Protection; Appointment Of Representation; Disqualification Of Officers; Public Debt; Enforcement

Section 1. All persons born or naturalized in the United States, and subject to the jurisdiction thereof, are citizens of the United States and of the State wherein they reside. No State shall make or enforce any law which shall abridge the privileges or immunities of citizens of the United States; nor shall any State deprive any person of life, liberty, or property, without due process of law; nor deny to any person within its jurisdiction the equal protection of the laws.

Section 2. Representatives shall be apportioned among the several States according to their respective numbers, counting the whole number of persons in each State, excluding Indians not taxed. But when the right to vote at any election for the choice of electors for President and Vice President of the United States, Representatives in Congress, the Executive and Judicial officers of a State, or the members of the Legislature thereof, is denied to any of the male inhabitants of such State, being twenty-one years of age, and citizens of the United States, or in any way abridged, except for participation in rebellion, or other crime, the basis of representation therein shall be reduced in the proportion which the number of such male citizens shall bear to the whole number of male citizens twenty-one years of age in such State.

Section 3. No person shall be a Senator or Representative in Congress, or elector of President and Vice President, or hold any office, civil or military, under the United States, or under any State, who, having previously taken an oath, as a member of Congress, or as an officer of the United States, or as a member of any State legislature, or as an executive or judicial officer of any State, to support the Constitution of the United States, shall have engaged in insurrection or rebellion against the same, or given aid or comfort to the enemies thereof. But Congress may by a vote of two-thirds of each House, remove such disability.

Section 4. The validity of the public debt of the United States, authorized by law, including debts incurred for payment of pensions and bounties for services in suppressing insurrection or rebellion, shall not be questioned. But neither the United States nor any State shall assume or pay any debt or obligation incurred in aid of insurrection or rebellion against the United States, or any claim for the loss or emancipation of any slave; but all such debts, obligations and claims shall be held illegal and void.

Section 5. The Congress shall have power to enforce, by appropriate legislation, the provisions of this article.

Amendment XV. Universal Male Suffrage

Section 1. The right of citizens of the United States to vote shall not be denied or abridged by the United States or by any State on account of race, color, or previous condition of servitude.

Section 2. The Congress shall have power to enforce this article by appropriate legislation.

Amendment XVI. Income Tax

The Congress shall have power to lay and collect taxes on incomes, from whatever source derived, without apportionment among the several States, and without regard to any census or enumeration.

Amendment XVII. Popular Election of Senators

The Senate of the United States shall be composed of two Senators from each State, elected by the people thereof, for six years; and each Senator shall have one vote. The electors in each State shall have the qualifications requisite for electors of the most numerous branch of the State legislatures. When vacancies happen in the representation of any State in the Senate, the executive authority of such State shall issue writs of election to fill such vacancies: Provided, That the legislature of any State may empower the executive thereof to make temporary appointments until the people fill the vacancies by election as the legislature may direct. This amendment shall not be so construed as to affect the election or term of any Senator chosen before it becomes valid as part of the Constitution.

Amendment XVIII. Liquor Prohibition [Repealed]

Amendment XIX. Woman Suffrage

The right of citizens of the United States to vote shall not be denied or abridged by the United States or by any State on account of sex.

Congress shall have power to enforce this article by appropriate legislation.

Amendment XX. Lame Duck Amendment

Section 1. The terms of the President and Vice President shall end at noon on the 20th day of January, and the terms of Senators and Representatives at noon on the 3d day of January, of the years in which such terms would have ended if this article had not been ratified; and the terms of their successors shall then begin.

Section 2. The Congress shall assemble at least once in every year, and such meeting shall begin at noon on the 3d day of January, unless they shall by law appoint a different day.

Section 3. If, at the time fixed for the beginning of the term of the President, the President elect shall have died, the Vice President elect shall become President. If a President shall not have been chosen before the time fixed for the beginning of his term, or if the President elect shall have failed to qualify, then the Vice President elect shall act as President until a President shall have qualified; and the Congress may by law provide for the case wherein neither a President elect nor a Vice President elect shall have qualified, declaring who shall then act as President, or the manner in which one who is to act shall be selected, and such person shall act accordingly until a President or Vice President shall have qualified.

Section 4. The Congress may by law provide for the case of the death of any of the persons from whom the House of Representatives may choose a President whenever the right of choice shall have devolved upon them, and for the case of the death of any of the persons from whom the Senate may choose a Vice President whenever the right of choice shall have devolved upon them.

Section 5. Sections 1 and 2 shall take effect on the 15th day of October following the ratification of this article.

Section 6. This article shall be inoperative unless it shall have been ratified as an amendment to the Constitution by the legislatures of three-fourths of the several States within seven years from the date of its submission.

Amendment XXI. Repeal of Prohibition Amendment

Section 1. The eighteenth article of amendment to the Constitution of the United States is hereby repealed.

Section 2. The transportation or importation into any State, Territory, or possession of the United States for delivery or use therein of intoxicating liquors, in violation of the laws thereof, is hereby prohibited.

Section 3. This article shall be inoperative unless it shall have been ratified as an amendment to the Constitution by conventions in the several States, as provided in the Constitution, within seven years from the date of the submission hereof to the States by the Congress.

Amendment XXII. Limitation on Presidential Terms

Section 1. No person shall be elected to the office of the President more than twice, and no person who has held the office of President, or acted as President, for more than two years of a term to which some other person was elected President shall be elected to the office of the President more than once. But this Article shall not apply to any person holding the office of President when this Article was proposed by the Congress, and shall not prevent any person who may be holding the office of President, or acting as President, during the term within which this Article becomes operative from holding the office of President or acting as President during the remainder of such term.

Section 2. This article shall be inoperative unless it shall have been ratified as an amendment to the Constitution by the legislatures of three-fourths of the several States within seven years from the date of its submission to the States by the Congress.

Amendment XXIII. Presidential Electors for District of Columbia

Section 1. The District constituting the seat of Government of the United States shall appoint in such manner as the Congress may direct: A number of electors of President and Vice President equal to the whole number of Senators and Representatives in Congress to which the District would be entitled if it were a State, but in no event more than the least populous State; they shall be in addition to those appointed by the States, but they shall be considered, for the purposes of the election of President and Vice President, to be electors appointed by a State; and they shall meet in the District and perform such duties as provided by the twelfth article of amendment.

Section 2. The Congress shall have power to enforce this article by appropriate legislation.

Amendment XXIV. Qualifications of Electors; Poll Tax

Section 1. The right of citizens of the United States to vote in any primary or other election for President or Vice President, for electors for President or Vice President, or for Senator or Representative in Congress, shall not be denied or abridged by the United States or any State by reason of failure to pay any poll tax or other tax.

Section 2. The Congress shall have power to enforce this article by appropriate legislation.

Amendment XXV. Succession to Presidency and Vice Presidency; Disability of President

Section 1. In case of the removal of the President from office or of his death or resignation, the Vice President shall become President.

Section 2. Whenever there is a vacancy in the office of the Vice President, the President shall nominate a Vice President who shall take office upon confirmation by a majority vote of both Houses of Congress.

Section 3. Whenever the President transmits to the President pro tempore of the Senate and the Speaker of the House of Representatives his written declaration that he is unable to discharge the powers and duties of his office, and until he transmits to them a written declaration to the contrary, such powers and duties shall be discharged by the Vice President as Acting President.

Section 4. Whenever the Vice President and a majority of either the principal officers of the executive departments or of such other body as Congress may by law provide, transmit to the President pro tempore of the Senate and the Speaker of the House of Representatives their written declaration that the President is unable to discharge the powers and duties of his office, the Vice President shall immediately assume the powers and duties of the office as Acting President.

Thereafter, when the President transmits to the President pro tempore of the Senate and the Speaker of the House of Representatives his written declaration that no inability exists, he shall resume the powers and duties of his office unless the Vice President and a majority of either the principal officers of the executive department or of such other body as Congress may by law provide, transmit within four days to the President pro tempore of the Senate and the Speaker of the House of Representatives their written declaration that the President is unable to discharge the powers and duties of his office. Thereupon Congress shall decide the issue, assembling within forty-eight hours for that purpose if not in session. If the Congress, within twenty-one days after receipt of the latter written declaration, or, if Congress is not in session, within twenty-one days after Congress is required to assemble, determines by two-thirds vote of both Houses that the President is unable to discharge the powers and duties of his office, the Vice President shall continue to discharge the same as Acting President; otherwise, the President shall resume the powers and duties of his office.

Amendment XXVI. Right to Vote; Citizens Eighteen Years of Age or Older

Section 1. The right of citizens of the United States, who are eighteen years of age or older, to vote shall not be denied or abridged by the United States or by any State on account of age.

Section 2. The Congress shall have power to enforce this article by appropriate legislation.

Amendment XXVII. Compensation of Senators and Representatives

No law, varying the compensation for the services of the Senators and Representatives, shall take effect, until an election of Representatives shall have intervened.

TABLE OF CONTENTS

VOLUME 1

PART ONE

THE SOCIETAL INTERESTS IN COMMUNICATION, ASSOCIATION AND RELIGION

CHAPTER ONE

Introduction and the Search for Doctrine

CHAPTER TWO

The Process of Adjudicating First Amendment Cases

CHAPTER THREE

Pervasive Principles

CHAPTER FOUR

The Supreme Court's Triad of Expressions, the "Pure," the "Not-So-Pure" and the "Impure"

PART TWO

RESOLVING CLASHES BETWEEN SOCIETAL INTERESTS IN FIRST AMENDMENT FREEDOMS AND OTHER IMPORTANT SOCIETAL INTERESTS

CHAPTER FIVE

Society's Interest in Protecting Peace, Good Order and Safety

CHAPTER SIX

Balancing Societal Interests in First Amendment Freedoms With the Societal Interest in Protecting Private Reputation

---

CHAPTER SEVEN

Balancing Societal Interests in First Amendment Freedoms With the Societal Interest in Personal Privacy

---

CHAPTER EIGHT

Reconciling Societal Interest in First Amendment Freedoms With the Interest in Safeguarding the Public Health

---

CHAPTER NINE

Balancing Societal Interests in First Amendment Freedoms With the Societal Interest in Protecting Public Morality

CHAPTER TEN

The Societal Interest in Protecting the Security of the State as Limitative of First Amendment Freeedoms

I. The War Effort and Preparedness Cases

CHAPTER ELEVEN

Society's Interest in Safeguarding the Integrity of the Judicial Process

CHAPTER TWELVE

Safeguarding the Electoral Process

CHAPTER THIRTEEN

Interest in the Good Administration of Government

CHAPTER FOURTEEN

First Amendment Freedoms and Other Opposed Interests

PART THREE

RECONCILING THE SOCIETAL INTERESTS IN THE INTEGRITY AND PRIVACY OF THE INDIVIDUAL WITH OTHER IMPORTANT INTERESTS OF SOCIETY

CHAPTER FIFTEEN

Sacrifices in the Names of Health, Morality and Public Safety

CHAPTER SIXTEEN

Unreasonable Searches and Seizures of Property

CHAPTER SEVENTEEN

Protection from Unreasonable Searches and Seizures of the Person

CHAPTER EIGHTEEN

The Privilege Against Self-Incrimination

CHAPTER TWENTY-ONE

Freedom of Enterprise

CHAPTER TWENTY-TWO

Freedom of Contract

PART FIVE

THE REMAINING LIBERTIES AND FREEDOMS

CHAPTER TWENTY-THREE

The Liberties

CHAPTER TWENTY-FOUR

Freedom From an Establishment of Religion

I. In General

II. Aid to Churches

VOLUME 2

PART SIX

THE SOCIETAL INTERESTS IN EQUALITY

CHAPTER TWENTY-FIVE

Framework for Equal Protection Analysis

CHAPTER TWENTY-EIGHT

Discrimination Based Upon Gender, Sexual Orientation or Legitimacy

I. Gender Discrimination

CHAPTER TWENTY-NINE

Discrimination Which Impinges Upon Fundamental Interests

CHAPTER THIRTY

Social and Economic Regulations

THIRTY-ONE

Slavery and Involuntary Servitude

PART SEVEN

THE SOCIETAL INTERESTS IN CIVIL JUSTICE

CHAPTER THIRTY-FOUR

Jurisdiction of State Courts

CHAPTER THIRTY-FIVE

Procedural Due Process

I. In General

II. Elements of Process

III. Protected Property and Liberty Interests

CHAPTER THIRTY-SIX

Persons Subject to Involuntary Civil Commitment

I. In General

CHAPTER THIRTY-SEVEN

Citizenship and Alienage

I. Right to Citizenship

II. Due Process Rights of Aliens

PART EIGHT

THE RIGHT TO CRIMINAL JUSTICE

CHAPTER THIRTY-EIGHT

Constitutional Limits on Criminal Law Legislation

I. The Need for Clarity in Criminal Statutes

CHAPTER THIRTY-NINE

Pre-trial Rights of Criminal Defendants

I. Constitutional Protection for Criminal Defendants in State Court

II. Grand Jury Indictment

IV. Right to Trial by Jury

V. Right to an Impartial and Representative Tribunal

VI. Joinder and Severance of Parties and Charges

VII. Freedom from Double Jeopardy

CHAPTER FORTY-ONE

Post-Conviction Constitutional Rights

I. Sentencing and Punishment in Non-Capital Cases

II. The Death Penalty

III. Appellate Review of Criminal Convictions

IV. Habeas Corpus

V. Harmless Error

VI. Rights Associated with Probation or Parole

VII. The Right of Prisoners to be Free from Cruel and Unusual Punishment

CHAPTER FORTY-TWO

Constitutional Rights of Defendants in Special Forums

I. Contempt of Court and Legislature

II. Constitutional Rights of Juvenile Defendants

III. Rights of Persons Subject to Punishment by the Military

VOLUME 3

PART NINE

FEDERALISM

CHAPTER FORTY-THREE

Powers and Limitations of State Governments

I. Introduction

II. Express Limitations

CHAPTER FORTY-FOUR

The Powers of Congress

I. Introduction

CHAPTER FORTY-SEVEN

The Powers of the President

CHAPTER FORTY-EIGHT

The Structure and Jurisdiction of Federal Courts

I. The Federal Court System

II. Subject Matter Jurisdiction of Federal Courts

III. Appellate Jurisdiction of the United States Supreme Court

IV. Relationship of State and Federal Trial Courts

VIII. Refusal to Adjudicate Political Questions

PART ELEVEN

CONSTITUTIONAL LITIGATION

CHAPTER FORTY-NINE

Enforcement of Constitutional Rights

I. Introduction

II. Liability Based Upon Federal Civil Rights Statutes

III. Liability Based Upon Other Federal Statutes

IV. Attorneys' Fees

V. Actions Against Federal Agents

CHAPTER FIFTY

Judicial Review of Constitutional Issues

I. Introduction

II. The Context of Constitutional Litigation

III. The Scope of Judicial Authority to Interpret the Constitution

IV. Sources for Constitutional Adjudication

TABLE OF CASES
INDEX

PART ONE

THE SOCIETAL INTERESTS IN COMMUNICATION, ASSOCIATION AND RELIGION

CHAPTER ONE

Introduction and the Search for Doctrine

§ 1.00. Introduction
§ 1.01. The right of petition
§ 1.02. Freedom of association
§ 1.03. The search for the proper method to adjudicate First Amendment cases

---

§ 1.00. Introduction

The First Amendment specifically makes binding upon the federal government freedoms of speech, press, assembly, and religion, and these freedoms are binding upon the states through the Due Process Clause of the Fourteenth Amendment. Additionally, the First Amendment enshrines the right "to petition the government for a redress of grievances,"[1] and since 1952 the United States Supreme Court has held that freedom of association is a First Amendment value, protectable against infringement by both state and federal governments.[2]

The generation of America's Founding Fathers saw the nature of men and women as social, political, communicative, and spiritual beings, and from such natures they deduced all the aforementioned rights as "natural," with concomitant acceptance that man is not made for the state, but rather the state is designed to effectively protect the individual in his "natural rights."[3] It is a commonplace

---

1. The right of petition is discussed in § 1.01.

2. The freedom of association is treated in § 1.02.

3. Antieau, *Rights of Our Fathers* (Coiner Publications, Vienna, Virginia, 1968).

1

that the natural rights of the constitutional generation became the "fundamental rights" of today's constitutional law. In 1945 the Supreme Court made reference to "a 'fundamental right,' which used to be called a 'natural right' of the individual."[4]

There are very important societal interests in protecting and encouraging all the First Amendment freedoms. Our society is interested in seeing that all citizens have access to new ideas, so that our people may better govern themselves, may function economically more productively, and may obtain temporal and spiritual happiness more readily and more fully. In a representative society, it is imperative that all avenues of communication be kept open between the citizens and their representatives in government, as well as their public servants. When measures are proposed by their representatives in federal and state legislatures, citizens must have adequate opportunity to discuss them before adoption. United States Chief Justice Charles Evans Hughes, speaking for the Supreme Court in 1931, stated that "it is essential to the security of the Republic" that there be "opportunity for free political discussion to the end that government may be responsible to the will of the people."[5] California Supreme Court Justice Stanley Mosk echoed this in 1985: "The constitutional right of free expression is an essential ingredient of our democratic society. . . . The airing of opposite views is fundamental to an informed electorate and through it, a free society."[6]

Our society is premised upon the twin propositions that ultimate political power belongs to the people, and that exposure to the marketplace of thought is necessary to test the validity and desirability of all new ideas, especially those relevant to how we should govern ourselves. Ever worth recalling are the illuminating words of United States Supreme Court Justice John Harlan, who wrote in 1971 with reference to First Amendment freedom of expression:

> It is designed and intended to remove governmental restraint upon the arena of public discussion, putting the decision as to what views shall be voiced largely into the hands of each of us, in the hope that use of such freedom will ultimately produce a more capable citizenry and more perfect polity, and in the belief that no other approach could comport with the premise

4. Chase Securities Corp. v. Donaldson, 325 U.S. 304, 314, 65 S. Ct. 1137, 89 L. Ed. 1628 (1945).

5. Stromberg v. People of State of Cal., 283 U.S. 359, 51 S. Ct. 532, 75 L. Ed. 1117, 1123, 73 A.L.R. 1484 (1931).

6. Spiritual Psychic Science Church of Truth, Inc. v. Azusa, 39 Cal. 3d 501, 217 Cal. Rptr. 225, 703 P.2d 1119, 1124 (1985).

of individual dignity and choice upon which our political system rests.[7]

As our society has matured, we have realized that the First Amendment freedoms are beyond being individual rights of citizens, and are the basic values or interests of a free society. Accordingly, the task of a constitutional court is to balance these with the other most important interests of the society, remembering always what the Supreme Court said in 1979, that "the values enshrined in the First Amendment plainly rank high in the scale of our national values."[8]

§ 1.01. The right of petition

In a society that is both democratic and representative, there is a strong societal interest in assuring that individual citizens enjoy an almost unrestricted constitutional right to petition their public servants in all branches and on all levels of government.

The English people in their 1692 Declaration of Rights asserted the right of unrestrained petition of all people against public grievances. In America, Thomas Jefferson asserted the people's natural right to communicate with their elected representatives,[9] and his fellow Virginian, George Mason, fully agreed that by nature men have a "right to instruct their representatives."[10] Francis Lieber wrote that "the right of petitioning is indeed a necessary consequence of the right of free speech and deliberation—a simple, primitive and natural right."[11]

By the Nineteenth Century the right was fully acknowledged by the United States Supreme Court. The Court in the 1876 case *United States v. Cruikshank* stated:

> The right of the people peaceably to assemble for the purpose of petitioning Congress for a redress of grievances, or for anything else connected with the powers or duties of the national government, is an attribute of national citizenship and, as such, under the protection of, and guaranteed by, the United States. The very idea of a government, republican in form,

---

7. Cohen v. California, 403 U.S. 15, 24, 91 S. Ct. 1780, 29 L. Ed. 2d 284, 293 (1971).

8. N.L.R.B. v. Catholic Bishop of Chicago, 440 U.S. 490, 99 S. Ct. 1313, 59 L. Ed. 2d 533, 541 (1979).

9. Letter to James Monroe, Sept. 7, 1797, in *Writings* (Ford ed. 1904-05) VIII, 339.

10. Kate Mason Rowland, *Life of George Mason* (New York, 1892) II, 447.

11. Lieber, *Civil Liberty and Self-Government,* c. 12.

implies a right on the part of its citizens to . . . petition for a redress of the government.

The court significantly added that this right of petitioning federal officials is the type of right that Congress clearly has power to protect as against private individuals as well as public officials—"state action" being irrelevant to this right.[12]

The Supreme Court again in 1972 honored the right of petition and added that, in the case of prisoners, it includes a right to petition the courts for relief. Said the Court: "Persons in prison, like other individuals, have the right to petition the Government for redress of grievances which, of course, includes access of prisoners to the courts for the purpose of presenting their complaints."[13]

Over dissents of Justices Brennan, Stewart and Stevens (Marshall, J. not participating) the Supreme Court held valid a Navy and Marine Corps regulation requiring personnel to secure command approval before circulating petitions addressed to their members in Congress. This was a most unfortunate ruling, hardly likely to persuade members of the military that the land for which they fight is a society that treasures First Amendment freedoms.[14]

The right of petition embraces a right to circulate petitions for signature.[15] Citizens are not to be penalized for exercising their right of petition. The Pennsylvania Supreme Court has held that a labor union could not oust from membership a worker who had signed a petition to the legislature requesting it to repeal the Full Crew Law. "The right of petition," said the Court, "cannot lawfully be infringed, even momentarily by individuals, any more than by the state itself." It added: "The Constitution does not confer the right, but guarantees its free exercise without let or hindrance from those in authority at all times, under any and all circumstances, and . . . it is apparent that such a prerogative can neither be denied by others nor surrendered by the citizen himself."[16]

Notwithstanding the federal constitutional right of petition, the Supreme Court has ruled that a citizen can be prosecuted for libel when communicating with a public official (the President) he utters defamatory remarks about another person, which remarks are

---

12. U.S. v. Cruikshank, 92 U.S. 542, 23 L. Ed. 588 (1875).

13. Cruz v. Beto, 405 U.S. 319, 92 S. Ct. 1079, 31 L. Ed. 2d 263 (1972).

14. Secretary of Navy v. Huff, 444 U.S. 453, 100 S. Ct. 606, 62 L. Ed. 2d 607 (1980).

15. Yancey v. Commonwealth, 135 Ky. 207, 122 S.W. 123 (1909).

16. Spayd v. Ringing Rock Lodge No. 665, Brotherhood of Railroad Trainmen of Pottstown, 270 Pa. 67, 113 A. 70, 14 A.L.R. 1443 (1921).

known to be false or without probable cause or without checking for their truth by means at hand. There was no dissent.[17]

A Wisconsin Court informs us that the right of petition has "never included the right to influence the decision of a court through the medium of a petition."[18]

§ 1.02. Freedom of association

While freedom of association is not explicitly mentioned in the First Amendment, the United States Supreme Court since 1958 has held that this right is entitled to the protection of the First and Fourteenth Amendments. In that year the Court held that the freedom of association of members of the National Association for the Advancement of Colored People outweighed an interest of Alabama in seeking to compel disclosure of membership lists when it was clear that divulgence of such lists would expose members to economic reprisals, loss of employment, threats of physical harm, etc.[19]

Two years later the Court comparably ruled that cities could not compel local branches of the N.A.A.C.P. to divulge their membership lists. The Court stated that where governmental controls upon association are at issue, they can be sustained "only upon showing a subordinating interest which is compelling."[20] In 1963 the Court reaffirmed that associational privacy was an important First Amendment value, adding that not only must an opposed societal interest be "compelling," but the government seeking to expose memberships in associations must "convincingly show a substantial relation between the information sought and the compelling State interest."[21] In 1928, before the Court appreciated freedom of association as a valuable First Amendment right, it had sustained a state law requiring a local chapter of the Ku Klux Klan to divulge its membership,[22] and language of the Court in the 1963 *Gibson* case indicates the Court would likely again sustain such a control if a governmental

---

17. McDonald v. Smith, 472 U.S. 479, 105 S. Ct. 2787, 86 L. Ed. 2d 384, 17 Fed. R. Evid. Serv. (LCP) 1041 (1985).

18. In re Stolen, 193 Wis. 627, 216 N.W. 127, 55 A.L.R. 1355 (1927).

19. National Ass'n for Advancement of Colored People v. State of Ala., ex rel. Patterson, 357 U.S. 449, 78 S. Ct. 1163, 2 L. Ed. 2d 1488 (1958).

20. Bates v. City of Little Rock, 361 U.S. 516, 80 S. Ct. 412, 4 L. Ed. 2d 480 (1960).

21. Gibson v. Florida Legislative Investigation Committee, 372 U.S. 539, 83 S. Ct. 889, 9 L. Ed. 2d 929 (1963).

22. People of State of New York ex rel. Bryant v. Zimmerman, 278 U.S. 63, 49 S. Ct. 61, 73 L. Ed. 184, 62 A.L.R. 785 (1928).

entity is prepared to clearly prove a substantial relationship between its demand and a societal interest either in national security or safety and order.

In 1964 the Supreme Court held that First Amendment freedom of association will prevent a state from ousting an organization such as the N.A.A.C.P., unless it can provide clear proof that a compelling interest advanced in support of such action cannot be protected adequately by lesser sacrifice of associational freedom.[23] Eight years later the Court held that a student organization at a state college cannot be banned from the campus, or denied recognition, because the college administration disagrees with the group's views or philosophy.[24]

Where a strong societal interest, such as eliminating discrimination against women, is present in opposition to associational claims, the Court has indicated that it will extend freedom of association protection only to an association which "is sufficiently personal or private to warrant constitutional protection," which involves a consideration of factors such as size, purpose, selectivity, and whether others are excluded from critical aspects of the relationship.[25]

§ 1.03. The search for the proper method to adjudicate First Amendment cases

During the nineteenth century the United States Supreme Court developed no distinctive method for the adjudication of constitutional cases involving clashes between the First Amendment and other substantial interests of society. During most of this period, when all First Amendment cases before the Court involved congressional infringements upon these interests, the Supreme Court was willing to sustain such governmental restraints upon freedom whenever the judges agreed with the Congress that the controls were reasonable[26] with, in effect, a presumption of reasonableness. This was the view, too, of contemporary scholars. Joseph Story, a distinguished law professor and later Supreme Court Justice, wrote in 1833 that

---

23. National Ass'n for Advancement of Colored People v. Alabama ex rel. Flowers, 377 U.S. 288, 84 S. Ct. 1302, 12 L. Ed. 2d 325 (1964).

24. Healy v. James, 408 U.S. 169, 92 S. Ct. 2338, 33 L. Ed. 2d 266 (1972).

25. Board of Directors of Rotary Intern. v. Rotary Club of Duarte, 481 U.S. 537, 107 S. Ct. 1940, 95 L. Ed. 2d 474 (1987).

26. E.g. Reynolds v. U.S., 98 U.S. 145, 25 L. Ed. 244 (1878); Davis v. Beason, 133 U.S. 333, 10 S. Ct. 299, 33 L. Ed. 637 (1890).

freedom of communication under the Constitution ended when it began to disturb the peace.[27]

It was 1919 when Justice Oliver Wendell Holmes provided the first serious effort of a Supreme Court justice to doctrinally state the method for determining when the basic societal interests in the First Amendment might properly be temporarily limited by the legitimate demands of other substantial societal interests. Writing for the Court in sustaining another conviction for speech violative of an act of Congress, Justice Holmes told his colleagues on the bench and the larger American community that whenever First Amendment rights are at issue, "the question in every case is whether the words are used in such circumstances and are of such a nature as to create a clear and present danger that they will bring about the substantive evils that Congress has a right to prevent."[28]

During the 1930s the judicial philosophy of "interessenjurisprudenz" or the jurisprudence of interests, originated by the German scholar Rudolf vonJhering, was seen by Roscoe Pound and other American scholars to provide a distinct advantage in adjudicating constitutional law controversies. In 1940 members of the Supreme Court, in a case involving the clash between substantial interests in speech and religion on one hand, and the interest in peace and safety on the other, saw that the task was one of balancing and reconciling such interests, if possible. Setting aside a conviction of a Jehovah's Witness for seeking converts on a Connecticut street, the Court stated that it would allow governmental controls upon First Amendment freedoms only by "a statute narrowly drawn to define and punish specific conduct and constituting a clear and present danger to a substantial interest of the state."[29] It was then, hopefully for all time, established that only a "substantial" interest of the society deserves to be put on the scales in opposition to the interest in First Amendment freedoms, and that even then any legislative control must be "narrowly drawn" to protect the opposed substantial interest, with the least impingement upon First Amendment values.

When a court faces the task of constitutional adjudication involving the First Amendment freedoms, in the great majority of instances, it will be well-advised to:

(a) ensure that the governmental entity has power under its governing law to enact an ordinance or statute restricting First Amendment freedoms in the particular manner;

---

27. Joseph Story, *Commentaries on the Constitution* (1st ed., Boston, 1933) vol. III, pp. 732-33.

28. Schenck v. U.S., 249 U.S. 47, 39 S. Ct. 247, 63 L. Ed. 470 (1919).

29. Cantwell v. State of Connecticut, 310 U.S. 296, 60 S. Ct. 900, 84 L. Ed. 1213, 128 A.L.R. 1352 (1940).

(b) make certain that the basis for the legislation impacting upon such freedoms is a very important societal interest;

(c) comprehend that it is not balancing a citizen's personal right to communicate or to worship, but societal interests in the First Amendment freedoms;

(d) discover whether the legislation affecting First Amendment freedoms is "content neutral";

(e) ascertain that the locus of the expressive activity is not a private forum;

(f) inquire if the legislation is so vague that a citizen of average understanding could not contemplate its meaning;

(g) discover whether the public official charged with granting or denying permits and licenses has been given clear standards to confine his discretion;

(h) be convinced the legislation affecting First Amendment freedoms is narrowly tailored to reach only that expression which impacts upon the opposed interest—that the legislation does not suffer from overbreadth;

(i) ascertain with certainty whether banning or limiting a First Amendment freedom will advance or protect the opposed substantial societal interest;

(j) decide whether the means chosen to protect the opposed interest are the least restrictive of First Amendment freedoms that will accomplish the object;

(k) resolve whether the legislation leaves open adequate opportunity for the First Amendment freedoms to be exercised in the area;

(l) inquire whether the First Amendment expression being banned or limited would clearly and unequivocally, presently or imminently, seriously and substantially harm the interest advanced by the state, if not stopped;

(m) determine if the statute in effect imposes unconstitutional conditions upon a citizen's lawful exercise of a basic right;

(n) weigh the evidence at trial to see that the crime charged has been proved by the state; and

(o) be ever cognizant of the words of Justice Rutledge in *Thomas v. Collins*[30] that here we are balancing other interests with "the preferred place given in our scheme to the great, the indispensable democratic freedoms secured by the First Amendment."

There is an occasional temptation for justices to avoid meticulous examinations, such as indicated by the foregoing, and to simply

---

30. Thomas v. Collins, 323 U.S. 516, 65 S. Ct. 315, 89 L. Ed. 430, 440 (1945).

retreat into the time-dishonored "reasonable" test as determinative of the constitutionality of governmental bans and controls upon all forms of First Amendment expression; and this is compounded readily by the justices who have an inadequate appreciation of First Amendment values, since the "reasonableness" standard almost automatically results in sustaining virtually any policy controls over expression and communication, as American history well attests. As we move toward the traditional topical approach to the common instances in which courts have adjudicated clashes between First Amendment freedoms and various other societal interests, one should ask if the occasions when these justices would carve out exceptions to the foregoing list are, in the particular instance, meritorious.

CHAPTER TWO

The Process of Adjudicating First Amendment Cases

§ 2.00.   Principles of adjudication

---

§ 2.00. Principles of adjudication

First, to sustain any governmental limitation upon the First Amendment freedoms, it behooves a constitutional court to ascertain that the regulation is within the power of the governmental entity to impose such a control. Most of the attempted restraints upon First Amendment freedom have come from local governments, none of which have sovereign powers and all of which are confined by limitations contained in state constitutions and statutes. The United States Supreme Court has aptly warned that when governmental controls upon First Amendment freedoms come to a court, it is desirable first to ascertain if the public agency had power under its appropriate laws to enact the controls.[1]

Second, no purely private right or interest ever deserves to be placed on the scales with First Amendment freedoms in constitutional adjudication. The opposed claim must be a public interest, and no insignificant public interest ever qualifies.[2] Any tribunal, states the Supreme Court, "has the duty . . . to assess the substantiality of the governmental interest asserted."[3] In the Court's words, "only those interests of the highest order" deserve in constitutional adjudication to be placed on scales in opposition to the First Amendment freedoms.[4] The kind of societal interest that is deemed by the Court to be qualified to be placed on scales in opposition to First Amendment values is one described by that tribunal

---

1. U.S. v. O'Brien, 391 U.S. 367, 88 S. Ct. 1673, 20 L. Ed. 2d 672, 680 (1968).

2. Brown v. Hartlage, 456 U.S. 45, 102 S. Ct. 1523, 71 L. Ed. 2d 732 (1982).

3. City of Newport, Ky. v. Iacobucci, 479 U.S. 92, 107 S. Ct. 383, 93 L. Ed. 2d 334, 341 (1986) (Stevens, J. and Brennan, J.).

4. Hobbie v. Unemployment Appeals Com'n of Florida, 480 U.S. 136, 107 S. Ct. 1046, 94 L. Ed. 2d 190 (1987).

as "a substantial and important societal interest."[5] The Court has emphasized that, in opposition to First Amendment interests, only "substantial,"[6] "compelling,"[7] "important,"[8] "strong,"[9] "paramount,"[10] "subordinating,"[11] and "cogent"[12] societal interests qualify to be judged with First Amendment values. The Court has further ruled that the burden is upon the state to show such an interest.[13] With a good deal less illumination, the Court has said on occasion that an "overriding" interest can outweigh First Amendment interests.[14]

Third, persons adjudicating First Amendment freedoms must remember always that the balancing is between two societal interests, not between a plaintiff's private rights or interests versus interests of the "state" or the "government." In 1968 the Supreme Court ill-advisedly said that "the problem . . . is to arrive at a balance between the interests of the *teacher* . . . and the interest of the State

---

5. Seattle Times Co. v. Rhinehart, 467 U.S. 20, 104 S. Ct. 2199, 38, 81 L. Ed. 2d 17 (1984).

6. Procunier v. Martinez, 416 U.S. 396, 94 S. Ct. 1800, 40 L. Ed. 2d 224, 71 Ohio Op. 2d 139 (1974) (overruled on other grounds by, Thornburgh v. Abbott, 490 U.S. 401, 109 S. Ct. 1874, 104 L. Ed. 2d 459 (1989)); Clark v. Community for Creative Non-Violence, 468 U.S. 288, 104 S. Ct. 3065, 82 L. Ed. 2d 221 (1984); Ward v. Rock Against Racism, 491 U.S. 781, 109 S. Ct. 2746, 105 L. Ed. 2d 661 (1989); Bolger v. Youngs Drug Products Corp., 463 U.S. 60, 103 S. Ct. 2875, 77 L. Ed. 2d 469 (1983).

7. Williams v. Rhodes, 393 U.S. 23, 89 S. Ct. 5, 21 L. Ed. 2d 24, 45 Ohio Op. 2d 236 (1968); Pacific Gas and Elec. Co. v. Public Utilities Com'n of California, 475 U.S. 1, 106 S. Ct. 903, 89 L. Ed. 2d 1 (1986); Jenness v. Fortson, 403 U.S. 431, 91 S. Ct. 1970, 29 L. Ed. 2d 554 (1971); Bates v. City of Little Rock, 361 U.S. 516, 80 S. Ct. 412, 4 L. Ed. 2d 480 (1960); Boos v. Barry, 485 U.S. 312, 108 S. Ct. 1157, 99 L. Ed. 2d 333 (1988).

8. Procunier v. Martinez, 416 U.S. 396, 94 S. Ct. 1800, 40 L. Ed. 2d 224, 71 Ohio Op. 2d 139 (1974) (overruled on other grounds by, Thornburgh v. Abbott, 490 U.S. 401, 109 S. Ct. 1874, 104 L. Ed. 2d 459 (1989)).

9. Sherbert v. Verner, 374 U.S. 398, 83 S. Ct. 1790, 10 L. Ed. 2d 965, 973 (1963).

10. Thomas v. Collins, 323 U.S. 516, 65 S. Ct. 315, 89 L. Ed. 430, 440 (1945).

11. Bates v. City of Little Rock, 361 U.S. 516, 80 S. Ct. 412, 4 L. Ed. 2d 480, 486 (1960).

12. Bates v. City of Little Rock, 361 U.S. 516, 80 S. Ct. 412, 4 L. Ed. 2d 480, 486 (1960).

13. First Nat. Bank of Boston v. Bellotti, 435 U.S. 765, 98 S. Ct. 1407, 55 L. Ed. 2d 707 (1978).

14. Bob Jones University v. U.S., 461 U.S. 574, 103 S. Ct. 2017, 76 L. Ed. 2d 157, 10 Ed. Law Rep. 918 (1983).

. . . "[15] Such a perversion of the jurisprudence of interests must scrupulously be avoided. The interests to be balanced in this area are always two *societal* interests, not private interests and not state/governmental interests but two most important interests of a free, democratic society.

Fourth, the overwhelming weight of authority holds that governmental controls furthering interests in opposition to First Amendment interests will generally only be constitutional when they are "content neutral," that is when they contain no "content discrimination." The Supreme Court has often affirmed that a governmental regulatory measure affecting First Amendment freedom is to be voided unless "the governmental interest is unrelated to the suppression of free expression."[16] In 1992 the Court held unconstitutional a "hate ordinance" because "it prohibits otherwise permitted speech solely on the basis of the subjects the speech addresses."[17] The same year the Court emphasized that "any permit scheme controlling the time, place and manner of speech must not be based on the content of the message . . . and the amount of the fee cannot be tied, even indirectly, to the content of the speech."[18] One exception exists where "commercial speech" is involved, since such communications are customarily preferential, and a few more exceptions have been permitted where the Court is placing utterances outside constitutional protection because of their content: for example, libel, obscenities, and "fighting words." The Court explains that "with respect to non-commercial speech, this Court has sustained content-based restrictions only in the most extraordinary circumstances."[19]

Fifth, there are limits to where First Amendment freedoms can be exercised. They cannot ordinarily be exercised on private properties, unless such have been dedicated to public use. Furthermore, of recent vintage is the proposition that governmental properties cannot be used for such freedoms, where, unlike parks, common grounds, and streets and sidewalks, which traditionally have been committed to speech and assembly, they are not public forums but edifices and things, like rapid transit cars, held in a "proprietary"

---

15. Pickering v. Board of Ed. of Tp. High School Dist. 205, Will County, Illinois, 391 U.S. 563, 88 S. Ct. 1731, 20 L. Ed. 2d 811, 817 (1968).

16. U.S. v. O'Brien, 391 U.S. 367, 88 S. Ct. 1673, 20 L. Ed. 2d 672 (1968).

17. R.A.V. v. City of St. Paul, Minn., 505 U.S. 377, 112 S. Ct. 2538, 120 L. Ed. 2d 305 (1992).

18. Forsyth County, Ga. v. Nationalist Movement, 505 U.S. 123, 112 S. Ct. 2395, 120 L. Ed. 2d 101, 75 Ed. Law Rep. 29 (1992).

19. Bolger v. Youngs Drug Products Corp., 463 U.S. 60, 103 S. Ct. 2875, 77 L. Ed. 2d 469, 476 (1983).

role, wherein government service would be harmed by a particular exercise of First Amendment freedoms. This is treated at length in § 3.03.

Sixth, due process of law demands that every statute or ordinance denying or limiting First Amendment freedoms be drafted so that any member of the community of ordinary intelligence can readily comprehend it, and this principle of law is customarily applied with strictness to legislation impacting upon First Amendment freedoms. The vice of vagueness is examined fully in § 3.01.

Seventh, any statute or ordinance which seeks to restrict First Amendment freedoms by either license or permit requirements will be unconstitutional if it fails to provide very clear and adequate standards which will confine the area of discretion allowed the public official charged with granting the authorization. This is dealt with in § 3.07.

Eighth, due process of law clauses in the Fifth and Fourteenth Amendments require the judicial voiding of governmental controls of all constitutional rights when the legislation suffers from the vice of overbreadth, that is, when governmental limitations upon constitutional freedoms are not narrowly tailored to reach only the specific aspect of the right allegedly harming the opposed societal interest. These correlative doctrines have always been applied most readily by the Supreme Court when legislation impacts upon First Amendment freedoms. This is covered in § 3.02.

Ninth, individuals and corporations subjected to governmental controls on their exercise of First Amendment freedoms at times become upset that their class has been singled out for restraint, while others whom they believe are in the same position are not subjected to comparable controls, and they then make an attack upon the control, alleging that it should be constitutionally voided for "underinclusiveness." Illustratively, when Michigan forbade corporations from making expenditures out of company funds in connection with state candidate elections, but did not impose similar controls upon unincorporated labor unions, the Michigan Chamber of Commerce, a local corporation, brought a constitutional attack upon the statute, charging underinclusiveness. The statute permitted corporations wishing to make independent expenditures in support of candidates to do so through segregated funds or political action committees, instead of through directing funds through their corporate treasuries. The Supreme Court sustained the distinction, finding in this area "a crucial difference between unions and corporations." Justice Brennan in his concurring opinion saw a second aspect of "underinclusiveness" present under the statute. He observed: "The Michigan law is concededly 'underinclusive' insofar as it does not bar other types of political expenses [by a corporation] to which a dissenting Chamber member or corporate shareholder might object," and he added that corporations were free, for example, to use general treasury funds to support a proposed initiative or a state referendum. "Underinclusiveness" claims, the Court pointed out, do not require voiding distinctions in statutes seen as reasonable by legislatures and the Court.[20] An "underinclusiveness" claim by individuals restricted in their First Amendment freedoms is basically an assertion that they are not being treated equally among equals, a proposition that raises equal protection of the laws issues, the Equal Protection Clause being binding upon all state actions impacting upon First Amendment freedoms. First Amendment claims of underinclusiveness have not fared well with the Court.

Tenth, even though an interest is both a societal one and a "compelling" or "substantial" one, statutes seeking to protect such interests will be held unconstitutional where banning the proscribed exercise of First Amendment freedoms does not advance the proffered interest. Distinguished here from the overbroad statute is the type of legislation which defines with clarity and specificity the exercise of First Amendment freedoms to be restricted but which does not advance the opposed societal interest. The Supreme Court has stated that the procedure for adjudicating First Amendment cases is to initially make sure that the opposed interest is compelling: "If so, we must then determine whether the regulation directly advances the governmental interest asserted."[21] Three years after the case in which it made that statement, when the Court had before it a clearly stated and narrowly drawn statute closing criminal proceedings to the public, the Court voided the limitation on the First Amendment right to know about public affairs, and held that "the proceedings cannot be closed unless specific, on the record, findings are made demonstrating that closure is essential to preserve higher values." The Court further explained that anyone seeking closure must show a substantial probability that the defendant's rights to a fair trial will be denied by publicity that closure would prevent and that reasonable alternatives to closure cannot adequately protect a defendant's fair trial rights.[22]

In 1971 the Court held that when a state seeks to inquire into an

---

20. Austin v. Michigan Chamber of Commerce, 494 U.S. 652, 110 S. Ct. 1391, 108 L. Ed. 2d 652, 658, 675 (1990).

21. Bolger v. Youngs Drug Products Corp., 463 U.S. 60, 103 S. Ct. 2875, 77 L. Ed. 2d 469 (1983).

22. Press-Enterprise Co. v. Superior Court of California for Riverside County, 478 U.S. 1, 106 S. Ct. 2735, 92 L. Ed. 2d 1 (1986).

individual's beliefs and associations, it has the clear burden of proving that the inquiry is necessary to protect a legitimate state interest.[23] Seven years later the Court again stressed that when First Amendment freedoms are being limited by legislation, the government has the burden of making a clear showing that, when unregulated, the expressive conduct jeopardized the asserted interest.[24] In 1980 the Court ruled that a state cannot completely ban all promotional advertising by a public utility, since this was not, according to the Court, necessary to protect a legitimate interest in energy conservation. We must ask, said the Court, "whether the regulation directly advances the governmental interest asserted."[25] Comparably, in 1981, the Court reminded us that a ban upon First Amendment activity is only valid when the opposed interest proffered by a government is directly furthered by the legislation.[26]

Eleventh, statutes attempting to deny or limit the exercise of First Amendment freedoms, even in a worthy cause for a substantial societal interest, should be voided if they do not employ the means least restrictive of First Amendment freedoms while protecting the opposed interest—the "less drastic" rule. In dozens of cases the Supreme Court has voided statutes and ordinances protective of other societal interests because the provisions failed to utilize less drastic means, means less oppressive of First Amendment freedoms which would still be adequate to protect the opposed interest.[27] In voiding an ordinance regulating solicitation by a charitable organization, the Court in 1980 explained that the local government's "interest in preventing fraud can be better served by measures less

---

23. Baird v. State Bar of Arizona, 401 U.S. 1, 91 S. Ct. 719, 27 L. Ed. 2d 639 (1971).

24. In re Primus, 436 U.S. 412, 98 S. Ct. 1893, 56 L. Ed. 2d 417 (1978).

25. Consolidated Edison Co. of New York, Inc. v. Public Service Commission of New York, 447 U.S. 530, 100 S. Ct. 2326, 65 L. Ed. 2d 319 (1980). And cf. Thomas v. Collins, 323 U.S. 516, 65 S. Ct. 315, 89 L. Ed. 430, 445 (1945): "Whatever occasion would restrain orderly discussion and persuasion . . . must have clear support in public danger, actual or impending. Only the gravest abuses, endangering paramount interests give occasion for permissible limitation."

26. Metromedia, Inc. v. City of San Diego, 453 U.S. 490, 101 S. Ct. 2882, 69 L. Ed. 2d 800 (1981).

27. Aptheker v. Secretary of State, 378 U.S. 500, 84 S. Ct. 1659, 12 L. Ed. 2d 992 (1964); National Ass'n for Advancement of Colored People v. Alabama ex rel. Flowers, 377 U.S. 288, 84 S. Ct. 1302, 12 L. Ed. 2d 325 (1964); Shelton v. Tucker, 364 U.S. 479, 81 S. Ct. 247, 5 L. Ed. 2d 231 (1960); Lovell v. City of Griffin, Ga., 303 U.S. 444, 58 S. Ct. 666, 82 L. Ed. 949 (1938); R.A.V. v. City of St. Paul, Minn., 505 U.S. 377, 112 S. Ct. 2538, 120 L. Ed. 2d 305 (1992).

intrusive than a direct prohibition on solicitation."[28] The following year the Court comparably affirmed that it has a duty "to assess the substantiality of the government interests asserted and determine whether those interests could be served by means that would be less intrusive on activity protected by the First Amendment."[29] In 1989 the Court once again emphasized that the means employed must normally be the ones "least harmful" to First Amendment interests, while sufficient to protect the opposed interest.[30]

When what the Court characterizes as "pure speech" is not being denied or controlled, but only a First Amendment value the members of the Court deem of secondary importance in the world of the First Amendment, such as "commercial speech," the Court is inclined to accept as constitutional a government regulation necessary for an opposed important interest, even if it does not honor the least restrictive means test, so long as it is deemed reasonable and seems narrowly tailored to achieve the desired objective.[31]

Twelfth, the existence or nonexistence of adequate alternative avenues of communication for persons being subjected to legislation protective of other interests must be examined. The Supreme Court stated in 1992 that before any permit scheme controlling time, place, or manner of speech will be upheld, the legislation "must leave open alternatives for communication."[32] The Court's protection for citizens walking in the community with signs expressing what they desire or despise has a foundation in the realization that persons without ownership of newspapers, television stations, or other media really have no adequate alternative means of exercising their First Amendment freedoms.[33] It is comparably true for persons distributing handbills.[34]

Correlatively, the Court is more apt to sustain interests other than

28. Village of Schaumburg v. Citizens for a Better Environment, 444 U.S. 620, 100 S. Ct. 826, 63 L. Ed. 2d 73 (1980).

29. Schad v. Borough of Mount Ephraim, 452 U.S. 61, 70, 101 S. Ct. 2176, 68 L. Ed. 2d 671 (1981).

30. Board of Trustees of State University of New York v. Fox, 492 U.S. 469, 109 S. Ct. 3028, 106 L. Ed. 2d 388, 54 Ed. Law Rep. 61 (1989).

31. Board of Trustees of State University of New York v. Fox, 492 U.S. 469, 109 S. Ct. 3028, 106 L. Ed. 2d 388, 54 Ed. Law Rep. 61 (1989).

32. Forsyth County, Ga. v. Nationalist Movement, 505 U.S. 123, 112 S. Ct. 2395, 120 L. Ed. 2d 101, 75 Ed. Law Rep. 29 (1992).

33. Talley v. California, 362 U.S. 60, 80 S. Ct. 536, 4 L. Ed. 2d 559 (1960); U.S. v. Grace, 461 U.S. 171, 103 S. Ct. 1702, 75 L. Ed. 2d 736 (1983); Lovell v. City of Griffin, Ga., 303 U.S. 444, 58 S. Ct. 666, 82 L. Ed. 949 (1938).

34. Schneider v. State of New Jersey, Town of Irvington, 308 U.S. 147, 60 S. Ct. 146, 84 L. Ed. 155 (1939).

those inherent in the First Amendment when it is clear that the persons basing claims upon that Amendment have adequate opportunities to express and communicate their thoughts.[35] Thus, in 1974 the Court sustained California's prison regulations denying prisoners the opportunity to have visits from newsmen, thus denying news reporters the opportunity to interview particular prisoners chosen by them. The Court stated: "We regard the available alternative means of communication as a relevant factor in a case such as this where we are called upon to balance First Amendment rights against governmental interests."[36] In 1983 the Court emphasized that "substantial alternative channels" of communication were open to other teachers' organizations protesting a collective bargaining agreement giving to one teachers' organization the exclusive use of the inter-school mail system and the teachers' mail system, and held that such arrangement accordingly did not violate either the First Amendment or the Equal Protection Clause.[37] The following year, the existence of "ample alternative channels for communication of information" by persons desiring to call attention to the plight of the homeless in Washington, D.C. influenced the Court to sustain a National Park Service ban on sleeping in Lafayette Park and on the Mall.[38] The same year, in passing upon the validity of a ban upon using utility poles for posting signs, the Court re-emphasized that "a restriction on expressive activity may be invalid if the remaining modes of communication are inadequate."[39]

Thirteenth, expressive communications are not punishable under the First Amendment and the Due Process of Law Clauses, even where the opposed interest is "substantial" and the criminal stature is "narrowly tailored" and carefully drafted, so long as the conduct under the First Amendment does not pose a real, immediate, certain, and substantial threat to the opposed interest. In the 1940's the Supreme Court regularly held that manifestations of First Amendment freedoms were not punishable unless it was proven that the expression constituted a clear and present danger of a substantive

---

35. Frisby v. Schultz, 487 U.S. 474, 108 S. Ct. 2495, 101 L. Ed. 2d 420 (1988).

36. Pell v. Procunier, 417 U.S. 817, 94 S. Ct. 2800, 41 L. Ed. 2d 495, 71 Ohio Op. 2d 195 (1974).

37. Perry Educ. Ass'n v. Perry Local Educators' Ass'n, 460 U.S. 37, 103 S. Ct. 948, 74 L. Ed. 2d 794, 9 Ed. Law Rep. 23 (1983).

38. Clark v. Community for Creative Non-Violence, 468 U.S. 288, 104 S. Ct. 3065, 82 L. Ed. 2d 221 (1984).

39. Members of City Council of City of Los Angeles v. Taxpayers for Vincent, 466 U.S. 789, 104 S. Ct. 2118, 80 L. Ed. 2d 772 (1984).

evil.[40] James Madison had written that the exercise of religious liberty was not to be interfered with by the state, unless "the preservation of equal liberty and the existence of the state be manifestly endangered,"[41] and it has increasingly been appreciated in free societies that First Amendment freedoms are not to be suppressed or punished unless there is clear proof that such expression will, not conjecturally, but certainly; not insignificantly, but gravely, impact upon a substantial societal interest, not of the government, but of society; not in the distant future, but immediately. While the clear and present danger language is currently used only infrequently, these principles remain viable.[42]

Fourteenth, whenever an individual in the United States is by law possessed of a particular entitlement, such as to public employment, governmental entities cannot condition this upon renunciation of any First Amendment rights—the doctrine of unconstitutional conditions, which is stated more fully in § 3.04.

Finally, convictions for exercising First Amendment freedoms, even under well-intended statutes, must be set aside where the record is totally devoid of evidentiary support to prove the alleged crime. Due process of law does not allow depriving an individual of his liberty under such conditions. When in 1969 the Supreme Court could find no proof in the record that the petitioners' conduct had been disorderly, the Court promptly reversed the conviction of marchers for disorderly conduct.[43]

---

40. "Whatever occasion would restrain orderly discussion and persuasion . . . must have clear support in public danger, actual or impending. Only the gravest abuses, endangering paramount interests, give occasion for permissible limitation." Thomas v. Collins, 323 U.S. 516, 65 S. Ct. 315, 89 L. Ed. 430, 445 (1945).

41. Irving Brant, James Madison, *Virginia Revolutionary* (Indianapolis 1941) 246.

42. City of Houston, Tex. v. Hill, 482 U.S. 451, 107 S. Ct. 2502, 96 L. Ed. 2d 398 (1987).

43. Gregory v. City of Chicago, 394 U.S. 111, 89 S. Ct. 946, 22 L. Ed. 2d 134 (1969).

CHAPTER THREE

Pervasive Principles

---

§ 3.00. Introduction

As this treatise soon develops, First Amendment freedoms have to be balanced and reconciled with a host of societal interests, including interests in: peace, good order, and safety; protecting public morality; protecting private reputation; safeguarding the privacy of the individual; protecting the public health; and assuring the safety of political states. There are a number of pervasive principles in First Amendment cases that apply regardless of which important societal interest is posed in juxtaposition to speech, press, association, assembly, religion, and petition. They are examined in Chapter Three.

§ 3.01. The vice of vagueness

It is a prime principle of constitutional law that every statute or ordinance affecting the lives, liberties, or property of individuals in the United States must be carefully drafted so that a person of ordinary intelligence in the community can readily learn of the scope of the statute or ordinance. This principle of clarity, outlawing the vice of vagueness, is especially demanding where First Amendment freedoms are at risk from governmental controls.[1] The United States Supreme Court stated in 1959: "Certainty is all the

---

1. Herndon v. Lowry, 301 U.S. 242, 57 S. Ct. 732, 81 L. Ed. 1066 (1937); Joseph Burstyn, Inc. v. Wilson, 343 U.S. 495, 72 S. Ct. 777, 96 L. Ed. 1098 (1952); Rabe v. Washington, 405 U.S. 313, 92 S. Ct. 993, 31 L. Ed. 2d 258 (1972); Smith v. Goguen, 415 U.S. 566, 94 S. Ct. 1242, 39 L. Ed. 2d 605 (1974); Strom-

more essential when vagueness might induce individuals to forego their rights of speech, press, and association for fear of violating an unclear law."[2] The Court again in 1982 emphasized that the "most important factor affecting the clarity that the Constitution demands of a law is whether it threatens to inhibit the exercise of constitutionally protected rights. If, for example, the law interferes with the right of free speech or of association, a more stringent vagueness test should apply."[3]

Illustratively, the Court in 1971 held void for vagueness an ordinance making it "unlawful for three or more persons to assemble, except at a public meeting of citizens, on any of the sidewalks, street corners, vacant lots, or mouths of alleys, and there conduct themselves in a manner annoying to persons passing by, or occupants of adjacent buildings."[4]

In 1976 the Court held unconstitutionally vague an ordinance requiring advance notice to a police department of "any person desiring to canvass, solicit or call from house to house for a recognized charitable . . . or political campaign or cause . . . in writing, for identification only."[5]

In voiding a statute prohibiting the sale of "any magazine . . . which would appeal to the lust of persons under the age of 18 years or to their curiosity to sex, or to the anatomical differences between the sexes," the Court in 1968 held that controls on printed matter to protect the public morality will be unconstitutional when they are so vague and uncertain that publishers and retailers do not know what is legal and what is forbidden.[6] The same year, in voiding for vagueness a statute regulating films, the Court once again emphasized its general rule that "the vice of vagueness is particularly pronounced where expression is sought to be subjected to licensing."[7]

---

berg v. People of State of Cal., 283 U.S. 359, 51 S. Ct. 532, 75 L. Ed. 1117, 73 A.L.R. 1484 (1931).

2. Scull v. Com. of Va. ex rel. Committee on Law Reform and Racial Activities, 359 U.S. 344, 79 S. Ct. 838, 3 L. Ed. 2d 865 (1959).

3. Village of Hoffman Estates v. Flipside, Hoffman Estates, Inc., 455 U.S. 489, 102 S. Ct. 1186, 71 L. Ed. 2d 362 (1982).

4. Coates v. City of Cincinnati, 402 U.S. 611, 91 S. Ct. 1686, 29 L. Ed. 2d 214, 58 Ohio Op. 2d 481 (1971).

5. Hynes v. Mayor and Council of Borough of Oradell, 425 U.S. 610, 96 S. Ct. 1755, 48 L. Ed. 2d 243 (1976).

6. Rabeck v. New York, 391 U.S. 462, 88 S. Ct. 1716, 20 L. Ed. 2d 741 (1968).

7. Interstate Circuit, Inc. v. City of Dallas, 390 U.S. 676, 88 S. Ct. 1298, 20 L. Ed. 2d 225 (1968).

§ 3.02. The vice of overbreadth

Courts have long held void under the Due Process Clauses of the Fifth and Fourteenth Amendments governmental regulations of any federal constitutional rights, whenever governmental control, by law or permit, suffers from the vice of overbreadth, that is, when a governmental limitation has not been carefully drawn and narrowly tailored to reach only the specific vice perceived. This constitutional doctrine is at its most exacting when legislation affecting First Amendment freedoms is involved.[8] In 1971 the United States Supreme Court held unconstitutionally broad, because it authorized punishment of protected speech, an ordinance making it "unlawful for three or more persons to assemble, except at a public meeting of citizens, on any of the sidewalks, street corners, vacant lots, or mouths of alleys, and there conduct themselves in a manner annoying to persons passing by, or occupants of adjacent buildings." The Court added that "mere public intolerance or animosity cannot be the basis for abridgment of First Amendment freedoms."[9] The following year the Court held unconstitutional as impermissibly broad a statute providing that "any person who shall, without provocation, use to or of another, and in his presence . . . opprobrious words or abusive language, tending to cause a breach of the peace . . . shall be guilty of a misdemeanor." In this area of First Amendment freedoms, the Court states that "a statute must be carefully drawn or be authoritatively construed to punish only unprotected speech and not be susceptible of application to protected expression." It is not necessary that the person attacking the statute demonstrate that his own conduct could not be regulated by a statute drawn with the requisite narrow specificity, since, said the Court, "persons whose expression is constitutionally protected may well refrain from exercising their rights for fear of criminal sanctions provided by a statute susceptible of application to protected expression."[10]

The next year, when a statute too broadly restricted the political opportunities of public servants, it was held unconstitutional by the Court. Said Justice White for the Court:

---

8. Brandenburg v. Ohio, 395 U.S. 444, 89 S. Ct. 1827, 23 L. Ed. 2d 430, 48 Ohio Op. 2d 320 (1969); Coates v. City of Cincinnati, 402 U.S. 611, 91 S. Ct. 1686, 29 L. Ed. 2d 214, 58 Ohio Op. 2d 481 (1971); Boos v. Barry, 485 U.S. 312, 108 S. Ct. 1157, 99 L. Ed. 2d 333 (1988); Simon & Schuster, Inc. v. Members of New York State Crime Victims Bd., 502 U.S. 105, 112 S. Ct. 501, 116 L. Ed. 2d 476 (1991).

9. Coates v. City of Cincinnati, 402 U.S. 611, 91 S. Ct. 1686, 29 L. Ed. 2d 214, 58 Ohio Op. 2d 481 (1971).

10. Gooding v. Wilson, 405 U.S. 518, 92 S. Ct. 1103, 31 L. Ed. 2d 408 (1972).

> It has long been recognized that the First Amendment needs
> breathing space and that statutes attempting to restrict or
> burden the exercise of First Amendment rights must be nar-
> rowly drawn and represent a considered legislative judgment
> that a particular mode of expression has to give way to other
> compelling needs of society. . . . In such cases, it has been the
> judgment of this Court that the possible harm to society in
> permitting some unprotected speech to go unpunished is
> outweighed by the possibility that protected speech of others
> may be muted and perceived grievances left to fester because of
> the possible inhibitory effects of overly broad statutes.

Justice White added that the Court in this situation has expanded
the rules of standing to readily permit suit "because of a judicial
prediction or assumption that the statute's very existence may cause
others not before the court to refrain from constitutionally protected
speech or expression."[11]

In 1974 the Court voided as "constitutionally overbroad and
therefore as facially invalid because susceptible of application to
protected speech" an ordinance that provided: "It shall be unlawful
and a breach of the peace to curse or revile or to use obscene or opprobrious language toward or with reference to any member of the
city police while in the actual performance of his duties." The
proscription of "opprobrious" language was broader than the earlier
upheld banning of "fighting words," and the Court held the statute
unconstitutional.[12]

Six years later the Court reaffirmed that "where a government
restricts the speech of a private person, the state action may be
sustained only if the government can show that the regulation is a
precisely drawn means of serving a compelling state interest."[13] In
1983 the Court added that it must always ask "whether [any legislation affecting First Amendment freedoms] is not more extensive
than necessary to serve the governmental interest asserted."[14] It follows that any license or permit scheme controlling First Amend-

---

11. Broadrick v. Oklahoma, 413 U.S. 601, 93 S. Ct. 2908, 37 L. Ed. 2d 830
(1973).

12. Lewis v. City of New Orleans, 415 U.S. 130, 94 S. Ct. 970, 39 L. Ed. 2d 214
(1974).

13. Consolidated Edison Co. of New York, Inc. v. Public Service Commission
of New York, 447 U.S. 530, 100 S. Ct. 2326, 65 L. Ed. 2d 319 (1980).

14. Bolger v. Youngs Drug Products Corp., 463 U.S. 60, 103 S. Ct. 2875, 77 L.
Ed. 2d 469 (1983).

ment interests "must be narrowly tailored to serve significant interests."[15]

The Supreme Court ruled in 1989 that a governmental restriction on commercial speech is valid, even if it goes beyond the least restrictive means to achieve the desired end, so long as it is reasonable and narrowly tailored to achieve the desired objective.[16] The Court had earlier considered it inappropriate to apply the overbreadth doctrine in a case dealing with advertising by professional people since, as commercial speech, it is unlikely to be crushed by overbroad regulation.[17] Justice Stevens, speaking for the Court, confided that "the concept of 'substantial overbreadth' is not readily reduced to an exact definition."[18] A defendant's standing to challenge a statute on First Amendment grounds does not depend upon whether his own activity is shown to be constitutionally privileged. The Court reports that it "consistently has permitted attacks on overly broad statutes with no requirement that the person making the attack demonstrate that his own conduct could not be regulated by a statute drawn with the requisite narrow specificity."[19]

The Court has held the First Amendment overbreadth doctrine inapplicable to advertising by professional groups, such as lawyers.[20]

§ 3.03. Forum analysis

First Amendment rights are made applicable to the states by the Due Process Clause of the Fourteenth Amendment, and that Amendment is applicable only where there is "state action." This can be found from governments dedicating properties to First Amendment activities, as has traditionally been the case with parks, sidewalks, streets, and the like. At times state action can be found from private owners committing various properties to common use, but generally there is no state action by private owners of property. In 1972, the United States Supreme Court held that union organizers soliciting new members had no First Amendment right to

---

15. Forsyth County, Ga. v. Nationalist Movement, 505 U.S. 123, 112 S. Ct. 2395, 120 L. Ed. 2d 101, 75 Ed. Law Rep. 29 (1992).

16. Board of Trustees of State University of New York v. Fox, 492 U.S. 469, 109 S. Ct. 3028, 106 L. Ed. 2d 388, 54 Ed. Law Rep. 61 (1989).

17. Bates v. State Bar of Arizona, 433 U.S. 350, 97 S. Ct. 2691, 53 L. Ed. 2d 810, 51 Ohio Misc. 1, 5 Ohio Op. 3d 60 (1977).

18. Members of City Council of City of Los Angeles v. Taxpayers for Vincent, 466 U.S. 789, 104 S. Ct. 2118, 80 L. Ed. 2d 772, 783 (1984).

19. Bigelow v. Virginia, 421 U.S. 809, 95 S. Ct. 2222, 44 L. Ed. 2d 600 (1975).

20. Shapero v. Kentucky Bar Ass'n, 486 U.S. 466, 108 S. Ct. 1916, 100 L. Ed. 2d 475 (1988).

conduct their operations on a parking lot belonging to a large hardware store. The Court said that it is only when private property "has assumed to some significant degree the functional attributes of public property devoted to public use" that it becomes a public forum.[21] The same year, the Court ruled that a large private shopping center could, whenever it desired, ban distribution of literature unrelated to the affairs of stores within the center, anywhere on its private property. The Court held that, when First Amendment rights are sought to be protected under the Fourteenth Amendment Due Process Clause, the traditional concept of "state action" must be present.[22]

Two earlier cases had held that privately-owned properties could be brought within the Fourteenth Amendment. In 1946 the Supreme Court had ruled that a company town in Alabama must honor First Amendment freedoms and could not punish a religious group for distributing religious literature therein. Justice Black for the Court said: "Whether a municipality or a corporation owns or possesses the town, the public in either case has an identical interest in the functioning of the community in such manner that the channels of communication remain free." Justice Black added: "The more an owner, for his advantage, opens up his property for use by the public in general, the more do his rights become circumscribed by the constitutional rights of those who use it."[23] Then, in 1968, the Court held that picketing of a store in a large shopping center, for alleged unfair labor practices, could not be entirely banned by the owners of a shopping center, which had become, in effect, a community area. The Court recognized, however, that some controls on the picketing would be permissible.[24] The Court held in 1974 that, where governmental entities operate public buses, they have broad powers to control even freedom of expression on such carriers, and ruled that a city could accept commercial advertising generally on buses while refusing to accept an advertisement from a candidate for public office. With Justice Douglas concurring on other grounds, Justices Brennan, Marshall, Powell and Stewart dissented, maintaining that the city had established "a public forum for communication," and, accordingly, it should not be permitted to refuse such advertisements without providing proof of a substantial interest

---

21. Central Hardware Co. v. N.L.R.B., 407 U.S. 539, 92 S. Ct. 2238, 33 L. Ed. 2d 122 (1972).

22. Lloyd Corp., Limited v. Tanner, 407 U.S. 551, 92 S. Ct. 2219, 33 L. Ed. 2d 131 (1972).

23. Marsh v. State of Ala., 326 U.S. 501, 66 S. Ct. 276, 90 L. Ed. 265 (1946).

24. Amalgamated Food Emp. Union Local 590 v. Logan Valley Plaza, Inc., 391 U.S. 308, 88 S. Ct. 1601, 20 L. Ed. 2d 603, 45 Ohio Op. 2d 181 (1968).

requiring protection.[25] The Court also recognizes that where military installations are "closed posts," and the authorities have not abandoned their right to regulate, the distribution of literature and making political speeches can be forbidden and punished.[26]

In 1977 the Court held that a prison, like a military base, is not a public forum and, applying a "reasonableness" test, sustained prison regulations forbidding prisoners to solicit other prisoners for a union and banning union meetings.[27] Ten years later the Court ruled five-to-four that jails and penitentiaries are not ordinarily "public forums," and held that it is sufficient in such institutions that regulations are "reasonably related to legitimate penological interests." Justices Brennan, Marshall, Blackmun and Stevens dissented, condemning the old "reasonableness" test that has traditionally failed adequately to protect First Amendment values.[28]

In 1984 the Court sustained a municipal ordinance prohibiting posting signs on public property, and held that public utility poles were not within the "public forum" doctrine. The district court had found that the signs were removed "without regard to their content" and had found a "legitimate and compelling interest" in controlling "clutter and visual blight." The Court noted that such utility poles are not traditionally recognized as a forum for public communication.[29] In 1993, however, the Court ruled violative of the First Amendment Cincinnati's attempt to ban businesses from distributing commercial publications through freestanding newsracks on public property. Such uses, said the Court, "continue to play a significant role in the dissemination of protected speech."[30]

Streets, sidewalks, and parks have traditionally in the western world been used as public fora for communicative and religious freedoms. In 1951 the Supreme Court said:

> In considering the right of a municipality to control the use of public streets for the expression of religious views, we start with the words of Justice Roberts that "wherever the title of streets

---

25. Lehman v. City of Shaker Heights, 418 U.S. 298, 94 S. Ct. 2714, 41 L. Ed. 2d 770 (1974).

26. Greer v. Spock, 424 U.S. 828, 96 S. Ct. 1211, 47 L. Ed. 2d 505 (1976).

27. Jones v. North Carolina Prisoners' Labor Union, Inc., 433 U.S. 119, 97 S. Ct. 2532, 53 L. Ed. 2d 629 (1977).

28. O'Lone v. Estate of Shabazz, 482 U.S. 342, 107 S. Ct. 2400, 96 L. Ed. 2d 282 (1987).

29. Members of City Council of City of Los Angeles v. Taxpayers for Vincent, 466 U.S. 789, 104 S. Ct. 2118, 80 L. Ed. 2d 772 (1984).

30. City of Cincinnati v. Discovery Network, Inc., 507 U.S. 410, 113 S. Ct. 1505, 123 L. Ed. 2d 99 (1993).

and public parks may rest, they have immemorially been held in trust for the use of the public and, time out of mind, have been used for purposes of assembly, communicating thoughts between citizens, and discussing public questions." [quoting Hague v. CIO, 307 U.S. 496, 59 S. Ct. 954, 83 L. Ed. 1423 (1939)].[31]

In 1988 the Supreme Court reminded us that it had repeatedly indicated that the public streets and sidewalks are the "archetype of a traditional public forum." It recorded that "time out of time public streets and sidewalks have been used for public assembly and debate, the hallmarks of a traditional public forum." It added: "A public street does not lose its status as a traditional public forum simply because it runs through a residential neighborhood," stating that "all public streets [these quintessential public fora] are held in the public trust as properly considered public fora."[32]

In 1990 the Court, in an opinion by Justice O'Connor, with Chief Justice Rehnquist and Justices White and Scalia joining, and with Justice Kennedy concurring, held that a United States Post Office regulation prohibiting solicitation of alms and contributions on postal premises was valid as applied to workers for the Democratic Party soliciting funds, selling books and newspaper descriptions, and distributing political literature on the sidewalk in front of the Bowie, Maryland post office. The part of the sidewalk involved led only from the post office parking lot to the front door, and it had not been dedicated to expressive activities, so the Court declared that it was not a public forum and hence was subject to reasonable controls by the government. Justice Kennedy, concurring, stated that it was not necessary to determine whether the sidewalk was a public or a non-public forum, since the regulation was a reasonable time, place, and manner restriction of protected expression. His remarks seemingly indicate his willingness to allow public forums to be controlled as to time, place, and manner of expression, by the old, discredited "reasonableness" test.[33]

In 1992 the Court, in an opinion by the Chief Justice, joined by Justices White, O'Connor, Scalia and Thomas, held that the New York Port Authority was not a public forum, but an institution held by the local government as a "proprietor," and ruled that solicitation by a religious group could be banned from the airports in the

---

31. Kunz v. People of State of New York, 340 U.S. 290, 293, 71 S. Ct. 312, 95 L. Ed. 280, 283 (1951).

32. Frisby v. Schultz, 487 U.S. 474, 108 S. Ct. 2495, 101 L. Ed. 2d 420, 428 (1988).

33. U.S. v. Kokinda, 497 U.S. 720, 110 S. Ct. 3115, 111 L. Ed. 2d 571 (1990).

New York City area, which the Port Authority owned and operated. The Chief Justice said that "where the government is acting as a proprietor, managing its internal operations, rather than acting as a lawmaker with the power to regulate or license, its actions will not be subjected to the heightened reviews to which its actions as a lawmaker may be judged." In such "proprietary" instances, the Chief Justice added, "the challenged regulation need only be reasonable, as long as the regulation is not an effort to suppress the speaker's activity due to disagreement with the speaker's views."[34] Justices Kennedy, Blackmun, Stevens and Souter refused to accept the "proprietary" doctrine, stating that "it leaves the government with almost unlimited authority to restrict speech on its property by doing nothing more than activating a non-speech related principle for the area." Justice Kennedy added that he believed non-speech elements of expressive conduct can be subjected to reasonable restrictions on time, place and manner.[35]

Both the Rehnquist and Kennedy views are portentous. With an increasing government ownership of property in the country, the reader may well join Justices Kennedy, Blackmun, Stevens and Souter in being alarmed that soon their five colleagues will widely and recklessly embark upon labeling other government-owned structures and facilities as "proprietary"; for example, schools, auditoria, stadiums, theaters, convention centers etc., with their concomitant notion that all government controls upon First Amendment freedoms will survive so long as they appear "reasonable" to five justices. As to Justice Kennedy's willingness to expose all "non-speech" elements of communication to any "reasonable" time, place, and manner controls, virtually all forms of silent expression, such as wearing a yarmulke or a black armband in mourning at a public forum, are in grave danger of being exposed to governmental restrictions under the old "reasonableness" norm, which has provided virtually no protection for First Amendment values in the past.

§ 3.04. Unconstitutional conditions

In 1926 the United States Supreme Court stated that "the power of the state . . . is not unlimited; and one of the limitations is that it may not impose conditions which require the relinquishment of constitutional rights" as a qualification upon receiving permits. The Court added: "If so, constitutional guaranties, so carefully

---

34. International Soc. for Krishna Consciousness, Inc. v. Lee, 505 U.S. 672, 112 S. Ct. 2701, 2705-06, 120 L. Ed. 2d 541 (1992).

35. International Soc. for Krishna Consciousness, Inc. v. Lee, 505 U.S. 672, 112 S. Ct. 2701, 2713, 120 L. Ed. 2d 541 (1992).

safeguarded against direct assault, are open to destruction by the indirect but no less effective process of requiring a surrender, which, though in form voluntary, lacks none of the elements of compulsion."[36]

Then, in 1943 the Court held that the right of children to a public school education could not be conditioned upon their renouncing their religious faith and agreeing to salute the flag.[37] Nine years later, the Court voided a loyalty oath as a condition of public employment. Noting that it need not pause to consider whether an abstract right to public employment exists, the Court found it sufficient to say that constitutional protection does extend to the public servant whose exclusion pursuant to a statute is patently arbitrary or discriminatory. The Court pointed out that it is obvious that Congress could not pass a law providing, for example, "that no federal employee shall attend mass or take any active part in missionary work."[38]

In 1961, quoting the sentence above from *Wieman v. Updegraff,* the Court held that the holding of public office can not be conditioned upon some religious belief or lack thereof. The Court stated: "The fact that a person is not compelled to hold public office cannot possibly be an excuse from barring him from office by state-imposed criteria forbidden by the Constitution."[39] Two years later the Court ruled that a state could not deny Seventh Day Adventists their unemployment compensation because they could not, because of their religious faith, labor on Saturdays. Justice Brennan for the Court said: "It is too late in the day to doubt that the liberties of religion and expression may be infringed by the denial of or placing of conditions upon a benefit or privilege."[40]

Four years later the Court voided a state statute conditioning employment as a teacher in the public schools upon her giving up membership in a listed organization, when there was no proof showing she was committed to furthering the organization's unlawful aims. Repeating what the Court of Appeals for the Second Circuit had said in this case, the Supreme Court echoed: "The theory that public employment may be denied altogether or may be subjected to

36. Frost v. Railroad Commission of State of Cal., 271 U.S. 583, 593-94, 46 S. Ct. 605, 70 L. Ed. 1101, 47 A.L.R. 457 (1926).

37. West Virginia State Board of Education v. Barnette, 319 U.S. 624, 63 S. Ct. 1178, 87 L. Ed. 1628, 147 A.L.R. 674 (1943).

38. Wieman v. Updegraff, 344 U.S. 183, 73 S. Ct. 215, 97 L. Ed. 216, 222 (1952).

39. Torcaso v. Watkins, 367 U.S. 488, 81 S. Ct. 1680, 6 L. Ed. 2d 982, 987 (1961).

40. Sherbert v. Verner, 374 U.S. 398, 83 S. Ct. 1790, 10 L. Ed. 2d 965 (1963).

any conditions regardless of how unreasonable, has been uniformly rejected."[41] The following year, the Court voided the firing of a teacher who had written a letter to a newspaper criticizing the record of the board of education in its handling of a proposed bond issue, which letter had not interfered with the teacher's performance of his duties nor impaired the general operation of the school system. The Court stated:

> To the extent that the Illinois Supreme Court opinion may be read to suggest that teachers may be compelled to relinquish the First Amendment rights they would otherwise enjoy as citizens to comment on matters of public interest in connection with the operation of the public schools in which they work, it proceeds on a premise that has been unequivocally rejected in a number of prior decisions of this Court.[42]

However, over claimed facial unconstitutionality, the Supreme Court in 1991 sustained a federal spending program forbidding personnel opting for the program to counsel abortion as a method of family planning, from referring pregnant women to abortion counselors or doctors, and from even indirectly promoting abortion. The Court held that unless the government creates an "unconstitutional condition," as defined by prior cases, "when the government appropriates public funds to establish a program, it is entitled to define the limits of that program." The Court added:

> The Government can, without violating the Constitution, selectively fund a program to encourage certain actions it believes to be in the public interest, without at the same time funding alternative programs which seek to deal with the problem in another way.

As to "unconstitutional conditions," the Court explained these were different, since they all involved "situations in which the government has placed a condition on the recipient of the subsidy, rather than on a particular program or service." In dissent, Justices Blackmun, Marshall and Stevens pointed out this was the first time the Court has ever upheld a viewpoint-based suppression of speech solely because it was imposed on those dependent upon the government for economic support.[43]

---

41. Keyishian v. Board of Regents of University of State of N. Y., 385 U.S. 589, 87 S. Ct. 675, 17 L. Ed. 2d 629, 642 (1967).

42. Pickering v. Board of Ed. of Tp. High School Dist. 205, Will County, Illinois, 391 U.S. 563, 88 S. Ct. 1731, 20 L. Ed. 2d 811 (1968).

43. Rust v. Sullivan, 500 U.S. 173, 111 S. Ct. 1759, 114 L. Ed. 2d 233 (1991).

§ 3.05. Time, place, and manner controls

Thirty years ago in the infancy of the time, place, and manner doctrine, it was not to be applicable to "pure speech" or expressions of ideas at the core of the First Amendment. Justice Goldberg for the Court in 1965 made it clear that *"secondary* forms of expression" were to be the victims of the principle. He stated: "We emphatically reject the notion urged by the appellant that the First and Fourteenth Amendments afford the same kind of freedom to those who would communicate ideas by conduct such as patrolling, marching, and picketing on streets and highways, as these Amendments afford to those who communicate ideas by pure speech."[44]

Assuming we could agree on which forms of expression are "secondary" or of lesser value than "pure speech," it might be appropriate to apply the time, place and manner doctrine in balancing the competing societal interests. In 1987 the Court held that the First Amendment protected from dismissal a clerical employee in a county constable's office who heard of the attack upon President Reagan and said: "If they go for him again, I hope they get him." The Court stated that "the manner, time and place of the employee's expression are relevant, as is the context in which the dispute arose." Chief Justice Rehnquist, and Justices O'Connor, Scalia and White dissented, thinking the speech here was not "of public concern" and consequently easily outweighed by the opposing public interests.[45]

The danger to our First Amendment society lies in the apparent willingness of a majority of the present Supreme Court to transfer the time, place and manner doctrine from "secondary" forms of communication[46] to all protected expression. In 1983 the Court, in an opinion by Justice White, held unconstitutional an enactment in effect banning the distribution of leaflets on sidewalks embraced within the Supreme Court grounds, but by way of dictum volunteered that reasonable time, place, and manner restrictions would survive.[47] That same year the Court stated: "The state may also enforce regulations of the time, place and manner which are content

---

44. Cox v. State of Louisiana, 379 U.S. 536, 555, 85 S. Ct. 466, 13 L. Ed. 2d 487 (1965).

45. Rankin v. McPherson, 483 U.S. 378, 107 S. Ct. 2891, 97 L. Ed. 2d 315 (1987).

46. Cox v. State of New Hampshire, 312 U.S. 569, 61 S. Ct. 762, 85 L. Ed. 1049, 133 A.L.R. 1396 (1941) (a parade); Cox v. State of Louisiana, 379 U.S. 536, 85 S. Ct. 466, 13 L. Ed. 2d 487 (1965) (a parade and demonstration); Clark v. Community for Creative Non-Violence, 468 U.S. 288, 104 S. Ct. 3065, 82 L. Ed. 2d 221 (1984) (sleeping in a park); Adderley v. State of Fla., 385 U.S. 39, 87 S. Ct. 242, 17 L. Ed. 2d 149 (1966) (trespass upon jail grounds).

47. U.S. v. Grace, 461 U.S. 171, 103 S. Ct. 1702, 1707, 75 L. Ed. 2d 736 (1983).

neutral and narrowly tailored to serve a significant interest, and leave open ample alternative channels of communication."[48] The following year, Justice White, speaking for the Court in holding valid a federal ban on sleeping in Washington parks in its application to persons protesting unconcern for the homeless in America, said:

> Expression, whether oral or written, or symbolized by conduct, is subject to reasonable time, place and manner restrictions [so long as,] without reference to the content of the regulated speech, they are narrowly tailored to serve a significant government interest, and they leave open ample alternative channels for communication of information.[49]

Note that the new Time, Place or Manner doctrine seemingly now would extend to all First Amendment protected freedom, "whether oral or written, or symbolized by conduct." During the same term, the Court held that a federal statute allowing photographic reproduction of United States currency for "philatelic, numismatic, educational, historical or newsworthy purposes," as an exception to an otherwise universal statutory prohibition on such reproduction, was not a valid time, place, and manner regulation because it discriminated on the basis of content.[50]

Six years later, the Court allowed New York City to cope with noise in Central Park produced by rather loud musicians. Justice Kennedy, after quoting the foregoing statement of Justice White, added that "a regulation of the time, place or manner of protected speech must be narrowly tailored to serve the government's legitimate, content-neutral interests, but . . . it need not be the least restrictive or least intrusive means of doing so,"[51] thus further chipping away at the constitutional protection previously provided for First Amendment freedoms. In dissent, Justice Marshall, Brennan and Stevens saw this, urging that even controls on secondary expressive forms must be narrowly tailored.

In 1992 the Court reaffirmed that "any permit scheme controlling the time, place and manner of speech must not be based on the content of the message, must be narrowly tailored to serve significant government interests, and must leave open alternatives for com-

---

48. Perry Educ. Ass'n v. Perry Local Educators' Ass'n, 460 U.S. 37, 45, 103 S. Ct. 948, 74 L. Ed. 2d 794, 9 Ed. Law Rep. 23 (1983).

49. Clark v. Community for Creative Non-Violence, 468 U.S. 288, 293, 104 S. Ct. 3065, 82 L. Ed. 2d 221 (1984).

50. Regan v. Time, Inc., 468 U.S. 641, 104 S. Ct. 3262, 82 L. Ed. 2d 487 (1984).

51. Ward v. Rock Against Racism, 491 U.S. 781, 109 S. Ct. 2746, 105 L. Ed. 2d 661 (1989).

munication," and held unconstitutional an assembly and parade permit ordinance which allowed a government official to vary the fee to reflect the estimated cost of maintaining public order. There can be no "unbridled discretion in a government official" in permit and license legislation, because "the peril is too great, and the amount of the fee cannot be tied, even indirectly, to the content of the speech."[52]

What we are facing, then, is the possibility of a time, place and manner doctrine applicable to the finest kind of communication protected by the First Amendment, with no longer a need to require the government to utilize the least restrictive means of protecting its opposed interests, so long as the inroad upon freedom of expression is content-neutral, the opposed interest is "significant," ample alternative channels of communication are available, and the Court sees the regulation as "reasonable."[53] The principle is a well-veiled return to the test of "reasonableness," which for decades virtually emasculated the First Amendment freedoms. What will be left is a naked right to publish, to preach, to associate, to assemble, to petition, to speak—with virtually unlimited regulatory power at all levels of government on its actual exercise.

§ 3.06. Prior restraints upon the First Amendment freedoms

In 1931 the United States Supreme Court wrote: "The fact that for approximately one hundred and fifty years there has been almost an entire absence of attempt to impose previous restraints upon publications relating to the malfeasance of public officers is significant of the deep-seated conviction that such restrictions would violate constitutional right. . . . The general principle that the constitutional guaranty of the liberty of the press gives immunity from previous restraints has been approved in many decisions under the provisions of state constitutions. . . . Subsequent punishment for such abuses as may exist is the appropriate remedy, consistent with constitutional privilege." The Court held unconstitutional a state statute that authorized the county attorney to enjoin publication of any "malicious, scandalous and defamatory" publication.[54]

However, in 1957 the Court upheld a state statute providing that

---

52. Forsyth County, Ga. v. Nationalist Movement, 505 U.S. 123, 112 S. Ct. 2395, 120 L. Ed. 2d 101, 75 Ed. Law Rep. 29 (1992).

53. "The nature of a place, the pattern of its normal activities, dictate the kinds of regulations of time, place and manner that are reasonable." Grayned v. City of Rockford, 408 U.S. 104, 116, 92 S. Ct. 2294, 33 L. Ed. 2d 222 (1972).

54. Near v. State of Minnesota ex rel. Olson, 283 U.S. 697, 51 S. Ct. 625, 75 L. Ed. 1357 (1931).

a distributor of books was entitled to a trial on the issues within one day after joinder of issue and requiring a decision to be rendered by the court within two days of the conclusion of the trial. In the *Kingsley Books* case the distributor consented to the granting of an injunction pendente lite, and the judge at trial, sitting in equity, found the books to be obscene and ordered their surrender. The Court, in a five-to-four ruling, affirmed, pointing out that protection even as to previous restraints is not an absolute. Among the dissenters, Justices Black and Douglas said that the opportunity of a judge to issue even an injunction pendente lite, without any hearing and without any finding on the issue of obscenity, should be unconstitutional.[55]

Six years later the Court ruled unconstitutional a Rhode Island practice whereby a state commission notified book dealers that certain designated books and magazines were objectionable for sale or display to youths under 18. The book dealers were told the lists had been given to the local police, and soon local police visited the bookstore. Justice Brennan, speaking for the Court said:

> The Fourteenth Amendment requires that regulation by the States of obscenity conform to procedures that will ensure against the curtailment of constitutionally protected expression, which is often separated from obscenity only by a dim and uncertain line. It is characteristic of the freedom of expression in general that they are vulnerable to gravely damaging yet barely visible encroachments. Our insistence that regulation of obscenity scrupulously embody the most rigorous procedural safeguards is therefore but a special instance of the larger principle that the freedoms of expression must be ringed about with adequate bulwarks. . . . Any system of prior restraints of expression comes to this Court bearing a heavy presumption against its constitutional validity. We have tolerated such a system only where it operated under judicial superintendence and assured an almost immediate judicial determination of the validity of the restraint [citing *Kingsley Books v. Brown*].[56]

In 1965 the Court invalidated a state's practice of dealing with obscene films because of procedural inadequacies which often kept films off the market for as long as six months before a definitive ruling was had. Said the Court:

---

55. Kingsley Books, Inc. v. Brown, 354 U.S. 436, 77 S. Ct. 1325, 1 L. Ed. 2d 1469, 14 Ohio Op. 2d 471 (1957).

56. Bantam Books, Inc. v. Sullivan, 372 U.S. 58, 83 S. Ct. 631, 9 L. Ed. 2d 584, 590-91 (1963).

> [W]e hold that a noncriminal process which requires the prior
> submission of a film to a censor avoids constitutional infirmity
> only if it takes place under procedural safeguards designed to
> obviate the dangers of a censorship system. First, the burden of
> proving that the film is unprotected expression must rest on the
> censor. . . . Second, while the State may require advance
> submission of all films, in order to proceed effectively to bar all
> showings of unprotected films, the requirement cannot be
> administered in a manner which would lend an effect of finality
> to the censor's determination whether a film constitutes
> protected expression. . . . To this end, the exhibitor must be
> assured, by statute or authoritative judicial construction, that
> the censor will, within a specified brief period, either issue a
> license or go to court to restrain showing the film. Any restraint
> imposed in advance of a final judicial determination on the
> merits must similarly be limited to preservation of the status
> quo for the shortest fixed period compatible with sound judicial
> resolution. . . . [T]he procedure must also assure a prompt
> final judicial decision, to minimize the deterrent effect of an
> interim and possibly erroneous denial of a license.[57]

Three years later these rulings were followed in *Teitel Film
Corporation v. Cusack*,[58] and in 1971 the Court comparably
invalidated a federal law giving the Postmaster General power to
hold up mail being received by a person pending determination of
obscenity.[59]

Under ordinary circumstances courts cannot issue orders banning
the exercise of First Amendment freedoms, such as rallies and public
meetings, without notice to the citizens affected. Said the Supreme
Court in 1968: "There is a place in our jurisprudence for an ex parte
issuance, without notice, of temporary restraining orders of a short
duration, but there is no place within the area of basic freedom
guaranteed by the First Amendment for such orders where no showing is made that it is impossible to serve or to notify the opposing
parties and to give them an opportunity to participate."[60]

Two years later the Court dismissed for want of a substantial
federal question an appeal from a conviction under a Philadelphia

---

57. Freedman v. State of Md., 380 U.S. 51, 85 S. Ct. 734, 13 L. Ed. 2d 649, 655
(1965).

58. Teitel Film Corp. v. Cusack, 390 U.S. 139, 88 S. Ct. 754, 19 L. Ed. 2d 966
(1968).

59. Blount v. Rizzi, 400 U.S. 410, 91 S. Ct. 423, 27 L. Ed. 2d 498 (1971).

60. Carroll v. President and Com'rs of Princess Anne, 393 U.S. 175, 89 S. Ct.
347, 21 L. Ed. 2d 325 (1968).

ordinance which empowered the mayor to declare a state of emergency and ban meetings in any outdoor place. The mayor had banned meetings of twelve or more. When the petitioners met they were convicted despite the fact that the three meetings involved were peaceful, orderly, and noninflammatory. None of the meetings them interfered with traffic and none violated any law save for the proclamation of the mayor. Justice Douglas in dissent pointed out that the appellants' claim that the ordinance and the proclamation were overbroad raised substantial constitutional questions.[61]

Observing that "any prior restraint on expression comes to this Court with a heavy presumption against its constitutional validity," the Supreme Court in 1971 set aside a state court injunction enjoining a group from distributing literature anywhere in a city.[62] The same year the Court denied the federal government an injunction against the *Washington Post* and the *New York Times* which were about to print a classified study entitled "History of U.S. Decision Making Process on Viet Nam Policy" (the Pentagon Papers), the per curiam opinion indicating that the government had not met the heavy burden upon those who would impose a prior restraint upon the press. Justice Brennan in his concurring opinion stated that the First Amendment "tolerates absolutely no prior judicial restraints of the press predicated upon surmise or conjecture that untoward consequences may result." He acknowledged "that there is a single, extremely narrow class of cases in which the First Amendment's ban on prior judicial restraint may be overridden," that is, when the nation is at war.[63]

In 1973 the Court held that a judicial officer authorized to issue warrants, who has viewed a film and concluded that it is obscene, can issue a constitutionally valid warrant for the film's seizure as evidence in a prosecution against the exhibitor, without conducting first an adversary hearing on the issue of probable obscenity.[64] Two years later, the Court ruled that a government cannot ban a production for the stage, without first providing all the procedural safeguards necessary when films are subjected to prior restraints.[65]

The following year the Court ruled unconstitutional a "gag order"

---

61. Stotland v. Pennsylvania, 398 U.S. 916, 90 S. Ct. 1552, 26 L. Ed. 2d 83 (1970).

62. Organization for a Better Austin v. Keefe, 402 U.S. 415, 91 S. Ct. 1575, 29 L. Ed. 2d 1 (1971).

63. New York Times Co. v. U.S., 403 U.S. 713, 91 S. Ct. 2140, 29 L. Ed. 2d 822 (1971).

64. Heller v. New York, 413 U.S. 483, 93 S. Ct. 2789, 37 L. Ed. 2d 745 (1973).

65. Southeastern Promotions, Ltd. v. Conrad, 420 U.S. 546, 95 S. Ct. 1239, 43 L. Ed. 2d 448 (1975).

imposed by a trial court judge preventing publishers from printing before trial incriminating statements made by the accused or other matter "strongly implicative" of him. Chief Justice Burger for the Court stated: "Prior restraints on speech and publication are the most serious and the least tolerable infringement on First Amendment rights. . . . We cannot say on the record that alternatives to a prior restraint on petitioners would not have sufficiently mitigated the adverse effects of pretrial publicity so as to make prior restraints unnecessary. Nor can we conclude that the restraining order actually entered would serve its intended purpose. Reasonable minds can have few doubts about the gravity of the evil pretrial publicity can work, but the probability that it would do so here was not demonstrated with the degree of certainty our cases on prior restraint require." After noting that "an accused's right to a fair trial may be adequately assured through methods that do not infringe First Amendment values," Justice Brennan in a concurring opinion added that "at least in the context of prior restraints on publication, the decision of what, when, and how to publish is for editors, not judges."[66] The *Nebraska Press* case was followed the next year when a state court endeavored to stop publication of information about a juvenile delinquency proceeding.[67]

In 1983 Justice Brennan, as the supervising Circuit Justice, set aside a judge's "gag order" which after selection of a trial jury permanently restrained publication of the names and addresses of jurors in the trial. Justice Brennan wrote: "We have recognized the special importance of swift action to guard against the threat to First Amendment values posed by prior restraints. . . . It is clear that even a short-lived 'gag' order in a case of wide-spread concern to the community constitutes a substantial prior restraint and causes irreparable damage to First Amendment interests as long as it remains in effect." Justice Brennan observed that "It hardly requires repetition that any system of prior restraints of expression comes to the Court bearing a heavy presumption against its constitutional validity, and that the state carries a heavy burden of showing justification for the imposition of such a restraint." Justice Brennan assumed for purposes of argument only that the state has "a compelling interest in keeping personal information about jurors confidential in an appropriate case, either to assure the defendant a fair trial, or to protect the privacy of jurors," However, the Justice noted that

66. Nebraska Press Ass'n v. Stuart, 427 U.S. 539, 96 S. Ct. 2791, 49 L. Ed. 2d 683 (1976).

67. Oklahoma Pub. Co. v. District Court In and For Oklahoma County, 430 U.S. 308, 97 S. Ct. 1045, 51 L. Ed. 2d 355 (1977).

that far more justification than appeared on the record in the current case would be necessary to show that a categorical, permanent prohibition against publishing information already in the public record was "narrowly tailored to serve that interest," if indeed any justification would suffice to sustain a permanent order. He forecast that the Supreme Court would probably reverse this permanent prohibition against publishing information already in the public record, explaining "We have not permitted restriction on the publication of information that would have been available to any member of the public who attended an open proceeding in a criminal trial, even for the obviously sympathetic purpose of protecting the privacy of rape victims" [citing cases]. Quoting from *Globe Newspaper Co. v. Superior Court,*[68] Justice Brennan stated: "In an extraordinary case such a restriction might be justified, but the justification must be addressed on a case-by-case basis, with all interested parties given the opportunity to participate, and less restrictive alternatives must be adopted, if feasible."[69]

§ 3.07. Licenses and permits

When a government seeks to control First Amendment freedoms by licenses or permits, clear and adequate standards must be provided for the public servant charged with granting or denying such an authorization. The danger of censorship by public officials is so great that the vice-of-vagueness doctrine must readily be applied to void legislation without standards, or with only inexact or fragmentary standards to control official behavior.

In 1936 the United States Supreme Court held invalid on its face an ordinance prohibiting the distribution of literature of any kind at any time or place without a permit from the city manager, who was given no standards to apply in granting or refusing the permit. The Court stated:

> Whatever the motive which influenced its adoption, its character is such that it strikes at the very foundation of the freedom of the press by subjecting it to license and censorship. . . . While this freedom from previous restraint upon publication cannot be regarded as exhausting the guaranty of liberty, the prevention of that restraint was a leading purpose in the adoption of the constitutional provision. Legislation of the type

---

68. Globe Newspaper Co. v. Superior Court for Norfolk County, 457 U.S. 596, 102 S. Ct. 2613, 73 L. Ed. 2d 248 (1982).

69. Capital Cities Media, Inc. v. Toole, 463 U.S. 1303, 103 S. Ct. 3524, 77 L. Ed. 2d 1284, 1287-89 (1983).

of the ordinance in question would restore the system of license and censorship in its boldest form.[70]

The following year the Court voided on its face an ordinance requiring a permit for public assemblies upon the streets and vesting in the city's director of public safety power to refuse the permit when "he believes it proper to refuse the issuance thereof; provided, however that said permit shall only be refused for the purpose of preventing riots, disturbances or disorderly assemblage."[71]

The next year the Court held void a law requiring persons soliciting on the streets for religious or charitable causes to secure a certificate, which could be denied by a public servant unless he believed "such cause a religious one or is a bonafide object of charity or philanthropy and conforms to reasonable standards of efficiency and integrity." The Court stated: "To condition the solicitation of aid for the perpetuation of religious views upon a license, the grant of which rests in the exercise of a determination by state authority as to what is a religious cause, is to lay a forbidden burden upon the exercise of liberty protected by the Constitution."[72]

In 1941 the Court upheld the requirement of a license for groups contemplating parades. The state court had said that notice in advance was necessary so that the city could provide adequate police protection, and had held that the statute required the permit to be granted to any group whenever "the convenience of the public in the use of the streets would not thereby be unduly disturbed."[73]

When the Supreme Court in 1951 voided a conviction for speaking without a permit, because the governing statute did not have adequate standards, the Court recalled: "We have consistently condemned licensing systems which vest in an administrative official discretion to grant or withhold a permit upon broad criteria unrelated to proper regulation of public places."[74]

In 1969 the Court held invalid an ordinance requiring a permit for any public demonstration, and giving to members of a city commission absolute power to refuse a parade permit whenever they thought

---

70. Lovell v. City of Griffin, Ga., 303 U.S. 444, 58 S. Ct. 666, 82 L. Ed. 949, 954 (1938).

71. Hague v. Committee for Indus. Organization, 307 U.S. 496, 59 S. Ct. 954, 83 L. Ed. 1423 (1939).

72. Cantwell v. State of Connecticut, 310 U.S. 296, 60 S. Ct. 900, 84 L. Ed. 1213, 1219, 128 A.L.R. 1352 (1940).

73. Cox v. State of New Hampshire, 312 U.S. 569, 61 S. Ct. 762, 85 L. Ed. 1049, 133 A.L.R. 1396 (1941).

74. Kunz v. People of State of New York, 340 U.S. 290, 71 S. Ct. 312, 95 L. Ed. 280 (1951).

"the public welfare, peace, safety, health, decency, good morals or convenience required that it be refused." The Court said:

> A law subjecting the exercise of First Amendment freedoms to the prior restraint of a license, without narrow, objective, and definite standards to guide the licensing authority, is unconstitutional . . . our decisions have made it clear that a person faced with such an unconstitutional licensing law may ignore it and engage with impunity in the exercise of the right of free expression for which the law purports to require a license.[75]

In 1988 the Court held void an ordinance requiring newspaper publishers to secure a permit before they placed coin-operated dispensing machines on the municipal sidewalks, because the authorities charged with granting or denying such permits were given unbridled power to refuse such permits. In such cases, the Court reminded us, one subject to a law without adequate standards for officials may challenge it facially without the necessity of first applying for, and then being denied, a license or permit.[76]

Two years later, in an opinion of the Court by Justice O'Connor, joined by Justices Stevens and Kennedy, an ordinance regulating sexually-oriented businesses by licensing was voided because no time was prescribed within which applications for licenses must be acted upon. In such a licensing regulation, there must be, said the Court, "an effective limitation on the time within which the licensor's decision must be made." Additionally, the ordinance was unconstitutional because it failed "to provide an avenue for prompt judicial review so as to minimize suppression of speech in the event of a license denial." These three Justices felt that a city should not have to bear the burden of going to court to effect the denial of a license application, nor bear the burden of proof once in court. Justices Brennan, Marshall and Blackmun disagreed with the burden comments.[77]

Reaffirming two years later that "any permit scheme controlling the time, place and manner of speech must not be based on the content of the message, must be narrowly tailored to serve significant governmental interests and must leave open alternatives for communication," the Supreme Court held unconstitutional an assembly

---

75. Shuttlesworth v. City of Birmingham, Ala., 394 U.S. 147, 89 S. Ct. 935, 22 L. Ed. 2d 162 (1969).

76. City of Lakewood v. Plain Dealer Pub. Co., 486 U.S. 750, 108 S. Ct. 2138, 100 L. Ed. 2d 771 (1988).

77. FW/PBS, Inc. v. City of Dallas, 493 U.S. 215, 110 S. Ct. 596, 107 L. Ed. 2d 603 (1990).

and parade permit ordinance which allowed a government official to vary the fee to reflect the estimated cost of maintaining public order. There can be no "unbridled discretion in a government official," said the Court, because the peril of censorship is too great, and the amount of a fee cannot be tied, even indirectly, to the content of the speech.[78]

The Court held in 1953 that, where a state supreme court has ruled that it is obligatory upon a city to issue a license for religious services, persons desiring to use a park for such occasions have to pursue their remedies in the state courts for a license required by ordinance and arbitrarily or unreasonably denied by municipal officials. Failing to pursue such remedies and meeting in the park without a license, they could be convicted.[79]

When permits or licenses affecting exercise of First Amendment freedoms are denied unlawfully, mandamus or its local equivalent is customarily available to force the appropriate public official to grant the license or permit.[80]

Even where First Amendment freedoms are involved, governments can utilize permit and license requirements if (a) a significant societal interest would otherwise be seriously and imminently harmed; (b) no other method of adequately protecting that interest with less impact upon the First Amendment exists; (c) alternative avenues of expression are available for citizens seeking to express their First Amendment freedoms; (d) the legislation is narrowly tailored to reach only those aspects of the exercise of First Amendment rights which endanger the opposed societal interest; (e) there is an effective limitation on the time within which the licensor's decision must be made; (f) there is an opportunity for prompt judicial review of license or permit denials; (g) the burden is on the government to show why First Amendment values must be sacrificed in the particular instance; and (h) judicial review must be completed within a relatively short period of time.

Equal protection of the laws is involved when a government unfairly discriminates against either an individual or a group in

---

78. Forsyth County, Ga. v. Nationalist Movement, 505 U.S. 123, 112 S. Ct. 2395, 120 L. Ed. 2d 101, 75 Ed. Law Rep. 29 (1992).

79. Poulos v. State of N.H., 345 U.S. 395, 73 S. Ct. 760, 97 L. Ed. 1105, 30 A.L.R.2d 987 (1953).

80. People ex rel. Doyle v. Atwell, 232 N.Y. 96, 133 N.E. 364, 25 A.L.R. 107 (1921).

denying permits or licenses to exercise any of the First Amendment
freedoms.[81]

81. Niemotko v. State of Md., 340 U.S. 268, 71 S. Ct. 325, 95 L. Ed. 267, 271
(1951) (Jehovah's Witnesses denied use of park).

CHAPTER FOUR

The Supreme Court's Triad of Expressions, the "Pure," the "Not-So-Pure" and the "Impure"

---

§ 4.00. The impure

Albert Putney wrote in 1908 that Americans had traditionally considered undeserving of constitutional protection four forms of expression: "indecent" matter, libel and slander, blasphemy, and polygamy.[1] In 1957 the United States Supreme Court pointed out that of the fourteen states which had ratified the Constitution by 1792, "thirteen provided for the prosecution of libel, and all of them made either blasphemy or profanity, or both, statutory crimes," adding that in 1712 Massachusetts had made it criminal to publish "any filthy, obscene, or profane song, pamphlet, libel or mock sermon." On that occasion the Supreme Court ruled that obscenity is not deserving of constitutional protection, and gave us a suggestion of which forms of expression would be unprotected under the First Amendment—those, in the words of the Court, "utterly without redeeming social importance."[2] In the *Roth* case Justices Douglas and Black, in an opinion by the former, denied that any communication was beyond First Amendment protection, and they doubted that the members of the Court could wisely determine which utterances in society would have "no redeeming social importance."

Child pornography is sufficiently impure as to be beyond the protection of the First Amendment. In 1982 the Supreme Court

---

1. Albert Putney, *The United States Constitutional History and Law* (Chicago 1908) 361-62.

2. Roth v. U.S., 354 U.S. 476, 77 S. Ct. 1304, 1 L. Ed. 2d 1498, 14 Ohio Op. 2d 331 (1957).

stated that it recognized child pornography "as a category of material outside the protection of the First Amendment."[3]

In 1942 the Court had held that a state could ban and punish "words likely to cause the average addressee to fight," giving birth to the "fighting words" doctrine, and removing such utterances from First Amendment protection. In that case a Jehovah's Witness had told a town marshal: "You are a God-damned racketeer" and "a damned fascist," whereupon he was arrested. Speaking for the Court, Justice Murphy said:

> There are certain well-defined and narrowly limited classes of speech, the prevention and punishment of which have never been thought to raise any Constitutional problem. These include the lewd and obscene, the profane, the libelous, and the insulting or "fighting" words—those which by their very utterance inflict injury or tend to incite an immediate breach of the peace. It has been well observed that such utterances are no essential part of any exposition of ideas, and are of such light social value as a step to truth that any benefit that may be derived from them is clearly outweighed by the social interest in order and morality.[4]

It is suggested that the decision was unfortunate. "Fighting words" have been employed by presidents unappreciative of the work of certain music critics. Furthermore, the concept is so vague and unclear that no lawyer can adequately guide a client contemplating public speech. Today few, if any, Americans would fight when referred to as a "Mugwump." Should someone feel compelled to fight, society would do well to punish not the verbal, but the violent.

There is Supreme Court dictum in *Brandenburg v. Ohio* in 1969 that advocacy of the use of force or of a violation of the law "where such advocacy is directed to inciting or producing imminent lawless action and is likely to incite or produce such action," is not protected by the First Amendment.[5] The words have been approvingly quoted on a number of subsequent occasions.

Defamatory utterances and publications have been punishable for centuries, both at the common law and by statutes. The Supreme Court in 1922 found nothing in the First Amendment to prevent a

---

3. New York v. Ferber, 458 U.S. 747, 102 S. Ct. 3348, 73 L. Ed. 2d 1113 (1982).

4. Chaplinsky v. State of New Hampshire, 315 U.S. 568, 62 S. Ct. 766, 86 L. Ed. 1031, 1034-35 (1942).

5. Brandenburg v. Ohio, 395 U.S. 444, 89 S. Ct. 1827, 23 L. Ed. 2d 430, 434, 48 Ohio Op. 2d 320 (1969).

prosecution for libel.[6] Twenty years later the Court repeated that the "libelous" was not protected,[7] and again in 1952 the Court reaffirmed that "libelous utterances [are] not within the area of constitutionally protected speech."[8]

Undeserving of First Amendment protection, holds the Supreme Court, is "coercive speech." In 1969 the Court so characterized utterances by a business firm threatening reprisals or economic retaliation if the employees voted to unionize. The Court, however, recognized that "an employer's free speech right to communicate his views to his employees is firmly established," adding: "[t]hus, an employer is free to communicate to his employees any of his general views about unionism or any of his specific views about a particular union, so long as the communications do not contain a 'threat of reprisal or force or promise of benefit.' He may even make a prediction as to the precise effects he believes unionization will have on his company. In such a case, however, the prediction must be carefully phrased on the basis of objective fact to convey an employer's belief as to demonstrable probable consequences beyond his control or to convey a management decision already arrived at to close the plant in case of unionization."[9]

Secondary picketing, away from the immediate locus of an industrial dispute, is not protected communication under the First Amendment. In 1992 the Supreme Court reminded us the Court had "consistently rejected the claim that secondary picketing by labor unions in violation of [the National Labor Relations Act] is protected activity under the First Amendment." After noting that secondary picketing is not protected, the Court added: "It would seem even clearer that conduct designed not to communicate but to coerce merits still less consideration under the First Amendment." It then ruled beyond protection of the Amendment an attempted boycott by a labor union against a neutral party.[10]

---

6. Balzac v. Porto Rico, 258 U.S. 298, 42 S. Ct. 343, 66 L. Ed. 627 (1922).

7. Chaplinsky v. State of New Hampshire, 315 U.S. 568, 62 S. Ct. 766, 86 L. Ed. 1031 (1942).

8. Beauharnais v. People of State of Ill., 343 U.S. 250, 72 S. Ct. 725, 96 L. Ed. 919, 932 (1952).

9. N. L. R. B. v. Gissel Packing Co., 395 U.S. 575, 89 S. Ct. 1918, 23 L. Ed. 2d 547 (1969).

10. International Longshoremen's Ass'n, AFL-CIO v. Allied Intern., Inc., 456 U.S. 212, 227, 102 S. Ct. 1656, 72 L. Ed. 2d 21 (1982) (citing American Radio Ass'n, AFL-CIO v. Mobile S.S. Ass'n, Inc., 419 U.S. 215, 95 S. Ct. 409, 42 L. Ed. 2d 399 (1974); N. L. R. B. v. Retail Store Emp. Union, Local 1001, 447 U.S. 607, 100 S. Ct. 2372, 65 L. Ed. 2d 377 (1980)).

Threatening letters do not deserve First Amendment protection,[11] nor do treasonous speech or publications.[12] Comparably devoid of constitutional protection are certain kinds of prisoners' mail, such as "letters concerning escape plans or containing other information concerning proposed criminal activity, whether within or without the prison [as well as] encoded messages."[13] In 1989 the Supreme Court ruled that dancing by large numbers of patrons of a dance hall was not the kind of expressive conduct entitled to First Amendment protection.[14]

Content has been the prime determinant that certain expressions and communications are not entitled to First Amendment freedoms. Nevertheless, it should be appreciated that factors of both time and place can convert protected speech into "impure" speech not protected by the First and Fourteenth Amendments. In 1919, Justice Holmes, speaking for the Court, said: "When a nation is at war many things that might be said in time of peace are such a hindrance to its effort that their utterance will not be endured so long as men fight and that no Court could regard them as protected by any constitutional right."[15] In 1931, Chief Justice Hughes, speaking for the Court, quoted the above and then added: "No one would question but that a government might prevent actual obstruction to its recruiting service or the publication of the sailing dates of transports or the number and location of troops . . . "[16] Quoting this, Justice Stevens, speaking for the Court in 1976, stated: "The question whether speech is, or is not, protected by the First Amendment often depends on the context of the speech."[17]

Illustratively, while "vulgar" remarks have never been held without constitutional protection when uttered in public or in the White House, in 1986 the Court allowed school officials to suspend from school a student who had used such speech, on the premise

11. Watts v. U.S., 394 U.S. 705, 89 S. Ct. 1399, 22 L. Ed. 2d 664 (1969).

12. "Trafficking with the enemy, in whatever form, is wholly outside the shelter of the First Amendment. Congress may make criminal any type of dealing with the enemy . . . "; Chandler v. U.S., 171 F.2d 921, 939 (1st Cir. 1948).

13. Procunier v. Martinez, 416 U.S. 396, 94 S. Ct. 1800, 40 L. Ed. 2d 224, 240, 71 Ohio Op. 2d 139 (1974) (overruled on other grounds by, Thornburgh v. Abbott, 490 U.S. 401, 109 S. Ct. 1874, 104 L. Ed. 2d 459 (1989)).

14. City of Dallas v. Stanglin, 490 U.S. 19, 109 S. Ct. 1591, 104 L. Ed. 2d 18 (1989).

15. Schenck v. U.S., 249 U.S. 47, 39 S. Ct. 247, 63 L. Ed. 470 (1919).

16. Near v. State of Minnesota ex rel. Olson, 283 U.S. 697, 51 S. Ct. 625, 75 L. Ed. 1357 (1931).

17. Young v. American Mini Theatres, Inc., 427 U.S. 50, 96 S. Ct. 2440, 49 L. Ed. 2d 310, 323-24 (1976).

that it undermined the school's basic educational function. Justices Stevens and Marshall in dissent noted that on the facts the student's use of the words had not been disruptive of the educational program and that the student could not have known from the school rules that his expression was forbidden.[18]

§ 4.01. Pure speech

We turn to the "pure" speech categorization used by the Supreme Court,[19] while questioning whether such categorization is commonly a useful tool in the pursuit of wisdom. Apparently, expression is at its purist when it is, in the language of the Court, core political speech.[20] In 1988, as the Court voided a statute making it a crime to pay persons to circulate initiative petitions, the Court explaining: "The circulation of a petition involves the type of interactive communication concerning political change that is appropriately described as 'core political speech,'" adding that such a statute "trenches upon an area in which the importance of First Amendment protection is 'at the zenith.'"[21] In 1968, the Court had voided an election law making it virtually impossible for third parties to find a place on ballots, the Court speaking of "the right of individuals to associate for the advancement of political beliefs [as] among our most precious freedoms."[22]

Where "pure speech" is involved, this is not limited by the Supreme Court to oral and written communications. In 1976 the Court held that the use of funds to support a candidate for political office is "speech" and added that independent campaign expenditures constitute "political expression 'at the core of our political process and of the First Amendment freedoms.'"[23]

Where the topic involved is "politics," that is, the kind of government and laws we should be having, expressive conduct manifesting a citizen's views deserves protection. When a young man burned the United States flag in public to show his opposition to the government's policies of the moment, the Supreme Court in 1989 set aside

---

18. Bethel School Dist. No. 403 v. Fraser, 478 U.S. 675, 106 S. Ct. 3159, 92 L. Ed. 2d 549, 32 Ed. Law Rep. 1243 (1986).

19. Rankin v. McPherson, 483 U.S. 378, 107 S. Ct. 2891, 97 L. Ed. 2d 315 (1987).

20. Bigelow v. Virginia, 421 U.S. 809, 95 S. Ct. 2222, 44 L. Ed. 2d 600 (1975).

21. Meyer v. Grant, 486 U.S. 414, 108 S. Ct. 1886, 100 L. Ed. 2d 425, 435 (1988).

22. Williams v. Rhodes, 393 U.S. 23, 89 S. Ct. 5, 21 L. Ed. 2d 24, 45 Ohio Op. 2d 236 (1968).

23. Buckley v. Valeo, 424 U.S. 1, 96 S. Ct. 612, 46 L. Ed. 2d 659, 699 (1976).

his conviction. The Court ruled that a state "may not . . . proscribe particular conduct because it has expressive elements."[24] The next year the Court again voided a conviction of a citizen who burned the flag to show dissatisfaction with those temporarily in control of the federal government, the Court ruling that Congress cannot "criminally proscribe expressive conduct because of its likely communicative impact." Justice Brennan for the Court observed: "Punishing desecration of the flag dilutes the very freedom that makes this emblem so revered, and worth revering." While Justices Stevens, White, O'Connor and the Chief Justice dissented, they admitted that "reasonable judges may differ with respect to" the interest-balancing required in a case such as this.[25]

On occasion the Supreme Court has acknowledged, and properly, that the area of expression deserving of maximum First Amendment protection is broader than "political speech." In 1968 the Court ruled that we must have "free and uninhibited debate on matters of public concern,"[26] and the following year the Court reaffirmed "our profound commitment to the principles that debate on public issues should be uninhibited, robust and wide-open."[27] In 1943, when a citizen had spoken out against compulsory flag salutes and added that it is wrong to kill, his conviction was set aside by the Court, which could find no threat of "any clear and present danger to the institutions or government."[28] In 1983 the Court described the kind of expression most deserving of constitutional protection as that "relating to any matter of political, social or other concerns of the community."[29]

Just as in designating speech as impure, or beyond the pale, so, too, in defining the purity of preferred speech, note that the principal determining factor is content.

While engaged in categorizing some forms of expression as preferred under the First Amendment, the Court does well at times to acknowledge, with the American founding fathers,[30] that such components as freedom of speech and press are intended primarily

---

24. Texas v. Johnson, 491 U.S. 397, 109 S. Ct. 2533, 105 L. Ed. 2d 342 (1989).

25. U.S. v. Eichman, 496 U.S. 310, 110 S. Ct. 2404, 110 L. Ed. 2d 287 (1990).

26. Pickering v. Board of Ed. of Tp. High School Dist. 205, Will County, Illinois, 391 U.S. 563, 88 S. Ct. 1731, 20 L. Ed. 2d 811, 820 (1968).

27. Watts v. U.S., 394 U.S. 705, 89 S. Ct. 1399, 22 L. Ed. 2d 664, 667 (1969).

28. Taylor v. State of Mississippi, 319 U.S. 583, 63 S. Ct. 1200, 87 L. Ed. 1600 (1943).

29. Connick v. Myers, 461 U.S. 138, 103 S. Ct. 1684, 75 L. Ed. 2d 708 (1983).

30. Antieau, *Rights of Our Fathers* (Coiner Publications, Vienna, Virginia, 1968) 65 (John Adams), 67 (Jefferson).

not for the protection of speakers and publishers, but for the citizens of a free republic,[31] that their right to know must be respected—on everything political and on the world beyond politics, including matters of economic, social, scientific, literary, philosophical, artistic, or theological importance, ad infinitum. The Court must be recalled to its own language in 1969 when it stated: "It is well established that the Constitution protects the right to receive information and ideas. This right to receive information and ideas, regardless of their social worth, is fundamental to our free society."[32]

§ 4.02. The "not-so-pure" expressions

Supreme Court Justices acknowledge, seemingly reluctantly, that while certain expressions and communications cannot be completely stripped of First Amendment protections, these categories of speech are not going to be protected as thoroughly as their favorite "political" discussions.

In 1976 the Court held valid an ordinance requiring adult theaters to be situated beyond 500 feet from any residential zone and also beyond a 1,000 feet from any two other "regulated uses." Speaking for the Court, Justice Stevens wrote:

> Even though we recognize that the First Amendment will not tolerate the total suppression of erotic materials that have some arguably artistic value, it is manifest that society's interest in protecting this type of expression is of a wholly different, and lesser, magnitude than the interest in untrammeled political debate.[33]

Comparably, in 1941, the Supreme Court, in upholding a permit requirement for a parade by Jehovah's Witnesses, stated:

> We emphatically reject the notion urged here that the First and Fourteenth Amendments afford the same kind of freedom to those who would communicate by conduct, such as patrolling,

---

31. Smith v. People of the State of California, 361 U.S. 147, 80 S. Ct. 215, 4 L. Ed. 2d 205, 14 Ohio Op. 2d 459 (1959); Kingsley Intern. Pictures Corp. v. Regents of University of State of N.Y., 360 U.S. 684, 79 S. Ct. 1362, 3 L. Ed. 2d 1512 (1959).

32. Stanley v. Georgia, 394 U.S. 557, 89 S. Ct. 1243, 22 L. Ed. 2d 542, 549 (1969).

33. Young v. American Mini Theatres, Inc., 427 U.S. 50, 96 S. Ct. 2440, 49 L. Ed. 2d 310, 324 (1976).

marching and picketing on streets and highways, as these amendments afford to those who communicate by pure speech.[34]

Content of the expression or communication also plays a part in deciding whether it is a "not-so-pure" exercise of First Amendment freedom and, accordingly, deserving of somewhat lesser respect. Illustratively, when a public employee claimed that her First Amendment rights were denied where she was discharged because she circulated a petition at work, the Supreme Court in 1983 analyzed the petition, concluded that it was almost entirely devoted to the employee's private concerns, and reversed a judgment in the employee's favor. The Court noted its "long-standing recognition that the First Amendment's primary aim is the full protection of speech upon public concern," and ruled that "private" speech was far less deserving of that kind of protection. Said the Court:

> When employee expression cannot be fairly considered as relating to any matter of political, social or other concern to the community, government officials should enjoy wide latitude in managing their affairs, without intrusive oversight by the judiciary in the name of the First Amendment.[35]

Four years later four Supreme Court Justices described as "not of public concern" and easily outweighed by opposed societal interests remarks made in private by an individual after the attempted assassination of President Reagan that "If they go for him again, I hope they get him."[36]

While "pure" symbolic acts, such as patriotically saluting the flag or standing at attention during the playing of the national anthem, would readily be acknowledged as protected expressive conduct by the Court, the impression lingers that, to most members of the present tribunal, when freedom is manifested by action it is metamorphosed with alarming celerity into a very questionable First Amendment right. "We cannot," remarked the Court in 1968, "accept the view that an apparently limitless variety of conduct can be labelled 'speech' whenever the person engaging in the conduct intends thereby to express an idea."[37]

---

34. Cox v. State of New Hampshire, 312 U.S. 569, 61 S. Ct. 762, 85 L. Ed. 1049, 133 A.L.R. 1396 (1941).

35. Connick v. Myers, 461 U.S. 138, 103 S. Ct. 1684, 75 L. Ed. 2d 708 (1983).

36. Rankin v. McPherson, 483 U.S. 378, 107 S. Ct. 2891, 97 L. Ed. 2d 315 (1987).

37. U.S. v. O'Brien, 391 U.S. 367, 88 S. Ct. 1673, 20 L. Ed. 2d 672, 679 (1968).

§4.03. Commercial speech

Although the United States Supreme Court in 1942 ruled that "commercial" literature could be completely banned from a municipality,[38] the decision was unfortunate. There is nothing sinister about the distribution of newspapers and other printed matter sufficient to justify complete elimination from a city. The prime purpose of the First Amendment is to safeguard the right of the citizenry to read, and it should be obvious that even commercial publications contain much information and ideas to which the people are entitled.

In 1976 the Supreme Court repudiated the holding in *Valentine v. Chrestensen*. Emphasizing "the consumer's interest in the free flow of commercial information," the Court voided a statute prohibiting pharmacists from advertising the price of prescription drugs. "Commercial speech, like other varieties, is protected," said the Court, adding, however, that it can be regulated in some ways, and even prohibited when "false or misleading" or when actions urged in an advertisement are themselves illegal.[39]

The following year the Court held invalid as violative of the First Amendment a state ban upon lawyer advertising but repeated that "false, deceptive, or misleading" advertisements would be subject to control. The Court added: "As with other species of speech, it follows as well that there may be reasonable restrictions on time, place and manner of advertising."[40] The next year the Court reported that it had "afforded commercial speech a limited measure of protection, commensurate with its subordinate position in the scale of First Amendment values, while allowing modes of regulation that might be impermissible in the realm of non-commercial expression."[41] In 1982, the Court ruled that the First Amendment prohibits a state bar from banning non-misleading advertising by lawyers showing their specializations and listing the jurisdictions in which they are licensed to practice.[42]

The following year the Supreme Court indicated that "communications can constitute 'commercial speech' notwithstanding that they

---

38. Valentine v. Chrestensen, 316 U.S. 52, 62 S. Ct. 920, 86 L. Ed. 1262 (1942).

39. Virginia State Bd. of Pharmacy v. Virginia Citizens Consumer Council, Inc., 425 U.S. 748, 96 S. Ct. 1817, 48 L. Ed. 2d 346 (1976).

40. Bates v. State Bar of Arizona, 433 U.S. 350, 97 S. Ct. 2691, 53 L. Ed. 2d 810, 51 Ohio Misc. 1, 5 Ohio Op. 3d 60 (1977).

41. Ohralik v. Ohio State Bar Ass'n, 436 U.S. 447, 98 S. Ct. 1912, 56 L. Ed. 2d 444 (1978).

42. In re R. M. J., 455 U.S. 191, 102 S. Ct. 929, 71 L. Ed. 2d 64 (1982).

contain discussions of important public issues."[43] In 1985 the Court held that commercial speech that is not false or deceptive and does not concern unlawful activities may be restricted only in the service of a substantial interest, and only by means that directly advance that interest. The Court there voided disciplinary action against a lawyer who had used newspaper advertising, and it found equally wanting a ban upon the use of illustrations in such advertising by lawyers. However, the Court sustained application of a requirement that an attorney advertising his availability on a contingent fee basis disclose that clients will have to pay costs if their lawsuits are unsuccessful. It will be sufficient, added the Court that "disclosure requirements are reasonably related to the State's interest in preventing deception of consumers."[44] Reaffirming that lawyer advertising is in the category of constitutionally protected commercial speech, the Court in 1988 voided a state ban upon lawyers soliciting business by sending truthful and nondeceptive letters to potential clients known to face particular legal problems.[45]

In 1989 the Supreme Court sustained a ban by a state university of most private commercial enterprises on the campus, upholding action against a woman who desired to peddle "tupperware" at meetings held in dormitory rooms. The Court ruled that a governmental restriction on commercial speech is valid even if it goes beyond the least restrictive means to achieve a worthy interest of the government. In dissent, Justices Blackmun, Brennan and Marshall stated that the least restrictive means doctrine should be equally applicable to commercial speech.[46]

In voiding a state statute prohibiting the advertisement of retail liquor prices except at the place of sale, the Court described the statute as "a blatant prohibition against truthful, nonmisleading speech about a lawful product" that is "unrelated to consumer protection." While noting that a "reasonable fit" rule generally applies in commercial speech cases, the Court held there was no such fit between the state's abridgment of speech and its temperance goal. Of broader significance, the Court informed us that "the Twenty-first Amendment does not qualify the constitutional prohibition

---

43. Bolger v. Youngs Drug Products Corp., 463 U.S. 60, 67-68, 103 S. Ct. 2875, 77 L. Ed. 2d 469 (1983).

44. Zauderer v. Office of Disciplinary Counsel of Supreme Court of Ohio, 471 U.S. 626, 105 S. Ct. 2265, 85 L. Ed. 2d 652 (1985).

45. Shapero v. Kentucky Bar Ass'n, 486 U.S. 466, 108 S. Ct. 1916, 100 L. Ed. 2d 475 (1988).

46. Board of Trustees of State University of New York v. Fox, 492 U.S. 469, 109 S. Ct. 3028, 106 L. Ed. 2d 388, 54 Ed. Law Rep. 61 (1989).

against laws abridging the freedom of speech embraced in the First Amendment."[47]

The Court held in 1997 that the First Amendment's freedom of speech provision was not violated by the Agricultural Marketing Agreement Act, which authorized the Secretary of Agriculture to impose marketing orders on defined products, and included provisions imposing assessments upon all members of a marketing group benefitted by generic advertising, such as that beneficial to peach and nectarine growers. Four dissenters asserted that laws requiring individuals to engage in or pay for expressive activities are to be held constitutional only under the same rules applicable to individuals voluntarily engaging in First Amendment activities: namely, the government's interest must be substantial, and the regulation must directly advance such interest and be narrowly tailored to serve it.[48]

§ 4.04. Expressive conduct—symbolic acts

For over a half century the United States Supreme Court has acknowledged that symbolic actions conveying legal messages are protected by the First Amendment. In 1931 the Court held unconstitutional a state statute which made it a crime to display a flag "as a sign, symbol or emblem of opposition to organized government," which the state court interpreted to cover peaceful and orderly opposition by legal means to some state policy. Said the Court:

> The maintenance of the opportunity for free political discussion to the end that government may be responsive to the will of the people and that changes may be obtained by lawful means, an opportunity essential to the security of the Republic, is a fundamental principle of our constitutional system.[49]

Correlatively, governments cannot require adults or children to perform symbolic acts expressing particular sentiments, to which they have religious or philosophical objections. When in 1943 West Virginia attempted to exclude from the public schools children who could not in conscience participate in a flag salute, the Supreme Court voided the statute. Justice Jackson, speaking for the Court, said:

---

47. 44 Liquormart, Inc. v. Rhode Island, 116 S. Ct. 1495, 134 L. Ed. 2d 711 (U.S. 1996).

48. Glickman v. Wileman Bros. & Elliott, Inc., 117 S. Ct. 2130, 138 L. Ed. 2d 585 (U.S. 1997).

49. Stromberg v. People of State of Cal., 283 U.S. 359, 51 S. Ct. 532, 75 L. Ed. 1117, 73 A.L.R. 1484 (1931).

> If there is any fixed star in our constitutional constellation, it is that no official, high or petty, can prescribe what shall be orthodox in politics, nationalism, religion, or any other matters of opinion or force citizens to confess by word or act their faith therein.[50]

In 1966 the Court held constitutional a sit-in at a public library to encourage desegregation, finding it to be a symbolic act protected by the First Amendment. The Court clearly stated that First Amendment rights "are not confined to verbal expression. They embrace appropriate types of action which certainly include the right in a peaceable and orderly manner to protest by silent and reproachful presence, in a place where the protestant has every right to be, the unconstitutional segregation of public facilities."[51]

However, blanket protection for peaceful symbolic acts ended abruptly in 1968 when a person who burned his Selective Service registration certificate on the steps of a courthouse was convicted of violating an act of Congress and the Supreme Court sustained the conviction, stating, inter alia: "We cannot accept the view that an apparently limitless variety of conduct can be labelled 'speech' whenever the person engaged in the conduct intends thereby to express an idea." The Court observed, without citations, that it "has held that when 'speech' and 'nonspeech' elements are combined in the same course of conduct, a sufficiently important governmental interest in regulating the nonspeech element can justify incidental limitations on First Amendment freedoms." The appropriate rule in "speech plus" situations, thought the Court, should be this:

> A government regulation is sufficiently justified if it is within the constitutional power of the government; if it furthers an important or substantial governmental interest; if the governmental interest is unrelated to the suppression of free expression; and if the incidental restriction on alleged First Amendment freedom is no greater than is essential to the furtherance of that interest.[52]

Justice Harlan, in a concurring opinion, explained that the Court's ruling: "does not foreclose consideration of First Amendment claims in those rare instances when an 'incidental' restriction upon expres-

---

50. West Virginia State Board of Education v. Barnette, 319 U.S. 624, 642, 63 S. Ct. 1178, 87 L. Ed. 1628, 147 A.L.R. 674 (1943).

51. Brown v. State of La., 383 U.S. 131, 86 S. Ct. 719, 15 L. Ed. 2d 637, 645 (1966).

52. U.S. v. O'Brien, 391 U.S. 367, 88 S. Ct. 1673, 20 L. Ed. 2d 672, 680 (1968).

sion, imposed by a regulation which furthers an 'important or substantial' governmental interest and satisfies the Court's other criteria, in practice has the effect of entirely preventing a 'speaker' from reaching a significant audience with whom he could not otherwise lawfully communicate. This is not such a case, since O'Brien manifestly could have conveyed his message in many ways other than by burning his draft card." It is suggested that the ruling of the Court is unworthy. In balancing societal interests, First Amendment values demand proof that the opposed societal (not "governmental") interest would be seriously impaired by the form of expression, and surely the draft would have gone on without material impairment after the burning of the draft card.

The following year, when a person burned the American flag after hearing that the civil rights leader, James Meredith, had been shot and killed in Mississippi, and then shouted: "If they did that to Meredith, we don't need an American flag," the Court set aside a conviction after concluding that the malicious mischief charge against the defendant could have been based entirely on his words. In dissent Chief Justice Warren, as well as Justices Black, White and Fortas believed that the real issue was burning the flag, which they viewed as an unprotected symbolic act.[53]

That same year (1969) the Court voided a school board suspension of a student for wearing a black armband to school to express his opposition to the Vietnam war. The Court stated that "the wearing of an armband for the purpose of expressing certain views is the type of symbolic act that is within the Free Speech Clause of the First Amendment." Such act, said the Court, "was closely akin to 'pure speech' which, we have repeatedly held, is entitled to comprehensive protection under the First Amendment." By way of dictum, however, the Court volunteered that it "read the First Amendment to permit reasonable regulation of speech-connected activities in carefully restricted circumstances."[54] If symbolic acts are closely akin to pure speech, it nevertheless appears the Court unfortunately is willing to allow any regulation so long as "reasonable," a test long ago found unworthy and insufficiently protective of First Amendment values.

In 1974 the Supreme Court reversed a conviction of a college student who hung a United States flag upside down outside his apartment window, with a peace symbol of black tape attached to the flag. Said the Court: "Given the protected character of his

---

53. Street v. New York, 394 U.S. 576, 89 S. Ct. 1354, 22 L. Ed. 2d 572 (1969).

54. Tinker v. Des Moines Independent Community School Dist., 393 U.S. 503, 89 S. Ct. 733, 21 L. Ed. 2d 731, 49 Ohio Op. 2d 222 (1969).

expression and in light of the fact that no interest the State may have in preserving the physical integrity of a privately-owned flag was significantly impaired on these facts, the conviction must be invalidated."[55]

In 1989 the Court reminded us that the term "speech" as used in the First Amendment has, for a long time, been understood to protect expression in forms other than the spoken or written word, and ruled that a state can not convict a person for burning the flag. A state, ruled the Court, "may not . . . proscribe particular conduct because it has expressive elements," and held that public protest by burning the United States flag cannot be punished as a crime.[56] The following year, when the government acknowledged that a defendant's conduct in burning the flag constituted expressive conduct, and the Court found that the government's asserted interest is related to the suppression of free expression, the Court held that Congress cannot "criminally proscribe expressive conduct because of its likely communicative impact," and ruled violative of the First Amendment the Congressional Flag Protection Act of 1989 when used as a basis for prosecution of a citizen who burned a flag to express his dissatisfaction with the government. Said Justice Brennan for the Court: "Punishing desecration of the flag dilutes the very freedom that makes this emblem so revered, and worth revering."[57]

---

55. Spence v. State of Wash., 418 U.S. 405, 94 S. Ct. 2727, 41 L. Ed. 2d 842 (1974).

56. Texas v. Johnson, 491 U.S. 397, 109 S. Ct. 2533, 105 L. Ed. 2d 342 (1989).

57. U.S. v. Eichman, 496 U.S. 310, 110 S. Ct. 2404, 110 L. Ed. 2d 287 (1990).

PART TWO

RESOLVING CLASHES BETWEEN SOCIETAL INTERESTS IN FIRST AMENDMENT FREEDOMS AND OTHER IMPORTANT SOCIETAL INTERESTS

CHAPTER FIVE

Society's Interest in Protecting Peace, Good Order and Safety

§ 5.19. Legislative power of Congress under the Fourteenth
Amendment relative to First Amendment

---

§ 5.00. Distributing literature

Local communities at times feel that they have worthy interests in
protecting their streets and sidewalks from being littered with cast
aside handbills and tracts, in protecting the purse of their people
from charges and contributions often connected with the proffer of
sundry forms of literature, and in protecting the citizens from being
annoyed by distributors of printed matter.

The conflict between such interests and the societal interest in
freedom of communication has now been resolved by the United
States Supreme Court in a number of instances. In 1938 the Court
held invalid on its face an ordinance prohibiting the distribution of
literature of any kind at any time or place without a permit from
the city manager, who was given no standards to apply in granting
or denying the license.[1] The following year the Court passed upon
four ordinances from various parts of the country, in a case reported
as *Schneider v. Town of Irvington,* and ruled that local communities
cannot completely prohibit the distribution of religious, economic,
or philosophical literature upon their streets. "The streets are natural
and proper places for the dissemination of information and opinion,"
said the Court. The Court added:

> We are of opinion that the purpose to keep the streets clean
> and of good appearance is insufficient to justify an ordinance
> which prohibits a person rightfully on a public street from
> handing literature to one willing to receive it. Any burden
> imposed upon the city authorities in cleaning and caring for the
> streets as an indirect consequence of such distribution results
> from the constitutional protection of the speech and press. This
> constitutional protection does not deprive a city of all power to
> prevent littering. Among these is the punishment of those who
> actually throw papers on the streets.

By way of dictum, the Court added:

> Municipal authorities, as trustees for the public, have the duty
> to keep their communities' streets open and available for move-
> ment of people and property, the primary purpose to which the

---

1. Lovell v. City of Griffin, Ga., 303 U.S. 444, 58 S. Ct. 666, 82 L. Ed. 949,
954 (1938).

---

streets are dedicated. So long as legislation to this end does not abridge the constitutional liberty of one rightfully on the street to impart information through speech or the distribution of literature, it may lawfully regulate the conduct of those using the streets. For example, a person could not exercise this liberty by taking his stand in the middle of a crowded street, contrary to traffic regulations, and maintain his position to the stoppage of all traffic; a group of distributors could not insist upon a constitutional right to form a cordon across the street and to allow no pedestrian to pass who did not accept a tendered leaflet; nor does the guarantee of freedom of speech or of the press deprive a municipality of power to enact regulations against throwing literature broadcast in the streets.[2]

In 1942 the Supreme Court ill-advisedly ruled that "commercial literature" could be completely banned from a municipality.[3] The prime purpose of the constitutional freedom of the press is to honor the right of the citizen to know, to have information and ideas, and it is clear by now that "commercial" publications provide such material. In 1976 the decision in *Valentine v. Chrestensen* was, in effect, overruled, and it was established that commercial speech deserves at least some degree of constitutional protection.[4] The following year, the Court held that a wholesale ban on advertising violated both the public's right to know and the First Amendment rights of lawyers who desired to advertise. The Court indicated that, while professional advertising may be closely yet reasonably regulated, attorneys cannot be prevented from indicating the prices at which they will perform routine legal services in public advertisements. Interestingly, the overbreadth doctrine was considered inappropriate to apply to instances of professional advertising since, as commercial speech, it is unlikely to be crushed by overbroad regulation. After carefully examining the advertisement, the Court ruled it could not be suppressed.[5]

The Supreme Court held in 1989 that a governmental restriction on commercial speech is valid even it goes beyond the least restric-

---

2. Schneider v. State of New Jersey, Town of Irvington, 308 U.S. 147, 60 S. Ct. 146, 84 L. Ed. 155, 166 (1939).

3. Valentine v. Chrestensen, 316 U.S. 52, 62 S. Ct. 920, 86 L. Ed. 1262 (1942).

4. Virginia State Bd. of Pharmacy v. Virginia Citizens Consumer Council, Inc., 425 U.S. 748, 96 S. Ct. 1817, 48 L. Ed. 2d 346 (1976).

5. Bates v. State Bar of Arizona, 433 U.S. 350, 97 S. Ct. 2691, 53 L. Ed. 2d 810, 51 Ohio Misc. 1, 5 Ohio Op. 3d 60 (1977).

tive means to achieve the desired end, if it is reasonable and narrowly tailored to achieve the desired objective.[6]

Observing that "any prior restraint on expression comes to this Court with a heavy presumption against its constitutional validity," the Court in 1971 set aside a state court injunction restraining a community organization from distributing literature anywhere in a particular city. The organization had distributed pamphlets criticizing a real estate broker's practices that the organization claimed constituted "blockbusting" or "panic peddling."[7] In 1983 the Court held unconstitutional a federal statute in effect banning the distribution of leaflets on sidewalks surrounding the grounds of the Supreme Court. By way of dictum, the Court indicated that reasonable time, place, and manner restrictions on distribution would be valid.[8]

The Supreme Court has held violative of the First Amendment Cincinnati's refusal to allow a business to distribute commercial publications through freestanding newsracks located on public property. The Court in 1993 indicated that in such cases the city has the burden to establish a reasonable fit between its legitimate interests in safety and esthetics and its enactment of a limited and selective prohibition of newsracks as the means chosen to serve these interests. Newsracks on public property, said the Court, "continue to play a significant role in the dissemination of protected speech." Justice Blackmun, concurring, would have preferred a rule giving commercial speech full First Amendment protection.[9]

The United States has a long history of using and treasuring anonymous publications. The Supreme Court in 1960 declared void on its face an ordinance prohibiting the distribution of handbills that did not have printed on the cover or the face thereof the names and addresses of the persons preparing and distributing the handbills. Justice Black, author of the opinion for the Court, reminded us that "anonymous pamphlets, leaflets, brochures and even books have played an important role in the progress of mankind," and added that "identification and fear of reprisal might deter perfectly peaceful discussions of public matters of importance." He recalled that the arguments favoring ratification of our Constitution were published under fictitious names, as was the case with the

---

6. Board of Trustees of State University of New York v. Fox, 492 U.S. 469, 109 S. Ct. 3028, 106 L. Ed. 2d 388, 54 Ed. Law Rep. 61 (1989).

7. Organization for a Better Austin v. Keefe, 402 U.S. 415, 91 S. Ct. 1575, 29 L. Ed. 2d 1 (1971).

8. U.S. v. Grace, 461 U.S. 171, 103 S. Ct. 1702, 75 L. Ed. 2d 736 (1983).

9. City of Cincinnati v. Discovery Network, Inc., 507 U.S. 410, 113 S. Ct. 1505, 123 L. Ed. 2d 99 (1993).

Federalist Papers. He recalled for us that "persecuted groups and sects from time to time throughout history" have utilized anonymous publications to criticize suppressive laws and practices by those in power.[10]

In 1995 the Supreme Court voided as violative of the First Amendment a state statute prohibiting the distribution of anonymous campaign literature. Communications discussing public issues and the qualifications of candidates, said the Court, are "the core of the protection afforded by the First Amendment," and all restraints on them will be subject to exacting scrutiny. The Court reported generally that "the anonymity of an author is not ordinarily a sufficient reason to exclude [the author's] work product from the protection of the First Amendment."[11]

§ 5.01. Parading and marching

Many religious groups, such as the Salvation Army, as well as other organizations, have utilized parades and marches as part of their proselytizing activities and social protests. Signs, placards, and banners carried in such processions can be communicative and informative to bystanders. On the other hand, local communities think at times that such activity is inconsistent with other interests, insofar as it can cause inconvenience, noise, traffic disruptions, and breaches of the peace.

In 1941 the United States Supreme Court sustained a licensing requirement as a precondition to parades. In so doing, it upheld the conviction of Jehovah's Witnesses who in 4 or 5 groups of 15 to 20 marched single file down a sidewalk in Manchester, New Hampshire, in the early evening hours. The state court had noted that advance notice of a parade was necessary so as to afford opportunity for proper policing, and had interpreted the statute as giving all citizens the right to a parade license without arbitrary interference by any public official whenever "the convenience of the public in the use of the streets would not thereby be unduly disturbed." In an opinion by Chief Justice Hughes, the Court stated:

> The authority of a municipality to impose regulations in order to assure the safety and convenience of the people to the use of public highways has never been regarded as inconsistent with civil liberties but rather as one of the means of safeguarding the

---

10. Talley v. California, 362 U.S. 60, 80 S. Ct. 536, 538-39, 4 L. Ed. 2d 559 (1960).

11. McIntyre v. Ohio Elections Com'n, 514 U.S. 334, 115 S. Ct. 1511, 131 L. Ed. 2d 426, 439, 440, 446 (1995).

good order upon which they ultimately depend. The control of travel on the streets of cities is the most familiar illustration of this recognition of social need. Where a restriction of the use of highways in that relation is designed to promote the public convenience in the interest of all, it cannot be disregarded by the attempted exercise of some civil right which in other circumstances would be entitled to protection. One would not be justified in ignoring the familiar red traffic light because he thought it his religious duty to disobey the municipal command or sought by that means to direct public attention to an announcement of his opinions.

The Court additionally held that a license fee reasonably limited to the cost of policing the occasion, and not as a revenue measure, was not contrary to the Constitution.[12]

In 1969 the Court held invalid an ordinance requiring a permit for a parade or procession or other public demonstration and giving to members of a city commission absolute power to refuse a parade permit whenever they thought "the public welfare, peace, safety, health, decency, good order, morals or convenience required that it be refused." The Court stated: "A law subjecting the exercise of First Amendment freedoms to the prior restraint of a license, without narrow, objective and definite standards to guide the licensing authority, is unconstitutional." The Court added: "Our decisions have made clear that a person faced with such an unconstitutional licensing law may ignore it and engage with impunity in the exercise of the right of free expression for which the law purports to require a license."[13]

State courts have overwhelmingly held that local governments cannot totally ban all parades and marches on the public streets and sidewalks. The Illinois Supreme Court is typical in stating:

Parades and processions on the streets of a city are not necessarily productive of danger and disorder so as to render them per se the creators of public disturbance; nor are they necessarily nuisances. There is no authority, therefore, in the municipal corporations to suppress such demonstrations of all kinds, at all times, and under all circumstances. Citizens have the constitutional right of "pursuing their own happiness," and on suitable occasions, and for lawful purposes, and in a peaceable manner

---

12. Cox v. State of New Hampshire, 312 U.S. 569, 61 S. Ct. 762, 85 L. Ed. 1049, 1052-53, 133 A.L.R. 1396 (1941).

13. Shuttlesworth v. City of Birmingham, Ala., 394 U.S. 147, 89 S. Ct. 935, 22 L. Ed. 2d 162 (1969).

they may gather together in street parades and processions, if they so desire, or provided they do not disturb or threaten the public peace, or substantially interfere with the rights of others.[14]

There is some support for the proposition that parades of masked individuals in the public streets can be outlawed.[15]

Where permits or licenses are demanded for parades and marches, they cannot be denied arbitrarily, that is, they cannot be refused unless it is certain that the contemplated procession will clearly and imminently seriously interfere with another societal interest, such as preservation of peace, good order, and safety:

> It is also well established that peaceful, orderly expressions of views—through marches, demonstrations or otherwise—cannot be prohibited, or otherwise interfered with merely because the views expressed may be so unpopular at the time as to stir the public to anger, invite dispute, and thus create, or appear to the public authorities to create, unrest or even disturbance. . . . Under such circumstances suppression by public authorities or police of the right of free speech and assembly cannot be made an easy substitute for the performance of their duty to maintain order by taking such steps as may be reasonably necessary and feasible to protect peaceable, orderly speakers, marchers or demonstrators in the exercise of their rights against violence or disorderly retaliation or attack at the hands of those who may disagree and object.[16]

A disorderly conduct conviction of marchers was reversed by the Supreme Court in 1969 when it could find no proof in the record that the petitioners' conduct was disorderly. The Court reminded us that such convictions, when so totally devoid of evidentiary support, violate due process of law.[17]

When Massachusetts courts, applying a statute forbidding discrimination in places of public accommodation on the basis of sexual orientation, had held that a group of individuals of Irish ancestry could not exclude from a St. Patrick's Day parade another group of Irish ancestry who identified themselves as gay and lesbian, the United States Supreme Court reversed. In an unanimous opinion,

---

14. City of Chicago v. Trotter, 136 Ill. 430, 26 N.E. 359 (1891).

15. City of Pineville v. Marshall, 222 Ky. 4, 299 S.W. 1072 (1927).

16. Hurwitt v. City of Oakland, 247 F. Supp. 995, 1000-01 (N.D. Cal. 1965).

17. Gregory v. City of Chicago, 394 U.S. 111, 89 S. Ct. 946, 22 L. Ed. 2d 134 (1969).

the Court ruled that a state may not require a group sponsoring a parade to allow among the marchers another group with a message the organizing group did not want to convey. There is, said the Court, a fundamental right of protection under the First Amendment of the principle that "a speaker has the autonomy to choose the content of his own message."[18]

§ 5.02. Picketing, boycotts, and demonstrations

Picketing can be a lawful form of communication. However, local communities have at times thought that picketing can jeopardize societal interests in peace, good order, and safety, by leading to altercations between pickets and employers, between pickets and workers, between pickets and persons making deliveries, as well as between pickets and customers who are not inclined to honor a picket line.

In 1940, for the first time, the United States Supreme Court ruled that picketing was a form of expression and as such to be protected under the First Amendment. In the *Thornhill* case the Court held that absolute bans upon picketing in a community were unconstitutional, and this remains the law today. In so holding, the Court applied its then prevalent clear and present danger test, finding no such peril from the facts of the case.[19] Initially the Court gave local communities a good deal of leeway in controlling picketing under an "unlawful purpose" doctrine.[20]

In 1968 the Court held that peaceful picketing could not be completely banned by owners of a large shopping center, where the center was generally open to all the public and served the function of a community business area, bringing it within the concept of "state action," and making the Fourteenth Amendment applicable. Said the Court: "Peaceful picketing carried on in a location open generally to the public is, absent other factors involving the purpose or manner of that picketing, protected by the First Amendment."[21]

Four years later, however, the Court ruled that the principle of *Logan Valley* did not give to union organizers soliciting members

---

18. Hurley v. Irish-American Gay, Lesbian and Bisexual Group of Boston, 515 U.S. 557, 115 S. Ct. 2338, 132 L. Ed. 2d 487 (1995).

19. Thornhill v. State of Alabama, 310 U.S. 88, 60 S. Ct. 736, 84 L. Ed. 1093 (1940).

20. Hughes v. Superior Court of Cal. in and for Contra Costa County, 339 U.S. 460, 70 S. Ct. 718, 42, 94 L. Ed. 985, 42 Ohio Op. 80, 57 Ohio L. Abs. 298 (1950).

21. Amalgamated Food Emp. Union Local 590 v. Logan Valley Plaza, Inc., 391 U.S. 308, 88 S. Ct. 1601, 20 L. Ed. 2d 603, 45 Ohio Op. 2d 181 (1968).

the right to conduct their activities on the parking lot of a large hardware store. It is only when private property "has assumed to some significant degree the functional attributes of public property devoted to public use," held the Court, that it qualifies as "state action" and subject to the Fourteenth Amendment.[22] The same year the Court, in a five-to-four decision, held that a large, privately-owned shopping center with 60 commercial tenants and 50 acres of land could, whenever it desired, ban the distribution on its premises of literature unrelated to the affairs of stores within the shopping center. The four dissenters found no constitutional difference in the fact that here speech was directed at topics of general interest, whereas the speech in *Logan Valley* was directed to the activities of a store in that shopping center. The majority opinion indicated that a store, as private property, does not assume significant public attributes because the public generally is invited to use it for designated purposes and, further, that size alone does not bring it within the *Logan Valley* concept.[23]

Beginning in 1949 the Supreme Court has generally refrained from applying the clear and present danger formula in picketing cases. Rather, in that year the Court began allowing states and their political subdivisions to ban picketing for "unlawful purposes."[24] The Court has accorded to state legislatures and courts a good deal of deference on what are proper "unlawful purposes." Many of the decisions, it is suggested, represent totally unwarranted and unnecessary abridgment of communicative freedoms, where on the facts there was nothing approximating a clear and present danger of substantive evil from the activities of the citizens involved.[25]

Picketing has been looked upon by the Court as something less deserving of constitutional protection than what it refers to, somewhat vaguely, as "pure speech." Illustratively, in 1965, the Court stated:

> We emphatically reject the notion urged by appellant that the First and Fourteenth Amendments afford the same kind of freedom to those who would communicate by conduct such as

22. Central Hardware Co. v. N.L.R.B., 407 U.S. 539, 92 S. Ct. 2238, 33 L. Ed. 2d 122 (1972).

23. Lloyd Corp., Limited v. Tanner, 407 U.S. 551, 92 S. Ct. 2219, 33 L. Ed. 2d 131 (1972).

24. Giboney v. Empire Storage & Ice Co., 336 U.S. 490, 69 S. Ct. 684, 93 L. Ed. 834 (1949).

25. E.g., Hughes v. Superior Court of Cal. in and for Contra Costa County, 339 U.S. 460, 70 S. Ct. 718, 94 L. Ed. 985, 42 Ohio Op. 80, 57 Ohio L. Abs. 298 (1950).

patrolling, marching, and picketing on streets and highways, as these amendments afford to those who communicate by pure speech.[26]

That same year, the Court reversed a conviction of individuals who had picketed near a courthouse because local officials had led the demonstrators to believe they could legally assemble where they did. The Court, however, indicated with clarity that statutes and ordinances can constitutionally keep demonstrators away from courthouses when judicial business is under way. Said the Court: "A narrowly drawn statute such as the one under review is obviously a safeguard both necessary and appropriate to vindicate the State's interest in assuring justice under law."[27]

In 1968 the Supreme Court upheld, over claims of vagueness, a state statute prohibiting "picketing in such a manner as to obstruct or unreasonably interfere with free ingress or egress to and from any country courthouses" and other public buildings. Said the Court: "Any chilling effect on the picketing as a form of protest and expression that flows from good-faith enforcement of this valid statute would not, of course, constitute that enforcement an impermissible invasion of protected freedoms." Relief under this ruling requires proof by plaintiffs "that the statute was enforced against them with no expectation of convictions but only to discourage exercise of protected rights."[28]

Violent picketing can be banned and punished.[29] Furthermore, picketing can be limited to the scenes of industrial or other disputes.[30] The Court in 1973 held not preempted by the National Labor Relations Act nor the First Amendment Alabama's enjoining of peaceful, but secondary, picketing by American seamen at Mobile docks protesting the use of foreign carriers at wages substantially lower than those paid American seamen.[31]

Not facially invalid was an ordinance banning picketing "before or about" any residence, ruled the Supreme Court in 1988. An anti-abortion group had picketed the residence of a medical doctor who

---

26. Cox v. State of Louisiana, 379 U.S. 536, 85 S. Ct. 453, 13 L. Ed. 2d 471, 474 (1965).

27. Cox v. State of La., 379 U.S. 559, 85 S. Ct. 476, 13 L. Ed. 2d 487 (1965).

28. Cameron v. Johnson, 390 U.S. 611, 88 S. Ct. 1335, 20 L. Ed. 2d 182 (1968).

29. Milk Wagon Drivers Union of Chicago, Local 753 v. Meadowmoor Dairies, 312 U.S. 287, 61 S. Ct. 552, 85 L. Ed. 836, 132 A.L.R. 1200 (1941).

30. Carpenters and Joiners Union of America, Local No. 213 v. Ritter's Cafe, 315 U.S. 722, 62 S. Ct. 807, 86 L. Ed. 1143 (1942).

31. American Radio Ass'n, AFL-CIO v. Mobile S.S. Ass'n, 419 U.S. 215, 95 S. Ct. 409, 42 L. Ed. 2d 399 (1974).

was thought to do abortions in other communities nearby. The public streets, acknowledged the Court, are "the archetype of a traditional public forum," but emphasized that the law recognizes a substantial interest in protecting privacy, and, further, that the protesters had ample alternative channels of communication. In dissent, Justices Brennan, Marshall and Stevens found the ordinance overbroad and not as narrowly tailored as it could have been with more exact and limited size, time, volume, etc., controls.[32]

The Court ruled in 1969 that peaceful picketing by railroad employees, whether primary or secondary, cannot be proscribed by the states until Congress acts.[33]

Pickets can be prohibited from obstructing the free use of the streets and sidewalks adjacent to an establishment being picketed, and from interfering with free ingress and egress to and from that property.[34]

The Supreme Court has held unconstitutional, as violative of equal protection of the laws, an ordinance prohibiting picketing near schools but permitting labor picketing when a school is involved in a labor dispute.[35]

Secondary boycotts have been banned by Congress in the field of labor relations in the National Labor Relations Act § 8(b)(4)(B), and application of that statute does not violate the First Amendment rights of unions or their members. The Supreme Court stated in 1982: "Undoubtedly many secondary boycotts have the object of freeing employees from handling goods from an objectionable source. Nevertheless, when a purely secondary boycott reasonably can be expected to threaten neutral parties with ruin or substantial loss . . . application of 8(b)(4) will not infringe the First Amendment rights of the ILA [International Longshoremen's Assn.] and its members." The Court added: "We have consistently rejected the claim that secondary picketing by labor unions in violation of 8(b)(4) is protected activity under the First Amendment. It would seem even clearer that conduct designed not to communicate but to coerce merits still less consideration under the First Amendment. There are many ways in which a union and its individual members may express

32. Frisby v. Schultz, 487 U.S. 474, 108 S. Ct. 2495, 101 L. Ed. 2d 420 (1988).

33. Brotherhood of R.R. Trainmen v. Jacksonville Terminal Co., 394 U.S. 369, 89 S. Ct. 1109, 22 L. Ed. 2d 344 (1969).

34. Youngdahl v. Rainfair, Inc., 355 U.S. 131, 78 S. Ct. 206, 2 L. Ed. 2d 151 (1957).

35. Police Dept. of City of Chicago v. Mosley, 408 U.S. 92, 92 S. Ct. 2286, 33 L. Ed. 2d 212 (1972).

their opposition to Russian foreign policy without infringing upon the rights of others."[36]

Boycotts, not of labor strife origins, but of persons desiring to express their views on political, economic, or social matters of public concern stand on a different level. In the same year as the foregoing decision, the Supreme Court ruled that a boycott by African Americans of white merchants in the community, designed to achieve racial equality and integration, was protected by constitutional rights of speech, assembly, association, and petition. Fully protected by the First Amendment, said the Court, are persons who peacefully seek "to bring about political, social and economic change" by boycott.[37] When anti-abortion demonstrators were protesting around an abortion clinic, a state court enjoined the demonstrators from blocking or interfering with public access to the clinic, and from physically abusing persons entering or leaving it. Later, when the demonstrators continued, the court issued an amended order excluding the demonstrators from a 36-foot buffer zone around the clinic driveway and entrances, as well as private property on the back and side of the clinic. The order also banned excessive noise, and displaying "images observable" to persons in the clinic; as well as creating a 300-foot buffer zone around the clinic in which demonstrators were not to approach persons unless they "indicated a desire to communicate." The Supreme Court in 1994 held constitutional the buffer zone around the entrance to the clinic, indicating that this "burdens no more speech than necessary to accomplish the governmental interest at stake." However, it voided that part of the order applicable to the back and side of the clinic, since it burdened "more speech than necessary to protect access to the clinic." The noise restrictions were sustained since necessary to protect the health and well-being of the occupants of the clinic. However, the ban on showing "images observable" outside the clinic was voided since patients and others in the clinic could adequately protect themselves by pulling down the shades. Unconstitutional was the ban upon approaching persons within 300 feet of the clinic, since it "burdens more speech than is necessary to prevent intimidation and to ensure access to the clinic." Also voided was a provision prohibiting picketing, demonstrating and using sound amplification equipment within 300 feet of the residences of the clinic staff, since the Court concluded banning pickets from a

---

36. International Longshoremen's Ass'n, AFL-CIO v. Allied Intern., Inc., 456 U.S. 212, 227, 102 S. Ct. 1656, 72 L. Ed. 2d 21 (1982).

37. N. A. A. C. P. v. Claiborne Hardware Co., 458 U.S. 886, 102 S. Ct. 3409, 73 L. Ed. 2d 1215, 1235 (1982).

much smaller zone would have sufficed. A provision of the order prohibiting respondents from acting in concert with others to close off the sole access to streets on which employees of the clinic lived was attacked by respondents as violating their freedom of association, but the Supreme Court explained that "The freedom of association protected by the First Amendment does not extend to joining with others for the purpose of depriving third parties of their lawful rights."[38]

Three years later the Court had before it a temporary restraining order enjoining anti-abortion protesters from physically blockading clinics providing access to family planning and abortion services, physically abusing or tortiously harassing anyone entering or leaving the clinics, or "demonstrating within 15 feet of any person entering or leaving the clinics." As an exception to this 15-foot "buffer zone," the restraining order allowed two sidewalk counselors to "have a conversation of a non-threatening nature" with persons leaving or entering the clinic. If the individuals indicated they did not want such counseling, however, the counselors had to "cease and desist" their efforts. The Court struck down the floating buffer zones around people entering and leaving the clinics because "they burden more speech than is necessary to serve the relevant governmental interests." Comparably, the Court voided a 15-foot buffer zone around vehicles entering or leaving the area. However, the Court upheld fixed buffer zones around the doorways, driveways, and driveway entrances. "These buffer zones," said the Court, "are necessary to ensure that people and vehicles trying to enter or exit the clinic property or clinic parking lots can do so."[39]

The petitioners argued unsuccessfully that the term "demonstrating" in the order was impermissibly vague, but the Court held that when the injunction was read as a whole, persons "of ordinary intelligence" had been given "a reasonable opportunity to know what is prohibited." The Court concluded by reminding us that in America there is no constitutional basis of any generalized right "to be left alone" on a public street or sidewalk and that "the entire exception for sidewalk counselors was an effort to enhance the petitioners' speech rights." Once again the Court repeated what it had said twice before, "that in public debate our own citizens must tolerate insulting, and even outrageous, speech in order to provide adequate

38. Madsen v. Women's Health Center, Inc., 512 U.S. 753, 114 S. Ct. 2516, 129 L. Ed. 2d 593 (1994).

39. Schenck v. Pro-Choice Network Of Western New York, 117 S. Ct. 855, 137 L. Ed. 2d 1 (U.S. 1997).

breathing space to the freedoms protected by the First Amendment."[40]

§ 5.03. Meetings

Meetings on the public streets and sidewalks have long been popular forms of association and communication. However, states and cities at times believe such gatherings can jeopardize the public interests in pedestrian safety, vehicular traffic control, and, because such meetings have at times ended in violence, the more general interest in preserving the peace, good order, and safety.

The Supreme Court has aptly said: "In considering the right of a municipality to control the use of public streets for the expression of religious views, we start with the words of Justice Roberts that 'Wherever the title of streets and public parks may rest, they have immemoriably been held in trust for the use of the public and, time out of mind, have been used for purposes of assembly, communicating thoughts between citizens, and discussing public questions.' Hague v. C. I. O., 307 U.S. 496, 515 (1939)."[41]

In the *Hague* Case the Supreme Court had, in 1939, for the first time held that freedom of assembly was a fundamental right made binding upon the states and their political subdivisions by the Fourteenth Amendment. In that case the Court held void on its face a Jersey City ordinance requiring a permit for public assemblies on the streets and vesting in the city's director of public safety authority to refuse such permit when "he believes it proper to refuse the issuance thereof; provided, however, that such permit shall only be refused for the purpose of preventing riots, disturbances or disorderly assemblages."[42] However, the same year, the Court by way of dictum suggested that "a person could not exercise this liberty by taking his stand in the middle of a crowded street, contrary to traffic regulations, and maintain his position to the stoppage of all traffic; a group of distributors could not insist upon a constitutional right to form a cordon across the street and to allow no pedestrian to pass who did not accept a tendered leaflet . . ."[43]

In 1970 the Supreme Court voided the conviction of anti-Vietnam

40. Schenck v. Pro-Choice Network Of Western New York, 117 S. Ct. 855, 137 L. Ed. 2d 1 (U.S. 1997).

41. Kunz v. People of State of New York, 340 U.S. 290, 71 S. Ct. 312, 95 L. Ed. 280, 283 (1951).

42. Hague v. Committee for Indus. Organization, 307 U.S. 496, 59 S. Ct. 954, 83 L. Ed. 1423 (1939).

43. Schneider v. State of New Jersey, Town of Irvington, 308 U.S. 147, 60 S. Ct. 146, 84 L. Ed. 155, 163-64 (1939).

War protesters who had been meeting on a public street in Baltimore, under an ordinance banning "acting in a disorderly manner" etc. The Court indicated that under this provision the defendants could have been convicted at trial "simply because they advocated unpopular ideas." It is not sufficient to deprive a person in the United States of his liberty simply by proving that his views were offensive to some of his listeners.[44]

It is well-established that an enactment requiring permits for meetings will be voided by the Supreme Court whenever it fails to provide adequate standards to the public servants charged with administering the provision. In the 1951 *Kunz* case, the Court reversed the conviction of a Baptist minister for speaking without a permit, when the ordinance requiring the permit failed to provide clear and adequate standards. The Court noted:

> We have consistently condemned the licensing systems which vest in an administrative official discretion to grant or withhold a permit upon broad criteria unrelated to proper regulation of public places.[45]

Reaffirming in 1992 that "any permit scheme controlling the time, place and manner of speech must not be based on the content of the message, must be narrowly tailored to serve significant government interests, and must leave open alternatives for communication," the Supreme Court held unconstitutional an assembly and parade permit ordinance which allowed a government official to vary the fee for the permit to reflect the official's estimated cost of maintaining order. There can be no "unbridled discretion in a government official" to deny permits where First Amendment freedoms are involved because the peril of censorship is too great, and the amount of a required fee cannot be tied, even indirectly, to the content of a communication.[46]

The Supreme Court has a number of times emphasized that neither states nor cities can make criminal the peaceful expression of unpopular views at meetings in the public streets.[47] In 1965 the Court found unconstitutionally vague and broad a state statute which allowed criminal punishment of citizens for activity which

---

44. Bachellar v. Maryland, 397 U.S. 564, 90 S. Ct. 1312, 25 L. Ed. 2d 570, 52 Ohio Op. 2d 200 (1970).

45. Kunz v. People of State of New York, 340 U.S. 290, 71 S. Ct. 312, 95 L. Ed. 280 (1951).

46. Forsyth County, Ga. v. Nationalist Movement, 505 U.S. 123, 112 S. Ct. 2395, 120 L. Ed. 2d 101, 75 Ed. Law Rep. 29 (1992).

47. E.g., Henry v. City of Rock Hill, 376 U.S. 776, 84 S. Ct. 1042, 12 L. Ed. 2d 79 (1964).

was such as "to agitate, to arouse from a state of repose, to molest, to interrupt, to hinder, to disquiet." Said the Court: "the statute is unconstitutional in that it sweeps within its broad scope some activities that are constitutionally protected free speech and assembly. Maintenance of the opportunity for free political discussion is a basic tenet of our democracy." The Court added: "Constitutional rights may not be denied simply because of hostility to their assertion or exercise."[48]

Three years later the Court ruled that courts cannot issue orders banning rallies and public meetings without notice to the citizens affected, under ordinary circumstances. Said the Court:

> There is a place in our jurisprudence for ex parte issuance, without notice, of temporary restraining orders of short duration, but there is no place within the area of basic freedoms guaranteed by the First Amendment for such orders where no showing is made that it is impossible to serve or to notify the opposing parties and to give them an opportunity to participate.[49]

In 1982 the Court ruled that a boycott of white merchants in a community, designed to achieve racial equality and integration, was protected by constitutional rights of speech, assembly, association, and petition. The fact that some members of the boycotting groups engaged in illegal and unprotected conduct was held insufficient to render all members participating in peaceful political activity liable for civil damages for loss of business. However, the Court added that the members of the boycott who engaged in violent conduct could be held liable for injuries they caused, and that the leader of such a meeting could be held liable if he authorized, directed, or ratified specific tortious conduct.[50]

In 1965 the Court suggested that certain types of governmental controls upon meetings in the streets are constitutional. The Court stated:

> The control of traffic on the streets is a clear example of governmental responsibility to insure the necessary order. A restriction in that relation, designed to promote the public convenience in the interest of all, and not susceptible of abuses

---

48. Cox v. State of Louisiana, 379 U.S. 536, 85 S. Ct. 453, 13 L. Ed. 2d 471 (1965).

49. Carroll v. President and Com'rs of Princess Anne, 393 U.S. 175, 89 S. Ct. 347, 21 L. Ed. 2d 325 (1968).

50. N. A. A. C. P. v. Claiborne Hardware Co., 458 U.S. 886, 102 S. Ct. 3409, 73 L. Ed. 2d 1215 (1982).

of discriminatory application, cannot be disregarded by the attempted exercise of some civil right which, in other circumstances, would be entitled to protection. . . . Governmental authorities have the duty and responsibility to keep their streets open and available for movement. A group of demonstrators could not insist upon the right to cordon off a street or entrance to a public or private building and allow no one to pass who did not agree to listen to their exhortations.[51]

Five years later, the Court dismissed for want of a substantial federal question an appeal from convictions under a Philadelphia ordinance which empowered the mayor to declare a state of emergency and ban meetings in every outdoor place. The mayor had banned meetings of 12 or more, and when that many individuals met they were convicted despite the fact that the three meetings involved were peaceful, orderly, and noninflammatory. None of the meetings involved interfered with traffic and none of them violated any law, save for the mayoral proclamation. In dissent, Justice Douglas pointed out that appellants' claim that the ordinance and proclamation were overbroad raised substantial constitutional questions.[52]

State courts have generally upheld local ordinances prohibiting obstruction of the streets and sidewalks and requiring crowds to disperse and move on upon the command of a police officer "whenever the free passage of any street or sidewalk shall be obstructed."[53] State courts have also held that where the activity of persons assembling in the streets actually constitutes a breach of the peace or disorderly conduct, participants can be punished under properly drawn legislation.[54]

Ordinances prohibiting meetings in the public streets must be carefully drawn, avoiding the vices both of vagueness and overbreadth, and leaving adequate alternative opportunities for speech, association, assembly, and petition. In 1971 the Supreme Court held unconstitutional for vagueness a municipal ordinance making it "unlawful for three or more persons to assemble except at a public meeting of citizens, on any of the sidewalks, street corners, vacant

51. Cox v. State of Louisiana, 379 U.S. 536, 85 S. Ct. 453, 13 L. Ed. 2d 471, 484 (1965).

52. Stotland v. Pennsylvania, 398 U.S. 916, 90 S. Ct. 1552, 26 L. Ed. 2d 83 (1970).

53. In re Garrison, 18 Cal. App. 2d 495, 64 P.2d 1007 (1st Dist. 1937); Com. v. Surridge, 265 Mass. 425, 164 N.E. 480, 62 A.L.R. 402 (1929); City of Tacoma v. Roe, 190 Wash. 444, 68 P.2d 1028 (1937).

54. City of Cleveland Heights v. Christie, 128 Ohio St. 297, 190 N.E. 770 (1934); Ponchatoula v. Bates, 173 La. 824, 138 So. 851 (1931).

lots, or mouths of alleys, and there conduct themselves in a manner annoying to persons passing by, or occupants of adjacent buildings." Reminding us that "mere public intolerance or animosity cannot be the basis for abridgment of First Amendment freedoms, the Court further held that the ordinance was unconstitutionally broad because it authorized the punishment of constitutionally protected conduct."[55] In voiding an ordinance making it unlawful to assemble "for the purpose of breaking down law enforcement," a New York court aptly explained: "It is almost impossible to envisage where the heritage of protest ends and the violation of this ordinance begins. . . . Such dragnets must be declared void."[56]

§ 5.04. Addressing groups and individuals

At times communities are concerned with avoiding violence on streets and sidewalks that occasionally follows provocative language, forestalling riots triggered at times by speakers on the walks and streets, and protecting pedestrians from being forced off the walks into the path of vehicular traffic on the streets by crowds gathered to hear speakers. These valid interests must be reconciled with the societal interests embodied in the First Amendment.

In 1940 a Jehovah's Witnesses minister went into a predominantly Catholic neighborhood in New Haven, Connecticut and played a record attacking the Catholic faith on a portable phonograph. When some listeners became highly offended, considered assaulting the evangelist, and told him to leave their presence, he took his phonograph and proceeded down the street. His subsequent conviction was reversed by the Supreme Court, which stated:

> Although the contents of the record not unnaturally aroused animosity, we think that, in the absence of a statute narrowly drawn to define and punish specific conduct as constituting a clear and present danger to a substantial interest of the State, the petitioner's communication, embodied in the light of the constitutional guarantees, raised no such clear and present menace to public peace and order as to render him liable to conviction of the common law offense in question.

The Court here ably expressed the judicial function in cases where the First Amendment freedoms of religion and expression clash with society's interest in keeping the peace and good order. The Court said:

---

55. Coates v. City of Cincinnati, 402 U.S. 611, 91 S. Ct. 1686, 29 L. Ed. 2d 214, 58 Ohio Op. 2d 481 (1971).

56. American Civil Liberties Union v. Town of Cortlandt, 109 N.Y.S.2d 165, 169 (Sup. Ct. 1951).

Decision as to the lawfulness of the conviction demands the weighing of two conflicting interests. The fundamental law declares the interest of the United States that the free exercise of religion be not prohibited and that freedom to communicate information and ideas be not abridged. The State of Connecticut has an obvious interest in the preservation and protection of peace and good order within her borders. We must determine whether the alleged protection of the State's interest . . . has been pressed in this instance, to a point where it has come into fatal collision with the overriding interest protected by the federal compact.[57]

Two years later the Court ruled that the states and their political subdivisions could punish "the use in a public place of words likely to cause a breach of the peace." According to the state court's interpretation of the applicable statute, "fighting words" were the only ones banned. In the case before the Court a Jehovah's Witness had been arrested by a city marshal for distributing religious literature on the streets, whereupon the minister told the marshal: "You are a God-damned racketeer" and "a damned fascist," which resulted in his arrest and prosecution. For the Supreme Court, Justice Murphy wrote:

There are certain well-defined and narrowly limited classes of speech which have never been thought to raise any Constitutional problem. These include the lewd and obscene, the libelous, and the insulting or "fighting" words—those which by their very utterance inflict injury or tend to incite an immediate breach of the peace. It has been well observed that such utterances are no essential part of any exposition of ideas, and are of such slight social value as a step to truth that any benefit that may be derived from them is clearly outweighed by the social interest in order and morality.[58]

It is suggested that the creation of a "fighting words" exception to First Amendment protections was wrong. "Fighting words" have been used not only by American presidents but by many other citizens, and they are a traditional aspect of our communicative freedom. Furthermore, the concept is so vague that no lawyer can adequately guide his client contemplating a speech, especially a political speech. Additionally, the assumption by the Court that

---

57. Cantwell v. State of Connecticut, 310 U.S. 296, 60 S. Ct. 900, 84 L. Ed. 1213, 1219-20, 128 A.L.R. 1352 (1940).

58. Chaplinsky v. State of New Hampshire, 315 U.S. 568, 62 S. Ct. 766, 86 L. Ed. 1031, 1036 (1942).

fighting words generally lead to breaches of the peace must be seriously questioned. If fisticuffs break out, the larger interests of a free society are better served by chastising the violent rather than the verbal.

Since 1951 the Supreme Court has indicated that states and their political subdivisions may prohibit incitement to riot, and may punish individuals who speak on sidewalks and streets so as to incite the audience to riot. In the *Feiner* case of that year, the Court upheld a conviction for disorderly conduct of a person who spoke from a box on a sidewalk, using a loudspeaker system, when he, in the language of the Court, "gave the impression he was endeavoring to arouse the Negro people against the Whites, urging that they rise up in arms and fight for equal rights," and then refused to alight from the box, when so ordered by a policeman. The Court said that it "respects as it must, the interest of the community in maintaining peace and order on the streets." According to the Court, communities can punish "when, as here, the speaker passes the bounds or argument or persuasion and undertakes incitement to riot."[59] Justices Black, Minton and Douglas dissented, with Justice Black stating:

> The police of course have power to prevent breaches of the peace. But if, in the name of preserving order, they even can interfere with a lawful public speaker, they first must make all reasonable efforts to protect him. Here the policemen did not even try to protect petitioner's right to talk, even to the extent of arresting the man who threatened to interfere. Instead, they shirked that duty and acted only to suppress the right to speak.

It is suggested that the case was wrongly decided. It is simply impossible for a layman to know when he "passes the bounds of argument or persuasion and undertakes incitement to riot." It is impossible for a lawyer to give counsel to a client in this situation, it is not possible for a policeman on the beat to make just and consistent decisions in this area, and it is even more impossible for a jury some months later to capture the milieu of the moment in judging whether information or incitement was said. If members listening voluntarily to a public speaker do not care for what he is saying, they can easily move on. It is the proper function of the police to protect speakers with unpopular messages and annoying deliveries, and to move along those who would deny First Amendment freedoms by themselves indulging in violence or threatening the same.

Happily, the Supreme Court soon began moving away from its approach and language in *Feiner*. In 1964 the Court ruled that local

---

59. Feiner v. New York, 340 U.S. 315, 71 S. Ct. 303, 95 L. Ed. 295 (1951).

communities cannot convict public speakers simply because "their speech stirred people to anger, invited public dispute, or brought about a condition of unrest." "A conviction resting on any of these grounds may not stand," stated the Court, reminding us that "The Fourteenth Amendment does not permit a state to make criminal the peaceful expression of unpopular views."[60] The following year, the Court emphasized that speakers cannot be put in jail under a breach of peace statute that made it unlawful "to agitate, to arouse from a state of repose, to molest, to interrupt, to hinder, to disquiet." "The statute is unconstitutional," said the Court, "in that it sweeps within its broad scope activities that are constitutionally protected free speech and assembly. Maintenance of the opportunity for free political discussion is a basic tenet of our democracy." With sagacity the Court added: "Constitutional rights may not be denied simply because of hostility to their assertion or exercise."[61]

If members of a mob have vowed beforehand that they will indulge in violence when certain individuals speak in their area on controversial topics, it should be obvious that any such speaker would "incite to riot" simply by climbing on a box and beginning to read the Bill of Rights. Local authorities can, of course, warn such a speaker that they may not be able to protect him, but the obligation of the authorities is first and foremost to suppress violence from members of a mob who would deny freedom of speech and, at times, religious freedom.

In 1972 the Supreme Court held unconstitutional as impermissibly broad a statute which provided that: "Any person who shall, without provocation, use to or of another, and in his presence . . . opprobrious words or abusive language, tending to cause a breach of the peace . . . shall be guilty of a misdemeanor." The Court reminds us that it is not necessary that the person attacking the ordinance demonstrate that his own conduct could not be regulated by a statute drawn with the requisite narrow specificity, since "persons whose expression is constitutionally protected may well refrain from exercising their rights for fear of criminal sanctions provided by a statute susceptible of application to protected expression." In this area, the Court explained, a "statute must be carefully drawn or be

---

60. Henry v. City of Rock Hill, 376 U.S. 776, 84 S. Ct. 1042, 12 L. Ed. 2d 79, 81 (1964).

61. Cox v. State of Louisiana, 379 U.S. 536, 85 S. Ct. 453, 13 L. Ed. 2d 471, 482-83 (1965).

authoritatively construed to punish only unprotected speech and not be susceptible of application to protected expression."[62]

Two years later, the Court concluded that an ordinance was susceptible of application to protected speech and therefore ruled that it was constitutionally overbroad and therefore was facially invalid. The Court again ruled that the proscription of "opprobrious" language is broader than the banning of "fighting words" and is unconstitutional.[63] In 1987 the Court repeated that restraints upon First Amendment activities cannot "reach a substantial amount of constitutionally protected conduct." The Court then held unconstitutionally broad an ordinance which would have punished any person who by words alone "interrupts any policeman in the execution of his duty." Remarking that "the First Amendment protects a significant amount of verbal criticism and challenge directed at police officers" so long as a clear and present danger of substantive evil is not thereby created, the Court added generally: "The freedom of individuals verbally to oppose a challenged police officer without thereby risking arrest is one of the principal characteristics by which we distinguish a free nation from a police state."[64]

The Supreme Court has said that "the constitutional guarantees of free speech and free press do not permit a State to forbid or proscribe advocacy of the use of force or of law violation except where such advocacy is directed to inciting or producing immediate lawless action and is likely to incite or produce such action."[65] In 1973 the Court in a per curiam decision reversed the conviction of a participant in an anti-war demonstration who, within hearing of a sheriff, said: "We'll take the fucking street again." The Court stated that the words did not fall within any of the limited classes of speech which are punishable.[66]

§ 5.05. Activities on public grounds

Communities have valid interests in keeping quiet the grounds around public buildings, such as schools, courts, and legislative halls; in making parks a haven for those who would relax; in conserving the beauty of the parks; and in outlawing violence in the parks.

---

62. Gooding v. Wilson, 405 U.S. 518, 92 S. Ct. 1103, 31 L. Ed. 2d 408 (1972).

63. Lewis v. City of New Orleans, 415 U.S. 130, 94 S. Ct. 970, 39 L. Ed. 2d 214 (1974).

64. City of Houston, Tex. v. Hill, 482 U.S. 451, 107 S. Ct. 2502, 96 L. Ed. 2d 398 (1987).

65. Brandenburg v. Ohio, 395 U.S. 444, 89 S. Ct. 1827, 23 L. Ed. 2d 430, 434, 48 Ohio Op. 2d 320 (1969).

66. Hess v. Indiana, 414 U.S. 105, 94 S. Ct. 326, 38 L. Ed. 2d 303 (1973).

The United States Supreme Court set aside a disorderly conduct conviction of Jehovah's Witnesses who used a park in a Maryland city without a permit from the mayor. No ordinance required a permit, but local custom decreed that persons contemplating such use of a park apply to the mayor, who in this case refused permission. There was no evidence of any misbehavior by the group, the alleged offense of disorderly conduct being based solely on the use of the park without the permit. The Supreme Court stated: "The lack of standards in the license-issuing 'practice' renders that 'practice' a prior restraint in contravention of the Fourteenth Amendment, and . . . the completely arbitrary and discriminatory refusal to grant the permits was a denial of equal protection."[67]

Two years later the Court voided another conviction of Jehovah's Witnesses for speaking in a public park, and held invalid an ordinance prohibiting religious meetings in any public park when, on oral argument, the attorney general of the state admitted that other faiths could hold religious services in the park without being deemed to violate the ordinance. Said the Supreme Court: "That broad concession . . . is fatal to [the state's] case. For it plainly shows that a religious service of Jehovah's Witnesses is treated differently than a religious service of other sects. That amounts to the state preferring some religious groups over this one."[68]

The same year the Court ruled that Jehovah's Witnesses, as well as others, who desired to use a public park had to pursue their remedies in the applicable state courts to obtain a license required by statute or ordinance and arbitrarily or unreasonably refused by local authorities. Failing to pursue such remedies and meeting in a park without the license, the citizens could be convicted criminally for violating the law. The state supreme court had held that the ordinance made it obligatory upon the city to grant a license for such religious services and, as so interpreted, the ordinance was valid. The Supreme Court majority said:

> The principles of the First Amendment are not to be treated as a promise that everyone with opinions or beliefs to express may gather around him at any public place and at any time a group for discussion or instruction. It is a non sequitur to say that First Amendment rights may not be regulated because they hold a preferred position in the hierarchy of the constitutional guarantees of the incidents of freedom. This Court has never so

67. Niemotko v. State of Md., 340 U.S. 268, 71 S. Ct. 325, 95 L. Ed. 267, 271 (1951).

68. Fowler v. State of R.I., 345 U.S. 67, 73 S. Ct. 526, 97 L. Ed. 828, 830-31 (1953).

held and indeed has definitely indicated the contrary. It has indicated approval of reasonable nondiscriminatory regulations by governmental authority that preserves peace, order and tranquillity without deprivation of the First Amendment guarantees of free speech, press and the exercise of religion. When considering specifically the regulation of the use of public parks, the Court has taken the same position.[69]

Justice Douglas, speaking also for Justice Black, stated in dissent:

The vice of a statute, which exacts a license for the right to make a speech, is that it adds a burden to the right. The burden is the same when the officials administering the licensing system withhold the license and require the applicant to spend months or years in the courts in order to win a right which the Constitution says no government shall deny.[70]

Legislation that is void on its face, and has not been authoritatively narrowed to constitutional clarity by state high courts, should, when violative of First Amendment freedoms, be held unconstitutional by federal courts at the first opportunity. It hardly serves the Constitution for a court to conclude after an election is over that desired political speech should have been permitted.

In 1969 the Supreme Court ruled in effect that a person faced with an ordinance that was unconstitutional because of the absence of adequate standards for the public official charged with granting or denying a permit could disregard the ordinance and, in a subsequent criminal prosecution, defend on the ordinance's unconstitutionality. Said the Court: "Our decisions have made clear that a person faced with such an unconstitutional licensing law may ignore it and engage with impunity in the exercise of the right of free expression for which the law purports to require a license." Justice Harlan, in his concurring opinion, stressed that the local law did not provide "sufficiently expedited procedures for the consideration of parade permits."[71] Any permit ordinance limiting First Amendment freedoms should be unconstitutional if it does not provide for easy, expeditious, and inexpensive mandamus actions, or their equivalent, to compel the issuance of a permit unconstitutionally withheld.

---

69. Poulos v. State of N.H., 345 U.S. 395, 73 S. Ct. 760, 97 L. Ed. 1105, 1114-15, 30 A.L.R.2d 987 (1953).

70. Poulos v. State of N.H., 345 U.S. 395, 73 S. Ct. 760, 97 L. Ed. 1105, 1123, 30 A.L.R.2d 987 (1953).

71. Shuttlesworth v. City of Birmingham, Ala., 394 U.S. 147, 89 S. Ct. 935, 22 L. Ed. 2d 162 (1969).

When, in 1963 the Court ruled that African American young men could not be arrested and convicted for playing in a "white" park, it re-emphasized that "the possibility of disorder by others would not justify exclusion of the petitioners from the park."[72] The same year the Court had held that state and local governments cannot ordinarily punish persons for orderly and peaceful gatherings on state house grounds, even when the gatherers carry placards protesting such things as racial segregation. It is not enough, repeated the Court, that the parade and speeches stir people to anger, invite public dispute, or bring about a condition of unrest. "A conviction resting on any of these grounds may not stand," announced the Court. Said the Court by way of dictum: "If . . . petitioners had been convicted upon evidence that they had violated a law regulating traffic, or had disobeyed a law reasonably limiting the periods during which the State House grounds were open to the public, this would be a different case."[73]

In 1966 the Court had affirmed the conviction of some African American college students under a trespass statute, for having demonstrated peaceably on the grounds of a county jail, after having been ordered by the sheriff to leave. The five-to-four majority opinion believed that the trespass statute gave adequate guidance to those who would be law-abiding, and distinguished the earlier *Edwards* case by remarking that state house grounds are generally open to the public, whereas "jails, built for security purposes, are not." The majority opinion rejected the notion "that people who want to propagandize protests or views have a constitutional right to do so whenever and however and wherever they please."[74] Chief Justice Warren, Justices Brennan, Fortas and Douglas dissented, stressing that the petitioners had been peaceable and caused no interference with persons or vehicles going into or coming out from the jail. The custodian of public property should not, according to these Justices, be able by his simple fiat to convert a peaceable demonstration into a crime.

The following year, in another five-to-four decision, the Supreme Court sustained a contempt conviction of eight African American ministers for violating an ex parte injunction, issued without notice or hearing, restraining them and others from conducting parades and processions without a permit required by an ordinance—an

---

72. Wright v. State of Ga., 373 U.S. 284, 83 S. Ct. 1240, 10 L. Ed. 2d 349 (1963).

73. Edwards v. South Carolina, 372 U.S. 229, 83 S. Ct. 680, 9 L. Ed. 2d 697, 703 (1963).

74. Adderley v. State of Fla., 385 U.S. 39, 87 S. Ct. 242, 247, 17 L. Ed. 2d 149 (1966).

ordinance which in all likelihood was unconstitutional. The Court said:

> We have consistently recognized the strong interest of state and local governments in regulating the use of their streets and other public places. When protest takes the form of mass demonstrations, parades, or picketing on the public streets and sidewalks, the free passage of traffic and the prevention of public disorder and violence become important objects of legitimate state concern.[75]

Acknowledging that "the breadth and vagueness of the injunction would also unquestionably be subject to substantial constitutional question," the Court held that "the way to raise that question was to apply to the Alabama courts to have the injunction modified or dissolved." The Chief Justice, as well as Justices Brennan, Douglas and Fortas dissented. After characterizing the ordinance as "patently unconstitutional on its face" for giving unfettered discretion to a local official to deny permits, the Chief Justice stated:

> It shows no disrespect for law to violate a statute on the ground that it is unconstitutional and then to submit one's case to the courts with the willingness to accept the penalty if the statute is to be held valid.

Pointing out that "the ex parte injunction has a long and odious history in this country, and its susceptibility to misuse is all too apparent from the facts of the case," the Chief Justice and the other dissenters aptly pointed out "the power to nullify the United States Constitution by the simple process of incorporating its unconstitutional criminal statutes into judicial decrees."[76]

In 1981 the Supreme Court upheld the action of a state fair in limiting solicitation of funds by a religious group to assigned locations. The Court indicated that it will sustain time, place and manner regulations of First Amendment activities when the controls serve a significant governmental interest, and the protection of the safety and convenience of the other individuals attending the fair was held to be such an interest. Justices Brennan, Stevens and Marshall dissented in part because the regulation involved could readily have been drafted with less restriction on the distribution of

---

75. Walker v. City of Birmingham, 388 U.S. 307, 87 S. Ct. 1824, 1830, 18 L. Ed. 2d 1210 (1967).

76. Walker v. City of Birmingham, 388 U.S. 307, 87 S. Ct. 1824, 1839, 18 L. Ed. 2d 1210 (1967).

literature.[77] Three years later, while acknowledging that sleeping in Lafayette Park and on the Mall in Washington, D.C. was a communicative aspect of a demonstration seeking to find help for the homeless, the Court nevertheless ruled that a ban upon such activity did not violate the First Amendment, since the majority believed that maintaining those sites in an attractive and intact condition was a substantial governmental interest, and that there were "ample alternative channels for communication of information" available to the protesters. In dissent, Justices Marshall and Brennan found no substantial governmental interest present, and concluded that this was not a reasonable time, place and manner restriction.[78]

While readily acknowledging in 1989 that "music, as a form of expression and communication, is protected under the Fourteenth Amendment," the Supreme Court added that the "government has a substantial interest in protecting its citizens from unwanted noise," and held that this societal interest justified New York City in requiring that performers at a band shell in Central Park use sound equipment and a sound technician provided by the City. The Court found the regulation was "narrowly tailored to serve a significant government interest." In dissent, Justices Marshall, Brennan and Stevens took the view that the ordinance imposed a prior restraint, and that constitutionally required procedural safeguards were not present.[79]

The Supreme Court in 1972 had held constitutional an anti-noise ordinance which provided:

> No person, while on public or private grounds adjacent to any building in which a school or any class thereof is in session, shall wilfully make or assist in the making of any noise or diversion which disturbs or tends to disturb the peace or good order of such school session or class thereof.[80]

A state cannot on Establishment Clause grounds forbid the Ku Klux Klan to erect a cross in a public park facing the state capitol, when the park has been dedicated as a public forum. The Court noted that "The right to use government property for one's private expression depends upon whether the property has been by law or tradition given the status of a public forum, or rather has been

---

77. Heffron v. International Soc. for Krishna Consciousness, Inc., 452 U.S. 640, 101 S. Ct. 2559, 69 L. Ed. 2d 298 (1981).

78. Clark v. Community for Creative Non-Violence, 468 U.S. 288, 104 S. Ct. 3065, 82 L. Ed. 2d 221 (1984).

79. Ward v. Rock Against Racism, 491 U.S. 781, 109 S. Ct. 2746, 105 L. Ed. 2d 661 (1989).

80. Grayned v. City of Rockford, 408 U.S. 104, 92 S. Ct. 2294, 33 L. Ed. 2d 222 (1972).

reserved for specific official uses," adding that while "a State's right to limit protected expressive activities is sharply circumscribed, it may impose reasonable content-neutral time, place and manner restrictions, but it may regulate expressive content only if such a restriction is necessary and narrowly drawn, to serve a compelling state interest." Remarking that there is "no doubt that compliance with the Establishment Clause is a state interest sufficiently compelling to justify content-based restrictions on speech," the Court nevertheless held that "religious expression cannot violate the Establishment Clause where it is (1) purely private, and (2) occurs in a traditional or designated public forum and open to all on equal terms." The opinion of the Court indicated that "private religious expression secures preferential treatment under the Free Expression Clause."[81]

Worth long honoring is a decision by the United States Court of Appeals for the Eighth Circuit holding that a group of Jehovah's Witnesses were entitled to an injunction against interference with their bible meeting in a public park and to a declaratory judgment that they had a constitutional right to be there and to be protected by the police in their exercise of First Amendment freedoms. Judge Sanborn wrote for the Court:

> The theory that a group of individuals may be deprived of their constitutional rights of assembly, speech and worship if they have become so unpopular with, or offensive to, the people of a community that their presence in a public park to deliver a bible lecture is likely to result in riot and bloodshed, is interesting but somewhat difficult to accept. Under such a doctrine, unpopular political, racial and religious groups might find themselves virtually inarticulate. Certainly the fundamental rights to assemble, to speak, and to worship cannot be abridged merely because persons threaten to stage a riot or because peace officers believe or are afraid that breaches of the peace will occur if the rights are exercised.

> We are convinced that evidence of unconfirmed rumors, talk, and fears cannot form the basis of a finding of the existence of such a clear and present danger to the State as to justify a deprivation of fundamental and essential constitutional rights. . . . The only sound way to enforce the law is to arrest and prosecute those who violate the law. The Jehovah's Witnesses were at all times acting lawfully, and those who attacked them,

---

81. Capitol Square Review and Advisory Bd. v. Pinette, 515 U.S. 753, 115 S. Ct. 2440, 132 L. Ed. 2d 650 (1995).

for the purpose of preventing them from holding their religious meeting . . . were acting unlawfully and without any legal justification for their conduct.[82]

The New Hampshire Supreme Court adds: "When peaceful, orderly public comment is involved, the police have a duty to take reasonable affirmative steps to insure the maintenance of the protestors' rights to freedom of speech and expression."[83]

Complete state or municipal bans upon the use of public parks for religious meetings or other matters of public concern are invalid. The Wisconsin Supreme Court has said this well:

> Government may, in the interests of public order, safety and the equitable sharing of facilities, exercise reasonable control over when, where and under what conditions public meetings may be held on public property; but to deny to the people all use of the people's property for the public discussion of specified subjects is an unconstitutional interference of rights expressly guaranteed by both state and federal constitutions.[84]

Any legislation seeking to deny public use of the public parks for matters of public concern must avoid the twin vices of vagueness and overbreadth, must serve a substantial societal interest in need of such protection, one that would clearly and imminently be endangered by the exercise of First Amendment freedoms of communication, assembly and worship, and must provide clear and adequate standards for the public official charged with granting or denying a permit, with adequate alternatives available to the public denied the use of a park, and with easy, inexpensive, and prompt judicial review from refusal of permits or other authorizations. Absent specified methods of appeal, injunctions are available to restrain government personnel from interfering with the holding of public meetings.

The Supreme Court in 1988 held void a municipal ordinance requiring newspapers to secure a permit in order to place coin-operated dispensing devices on city sidewalks, because municipal authorities had unbridled discretion to refuse such permits. To be constitutional, said the Court, such a law "must have a close enough nexus to expression, or to conduct commonly associated with expression." Justices White, Stevens and O'Connor dissented, deeming the "close nexus" test too broad and concluding that significant interests

---

82. Sellers v. Johnson, 163 F.2d 877 (C.C.A. 8th Cir. 1947).

83. State v. Nickerson, 120 N.H. 821, 424 A.2d 190 (1980).

84. Milwaukee County v. Carter, 258 Wis. 139, 45 N.W.2d 90 (1950).

of cities, such as insuring the safety of pedestrians using sidewalks, justify regulating the placement of newsracks on the public sidewalks.[85]

Five years later the Court held violative of the First Amendment Cincinnati's refusal to allow a business to distribute commercial publications through freestanding newsracks located on public property. The Court indicated that in such cases the city has the burden to establish a reasonable fit between its legitimate interests in safety and esthetics and its choice of a limited and selective prohibition of newsracks as the means chosen to serve these interests. Newsracks on public property, said the Court, "continue to play a significant role in the dissemination of protected speech."[86]

§ 5.06. Activities in and around buildings open to the public generally

Even where activity within the protection of the First Amendment occurs in private halls, auditoria, and churches, local communities have an interest in protecting society from undue noise and from outbreaks of violence.

In 1940 the United States Supreme Court reversed the conviction of a speaker who gave an address in a Chicago auditorium, with 800 persons assembled inside the building and over a thousand gathered outside the auditorium to protest the talk. As a result of a disturbance outside the hall at the end of the meeting, the speaker was charged with disorderly conduct. The jury was told it could convict him, under a local ordinance, if his speech "stirs the public to anger, invites dispute, brings about a condition of unrest or creates a disturbance, or if it molests the inhabitants in the enjoyment of peace and quiet by arousing alarm." This was error, the Court held, stating: "A conviction resting on any of those grounds may not stand." Justice Douglas spoke for the Court, as follows:

> The vitality of civil and political institutions in our society depends on free discussion . . . it is only through free debate and free exchange of ideas that government remains responsive to the will of the people and peaceful change is effected. The right to speak freely and to promote diversity of ideas and programs is therefore one of the chief distinctions that set us apart from the totalitarian regimes.

---

85. City of Lakewood v. Plain Dealer Pub. Co., 486 U.S. 750, 108 S. Ct. 2138, 100 L. Ed. 2d 771 (1988).

86. City of Cincinnati v. Discovery Network, Inc., 507 U.S. 410, 113 S. Ct. 1505, 123 L. Ed. 2d 99 (1993).

Accordingly a function of free speech under our system is to invite dispute. It may indeed best serve its high purpose when it induces a condition of unrest, creates dissatisfaction with conditions as they are, or even stirs people to anger. Speech is often provocative and challenging. It may strike at prejudice and preconceptions and have profound unsettling effects as it presses for acceptance of an idea. That is why speech, though not absolute, is nevertheless protected against censorship or punishment, unless shown likely to produce a clear and present danger of a substantive evil that rises above public inconvenience, annoyance or unrest.[87]

In another Supreme Court decision involving speech and assembly in a hall, where a union rented the city hall, the Court ruled that a national organizer speaking there could not be exposed to a license or registration requirement as a prerequisite to the speech. The Court stated: "A requirement that one must register before he undertakes to make a public speech or enlist support for a lawful movement is quite incompatible with the requirements of the First Amendment."[88]

State court decisions have permitted punishment of individuals meeting in private buildings when they became unduly noisome and boisterous,[89] and at times church services have been deemed public nuisances when they were conducted with such noise as to greatly disturb the neighborhood.[90]

Local communities have at times thought that their interest in peace and good order was affronted by "sit-ins" at stores, restaurants, bus terminals, and various other facilities. At one time the presence in such places of African Americans was disturbing to some whites and likely their attempted patronage could produce some violence. Nevertheless, the United States Supreme Court has made it clear that peaceful, orderly "sit-ins" are forms of communication protected by the First Amendment.

In 1961, the Court set aside the conviction of African Americans for disturbing the peace after they quietly sat in at a "white" lunch counter. Said the Court: "The convictions in these cases are so totally devoid of evidentiary support as to render them unconstitutional under the Due Process Clause of the Fourteenth Amend-

---

87. Terminiello v. City of Chicago, 337 U.S. 1, 69 S. Ct. 894, 93 L. Ed. 1131, 1134-35 (1949).

88. Thomas v. Collins, 323 U.S. 516, 65 S. Ct. 315, 89 L. Ed. 430 (1945).

89. Village of Vicksburg v. Briggs, 102 Mich. 551, 61 N.W. 1 (1894).

90. Morison v. Rawlinson, 193 S.C. 25, 7 S.E.2d 635 (1940).

ment."[91] The following year the Court held that African Americans could not constitutionally be convicted of breach of the peace for quietly going into the "white" waiting room at an interstate bus terminal while waiting for their bus.[92] Where persons have a constitutional right to be present in a certain locus, they cannot be convicted of breach of the peace, disorderly conduct, rioting or anything else for quietly exercising their constitutional rights under the First Amendment. Since no state or local legislation can require racial segregation in public facilities, African Americans cannot be punished for disregarding such unconstitutional enactments.[93]

The Supreme Court has reversed the conviction of individuals who "sat in" at a drug store, where the local statute made it a misdemeanor to *enter* another's property after a notice prohibited such entry. The Court ruled that for the South Carolina courts to interpret the statute as making criminal *sitting in* at a store's lunch counter, when they were more than welcome at the other departments of the store, violated the well-established doctrine that "a criminal statute must give fair warning of the conduct which it prohibits."[94]

The Court has also ruled that the federal Civil Rights Act of 1964 prevents states and communities from prosecuting persons for sit-ins at restaurants covered by the act, even *previous* to passage of the act. Justices Black, Harlan, Stewart and White dissented.[95]

§ 5.07. Activities in government-owned public buildings and conveyances

In 1966 the United States Supreme Court ruled that African Americans could not be convicted under a state breach of peace statute for having peacefully and quietly "sat-in" at a public library to protest what they thought were denials of facilities to African Americans citizens. At the threshold the Court ruled that "petitioners cannot constitutionally be convicted merely because they did not

---

91. Garner v. State of La., 368 U.S. 157, 82 S. Ct. 248, 7 L. Ed. 2d 207, 219 (1961). Note also: Barr v. City of Columbia, 378 U.S. 146, 84 S. Ct. 1734, 12 L. Ed. 2d 766 (1964).

92. Taylor v. State of La., 370 U.S. 154, 82 S. Ct. 1188, 8 L. Ed. 2d 395 (1962).

93. Shuttlesworth v. City of Birmingham, Ala., 373 U.S. 262, 83 S. Ct. 1130, 10 L. Ed. 2d 335 (1963). Note also: Boynton v. Com. of Va., 364 U.S. 454, 81 S. Ct. 182, 5 L. Ed. 2d 206 (1960).

94. Bouie v. City of Columbia, 378 U.S. 347, 84 S. Ct. 1697, 12 L. Ed. 2d 894 (1964).

95. Hamm v. City of Rock Hill, 379 U.S. 306, 85 S. Ct. 384, 13 L. Ed. 2d 300 (1964).

comply with an order to leave the library." Then, referring to the First Amendment rights, the Court said:

> As this Court has repeatedly stated, these rights are not confined to verbal expression. They embrace appropriate types of action which certainly include the right in a peaceable and orderly manner to protest by silent and reproachful presence, in a place where the protestant has every right to be, the unconstitutional segregation of public facilities. Accordingly, even if the accused action were within the scope of the statutory instrument, we would be required to assess the constitutional impact of its application, and we would have to hold that the statute cannot constitutionally be applied to punish actions in the circumstances of the case.[96]

Three years later the Court held unconstitutional a school district rule forbidding the wearing of black arm bands in school as a protest to the Vietnam War. The Court stated that "the wearing of an armband for the purpose of expressing certain views is the type of symbolic act that is within the Free Speech Clause of the First Amendment." After noting that there was no evidence whatsoever that the defendants' conduct interfered with the work of the school, the Court said: "In order for the State in the person of school officials to justify prohibition of a particular expression of opinion, it must be able to show that its action was caused by something more than a mere desire to void the discomfort and unpleasantness that always accompany an unpopular viewpoint. Certainly where there is no finding and no showing that engaging in the forbidden right would 'materially and substantially interfere with the requirements of appropriate discipline in the operation of the school,' the prohibition cannot be sustained." However, by way of dictum, the Court added: "But conduct by the student, in class or out of it, which for any reason—whether it stems from time, place or type of behavior—materially disrupts classwork or involves substantial disorder or invasion of the rights of others is, of course, not immunized by the constitutional guarantee of freedom of speech."[97]

Although a school activity in elementary or secondary schools is primarily communicative or expressive, the Supreme Court in 1988 held it is subject to reasonable regulation, including censorship of school papers, when the activity is seen as "part of the school curriculum," and the actions of school authorities "are reasonably

---

96. Brown v. State of La., 383 U.S. 131, 86 S. Ct. 719, 15 L. Ed. 2d 637 (1966).

97. Tinker v. Des Moines Independent Community School Dist., 393 U.S. 503, 89 S. Ct. 733, 21 L. Ed. 2d 731, 49 Ohio Op. 2d 222 (1969).

related to legitimate pedagogical concerns." In dissent, Justices Brennan, Marshall and Blackmun asserted that "the censorship served no legitimate pedagogical purpose" and stated further that the First Amendment prohibits "censorship of any student expression that neither disrupts classwork nor invades the rights of others, and . . . any censorship that is not narrowly tailored to serve its purpose."[98]

In 1992 the Supreme Court invalidated as violative of the First Amendment a ban on distribution of religious literature by the International Society for Krishna Consciousness at airports operated by the Port Authority of New York and New Jersey (La Guardia, Kennedy, and Newark Airports). In a companion case, a ban upon soliciting funds at the airport by the same group was sustained. While Justices Kennedy, Blackmun, Stevens and Souter disagreed with the majority in the latter case in their belief that a publicly-owned airport terminal is a public forum, they would also have sustained the ban upon solicitation as reasonable. Justice Kennedy stated the rule that "nonspeech elements of expressive conduct can be subject to reasonable restrictions on time, place, and manner."[99]

In an opinion by Justice Blackmun, joined by Chief Justice Burger and Justices White and Rehnquist, the Supreme Court in 1974 held that a candidate for public office had no right to have a local government, which operated a rapid transit system and accepted commercial advertising generally on the system's cars, accept his paid political advertising for advertising space on the cars. The opinion for the Court indicated that the denial was not arbitrary, capricious, or invidious. Justice Douglas concurred, to provide a majority, because he believed that such a candidate has no constitutional right "to spread his message before this captive audience." Justices Brennan, Marshall, Powell and Stewart dissented, finding no substantial societal interest justifying such abridgment "once a public form for communication has been established," and suggesting there is really no "captive audience" since any rider of the cars need only glance away.[1]

Activities at jails and penitentiaries are treated in the following section.

---

98. Hazelwood School Dist. v. Kuhlmeier, 484 U.S. 260, 108 S. Ct. 562, 98 L. Ed. 2d 592, 43 Ed. Law Rep. 515 (1988).

99. Lee v. International Soc. for Krishna Consciousness, Inc., 505 U.S. 830, 112 S. Ct. 2709, 120 L. Ed. 2d 669 (1992); International Soc. for Krishna Consciousness, Inc. v. Lee, 505 U.S. 672, 112 S. Ct. 2701, 120 L. Ed. 2d 541 (1992).

1. Lehman v. City of Shaker Heights, 418 U.S. 298, 94 S. Ct. 2714, 41 L. Ed. 2d 770 (1974).

§ 5.08. Activities in penal institutions

In 1974 the Supreme Court ruled that censorship of prison mail did not violate the First Amendment, so long as the following criteria are met:

First, the regulation or practice in question must further an important or substantial interest unrelated to the suppression of expression. . . . Second, the limitation of First Amendment freedoms must be no greater than is necessary or essential to the protection of the particular governmental interest involved. Thus, a restriction on inmate correspondence that furthers an important or substantial interest of penal administration will nevertheless be invalid if its sweep is unnecessarily broad.

The Court recognized that there are legitimate interests at stake, including "the preservation of internal order and discipline, the maintenance of institutional security against escape or unauthorized entry, and the rehabilitation of prisoners." By way of dictum the Court indicated:

Perhaps the most obvious example of justifiable censorship of prisoner mail would be refusal to send or deliver letters concerning escape plans or containing other information concerning proposed criminal activity, whether within or without the prison. Similarly, prison officials may properly refuse to transmit encoded messages.

The Court added, however, that "the decision to censor or withhold delivery of a particular letter must be accompanied by minimum procedural safeguards. . . . The District Court required that an inmate be notified of the rejection of a letter written by or addressed to him, that the author of that letter be given a reasonable opportunity to protest that decision, and that complaints be referred to a prison official other than the person who originally disapproved the correspondence. These requirements do not appear to be unduly burdensome."[2]

The Court in 1979 held valid a prison ban upon the receipt of hardcover books which were not sent directly from publishers, book clubs, or book stores, as not violating the First Amendment rights of prisoners, and held that pretrial detainees can be denied the receipt of packages except for one at Christmas, can be subject to room searches out of sight of the occupants, can be subjected to

---

2. Procunier v. Martinez, 416 U.S. 396, 94 S. Ct. 1800, 40 L. Ed. 2d 224, 71 Ohio Op. 2d 139 (1974) (overruled on other grounds by, Thornburgh v. Abbott, 490 U.S. 401, 109 S. Ct. 1874, 104 L. Ed. 2d 459 (1989)).

visual body inspections after visits from outsiders, and can be subjected to "double bunking." Generally, the Court indicated that it will not set aside conditions imposed by jailers or prison officials unless they "amount to punishment."[3]

In 1974 the Supreme Court sustained a federal rule generally banning face-to-face interviews between the press and designated prisoners, so long as the prisoners had adequate alternative means of communicating with the press. The practice of interviewing and reporting names, said the Court, "became the source of severe disciplinary problems." Justices Powell, Brennan, and Marshall dissented, with Justice Powell stating that the Federal Bureau of Prisons' "absolute prohibition of prisoner-press interviews negates the ability of the press to discharge that function and thereby substantially impairs the right of the people to a free flow of information and ideas on the conduct of their Government. The underlying right is the right of the public generally."[4] The Court has also held valid prison regulations denying prisoners the opportunity to have newsmen visit them, and correlatively denying news reporters the opportunity to interview particular prisoners chosen by them. The Court said: "We regard the available alternative means of communications as a relevant factor in a case such as this where we are called upon to balance First Amendment rights against legitimate governmental interests," and found communications by mail to be an adequate alternative for a prisoner desiring to communicate. The Court then added: "The Constitution does not . . . require government to accord the press special access to information not shared by members of the public generally."[5]

In 1977 the Court upheld a ban upon meetings by a prisoners' union, as well as solicitation for such a union and denial of bulk mailing privileges to the union. Holding that the prison was not a public forum, the Court held that it was enough that prison regulations were reasonable regulations that rationally furthered the permissible objectives of security and order.[6]

A year later the Court held that the news media do not have a constitutional right, over and above that of other persons, to interview jail inmates and to make sound recordings, films, and

---

3. Bell v. Wolfish, 441 U.S. 520, 99 S. Ct. 1861, 60 L. Ed. 2d 447 (1979).

4. Saxbe v. Washington Post Co., 417 U.S. 843, 94 S. Ct. 2811, 41 L. Ed. 2d 514 (1974).

5. Pell v. Procunier, 417 U.S. 817, 94 S. Ct. 2800, 41 L. Ed. 2d 495, 71 Ohio Op. 2d 195 (1974).

6. Jones v. North Carolina Prisoners' Labor Union, Inc., 433 U.S. 119, 97 S. Ct. 2532, 53 L. Ed. 2d 629 (1977).

photographs for publication and broadcasting. Said the Court: "Neither the First Amendment nor the Fourteenth Amendment mandates a right of access to government information or sources of information within the government's control." Justices Marshall and Blackmun did not participate, while Justices Stevens, Brennan and Powell dissented, stating that an arbitrary cutting off of the flow of information on public concerns violates the First Amendment.[7]

In 1984 the Court ruled that pretrial detainees, even low-risk detainees, have no constitutional right to contact visits from their spouses, relatives, children, or friends.[8]

The Court now holds that First Amendment rights of prisoners to receive publications from the outside can be regulated whenever regulations are reasonably related to legitimate penological interests. This requires that the governmental objective underlying the regulations at issue be legitimate and neutral, and that the regulations be rationally related to that objective. Justices Stevens, Brennan and Marshall objected to "the feeble protection provided by a reasonableness standard."[9] The Court has held that prison authorities can open mail from a prisoner's attorney, in looking for contraband, so long as the prisoner is present and there is no reading of the mail by prison personnel.[10]

The Court has described as "indisputable that indigent inmates must be provided with paper and pen to draft legal documents, with notarial services to authenticate them, and with stamps to mail them,"[11] and has held that states may not prohibit inmates from conducting litigation of their own or for rendering assistance to other inmates, or punish them for doing so, in the absence of any other adequate source of legal aid.[12] Prisoners also have a constitutional right, in the language of the Court, to "adequate law libraries or adequate assistance from persons trained in the law."[13]

The property rights of prisoners must be respected by prison authorities.

---

7. Houchins v. KQED, Inc., 438 U.S. 1, 98 S. Ct. 2588, 57 L. Ed. 2d 553 (1978).

8. Block v. Rutherford, 468 U.S. 576, 104 S. Ct. 3227, 82 L. Ed. 2d 438 (1984).

9. Thornburgh v. Abbott, 490 U.S. 401, 109 S. Ct. 1874, 104 L. Ed. 2d 459 (1989).

10. Wolff v. McDonnell, 418 U.S. 539, 94 S. Ct. 2963, 41 L. Ed. 2d 935, 71 Ohio Op. 2d 336 (1974).

11. Bounds v. Smith, 430 U.S. 817, 97 S. Ct. 1491, 52 L. Ed. 2d 72, 81 (1977).

12. Johnson v. Avery, 393 U.S. 483, 89 S. Ct. 747, 21 L. Ed. 2d 718 (1969).

13. Weddle v. Director, Patuxent Institution, 405 U.S. 1036, 92 S. Ct. 1318, 31 L. Ed. 2d 577 (1972).

Prisoners do not leave behind their freedom of religion when they enter prisons, but in 1987 the Supreme Court held that it is sufficient if prison regulations affecting the religious beliefs of inmates are "reasonably related to legitimate penological interests." So stating, five justices in the majority were willing to sustain regulations which prevented the return of Muslim prisoners from a distant work camp in time for their weekly services. Justices Brennan, Marshall, Blackmun, and Stevens all dissented, condemning the "reasonable" test where constitutional rights were affected, and affirming that government must in these instances show that less extreme measures would not serve the purpose, and stating also that the government must show the restrictions "are necessary to further an important governmental interest and that these restrictions are not greater than necessary to achieve the prison objective."[14]

The Supreme Court held in 1980 that the Fourteenth Amendment Due Process Clause does not require the invalidation of a state statute granting absolute immunity to public employees who make parole release determinations, and that 42 U.S.C.A. § 1983 is not violated when an individual released on parole inflicts harm upon a person.[15]

§ 5.09. Protecting against fraud and deception—fortune-telling

Concern for the financial safety of the people has prompted a number of governments to prohibit fortune-telling and spiritualistic seances for gain. Where money passes hands, most courts have sustained the convictions of fortune-tellers and spiritualists, even when they defended on freedoms of speech and religion,[16] privileges and immunities, and due process of law.[17]

Illustrative is a 1976 California Court of Appeals case which denied habeas corpus when a jury had found that the petitioner had taken fees for fortune-telling in violation of a Los Angeles ordinance. Said the Court: "It is within the police power of the municipality and province of the legislative body to determine that the business

---

14. O'Lone v. Estate of Shabazz, 482 U.S. 342, 107 S. Ct. 2400, 96 L. Ed. 2d 282 (1987).

15. Martinez v. State of Cal., 444 U.S. 277, 100 S. Ct. 553, 62 L. Ed. 2d 481 (1980).

16. People v. Ashley, 184 A.D. 520, 172 N.Y.S. 282, 286 (2d Dep't 1918); McMasters v. State, 21 Okla. Crim. 318, 207 P. 566, 29 A.L.R. 292 (1922); Dill v. Hamilton, 137 Neb. 723, 291 N.W. 62, 129 A.L.R. 743 (1940).

Annotation, Regulation of Astrology, Clairvoyancy, Fortune-Telling and the Like, 91 A.L.R. 3d 766.

17. Davis v. State, 118 Ohio St. 25, 6 Ohio L. Abs. 61, 160 N.E. 473 (1928).

of fortune-telling is inherently deceptive and that its regulation or prohibition is required to protect the gullible, superstitious or unwary."[18]

However, in 1985 the California Supreme Court, in an opinion by Justice Mosk, held that a ban on fortune-telling etc. was unconstitutional under the California Constitution, Article I, Section 2 (the free speech provision) which, the Court indicated, provides broader protection for this freedom than does the federal constitution. Justice Mosk said: "It is manifest that speech does not lose its protected character when it is engaged in for profit," and then added: "The act of fortune-telling . . . involves the passing of ideas and information, some valid, some questionable, some false—between the fortune teller and client." To outlaw because money was charged would soon result in outlawing lectures when a charge was made for attendance, said Justice Mosk. He added: "The constitutional right of free expression is an essential ingredient of our democratic society. . . . The airing of opposite views is fundamental to an informed electorate and through it, a free society."[19]

A New Jersey court has also reversed the conviction of a "medium" for fortune-telling when it concluded that the act was part of a religious service, in which freedom to participate was guaranteed by the state constitution.[20]

§ 5.10. —mail frauds

In 1892 the United States Supreme Court held that a Congressional act banning lotteries' use of the mails did not violate freedom of the press.[21]

The Court in 1944 reversed the decision of a federal court of appeals which had set aside a conviction under the mail fraud statute of a person who had been soliciting funds for the "I Am" movement. The truth of the defendant's religious beliefs could not be submitted to the jury, the trial court had ruled, and this was affirmed by the Supreme Court. The trial court, in the language of Justice Stone's dissenting opinion, "submitted to the jury the single issue whether petitioners honestly believed [some allegedly religious experiences] had occurred, with the instruction that if the jury did not so find, then it should return a verdict of guilty." The jury

---

18. In re Bartha, 63 Cal. App. 3d 584, 134 Cal. Rptr. 39, 45, 91 A.L.R.3d 759 (2d Dist. 1976) (citing cases).

19. Spiritual Psychic Science Church of Truth, Inc. v. Azusa, 39 Cal. 3d 501, 217 Cal. Rptr. 225, 703 P.2d 1119, 1123-24 (1985).

20. State v. De Laney, 1 N.J. Misc. 619, 122 A. 890 (Sup. Ct. 1923).

21. Ex parte Rapier, 143 U.S. 110, 12 S. Ct. 374, 36 L. Ed. 93, 102 (1892).

returned a verdict of guilty. Justice Jackson in dissent said: "I would dismiss the indictment and have done with this business of judicially examining other peoples' faiths."[22]

The following year the United States Court of Appeals for the Seventh Circuit ruled that a person who urged his followers to invest in a faith known as "neology" could be convicted under the mail fraud statute. The jury had properly been told that "if you believe they are matters of religion you are not to question the truth or falsity of such beliefs."[23]

The Supreme Court ruled in 1948 that the mail fraud statutes could be applied to publishers without violating freedom of the press. Said Justice Black for the Court: "A contention cannot be seriously considered which assumes that freedom of the press includes a right to raise money to promote circulation by deception of the public."[24]

§ 5.11. —solicitation of funds

Governments believe they have an interest in protecting the public from frauds, as well as from annoyances, which justifies some controls upon both individuals and groups, even religious organizations such as the Salvation Army, when they are engaged in soliciting funds from citizens.

In the 1940 case of *Cantwell v. Connecticut* the Supreme Court voided a law requiring of Jehovah's Witnesses and others soliciting funds on the streets for religious or charitable purposes a certificate which could be denied by a public official unless he believed "such cause is a religious one or is a bona fide object of charity or philanthropy, and conforms to reasonable standards of efficiency and integrity." The Court stated:

> To condition the solicitation of aid for the perpetuation of religious views or systems upon a license, the grant of which rests in the determination by state authority as to what is a religious cause, is to lay a forbidden burden upon the exercise of liberty protected by the Constitution.

However, by way of dictum the Court added:

> The general regulation, in the public interest, of solicitation, which does not involve any religious test and does not unreason-

---

22. U.S. v. Ballard, 322 U.S. 78, 64 S. Ct. 882, 88 L. Ed. 1148, 1158 (1944).

23. U.S. v. Carruthers, 152 F.2d 512 (C.C.A. 7th Cir. 1945).

24. Donaldson v. Read Magazine, 333 U.S. 178, 68 S. Ct. 591, 598, 92 L. Ed. 628, 641 (1948).

ably obstruct or delay the collection of funds, is not open to any constitutional objection, even though the collection is for a religious purpose. Such regulation would not constitute a prohibited previous restraint on the free exercise of religion or interpose an inadmissible obstacle to its exercise. . . . Without doubt, a State may protect its citizens from fraudulent solicitation by requiring a stranger in the community, before permitting him publicly to solicit funds for any purpose, to establish his identity and his authority to act for the cause which he purports to represent. The State is likewise free to regulate the time and manner of solicitation generally, in the interest of public safety, peace, comfort or convenience.[25]

Five years later, in *Thomas v. Collins,* the Court by way of dictum added: "Once the speaker . . . undertakes the collection of funds or securing subscriptions, he enters a realm where reasonable regulation or identification requirement may be imposed."[26] In 1948 the Court added: "A contention cannot be seriously considered which assumes that freedom of the press includes a right to raise money to promote circulation [of a magazine] by deception of the public."[27]

In 1990 the Court held that a Post Office regulation could prohibit workers for the Democratic party from "solicitation of alms and contributions" on the sidewalk in front of the Bowie, Maryland post office. The opinion of the Court pointed out that such sidewalk was not a public forum, since it led only from the parking lot to the front door of the post office, and was not dedicated to any expressive activities. Accordingly, it was to be judged under rules for "nonpublic fora," which meant a reasonableness test. Justice Kennedy, concurring, indicated that there was no discrimination on the basis of content and that the regulation was narrowly drawn to serve an important governmental interest and still allowed the party to engage in a broad range of action to express the views of the party. Justice Kennedy believed it was not necessary to decide if it was a public or nonpublic forum, since it was a reasonable time, place, and manner restriction of protected expression. Justices Brennan, Marshall and Stevens dissented, as did Justice Blackmun in part. They wrote that the Court has "never applied a 'reasonable' test to speech in a place where government property was open to the public," and that to validate such a restriction the government must

---

25. Cantwell v. State of Connecticut, 310 U.S. 296, 60 S. Ct. 900, 84 L. Ed. 1213, 128 A.L.R. 1352 (1940).

26. Thomas v. Collins, 323 U.S. 516, 65 S. Ct. 315, 89 L. Ed. 430 (1945).

27. Donaldson v. Read Magazine, 333 U.S. 178, 68 S. Ct. 591, 92 L. Ed. 628, 642 (1948).

show a compelling interest, plus a narrowly-drawn control. They would find unconstitutional any attempt to distinguish between soliciting and other forms of speech, and observed that "any restriction on speech, the application of which turns on the substance of the speech, is content-based, no matter what the government's interest may be." To them a ban upon asking for financial support of the Democratic Party was clearly content-based.[28]

Two years later the Court held that a public airport terminal operated by the New York Port Authority was not a public forum and that solicitation of funds there by the International Society for Krishna Consciousness could be banned. Justices Kennedy, Blackmun, Stevens and Souter concurred, disagreeing with the holding that the airport was not a public forum but taking the view that that reasonable controls of solicitation of funds, which they viewed as a "non-speech" activity, were valid.[29] In a companion ruling the same day, the Court held that a ban upon the same group's distribution of religious literature at the same airport terminal was unconstitutional. It was a per curiam decision for reasons given by Justices O'Connor, Kennedy, Souter and Blackmun. Justices Souter, with whom Justices Blackmun and Stevens agreed, said: "We have held the solicitation of money by charities to be fully protected as the dissemination of ideas. . . . One cannot provide government with plenary authority to ban solicitations just because it could be fraudulent." Justice Kennedy, in an opinion joined by Justices Blackmun, Souter, and Stevens saw the airport as a public forum, and would deny any notion of giving a governmental body greater powers to limit First Amendment freedoms as a proprietor rather than as a regulator. "It leaves the government with almost unlimited authority to restrict speech on its property by doing nothing more than attributing a non-speech related purpose for the area." His opinion, however, would acknowledge that non-speech elements of expressive conduct can be subject to reasonable restrictions on time, place, and manner.[30]

Even though a statute prohibiting solicitations by charitable organizations whose costs of soliciting were over 25% had a provision for waiver "where the 25% limitation would effectively prevent the charitable organization from raising contributions," the Supreme Court, in a suit brought by a "professional" fund-raiser, invalidated

---

28. U.S. v. Kokinda, 497 U.S. 720, 110 S. Ct. 3115, 111 L. Ed. 2d 571 (1990).

29. International Soc. for Krishna Consciousness, Inc. v. Lee, 505 U.S. 672, 112 S. Ct. 2701, 120 L. Ed. 2d 541 (1992), concurring opinion at 112 S. Ct. 2711.

30. Lee v. International Soc. for Krishna Consciousness, Inc., 505 U.S. 830, 112 S. Ct. 2709, 120 L. Ed. 2d 669 (1992).

the statute as violative of the First Amendment. Interestingly, the Court ruled that where a plaintiff was protecting First Amendment interests, the tribunal was liberal in according standing to parties not primarily affected by legislation, so long as they could show "injury in fact" and could be expected to properly frame the issues in the case.[31]

Legislation controlling solicitation becomes unconstitutional when it suffers from the vice of vagueness. In 1976, while recognizing that municipalities can generally protect citizens against fraud and undue annoyance, the Supreme Court held unconstitutionally vague an ordinance requiring advance notice to the police department by "any person desiring to canvass, solicit or call from house to house for a recognized charitable . . . or political campaign or cause . . . in writing for identification only."[32] In 1980, the Court acknowledged that a city can regulate solicitation in such a manner as not to intrude upon communicative rights, but added that charitable solicitation in residential neighborhoods is protected by the First Amendment. The Court held void an ordinance prohibiting the solicitation of contributions by charitable organizations that did not use at least 75% of their receipts for "charitable purposes," those being defined to exclude expenses of soliciting, salaries, overhead, and other administrative expenses. The Court held that the government's "interest in preventing fraud can be better served by measures less intrusive than a direct prohibition on solicitation."[33]

In 1988 the Court ruled unconstitutional as violative of freedom of speech a North Carolina statute requiring licenses for fund-raisers for charities, and requiring that prior to any appeal for funds the fund-raisers must disclose the percentage of gross receipts actually turned over to charities from funds collected in the state, with detailed provisions that fees up to 20% could be deemed reasonable, with solicitors having the burden of showing reasonableness of fees above 20%, and with a statutory provision that fees exceeding 35% were presumed to be unreasonable. Concluding that the fund-raising control was "content-based," the Court applied to the legislation the exacting scrutiny test. Because the licensing statute permitted delays without limit in deciding whether to grant or deny the license, the Court ruled it unconstitutional. Chief Justice Rehnquist and Justice O'Connor dissented, being of the belief that the disclosure provi-

---

31. Secretary of State of Md. v. Joseph H. Munson Co., Inc., 467 U.S. 947, 104 S. Ct. 2839, 81 L. Ed. 2d 786 (1984).

32. Hynes v. Mayor and Council of Borough of Oradell, 425 U.S. 610, 96 S. Ct. 1755, 48 L. Ed. 2d 243 (1976).

33. Village of Schaumburg v. Citizens for a Better Environment, 444 U.S. 620, 100 S. Ct. 826, 63 L. Ed. 2d 73 (1980).

sions were reasonable and the fee provisions narrowly tailored to accomplish a legitimate end.[34]

In 1993 the Court acknowledged that there is a substantial interest in communication, as well as substantial interests in preventing fraud and in protecting the privacy of individuals subjected to solicitations. It then added that in cases of commercial speech, it would ask if the speech concerned lawful activity and was not misleading; then, where both opposed interests are substantial, whether the regulation directly advances the governmental interests asserted, and whether it is not more extensive than is necessary to serve that interest. It held that a state law banning direct, uninvited solicitations by certified public accountants seeking new business was not necessary to protect the interests advanced, and did not serve these purposes in a direct and material manner, and hence was unconstitutional under the First Amendment.[35]

A federal statute allowing photographic reproduction of United States currency for philatelic, numismatic, educational, historical or newsworthy purposes, as an exception to the otherwise universal statutory prohibition on reproductions of currency was voided by the Court as not a valid time, place and manner regulation because it discriminated on the basis of content.[36]

§ 5.12. —soliciting members for organizations

Governmental bodies have often felt that they have an interest in discouraging membership in certain organizations such as the Ku Klux Klan and the Communist Party. In addition, they have at times taken action designed to prevent initiation fees and dues from being drained off for the personal advantage of solicitors.

In 1945 the United States Supreme Court ruled that a state could not punish a labor union official for speaking at a labor meeting and soliciting new members without an organizer's card issued by a public official. Although the meeting occurred within a city hall, it can be assumed that the same registration requirement would be equally unconstitutional if the organizational activity occurred upon the public streets or in a public park or, for that matter, in private halls. Said the Court: "A requirement that one must register before he undertakes to make a public speech to enlist support for a lawful

---

34. Riley v. National Federation of the Blind of North Carolina, Inc., 487 U.S. 781, 108 S. Ct. 2667, 101 L. Ed. 2d 669 (1988); Regan v. Time, Inc., 468 U.S. 641, 104 S. Ct. 3262, 82 L. Ed. 2d 487 (1984).

35. Edenfield v. Fane, 507 U.S. 761, 113 S. Ct. 1792, 123 L. Ed. 2d 543 (1993).

36. Regan v. Time, Inc., 468 U.S. 641, 104 S. Ct. 3262, 82 L. Ed. 2d 487 (1984).

movement is quite incompatible with the requirements of the First Amendment." The Court then added:

> The usual presumption supporting legislation is balanced by the preferred place given in our scheme to the great, the fundamental democratic freedoms secured by the First Amendment. That priority gives these liberties a sanctity and a sanction not permitting dubious intrusions. For these reasons any attempt to restrict those liberties must be justified by clear public interest, threatened not doubtfully or remotely, but by clear and present danger. The rational connection between the remedy provided and the evil to be curbed, which in other contexts might support legislation against attack on due process grounds, will not suffice. These rights rest on firmer foundation. Accordingly, whatever occasion would restrain orderly discussion and persuasion . . . must have clear support in public danger, actual or impending. Only the gravest abuses, endangering paramount interests, give occasion for permissible limitation. It is therefore in our tradition to allow the widest room for discussion, the narrowest range for its restriction, particularly when this right is exercised in conjunction with peaceable assembly.[37]

In 1958 the Court again invalidated an ordinance requiring a permit from a mayor and council before a union organizer or any other person could solicit membership for any organization requiring dues, where the ordinance lacked adequate standards to guide and control the public officials. Under the ordinance, the permit could be denied after considering "the character of the applicant, the nature of the organization for which members are desired to be solicited, and its effects upon the general welfare of the citizens of the City of Baxley." The Supreme Court ruled:

> These criteria are without semblance of definitive standards or other controlling guides governing the action of the mayor and Council in granting or withholding a permit. It is thus plain that they act in this respect in their uncontrolled discretion.

> It is settled by a long line of recent decisions of this Court that an ordinance which, like this one, makes the peaceful enjoyment of freedoms which the constitution guarantees contingent upon the uncontrolled will of an official—as by requiring a permit or license which may be granted or withheld in the

---

37. Thomas v. Collins, 323 U.S. 516, 65 S. Ct. 315, 89 L. Ed. 430, 440, 445 (1945).

discretion of such official—is an unconstitutional censorship or prior restraint upon the enjoyment of those freedoms.[38]

Stating that the "fact of confinement and the needs of the penal system impose limitations on constitutional rights, including those derived from the First Amendment," the Supreme Court upheld regulations which prohibited prisoners from soliciting other prisoners for union membership, barred union meetings within prison confines, and prohibited the utilization of bulk mailing privileges by the union. Finding that the regulations rationally furthered the permissible objectives of security and order, the Court ruled that the authorities were not required to make a demonstrable showing that the unions were harmful prior to restricting prisoners' First Amendment rights, since federal courts are obliged to pay deference to the informed discretion of prison officials unless it can be shown that their actions are unreasonable. The fact that both meeting and bulk mailing privileges were extended to other organizations did not offend the equal protection clause since a prison, like a military base, is not a public forum and therefore authorities are justified in making reasonable regulations regarding who will be allowed to speak. Justices Brennan and Marshall in dissent insisted that the basic mode of First Amendment analysis requiring that restrictions on speech be supported by "reasons imperatively justifying the particular deprivation" should not be altered simply because the First Amendment claimants are incarcerated.[39]

§ 5.13. Advertising

For decades it has been recognized that advertising is a form of lawful commercial speech,[40] the Court holding in 1976 that the consumer's interest in the free flow of commercial information merits constitutional protection for advertising, so long as it is not "false or misleading."[41] The following year the Court held that attorneys cannot be prevented from advertising the prices they charge for the performance of routine legal services.[42] That year, too, the Court voided a municipal ban on "For Sale" signs on residential proper-

---

38. Staub v. City of Baxley, 355 U.S. 313, 78 S. Ct. 277, 2 L. Ed. 2d 302, 311 (1958).

39. Jones v. North Carolina Prisoners' Labor Union, Inc., 433 U.S. 119, 97 S. Ct. 2532, 53 L. Ed. 2d 629 (1977).

40. Bigelow v. Virginia, 421 U.S. 809, 95 S. Ct. 2222, 44 L. Ed. 2d 600 (1975).

41. Virginia State Bd. of Pharmacy v. Virginia Citizens Consumer Council, Inc., 425 U.S. 748, 96 S. Ct. 1817, 48 L. Ed. 2d 346 (1976).

42. Bates v. State Bar of Arizona, 433 U.S. 350, 97 S. Ct. 2691, 53 L. Ed. 2d 810, 51 Ohio Misc. 1, 5 Ohio Op. 3d 60 (1977).

ties, concluding that the municipal interest in avoiding "white flight" was outweighed by First Amendment values.[43]

In 1980 the Court reminded us that advertising must concern "lawful activity" to be accorded First Amendment protections, and held that First Amendment rights were violated when a state completely banned all promotional advertising by a public utility. The Court explained that in these cases it must ask "whether the asserted governmental interest [in opposition to communication] is substantial . . . [then] we must ask whether the regulation directly advances the substantial government interest asserted and whether it is not more extensive than is necessary to serve that interest."[44]

Signs are traditional means of conveying information and are protected under the First Amendment, subject to regulation and prohibition under general principles applicable to that Amendment. Finding that there were less restrictive means that would adequately serve the government's legitimate interests, the Supreme Court in 1988 voided a provision of the District of Columbia Code which prohibited the display of any sign within 500 feet of a foreign embassy, if the sign tended to bring the foreign embassy into "public odium" or "public disrepute."[45]

In 1981 the Court, in a plurality opinion, held unconstitutional an ordinance prohibiting off-site billboards from carrying even non-commercial messages while allowing on-site billboards to carry commercial advertisements. The opinion of the Court reaffirmed the propriety of earlier rulings allowing the prohibition of off-site billboards.[46]

§ 5.14. Zoning controls and other land use restraints affecting First Amendment freedoms

Attempts to zone out either churches or church-related schools from an entire municipal corporation have been invalidated.[47] The better view is that attempts to zone churches and synagogues out of residential districts are unconstitutional. The New York high court states:

---

43. Linmark Associates, Inc. v. Willingboro Tp., 431 U.S. 85, 97 S. Ct. 1614, 52 L. Ed. 2d 155 (1977).

44. Central Hudson Gas & Elec. Corp. v. Public Service Commission of New York, 447 U.S. 557, 100 S. Ct. 2343, 65 L. Ed. 2d 341 (1980).

45. Boos v. Barry, 485 U.S. 312, 108 S. Ct. 1157, 99 L. Ed. 2d 333 (1988).

46. Metromedia, Inc. v. City of San Diego, 453 U.S. 490, 101 S. Ct. 2882, 69 L. Ed. 2d 800 (1981).

47. Mooney v. Village of Orchard Lake, 333 Mich. 389, 53 N.W.2d 308 (1952); North Shore Unitarian Soc. v. Village of Plandome, 200 Misc. 524, 109 N.Y.S.2d 803 (Sup. Ct. 1951).

It is well established in this country that a zoning ordinance may not wholly exclude a church or synagogue from any residential district. Such a provision is stricken on the ground that it bears no substantial relation to the public health, safety, morals, peace or general welfare of the community.[48]

Permits have been required before churches could build in residential zones, but they cannot be denied arbitrarily.[49] However, some courts have sustained denials of such permits where it was clear that the erection of such an edifice would occasion severe traffic congestion and hazards in the neighborhood, or would greatly depreciate the value of residences in the neighborhood.[50]

When public schools are permitted in an area, the exclusion of church-related schools from the area is generally deemed unreasonable and invalid,[51] although there is some authority to the contrary.[52]

Church-related institutions, such as hospitals, orphanages, and seminaries have at times been permitted in residential zones,[53] but there is also contra authority.[54]

When a church was banned from a downtown business district, the case was remanded by the Court of Appeals for the Eighth Circuit to the district court, with summary judgment for the city reversed, and the city given an opportunity to prove that the church

---

48. Diocese of Rochester v. Planning Bd. of Town of Brighton, 1 N.Y.2d 508, 154 N.Y.S.2d 849, 136 N.E.2d 827, 834 (1956).

Semble: Community Synagogue v. Bates, 1 N.Y.2d 445, 154 N.Y.S.2d 15, 136 N.E.2d 488 (1956).

Contra: Miami Beach United Lutheran Church of the Epiphany v. City of Miami Beach, 82 So. 2d 880 (Fla. 1955); Corporation of Presiding Bishop of Church of Jesus Christ of Latter-Day Saints v. City of Porterville, 90 Cal. App. 2d 656, 203 P.2d 823 (4th Dist. 1949).

49. Redwood City Co. of Jehovah's Witnesses v. City of Menlo Park, 167 Cal. App. 2d 686, 335 P.2d 195 (1st Dist. 1959).

50. Milwaukie Co. of Jehovah's Witnesses v. Mullen, 214 Or. 281, 330 P.2d 5, 74 A.L.R.2d 347 (1958); Miami Beach United Lutheran Church of the Epiphany v. City of Miami Beach, 82 So. 2d 880 (Fla. 1955).

51. Catholic Bishop of Chicago v. Kingery, 371 Ill. 257, 20 N.E.2d 583 (1939).

52. State ex rel. Wisconsin Lutheran High School Conference v. Sinar, 267 Wis. 91, 65 N.W.2d 43 (1954).

53. Concordia Collegiate Institute v. Miller, 301 N.Y. 189, 93 N.E.2d 632, 21 A.L.R.2d 544 (1950); Daughters of St. Paul, Inc. v. Zoning Bd. of Appeals of Town of Trumbull, 17 Conn. App. 53, 549 A.2d 1076 (1988) (sustaining grant of special exception for convent).

54. Yanow v. Seven Oaks Park, Inc., 11 N.J. 341, 94 A.2d 482, 36 A.L.R.2d 639 (1953).

would displace economic activity hoped for, to a greater extent than other non-commercial uses permitted in the business district.[55]

When zoning ordinances restrict the location of adult theaters, leaving reasonable alternative avenues of communication, and serving a substantial societal interest, they are constitutional although impacting upon freedom of expression. In 1976, the Supreme Court upheld, over a First Amendment argument, an ordinance prohibiting locating an adult theater within 1,000 feet of any two other regulated uses or within 500 feet of any residential zone. The Court was "not persuaded that [such] ordinances will have a significant deterrent effect on the exhibition of films protected by the First Amendment." Justice Stevens for the Court added: "Even though we recognize that the First Amendment will not tolerate the total suppression of erotic materials that have some arguably artistic value, it is manifest that society's interest in protecting this type of expression is of a wholly different, and lesser magnitude than the interest in untrammeled political debate."[56] Ten years later the Court sustained an ordinance banning adult theaters within 1,000 feet of any residential zone, single- or multiple-family dwelling, church, park or school.[57]

In 1994 the Court voided an attempt by a municipality to ban "almost all residential signs" in application to a homeowner who had been refused permission to exhibit an 8-1/2 by 11 inch sign with the words "For Peace in the Gulf" in her second-story window. The opinion indicates a continuing judicial respect for the prime kind of communication, that on political concerns.[58]

§ 5.15. First Amendment issues where labor relations are involved

While the Supreme Court in 1977 found no constitutional barrier to an agency shop agreement between a municipality and a teachers' union insofar as the agreement required *every* employee in the unit to pay a service fee to defray costs of collective bargaining, contract administration and grievance adjustment, the Court ruled that the union could not collect from dissenting non-union employees any

---

55. Cornerstone Bible Church v. City of Hastings, 948 F.2d 464 (8th Cir. 1991).

56. Young v. American Mini Theatres, Inc., 427 U.S. 50, 96 S. Ct. 2440, 49 L. Ed. 2d 310 (1976).

57. City of Renton v. Playtime Theatres, Inc., 475 U.S. 41, 106 S. Ct. 925, 89 L. Ed. 2d 29 (1986).

58. City of Ladue v. Gilleo, 512 U.S. 43, 114 S. Ct. 2038, 129 L. Ed. 2d 36 (1994).

sums for the support of ideological causes not germane to its duties as the collective-bargaining agent.[59]

Remarking that "substantial alternative channels" were open to other teachers' organizations, the Court held valid a collective bargaining agreement giving to one teachers' organization the exclusive use of its inter-school mail system and the teachers' mailboxes, finding no violation of either the First Amendment or the Equal Protection Clause. Justices Brennan, Marshall and Stevens aptly pointed out in dissent that public bodies cannot engage in viewpoint discrimination such as this where, as here, there is no discernible state interest to justify the discrimination.[60]

The Court has sustained over First Amendment objections an employee arrangement under which workers were not compelled to join a union, but were obligated to pay an "agency fee" equivalent to membership dues, with a limited rebate provision. The Court ruled that the governing statute did not permit inclusion of the "agency fee" in sums used in organizing efforts by the union or for litigation unrelated to the non-union employees' bargaining unit.[61]

Since requiring non-union employees to support their collective bargaining representative has an impact upon their First Amendment interests, the Court held in 1986 that the First Amendment requires procedural safeguards to be carefully tailored to minimize this infringement. Adequate information must be provided initially to the non-union employees to enable them to ascertain whether the charges imposed upon them are valid. Furthermore, there must be a reasonably prompt decisionmaker. Amounts reasonably in dispute must be placed in escrow until the decision.[62]

The Court in 1987 reaffirmed that, where a worker's speech is a matter of public concern there must be a balancing of societal interests involved, and held that the First Amendment protected from dismissal a clerical employee in a county constable's office, when the employee, hearing of the attack on President Reagan's life, said: "If they go for him again, I hope they get him." The Court stated that "the manner, time and place of the employee's expression are relevant, as is the context in which the dispute arose," and noted that the employee's remark had been made under conditions

---

59. Abood v. Detroit Bd. of Ed., 431 U.S. 209, 97 S. Ct. 1782, 52 L. Ed. 2d 261 (1977).

60. Perry Educ. Ass'n v. Perry Local Educators' Ass'n, 460 U.S. 37, 103 S. Ct. 948, 74 L. Ed. 2d 794, 9 Ed. Law Rep. 23 (1983).

61. Ellis v. Brotherhood of Ry., Airline and S.S. Clerks, Freight Handlers, Exp. and Station Employees, 466 U.S. 435, 104 S. Ct. 1883, 80 L. Ed. 2d 428 (1984).

62. Chicago Teachers Union, Local No. 1, AFT, AFL-CIO v. Hudson, 475 U.S. 292, 106 S. Ct. 1066, 89 L. Ed. 2d 232, 30 Ed. Law Rep. 649 (1986).

where it did not interfere with the work of others, because it was not heard by the public, and it did not provide any likelihood of diminished law enforcement by the speaker. In dissent, the Chief Justice, Justices Scalia, White and O'Connor thought the speech was not "of public concern" and consequently any interest in freedom of expression was outweighed by the constable's interest in maintaining a public image and *esprit de corps.*[63]

In 1991 the Supreme Court announced that for charges to be imposed by labor unions upon dissenting employees, "the chargeable activities must (1) be germane to collective bargaining activity, (2) be justified by the government's vital policy interest in labor peace and avoiding 'free riders' and (3) not significantly add to the burden of free speech that is inherent in . . . the agency or union shop." The Court held that the First Amendment rights of members dissenting from the majority in a public sector union prevent them from being "charged over their objection for lobbying activities that do not concern legislative ratification of, or fiscal appropriations for, their collective bargaining." However, the Court held that a union could charge dissenters for such costs as preparing for a potential strike, that had value in bargaining. It added: "A local bargaining representative may charge objecting employees for their proportionate share of the costs associated with otherwise chargeable activities of its state and national affiliates, even if those activities were not performed for the direct benefit of the objecting employees' bargaining unit."[64]

§ 5.16. The public's constitutional right of access to information and ideas

The United States Supreme Court has frequently acknowledged that the First Amendment protects a right to know, that is, a right of access to both information and ideas. In 1969 the Court stated that "it is now well established that the Constitution protects the right to receive information and ideas. . . . This right to receive information and ideas, regardless of their social worth, is fundamental to our free society."[65]

Again, seven years later, the Court recognized that in First Amendment situations it is not always the right of speakers and writers that is the paramount First Amendment value to a protected,

---

63. Rankin v. McPherson, 483 U.S. 378, 107 S. Ct. 2891, 97 L. Ed. 2d 315 (1987).

64. Lehnert v. Ferris Faculty Ass'n, 500 U.S. 507, 111 S. Ct. 1950, 114 L. Ed. 2d 572, 67 Ed. Law Rep. 421 (1991).

65. Stanley v. Georgia, 394 U.S. 557, 89 S. Ct. 1243, 22 L. Ed. 2d 542 (1969).

but rather the right of recipient consumers and citizens to information that is being vindicated.[66]

Equally significant is the constitutional right to be free from ideas noisily imposed upon unreceptive citizens.[67]

In 1997 the Supreme Court sustained a federal law requiring all cable operators with more than 12 channels to set aside one-third of their channel capacity for local broadcasters. The Court found that important governmental interests served by this legislation were (1) preserving the benefits of free, over-the-air local broadcast television, (2) promoting the widespread dissemination of information from a multiplicity of sources, and (3) promoting fair competition in the market for television programming. The burden upon cable operators, concluded the Court, was only "modest." Justice Breyer, concurring in part, wrote:

> The statute's basic non-economic purpose is to prevent too precipitous a decline in the quality and quantity of programming choice for an existing non-cable subscribing segment of the public, [as well as] to facilitate the public discussion and informed deliberation [which] the First Amendment seeks to achieve . . . [this being] a governmental purpose of the highest scrutiny.

The Justices in the majority saw this as a "content-neutral" governmental control affecting First Amendment matters and, as to this, Justice Kennedy wrote: "Content neutral regulations do not pose the same inherent dangers to free expression and thus are subject to a less rigorous analysis, which afford the Government latitude in designing a regulatory solution." Furthermore, he concluded the evidence indicated "the actual effects are modest." Broadly speaking, he added, "[j]udgments about how competing economic interests are to be reconciled in the complex and fast-changing field of television are for Congress to make." Justice Breyer, in concurring thought it was enough that the Court gave "intermediate scrutiny" to the federal legislation.

In dissent, Justices O'Connor, Scalia, Thomas and Ginsburg opposed "intermediate scrutiny" in the case, being unwilling to describe the problem as "content neutral." They saw the "must

---

66. Virginia State Bd. of Pharmacy v. Virginia Citizens Consumer Council, Inc., 425 U.S. 748, 96 S. Ct. 1817, 48 L. Ed. 2d 346 (1976).

67. Ward v. Rock Against Racism, 491 U.S. 781, 109 S. Ct. 2746, 105 L. Ed. 2d 661 (1989).

carry" provisions of the Act as subject to strict scrutiny which would invalidate the legislation.[68]

§ 5.17. Balancing First Amendment interests with the interest in educational and aesthetic values

The Supreme Court has held that freedom of religion was violated by a state statute requiring Amish children to attend high schools over their religious objections. Chief Justice Berger stated: "a state's interest in universal education, however highly we rank it, is not totally free from a balancing process when it impinges on other fundamental rights and interests, such as those specifically protected by the Free Exercise Clause of the First Amendment and the traditional interest of parents with respect to the religious upbringing of their children, so long as they . . . prepare them for additional obligations."[69]

Two years later the Supreme Court held that a societal interest in aesthetics may at times outweigh the societal interest in freedom of communication. Valid was a Los Angeles ordinance prohibiting the posting of signs on public property, such as utility poles, when applied to signs advocating the election of a candidate for the city council. The Court acknowledged that "restrictions on expressive activity may be invalid if the remaining modes of communication are inadequate," and professed to follow the orthodox test requiring the finding of an opposed societal interest unrelated to the suppression of free expression and an incidental restriction on expression no greater than essential to the furtherance of that interest. In dissent, Justices Brennan, Marshall and Blackmun acknowledged that the judicial task is one of balancing opposed societal interests in expression and aesthetics, but stressed the Court should "require the government to provide tangible proof of the legitimacy and substantiality of its aesthetic objective."[70]

§ 5.18. Balancing First Amendment interests with the interest in effective law enforcement

In 1972 the United States Supreme Court wrote that there is a strong societal interest in "fair and effective law enforcement aimed at providing security for the person and property of the individual"

---

68. Turner Broadcasting System, Inc. v. F.C.C., 117 S. Ct. 1174, 137 L. Ed. 2d 369 (U.S. 1997).

69. Board of Educ., Island Trees Union Free School Dist. No. 26 v. Pico, 457 U.S. 853, 102 S. Ct. 2799, 8, 73 L. Ed. 2d 435, 4 Ed. Law Rep. 1013 (1982).

70. Members of City Council of City of Los Angeles v. Taxpayers for Vincent, 466 U.S. 789, 104 S. Ct. 2118, 80 L. Ed. 2d 772 (1984).

and that such enforcement "is a fundamental function of government." The Court ruled that where the burden on news gathering from the absence of "a newsman's privilege" was uncertain, newspaper reporters, like other citizens, would have to respond to grand jury summonses and divulge what they knew about crimes being committed. The Court said: "We cannot accept the argument that the public interest in possible future news about crime from undisclosed, unverified sources must take precedence over the public interest in pursuing and prosecuting those crimes reported to the press by informants and in thus deterring the commission of such crimes in the future." There was, said the Court, an overriding and compelling state interest here that outweighed claims of the newspaper reporters. There were four dissenters, with Justice Stewart writing that "the First Amendment interests . . . to insure nothing less than democratic decision making through the free flow of information to the public outweighs the interest in securing the names of reporters' informers."[71]

While holding constitutional "on its face" a federal statute making it a crime to unwillingly and willfully make a threat against the President, the Supreme Court in 1969 ordered the acquittal of a defendant when it found his language did not constitute a "true threat." The Court reaffirmed "the profound national commitment to the principle that debate on public issues should be uninhibited, robust and wide-open, and that it may well include vehement, caustic and sometimes unpleasantly sharp attacks on government and school officials."[72]

But in 1983 the Supreme Court allowed the sentencing judge to take into account a defendant's animus toward his victim. The Court held that the Constitution did not prohibit state trial court, in making a sentencing decision following the defendant's first-degree murder conviction, from taking into account the elements of racial hatred in the murder.[73]

The Supreme Court has said by way of dictum that "the Constitution does not erect a *per se* barrier to the admission of evidence concerning one's beliefs and associations at sentencing simply because these beliefs and associations are protected by the First Amendment," and that "a defendant's membership in an organization that endorses the killing of any identifiable group, for example, might be relevant to a jury's inquiry into whether the defendant will be dangerous in the future." However, in the case at bar the Court

---

71. Branzburg v. Hayes, 408 U.S. 665, 92 S. Ct. 2646, 33 L. Ed. 2d 626 (1972).

72. Watts v. U.S., 394 U.S. 705, 89 S. Ct. 1399, 22 L. Ed. 2d 664 (1969).

73. Barclay v. Florida, 463 U.S. 939, 103 S. Ct. 3418, 77 L. Ed. 2d 1134 (1983).

held violative of the First Amendment, in its application to the states, the government's use in a capital sentencing proceeding of evidence that the defendant belonged to a white racist organization, when the beliefs of such organization had no relevance in the instant case. A defendant's abstract beliefs, however obnoxious to most people, may not be taken into consideration by a sentencing judge, said the Court.[74]

When the leader of a group of young African American men and boys told the group, as a young white boy approached, "There goes a white boy, go get him," the young African American man's sentence for aggravated battery was enhanced under a Wisconsin statute authorizing a sentence for aggravated battery whenever a defendant in committing a crime selected a victim because of race, religion, color, disability, sexual orientation, national origin, or ancestry. When the defendant appealed his increased sentence on First Amendment grounds, arguing that he was punished for what he thought and said, the Wisconsin Supreme Court reversed his enhanced penalty on the ground that the statute "violates the First Amendment directly by punishing what the legislature has deemed to be offensive conduct." The United States Supreme Court reversed the Wisconsin tribunal, repeating what it had said in *Dawson,* that "the Constitution does not erect a per se barrier to the admission of evidence concerning one's beliefs and associations at sentencing simply because those beliefs and associations are protected by the First Amendment." It was for the Wisconsin Legislature, not the state's highest court, to decide as a general matter that bias-motivated offenses warrant greater maximum penalties across the board, ruled the Supreme Court, since "the primary responsibility for fixing criminal penalties lies with the legislature."[75]

§ 5.19. Legislative power of Congress under the Fourteenth Amendment relative to First Amendment

After the Supreme Court in 1990 refused to require states, in First Amendment Freedom of Religion cases, to show that regulatory controls were justified by a compelling public interest,[76] Congress passed the Religious Freedom Restoration Act, requiring states in resolving such First Amendment issues to honor the compelling

---

74. Dawson v. Delaware, 503 U.S. 159, 112 S. Ct. 1093, 117 L. Ed. 2d 309 (1992).

75. Wisconsin v. Mitchell, 508 U.S. 476, 113 S. Ct. 2194, 124 L. Ed. 2d 436 (1993).

76. Employment Div., Dept. of Human Resources of Oregon v. Smith, 494 U.S. 872, 110 S. Ct. 1595, 108 L. Ed. 2d 876 (1990).

interest test, as the Court had required in a number of cases before the 1990 decision. Specifically, the RFRA prohibited "[g]overnment" from "substantially burden[ing]" a person's exercise of religion even if the burden results from a rule of general applicability unless the government could demonstrate the burden "(1) is in furtherance of a compelling governmental interest; and (2) is the least restrictive means of furthering that . . . interest."[77]

RFRA's mandate applied to any branch of federal or state government, to all officials, and to other persons acting under color of law.[78] Its universal coverage included "all Federal and State law, and the implementation of that law, whether statutory or otherwise, and whether adopted before or after [RFRA's enactment]."[79]

In 1997, the Court, while acknowledging readily that Section Five of the Fourteenth Amendment was "a positive grant of legislative power to Congress," ruled that Congressional power under Section Five extends only to "enforcing" the provisions of the Amendment. It explained that "[l]egislation which alters the meaning of the Free Exercise Clause cannot be said to be enforcing the Clause." The Fourteenth Amendment, the Court said, means that there is a vast difference between "enforcing" First Amendment rights and establishing new First Amendment rights, not by constitutional amendment but by legislative acts. The Court determined that the RFRA contradicted principles necessary to maintain the separation of powers and the federal-state balance, addressed laws of general application that placed incidental burdens on religion that were not based on animus or hostility and did not indicate any widespread pattern of religious discrimination, and was not designed to identify and counteract state laws likely to be unconstitutional. In addition, the RFRA was out of proportion to its supposed remedial or preventative object, displaced laws and prohibited official actions in almost every level of government, and constituted considerable congressional intrusion into the states' traditional prerogatives and general authority to regulate.

The legislative power of Congress in the First Amendment area is thus not to be seen, in the language of the tribunal, as "definitional" but only as "remedial" and "preventative." The attempt of the Congress to change the burden of proof on states was seen as an

---

77. 42 U.S.C.A. § 2000bb-1.
78. 28 U.S.C.A. § 2000bb-2(1).
79. 28 U.S.C.A. § 2000bb-3(a).

impermissible change in the constitutional protection to be accorded by courts to religious freedom.[80]

80. City of Boerne v. Flores, 117 S. Ct. 2157, 138 L. Ed. 2d 624 (U.S. Sup. Ct. 1997).

CHAPTER SIX

Balancing Societal Interests in First Amendment Freedoms With the Societal Interest in Protecting Private Reputation

---

§ 6.00. Introduction

The common law has long recognized a societal interest in protecting the good name and reputation of individuals, and the United States Supreme Court as early as 1922 indicated that there was to be no blanket First Amendment protection from either civil action or criminal prosecution for those who defame others.[1] In 1942 the Court indicated that the libelous was beyond the pale.[2] and 10 years later the Court again spoke of "libelous utterances" as "not being within the area of constitutionally protected speech."[3]

While no longer speaking in absolutes, the Supreme Court still recognizes "important social values . . . underlie the law of defamation," and acknowledges that "[s]ociety has a pervasive and strong interest in preventing and redressing attacks upon reputation."[4] In

---

1. Balzac v. Porto Rico, 258 U.S. 298, 42 S. Ct. 343, 66 L. Ed. 627 (1922).

2. Chaplinsky v. State of New Hampshire, 315 U.S. 568, 62 S. Ct. 766, 86 L. Ed. 1031, 1034-35 (1942).

3. Beauharnais v. People of State of Ill., 343 U.S. 250, 72 S. Ct. 725, 96 L. Ed. 919, 932 (1952).

4. Rosenblatt v. Baer, 383 U.S. 75, 86, 86 S. Ct. 669, 15 L. Ed. 2d 597 (1966).

1974 the Court explained that the "legitimate state interest underlying the law of libel is the compensation of individuals for the harm inflicted on them by defamatory falsehood."[5]

§ 6.01. Defamation of public figures

In 1964 in *New York Times v. Sullivan,* the Supreme Court ruled that a civil suit could be authorized by the states for defamation of public figures only if the statement was both false and made with actual malice, "that is, with knowledge that it was false or with reckless disregard of whether it was false or not." The Court explained that cases such as this must be considered "against the background of a profound national commitment to the principle that debate on public issues should be uninhibited, robust and wide-open, and that it may include vehement, caustic and sometimes unpleasantly sharp attacks on government and public officials."[6]

At the following term, the Court held that actual malice must also be proved in a criminal prosecution for defamation of a public official regarding his official conduct.[7]

In 1966 the Supreme Court reversed a state court judgment for a county employee who was in charge of a recreation area and who had allegedly been libeled by a local newspaper. The Court found objectionable the fact that the trial judge had authorized the jury to award the public employee a recovery without regard to evidence that the asserted implication of the column was made specifically of and concerning him. Said the Court:

> A theory that the column cast indiscriminate suspicion on the members of the group responsible for the conduct of this governmental operation is tantamount to a demand for recovery based on libel of government, and therefore is constitutionally insufficient.

The Court further ruled that the "public official" designation "applies at the very least to those among the hierarchy of government employees who have, or appear to the public to have, substantial responsibility for or control over the conduct of governmental affairs." The Court reminds us that in the *New York Times* case it had

---

5. Gertz v. Robert Welch, Inc., 418 U.S. 323, 94 S. Ct. 2997, 41 L. Ed. 2d 789 (1974).

6. New York Times Co. v. Sullivan, 376 U.S. 254, 84 S. Ct. 710, 11 L. Ed. 2d 686, 95 A.L.R.2d 1412 (1964).

7. Garrison v. State of La., 379 U.S. 64, 85 S. Ct. 209, 13 L. Ed. 2d 125 (1964); Gibson v. Lockheed Aircraft Service, 350 U.S. 356, 76 S. Ct. 366, 100 L. Ed. 395 (1956).

expressed "a profound national commitment to the principle that debate on public issues should be uninhibited, robust and wide-open, and that such debate may well include vehement, caustic and sometimes unpleasantly sharp attacks on government and public officials." The Court added:

> There is, first, a strong interest in debate on public issues, and, second, a strong interest in debate about those persons who are in a position significantly to influence the resolution of those issues. Criticism of government is at the very center of the constitutionally protected area of free discussion. Criticism of those responsible for government operations must be free, lest criticism of government itself be penalized.[8]

In 1968 the Supreme Court, in finding no actual malice in a case before it, stated:

> Reckless conduct is not measured by whether a reasonably prudent man would have published or would have investigated before publishing. There must be sufficient evidence to permit the conclusion that the defendant in fact entertained serious doubts as to the truth of his publication. Publishing with such doubts shows reckless disregard for truth or falsity and demonstrates actual malice.

The Court explained:

> Concededly, the reckless disregard standard may permit recovery in fewer situations than would a rule that publishers must satisfy the standard of the reasonable man or the prudent publisher . . . the stake of the people in public business and the conduct of public officials is so great that neither the defense of truth nor the standard of ordinary care would protect against self-censorship and thus adequately implement First Amendment policies.

By way of dictum, the Court added:

> The defendant in a defamation action brought by a public official cannot, however, automatically insure a favorable verdict by testifying that he published with a belief that the statements were true. The finder of fact must determine whether the publication was indeed made in good faith. Professions of good faith will be unlikely to prove persuasive, for example, where a story is fabricated by the defendant, is the product of his

---

8. Rosenblatt v. Baer, 383 U.S. 75, 86 S. Ct. 669, 675-76, 15 L. Ed. 2d 597 (1966).

imagination, or is based wholly on an unverified anonymous telephone call. Nor will they be likely to prevail when the publisher's allegations are so inherently improbable that only a reckless man would have put them in circulation. Likewise, recklessness may be found where there are obvious reasons to doubt the veracity of the informant or the accuracy of his report.[9]

That year the Court ruled that a public school teacher could not be discharged for a letter to a newspaper criticizing school officials, absent proof of false statements that were knowingly or recklessly made. Said the Court: "In a case such as this, absent proof of false statements knowingly or recklessly made by him, a teacher's exercise of the right to speak on issues of public importance may not furnish the basis for his dismissal from public employment."[10]

Three years later the Supreme Court held that as a matter of constitutional law a charge of criminal conduct, no matter how remote in time or place, can never be irrelevant to an official's or a candidate's fitness for office for purposes of application of the "knowing falsehood or reckless disregard" rule of *New York Times v. Sullivan*.[11] That year, too, the Court ruled that the omission of the word "alleged" by a reporter in a news story was not enough to create a jury issue of "malice" under the *New York Times* rule.[12]

Where the *New York Times* clear and convincing evidence requirement is applicable, a court on summary judgment motion can hold for the defendant if the evidence on the record cannot support a reasonable jury finding that the plaintiff has shown actual malice by clear and convincing evidence.[13]

A candidate for public office is embraced within the "public officer" rule under the *New York Times* applicability to defamations.[14]

§ 6.02. Defamation of "public figures" who are not public officials

Three years after *New York Times v. Sullivan* the United States

---

9. St. Amant v. Thompson, 390 U.S. 727, 88 S. Ct. 1323, 20 L. Ed. 2d 262 (1968).

10. Pickering v. Board of Ed. of Tp. High School Dist. 205, Will County, Illinois, 391 U.S. 563, 88 S. Ct. 1731, 20 L. Ed. 2d 811 (1968).

11. Monitor Patriot Co. v. Roy, 401 U.S. 265, 91 S. Ct. 621, 28 L. Ed. 2d 35 (1971).

12. Time, Inc. v. Pape, 401 U.S. 279, 91 S. Ct. 633, 28 L. Ed. 2d 45 (1971).

13. Anderson v. Liberty Lobby, Inc., 477 U.S. 242, 106 S. Ct. 2505, 91 L. Ed. 2d 202, 4 Fed. R. Serv. 3d (LCP) 1041 (1986).

14. Ocala Star-Banner Co. v. Damron, 401 U.S. 295, 91 S. Ct. 528, 28 L. Ed. 2d 57 (1971).

Supreme Court, in consolidated cases of *Curtis Publishing Co. v. Butts* and *Associated Press v. Walker*,[15] extended the scope of the *New York Times* rule to media defendants when sued for defamation by "public figures" who are not public officials—in one case a well-known football coach and in the other a person widely recognized during the desegregation years. Under the *New York Times* test, the Court ruled, a public figure may recover damages for a defamatory falsehood whose substance makes substantial danger to his reputation apparent, only "on a showing of highly unreasonable conduct constituting an extreme departure from the standards of investigation and reporting ordinarily adhered to by responsible publishers."[16] Misconduct sufficient to justify the award of compensatory damages under the foregoing test also justifies the award of punitive damages against the publisher, subject to the limitation that such award is not demonstrated to be founded on mere prejudice of the jury.[17] In his concurring opinion, Chief Justice Warren explained that "public figures" are non-public officers who "are nevertheless involved in the resolution of important public questions or by reason of their fame shape events in areas of concern to society at large."[18]

In 1979 the Supreme Court held that a particular citizen was not a "public figure" since he "did not thrust himself or his views into public controversy to influence others." The Court added: "Clearly those charged with defamation cannot, by their own conduct, create their own defense by making the claimant a public figure."[19] The same year the Court observed generally that a person who engages in criminal activity does not automatically become a public figure, and then held that a person held in contempt for failing to respond to a grand jury subpoena was not a public figure, since his activities were "in no way calculated to draw attention to himself." Accordingly, to recover for defamation it was not necessary for the plaintiff to prove the defendant acted with malice.[20] The Court stated in 1974:

---

15. Curtis Pub. Co. v. Butts, 388 U.S. 130, 87 S. Ct. 1975, 18 L. Ed. 2d 1094 (1967).

16. Curtis Pub. Co. v. Butts, 388 U.S. 130, 87 S. Ct. 1975, 18 L. Ed. 2d 1094 (1967).

17. Curtis Pub. Co. v. Butts, 388 U.S. 130, 87 S. Ct. 1975, 18 L. Ed. 2d 1094 (1967).

18. Curtis Pub. Co. v. Butts, 388 U.S. 130, 87 S. Ct. 1975, 18 L. Ed. 2d 1094 (1967).

19. Hutchinson v. Proxmire, 443 U.S. 111, 99 S. Ct. 2675, 61 L. Ed. 2d 411 (1979).

20. Wolston v. Reader's Digest Ass'n, Inc., 443 U.S. 157, 99 S. Ct. 2701, 61 L. Ed. 2d 450 (1979).

For the most part those who attain this status ("public figures") have assumed roles of especial prominence in the affairs of society. Some occupy positions of such pervasive power and influence that they are deemed public figures for all purposes. More commonly, those claimed as public figures have thrust themselves to the forefront of particular public controversies in order to influence the resolution of the issues involved.[21]

In 1970 the Court held that public figures cannot recover in libel unless they can show that the defamatory matter was not only false, but was uttered with actual malice—that is, with knowledge that it was false or with reckless disregard of whether it was false or not.[22]

In 1979 the Supreme Court ruled a plaintiff, suing the media for defamation in having falsely and maliciously portrayed him as a liar, was a "public figure" and had to prove reckless disregard for the truth, that is, that the defendant producer-editor for the Columbia Broadcasting System in fact entertained serious doubts as to the truth of his publication. The Court said the defendant had no absolute privilege to be free from answering discovery questions by the plaintiff about the editorial processes, including thoughts, opinions, and conclusions with respect to the material gathered by him and about his conversations with his editorial colleagues. In dissent, Justices Brennan, Stewart and Marshall took the position that a limited privileges with "some incidental sacrifice" of evidentiary material, is necessary to protect the societal values served by a free media. Although they agreed that a privilege should not shield editors' "mental processes," they urged that predecisional communications among editors should be protected by a privilege, which would yield if a public figure plaintiff made a prima facie case of defamatory falsehood.[23]

Five years later, the Court reaffirmed that the First Amendment precludes recovery by "public figures" unless the plaintiff proves by clear and convincing evidence that the defendant made a false disparaging statement with actual malice. The Court emphasized that in defamation cases, as in all the First Amendment areas where the Court has under certain circumstances permitted civil or criminal punishment for expression, it and other appellate courts are required to conduct an independent review of the record "both to be

---

21. Gertz v. Robert Welch, Inc., 418 U.S. 323, 94 S. Ct. 2997, 41 L. Ed. 2d 789, 808 (1974).

22. Greenbelt Co-op. Pub. Ass'n v. Bresler, 398 U.S. 6, 90 S. Ct. 1537, 26 L. Ed. 2d 6 (1970).

23. Herbert v. Lando, 441 U.S. 153, 99 S. Ct. 1635, 60 L. Ed. 2d 115, 3 Fed. R. Evid. Serv. (LCP) 822 (1979).

sure that the speech in question actually falls within the unprotected category and to confine the perimeters of any unprotected category within the acceptably narrow limits in an effort to ensure that protected expression will not be prohibited."[24]

In 1988 the Court held that a public figure plaintiff seeking damages for emotional distress arising from publication of a defamatory falsehood could recover only if the statement was made with knowledge that it was false or with reckless disregard of whether it was false or not. The Court observed that First Amendment values require that even "outrageous" cartoons are entitled to the protection of this rule.[25] The following year, the Court ruled that whether a defendant has been guilty of malice is a question of law, and applying the actual malice rule, concluded that malice was present in the instant case.[26]

In 1990 the Supreme Court ruled that where a connotation that the plaintiff committed perjury is sufficiently factual to be susceptible of being proven true or false, there is no "opinion" exemption from libel actions under the First Amendment. However, the Court carefully added that "a statement of opinion relating to matters of public concern which does not contain a probably false factual connotation will receive a full constitutional protection."[27]

§ 6.03. Defamation suits by private persons against the media

In 1971 in *Rosenbloom v. Metromedia,* eight Justices (Douglas, J. not participating) wrote five separate opinions, none of which commanded more than three votes. The plurality opinion of Justice Brennan, the Chief Justice, and Justice Blackmun held that the *New York Times* rule should apply even when private citizens sue the media for defamation so long as "the utterance involved concerns an issue of public or general concern."[28] Three years later, however, when a private citizen sued for libel against a publisher who had falsely said that the plaintiff had a criminal record and was a communist, the Court declined to extend the *New York Times* rule to

---

24. Bose Corp. v. Consumers Union of U.S., Inc., 466 U.S. 485, 104 S. Ct. 1949, 80 L. Ed. 2d 502 (1984).

25. Hustler Magazine v. Falwell, 485 U.S. 46, 108 S. Ct. 876, 99 L. Ed. 2d 41 (1988).

26. Harte-Hanks Communications, Inc. v. Connaughton, 491 U.S. 657, 109 S. Ct. 2678, 105 L. Ed. 2d 562 (1989).

27. Milkovich v. Lorain Journal Co., 497 U.S. 1, 110 S. Ct. 2695, 111 L. Ed. 2d 1, 60 Ed. Law Rep. 1061 (1990).

28. Rosenbloom v. Metromedia, Inc., 403 U.S. 29, 91 S. Ct. 1811, 29 L. Ed. 2d 296 (1971).

suits by private individuals. The Court held that so long as the states do not impose liability without fault, they may define for themselves the appropriate standard of liability for a publisher or broadcaster of a defamatory falsehood injurious to a private individual. The Court added, however, that a private defamation plaintiff who establishes liability under a less demanding standard than stated in *New York Times* may only recover such damages as are sufficient to compensate him for his actual injuries—not punitive damages.[29] The Court explained that "a legitimate state interest underlying the law of libel is the compensation of individuals for the harm inflicted on them by the defamatory falsehood," and added that a private person "has relinquished no part of his interest in the protection of his own good name, and consequently he has a more compelling call on the courts for redress of injury inflicted by defamatory falsehoods."[30]

In 1976 the Court reaffirmed its holding in *Gertz v. Welch,* supra, and ruled that the First Amendment does not prevent application of state law allowing a private individual to recover from a publisher for defamation where the defendant was negligent and the plaintiff can show actual injuries resulting from the defamation. Justice Brennan in dissent suggested that in reporting judicial proceedings of all kinds the press must be accorded a broad protection, and that the actual malice rule of *New York Times* would be appropriate.[31]

Ten years later the Court ruled that where a newspaper publishes a speech of public concern, a private-figure plaintiff cannot recover damages without also showing that the statements at issue are false. Under the First Amendment, the common-law presumption that defamatory speech is false cannot stand when a plaintiff seeks damages against a media defendant for speech of public concern. The Court reserved the question whether the new rule is to be applied to non-media defendants. Chief Justice Burger and Justices Stevens, White, and Rehnquist dissented, being of the view that a proper balancing of interests should here favor the interest in protecting individuals from defamatory falsehoods.[32]

Where a connotation that the plaintiff committed perjury is sufficiently factual to be susceptible of being proved true or false, there

---

29. Gertz v. Robert Welch, Inc., 418 U.S. 323, 94 S. Ct. 2997, 41 L. Ed. 2d 789 (1974).

30. Gertz v. Robert Welch, Inc., 418 U.S. 323, 94 S. Ct. 2997, 41 L. Ed. 2d 789 (1974).

31. Time, Inc. v. Firestone, 424 U.S. 448, 96 S. Ct. 958, 47 L. Ed. 2d 154 (1976).

32. Philadelphia Newspapers, Inc. v. Hepps, 475 U.S. 767, 106 S. Ct. 1558, 89 L. Ed. 2d 783 (1986).

is no "opinion" exemption from libel actions under the First Amendment. However, the Court indicated in 1990 that "a statement of opinion relating to matters of public concern which does not contain a provably false factual connotation will receive a full constitutional protection."[33]

The following year the Court indicated that "a deliberate alteration of the words uttered by a plaintiff does not equate with knowledge of falsity" for the purpose of *New York Times v. Sullivan,* unless the alternation results from the material change in the meaning conveyed by the statement. The Court added that an author is allowed "an interpretive license that is necessary when relying upon ambiguous sources," but noted further that where an author uses a quotation and a reasonable reader could conclude that the quote is a verbatim repetition of a statement of the speaker, such falsification is not permissible "interpretation" and that, if such alterations give a different meaning to a speaker's statements, bearing upon their defamatory character, then the device of quotations might well be critical in finding the words actionable.[34]

Libel actions under state law are preempted by federal law to the extent that a state seeks to make actionable defamatory statements in labor disputes which are published without knowledge of their falsity or reckless disregard for the truth.[35]

§ 6.04. Defamation suits by private individuals against non-media defendants

While the *New York Times* rule placed First Amendment limitations upon state and federal decisions to sustain awards or punishments against defamers, it is unlikely that the Supreme Court is prepared to interfere in the name of the Fourteenth Amendment when a state defines the circumstances under which private plaintiffs can recover in defamation from non-media defendants where the defamatory message has virtually no societal import. In 1985, when a private firm sued a private credit reporting agency for a report that was allegedly defamatory, the United States Supreme Court plurality opinion by Justice Powell, joined by Justices O'Connor and Rehnquist, held that a showing of actual malice is not necessary in such cases where the comment of the defendant was of no public

---

33. Milkovich v. Lorain Journal Co., 497 U.S. 1, 110 S. Ct. 2695, 111 L. Ed. 2d 1, 60 Ed. Law Rep. 1061 (1990).

34. Masson v. New Yorker Magazine, Inc., 501 U.S. 496, 111 S. Ct. 2419, 115 L. Ed. 2d 447 (1991).

35. Old Dominion Branch No. 496, Nat. Ass'n of Letter Carriers, AFL-CIO v. Austin, 418 U.S. 264, 94 S. Ct. 2770, 41 L. Ed. 2d 745 (1974).

concern. Chief Justice Burger and Justice White concurred. Even an award of presumed or punitive damages against the defendant in such cases does not violate the First Amendment. Said the Court: "In light of the reduced constitutional value of speech involving no matters of public concern, we hold that the state interest adequately supports awards of presumed and punitive damages—even absent a showing of 'actual malice.'"[36]

The following year, Justice O'Connor, in an opinion for the Court, observed "When the speech is of exclusively private concern and the plaintiff is a private figure, as in Dun and Bradstreet, the constitutional requirements do not necessarily force any change in at least some of the features of the common law landscape,"[37] which generally authorize compensatory and punitive damages in such instances, notwithstanding defense claims of freedom of expression.[38]

In a related statutory interpretation case, the Court held in effect in 1976 that a citizen's interest in his good name and reputation was not protectable in an action under 42 U.S.C.A. § 1983 alleging injury to his "liberty" nor "property," and, accordingly, that the citizen could not recover under that statute against a police chief who had falsely named him as an active shoplifter in a circular distributed to 800 merchants.[39]

§ 6.05. Anonymous publications

Because anonymous publications have often unfairly vilified and defamed innocent citizens, local communities have attempted to protect the interest in private reputation by suppressing anonymous handbills and tracts. The United States Supreme Court in 1960 in the *Talley* case declared void on its face a Los Angeles ordinance prohibiting the distribution of handbills that did not have printed on the cover or the face thereof the names and addresses of the parties preparing and distributing the handbills. The Court reasoned that identification of the parties might result in reprisals and fear of reprisals might deter the discussion of public matters of importance. Said the Court: "Anonymous pamphlets, leaflets, brochures and

---

36. Dun & Bradstreet, Inc. v. Greenmoss Builders, Inc., 472 U.S. 749, 105 S. Ct. 2939, 86 L. Ed. 2d 593 (1985).

37. Philadelphia Newspapers, Inc. v. Hepps, 475 U.S. 767, 106 S. Ct. 1558, 89 L. Ed. 2d 783 (1986).

38. E.g., Remington v. Bentley, 88 F. Supp. 166 (S.D.N.Y. 1949).

39. Paul v. Davis, 424 U.S. 693, 96 S. Ct. 1155, 47 L. Ed. 2d 405 (1976).

even books have played an important role in the progress of mankind."[40]

§ 6.06. Previous restraints upon defamatory publications

The United States Supreme Court has not permitted the states to enjoin the future publication of newspapers, magazines, and the like because previous issues have contained defamatory materials or because it is likely that future issues will contain defamatory materials. Freedom of the press, said the Supreme Court in the *Near* case,[41] especially means that ordinarily there will be no previous restraints upon publication.

State courts have held that local governments could not suppress publications by declaring them to be nuisances.[42] Nor can a municipal corporation forbid circulation within the community of a newspaper whose editorials and reporting have caused displeasure to local officials.[43]

The fact that some readers may threaten violence against a newspaper or its editor does not justify a local government in suppressing publication of the paper. A New Jersey court has said: "If the township may prevent the circulation of a newspaper for no reason other than that some of its inhabitants may violently disagree with it, and resent its circulation by resorting to physical violence, there is no limit to what may be prohibited."[44]

§ 6.07. Group libels and "hate ordinances"

A number of communities have believed that "race hate" literature and "group libels" untruthfully and unfairly brought the good name of members of various racial, religious, and ethnic groups into disrepute, that such propaganda in turn stimulates counter-racism and the like, and frequently results in violence. States and cities have, accordingly, enacted legislation to protect the reputation of racial, religious, and ethnic groups. For example, in 1952 the Supreme Court ruled on the constitutionality of an Illinois statute which made it a crime "for any person, firm or corporation to manufacture, sell, or offer for sale, advertise or publish, present or exhibit in any public place in this state any lithograph, moving

---

40. Talley v. California, 362 U.S. 60, 80 S. Ct. 536, 4 L. Ed. 2d 559, 563 (1960).

41. Near v. State of Minnesota ex rel. Olson, 283 U.S. 697, 51 S. Ct. 625, 75 L. Ed. 1357 (1931).

42. Ex parte Neill, 32 Tex. Crim. 275, 22 S.W. 923 (1893).

43. Star Co. v. Brush, 185 A.D. 261, 172 N.Y.S. 851 (2d Dep't 1918).

44. New Yorker Staats-Zeitung v. Nolan, 89 N.J. Eq. 357, 388, 105 A. 72 (1915).

picture, play, drama or sketch, which publication or exhibit portrays depravity, criminality, unchastity or lack of virtue of a class of citizens, of any race, color, creed or religion which said publication or exhibition exposes the citizens of any race, color, creed or religion to contempt, derision, or obloquy or which is productive of breach of the peace or riots." The Court sustained the Illinois statute when applied to an individual who distributed anti-African American literature on the streets of Chicago. The leaflets complained of also contained a petition calling on the Mayor and Council to "halt the further encroachment, harassment and invasion of white people, their property, neighborhoods and persons, by the Negro." This was a five-to-four decision, with the dissenters finding the prosecution impermissible because there was no clear and present danger of a substantive evil at this time and place from the conduct of the defendant. Justice Jackson, one of the dissenters, ably pointed out:

> Punishment of printed words, based on their tendency either to cause breach of the peace or injury to persons or groups, in my opinion, is justifiable only if the prosecution survives the "clear and present danger" test. It is the most just and workable standard yet evolved for determining criminality of words whose injurious or inciting tendencies are not demonstrated by the event but are ascribed to them on the basis of probabilities.[45]

It is suggested the *Beauharnais* case is wrongly decided. The ideas expressed in the leaflet may be antediluvian and the words utter drivel; yet it is a discussion of current problems and a petition to the individual's democratically elected public officials. On the facts shown there was not a clear and present danger of a substantive evil. The statute itself is an unjustified interference with the communicative process. The unpleasant impact upon the individual is so much more remote and attenuated than in the case of personal libels where the subject is named or clearly identified. Furthermore, if an African American accused the white race of being, let us say, "uncharitable," does our society have a pressing interest here that requires vindication by jailing the African American who would have violated the Illinois enactment in attributing "lack of virtue" to a covered group? Civil recoveries should be more than adequate recompense to any such covered group that feels it has been hurt. Any group contemplating using the power of the state to suppress or punish communication might well ask if anti-Semitism, racism,

---

45. Beauharnais v. People of State of Ill., 343 U.S. 250, 72 S. Ct. 725, 754, 96 L. Ed. 919, 952-53 (1952).

and bigotry can be effectively cured by incarceration or the threat thereof. Here, as elsewhere, we have committed our nation to the proposition that printing bad ideas will ultimately result in the triumph of responsive good ideas.

A federal court has held that a publisher who had run anti-Semitic articles was entitled to an injunction against Cleveland public officials who threatened his arrest if he continued such publication. The federal court stated:

> The necessary effect of such action is to censor in advance the contents of the newspaper, by preventing its sale in the same manner as all other newspapers are sold, so long as it contains articles of like character. . . . If it be assumed that the article might tend to excite others to breaches of the peace against people of the Jewish race, the reply is plain. It is the duty of all officials charged with preserving the peace to suppress firmly and promptly all persons guilty of disturbing it, and not to forbid innocent persons to exercise their lawful and equal rights.[46]

Although group libels for the time being can be criminally punished, the *Near* case[47] likely prevents state and federal courts from enjoining in advance future issues of racist publications.

When a St. Paul ordinance provided for the punishment of acts, such as burning crosses, which "arose anger, alarm, or resentment in others on the basis of race, color, creed, religion or gender," the Supreme Court found it fatally unconstitutional, ruling that there can be no "content discrimination" when a government goes about prohibiting speech. Justice Scalia for the Court wrote: "The First Amendment generally prevents government from proscribing speech or even expressive conduct because of disapproval of the ideas expressed. Content-based regulations are presumptively invalid." Although a Minnesota court had held that the ordinance was limited to "fighting words," the Supreme Court held that even as so applied it was defective because "it prohibits otherwise permitted speech solely on the basis of the subjects the speech addresses." The Court noted that the City had other adequate means of addressing the problem. While concurring in the result, Justices White, Blackmun, O'Connor and Stevens rejected the reasoning of the majority and

---

46. Dearborn Pub. Co. v. Fitzgerald, 271 F. 479, 481, 483 (N.D. Ohio 1921).

47. Near v. State of Minnesota ex rel. Olson, 283 U.S. 697, 51 S. Ct. 625, 75 L. Ed. 1357 (1931).

would have held the ordinance unconstitutional for its facial overbreadth.[48]

§ 6.08. Right of reply provisions

The United States Supreme Court in 1969 sustained a requirement of the Federal Communications Commission that a radio station provide a tape, transcript, or summary of a broadcast personally attacking a person, and provide such person with reply time whether or not the person could pay for it.[49] However, five years later the Court held unconstitutional a state's "right of reply" statute which provided that if a candidate for public office was assailed regarding his character or record, he had a right to demand that the newspaper print, free of cost, his reply to the newspaper's charges. The Court stated generally that the First Amendment outlaws "compulsion exerted by a government on a newspaper to print that which it would not otherwise print." Justices Brennan and Rehnquist, in their concurring opinion, emphasized that the ruling does not touch upon the constitutionality of "retraction statutes" applicable to persons defamed.[50]

In another instance of compulsion upon publishers, the Court held in 1986 that a state may not, absent proof of a compelling interest, impose upon a public utilities newsletter, included in the monthly billing envelope, a requirement to carry therein four months out of the year a message by an organization having views generally opposed to those of the utility. The Court emphasized that there is a constitutionally protected "freedom not to speak publicly," adding that "for corporations as for individuals the choice to speak includes within it the choice of what not to say." There was dictum, however, that "the State's interest may justify imposing on (a utility) the reasonable expenses of responsible groups that represent the public interest at rate-making proceedings."[51]

---

48. R.A.V. v. City of St. Paul, Minn., 505 U.S. 377, 112 S. Ct. 2538, 120 L. Ed. 2d 305 (1992).

49. Red Lion Broadcasting Co. v. F. C. C., 395 U.S. 367, 89 S. Ct. 1794, 23 L. Ed. 2d 371 (1969).

50. Miami Herald Pub. Co. v. Tornillo, 418 U.S. 241, 94 S. Ct. 2831, 41 L. Ed. 2d 730 (1974).

51. Pacific Gas and Elec. Co. v. Public Utilities Com'n of California, 475 U.S. 1, 106 S. Ct. 903, 89 L. Ed. 2d 1 (1986).

CHAPTER SEVEN

Balancing Societal Interests in First Amendment Freedoms With the Societal Interest in Personal Privacy

---

§ 7.00. Introduction

Our society is interested in protecting the privacy of the individual citizen from violation by way of intrusion into his home, publicizing his purely personal affairs, compelled divulgence of his views and beliefs which would expose the citizen to extra-legal sanctions, and from inroads into the individual's repose and relaxation. At times privacy interests, such as these and more, clash with the interests solemnly safeguarded in the First Amendment, and then constitutional adjudication demands skill and prudence in weighing, balancing, and reconciling these opposed societal values.

Privacy invasions by governmental searches and seizures are examined in Chapter 17.

§ 7.01. Protecting names of victims of crime

Local communities at times have felt that there is a legitimate interest in protecting the innocent victim of crimes, especially sex offenses, from identification in the public press. Wisconsin has such a statute, and its application has been upheld by the Supreme Court of that state in a very well-reasoned opinion.

Chief Justice Rosenberry, speaking for the Wisconsin Supreme Court in the *Evjue* case, stated:

This statute is intended to protect the victim from embarrassment and offensive publicity which no doubt have a strong tendency to affect her future standing in society. In addition to that it is a well known fact that many crimes of the character described go unpunished because the victim of the assault is unwilling to face the publicity which would follow prosecution. . . . there is a minimum of social value in the publication of the identity of a female in connection with such an outrage. . . . At most the publication of the identity of the female ministers to a morbid desire to connect the details of one of the most detestable crimes known to the law with the identity of the victim. When the situation of the victim of the assault and the handicap prosecuting officers labor under in such cases is weighed against the benefit of publishing the identity of the victim in connection with the details of the crime, there can be no doubt that the slight restriction of the freedom of the press prescribed by [the statute] is fully justified.[1]

In 1975 the Supreme Court held that the First Amendment proscribes imposition of civil liability in a privacy action predicated on the truthful publication of the name of a child who had been raped, when this matter was contained in an open judicial record.[2] Comparably, the Court held in 1989 that the First Amendment is violated by application of a statute prohibiting publication of the name of a rape victim, when a newspaper has obtained this information from a publicly released police report. Justice White, joined by the Chief Justice and Justice O'Connor, dissented, suggesting that we need a better judicial balancing of this clash between societal interests in privacy and communication.[3]

§ 7.02. Protecting the names of juveniles charged with offenses against the law

In 1977 the United States Supreme Court held that the First Amendment does not permit a state court to prohibit the publication of widely disseminated information, including the picture of a juvenile charged with an offense against the law, which information has been obtained at court proceedings open to the public.[4]

Two years later, the Court comparably held violative of the First

---

1. State v. Evjue, 253 Wis. 146, 33 N.W.2d 305, 13 A.L.R.2d 1201 (1948).

2. Cox Broadcasting Corp. v. Cohn, 420 U.S. 469, 95 S. Ct. 1029, 43 L. Ed. 2d 328 (1975).

3. The Florida Star v. B.J.F., 491 U.S. 524, 109 S. Ct. 2603, 105 L. Ed. 2d 443 (1989).

4. Oklahoma Pub. Co. v. District Court In and For Oklahoma County, 430 U.S. 308, 97 S. Ct. 1045, 51 L. Ed. 2d 355 (1977).

Amendment application of a statute making it a crime for a newspaper to publish, without the written approval of a juvenile court, the name of any youth charged as a juvenile offender, so long as the information is lawfully obtained.[5]

§ 7.03. Protection of individual privacy from governmental inquiries and surveillance

In 1972 the Supreme Court held that citizens opposed to the Army's gathering of intelligence data on civilians did not show that they had sustained, or were immediately in danger of sustaining, a direct injury as a result of the military's activities, and that "allegations of a subjective 'chill' are not an adequate substitute for a claim of specific objective harm or a threat of specific future harm." Justices Douglas, Marshall, Brennan and Stewart dissented.[6]

Five years later the Presidential Recording and Materials Act withstood constitutional challenge and was held not to constitute a violation of the separation of powers concept, intrusion into presidential privilege, or an invasion of the rights of association and privacy, or to constitute a bill of attainder. The Act provides for archival screening of Presidential materials, specifically those of Richard Nixon, by executive archivists to sort out purely private materials from those having national historic value and to make the latter available for use in judicial proceedings and accessible to the public except where national security dictates otherwise. Holding that, in light of the compelling public interest the Act was designed to serve, it operated in the least intrusive means possible, the Supreme Court discounted the claims of executive privilege and associational and privacy arguments made by the appellees. The Court held the Act did not constitute a bill of attainder, since the functional test of the existence of punishment directed at an identifiable individual is "whether the laws under challenge, viewed in terms of types and severity of punishment imposed, reasonably can be said to further nonpunitive legislative purposes." In dissent, Justices Burger and Rehnquist recognized a valid public interest in having information about the functioning of government, but felt that the Court should have examined more closely the appellant's asserted privacy violation. The President, they believed, should not be said to entirely relinquish his right to privacy when he assumes public office. The

---

5. Smith v. Daily Mail Publishing Co., 439 U.S. 963, 99 S. Ct. 448, 58 L. Ed. 2d 420 (1978).

6. Laird v. Tatum, 408 U.S. 1, 92 S. Ct. 2318, 33 L. Ed. 2d 154 (1972).

dissenters believed that the Act, by entrusting the responsibility to archivists, virtually insured, and needlessly so, the loss of privacy.[7]

The same year the Supreme Court upheld a state statute under which a form was required to be filed with the Public Health Commission indicating the name of the doctor prescribing drugs, the name of the pharmacist, the name, address and age of the patient, and the name of the drug, as well as the amount of dosage. Over claims of the physicians and patients that their "zone of privacy" was being unconstitutionally invaded, the Court in denying them relief indicated that any societal interest involved was not sufficiently invaded to constitute a constitutional violation.[8]

A 1983 decision by the Court of Appeals for the Fifth Circuit, on which *certiorari* was denied by the Supreme Court, held that police officers could be disciplined for cohabiting outside marriage. The Court of Appeals stated: "Police officers enjoy no constitutionally protected right to privacy against undercover and other investigations of their violations of department regulations."[9]

§ 7.04. Protecting privacy from commercial exploitation

The societal interest in protecting individual privacy finds expression at times in statutes authorizing civil causes of action, as well as criminal prosecutions, against persons and corporations who make use of the name or picture of a living person for purposes of advertising, trade, or profit without securing the individual's consent, or make such use of the name or picture of deceased persons without the consent of heirs.

Utah has such legislation, and it has been sustained by the United States Court of Appeals for the Tenth Circuit. When Warner Brothers made a film about the life of Jack Donahue, a recently deceased dancer and entertainer, without securing permission from his widow and children, the Court of Appeals acknowledged the validity of a statutory cause of action by Mrs. Donahue and the children. Said the Court, in reference to the filmmaker's claim of freedom of speech and press:

> The constitutional guarantee of free speech and free press in its full sweep does not undertake to create an inviolate asylum for unbridled appropriation or exploitation of the name, picture or personality of a deceased public figure for purely commercial

---

7. Nixon v. Administrator of General Services, 433 U.S. 425, 97 S. Ct. 2777, 53 L. Ed. 2d 867 (1977).

8. Whalen v. Roe, 429 U.S. 589, 97 S. Ct. 869, 51 L. Ed. 2d 64 (1977).

9. Shawgo v. Spradlin, 701 F.2d 470 (5th Cir. 1983).

purposes, or solely for purposes of trade, with the state powerless to enact appropriate forbidding or remedial legislation.[10]

In 1967 the Supreme Court reversed a recovery against a magazine under the New York "right of privacy" statute. The Court ruled:

that the constitutional protections for speech and press preclude the application of the New York statute to redress false reports of matters of public interest in the absence of proof that the defendant published the report with knowledge of its falsity or in reckless disregard of the truth.[11]

The Court explained: "Sanctions against either innocent or negligent misstatement would present a grave hazard of discouraging the press from exercising the constitutional guarantees."[12] Justices Black and Douglas, concurring, indicated their view that any recovery, even when there was malicious and reckless disregarding of the truth, would violate the First Amendment. The Chief Justice, as well as Justices Clark, Fortas and Harlan dissented. Chief Justice Warren said: "Privacy, then, is a basic right," and added that he felt that the trial judge's instructions satisfied the rule that "a verdict of liability could be predicated only on a finding of knowing or reckless falsity."[13]

In 1974 the Court sustained a judgment for a citizen placed in "false light" as the result of an invasion of her privacy by defendant's newspaper and reporter, when the trial judge instructed the jury that in light of *New York Times v. Sullivan* "liability could be imposed only if it concluded that the false statements . . . had been made with knowledge of their falsity or in reckless disregard of the truth."[14]

Three years later the Court ruled that the media do not, per se, possess the right to broadcast an entertainer's entire act without his consent, and the Court upheld a state law right of publicity against First and Fourteenth Amendment challenges. Though a state law right of publicity could not be construed to prevent the media from reporting the newsworthy facts about the act, it could prohibit the

---

10. Donahue v. Warner Bros. Pictures, 194 F.2d 6, 18 (10th Cir. 1952).

11. Time, Inc. v. Hill, 385 U.S. 374, 87 S. Ct. 534, 542, 17 L. Ed. 2d 456 (1967).

12. Time, Inc. v. Hill, 385 U.S. 374, 87 S. Ct. 534, 543, 17 L. Ed. 2d 456 (1967).

13. Time, Inc. v. Hill, 385 U.S. 374, 87 S. Ct. 534, 566-67, 17 L. Ed. 2d 456 (1967).

14. Cantrell v. Forest City Pub. Co., 419 U.S. 245, 95 S. Ct. 465, 42 L. Ed. 2d 419 (1974).

press from broadcasting it in its entirety and thus robbing the entertainer of the economic benefits of his activity. In dissent, Justices Powell, Brennan and Marshall insisted that the proper First Amendment analysis would focus not on the fact of the entire act being broadcast, but rather on the use made of the information by the network. They would have held that the First Amendment protects the media from a state-created right of publicity suit, provided that their use of the story is for news purposes and not "commercial exploitation."[15]

§ 7.05. Protecting the privacy of the householder

Solicitors and peddlers of printed matter frequently disturb householders in their repose. Such householders have been assaulted and exposed to disease; their down payments have mysteriously disappeared. Communities feel they have a legitimate interest in protecting householder privacy even against those who would distribute literature or call with religious messages.

In 1943 the United States Supreme Court invalidated a local ordinance forbidding anyone summoning the occupants of a residence to the door to receive advertisements, as applied to the free distribution of "dodgers" advertising a religious meeting. The principal objection of the Supreme Court to the ordinance was that "it substitutes the judgment of the community for the judgment of the individual householder." The Court added:

> Freedom to distribute information to every citizen wherever he desires to receive it is so clearly vital to the preservation of a free society that, putting aside reasonable police and health regulations of time and manner of distribution, it must be fully preserved.[16]

Eight years later, however, the Court sustained the more common "Green River" type ordinance which banned solicitors and peddlers, including those of printed matter, from invading the premises without the request or invitation of the householder. The Court there stated:

> Freedom of speech or press does not mean that one can talk or distribute where, when and how one chooses. Rights other than those of the advocates are involved. By adjustment of rights, we can have both full liberty of expression and an orderly life . . .

---

15. Zacchini v. Scripps-Howard Broadcasting Co., 433 U.S. 562, 97 S. Ct. 2849, 53 L. Ed. 2d 965, 5 Ohio Op. 3d 215 (1977).

16. Martin v. City of Struthers, Ohio, 319 U.S. 141, 143-44, 63 S. Ct. 862, 87 L. Ed. 1313, 1316-17 (1943).

This makes the constitutionality of Alexandria's ordinance turn upon a balancing of the conveniences between some householders' desire for privacy and the publisher's right to distribute publications in the precise way that those soliciting for him think brings the best results . . .

Subscriptions may be made by anyone interested in receiving the magazines without the annoyance of house-to-house canvassing. We think those communities that have found these methods of sale obnoxious may control them by ordinances. It would be, it seems to us, a misuse of the great guarantees of free speech and free press to use that guarantee to force a community to admit the solicitors of publications to the home premises of its residents. We see no abridgment of the principles of the First Amendment in this ordinance.[17]

In 1949, the Court had sustained the interest in protecting privacy and tranquility of homeowners from "loud and raucous" noises emitted from sound trucks.[18] And in 1970 the Court approved the power of the Post Office to exclude from homes materials the occupant did not want delivered to his dwelling.[19]

In 1978 the Court held that individuals are not required to welcome unwanted speech into their homes and that the government may protect this freedom; upheld was a ruling of the Federal Communications Commission prohibiting the radio broadcasting of indecent and filthy words, after a father and his young son were subjected to a barrage of such words.[20]

While in 1980 the Court was compelled by the Equal Protection Clause to invalidate an Illinois statute banning all picketing of residences and dwellings, but having an exception allowing peaceful picketing "of a place of employment involved in a labor dispute," the opinion of the Court strongly attested to its appreciation of the interest in privacy of the household, as sufficient with a properly drawn statute, to limit picketing. Justice Brennan, writing for the Court, announced: "We are not to be understood to imply that residential picketing is beyond the reach of uniform and nondiscrimi-

---

17. Breard v. City of Alexandria, La., 341 U.S. 622, 71 S. Ct. 920, 932-34, 95 L. Ed. 1233, 1247-50, 46 Ohio Op. 74, 62 Ohio L. Abs. 210, 35 A.L.R.2d 335 (1951).

18. Kovacs v. Cooper, 336 U.S. 77, 69 S. Ct. 448, 93 L. Ed. 513, 10 A.L.R.2d 608 (1949).

19. Rowan v. U.S. Post Office Dept., 397 U.S. 728, 90 S. Ct. 1484, 25 L. Ed. 2d 736 (1970).

20. F. C. C. v. Pacifica Foundation, 438 U.S. 726, 748-49, 98 S. Ct. 3026, 57 L. Ed. 2d 1073 (1978).

natory regulation . . . the right to communication is not limitless.
. . . We have often declared that a state or municipality may protect
individual privacy by enacting reasonable time, place and manner
regulations applicable to all irrespective of content." Justice Brennan added:

> Preserving the sanctity of the home, the one retreat to which
> men and women can repair to escape from the tribulations of
> their daily pursuits, is surely an important value. Our decisions
> reflect no lack of solicitude for the right of the individual "to be
> let alone" in the privacy of the home, "sometimes the last
> citadel of the tired, the weary and the sick." . . . The State's
> interest in protecting the well-being, tranquility, and privacy of
> the home is certainly of the highest order in a free and civilized
> society.[21]

Then, in 1988, the Court refused to find invalid on its face an
ordinance banning picketing "before or around" any residence.
Justice O'Connor began by noting that "the anti-picketing ordinance
operates at the core of the First Amendment by prohibiting [persons
wanting to protest the fact that a doctor residing at that location
had apparently performed abortions] from engaging in picketing on
an issue of public concern," and that "because of the importance of
uninhibited, robust and wide-open debate on public issues, we have
traditionally subjected restrictions on public issues picketing to careful scrutiny." Then Justice O'Connor recalled that "we have repeatedly held that individuals are not required to welcome unwanted
speech into their homes and that the government may protect this
freedom. . . . The First Amendment permits the government to
prohibit offensive speech as intrusive when the 'captive audience'
cannot avoid the objectionable speech." A resident in the community which enacted the ordinance, the Justice wrote, is "figuratively, and perhaps literally, trapped within the home and because of
the unique and subtle impact of such picketing is left with no ready
means of avoiding the unwanted speech."[22] Justices Brennan, Marshall and Stevens in dissent found the ordinance overbroad and not
so narrowly tailored as it could have been with more exact and
limited size, time, volume, etc., controls.

§ 7.06. Claims of "newsmen's privilege"

In 1972 the United States Supreme Court, in a five-to-four deci-

---

21. Carey v. Brown, 447 U.S. 455, 100 S. Ct. 2286, 65 L. Ed. 2d 263, 275-76
(1980).

22. Frisby v. Schultz, 487 U.S. 474, 108 S. Ct. 2495, 101 L. Ed. 2d 420, 428-29
(1988).

sion, held that there is no First Amendment privilege available to a reporter to refuse to answer questions of a grand jury and no privilege to refuse to appear before such a body. According to the majority opinion, the societal interest in "fair and effective law enforcement aimed at providing security for the person and property of the individual" is strong. It is "a fundamental function of government." When the burden on news gathering from the absence of a claimed "newsman's privilege" was in this case "uncertain," newspaper reporters, like other citizens, would have to respond to grand jury summonses and divulge what they knew about crimes being committed in the community. The Court explained that it "cannot accept the argument that the public interest in possible future news about crime from undisclosed, unverified sources must take precedence over the public interest in pursuing and prosecuting those crimes reported to the press by informants and in thus deterring the commission of such crimes in the future." Justice Powell, who constituted the fifth Justice by his concurring opinion, indicated that a case-to-case approach will be followed, with newsmen apparently being protected in some cases.

Justice Stewart's dissenting opinion for the four dissenters stated that "the First Amendment interests . . . to insure nothing less than democratic decision making through the free flow of information to the public" outweighs the interest in securing the names of reporters' informers.[23]

---

23. Branzburg v. Hayes, 408 U.S. 665, 92 S. Ct. 2646, 33 L. Ed. 2d 626 (1972).

CHAPTER EIGHT

Reconciling Societal Interest in First Amendment Freedoms With the Interest in Safeguarding the Public Health

---

§ 8.00. Protecting the health of children

State courts have ordered that medical care be administered to children, in the case of a life-threatening illness, over the religious objections of their parents.[1] Illustratively, in 1982 the Colorado Supreme Court ruled that the First Amendment was not violated by providing medical care and treatment to a child, determined by state authorities to be "neglected" by and dependent upon a mother who desired "faith healing" for the child. The court said: "When a minor suffers a life-threatening medical condition, due to a failure to comply with a program of medical treatment on religious conditions, [the statute] permits a finding of dependency and neglect and does not violate the constitutional provision protecting the free exercise of religion."[2]

An Ohio court tersely and accurately states: "When a child's right to live and his parents' religious beliefs collide, the former is paramount and the religious doctrine must give way."[3]

In an oft-cited 1955 case, the New York Court of Appeals affirmed a lower court ruling that an operation to correct a harelip

---

1.   People v. Pierson, 176 N.Y. 201, 68 N.E. 243 (1903).

2.   People in Interest of D. L. E., 645 P.2d 271 (Colo. 1982).

3.   In re Clark, 21 Ohio Op. 2d 86, 90 Ohio L. Abs. 21, 185 N.E.2d 128 (C.P. 1962).

and a cleft palate in a 14-year-old child was not precluded by the father's personal belief in mental healing, but where the child held the same belief in "forces in the universe," the court indicated that the final decision on the operation was to be left to the boy.[4]

Where parents refuse to authorize, on religious grounds, a blood transfusion for a child who is in grave danger of death without such assistance, state courts have held it proper to order such transfusions, even over religious opposition.[5] In 1967, a federal district court held valid a Washington state statute allowing a "dependent child" to have a blood transfusion over the objections of the child's parents where it "was or would be vital to save the life of the patient,"[6] and the United States Supreme Court affirmed per curiam in 1968.[7] In 1972 the Pennsylvania Supreme Court ruled that when a child's life is *not* at stake, the state does not have a sufficiently compelling interest to order a blood transfusion over the religious objections of the parents, but remanded the case to have the trial court ascertain and respect the wishes of the 16-year-old boy.[8]

States have a substantial interest in protecting both the physical and psychological health of children, and this justifies extensive controls upon individuals who would make and market pornographic pictures or movies involving children. The United States Supreme Court declared in 1982: "It is evidently beyond the need for elaboration that a State's interest in safeguarding the physical and psychological well-being of children is compelling." The Court said that the value of child pornography was "exceedingly modest if not de minimis" and said that it was classifying child pornography as a category of material outside the protection of the First Amendment, and the Court accordingly indicated that the states may criminalize the production and promotion by distribution of material depicting sexual conduct of children under 16. The societal interest in preventing sexual exploitation and abuse of children constitutes, according to the Court, a governmental objective of "surpassing importance." The Court rather readily dismissed a claim of overbreadth, finding

---

4. In re Seiferth, 309 N.Y. 80, 127 N.E.2d 820 (1955).

5. People ex rel. Wallace v. Labrenz, 411 Ill. 618, 104 N.E.2d 769, 30 A.L.R.2d 1132 (1952).

6. Jehovah's Witnesses in State of Wash. v. King County Hospital Unit No. 1 (Harborview), 278 F. Supp. 488 (W.D. Wash. 1967), judgment aff'd, 390 U.S. 598, 88 S. Ct. 1260, 20 L. Ed. 2d 158 (1968).

7. Jehovah's Witnesses in State of Washington v. King County Hospital Unit No. 1, 390 U.S. 598, 88 S. Ct. 1260, 20 L. Ed. 2d 158 (1968).

8. In re Green, 448 Pa. 338, 292 A.2d 387, 52 A.L.R.3d 1106 (1972).

the statute one "whose legitimate reach dwarfs its arguably impermissible application."[9]

Seven years later, when a state statute prohibiting adult photographs of children in the nude suffered from original overbreadth, but an amendment endeavored to save it by adding the requirement of lascivious intent, the Supreme Court remanded, with Justice O'Connor writing the opinion of the Court, joined by the Chief Justice and Justices White and Kennedy, indicating that the overbreadth issue was not moot. Justices Brennan, Marshall and Stevens dissented on the ground that the law was still overbroad. While Justices Scalia and Blackmun concurred in the result, they also believed the amendment to the statute did not remove the overbreadth defect.[10] In 1990 the Court re-emphasized that: "A State's interest in safeguarding the physical and psychological well-being of a minor is 'compelling' . . . the use of children as subjects of pornographic material is harmful to the psychological, emotional and mental health of the child." While stating that a state may punish the possessing or viewing of pictures of nude children who are neither the child nor a ward of the defendant, the Court had to order a new trial since it was unclear whether the state had properly proved scienter, a requirement of these cases, even though the trial attorney had adequately brought the attention of the court to this defect. Justices Brennan, Marshall and Stevens believed that the statute was overly broad and the test used by the state supreme court too vague, and they also saw the balancing of societal interests as inadequate on the facts.[11]

§ 8.01. Vaccination of adults

While claims based upon religious conscience were not argued to the Supreme Court in the 1905 case of *Jacobson v. Massachusetts,*[12] which sustained vaccination requirements generally when a disease of epidemic proportions is ravaging a community, it is conceivable, albeit unlikely, that the Court would exempt, because of religious beliefs, an individual from a general immunization program of a community. The Mississippi Supreme Court in 1979 stated that there was uniform agreement upholding statutes requiring im-

---

9. New York v. Ferber, 458 U.S. 747, 762, 102 S. Ct. 3348, 73 L. Ed. 2d 1113, 1122 (1982).

10. Massachusetts v. Oakes, 491 U.S. 576, 109 S. Ct. 2633, 105 L. Ed. 2d 493, 500 (1989).

11. Osborne v. Ohio, 495 U.S. 103, 110 S. Ct. 1691, 109 L. Ed. 2d 98 (1990).

12. Jacobson v. Commonwealth of Massachusetts, 197 U.S. 11, 25 S. Ct. 358, 49 L. Ed. 643 (1905).

munization against crippling and dangerous diseases, and so held. The United States Supreme Court denied certiorari.[13]

§ 8.02. Use of animals and drugs in religious services

Interests in freedom of religion and freedom of expression have clashed with the important societal interests in preserving health and safety when ministers and others utilize animals, snakes, drugs, etc., in religious services.

The clear weight of authority holds that governmental entities can prohibit and punish the use of dangerous snakes in public religious services, even over claims of infringement of religious liberty.[14]

Statutes and ordinances have at times banned the sacrifice of animals as part of religious services, but the United States Supreme Court in 1993 held violative of the First Amendment a municipal ordinance banning the "sacrifice of any animal" in the city. The Court heavily weighed the fact found by it that the ordinances had as their object the suppression of religion, and noted that reasonable alternatives short of prohibiting sacrifices were available to the city to protect its legitimate interests. Noting that there was no general ban on the killing of animals in the city, the Court indicated that "government, in the pursuit of legitimate interests, cannot in a selective manner impose burdens only on conduct initiated by religious belief." The Court advised that "all law that targets religious conduct for distinctive treatment, or advances legitimate governmental interests against conduct with a religious motivation, will survive strict scrutiny only in rare cases."[15]

While the California Supreme Court had ruled in 1964 that freedom of religion prevents a state from suppressing the use in Indian religious services of peyote, a narcotic root,[16] there are cases to the contrary,[17] and the United States Supreme Court ruled in 1990 that a state can deny unemployment benefits to persons dismissed from work because of religiously inspired use of peyote in violation of a general drug statute. The opinion of Justice Scalia, joined by four others, states that it is no longer necessary to prove that a compelling state interest outweighs the individual's interest when there is an "otherwise valid law that the state is free to

---

13. Brown v. Stone, 378 So. 2d 218 (Miss. 1979).

14. Hill v. State, 38 Ala. App. 404, 88 So. 2d 880 (1956).

15. Church of the Lukumi Babalu Aye, Inc. v. City of Hialeah, 508 U.S. 520, 113 S. Ct. 2217, 124 L. Ed. 2d 472 (1993).

16. People v. Woody, 61 Cal. 2d 716, 40 Cal. Rptr. 69, 394 P.2d 813 (1964).

17. Oliver v. Udall, 113 U.S. App. D.C. 212, 306 F.2d 819 (D.C. Cir. 1962); State v. Big Sheep, 75 Mont. 219, 243 P. 1067 (1926).

regulate." Justice O'Connor disagreed with this statement in her separate concurring opinion. Justices Brennan, Marshall and Blackmun dissented, indicating there was no compelling state interest here to justify denying the worker's expression of his religion.[18]

§ 8.03. Compulsory blood transfusions and other medical care

In 1956 a California appellate court ruled that the survivors of a worker could not get death benefits under the state workmen's compensation act, where the worker had refused to accept a blood transfusion because of his religious beliefs and consequently died. The California court remarked that the decedent "was free to believe and worship as he chose, and he was further free, if he so chose, to practice his belief; but if he exercised that choice and his death resulted from his choice, petitioners were not entitled, as a matter of right, to the benefits of the workmen's compensation laws."[19]

The Court of Appeals for the Second Circuit held in 1971 that a patient in a state hospital had a right, based upon freedom of religion, to be free from compulsory medication not imperatively needed to protect some other substantial interest of society, and the United States Supreme Court denied certiorari.[20] Other state and federal courts have held that adults in the exercise of their religious freedom have a constitutional right not to be subjected to blood transfusions, even if it may mean their death, so long at least as it is not outweighed by other valid interests of society, which may be present, for instance, if there are minor children dependent upon the individual.[21] While five years later a comparable Florida court held that "the right to refuse life-saving treatment will be overridden by a compelling state interest," such as the presence of children dependent upon the person, the Florida Supreme Court quashed the decision, holding that (1) a health care provider must comply with the wishes of a patient to refuse medical treatment unless ordered to do otherwise by court of competent jurisdiction; (2) a provider wishing to override a patient's decision to refuse medical treatment must immediately provide notice to the state attorney presiding in the circuit where the controversy arises, and to interested third parties known to the provider; and (3) there was no proof in the record that

18. Employment Div., Dept. of Human Resources of Oregon v. Smith, 494 U.S. 872, 110 S. Ct. 1595, 108 L. Ed. 2d 876 (1990).

19. Martin v. Industrial Acc. Commission, 147 Cal. App. 2d 137, 304 P.2d 828, 830 (2d Dist. 1956).

20. Winters v. Miller, 446 F.2d 65 (2d Cir. 1971).

21. In re Brooks' Estate, 32 Ill. 2d 361, 205 N.E.2d 435 (1965); Holmes v. Silver Cross Hospital of Joliet, Ill., 340 F. Supp. 125 (N.D. Ill. 1972).

abandonment of the patient's minor children would have occurred had the patient died after refusing medical treatment and, thus the heavy burden required to override the patient's constitutional right to refuse treatment was not satisfied.[22] On the other hand, a New York court in 1985 upheld a blood transfusion to a pregnant woman over her sincere religious objections.[23]

Remarking that "the principle that a competent person has a constitutionally protected liberty interest in refusing medical treatment may be inferred from our prior decisions," the Supreme Court in 1990 held that where a guardian seeks to discontinue nutrition and hydration of a person diagnosed to be in a persistent vegetative state, a state may refuse the guardian's request unless there is "clear and convincing" proof that this was the wish of the patient before becoming incompetent. Justice O'Connor concurring emphasized that, while it was undecided by the Court, an individual should be able to leave this decision to a proxy, such as a chosen attorney or family member. Justices Brennan, Blackmun, Marshall and Stevens dissented, indicating that the procedural obstacles violated the right of an individual to be free from unwanted nutrition and hydration, and that any state regulation must leave such decision to the "person whom the patient himself would most likely have chosen as proxy or leave the decision to the patient's family."[24]

§ 8.04. Compulsory physical examinations

Most states have required blood tests and physical examinations before issuing certificates to marry, and many states require some sort of physical examination as a prerequisite to entering state colleges. The United States Supreme Court has not yet passed upon the validity of such requirements when opposed by a citizen's freedom of religion. However, a Wisconsin court has held constitutional a requirement that all males secure a certificate indicating that they were free from venereal disease as a condition to the issuance of a marriage license. The court, in holding that this requirement in no way violated the petitioner's religious freedom, observed: "We know of no church which desires its ministers to profane the marriage tie

---

22. In re Dubreuil, 629 So. 2d 819 (Fla. 1993).

23. Crouse Irving Memorial Hosp., Inc. v. Paddock, 127 Misc. 2d 101, 485 N.Y.S.2d 443 (Sup. Ct. 1985).

24. Cruzan by Cruzan v. Director, Missouri Dept. of Health, 497 U.S. 261, 110 S. Ct. 2841, 111 L. Ed. 2d 224 (1990).

by uniting a man afflicted with a loathsome disease to an innocent woman."[25]

The Washington Supreme Court has sustained a regulation of the Board of Regents of the University of Washington requiring a chest X-ray as a condition of admission to that institution. Though an applicant found the practice objectionable to her faith as a Christian Scientist, the majority of the Court concluded there was a clear, present, grave and immediate danger to the health of all the students and faculty from the presence of a tubercular person.[26] The dissent characterized the application of the regulation to such cases as arbitrary and questioned whether a clear and present danger was really present.

In a somewhat comparable case, the Supreme Court of Florida has ruled that a state can hospitalize tubercular patients against their will. The court reflected: "Religious freedom cannot be used as a cloak for any person with a contagious or infectious disease to spread such disease because of his religion."[27]

§ 8.05. Fluoridation of water supplies

Lower court authority suggests that claims of freedom of religion will not prevail over the interest of society in endeavoring to minimize tooth decay. The Oregon Supreme Court has ruled that the fluoridation of the water supply by the city of Bend did not violate constitutional guarantees of religious liberty, observing: "The measure bears only remotely, if at all, upon the religious practices of any individual . . . it was adopted for the accomplishment of an end, concededly legitimate. . . . It is, therefore a valid exercise of the City's police power."[28] Future decisions are likely to follow this precedent.[29]

§ 8.06. Practice of the healing arts by religionists

Since the beginning of recorded history religious prophets and priests have healed and attempted to heal the sick. Although concededly the use of prayer for healing the sick could not be proscribed by any state authority, when individuals unlicensed to practice medicine perform surgery or prescribe medicine for ill persons, they

---

25. Peterson v. Widule, 157 Wis. 641, 147 N.W. 966, 977 (1914).

26. State ex rel. Holcomb v. Armstrong, 39 Wash. 2d 860, 239 P.2d 545 (1952).

27. Moore v. Draper, 57 So. 2d 648 (Fla. 1952).

28. Baer v. City of Bend, 206 Or. 221, 292 P.2d 134, 141 (1956) (noted in 55 Mich. L. Rev. 130).

29. Kraus v. City of Cleveland, 163 Ohio St. 559, 57 Ohio Op. 1, 127 N.E.2d 609 (1955).

are apt to run afoul of legislative controls over the practice of medicine.

Courts in a number of states have upheld convictions under statutes prescribing criminal penalties for the unlicensed practice of medicine, as against claims that such application of the statutes violated the defendant's religious liberty.[30]

Christian Scientists and some others are often expressly, or by judicial interpretation of statutes, exempted from state medical practice acts.[31]

§ 8.07. Regulating the sale of alcohol

Noting that the federal statute failed to directly advance a significant interest of the government, and that there were alternatives less intrusive on the First Amendment protection of communication, the Supreme Court in 1995 voided as violative of that Amendment provisions of a federal act prohibiting beer labels from showing the alcoholic content.[32]

Holding that a state ban on advertising the prices of liquor away from licensed premises was unconstitutional, the Court in 1996 readily acknowledged that restrictions are permissible to prevent misleading and untruthful advertising, but held that in this case the restraint was unrelated either to consumer protection or to reducing the consumption of alcohol in the state.[33]

The Supreme Court had in 1982 voided a state statute giving religious bodies veto power over individuals applying for liquor licenses in the immediate area. This, said the Court, had the effect of "advancing religion" in violation of the First Amendment.[34]

---

30. Fealy v. City of Birmingham, 15 Ala. App. 367, 73 So. 296 (1916); Smith v. People, 51 Colo. 270, 117 P. 612 (1911); State v. Verbon, 167 Wash. 140, 8 P.2d 1083 (1932); State v. Harrison, 260 Wis. 89, 50 N.W.2d 38 (1951).

31. People v. Cole, 219 N.Y. 98, 113 N.E. 790 (1916).

32. Rubin v. Coors Brewing Co., 514 U.S. 476, 115 S. Ct. 1585, 131 L. Ed. 2d 532 (1995).

33. 44 Liquormart, Inc. v. Rhode Island, 116 S. Ct. 1495, 134 L. Ed. 2d 711 (U.S. 1996).

34. Larkin v. Grendel's Den, Inc., 459 U.S. 116, 103 S. Ct. 505, 74 L. Ed. 2d 297 (1982).

CHAPTER NINE

Balancing Societal Interests in First Amendment Freedoms With the Societal Interest in Protecting Public Morality

---

§ 9.00. Introduction

Producers, distributors and exhibitors of films are all entitled to the protection of the First Amendment of the United States Constitution. So, too, are publishers, distributors, and vendors of books, magazines, newspapers and the like. Persons sermonizing or just speaking on the streets are entitled to constitutional free speech protection and, in the former case, to the protection flowing as well from freedom of religion.

The federal, state, and local governments have at times felt that certain written and spoken words tended to debase the public morality. Such concern has found expression in statutes and ordinances punishing profane language, in other provisions censoring films, in enactments punishing those who vend obscene literature, as well as some previous restraints upon such literature, in the policing of burlesque and other stage attractions, and in attempts to control the program content of radio and television.

§ 9.01. Material not obscene

In 1957 the United States Supreme Court ruled that a state could not punish a person who made available to the adult population of a community literature that would, according to the language of the statute, "manifestly tend to the corruption of the morals of youth." The Court said: "The incidence of this enactment is to reduce the adult population of Michigan to reading only what is fit for children." This, added the Court, "is to burn the house to roast the pig."[1]

The Court in 1994 made it clear that "non-obscene, sexually explicit materials, involving persons over the age of seventeen are protected by the First Amendment."[2]

Governmental regulations of printed matter to protect public morality are unconstitutional when they are so vague and uncertain that publishers and retailers cannot know what is legal and what is forbidden. Thus, in 1968 the Supreme Court voided a New York statute banning the sale of "any magazines . . . which would appeal to the lust of persons under the age of eighteen years or to their curiosity as to sex or to the anatomical differences between the sexes."[3]

In 1971 the Supreme Court ruled that a state could not punish under a statute forbidding "maliciously and willfully disturbing the peace or quiet of any neighborhood or person by offensive conduct," a young man who appeared in a county courthouse wearing, in protest against the military draft, a sweater with the words "Fuck the Draft" thereon. The Court applied its general rule voiding punishments for the contents of speech so long as the language is not within the limited exceptions.[4]

Two years later the Court held that a young woman could not be dismissed from a university for having used the word "mother-fucker" in an underground newspaper circulating on the campus. The Court emphasized that the First Amendment leaves no room for the operation of a dual standard in the academic community

---

1. Butler v. State of Mich., 352 U.S. 380, 77 S. Ct. 524, 1 L. Ed. 2d 412 (1957).

2. U.S. v. X-Citement Video, Inc., 513 U.S. 64, 115 S. Ct. 464, 130 L. Ed. 2d 372 (1994).

3. Rabeck v. New York, 391 U.S. 462, 88 S. Ct. 1716, 20 L. Ed. 2d 741 (1968).

4. Cohen v. California, 403 U.S. 15, 91 S. Ct. 1780, 29 L. Ed. 2d 284 (1971).

with respect to the content of speech, and held that the word was not obscene.[5]

Where matter had been ruled obscene in a previous civil suit to which the present defendant was not a party, the Supreme Court held that it was unconstitutional to deny the defendant in a criminal prosecution for selling obscene matter the opportunity to prove that the material was nonobscene.[6]

In 1962 the Court ruled that the Postmaster General could not ban from the mails magazines apparently of interest primarily to homosexuals. The opinion for the Court by Justice Harlan emphasized that publications cannot legally be "obscene" unless they possess the quality of "patent offensiveness," and that to be such they must go substantially beyond customary limits of candor in describing materials or events.[7]

The Court in 1982 affirmed a Court of Appeals' reversal of a District Court judgment which had dismissed a suit alleging that a school board, in removing "offensive," but concededly not obscene, books from school libraries, violated the First Amendment. The Supreme Court held that the evidence "does not foreclose the possibility that [the school board's] decision to remove the books rested decisively upon disagreement with constitutionally protected ideas in those books, or upon a desire . . . to impose upon the students . . . a political orthodoxy to which [the board members] and their constituents adhered."[8]

Nudity per se is not obscene. In 1972 the Supreme Court ruled that two pictures showing a nude man and woman embracing in a sitting position were not obscene, and that a poem giving an author's recollection of sexual intercourse amid a selection of other poems was not obscene. The Court ruled that whether the dominant theme of a publication appealed to prurient interest is a question of constitutional fact for the independent judgment of the Court.[9] The Supreme Court has reminded us that "all nudity cannot be deemed

5. Papish v. Board of Curators of University of Missouri, 410 U.S. 667, 93 S. Ct. 1197, 35 L. Ed. 2d 618 (1973).

6. McKinney v. Alabama, 424 U.S. 669, 96 S. Ct. 1189, 47 L. Ed. 2d 387 (1976).

7. Manual Enterprises, Inc. v. Day, 370 U.S. 478, 82 S. Ct. 1432, 8 L. Ed. 2d 639 (1962).

8. Board of Educ., Island Trees Union Free School Dist. No. 26 v. Pico, 457 U.S. 853, 102 S. Ct. 2799, 73 L. Ed. 2d 435, 4 Ed. Law Rep. 1013 (1982).

9. Kois v. Wisconsin, 408 U.S. 229, 92 S. Ct. 2245, 33 L. Ed. 2d 312 (1972).

obscene even as to minors."[10] Nevertheless, a badly divided Court in 1991 ruled that the First Amendment did not prevent a state from enforcing a public decency law to prevent nude dancing in public. The opinion for the Court saw the protection of order and morality as a "substantial" interest justifying this control upon expression. Justice Scalia, in his concurring opinion, necessary to provide a majority, opined that it was not necessary to find important public interests supporting such a law, where such legislation does not either directly or indirectly impede speech. Justice Souter, also necessary to provide a majority, in his concurring opinion remarked that "nudity is a condition, not an activity," repeating an earlier dictum that "not all dancing is entitled to First Amendment protection as an expressive activity." Justices White, Marshall, Blackmun and Stevens dissented, reaffirming that non-obscene nude dancing was protectable under the First Amendment, adding that there was here no narrowly drawn statute protective of a substantial public interest.[11]

Where ordinances restricting the location of adult theaters allow for reasonable alternative locations within the same community and serve a substantial societal interest, they have been upheld although impacting upon freedom of communication. In 1976 the Supreme Court sustained an ordinance prohibiting locating an adult theater within 1,000 feet of any two other regulated uses or within 500 feet of any residential zone,[12] and in 1986 it upheld prohibiting an adult theater within 1,000 feet of any residential zone, single- or multiple-family dwelling, church, park, or school. Justice Rehnquist for the Court held that the "content neutral" rule, permitting regulation of the time, place, and manner of expression so long as the regulating provision is designed to serve a substantial government interest and does not unreasonably limit alternative avenues of communication, would apply in this case, since the evil being controlled was not the nature of the films, but the impact of the theater upon residences and other named institutions.[13]

Child pornography, whether obscene or not, is not protected by the First Amendment. Accordingly governments may criminalize the production and distribution of material depicting sexual conduct

10. Erznoznik v. City of Jacksonville, 422 U.S. 205, 95 S. Ct. 2268, 45 L. Ed. 2d 125 (1975).

11. Barnes v. Glen Theatre, Inc., 501 U.S. 560, 111 S. Ct. 2456, 115 L. Ed. 2d 504 (1991).

12. Young v. American Mini Theatres, Inc., 427 U.S. 50, 96 S. Ct. 2440, 49 L. Ed. 2d 310 (1976).

13. City of Renton v. Playtime Theatres, Inc., 475 U.S. 41, 106 S. Ct. 925, 89 L. Ed. 2d 29 (1986).

by children under 16. The Supreme Court stated that the prevention of sexual exploitation and abuse of children constitutes a governmental objective of "surpassing importance." Rejecting a claim of overbreadth, the Court found the statute under review to be one "whose legitimate reach dwarfs its arguably impermissible applications."[14]

In a 1990 opinion of the Supreme Court, written by Justice O'Connor and joined by Justices Stevens and Kennedy, an ordinance regulating sexually-oriented businesses by licensing and regulation was voided because no time was prescribed within which applications for licenses had to be acted upon. There must be, said the opinion of the Court, "an effective limitation on the time within which the licensor's decision must be made." The Court further found unconstitutionality because the ordinance failed "to provide an avenue for prompt judicial review so as to minimize suppression of the speech in the event of license denial." These three Justices would hold that a city does not bear the burden of going to court to effect the denial of a license application, nor does it bear the burden of proof once in court. Justices Brennan, Marshall and Blackmun dissented, disagreeing with this novel view of burdens of proof.[15]

In another case, the First Amendment was held to be no bar to a closing order applicable to a bookstore that was also a place of prostitution and lewdness. The Court held that in such a situation there is no need to apply the *O'Brien* rule that limits a statute impacting upon freedom of communication to no more than what is necessary to serve its purpose, since the sexual activities punished had no element of protected expression. Justices Blackmun, Brennan and Marshall dissented, stating that when any book store is being closed by the government, only the least restrictive interference is constitutionally acceptable.[16]

§ 9.02. Obscene matter—subsequent punishment

A person who distributes, sells or offers for sale "obscene" literature can for such activity be criminally punished by the states in their attempt to protect the public morality. The United States Supreme Court in 1956 said: "In an unbroken series of cases extending over a long stretch of this Court's history, it has been accepted

---

14. New York v. Ferber, 458 U.S. 747, 102 S. Ct. 3348, 8, 73 L. Ed. 2d 1113 (1982).

15. FW/PBS, Inc. v. City of Dallas, 493 U.S. 215, 110 S. Ct. 596, 107 L. Ed. 2d 603 (1990).

16. Barnes v. Glen Theatre, Inc., 501 U.S. 560, 111 S. Ct. 2456, 115 L. Ed. 2d 504 (1991).

as a postulate that the primary requirements of decency may be enforced against obscene publications."[17] Later that term the Court decided the companion cases of *Roth v. United States* and *Alberts v. California,* holding that obscene literature is not entitled to constitutional protection so that the federal government can punish one who sends such material through the mails and the state and local governments can punish individuals who sell or possess for sale such literature. The Court indicated that literature would be obscene when "to the average person, applying contemporary community standards, the dominant theme of the material taken as a whole appeals to prurient interest."[18] Justices Douglas and Black dissented in an opinion by the former wherein it is said: "By these standards punishment is inflicted for thoughts provoked, not for overt acts nor antisocial conduct. This test cannot be squared with our decisions under the First Amendment. Even the ill-starred *Dennis* case conceded that speech to be punishable must have some relation to action which could be penalized by government."[19]

In 1987 the Supreme Court disavowed the popular understanding that, in allegedly obscene publications, the appeal to prurient interest and patent offensiveness were issues of fact to be decided by juries applying contemporary community standards, and ruled that the proper inquiry is whether a *reasonable* (not an ordinary) person would find serious literary, artistic, political or scientific value in the materials being questioned.[20]

Two years later the Court reversed a conviction for possessing obscene works for sale, ruling that no such legislation can constitutionally be applied unless it has as a necessary part of proof the fact that the distributor possess "scienter" of the nature of the work. Similarly, in 1989 the Court ordered a new trial for one convicted of possessing nude pictures of minors, when it was not clear that the state had properly proved scienter, the essential requirement.[21]

In 1966 the Court decided three cases which provide some additional guidance on when states can punish distributors of literature

---

17. Kingsley Books, Inc. v. Brown, 354 U.S. 436, 77 S. Ct. 1325, 1 L. Ed. 2d 1469, 14 Ohio Op. 2d 471 (1957).

18. Roth v. U.S., 354 U.S. 476, 77 S. Ct. 1304, 1 L. Ed. 2d 1498, 1509, 14 Ohio Op. 2d 331 (1957).

19. Roth v. U.S., 354 U.S. 476, 77 S. Ct. 1304, 1 L. Ed. 2d 1498, 1520, 14 Ohio Op. 2d 331 (1957).

20. Pope v. Illinois, 481 U.S. 497, 107 S. Ct. 1918, 95 L. Ed. 2d 439 (1987) (called into doubt by Pollard v. White, 119 F.3d 1430 (9th Cir. 1997).

21. Fort Wayne Books, Inc. v. Indiana, 489 U.S. 46, 109 S. Ct. 916, 103 L. Ed. 2d 34 (1989).

deemed dangerous to the public morality. In the *Memoirs* case, the Court through Justice Brennan stated that for literature to be obscene, "three elements must coalesce: it must be established that (1) the dominant theme of the material taken as a whole appeals to a prurient interest in sex; (2) the material is patently offensive because it affronts contemporary community standards relating to the description or representation of sexual matters; and (3) the material is utterly without redeeming social value."[22] The Massachusetts tribunal erred, said Justice Brennan, "in holding that a book need not be unqualifiedly worthless before it can be deemed obscene."

In the companion *Ginzburg* case the Court indicated that "commercial exploitation of erotica solely for the sake of their prurient appeal" will justify the federal and state governments in punishing the distributor, even though the work sold under some other circumstances might not be deemed obscene. Said the Court: "Where the purveyor's sole emphasis is on the sexually provocative aspects of his publications, that fact may be decisive in the determination of obscenity."[23] Justices Black, Douglas, Stewart and Harlan dissented. Said Justice Harlan:

> The First Amendment, in the obscenity area, no longer fully protects material on its face non-obscene, for such material must now also be examined in the light of the defendant's conduct, attitude, motives. This seems to me to be a mere euphemism for allowing punishment of a person who mails otherwise constitutionally protected material just because a jury or a judge may not find him or his business agreeable.[24]

In 1968 the Court held there can be a different standard of obscenity for material distributed to minors, and it affirmed the conviction of a person who had sold to a person under seventeen a "girlie" magazine that was not obscene for adults, because it had a predominant appeal to the prurient interests of minors, it was patently offensive to the prevailing standards of the adult community with respect to what was suitable material for minors, and it was utterly without redeeming social importance for minors. Scienter

---

22. A Book Named "John Cleland's Memoirs of a Woman of Pleasure" v. Attorney General of Com. of Mass., 383 U.S. 413, 86 S. Ct. 975, 16 L. Ed. 2d 1 (1966).

23. Ginzburg v. U.S., 383 U.S. 463, 86 S. Ct. 942, 16 L. Ed. 2d 31 (1966).

24. Ginzburg v. U.S., 383 U.S. 463, 86 S. Ct. 942, 16 L. Ed. 2d 31 (1966).

is a necessary provision for any statute under which such a conviction occurs.[25]

In 1972 the Court ruled that two pictures showing a nude man and woman embracing in a sitting position were not obscene, and that a poem giving the artist's recollection of sexual intercourse, amid a selection of other poems, was not obscene. The Court pointed out that whether the dominant theme of a publication appeals to prurient interest is a question of constitutional fact for the independent judgment of the Supreme Court.[26]

The following year the Court held that states can ban "works which depict or describe sexual conduct," but added by way of definition and limitation: "That conduct must be critically defined by the application of state law, as written or authoritatively construed. A state offense must also be limited to works which, taken as a whole, appeal to the prurient interest in sex, which portray sexual conduct in a patently offensive way, and which, taken as a whole, do not have serious literary, artistic, political or scientific value." The Court indicated it was isolating "hard core" pornography from expression protected by the First Amendment. Courts can apply local, rather than national, standards under this test. No longer is it necessary for a state to prove that a work is "utterly without redeeming social value."[27]

In 1974 the Court ruled that the *Miller* decision does not mean that a precise geographical area standard is required as a matter of law, and sustained a trial judge's instruction in a prosecution for mailing obscene materials that the jury was to determine by "contemporary standards of the community as a whole," which he defined as "standards generally held throughout this country." The trial judge had refused to allow the defendants to introduce evidence that similar materials were available on newsstands of the local community, and the Supreme Court sustained this, over dissents by Justices Brennan, Douglas, Marshall and Stewart.[28]

The same year, the Court viewed the film *Carnal Knowledge* and concluded that it was not obscene within the *Miller* test, there being no depiction of sexual conduct in a patently offensive way. The Court upheld the Georgia courts' rulings which had directed that

25. Ginsberg v. State of N. Y., 390 U.S. 629, 88 S. Ct. 1274, 20 L. Ed. 2d 195, 44 Ohio Op. 2d 339 (1968).

26. Kois v. Wisconsin, 408 U.S. 229, 92 S. Ct. 2245, 33 L. Ed. 2d 312 (1972).

27. Miller v. California, 413 U.S. 15, 93 S. Ct. 2607, 37 L. Ed. 2d 419 (1973).

28. Hamling v. U.S., 418 U.S. 87, 94 S. Ct. 2887, 41 L. Ed. 2d 590 (1974).

the jurors were to apply "community standards" without specifying which community.[29]

In another case from Georgia, the Supreme Court has held that no state can punish the mere possession of obscene matter within the privacy of the home.[30]

Where Illinois decisions had indicated clearly that sadomasochistic materials were embraced within its statutory ban on obscene publications, although these were not specifically enumerated in the statute, the Supreme Court sustained the application of the Illinois obscenity statute to individuals selling sadomasochistic materials.[31]

In determining whether publications are obscene and devoid of any redeeming social value, the Court held in 1977 that a jury can be permitted to consider the circumstances of sale and distribution to ascertain if the matter was commercially exploited solely for the sake of its prurient appeal,[32] and the following year, while holding that a trial court, in determining if obscenity exists, cannot include children within the concept of "the local community," the Court again ruled that trial courts can treat as relevant the methods of dissemination utilized by the distributor.[33]

In federal prosecutions for sending obscene matter through the mails, the triers of fact are not bound by definitions of the term "obscene" in legislation of the state where the mailing occurred.[34]

When Indiana law was amended to make obscenity violations predicate offenses to bring into play punishments under the state's anti-racketeering statute, the Supreme Court held that the statute, as so amended, was not unconstitutionally vague, and that its penalties were not so "draconian" as to violate the First Amendment.[35]

The Supreme Court has vacated and remanded a conviction under a statute prohibiting adult photographs of children in the nude, as applied to a father who had taken photographs of his 14-year-old stepdaughter. Justice O'Connor, who wrote the opinion for the Court, joined by Chief Justice Rehnquist and Justices White and Kennedy, ruled that the original overbreadth of the statute was made moot when the legislature added a requirement of lascivious

29. Jenkins v. Georgia, 418 U.S. 153, 94 S. Ct. 2750, 41 L. Ed. 2d 642 (1974).

30. Stanley v. Georgia, 394 U.S. 557, 89 S. Ct. 1243, 22 L. Ed. 2d 542 (1969).

31. Ward v. Illinois, 431 U.S. 767, 97 S. Ct. 2085, 52 L. Ed. 2d 738 (1977).

32. Splawn v. State of Cal., 431 U.S. 595, 97 S. Ct. 1987, 52 L. Ed. 2d 606 (1977).

33. Pinkus v. U.S., 436 U.S. 293, 98 S. Ct. 1808, 56 L. Ed. 2d 293 (1978).

34. Smith v. U.S., 431 U.S. 291, 97 S. Ct. 1756, 52 L. Ed. 2d 324 (1977).

35. Fort Wayne Books, Inc. v. Indiana, 489 U.S. 46, 109 S. Ct. 916, 103 L. Ed. 2d 34 (1989).

intent.[36] The following year the Court, while holding that a state may punish the possessing or viewing of pictures of nude minors who are neither the children nor wards of the defendant, held that a new trial was necessary where it was unclear whether the state had proved scienter, a requirement of the crime. Justices Brennan, Marshall and Stevens believed both that the statute was too broad and that the balancing of interests here was inadequate.[37]

Under the *Miller* rule, the prosecution need not present expert testimony that a publication is obscene.[38]

§ 9.03. —pre-trial restraints

In 1957 the United States Supreme Court upheld a New York statute which allowed the chief executive or legal officer of a municipality to go into court for an injunction pendente lite to restrain the distribution of publications alleged to be obscene. In the instant case, the judge issued an order to show cause within four days why the injunction pendente lite should not issue.

Under the New York statute the distributor was entitled to a trial on the issues within one day after joinder of issue, and a decision was rendered by the state court within two days of the conclusion of the trial. In the *Kingsley Books* case[39] the distributor consented to the granting of an injunction pendente lite, and the judge at trial, sitting in equity, found the books to be obscene and ordered their surrender. The Supreme Court affirmed, denying the claims of the publisher that this was an unconstitutional prior censorship. The Court pointed out that protection even as to previous restraints is not an absolute. Chief Justice Warren, as well as Justices Black, Brennan and Douglas dissented. The Chief Justice suggested that no book should be put on trial, but only "the conduct of the individual" in vending the book. Justice Brennan insisted upon the right to a jury trial, while Justices Black and Douglas believed that the opportunity of a New York judge to issue even an injunction pendente lite without a hearing and without any finding on the issue of obscenity was unconstitutional.

Six years later the Supreme Court ruled unconstitutional the Rhode Island practice wherein a state commission notified book dealers that certain designated books and magazines were objection-

---

36. Massachusetts v. Oakes, 491 U.S. 576, 109 S. Ct. 2633, 105 L. Ed. 2d 493 (1989).

37. Osborne v. Ohio, 495 U.S. 103, 110 S. Ct. 1691, 109 L. Ed. 2d 98 (1990).

38. Kaplan v. California, 413 U.S. 115, 93 S. Ct. 2680, 37 L. Ed. 2d 492 (1973).

39. Kingsley Books, Inc. v. Brown, 354 U.S. 436, 77 S. Ct. 1325, 1 L. Ed. 2d 1469, 14 Ohio Op. 2d 471 (1957).

able for sale or display to youths under 18, the book dealers were told the lists had been given to the local police, and soon local police dropped into the bookstore. Said Justice Brennan, speaking for the Court:

> The Fourteenth Amendment requires that regulation by the States of obscenity conform to procedures that will ensure against the curtailment of constitutionally protected expression, which is often separated from obscenity only by a dim and uncertain line. It is characteristic of the freedoms of expression in general that they are vulnerable to gravely damaging yet barely visible encroachments. Our insistence that regulations of obscenity scrupulously embody the most rigorous procedural safeguards, is therefore but a special instance of the larger principle that the freedoms of expression must be ringed about with adequate bulwarks . . .

> Any system of prior restrains of expression comes to this Court bearing a heavy presumption against its constitutional validity. We have tolerated such a system only where it operated under judicial superintendence and assured an almost immediate judicial determination of the validity of the restraint.[40] [citing *Kingsley Books,* supra]

A trial is not a constitutional requirement in a civil proceeding to determine obscenity vel non of written materials.[41]

To avoid constitutional infirmity, a scheme of administrative censorship must: (1) place the burdens of initiating judicial review and of proving that the material is unprotected expression on the censor; (2) require prompt judicial review—a final judicial determination on the merits within a specified, brief period—to prevent the administrative decision of the censor from achieving an effect of finality; and (3) limit to preservation of the status quo for the shortest fixed period compatible with sound judicial resolution any restraint imposed in advance of the final judicial determination.[42]

§ 9.04. Seizure by customs officials

Under the Tariff Act, publications that are obscene and immoral

---

40. Bantam Books, Inc. v. Sullivan, 372 U.S. 58, 83 S. Ct. 631, 9 L. Ed. 2d 584, 590-91, 593 (1963).

41. Alexander v. Virginia, 413 U.S. 836, 93 S. Ct. 2803, 37 L. Ed. 2d 993 (1973).

42. Blount v. Rizzi, 400 U.S. 410, 91 S. Ct. 423, 27 L. Ed. 2d 498 (1971).

can be seized by customs officers, after which proceedings in rem are instituted in the federal district courts. If the publication is found to be obscene, it is then destroyed.[43]

The United States Supreme Court has construed this Act to require that forfeiture proceedings be commenced within 14 days and completed within 60 days of their commencement, so long as the importer is not responsible for delays in administrative or judicial action.[44] As so construed, the federal government can ban the importation of obscene materials, with obscenity defined as in the *Miller* rule.[45] In a plurality opinion by Chief Justice Burger, Justices White, Brennan and Blackmun, it was held that there is no constitutional objection to the seizure at customs of obscene matter imported for the private use of the citizen. Justices Harlan and Stewart concurred because they viewed the importation as for commercial purposes. Justices Black, Douglas and Marshall dissented.[46]

§ 9.05. Exclusion of materials from mails and interstate commerce

Although a federal district court[47] and court of appeals[48] had ruled that nudist magazines could be kept from the mails, the action of the latter was reversed by the United States Supreme Court in 1958 in a per curiam opinion,[49] simply citing *Roth v. United States.*

In 1962 the Supreme Court ruled that the Postmaster General could not exclude from the mails magazines which did not qualify as "obscene," since they were not "so offensive on their face as to affront current community standards of decency."[50]

In 1970 the Court sustained an act of Congress under which

---

43. 19 U.S.C.A. § 1305.

44. U.S v. Thirty-Seven (37) Photographs, 402 U.S. 363, 91 S. Ct. 1400, 28 L. Ed. 2d 822 (1971).

45. U.S. v. 12 200-Foot Reels of Super 8mm. Film, 413 U.S. 123, 93 S. Ct. 2665, 37 L. Ed. 2d 500 (1973).

46. U.S. v. Thirty-Seven (37) Photographs, 402 U.S. 363, 91 S. Ct. 1400, 28 L. Ed. 2d 822 (1971).

47. Sunshine Book Co. v. Summerfield, 128 F. Supp. 564 (D.D.C. 1955), judgment aff'd, 101 U.S. App. D.C. 358, 249 F.2d 114 (D.C. Cir. 1957), judgment rev'd, 355 U.S. 372, 78 S. Ct. 365, 2 L. Ed. 2d 352 (1958).

48. Sunshine Book Co. v. Summerfield, 101 U.S. App. D.C. 358, 249 F.2d 114 (D.C. Cir. 1957), judgment rev'd, 355 U.S. 372, 78 S. Ct. 365, 2 L. Ed. 2d 352 (1958).

49. Sunshine Book Company v. Summerfield, 355 U.S. 372, 78 S. Ct. 365, 2 L. Ed. 2d 352 (1958).

50. Manual Enterprises, Inc. v. Day, 370 U.S. 478, 82 S. Ct. 1432, 1434, 8 L. Ed. 2d 639 (1962).

householders could protect themselves from matter they believe to be erotically arousing or sexually proactive. Under the statute, the Postmaster General was empowered, after receiving notice from the addressee, to issue an order to the sender to refrain from further mailings, and to delete the name of the addressee from all lists controlled by the sender. Here, the Court concluded, the interest in communication was outweighed by the interest in privacy.[51]

The following year the Supreme Court upheld the constitutionality of a criminal statute providing for the punishment of individuals who used the mails for the distribution of obscene materials, even when the addressee was a willing recipient.[52]

The same year the Court held violative of the First Amendment a Congressional act allowing the Postmaster General to stop the delivery of mail to a person when the Postmaster General concluded that the individual was using the mail for the distribution of obscene matter, since the statute did not provide the necessary procedural safeguards. The Court said:

> To avoid constitutional infirmity, a scheme of administrative censorship must place the burden of initiating judicial review and of proving that the material is unprotected expression on the censor, require prompt judicial review—a final judicial determination on the merits within a specified brief period—to protect the administrative decision of the censor from achieving an effect of finality, and limit to preservation of the status quo for the shortest, fixed period compatible with sound judicial resolution, any restraint imposed in advance of the final judicial determination.[53]

This rule is applicable throughout the entire area of administrative interference with First Amendment freedoms.

In 1983 the Court ruled that the First Amendment was violated by a federal statute prohibiting mailing to the public unsolicited advertisements for contraceptives. The Court observed: "We have never held the government itself can shut off the flow of mailings to protect those recipients who might potentially be offended." The Court emphasized that in First Amendment cases it had first to ascertain if the interest opposed to First Amendment freedoms was substantial. It added: "If so, we must then determine whether the regulation directly advances the governmental interest asserted, and

---

51. Rowan v. U.S. Post Office Dept., 397 U.S. 728, 90 S. Ct. 1484, 25 L. Ed. 2d 736 (1970).

52. U.S. v. Reidel, 402 U.S. 351, 91 S. Ct. 1410, 28 L. Ed. 2d 813 (1971).

53. Blount v. Rizzi, 400 U.S. 410, 91 S. Ct. 423, 27 L. Ed. 2d 498 (1971).

whether it is not more extensive than necessary to serve that interest."[54]

The United States government can punish the use of interstate commerce for the transmission of obscene materials.[55]

§ 9.06. Films—subsequent punishments

The United States Supreme Court in 1975 held unconstitutional under the First Amendment an ordinance prohibiting the display of nudity in films by a drive-in movie theater, when visible from a public street or place. The Court reminded us that "all nudity cannot be deemed obscene even as to minors." Its task, said the Court, is one of accommodating competing interests.[56]

Where a state statute declared any place exhibiting "lewd" films to be a "moral nuisance," and declared material to be "prurient" when it incited "to lust," the Supreme Court indicated that proper judicial review was not to void the entire statute, but only that part making criminal the handling of films that occasioned "lust." Since a clause in the statute equated "lewd" films with "obscene" films, that part of the statute was held valid.[57]

Statutes and ordinances attempting to punish the exhibition of obscene films will be invalidated when they are unconstitutionally vague. The Supreme Court has held impermissibly vague a state statute interpreted by the state courts as banning the showing at an outdoor theater of a film that the state court agreed could not be banned at an indoor theater.[58] Because of its vagueness a local ordinance requiring exhibitors to classify some films as "not suitable for young persons" was held unconstitutional by the Court. The term "likely to encourage sexual promiscuity" was found by the Court to be objectionably uncertain. "It could extend," said the Court, "depending upon one's moral judgment, from the obvious to any sexual contacts outside a marital relationship." The Court repeated its rule that "the vice of vagueness is particularly

---

54. Bolger v. Youngs Drug Products Corp., 463 U.S. 60, 103 S. Ct. 2875, 77 L. Ed. 2d 469 (1983).

55. U.S. v. Orito, 413 U.S. 139, 93 S. Ct. 2674, 37 L. Ed. 2d 513 (1973).

56. Erznoznik v. City of Jacksonville, 422 U.S. 205, 95 S. Ct. 2268, 45 L. Ed. 2d 125 (1975).

57. Brockett v. Spokane Arcades, Inc., 472 U.S. 491, 105 S. Ct. 2794, 86 L. Ed. 2d 394 (1985).

58. Rabe v. Washington, 405 U.S. 313, 92 S. Ct. 993, 31 L. Ed. 2d 258 (1972).

pronounced where expression is sought to be subjected to licensing."[59]

In 1972 the Supreme Court held that California could prevent the showing in bars of films which were not obscene under the orthodox *Roth* test, emphasizing the considerable power of regulation possessed by states over places dispensing alcoholic beverages.[60]

The Court held in 1993 that not violative of the First Amendment was federal punishment of a vendor of sexually explicit videotapes and magazines by forfeiture of the materials plus a fine of $100,000 and six years in prison. The forfeiture was held not to be a prior restraint, the Court noting that it was a consequence of illegal activity previously adjudicated by a Court. Justices Kennedy, Blackmun, Stevens and Souter dissented, asserting that the First Amendment forbids the permanent seizure of expressive materials without a judicial finding that the materials are obscene or of an otherwise unprotected character.[61]

§ 9.07. —previous censorship—substantive norms

In 1952 the Supreme Court for the first time, in the *Burstyn* case, ruled that the films were entitled to the protection of the First Amendment. The Court then held that no state could deny a license for the showing of a film on the ground it was "sacrilegious." The Court noted that it had "recognized many years ago that such a previous restraint is a form of infringement upon freedom of expression to be especially condemned." The New York court had held that films could be censored as sacrilegious when they "treated with contempt, mockery, scorn and ridicule" some religion. Said the Supreme Court: "This is far from the kind of narrow exception to freedom of expression which a state may carve out to satisfy the adverse demands of other interests of society. In seeking to apply the broad and all-inclusive definition of 'sacrilegious' given by the New York courts, the censor is set adrift upon a boundless sea amid a myriad of conflicting currents of religious views, with no charts but those provided by the most vocal and powerful orthodoxies. New York cannot vest such unlimited restraining control over motion pictures." The Court added that substantial problems of separa-

---

59. Interstate Circuit, Inc. v. City of Dallas, 390 U.S. 676, 88 S. Ct. 1298, 20 L. Ed. 2d 225 (1968).

60. California v. LaRue, 409 U.S. 109, 93 S. Ct. 390, 34 L. Ed. 2d 342 (1972).

61. Alexander v. U.S., 509 U.S. 544, 113 S. Ct. 2766, 125 L. Ed. 2d 441 (1993).

tion of church and state were present when a state began protecting any religious doctrine from real or imagined attacks.[62]

On a number of other occasions the Supreme Court has held that states and their political subdivisions cannot censor films for any reason other than obscenity. For instance, in 1952 the Court in a per curiam ruling voided a local ordinance which allowed a board of censors to refuse a permit for a film when it was "of the opinion" that the film was "of such character as to be prejudicial to the best interests of the people" of the city. Said Justice Douglas in a concurring opinion: "If a board of censors can tell the American people what it is in their best interests to see or to read or to hear, then thought is regimented, authority substituted for liberty, and the great purpose of the First Amendment to keep uncontrolled the freedom of expression defeated."[63]

Two years later the Supreme Court in a single per curiam opinion reversed Ohio's attempt to censor a film on the ground it was "harmful," and New York's attempt to censor a film on the ground it was "immoral" and "would tend to corrupt morals."[64]

The following year the Court invalidated an attempt by Kansas to censor a film under a statute allowing censorship if a film was "cruel, obscene, indecent or immoral, or such as tend to debase or corrupt morals."[65]

In 1959 the Court ruled that New York could not deny a license to a film because its subject matter was adultery presented as being right and desirable for certain people under certain circumstances. Said Justice Stewart for the Court:

> It is contended that the State's action was justified because the motion picture attractively portrays a relationship which is contrary to the moral standards, the religious precepts, and the legal code of its citizenry. This argument misconceives what it is that the Constitution protects. Its guarantee is not confined to the expression of ideas that are conventional or shared by a majority. It protects advocacy of the opinion that adultery may sometimes be proper, no less than advocacy of socialism or the

62. Joseph Burstyn, Inc. v. Wilson, 343 U.S. 495, 72 S. Ct. 777, 96 L. Ed. 1098 (1952).

63. Gelling v. State of Texas, 343 U.S. 960, 72 S. Ct. 1002, 96 L. Ed. 1359 (1952).

64. Superior Films, Inc. v. Department of Education of State of Ohio, Division of Film Censorship, 346 U.S. 587, 74 S. Ct. 286, 98 L. Ed. 329, 52 Ohio Op. 433, 67 Ohio L. Abs. 289 (1954).

65. Holmby Productions, Inc. v. Vaughn, 350 U.S. 870, 76 S. Ct. 117, 100 L. Ed. 770 (1955).

single tax. And in the realm of ideas it protects expression which is eloquent no less than that which is unconvincing.[66]

In 1961 the Supreme Court in a five-to-four decision indicated it will allow states and cites to impose censorship when limited to "obscene" films. In the *Times Film* case it was ruled that a Chicago ordinance permitting censorship of films when "immoral or obscene" was not void on its face. Chief Justice Warren, as well as Justices Black, Brennan and Douglas expressed their view that all censorship of the films is unconstitutional as a forbidden previous restraint upon communication.[67]

In 1964 the Court held that the film, *The Lovers,* was not obscene and accordingly could not be censored by the state of Ohio. Justice Brennan's opinion for the Court was joined in only by Justice Goldberg. They stated:

> The question of the proper standard for making this determination has been the subject of much discussion and controversy since our decision in Roth-Alberts seven years ago. Recognizing that the test for obscenity enunciated there—"whether to the average person, applying contemporary community standards, the dominant theme of the material taken as a whole appeals to prurient interests"—is not perfect, we think any substitute would raise equally difficult problems, and we therefore adhere to that standard. We would reiterate, however, our recognition in Roth that obscenity is excluded from the constitutional protection only because it is "utterly without redeeming social importance," and that the portrayal of sex, e.g., in art, literature and scientific works, is not itself sufficient reason to deny material the constitutional protection of freedom of speech and press. It follows that material dealing with sex in a manner that advocates ideas, or that has literary or scientific or artistic value or any other form of social importance, may not be branded as obscenity and denied the constitutional protection. Nor may the constitutional status of the material be made to turn on a "weighing" of its social importance against its prurient appeal, for a work cannot be proscribed unless it is "utterly" without social importance. It should also be recognized that the Roth standard requires in the first instance a finding that the material goes substantially beyond customary

---

66. Kingsley Intern. Pictures Corp. v. Regents of University of State of N.Y., 360 U.S. 684, 79 S. Ct. 1362, 1365, 3 L. Ed. 2d 1512 (1959).

67. Times Film Corp. v. City of Chicago, 365 U.S. 43, 81 S. Ct. 391, 5 L. Ed. 2d 403, 15 Ohio Op. 2d 254 (1961).

limits of candor in description or representation of such matters.[68]

In 1973 the Supreme Court upheld a Georgia civil statute enjoining the exhibition of obscene films,[69] wherein obscenity was defined as by the *Miller* case, that is, where (1) the work taken as a whole appeals to a prurient interest, (2) the work depicts or describes, in a patently offensive way, sexual conduct defined by the applicable state law, and (3) the work, taken as a whole, lacks serious literary, artistic, political or scientific value.[70]

The same year, a sheriff's seizure of a film being shown at a drive-in theater, because the sheriff deemed it obscene, was held unconstitutional by the Supreme Court, which observed that a "higher hurdle" exists in the evaluation of reasonableness when First Amendment values are at stake.[71]

§ 9.08. ——procedural requirements

In 1965 the United States Supreme Court invalidated Maryland's practice of dealing with obscene films because of procedural inadequacies which often kept films off the market for as long as six months before a definitive judicial ruling was had. The Court stated:

> We hold that a noncriminal process which requires the prior submission of a film to a censor avoids constitutional infirmity only if it takes place under procedural safeguards designed to obviate the dangers of a censorship system. First, the burden of proving that the film is unprotected expression must rest on the censor. . . . Second, while the State may require advance submission of all films, in order to proceed effectively to bar all showings of unprotected films, the requirement cannot be administered in a manner which would lend an effect of finality to the censor's determination whether a film constitutes protected expression. . . . To this end, the exhibitor must be assured, by statute or authoritative judicial construction, that the censor will, within a specified brief period, either issue a license or go to court to restrain showing the film. Any restraint imposed in advance of a final judicial determination on the merits must similarly be limited to preservation of the status

---

68. Jacobellis v. State of Ohio, 378 U.S. 184, 84 S. Ct. 1676, 1680, 12 L. Ed. 2d 793, 28 Ohio Op. 2d 101 (1964).

69. Paris Adult Theatre I v. Slaton, 413 U.S. 49, 93 S. Ct. 2628, 37 L. Ed. 2d 446 (1973).

70. Miller v. California, 413 U.S. 15, 93 S. Ct. 2607, 37 L. Ed. 2d 419 (1973).

71. Roaden v. Kentucky, 413 U.S. 496, 93 S. Ct. 2796, 37 L. Ed. 2d 757 (1973).

quo for the shortest period compatible with sound judicial resolution. . . . The procedure must also assure a prompt final judicial decision, to minimize the deterrent effect of an interim and possibly erroneous denial of a license.[72]

Absent the procedural safeguards spelled out in *Freedman v. Maryland,* a state statute is unconstitutional in authorizing prior restraints of indefinite duration on the exhibition of motion pictures, not adjudicated to be obscene, through the device of abating an adult theater as a public nuisance.[73]

The Supreme Court has held that the seizure of a film as allegedly obscene will be unlawful where the warrant was improperly issued, that is, was issued "solely upon the conclusory assertions of the police officer without any inquiry by the justice of the peace into the factual basis for the officers' conclusions." "This," said the Court, "was not a procedure 'designed to focus searchingly on the question of obscenity,' . . . and therefore fell short of constitutional requirements demanding necessary sensitivity to freedom of expression."[74] However, in rejecting the argument that an application for a warrant authorizing the seizure of books or films must be evaluated under a higher standard of probable cause than that used generally under the Fourth Amendment, the Court held that it is sufficient if a warrant for the seizure of books or films is supported by probable cause that the materials are obscene. The duty of a reviewing court is simply to ensure that the magistrate had a substantial basis for concluding that probable cause existed.[75]

§ 9.09. Stage and other public performances

While the United States Supreme Court had in 1957 affirmed per curiam[76] a ruling by the New Jersey Supreme Court[77] upholding a local ordinance which prohibited licensed theaters from presenting lewd, indecent, or obscene performances, and which also banned

---

72. Freedman v. State of Md., 380 U.S. 51, 85 S. Ct. 734, 13 L. Ed. 2d 649, 655 (1965).

73. Vance v. Universal Amusement Co., Inc., 445 U.S. 308, 100 S. Ct. 1156, 63 L. Ed. 2d 413 (1980).

74. Lee Art Theatre, Inc. v. Virginia, 392 U.S. 636, 88 S. Ct. 2103, 20 L. Ed. 2d 1313 (1968).

75. New York v. P.J. Video, Inc., 475 U.S. 868, 106 S. Ct. 1610, 89 L. Ed. 2d 871 (1986).

76. Adams Newark Theater Co v. City of Newark, 354 U.S. 931, 77 S. Ct. 1395, 1 L. Ed. 2d 1533 (1957).

77. Adams Newark Theatre Co. v. City of Newark, 22 N.J. 472, 126 A.2d 340 (1956), judgment aff'd, 354 U.S. 931, 77 S. Ct. 1395, 1 L. Ed. 2d 1533 (1957).

certain specific gestures as indecent, the United States Supreme Court in 1975 held that stage productions are entitled to the full protection of the First Amendment, and that a local government cannot ban a production without first providing all the procedural safeguards necessary when films are subjected to prior restraints.[78]

In 1981 the Supreme Court also held that a zoning ordinance banning from commercial districts all live entertainment, including nude dancing, was violative of the First Amendment.[79]

In 1981 and 1986, in two per curiam decisions, the Court upheld the power of a state and a city to prohibit nude or nearly nude dancing in local establishments licensed to sell liquor for consumption on the premises. Dissenting in the second case, Justice Stevens and Brennan appropriately advised that "The Court has a duty in this case to assess the substantiality of the governmental interests asserted and determine whether those interests could be served by means that would be less intrusive on activity protected by the First Amendment."[80]

In 1991 the Court ruled that the First Amendment does not prevent a state from enforcing a public decency law to prevent nude dancing in public. The Court noted that the protection of order and morality was a "substantial" interest justifying such control. In a concurring opinion, Justice Scalia indicated his belief that there should be no need to prove an important public interest in such a case where the law does not directly or indirectly impede speech. Justices White, Marshall, Blackmun, and Stevens dissented, stating the law was unconstitutional because there was not a narrowly drawn statute protecting a compelling interest, and reaffirming the rule that non-obscene nude dancing was protected by the First Amendment. Justice Souter in a concurring opinion remarked that "nudity is a condition, not an activity," and then repeated earlier dictum from the Court that "not all dancing is entitled to First Amendment protection as an expressive activity."[81]

§ 9.10. Television showings

In a five-to-four ruling in 1978 the United States Supreme Court

---

78. Southeastern Promotions, Ltd. v. Conrad, 420 U.S. 546, 95 S. Ct. 1239, 43 L. Ed. 2d 448 (1975).

79. Schad v. Borough of Mount Ephraim, 452 U.S. 61, 101 S. Ct. 2176, 68 L. Ed. 2d 671 (1981).

80. New York State Liquor Authority v. Bellanca, 452 U.S. 714, 69, 101 S. Ct. 2599, 69 L. Ed. 2d 357 (1981); City of Newport, Ky. v. Iacobucci, 479 U.S. 92, 107 S. Ct. 383, 93 L. Ed. 2d 334 (1986).

81. Barnes v. Glen Theatre, Inc., 501 U.S. 560, 111 S. Ct. 2456, 115 L. Ed. 2d 504 (1991).

majority held that both under the Federal Communications Act and the First Amendment, the Federal Communications Commission could regulate use on television of non-obscene words dealing with sex and excretion that were "vulgar," "offensive," and "shocking," and were heard by children, so long as these utterances were patently offensive. In dissent, Justices Brennan, Marshall, Stewart and White emphasized that the word "indecent" in the Act only applied to obscene words. Justices Brennan and Marshall further dissented on First Amendment grounds, urging that parents—not the government—are to determine what their children should hear, and that the ruling also prevented adults from hearing non-obscene telecasts.[82]

Faced in 1996 with provisions of a Congressional act supplemented by Federal Communications Commissions regulations, the Court, in an opinion by Justice Breyer, held constitutional under the First Amendment governmental authorization to cable system operators, concerned with protecting children from exposure to patently offensive sex-related materials, to screen out from leased access commercial channels programming that the cable operator "reasonably believes" is patently offensive, pursuant to a "written and published policy." Breyer's opinion on this was joined by Stevens, Souter and O'Connor. Justice Thomas, the Chief Justice and Justice Scalia concurred in this result.

Another provision of the statute, with its implementing regulations, required cable systems operators to place "patently offensive" leased channel programming on a separate channel; to block that channel, and to unblock that channel only upon written request of a subscriber's written request for access. Noting that there were other means available to protect children from "patently offensive" materials broadcast, such as a "lockbox" enabling parents to lock out programs they do not want their children to watch, the Court ruled that this provision was "overly restrictive," sacrificing First Amendment interests for too speculative a gain. Breyer's opinion was concurred in by Justices Stevens, Souter, O'Connor, Thomas and Kennedy, in whole or in part.

Also unconstitutional was a provision enabling cable operators to prevent transmission of "patently offensive programming" on public access channels. The Court believed that such channels, customarily owned by local governments, regularly protected children in the community, and that a veto power in the hands of absentee cable operators was unnecessary.

---

82. F. C. C. v. Pacifica Foundation, 438 U.S. 726, 98 S. Ct. 3026, 57 L. Ed. 2d 1073 (1978).

Throughout the case, Justices Kennedy and Ginsburg expressed their concern about the apparent willingness of the plurality to accord the Congress more leeway than usual in an area such as this where vast areas of new technologies were involved.[83]

§ 9.11. Blasphemous language

Although many of the decisions are quite old, there is a considerable body of law sustaining the power of states and their political subdivisions to punish individuals who utter blasphemous words, in spite of the defendants' claims that such punishment violated freedom of speech or freedom of religion.[84] Courts have, in so holding, remarked that blasphemy was offensive at the common law,[85] and that statutes prohibiting the utterance of such words antedated the federal and state constitutions.[86]

Decisions that convictions for blasphemy are constitutional have often been justified as necessary to preserve both public morality and the public peace. Chief Justice Kent of New York, holding that blasphemy was an abuse of rights of communication, stated: "We stand equally in need now as formerly of virtues which help to bind society together."[87] A Maine court felt that "the stability of government in no small measure depends upon the reverence and respect which a nation maintains toward its prevalent religion."[88] In 1967 the Pennsylvania Supreme Court held valid a punishment under a statute which provided: "Whoever wilfully and premeditatively

83. Denver Area Educational Telecommunications Consortium, Inc. v. F.C.C., 116 S. Ct. 2374, 135 L. Ed. 2d 888 (U.S. 1996).

84. State v. Mockus, 120 Me. 84 (1921); People v. Ruggles, 8 Johns. 290 (N.Y. Sup. Ct. 1811); Com. v. Kneeland, 37 Mass. 206, 20 Pick. 206 (1838); State v. Chandler, 2 Del. 553, 2 Harr. 553 (Gen. Sess. 1837); Updegraph v. Commonwealth, 11 Serg. & Rawle 394 (Pa. 1824); Young v. State, 78 Tenn. 165 (1882); Territory v. Kaaikaula, 22 Haw. 204, 1914 WL 1732 (1914); City of Georgetown v. Scurry, 90 S.C. 346, 73 S.E. 353 (1912); Goree v. State, 71 Ala. 7 (1881); Holmes v. State, 135 Ark. 187, 204 S.W. 846 (1918); Commonwealth v. Linn, 158 Pa. 22, 27 A. 843 (1893); Town of Torrington v. Taylor, 59 Wyo. 109, 137 P.2d 621 (1943); State v. Wiley, 76 Miss. 282, 24 So. 194 (1898); Holcomb v. Cornish, 8 Conn. 375 (1831); Roberts v. State, 120 Ga. 177, 47 S.E. 511 (1904); Gaines v. State, 75 Tenn. 410 (1881); Holcombe v. State, 5 Ga. App. 47, 62 S.E. 647 (1908); Stafford v. State, 91 Miss. 158, 44 So. 801 (1907).

85. People v. Ruggles, 8 Johns. 290 (N.Y. Sup. Ct. 1811); State v. Chandler, 2 Del. 553, 555, 2 Harr. 553 (Gen. Sess. 1837).

86. State v. Mockus, 120 Me. 84, 113 A. 39, 44 (1921); Com. v. Kneeland, 37 Mass. 206, 214, 217, 218, 20 Pick. 206 (1838); State v. Chandler, 2 Del. 553, 566-67, 2 Harr. 553 (Gen. Sess. 1837).

87. People v. Ruggles, 8 Johns. 290 (N.Y. Sup. Ct. 1811).

88. State v. Mockus, 120 Me. 84, 113 A. 39, 42 (1921).

blasphemes or speaks loosely and profanely of Almighty God, Jesus Christ, the Holy Spirit, or Scriptures of Truth" shall be exposed to criminal punishment.[89] The United States Supreme Court denied *certiorari.*[90]

Some decisions sustain blasphemy statutes only when the speaker intended to cause a breach of the peace and his utterance had that effect. "The only legitimate end of the prosecution," states the Delaware Court, "is to preserve the public peace."[91]

A Maryland appellate court in 1970 held unconstitutional a statute making it a crime to blaspheme or curse God or to utter profane words concerning Jesus Christ or the Trinity. Noting that the statute "was intended to protect and preserve and perpetuate the Christian religion," the Court ruled that "government must be neutral in matters of religion" and concluded that the statute was violative of both the Establishment Clause and the Freedom of Religion Clause of the First Amendment.[92]

§ 9.12. Use of cyberspace for materials possibly endangering the morality of children

The Telecommunications Act of 1996 made it criminal (1) to convey thereby or transmit any "communication which is obscene or indecent, knowing that the recipient of the communication is under 18 years of age" as well as (2) to use interactive computer facilities to display to children under 18 "any comment, request, suggestion, proposal, image, or other communication that, in context, depicts or describes, in terms patently offensive as measured by contemporary community standards, sexual or excretory activities or organs, regardless of whether the user of such service placed the call or initiated the communication."

The Act made defenses available to: (1) those who take "good faith, reasonable, effective and appropriate actions" to restrict access to the prohibited communications by a minor; and (2) those who restrict access to covered material by requiring certain designated forms of age proof, such as a verified credit card or an adult identification number or code. The chief judge of a three-judge district court had concluded that the affirmative defenses were not technologically or economically feasible for most providers, and the Supreme Court saw them comparably.

---

89. Com. ex rel. Brown v. Rundle, 424 Pa. 505, 227 A.2d 895 (1967).

90. Brown v. Pennsylvania, 387 U.S. 937, 87 S. Ct. 2066, 18 L. Ed. 2d 1002 (1967).

91. State v. Chandler, 2 Del. 553, 574, 2 Harr. 553 (Gen. Sess. 1837).

92. State v. West, 9 Md. App. 270, 263 A.2d 602, 41 A.L.R.3d 512 (1970).

The Supreme Court, while recognizing the importance of the societal interest in protecting children, held that the statute suffered from overbreadth and vagueness, impermissibly restricting First Amendment freedoms. Since the statute attempted to control the content of speech, the defenders in the case had a high burden of proving its constitutionality, the Court reminding us that "in the absence of evidence to the contrary, we presume that governmental regulation of the content of speech is more likely to interfere with the free exchange of ideas than to encourage it."[93]

93. Reno v. American Civil Liberties Union, 117 S. Ct. 2329, 138 L. Ed. 2d 874 (U.S. 1997).

CHAPTER TEN

The Societal Interest in Protecting the Security of the State as Limitative of First Amendment Freeedoms

I. The War Effort and Preparedness Cases

II. The Patriotism Cases

III. The "Subversive Organization" Cases

IV. The "Subversive Individual" Cases

I. The War Effort and Preparedness Cases

§ 10.00. First Amendment rights of servicemen

Courts have recognized that First Amendment protections are available to some extent to servicemen.[1] The Court of Military Appeals has held that "servicemen have all the protections of the Bill of Rights except such as are expressly or by necessary implication not applicable by reason of the peculiar circumstances of the military."[2]

However, there are a number of cases sustaining limitations upon First Amendment rights of servicemen. In 1969 the Court of Appeals for the Ninth Circuit held that an order to a draftee, in the process of induction, to refrain from soliciting signatures to a petition opposing the draft and the war in Vietnam, was not an impermissible intrusion upon his First Amendment rights.[3] The Court of Military Appeals has found without constitutional protection an offensive remark made by an officer about the President away from any military base and isolated from any military audience.[4] The decision has appropriately been criticized.[5]

A federal court in 1969 held that a post commander can ban publications from the post, but only when the specific publication presents a clear danger to the loyalty, discipline, or morale of the troops. The court additionally held that the post commander could bar assemblages on post "but only where it is reasonably possible that the meeting might represent a clear danger to military loyalty, discipline or morale of the military personnel at the post." The opinion suggested, however, that, when off the base, servicemen should be entitled to First Amendment rights, including "the right

---

1.   Dash v. Commanding General, Fort Jackson, S. C., 307 F. Supp. 849 (D. S.C. 1969), judgment aff'd, 429 F.2d 427 (4th Cir. 1970).

2.   U.S. v. Voorhees, 16 C.M.R. 83, 1954 WL 2431 (C.M.A. 1954); United States v. Jacoby, 29 CMB 244.

3.   Callison v. U.S., 413 F.2d 133 (9th Cir. 1969), judgment vacated on other grounds, 399 U.S. 526, 90 S. Ct. 2230, 26 L. Ed. 2d 776 (1970).

4.   U.S. v. Howe, 37 C.M.R. 429, 1967 WL 4286 (C.M.A. 1967).

5.   Kester, Soldiers who Insult the President, an Uneasy Look at Article 88 of the Uniform Code of Military Justice, 81 Harv. L. Rev. 1697 (1968).

of all other citizens to exercise the freedom to dissent and to criticize."[6]

In 1980 the Supreme Court, over dissents of Justices Brennan, Stewart and Stevens, with Justice Marshall not participating, held valid a Navy and Marine Corps regulation requiring personnel to secure command approval before circulating petitions addressed to members of Congress—a horribly unworthy ruling.[7] The same year, over dissents of Justices Brennan, Stewart and Stevens, with Justice Marshall abstaining, the Court held that the First Amendment was not violated by an Air Force regulation forbidding members from distributing within any installation printed or written material without permission of the commander, who was authorized to deny permission if he determined that distribution would result in "a clear danger to the loyalty, discipline, or morale of the members of the Air Force, or material interference with the accomplishment of a military mission." Justice Brennan pointed out that the regulations imposed a prior restraint, which is generally unconstitutional, that they did not provide procedures to protect permissible expression, and that there was no compelling public interest precisely protected by the regulation.[8]

The Supreme Court has not been very appreciative of the freedom of religion under the First Amendment for members of the military. In 1986 the Court held that the military's interest in uniformity of appearance of its personnel supported its ban upon the wearing of yarmulkes. The opinion of the Court, written by Justice Rehnquist and joined by the Chief Justice, held that the Air Force need not accommodate the religious practice of an Orthodox Jewish rabbi. Justices Stevens, White and Powell concurred. Justices Brennan, Marshall, Blackmun and O'Connor dissented, finding that "the Air Force has failed utterly to furnish a credible explanation why an exception to the dress code permitting Orthodox Jews to wear neat and conservative yarmulkes while in uniform is likely to interfere with its interest in discipline and uniformity" (Brennan, J.) and stating that the military, no more than the civil government, can subordinate freedom of religion without an interest of the highest order and limitation that is the least restrictive to serve such inter-

---

6. Dash v. Commanding General, Fort Jackson, S. C., 307 F. Supp. 849 (D. S.C. 1969), judgment aff'd, 429 F.2d 427 (4th Cir. 1970).

7. Secretary of Navy v. Huff, 444 U.S. 453, 100 S. Ct. 606, 62 L. Ed. 2d 607 (1980).

8. Brown v. Glines, 444 U.S. 348, 100 S. Ct. 594, 62 L. Ed. 2d 540 (1980).

est. (O'Connor, J.).[9]

§ 10.01. Speaking treason, urging surrender, or sowing disaffection, defeatism, or insubordination among the armed forces during hostilities

The treason statute provides that "Whoever, owing allegiance to the United States, levies war against them or adheres to their enemies, giving them aid and comfort within the United States or elsewhere, is guilty of treason. . . ."[10]

The Espionage Act of 1917 provided for the punishment of any one who "when the United States is at war, shall willfully cause or attempt to cause insubordination, disloyalty, mutiny, or refusal of duty, in the military or naval forces of the United States."[11]

The Alien Registration Act of 1940 made it unlawful "for any person, with intent to interfere with, impair or influence the loyalty, morale or discipline of the military or naval forces of the United States, (a) to advise, counsel, urge or in any manner cause insubordination, disloyalty, mutiny or refusal of duty by any member of the military or naval forces of the United States; or (b) to distribute any written or printed matter which advises, counsels, or urges the same."

When, during time of declared war, a United States citizen broadcasts propaganda for the enemy urging American troops to surrender, or sowing defeatism and discontent in their ranks, and it is possible for military personnel to hear the broadcasts, claims of freedom of expression will be no defense to criminal prosecutions. A United States court of appeals has said in the leading case:

> Trafficking with the enemy, in whatever form, is wholly outside the shelter of the First Amendment. Congress may make criminal any type of dealing with the enemy which in its judgment may have the potentiality of harm to our national interests, including acting as a commentator on the enemy's short wave station. Conviction could be had under such a criminal statute whether or not the prohibited acts, in the particular case, actually created any clear and present danger of substantial harm to the United States.[12]

In another case, where a member of the staff of the American

---

9. Goldman v. Weinberger, 475 U.S. 503, 106 S. Ct. 1310, 89 L. Ed. 2d 478 (1986).

10. 18 U.S.C.A. § 2381.

11. 50 U.S.C.A. § 33.

12. Chandler v. U.S., 171 F.2d 921, 939 (1st Cir. 1948). And cf. Gillars v. U.S., 87 U.S. App. D.C. 16, 182 F.2d 962 (D.C. Cir. 1950); Best v. U.S., 184 F.2d 131 (1st Cir. 1950).

embassy in Berlin remained behind in World War II and broadcast for the Germans, sowing discontent with the government of the United States and impairing the morale of the armed forces, he was subsequently convicted of treason, notwithstanding claims of freedom of expression. Said the Court: "The principle point advanced by the defendant is that the preparation and making of speeches does not, in itself, constitute treason. It is presumably contended that the defendant was exercising his right of freedom of speech guaranteed by the First Amendment. This position is not tenable. The right of freedom of speech is not unqualified or absolute. Actions may assume the form of oral pronouncements . . . words uttered with intent to betray one's country may well constitute treason. [13]

Even during wartime, however, neither diplomatic nor military policies of the administration are beyond criticism by the American people. The Supreme Court has well said: "We do not lose our right to condemn either measures or men because the country is at war."[14]

§ 10.02. Encouraging resistance to the draft—discouraging enlistments during wartime; conscientious objectors

The Espionage Act of 1917 made it a crime to "willfully obstruct the recruiting or enlistment service of the United States, to the injury of the service or of the United States."[15]

The first decision of the United States Supreme Court under this section of the statute was *Schenck v. United States* in 1919. There the Court upheld the conviction of a man who had mailed circulars to persons subject to the draft, urging them to assert their rights. So far as the opinion divulges, there was no proof of any interference with the draft from the circulars. The case is famous, not so much for the decision, as for the language of the Court. Said the Court, through Justice Holmes: "The question in every case is whether the words used are used in such circumstances and are of such a nature as to create a clear and present danger that they will bring about the substantive evils that Congress has a right to prevent."[16]

The second decision under this section, *Frohwerk v. United States,*[17] similarly sustained a conviction for violating the statute of an individual who had inserted several articles in a German-language newspaper in Missouri questioning both the propriety and constitutionality of World War I.

---

13. Burgman v. U.S., 88 U.S. App. D.C. 184, 188 F.2d 637 (D.C. Cir. 1951).

14. Frohwerk v. U.S., 249 U.S. 204, 39 S. Ct. 249, 251, 63 L. Ed. 561, 564 (1919).

15. 50 U.S.C.A. § 33.

16. Schenck v. U.S., 249 U.S. 47, 39 S. Ct. 247, 63 L. Ed. 470 (1919).

17. Frohwerk v. U.S., 249 U.S. 204, 39 S. Ct. 249, 63 L. Ed. 561 (1919).

A third decision, *Debs v. United States*,[18] also resulted in an affirmance of a conviction for attempting to obstruct recruiting and cause insubordination in the armed forces. Debs had spoken to the national convention of the Socialist Party, branding the war as a curse of capitalism.

In 1920 the Supreme Court also upheld the power of the states to punish persons who advocate that others should not enlist in the armed forces. Holmes concurred in the result, but Chief Justice White and Justice Brandeis dissented.[19]

The Selective Service Act of 1940 exposed to punishment any person who knowingly counseled, aided, or abetted another to evade registration or service.[20] Some members of the German-American Bund at the time of World War II published a "command" ordering its members within the reach of the Act to refuse to register, stating that "[e]very man, if he can, will refuse to do military duty until this law and all other laws of the country or the states which confine the citizenship rights of Bund members are revoked." The Bund was particularly objecting to the section of the act providing that Bund members were not to be hired by business or industry to replace anyone inducted into the armed services. The Supreme Court reversed the conviction. Justice Roberts stated:

> One with innocent motives, who honestly believes a law is unconstitutional and, therefore, not obligatory, may well counsel that the law shall not be obeyed; that its command shall be resisted until a court shall have held it valid, but this is not knowingly counseling, stealthily and by guile, to evade its command.[21]

Other convictions for violating the Act have been reversed, relying upon this interpretation.[22]

The Supreme Court has held that neither First Amendment freedom of religion nor establishment of religion clauses relieve objectors to particular wars from the obligations and responsibilities of military training and service. In holding that "relief for conscientious objectors is not mandated by the Constitution," the Court stated that "the Government's interest in procuring the manpower necessary for military purposes is very important," and added that Congress can refuse exemptions to conscientious objectors to

---

18. Debs v. U.S., 249 U.S. 211, 39 S. Ct. 252, 63 L. Ed. 566 (1919).

19. Gilbert v. State of Minn., 254 U.S. 325, 41 S. Ct. 125, 65 L. Ed. 287 (1920).

20. 50 U.S.C.A. § 311.

21. Keegan v. United States, 325 U.S. 478, 493-94, 65 S. Ct. 1203, 89 L. Ed. 1745, 1753-54 (1945).

22. Kiyoshi Okamoto v. U.S., 152 F.2d 905 (C.C.A. 10th Cir. 1945).

particular wars, while granting exemptions to those who oppose all wars.[23]

§ 10.03. Discouraging military service during peace time

In 1949 the United States Court of Appeals for the Tenth Circuit affirmed the conviction of a man who counselled his stepson to refuse to register for the draft, and who himself failed to register. Said the Court: "Freedom of religion and freedom of speech . . . may not be construed so as to prevent legislation necessary for national security."[24]

The same year the United States Court of Appeals for the Sixth Circuit affirmed a conviction of a dean at Bluffton College in Ohio for counseling and encouraging students not to register for selective service.[25] Of greater significance is the fact that the United States Supreme Court was equally divided in affirming the decision per curiam.[26]

The Supreme Court ruled in 1966 that a duly elected state legislator could not be denied his seat because he had spoken in opposition to the war in Vietnam and urged pacifist resistance to the selective service law. After noting that it was established "that Bond could not have been convicted for these statements consistently with the First Amendment,"[27] the Court emphasized that legislators must have all the rights of freedom of expression possessed by citizens generally. Said the Court:

> Legislators have an obligation to take positions on controversial political questions so that their constituents can be fully informed by them, and be better able to assess their qualifications for office; also so they may be represented in governmental debates by the person they have elected to represent them.[28]

There was no dissent.

§ 10.04. Publishing false statements with intent to interfere with the war effort

The Espionage Act of 1917 authorized the punishment of those

---

23. Gillette v. U.S., 401 U.S. 437, 91 S. Ct. 828, 28 L. Ed. 2d 168 (1971).

24. Warren v. U.S., 177 F.2d 596, 599 (10th Cir. 1949) (noted in 13 U Det LJ 88).

25. Gara v. U.S., 178 F.2d 38 (6th Cir. 1949), judgment aff'd, 340 U.S. 857, 71 S. Ct. 87, 95 L. Ed. 628 (1950) (noted in 12 Ohio St LJ 288).

26. Gara v. U.S., 340 U.S. 857, 71 S. Ct. 87, 95 L. Ed. 628 (1950).

27. Bond v. Floyd, 385 U.S. 116, 87 S. Ct. 339, 348, 17 L. Ed. 2d 235 (1966).

28. Bond v. Floyd, 385 U.S. 116, 87 S. Ct. 339, 349-50, 17 L. Ed. 2d 235 (1966).

who willfully published "false reports and statements with intent to interfere with the operation or success of the military or naval forces of the United States or to promote the success of its enemies."

The first case involving this section to come to the United States Supreme Court was *Schaefer v. United States.*[29] In that case the Court affirmed the conviction of three officers of a German language newspaper in Philadelphia for having printed inaccurate statements about the conduct of the war.

In the second case, *Pierce v. United States,*[30] the Supreme Court again sustained a conviction, this time of three Socialists who had printed and distributed an anti-war pamphlet. Justices Holmes and Brandeis dissented. They urged that the defendants should not be imprisoned for having written such things as: "Our entry into [the war] was determined by the certainty that if the allies do not win, J. P. Morgan's loans to the allies will be repudiated, and those American investors who bit on his promises would be hooked."

§ 10.05. Printing and publishing matters affecting national security

The United States Supreme Court in 1971 denied the federal government an injunction against the *New York Times* and the *Washington Post,* which were printing a "History of U.S. Decision-Making Process on Vietnam Policy" (the Pentagon Papers). The per curiam statement indicated that the government had not met the heavy burden upon anyone who would impose a prior restraint upon the press. Justices Black and Douglas in their concurring opinion suggested that such a restraint would never be constitutional. Justice Brennan acknowledged "that there is a single, extremely narrow class of cases in which the First Amendment's ban on prior judicial restraint may be overridden," and that was when the nation is at war. Justice Marshall believed that it would be "utterly inconsistent with the concept of separation of power for this Court to use its power of contempt to prevent behavior that Congress has specifically declined to prohibit."[31]

§ 10.06. Excluding from the mails publications deemed detrimental to the war effort

The Espionage Act of 1917 authorized the Postmaster General to

---

29. Schaefer v. U.S., 251 U.S. 466, 40 S. Ct. 259, 64 L. Ed. 360 (1920).

30. Pierce v. U.S., 252 U.S. 239, 40 S. Ct. 205, 64 L. Ed. 542 (1920).

31. New York Times Co. v. U.S., 403 U.S. 713, 91 S. Ct. 2140, 29 L. Ed. 2d 822 (1971).

exclude from the mails any publication violating the three sections of the act already discussed.

The story of the activities of the then Postmaster General has been well told by Professor Chafee and need not be narrated here.[32] Suffice it to note that the Postmaster General censored and suppressed publications such as the *Freeman's Journal* and the *Catholic Register* for printing such things as Jefferson's belief that Ireland should be a free republic.

In 1917 the Postmaster General denied the second class mailing rates to the *Milwaukee Leader* because of its opposition to the conduct of the war, and in 1921 this action was allowed to stand by the United States Supreme Court.[33] Justices Brandeis, Holmes and Clarke dissented.

§ 10.07. Dramatic portrayals tending to discredit the military

The United States Supreme Court ruled in 1970 that freedom of speech does not permit Congress in effect to make it a crime for an actor wearing a military uniform to say, during his performance, things critical of the conduct or policies of the armed forces. The Court stated: "an actor, like everyone else in our country, enjoys a constitutional right to freedom of speech, including the right openly to criticize the government during a dramatic performance."[34]

§ 10.08. Denying citizenship to applicants who will not agree to defend the country with arms

In 1929 and 1931 the United States Supreme Court ruled that an act of Congress providing that persons unwilling to defend the country with arms were ineligible for citizenship was constitutional.[35] However, in 1946, in *Girouard v. United States,*[36] the Court repudiated its earlier interpretation of the Congressional acts, and the Naturalization Act does not now automatically exclude from naturalization those unwilling for religious reasons to bear arms in

---

32. Chafee, *Free Speech in the United States,* Harvard U Press, Cambridge, 1941.

33. U.S. ex rel. Milwaukee Social Democratic Pub. Co. v. Burleson, 255 U.S. 407, 41 S. Ct. 352, 65 L. Ed. 704 (1921).

34. Schacht v. United States (1970) 398 US 58, 90 S Ct 1555, 26 L Ed 2d 44.

35. U.S. v. Schwimmer, 279 U.S. 644, 49 S. Ct. 448, 73 L. Ed. 889 (1929) (overruled in part by, Girouard v. U.S., 328 U.S. 61, 66 S. Ct. 826, 90 L. Ed. 1084 (1946)); U.S. v. Macintosh, 283 U.S. 605, 51 S. Ct. 570, 75 L. Ed. 1302 (1931) (overruled in part by, Girouard v. U.S., 328 U.S. 61, 66 S. Ct. 826, 90 L. Ed. 1084 (1946)).

36. Girouard v. U.S., 328 U.S. 61, 66 S. Ct. 826, 90 L. Ed. 1084 (1946).

defense of the nation. This is not, of course, to say that such persons have a constitutional right to be naturalized.

§ 10.09. Denying benefits to those who refuse military training

In 1934 the United States Supreme Court, in *Hamilton v. California,* upheld the denial of entrance to a state university of a student who would not, because of his religious principles, agree to participate in military training.[37] It is suggested the case is wrongly decided. Where a person and his parents contribute by taxation to the support of state colleges and universities, a court simply confuses the issues and indulges in ratiocination by labelling as "a privilege" the right to attend public institutions of learning. Society has no justification for compelling a person to give up his religious beliefs and principles, at least where, as here, their manifestation does not immediately imperil the survival of the political state.

More recently, the Maryland Court of Appeals has held that the University of Maryland's mandatory requirement that all physically able students take basic military training was not invalid as applied to students who, because of religious beliefs, were objectors to war.[38] The United States Supreme Court has held that there is no unconstitutional denial of religious liberty to a conscientious objector who was denied veterans' benefits under an act of Congress after he had served his alternate civilian duties, while draftees who did their military duty were given such benefits.[39]

§ 10.10. Burning draft registration papers

In 1968 the United States Supreme Court ruled that Congress can constitutionally provide for the punishment of those who burn their draft registration certificates. Without citing any cases, the opinion of the Court indicates that it "has held that when 'speech' and 'non-speech' elements are combined in the same course of conduct, a sufficiently important governmental interest in regulating the non-speech element can justify incidental limitations on First Amendment freedoms." So First Amendment freedoms are minimized by encouraging regulation of "related" conduct with "incidental" degradation of communicative values. The Court stated its new rule thus:

A government regulation is sufficiently justified if it is within

---

37. Hamilton v. Regents of the University of Calif., 293 U.S. 245, 55 S. Ct. 197, 79 L. Ed. 343 (1934).

38. Hanauer v. Elkins, 217 Md. 213, 141 A.2d 903 (1958), appeal dismissed, 358 U.S. 643, 79 S. Ct. 536, 3 L. Ed. 2d 567 (1959).

39. Johnson v. Robison, 415 U.S. 361, 94 S. Ct. 1160, 39 L. Ed. 2d 389 (1974).

the constitutional power of the Government, if it further an important or substantial governmental interest, if the governmental interest is unrelated to the suppression of free expression and if the incidental restriction on alleged First Amendment freedoms is no greater than is essential to the furtherance of that interest.

Justice John Harlan wrote a concurring opinion to explain that the Court's rule "does not foreclose consideration of First Amendment claims in those rare instances when an 'incidental' restriction upon expression, imposed by a regulation which furthers an important or substantial governmental interest and satisfies the Court's other criteria, in practice has the effect of entirely preventing a 'speaker' from reaching a significant audience with whom he could not otherwise lawfully communicate." He added: "This is not such a case, since O'Brien manifestly could have conveyed his message in many ways other than by burning his draft card."[40]

§ 10.11. First Amendment rights on military and naval installations

In 1961 the Supreme Court held that, without violating due process of law, persons deemed security risks by the commanding officer of a military or naval installation could summarily be ordered removed and excluded from those parts of the installation not open to the public, but in that case no First Amendment rights were involved.[41] Eleven years later the Court ruled in effect that, when a military base is open to the public generally, First Amendment rights apply there just as fully as though the base were a traditional municipality or a company town. Specifically, the Court held that the base commander could not order a citizen off of a public street simply because he was distributing peace leaflets.[42] However, in 1976 the Court held that military authorities have the right to ban political speeches and the distribution of leaflets at military posts unless they have abandoned their claim to so regulate, remarking that the distinction from *Flower v. United States* was that the authorities had in that case abandoned their claim to regulate.[43]

Over dissents of Justices Stevens, Brennan and Marshall, who found no Congressional authorization for punishment, the Supreme

---

40. U.S. v. O'Brien, 391 U.S. 367, 88 S. Ct. 1673, 20 L. Ed. 2d 672 (1968).

41. Cafeteria and Restaurant Workers Union, Local 473, AFL-CIO v. McElroy, 367 U.S. 886, 81 S. Ct. 1743, 6 L. Ed. 2d 1230 (1961).

42. Flower v. U.S., 407 U.S. 197, 92 S. Ct. 1842, 32 L. Ed. 2d 653 (1972).

43. Greer v. Spock, 424 U.S. 828, 96 S. Ct. 1211, 47 L. Ed. 2d 505 (1976).

Court held in 1985 that a person could be punished for visiting a military installation on an "open house day," when he had earlier been barred by the commanding officer of the post from reentry. Said the Court: "There is no generalized constitutional right to make political speeches or distribute leaflets on military bases even if they are generally open to the public." There is, however, dictum that "a commanding officer cannot exclude citizens from the base in a manner that is patently arbitrary or discriminatory."[44]

§ 10.12. Denying state bar membership to those who will not agree to defend the state with arms

In 1945 the United States Supreme Court in a five-to-four decision sustained the action of Illinois in refusing membership in the state bar to one, otherwise fully qualified, who was a conscientious objector to war.[45] There is no mention of the applicability of the clear and present danger test by either the majority of the court or the dissenters. Justices Black, Douglas, Murphy and Rutledge dissented.

It is suggested that the case is wrongly decided. The reliance placed by the majority upon the *Schwimmer* and *Macintosh* cases, already noted, cannot now be defended with the subsequent overruling of these two cases. More recently, too, the Supreme Court has held for the first time that no state can arbitrarily deny membership in the state bar to any applicant.[46] The state cannot in fairness penalize a man because of his religious beliefs by forcing him to change his views in order to practice law. There is no proof whatsoever that the administration of justice or even the security of the state will be gravely imperiled by the admission to practice of fully qualified persons whose religious beliefs will not permit them to bear arms in time of war.

II. The Patriotism Cases

§ 10.13. Showing contempt for the flag and the military

A Mississippi statute had made it a crime to use words which reasonably tended to create an attitude of stubborn refusal to salute, honor, or respect the flag of the United States. When an individual spoke against the flag salute and said it was wrong to fight, he was convicted under this statute. In 1943 the United States Supreme

---

44. U.S. v. Albertini, 472 U.S. 675, 105 S. Ct. 2897, 86 L. Ed. 2d 536 (1985).

45. In re Summers, 325 U.S. 561, 65 S. Ct. 1307, 89 L. Ed. 1795 (1945).

46. Schware v. Board of Bar Exam. of State of N.M., 353 U.S. 232, 77 S. Ct. 752, 1 L. Ed. 2d 796, 64 A.L.R.2d 288 (1957).

Court in *Taylor v. Mississippi* set aside the conviction. Justice Roberts, speaking for the Court, condemned the statute as applied because it punished the defendants "although what they communicated is not claimed or shown to have been done with evil or sinister purpose, to have advocated or incited subversive action against the nation or state, or to have threatened any clear and present danger to our institutions or our Government."[47]

The following year a state court ruled that a civil service commission could not refuse to appoint the highest applicant for a public post because he would not, because of conscience, give the flag salute.[48]

In 1969 the Supreme Court set aside a conviction under a state statute making it a crime to cast contempt upon the flag by words. The Court noted that the words were not an incitement to anything unlawful, nor were they "fighting words." The Court said: "We have no doubt that the constitutionally guaranteed 'freedom to be intellectually . . . diverse and even contrary' and the 'right to differ as to things that touch the heart of the existing order,' encompass the freedom to express publicly one's opinion about our flag, including those opinions which are defiant or contemptuous."[49]

Two years later, in a four-to-four decision without opinion, with Justice Douglas not participating, the Supreme Court affirmed a conviction under a state misuse of the flag statute of a person who displayed the flag in a manner suggesting a sexual organ.[50]

In 1974 a state flag misuse statute was held by the Court to be unconstitutionally vague when the state sought to punish, under a provision of the statute criminalizing one who "treats contemptuously the flag," a young man who had a small cloth version of the flag sewn to the seat of his trousers.[51] The same year the Court reversed the conviction of a college student who hung outside his apartment window a United States flag upside down, with a peace symbol of black tape attached to the flag. He had been charged with violating a state statute making it unlawful to attach designs, etc., to the flag. The Court stated: "Given the protected character of his expression and in light of the fact that no interest the State may

47. Taylor v. State of Mississippi, 319 U.S. 583, 589-90, 63 S. Ct. 1200, 87 L. Ed. 1600, 1606-07 (1943).

48. Morgan v. Civil Service Commission, 131 N.J.L. 410, 36 A.2d 898 (N.J. Sup. Ct. 1944).

49. Street v. New York, 394 U.S. 576, 89 S. Ct. 1354, 22 L. Ed. 2d 572 (1969).

50. Radich v. New York, 401 U.S. 531, 91 S. Ct. 1217, 28 L. Ed. 2d 287 (1971).

51. Smith v. Goguen, 415 U.S. 566, 94 S. Ct. 1242, 39 L. Ed. 2d 605 (1974).

have in preserving the physical integrity of a privately-owned flag was significantly impaired on these facts, the conviction must be invalidated." The Chief Justice, Justices White and Rehnquist dissented, suggesting that "the State has a valid interest in preserving the character of the flag," and can withdraw this "unique national symbol from the roster of materials that may be used as a background for communication."[52]

In 1989 the Supreme Court reminded us again that "a government may not prohibit the expression of an idea simply because society finds the idea offensive and disagreeable," and that the term "speech" as used in the First Amendment has, for a long time, been understood to protect expression in forms other than the spoken word. The Court ruled that a state cannot convict a person for burning the flag, under a statute forbidding "desecrating the flag." A state, said the Court, "may not . . . proscribe particular conduct because it has expressive elements." While admitting the government has an interest in encouraging proper treatment of the flag, the Court ruled that public protest by burning it cannot be made a crime. The Court explained: "The way to preserve the flag's special role is not to punish those who feel differently about these matters. It is to persuade them that they are wrong." The Chief Justice, Justice White, O'Connor and Stevens dissented.[53]

The following year, when the government admitted that the defendant's conduct in burning the flag constituted expressive conduct, and the Supreme Court found that the government's asserted interest was related to the suppression of free expression, the Court ruled that Congress cannot "criminally proscribe expressive conduct because of its likely communicative impact," and held that the Congressional Flag Protective Act of 1989 violated the First Amendment, when used as the basis of a prosecution of a citizen who burned a flag to show dissatisfaction with the government. For the Court, Justice Brennan stated: "Punishing desecration of the flag dilutes the very freedom that makes this emblem so revered and worth revering." While Justices Stevens, White, O'Connor and the Chief Justice dissented, they observed that "reasonable judges may differ with respect to" the interest balancing required in a case such as this.[54]

The Supreme Court has held that it violates freedom of speech for Congress in effect to make it a crime for an actor wearing a military

---

52. Spence v. State of Wash., 418 U.S. 405, 94 S. Ct. 2727, 41 L. Ed. 2d 842 (1974).

53. Texas v. Johnson, 491 U.S. 397, 109 S. Ct. 2533, 105 L. Ed. 2d 342 (1989).

54. U.S. v. Eichman, 496 U.S. 310, 110 S. Ct. 2404, 110 L. Ed. 2d 287 (1990).

uniform to say things during his performance critical of the conduct or policies of the military. Said the Court: "An actor, like everyone else in our country, enjoys a constitutional right to freedom of speech, including the right openly to criticize the Government during a dramatic performance."[55]

§ 10.14. Denial of educational opportunities to children who refuse, for religious reasons, to salute the flag

In 1943, in *West Virginia State Board of Education v. Barnette*,[56] the United States Supreme Court ruled that children could not be excluded from the public schools because they refused, due to religious beliefs, to engage in flag salutes.

§ 10.15. Banning the teaching of foreign languages

During World War I the state of Nebraska thought it necessary to ban the teaching of German in the public schools. In 1923 the prohibition came before the United States Supreme Court, which then ruled unconstitutional the Nebraska enactment.[57] The case is interesting because it in effect acknowledges a constitutional right to teach free from arbitrary restraints, the action having been brought by a schoolteacher. Furthermore, it illustrates how the prime rights—in this case, those of the children and parents—can at times be vindicated before the Supreme Court in actions brought by others.

Xenophobia breaks out from time to time in the American community. During the forties the Hawaiian territorial legislature forbade the teaching of Chinese and other foreign languages in the schools of Hawaii. A federal district court readily granted an injunction against the enforcement of the statute in 1947, noting that even the teaching of Greek and Latin would have been forbidden under the statute.[58]

III. The "Subversive Organization" Cases

§ 10.16. Requiring registration of subversive groups

In 1961 the United States Supreme Court ruled that the Communist Party could be compelled to register pursuant to an act of Congress requiring registration of all organizations substantially

---

55. Schacht v. U.S., 398 U.S. 58, 90 S. Ct. 1555, 26 L. Ed. 2d 44 (1970).

56. West Virginia State Board of Education v. Barnette, 319 U.S. 624, 63 S. Ct. 1178, 87 L. Ed. 1628, 147 A.L.R. 674 (1943).

57. Meyer v. Nebraska, 262 U.S. 390, 43 S. Ct. 625, 67 L. Ed. 1042, 29 A.L.R. 1446 (1923).

58. Mo Hock Ke Lok Po v. Stainback, 74 F. Supp. 852 (D. Haw. 1947), judgment rev'd on other grounds, 336 U.S. 368, 69 S. Ct. 606, 93 L. Ed. 741 (1949).

dominated by foreign powers. The case differs from previous cases involving the NAACP and labor unions, said the Supreme Court, "in the magnitude of the public interests which the registration and disclosure provisions are designed to protect and in the pertinence which registration and disclosure bear to the protection of those interests."[59] Justices Douglas and Brennan agreed that Congress has constitutional power to compel the Communist Party to register. Justice Black dissented, stating: "I would reverse this case and leave the Communists free to advocate their beliefs in proletarian dictatorship publicly and openly among the people of this country with full confidence that the people will remain loyal to any democratic government truly dedicated to freedom and justice . . ."[60]

Four years later, however, the Supreme Court voided a Louisiana statute making it a crime for a member of a Communist front organization to fail to register. The statute contained a presumption that organizations designated by the Attorney General of the United States, the Subversive Activities Control Board, "or any committee or subcommittee of the United States Congress" as a communist front organization was in fact such an organization. This was unconstitutional for two reasons, according to the Court. First, "the presumptions cast an impermissible burden upon the appellants to show that the organizations are not Communist fronts."[61] Secondly, "there is no requirement that the organization be so cited only after compliance with the procedural safeguards demanded by Anti-Fascist Committee v McGrath."[62]

Attempts of the states to compel subversive organizations to register may well be unconstitutional as impermissible invasions of a field preempted by the federal government.[63]

---

59. Communist Party of U.S. v. Subversive Activities Control Bd., 367 U.S. 1, 81 S. Ct. 1357, 6 L. Ed. 2d 625, 731 (1961).

60. Communist Party of U.S. v. Subversive Activities Control Bd., 367 U.S. 1, 81 S. Ct. 1357, 6 L. Ed. 2d 625, 687 (1961).

61. Dombrowski v. Pfister, 380 U.S. 479, 85 S. Ct. 1116, 14 L. Ed. 2d 22, 34 (1965) (citing Speiser v. Randall, 357 U.S. 513, 78 S. Ct. 1332, 2 L. Ed. 2d 1460, 1473 (1958)).

62. Dombrowski v. Pfister, 380 U.S. 479, 85 S. Ct. 1116, 14 L. Ed. 2d 22, 34 (1965); Joint Anti-Fascist Refugee Committee v. McGrath, 341 U.S. 123, 71 S. Ct. 624, 95 L. Ed. 817 (1951).

63. Cf. Albertson v. Millard, 106 F. Supp. 635 (E.D. Mich. 1952), especially dissent of Levin, J. at 647 (noted in 66 Harv L Rev 327 (1952)), vacated and remanded with directions to hold proceedings in abeyance a reasonable time pending construction of the statute by the Michigan courts, 345 U.S. 242, 73 S. Ct. 600, 97 L. Ed. 983 (1953).

§ 10.17. Organizing groups to overthrow the government by force or violence

In 1919 Anita Whitney participated in a convention in California called to organize a local branch of the Communist Labor Party. The convention went on record as being in favor of political strikes and the seizure of power. Ms. Whitney was charged with violating the California criminal syndicalism act, which made it unlawful to organize or assist in organizing any group assembled to advocate, teach, or aid and abet criminal syndicalism, that is, the violent overthrow of government or industry.

Ms. Whitney's conviction was sustained by the United States Supreme Court in an opinion characterizing her activity as an "abuse" of freedom and "tending" to evil, and her conviction as "not unreasonable or arbitrary." Justices Brandeis and Holmes concurred, but only because Ms. Whitney's counsel had failed at the trial court to demand a ruling on whether she had created a clear and present danger. There is some truly great language in the opinion of Justice Brandeis. He stated:

> Those who won our independence believed that the final end of the state was to make men free to develop their faculties; and that in its government the deliberative forces should prevail over the arbitrary. They valued liberty both as an end and as a means. They believed liberty to be the secret of happiness and courage to be the secret of liberty. They believed that freedom to think as you will and to speak as you think are means indispensable to the discovery and spread of political truth; that without free speech and assembly discussion would be futile; that with them, discussion affords ordinarily adequate protection against the dissemination of noxious doctrine; that the greatest menace to freedom is an inert people; that public discussion is a political duty; and that this should be a fundamental principle of the American government. They recognized the risks to which all human institutions are subject. But they knew that order cannot be secured merely through fear of punishment for its infraction; that it is hazardous to discourage thought, hope, and imagination; that fear breeds repression; that repression breeds hate; that hate menaces stable government; that the path of safety lies in the opportunity to discuss freely supposed grievances and proposed remedies; and that the fitting remedy for evil counsels is good ones. Believing in the power of reason as applied through public discussion, they eschewed silence coerced by law—the argument of force in its worst form. Recognizing the occasional tyrannies of govern-

ing majorities, they amended the Constitution so that free speech and assembly should be guaranteed.[64]

Justice Brandeis added:

> Those who won our independence by revolution were not cowards. They did not fear political change. They did not exalt order at the cost of liberty. To courageous, self-reliant men, with confidence in the power of free and fearless reasoning applied through the processes of popular government, no danger flowing from speech can be deemed clear and present, unless the incidence of the evil apprehended is so imminent that it may befall before there is opportunity for full discussion. If there be time to expose through discussion the falsehood and fallacies, to avert the evil by the processes of education, the remedy to be applied is more speech, not enforced silence. Only an emergency can justify repression. Such must be the rule if authority is to be reconciled with freedom. Such, in my opinion, is the command of the Constitution. It is, therefore, always open to Americans to challenge a law abridging free speech and assembly by showing that there was no emergency justifying it. . . . Among free men, the deterrents ordinarily to be applied to prevent crime are education and punishment for violations of the law, not abridgment of the rights of free speech and assembly.[65]

It should have been fairly obvious at the time that the security of neither the United States nor the State of California necessitated imprisoning Ms. Whitney. Indeed, within a few months she was pardoned by the Governor of California who remarked: "Miss Whitney, lifelong friend of the unfortunate, is not in any true sense a 'criminal,' and to condemn her, at sixty years of age, to a felon's cell is an action which is absolutely unthinkable."[66]

In 1927 the Supreme Court reversed a Kansas conviction of a person whose only misdeed was that he had recruited members for the Workers Industrial Union. Since there was no proof in the record that this organization ever advocated the violent overthrow

---

64. Whitney v. California, 274 U.S. 357, 47 S. Ct. 641, 71 L. Ed. 1095, 1105 (1927) (overruled in part by, Brandenburg v. Ohio, 395 U.S. 444, 89 S. Ct. 1827, 23 L. Ed. 2d 430, 48 Ohio Op. 2d 320 (1969)).

65. Whitney v. California, 274 U.S. 357, 47 S. Ct. 641, 71 L. Ed. 1095, 1106 (1927) (overruled in part by, Brandenburg v. Ohio, 395 U.S. 444, 89 S. Ct. 1827, 23 L. Ed. 2d 430, 48 Ohio Op. 2d 320 (1969)).

66. Chafee, *Freedom of Speech in the United States,* Harvard U Press, Cambridge (1941) p 353.

of the government, the man's conviction was, according to the Court, "an arbitrary and unreasonable exercise of the police power of the State, unwarrantably infringing the liberty of the defendant in violation of the Due Process Clause of the Fourteenth Amendment."[67]

The Supreme Court has now overruled *Whitney v. California* and holds that a state cannot punish the organization of a group devoted to advocacy of the use of force or of violation of the law to change the form of government. It is only incitement to imminent lawless action that can now be proscribed.[68]

The Alien Registration Act of 1940 provided: "It shall be unlawful for any person . . . to organize or help to organize any society, group, or assembly of persons who teach, advocate or encourage the overthrow or destruction of any government in the United States by force or violence. . . ." In 1951 the Supreme Court held that individuals could be punished for conspiring to organize the Communist Party as a group to teach and advocate the violent overthrow of government.[69] The Court did not determine that the defendants' activities caused a clear and present danger to the security of the nation. Rather, the majority of the Court accepted the Court of Appeals' reinterpretation of the test and adopted as the rule: "In each case courts must ask whether the gravity of the evil, discounted by its improbability, justifies such invasion of free speech as is necessary to avoid the danger."

Since, under the *Dennis* rule, the violent overthrow of the government will certainly be treated as a grave evil, the Court may be prepared to allow incarceration of those who associate and speak in this area, notwithstanding the existence of only remote and highly improbable dangers. It is suggested that the reformulation of the clear and present danger test is wrong. Not only does the reformulated test allow the danger to be distant and uncertain if the evil is great, but it demands no proof of causation between the acts charged and the substantive evil. The original principle demanded that the danger be imminent, clear, and certain, and that it be caused, not by others, but by the defendant. Both these aspects should be proved by the government before persons are removed from society for having spoken, written, or associated. Citizens should not be put in prison for having exercised their fundamental freedoms unless it is

---

67. Fiske v. State of Kansas, 274 U.S. 380, 47 S. Ct. 655, 71 L. Ed. 1108, 1111 (1927).

68. Brandenburg v. Ohio, 395 U.S. 444, 89 S. Ct. 1827, 23 L. Ed. 2d 430, 48 Ohio Op. 2d 320 (1969).

69. Dennis v. United States, 341 U.S. 494, 71 S. Ct. 857, 95 L. Ed. 1137 (1951).

imperatively necessary, that is, unless the voice of reason cannot prevail before an imminent crisis occurs.[70]

In 1957 the Court reversed the conviction of some of the second-ary leaders of the Communist Party for having organized a group to advocate and teach the violent overthrow of government. The Court ruled the trial court had erred in failing to distinguish between advocacy of abstract doctrine and advocacy of action. Speaking of the former, the Court said: "That sort of advocacy, even though uttered with the hope that it may ultimately lead to violent revolution, is too remote from concrete action to be regarded as the kind of indoctrination preparatory to action which was condemned in Dennis."[71] It is interesting that the Court, after reviewing the evidence against some of the defendants, ordered that they be acquitted. As to the others, the case was remanded for a new trial under proper instructions. Justices Black and Douglas, concurring and dissenting, said in the language of the former: "I would reverse every one of these convictions and direct that all the defendants be acquitted. In my judgment the statutory provisions on which these prosecutions are based abridge freedom of speech, press and assembly in violation of the First Amendment to the United States Constitution."[72]

§ 10.18. Membership in groups dedicated to the violent over-throw of the government

In 1961 the United States Supreme Court ruled that Congress could constitutionally punish members of organizations dedicated to the violent overthrow of the government, so long as they were "active" members—that is, members who knew the violent objectives of the group and had the specific intent to further those purposes. Said the Supreme Court majority:

> Little remains to be said concerning the claim that the statute infringes First Amendment freedoms. It was settled in Dennis that the advocacy with which we are here concerned is not constitutionally protected speech, and it was further established that a combination to promote such advocacy, albeit under the aegis of what purports to be a political party, is not such as-

---

70. Further reflections upon the *Dennis* case by the author are available in *Dennis v United States—Precedent, Principle or Perversion?*, 5 Vand L Rev 141 (1952).

71. Yates v. U.S., 354 U.S. 298, 77 S. Ct. 1064, 1078, 1 L. Ed. 2d 1356, 1376 (1957) (overruled on other grounds by, Burks v. U.S., 437 U.S. 1, 98 S. Ct. 2141, 57 L. Ed. 2d 1 (1978)).

72. Yates v. U.S., 354 U.S. 298, 77 S. Ct. 1064, 1087, 1 L. Ed. 2d 1356, 1386 (1957) (overruled on other grounds by, Burks v. U.S., 437 U.S. 1, 98 S. Ct. 2141, 57 L. Ed. 2d 1 (1978)).

sociation as is protected by the First Amendment. We can discern no reason why membership, when it constitutes a purposeful form of complicity in a group engaging in this same forbidden advocacy, should receive any greater degree of protection from the guarantees of that Amendment.[73]

Chief Justice Warren, as well as Justices Black, Brennan and Douglas, dissented. Said Justice Black: "The First Amendment absolutely forbids Congress to outlaw membership in a political party or similar association merely because one of the philosophical tenets of that group is that the existing government should be overthrown by force at some distant time in the future when circumstances may permit."[74]

On the same date the Court, with no dissent, reversed the conviction of a person for being a member of the Communist Party because the government had not proved in his case that the party was engaged in the advocacy of action to overthrow government by force "by the use of language reasonably and ordinarily calculated to incite persons to action" immediately or in the future. Said the Court:

> We held in Yates, and we reiterate now, that the mere abstract teaching of Communist theory, including the teaching of the moral propriety or even moral necessity for a resort to force and violence, is not the same as preparing a group for violent action and steeling it to such action. There must be some direct or circumstantial evidence of a call to violence now or in the future which is both sufficiently strong and sufficiently pervasive to lend color to the otherwise ambiguous theoretical material regarding Communist Party teaching, and to justify the inference that such a call to violence may fairly be imputed to the Party as a whole, and not merely to some narrow segment of it.

The Court added:

> There is danger that one in sympathy with the legitimate aims of such an organization, but not specifically intending to accomplish them by resort to violence, might be punished for his adherence to lawful and constitutionally protected purposes which he does not necessarily share.[75]

In 1965 the Court invalidated as unconstitutional on its face a

---

73. Scales v. U.S., 367 U.S. 203, 81 S. Ct. 1469, 1486, 6 L. Ed. 2d 782 (1961).
74. Scales v. U.S., 367 U.S. 203, 81 S. Ct. 1469, 1486, 6 L. Ed. 2d 782 (1961).
75. Noto v. U.S., 367 U.S. 290, 81 S. Ct. 1517, 1521, 6 L. Ed. 2d 836 (1961).

Louisiana statute making it a crime to contribute to the support of any "subversive organization" because the statute's definition of such organization was "unduly vague, uncertain and broad."[76]

§ 10.19. Denying the ballot to subversive political groups

A number of states in effect ban the use of the ballot to political parties and candidates who advocate the violent overthrow of the government, by requiring of the parties and candidates affidavits that they do not advocate such overthrow.[77] Some of the state statutes have been held unconstitutional by state courts under various clauses in the state constitutions.[78] Maryland's requirement of such an affidavit has been upheld by the United States Supreme Court in a per curiam opinion, which refers to the Maryland decision of *Shub v. Simpson*.[79]

> We read this decision to hold that to obtain a place on a Maryland ballot a candidate need only make an oath that he is not a person who is engaged in one way or another in the attempt to overthrow the government by force and violence, and that he is not knowingly a member of an organization engaged in such an attempt. At the bar of this Court, the Attorney General of the State of Maryland declared that he would advise the proper authorities to accept an affidavit in these terms as satisfying in full the statutory requirement. Under these circumstances and with this understanding, the judgment of the Maryland Court of Appeals is affirmed.[80]

When a state required of every political party an affidavit by the officers "that it does not advocate the overthrow of local, state or national government by force of violence," the Supreme Court in 1974 voided the statute because of "the principle that the constitutional guarantees of free speech and free press do not permit a State to forbid or prosecute advocacy of the use of force or of law violations except where such advocacy is directed to inciting or produc-

---

76. Dombrowski v. Pfister, 380 U.S. 479, 85 S. Ct. 1116, 14 L. Ed. 2d 22 (1965).

77. Note, 34 Va L Rev 450 (1948); Note, 25 Notre Dame Lawyer 319 (1949).

78. Communist Party of U.S. of America v. Peek, 20 Cal. 2d 536, 127 P.2d 889 (1942); Imbrie v. Marsh, 5 N.J. Super. 239, 68 A.2d 761 (App. Div. 1949), judgment aff'd, 3 N.J. 578, 71 A.2d 352, 18 A.L.R.2d 241 (1950); But note Field v. Hall, 201 Ark. 77, 143 S.W.2d 567 (1940), upholding the Arkansas statute.

79. Shub v. Simpson, 196 Md. 177, 76 A.2d 332 (1950).

80. Gerende v. Board of Sup'rs of Elections of Baltimore City, 341 U.S. 56, 71 S. Ct. 565, 95 L. Ed. 745 (1951).

ing imminent lawless action and is likely to incite or produce such action."[81]

§ 10.20. Regulating the use of the mails by subversive organizations

In 1965 the United States Supreme Court voided a federal statute providing that material thought by the Secretary of the Treasury to be "communist political propaganda" could be detained until specifically requested by the addressee. Said the Court:

> We rest on the narrow ground that the addressee in order to receive his mail must request in writing that it be delivered. This amounts in our judgment to an unconstitutional abridgment of the addressee's First Amendment rights. The addressee carries an affirmative obligation which we do not think the Government may impose on him. This requirement is almost certain to have a deterrent effect, especially as respects those who have sensitive positions. Their livelihood may be dependent on a security clearance. Public officials, like school-teachers who have no tenure, might think they would invite disaster if they read what the Federal Government says contains the seeds of treason.[82]

There was no dissent.

§ 10.21. Denying tax exemptions to subversive groups

In 1958 the United States Supreme Court indicated that if a state desired to deny tax exemptions to subversive organizations the state would have to "bear the burden of persuasion to show that the appellants engaged in criminal speech." The Court stated: "A discriminatory denial of a tax exemption for engaging in speech is a limitation on free speech . . . to deny an exemption to claimants who engage in certain forms of speech is in effect to penalize them for such speech."[83]

The Court added:

> When the constitutional right to speak is sought to be deterred

---

81. Communist Party of Indiana v. Whitcomb, 414 U.S. 441, 94 S. Ct. 656, 38 L. Ed. 2d 635 (1974).

82. Lamont v. Postmaster General of U.S., 381 U.S. 301, 85 S. Ct. 1493, 14 L. Ed. 2d 398, 402 (1965).

83. Speiser v. Randall, 357 U.S. 513, 78 S. Ct. 1332, 2 L. Ed. 2d 1460, 1468 (1958); First Unitarian Church of Los Angeles v. County of Los Angeles, 357 U.S. 545, 78 S. Ct. 1350, 2 L. Ed. 2d 1484 (1958).

by a state's general taxing program, due process demands that the speech be unencumbered until the state comes forward with sufficient proof to justify its inhibition.[84]

Justice Black said in a concurring opinion: "Advocacy which is in no way brigaded with action should always be protected by the First Amendment." With this Justice Douglas was in agreement.

§ 10.22. Compelling the production of membership lists by subversive organizations

In 1928 the United States Supreme Court upheld, as applied to a local chapter of the Ku Klux Klan, a New York statute requiring any unincorporated association which demanded an oath as a condition of membership to file with state officials copies of its constitution, bylaws, rules, regulations and oath of membership, together with a roster of its members and a list of officers. In the opinion, the Supreme Court took pains to emphasize the nature of the organization which New York was regulating. The Court stressed the particular character of the Klan's activities, involving acts of unlawful intimidation and violence, which the Court assumed was before the state legislature when it enacted the statute, and of which the Court itself took judicial notice.[85]

Thirty years later the Court had before it a situation where Alabama was interested in ascertaining whether a foreign corporation was unlawfully carrying on local activities within its borders while not qualified to do business in the manner required by Alabama law. Nevertheless, the Court denied Alabama a look at the membership lists of the National Association for the Advancement of Colored People. The Court recognized that a curbing of associational freedom would follow from the disclosure of the membership. The Court stated:

> It is hardly a novel perception that compelled disclosure of affiliation with groups engaged in advocacy may constitute as effective a restraint on freedom of association. . . . Petitioners made an uncontroverted showing that on past occasions revelations of the identity of its rank-and-file members has exposed these members to economic reprisal, loss of employment, threat of physical coercion, and other manifestations of hostility. Under these circumstances, we think it apparent that compelled

---

84. Speiser v. Randall, 357 U.S. 513, 78 S. Ct. 1332, 2 L. Ed. 2d 1460, 1473 (1958).

85. People of State of New York ex rel. Bryant v. Zimmerman, 278 U.S. 63, 49 S. Ct. 61, 73 L. Ed. 184, 62 A.L.R. 785 (1928).

disclosure of petitioner's Alabama membership is likely to affect adversely the ability of petitioner and its members to pursue their collective effort to foster beliefs which they admittedly have the right to advocate, in that it may induce members to withdraw from the Association and dissuade others from joining it because of fear of exposure of their beliefs shown through their associations and the consequences of this exposure.[86]

Then, when the Supreme Court found on the facts no important interest of the state that required divulging members names, it held the inquiry constitutionally impermissible. Said the Court:

We hold that the immunity from state scrutiny of membership lists which the Association claims on behalf of its members is here so related to the right of the members to pursue their lawful private interest privately and to associate freely with others in so doing as to come within the protection of the Fourteenth Amendment. And we conclude that Alabama has fallen short of showing a controlling justification for the deterrent effect on the free enjoyment of the right to associate which disclosure of membership lists is likely to have.[87]

Two years later the constitutional freedom of association was again made the basis for the Supreme Court's decision that a local branch of the NAACP could not be compelled to disclose its membership lists. The cities of Little Rock and North Little Rock, Arkansas, asserted the right to inspect such lists under municipal ordinances imposing occupational license taxes and requiring organizations operating within the municipality to furnish information to the city including a statement of the contributions received and by whom paid. The Court said: "Where there is a significant encroachment upon personal liberty, the State may prevail only upon showing a subordinating interest which is compelling." The Court found "no relevant correlation between the power of the municipalities to impose occupational license taxes and the compulsory disclosure and publication of the membership lists."[88]

In 1961 the Court said that "where it is shown . . . that disclosure of membership lists results in reprisals against and hostility to the members, disclosure is not required." So saying, the Court

---

86. National Ass'n for Advancement of Colored People v. State of Ala., ex rel. Patterson, 357 U.S. 449, 78 S. Ct. 1163, 2 L. Ed. 2d 1488, 1500 (1958).

87. National Ass'n for Advancement of Colored People v. State of Ala., ex rel. Patterson, 357 U.S. 449, 78 S. Ct. 1163, 1174, 2 L. Ed. 2d 1488 (1958).

88. Bates v. City of Little Rock, 361 U.S. 516, 80 S. Ct. 412, 4 L. Ed. 2d 480 (1960).

invalidated a Louisiana requirement that officers of local branches of the NAACP take an affidavit that none of the officers of its affiliates were members of a subversive organization. The Supreme Court observed: "It is not consonant with due process to require a person to swear to a fact that he cannot be expected to know or alternatively to refrain from a wholly lawful activity."[89]

Two years later the Court ruled that Florida could not compel the Miami branch of the NAACP to produce its membership lists. The Court began by observing that it "has repeatedly held that the rights of association are within the ambit of the constitutional protections afforded by the First and Fourteenth Amendments,"[90] adding "and it is equally clear that the guarantee encompasses protection of privacy of association."[91] "It is an essential prerequisite to the validity of an investigation which intrudes into the area of constitutionally protected rights of speech, press, association and petition," ruled the Supreme Court, "that the State convincingly show a substantial relation between the information sought and compelling State interest."[92] The Court distinguished previous decisions in which it had compelled individuals to talk about their own membership in the Communist Party. Said the Court: "The prior holdings that governmental interest in controlling subversion and the particular character of the Communist Party and its objectives outweigh the right of individual Communists to conceal party membership or affiliations by no means require the wholly different conclusion that other groups—concededly legitimate—automatically forfeit their rights to privacy of association simply because the general subject matter of the legislative inquiry is Communist subversive or infiltration."[93] The Court concluded:

> We rest our result on the fact that the record in this case is insufficient to show a substantial connection between the Miami branch of the NAACP and Communist activities which the respondent Committee itself concedes is an essential prerequisite to demonstrating the immediate, substantial and subordinating

---

89. Louisiana ex rel. Gremillion v. National Ass'n for the Advancement of Colored People, 366 U.S. 293, 81 S. Ct. 1333, 6 L. Ed. 2d 301, 303-04 (1961).

90. Gibson v. Florida Legislative Investigation Committee, 372 U.S. 539, 83 S. Ct. 889, 9 L. Ed. 2d 929, 934 (1963).

91. Gibson v. Florida Legislative Investigation Committee, 372 U.S. 539, 83 S. Ct. 889, 9 L. Ed. 2d 929, 934 (1963).

92. Gibson v. Florida Legislative Investigation Committee, 372 U.S. 539, 83 S. Ct. 889, 9 L. Ed. 2d 929, 934 (1963).

93. Gibson v. Florida Legislative Investigation Committee, 372 U.S. 539, 83 S. Ct. 889, 9 L. Ed. 2d 929, 934 (1963).

state interest necessary to sustain its right of inquiry into the membership lists of the association.[94]

Dictum in the *Gibson* case suggests that where there is a showing of "a substantial connection" between the investigated group and "Communist activities," it will be constitutionally permissible to require the production of its membership lists.

§ 10.23. Denying the use of public facilities to subversive groups

The United States Supreme Court has not yet ruled on whether local authorities may deny supposedly subversive groups access to public halls, auditoria, and the like. *DeJonge v. Oregon,*[95] however, suggests that even the Communist Party has a right to assemble peaceably and to discuss legal objectives and methods.

In 1936 a Catholic priest was denied the opportunity to use a Chicago stadium for a talk on "Social Justice," when the local authorities concluded it was "subversive and controversial" political propaganda, and the Illinois courts affirmed the action of the local authorities.[96]

In 1948, when a citizen brought action against the Board of Education of the City of New York to compel it to adopt a resolution denying the use of school buildings and grounds after hours to Communist, Nazi, and Facist groups, organizations fostering racial or religious intolerance, or "fronts" for the foregoing, the court denied relief, stressing the broad discretion customarily given to school authorities concerning the use of school properties by outside groups.[97]

Seven years later another New York court ruled that the local chapter of the Nationalist Party was not denied its constitutional rights of free speech and assembly by the refusal of fire district commissioners of permission to meet in the fire hall, even though the auditorium was customarily available to "residents and nonprofit organizations" of the district "for social and recreational purposes."[98]

The Supreme Court has held, one may recall here, that the public parks cannot be denied to the Jehovah's Witnesses for religious

---

94. Gibson v. Florida Legislative Investigation Committee, 372 U.S. 539, 83 S. Ct. 889, 9 L. Ed. 2d 929, 934 (1963).

95. De Jonge v. State of Oregon, 299 U.S. 353, 57 S. Ct. 255, 81 L. Ed. 278 (1937).

96. Coughlin v. Chicago Park Dist., 364 Ill. 90, 4 N.E.2d 1 (1936).

97. Stanton v. Board of Ed. of City of New York, 190 Misc. 1012, 76 N.Y.S.2d 559 (Sup. Ct. 1948).

98. Hooker v. Conte, 208 Misc. 188, 143 N.Y.S.2d 750 (Sup. Ct. 1955).

services when other faiths are permitted to use such parks.[99] It seems safe to suggest that any invidious discrimination in the use of public facilities, including halls and auditoria, will be unconstitutional as a violation both of the First Amendment and the Equal Protection Clause of the Fourteenth.

The Court has held that a student organization cannot be banned from a state college campus or exposed to nonrecognition, with concomitant impediments to free association, simply because of the views of a national organization with which the local is loosely affiliated, nor because of the administration's disagreement with the philosophy of the group. By dictum, however, the Court indicated that a group seeking recognition could be called upon to indicate its agreement to conform with reasonable standards respecting conduct.[1]

In 1962 a New York court indicated that public authorities who permit generally the use of school and other facilities cannot forbid such use by groups or individuals because their views are unpopular. Holding that Hunter College's facilities could not be denied to the *National Review* after a lecture by Jacques Soustelle, a French rightist, attacking France's Algerian policy, the court indicated that while there may be no duty to open the doors of schoolhouses to uses other than academic, once they are opened they must be opened under conditions consistent with constitutional principles.[2]

In 1946 a California court ruled that a local affiliate of the American Civil Liberties Union had a right to use school facilities which had generally been made available to the public, and held that school authorities need not make school buildings available to the public, but if they do, they cannot arbitrarily deny such use to any group.[3] In 1961 the same court held unconstitutional as violative of freedom of speech and assembly a statute prohibiting the use of school properties by subversive organizations and requiring applicants to sign statements that the property would not be used to accomplish the overthrow of the government by force.[4] Two years later the same court reaffirmed that local school authorities could

---

99. Fowler v. State of R.I., 345 U.S. 67, 73 S. Ct. 526, 97 L. Ed. 828 (1953).

1. Healy v. James, 408 U.S. 169, 92 S. Ct. 2338, 33 L. Ed. 2d 266 (1972).

2. Buckley v. Meng, 35 Misc. 2d 467, 230 N.Y.S.2d 924 (Sup. Ct. 1962).

3. Danskin v. San Diego Unified School Dist., 28 Cal. 2d 536, 171 P.2d 885 (1946).

4. American Civil Liberties Union of Southern Cal. v. Board of Ed. of City of Los Angeles, 55 Cal. 2d 167, 10 Cal. Rptr. 647, 359 P.2d 45, 94 A.L.R.2d 1259 (1961).

not require such statements.[5] The same year, however, the California court upheld a rule of the Los Angeles Board of Education requiring that any group requesting the use of school facilities sign a statement that the property would not be used for the commission of a crime, including the crime of criminal syndicalism.[6]

§ 10.24. Ousting unwanted organizations from the states

States have traditionally had power to oust foreign corporations from conducting business in the state unless statutory conditions have been met. However, in 1964 the United States Supreme Court ruled that Alabama could not oust the National Association for the Advancement of Colored People. It was not sufficient justification for the ouster that the NAACP had (1) financed the enrollment of African Americans at the University of Alabama, (2) furnished legal counsel to such applicants seeking admission, (3) supported the bus boycott in Montgomery, and (4) allegedly made false statements against state officials. Again, the Supreme Court affirmed that even though a governmental purpose, such as controlling foreign corporations in the state, is legitimate and substantial, the state cannot broadly stifle the fundamental freedoms when the purpose can be more narrowly achieved. The Court distinguished the NAACP from the KKK, which had been involved in the *Bryant* case, and noted that the latter decision was "based on the particular character of the ban's activities, involving acts of unlawful intimidation and violence." The Supreme Court observed that "This [*NAACP*] case, in truth, involves not the privilege of a corporation to do business in a State, but rather the freedom of individuals to associate for the collective advocacy of ideas."[7]

§ 10.25. Requiring affidavits that none of the officers of a group are subversive

In 1961 the United States Supreme Court ruled that a state cannot make the local branch officers of a national organization give an affidavit that none of the officers of its affiliates are members of a subversive organization. Said the Court: "It is not consonant with due process to require a person to swear to a fact that he cannot be

---

5. American Civil Liberties Union of Southern Cal. v. Board of Ed. of San Diego Unified School Dist., 59 Cal. 2d 224, 28 Cal. Rptr. 712, 379 P.2d 16 (1963).

6. American Civil Liberties U. of So. Cal. v. Board of Education, 59 Cal. 2d 203, 28 Cal. Rptr. 700, 379 P.2d 4 (1963).

7. National Ass'n for Advancement of Colored People v. Alabama ex rel. Flowers, 377 U.S. 288, 84 S. Ct. 1302, 1315, 12 L. Ed. 2d 325 (1964).

expected to know or alternatively to refrain from a wholly lawful activity."[8]

§ 10.26. Listing certain groups as subversives

In 1951, in *Joint Anti-Fascist Refugee Committee v. McGrath*[9] the Supreme Court ruled that the Attorney General could not list certain organizations as subversives without satisfying due process demands that they be given notice of the "branding" and a fair hearing with an opportunity to prove that they were neither subversive nor communist.

IV. The "Subversive Individual" Cases

§ 10.27. Advocating or inciting insurrection or the violent overthrow of the government

At the time of World War I, a New York statute provided:

> Criminal anarchy is the doctrine that organized government should be overthrown by force or violence, or by assassination of the executive head or of any of the executive officials of government, or by any unlawful means. The advocacy of such doctrine by word of mouth or writing is a felony.

In 1919 Ben Gitlow, business manager of *The Revolutionary Age,* a socialist publication, published therein the "Left Wing Manifesto" which called for mass political strikes and forecast "a revolutionary struggle against capitalism." For this he was charged with violating the above statute. The conviction was sustained by the United States Supreme Court in 1925, with Justices Brandeis and Holmes dissenting.[10] The New York courts and the Supreme Court majority rejected the clear and present danger test, with the high court stating that the criterion was inapplicable "where the legislative body itself has previously determined the danger of substantive evil arising from utterances of a specified character." The Supreme Court applied a "tendency" test, with some language suggestive of an "incitement" norm. Justices Holmes and Brandeis insisted upon the applicability of the clear and present danger test and found it not satisfied by the activity of Gitlow. They added:

***

8. Louisiana ex rel. Gremillion v. National Ass'n for the Advancement of Colored People, 366 U.S. 293, 81 S. Ct. 1333, 6 L. Ed. 2d 301, 303 (1961).

9. Joint Anti-Fascist Refugee Committee v. McGrath, 341 U.S. 123, 71 S. Ct. 624, 95 L. Ed. 817 (1951).

10. Gitlow v. People of State of New York, 268 U.S. 652, 45 S. Ct. 625, 69 L. Ed. 1138 (1925).

It is said that this manifesto was more than a theory, that it was an incitement. Every idea is an incitement. . . . The only difference between the expression of an opinion and an incitement in the narrower sense is the speaker's enthusiasm for the result. Eloquence may set fire to reason. But whatever may be thought of the redundant discourse before us, it had no chance of starting a present conflagration.

Following New York's success before the Supreme Court, a number of other states passed statutes making it a crime to incite insurrection. Thus, Georgia enacted a statute providing:

Any attempt, by persuasion or otherwise, to induce others to join in any combined resistance to the lawful authority of the State shall constitute an attempt to incite insurrection.

One Angelo Herndon was a paid organizer for the Communist Party who went to Georgia to enroll African Americans in the party. After his arrest for violating the above statute, his dwelling was searched and literature found that urged "self-determination for the Black Belt," as well as public relief. Conviction of Herndon in the Georgia courts was reversed by the United States Supreme Court.[11] It was not enough, said the Court, that Herndon's activities might have a dangerous tendency some time in the distant future, and the Court pointed out that convictions under such statutes can be constitutional only when the record contains proof that the defendant intended to induce resort to violence by his conduct. The Supreme Court stated:

The power of a state to abridge freedom of speech and of assembly is the exception rather than the rule and the penalizing even of utterances of a defined character must find its justification in a reasonable apprehension of danger to organized government. The judgment of the legislature is not unfettered. The limitation upon individual liberty must have appropriate relation to the safety of the state. Legislation which goes beyond this need violates the principle of the Constitution. . . . And, where a statute is so vague and uncertain as to make criminal an utterance or an act which may be innocently said or done with no intent to induce resort to violence or on the other hand may be said or done with a purpose violently to subvert government, a conviction under such a law cannot be sustained.

Seemingly, this put an end to the "Gitlow exception" to the clear and present danger test, that is, the notion that there is no need to

---

11. Herndon v. Lowry, 301 U.S. 242, 57 S. Ct. 732, 81 L. Ed. 1066 (1937).

satisfy the clear and present danger test when some legislative body has determined that a particular class of utterances is dangerous. In *Herndon* the Court added:

> The statute, as construed and applied, amounts merely to a dragnet which may enmesh anyone who agitates for a change of government if a jury can be persuaded that he ought to have foreseen his words would have some effect in the future conduct of others. No reasonably ascertainable standard of guilt is prescribed. So vague and indeterminate are the boundaries thus set to the freedom of speech and assembly that the law necessarily violates the guarantees of liberty embodied in the Fourteenth Amendment.

In 1957 the Supreme Court ruled that states can no longer punish those who within the state advocate the overthrow by violence of the government of the United States. This, the Court held, is a field preempted by the federal Congress.[12] Under narrowly drawn statutes, allowing convictions only when there is from the conduct of the defendant a clear and present danger of the violent overthrow of the state government, states can for the time being at least still punish individuals for speeches, printing, and associational activities.

The federal Alien Registration Act of 1940 provided:

> Sec. 2(a). It shall be unlawful for any person (1) to knowingly or willfully advocate, abet, advise, or teach the duty, necessity, desirability or propriety of overthrowing or destroying any government in the United States by force or violence, or by the assassination of any officer of any such government; (2) with the intent to cause the overthrow or destruction of any government in the United States, to print, publish, edit, issue, circulate, sell, distribute or publicly display any written or printed matter advocating, advising, or teaching the duty, necessity, desirability or propriety of overthrowing or destroying any government in the United States by force or violence.

Attempts and conspiracies were similarly made criminal. In the *Dennis* case[13] the Supreme Court, while sustaining a conviction for conspiring to advocate the violent overthrow of government, indicated that "discussions or teaching and advocacy in the realm of ideas" would not be punishable.

Then, in 1957, the Court ruled that advocacy and teaching of the

---

12. Com. of Pa. v. Nelson, 350 U.S. 497, 76 S. Ct. 477, 100 L. Ed. 640 (1956).
13. Dennis v. United States, 341 U.S. 494, 71 S. Ct. 857, 95 L. Ed. 1137 (1951).

forcible overthrow of government as an abstract principle, divorced from any effort to instigate action to that end, was permissible.[14] Although not a decision on the constitutional right of such speaker, the Court made it very clear that grave constitutional problems would be present if Congress attempted to punish persons for advocating and teaching principles divorced from action. The *Dennis* decision, said the Supreme Court, was limited to sustaining convictions where there was advocacy of concrete action for the forcible overthrow of the government.

In *Yates* the Court further explained its earlier *Dennis* holding. It stated:

> The essence of the Dennis holding was that indoctrination of a group in preparation for future violent action, as well as exhortation to immediate action, by advocacy found to be directed to action for the accomplishment of forcible overthrow, to violence as a rule or principle of action, and employing language of incitement, is not constitutionally protected when the group is of sufficient size and cohesiveness, is sufficiently oriented towards action, and other circumstances are such as reasonably to justify apprehension that action will occur.

The Court added:

> This is quite a different thing from the view of the District Court here that mere doctrinal justification of forcible overthrow is punishable per se under the Smith Act. That sort of advocacy, even though uttered with the hope that it may ultimately lead to violent revolution, is too remote from concrete action to be regarded as the kind of indoctrination preparatory to action which was condemned in Dennis.

In order to imprison persons for their advocacy of "subversive" ideas, the federal government will now have to prove that: (1) there was exhortation to action; (2) the language of incitement was employed; and (3) the audience or group was of sufficient size and cohesiveness and sufficiently oriented towards action, so that (4) circumstances are such as reasonably to justify apprehension that action of a very dangerous sort will follow.

§ 10.28. Flying the red flag

At one time 33 states had statutes providing for the punishment of

---

14. Yates v. U.S., 354 U.S. 298, 77 S. Ct. 1064, 1 L. Ed. 2d 1356 (1957) (overruled on other grounds by, Burks v. U.S., 437 U.S. 1, 98 S. Ct. 2141, 57 L. Ed. 2d 1 (1978)).

individuals who flew the red flag as a symbol of opposition to our form of government. The Michigan statute, for example, provided:

> Any person who shall display a red flag in any public parade or demonstration in this state is guilty of a felony. The use of such a flag at any such assembly, parade or demonstration shall be considered as prima facie evidence of its use as an emblem of anarchy.[15]

One can be somewhat amazed that the red flag, emblematic of the most totalitarian government known, is made punishable as a symbol of anarchy. However, such statutes have been upheld by the state courts.[16]

In 1931 the United States Supreme Court set aside a conviction under the California statute of a girl who flew the red flag at a summer camp, and indicated that states could not punish a person for displaying a red flag as a "symbol or emblem of opposition to organized government," since such opposition need not be by force. Opposition can be orderly, peaceful, and quite legal within the framework of a democratic society, and such type of opposition to government cannot be made criminal, according to the Court.[17]

§ 10.29. Assembly of criminal syndicalists and other "subversives"

In the 1930s Oregon made it a crime "to conduct and assist in conducting an assemblage" of Communist Party members, "which said assemblage of persons . . . did then and there . . . teach and advocate the doctrine of criminal syndicalism and sabotage." The Oregon Supreme Court had sustained the conviction of one De Jonge under the act for having assembled with fellow Communists at a meeting at which there was no urging of criminal syndicalism or anything else that was unlawful, the Oregon Court construing their statute to embrace such a situation.

De Jonge's conviction was reversed by the United States Supreme Court.[18] The high court was unanimous in ruling that "peaceable assembly for lawful discussion cannot be made a crime. The holding of meetings for peaceable political action cannot be proscribed.

---

15. Mich. Stat. Anno. § 28.237.

16. People v. Immonen, 271 Mich. 384, 261 N.W. 59 (1935) (noted in 6 Det L Rev 43).

17. Stromberg v. People of State of Cal., 283 U.S. 359, 51 S. Ct. 532, 75 L. Ed. 1117, 73 A.L.R. 1484 (1931).

18. De Jonge v. State of Oregon, 299 U.S. 353, 57 S. Ct. 255, 81 L. Ed. 278 (1937).

Those who assist in the conduct of such meetings cannot be branded as criminals on that score."

§ 10.30. Compelling persons to divulge their political beliefs and associations to more effectively protect national security

In 1947 a federal court of appeals affirmed the conviction of a man called before the House Committee on Un-American Activities who then refused to testify. Said the court:

> One need only recall the activities of the so-called fifth columns in various countries both before and during the late war to realize that the United States should be alert to discover and deal with the seeds of revolution within itself. And if there be any doubts on the score of the power and duty of the Government and Congress to do so, they may be resolved when it is remembered that one of the very purposes of the Constitution itself was to protect the country against danger from within as well as from without.[19]

Since then the Supreme Court has ruled that congressional committees which provide "immunity baths" can force a person to talk about his Communist Party associations, so long as the committee has "reasonable ground to suppose that the petitioner was an active Communist Party member" and "was an active Communist leader engaged primarily in propaganda activities."[20] First Amendment interests are outweighed here, according to the Court's majority, by the interests of society in giving the national legislature information as to the extent of the Communist threat. These have been five-to-four decisions, with the Chief Justice, Justices Black, Brennan and Douglas dissenting, so there is reason to doubt whether a Congressional committee can force some minister, lawyer, banker, or plain citizen with no attachment to the Communist apparatus to talk about his political beliefs or even his political associations.

In 1965 the Court held invalid as a denial of the privilege against self-incrimination the provision of the Subversive Activities Control Act requiring individual members of the Communist Party to register when the party failed to.[21]

---

19. U.S. v. Josephson, 165 F.2d 82 (C.C.A. 2d Cir. 1947).

20. Wilkinson v. U.S., 365 U.S. 399, 81 S. Ct. 567, 5 L. Ed. 2d 633 (1961); Braden v. U.S., 365 U.S. 431, 81 S. Ct. 584, 5 L. Ed. 2d 653 (1961); Barenblatt v. U.S., 360 U.S. 109, 79 S. Ct. 1081, 3 L. Ed. 2d 1115 (1959).

21. Albertson v. Subversive Activities Control Bd., 382 U.S. 70, 86 S. Ct. 194, 15 L. Ed. 2d 165 (1965).

§ 10.31. Enabling state legislative bodies to more effectively protect state security

In 1957 the United States Supreme Court set aside the conviction for contempt of a university professor who had already testified that he had never been a member of the Communist Party but refused to answer the question, "Do you believe in Communism?" or any other question concerning opinion or belief. The Court indicated that serious constitutional problems will exist if a state attempts, for instance, to compel a university professor to explain what he said in the classroom and to defend the utterance, or to compel a citizen to explain the extent of his support for an unpopular political party that has been lawfully on the ballot. Said the Court:

> The State Supreme Court thus conceded without extended discussion that petitioner's right to lecture and his right to associate with others were constitutionally protected freedoms which had been abridged through this investigation. These conclusions could not be seriously debated. Merely to summon a witness and compel him, against his will, to disclose the nature of his past expressions and associations is a measure of governmental interference in these matters. These are rights which are safeguarded by the Bill of Rights and the Fourteenth Amendment. We believe that there unquestionably was an invasion of petitioner's liberties in the areas of academic freedom and political expression—areas in which government should be extremely reticent to tread.[22]

Two years later, however, the Supreme Court in a five-to-four decision sustained the contempt conviction of the operator of a camp who refused to divulge to a New Hampshire investigator the names of members who attended a "World Fellowship" gathering. The Court noted that earlier-existing New Hampshire law required guests at such a public camp to register in a book open to public inspection by police officers, and that the information thus could hardly be deemed private. Said the Court: "This governmental interest [in self-preservation] outweighs individual rights in an associational privacy which were here tenuous at best."[23] Chief Justice Warren, as well as Justices Black, Brennan and Douglas dissented. Said Justice Brennan: "This record, I think, not only fails to reveal any interest of the State sufficient to subordinate appellant's

22. Sweezy v. State of N.H. by Wyman, 354 U.S. 234, 77 S. Ct. 1203, 1211, 1 L. Ed. 2d 1311, 1324 (1957).

23. Uphaus v. Wyman, 360 U.S. 72, 79 S. Ct. 1040, 1047, 3 L. Ed. 2d 1090 (1959).

constitutionally protected rights, but affirmatively shows that the investigatory objective was the impermissible one of exposure for exposure's sake."[24]

In 1960 the Supreme Court invalidated an Arkansas statute compelling teachers to disclose all organizations to which they belonged or to which they gave support within the previous five years. The demands were too great, said the Court, adding: "To compel a teacher to disclose his every associational tie is to impair that teacher's right of free association, a right closely allied to freedom of speech and a right which, like free speech, lies at the foundation of a free society."[25]

Three years later the Court held that Florida could not require a local branch of the NAACP to divulge its membership lists simply because Communism was the subject of the inquiry. Said the Court:

> The prior holdings that governmental interest in controlling subversion and the particular character of the Communist Party and its objectives outweigh the right of individual Communists to conceal party membership or affiliations by no means require the wholly different conclusion that other groups—concededly legitimate—automatically forfeit their rights to privacy of association simply because the general subject matter of the legislative inquiry is Communist subversion or infiltration.

There must be, then, a showing of a substantial connection between the local organization and Communist activities before the state has the right to inquire into membership lists of an association.[26]

In 1966 the Supreme Court ruled that a state could not punish a person for refusing to talk about his possible Communist connections before 1957. Said the Court: "New Hampshire's interest on the record is too remote and conjectural to override the guaranty of the First Amendment that a person can speak or not, as he chooses, free of all government compulsion."[27]

Thus, where freedom of speech with its embraced freedom of silence clashes with the interest of the state in ascertaining the extent of danger to the security of the state, the Supreme Court weighs the respective interests, with at times the former interests

---

24. Uphaus v. Wyman, 360 U.S. 72, 79 S. Ct. 1040, 1047, 3 L. Ed. 2d 1090 (1959).

25. Shelton v. Tucker, 364 U.S. 479, 81 S. Ct. 247, 5 L. Ed. 2d 231 (1960).

26. Gibson v. Florida Legislative Investigation Committee, 372 U.S. 539, 83 S. Ct. 889, 9 L. Ed. 2d 929 (1963).

27. DeGregory v. Attorney General of State of N. H., 383 U.S. 825, 86 S. Ct. 1148, 1152, 16 L. Ed. 2d 292 (1966).

prevailing, as in the *De Gregory, Shelton* and *Gibson* cases, and at other times the latter interest prevailing, as in *Uphaus v. Wyman.*

§ 10.32. Power of the executive to exclude aliens—conflicts with the First Amendment

The United States Supreme Court indicated in 1972 that the power of Congress to exclude aliens will seldom, if ever, be judicially reversed and that the Congress can confer conditional exercise of this power to the executive. The Court then held "that when the executive exercises this power negatively on the basis of a facially legitimate and bonafide reason, the courts will neither look behind the exercise of that discretion, nor test it by balancing its justification against the First Amendment interest of those who seek personal communication with the applicant." The Court left for another day the problem of executive action "for which no justification whatsoever is advanced." Justices Brennan and Marshall dissented, stating that "at least when the rights of Americans are involved, there is no basis for concluding that the power to exclude aliens is absolute," and recalling that, "It is established constitutional doctrine . . . that government may restrict First Amendment rights only if the restriction is necessary to further a compelling governmental interest." Justice Douglas also dissented.

It is suggested that foregoing holding was in error. Every American citizen has "a First Amendment right to receive information and ideas," as the majority had to acknowledge, and this most precious of rights is not to be negated without an overpowering societal interest that would clearly be imperiled by the communication. National security is simply not endangered even remotely by allowing American citizens to hear the views of the theoretical Marxists or "trickle down" economists, and no Attorney General should be allowed power to "protect" us from those who simply advocate ideas which many of us find quite disagreeable.[28]

§ 10.33. Deporting aliens who utter subversive thoughts, entertain subversive beliefs, or join subversive organizations

The constitutional right of a sovereign to deport aliens whom it finds distasteful has been pretty generally accepted, although no such specific power has been conferred upon the federal government.[29] Legislation has authorized the deportation of aliens who believe in the overthrow of government by force or violence, as well

---

28. Kleindienst v. Mandel, 408 U.S. 753, 92 S. Ct. 2576, 33 L. Ed. 2d 683 (1972).

29. Nishimura Ekiu v. U.S., 142 U.S. 651, 659, 12 S. Ct. 336, 35 L. Ed. 1146, 1149 (1892).

as those who become members of or affiliated with organizations that espouse such a belief. There are many additional grounds for deportation, including disbelief in all forms of organized government. Lower federal courts have sustained the permissibility of deportation for such grounds.[30] At times when we have felt specially insecure the government has indulged in mass arrests of aliens for deportation, as in January of 1919, when over 4,000 aliens were rounded up for deportation.[31]

In 1952 the Supreme Court upheld the deportation of aliens who at the time they entered or any time thereafter were members of an organization dedicated to the violent overthrow of the government.[32] At the same term, the Court said in a five-to-four decision that there was "no doubt that the doctrines and practices of communism clearly enough teach the use of force to achieve political control to give constitutional basis, according to any theory of reasonableness or arbitrariness, for Congress to expel known alien communists under its power to regulate the exclusion, admission and expulsion of aliens."[33] Two years later, the Court upheld the deportation of a man who had resided in the United States for 36 years, because he had been a member of the Communist Party from 1944 to 1946. The majority held the act authorizing such deportation was constitutional even though it did not require proof in individual cases that the alien knew of the party's dedication to violence at the time he was a member.[34] Justices Black and Douglas dissented, pointing out that at the time of the alien's membership, the Communist Party was a legal political organization on the ballot in California. They concluded: "he is being punished for what he once was, for a political faith he briefly expressed over six years ago and then rejected."

§ 10.34. Denial of benefits and opportunities to subversives— public employment

In 1952 the United States Supreme Court ruled that New York could make ineligible as a public school teacher one who advocates or teaches the overthrow of government by force and violence, or

---

30. Lopez v. Howe, 259 F. 401, 12 A.L.R. 192 (C.C.A. 2d Cir. 1919).

31. Chaffe, *Freedom of Speech in the United States,* Harvard U Press Cambridge, 1941, p. 196; and cf. Barkley, Jailing Radicals in Detroit, 110 Nation 136 (Jan. 31, 1920).

32. Harisiades v. Shaughnessy, 342 U.S. 580, 72 S. Ct. 512, 96 L. Ed. 586 (1952).

33. Carlson v. Landon, 342 U.S. 524, 72 S. Ct. 525, 96 L. Ed. 547 (1952).

34. Galvan v. Press, 347 U.S. 522, 74 S. Ct. 737, 98 L. Ed. 911 (1954).

who is knowingly a member of a group that is dedicated to the same.[35] The Court said:

> A teacher works in a sensitive area in a schoolroom. There he shapes the attitude of young minds towards the society in which they live. In this, the state has a vital concern. It must preserve the integrity of the schools. That the school authorities have the right and the duty to screen the officials, teachers, and employees as to their fitness to maintain the integrity of the schools as a part of ordered society, cannot be doubted.[36]

The New York civil service law was later amended to make ineligible for any position in the service of the state any individual who willfully and deliberately advocated, advised or taught the doctrine that government should be overthrown by force, who printed or sold any writing doing the same, or who was a member of any organization advocating the same. The act further provided that "membership in the communist party of the United States of America or the communist party of the state of New York shall constitute prima facie evidence of disqualification for appointment to or retention in any office or position in the service of the state or of any city or civil division thereof." In 1967 the Supreme Court voided this "Feinberg Law" with its requirement of dismissal for "treasonable or seditious utterances" which embraced, in the language of the Court, "advocacy of abstract doctrine" or even "mere expression of belief." The Court stressed the inhibiting effect on teachers of such broad attacks on subversion, and remarked:

> Our Nation is deeply committed to safeguarding academic freedom, which is of transcendent value to all of us and not merely to the teachers concerned. That freedom is therefore a special concern of the First Amendment, which does not tolerate laws that cast a pall of orthodoxy over the classroom.

The Court condemned the "overbreadth" of the New York legislation which barred "employment both for association which legitimately may be sanctioned and for association which may not be sanctioned consistently with First Amendment rights," again

---

35. Adler v. Board of Education of City of New York, 342 U.S. 485, 72 S. Ct. 380, 96 L. Ed. 517, 27 A.L.R.2d 472 (1952) (overruled in part by, Keyishian v. Board of Regents of University of State of N. Y., 385 U.S. 589, 87 S. Ct. 675, 17 L. Ed. 2d 629 (1967)).

36. Adler v. Board of Education of City of New York, 342 U.S. 485, 72 S. Ct. 380, 385, 96 L. Ed. 517, 524-25, 27 A.L.R.2d 472 (1952) (overruled in part by, Keyishian v. Board of Regents of University of State of N. Y., 385 U.S. 589, 87 S. Ct. 675, 17 L. Ed. 2d 629 (1967)).

reminding us that "legislation which sanctions membership unaccompanied by specific intent to further the unlawful goals of the organization or which is not active membership violates constitutional limitations."[37]

The Supreme Court has noted a number of times that the vice of vagueness is at its worst when First Amendment freedoms are concerned, because citizens restrict "their conduct to that which is unquestionably safe. Free speech may not be so inhibited." So stating, the Court invalidated a Washington loyalty oath as unconstitutionally vague. Statutes such as this, ruled the Court, cannot "require forswearing of an undefined variety of guiltless behavior."[38] More recently the Court has voided a Florida loyalty oath requirement which a public employee could not take safely if he had ever "supported," "advised," "counseled" or "influenced" the Communist Party. The "extraordinary ambiguity of the statutory language" violated the ban upon vagueness, said the Court.[39]

In 1952 the Court established for the first time that "constitutional protection does extend to the public servant whose exclusion pursuant to a statute is patently arbitrary or discriminatory." The Court at that time voided an Oklahoma loyalty oath because it had no "scienter" provision, ruling that an oath to be constitutional had to allow its taking by an employee who did not know he was a member of a subversive organization or who did not know of its subversive nature at the time he was a member. Said the Court:

> But membership may be innocent. A state servant may have joined a proscribed organization unaware of its activities and purposes. . . . At the time of affiliation, a group itself may be innocent, only later coming under the influence of those who would turn it toward illegitimate ends. . . . Indiscriminate classification of innocent with knowing activity must fall as an assertion of arbitrary power. The oath offends due process.[40]

In 1966 the Court invalidated Arizona's public employee loyalty oath as violative of freedom of association. The Court found especially objectionable the fact that nothing in the statute or oath "purports to exclude association by one who does not subscribe to

---

37. Keyishian v. Board of Regents of University of State of N. Y., 385 U.S. 589, 87 S. Ct. 675, 683, 686-87, 17 L. Ed. 2d 629 (1967).

38. Baggett v. Bullitt, 377 U.S. 360, 84 S. Ct. 1316, 12 L. Ed. 2d 377 (1964).

39. Cramp v. Board of Public Instruction of Orange County, Fla., 368 U.S. 278, 82 S. Ct. 275, 7 L. Ed. 2d 285 (1961).

40. Wieman v. Updegraff, 344 U.S. 183, 73 S. Ct. 215, 218-19, 97 L. Ed. 216, 221-23 (1952).

the organization's unlawful ends." It was not enough that the statute forbade membership with "knowledge of said unlawful purpose." The Court added: "A law which applies to membership without the specific intent to further the illegal aims of the organization infringes unnecessarily on protected freedoms. It rests on the doctrine of 'guilt by association' which has no place here."[41]

The Court has in effect held that public employees can be forced to divulge their associations with the Communist Party and, if they fail to respond to inquiries, can be dismissed. The Court has said: "As regards the question of public employees relative to Communist Party membership, it has already been held that the interest in not subjecting speech and association to the deterrence of subsequent disclosure is outweighed by the State's interest in ascertaining the fitness of the employee for the post he holds, and hence that such questioning does not infringe constitutional protections."[42] The Court has, in some five-to-four decisions, sustained the dismissal on grounds of "insubordination," "incompetency," and "doubtful trust and reliability" of public employees who refused to answer questions regarding their Communist Party affiliations, after having been ordered to respond by their superiors.[43] In the most important of the decisions, however, the Court divided four-to-four on the permissibility of a local government unit discharging a person for failure to answer questions regarding subversive association. According to the four who would affirm the dismissal, a state can fire a worker on the grounds of "insubordination for failure to give information which we have held that the State has a legitimate interest in securing."[44] Chief Justice Warren did not participate in the case, which arose from California.

The Supreme Court has not yet indicated the procedural safeguards to which a public employee is entitled when being dismissed as a security risk. In 1950 the Civil Service Commission wrote to a federal employee that it had information she was a member of the Communist Party, had attended meetings of the party, etc. She answered, but the regional board informed the federal security agency where she worked that she was disloyal and ineligible for federal employment. She demanded a hearing where

---

41. Elfbrandt v. Russell, 384 U.S. 11, 86 S. Ct. 1238, 16 L. Ed. 2d 321 (1966).

42. Konigsberg v. State Bar of Cal., 366 U.S. 36, 81 S. Ct. 997, 6 L. Ed. 2d 105, 118 (1961).

43. Lerner v. Casey, 357 U.S. 468, 78 S. Ct. 1311, 2 L. Ed. 2d 1423 (1958); Beilan v. Board of Public Ed., School Dist. of Philadelphia, 357 U.S. 399, 78 S. Ct. 1317, 2 L. Ed. 2d 1414 (1958).

44. Nelson v. Los Angeles County, 362 U.S. 1, 80 S. Ct. 527, 4 L. Ed. 2d 494 (1960).

she could cross-examine the persons who made such charges against her. This was denied, and the Court of Appeals affirmed.[45] The Supreme Court affirmed by an equally divided court.[46] By now, with the Court's increasing concern for procedural fairness, it can be anticipated that the rights demanded must be honored.

§ 10.35. —practice of law and medicine

In 1954 the United States Supreme Court allowed New York to suspend a medical doctor's right to practice for six months when, as head of an organization on the Attorney General's subversive list, he refused to produce documents before a congressional committee and for such refusal was convicted in a federal court. Under the New York practice, suspension was not automatic but followed only after a full hearing by 10 licensed doctors who recommended action to the Board of Regents. In sustaining the suspension, the Supreme Court majority remarked that "practice is a privilege."[47] Justices Black, Douglas and Frankfurter dissented, characterizing the suspension as "arbitrary" and violative of First Amendment rights. Justice Douglas said "Nothing in a man's political beliefs disables him from setting bones or removing ruptured appendixes, safely and efficiently," adding: "When a doctor cannot save lives in America because he is opposed to Franco in Spain, it is time to call a halt and look critically at the neurosis that has possessed us."[48]

The Supreme Court allowed states to deny membership in state bars to those applicants who had passed the examinations but who would not discuss with the bar officials their present membership in or affiliations with the Communist Party. Said the Court in the *Konigsberg* case:

> The Fourteenth Amendment's protection against arbitrary state action does not forbid a State from denying admission to a bar applicant so long as he refuses to provide unprivileged answers to questions having a substantial relevance to his qualifications. . . . Whenever, in such a context, these protections are asserted against the exercise of valid governmental powers a reconciliation must be effected, and that perforce requires an appropriate weighing of the respective interests involved.

---

45. Bailey v. Richardson, 86 U.S. App. D.C. 248, 182 F.2d 46 (D.C. Cir. 1950), judgment aff'd by equally divided Supreme Court, 341 U.S. 918, 71 S. Ct. 669, 95 L. Ed. 1352 (1951).

46. Bailey v. Richardson, 341 U.S. 918, 71 S. Ct. 669, 95 L. Ed. 1352 (1951).

47. Barsky v. Board of Regents of University, 347 U.S. 442, 74 S. Ct. 650, 98 L. Ed. 829 (1954).

48. Barsky v. Board of Regents of University, 347 U.S. 442, 474, 74 S. Ct. 650, 98 L. Ed. 829, 850 (1954).

After noting that the Court had earlier held that public employees could be compelled to talk about their Communist associations, the Court added:

> With respect to this same question of Communist Party membership, we regard the State's interest in having lawyers who are devoted to the law in its broadest sense, including not only its substantive provisions, but also its procedures for orderly change, as clearly sufficient to outweigh the minimal effect upon free association occasioned by compulsory disclosure in the circumstances here presented.[49]

Chief Justice Warren, as well as Justices Black, Brennan and Douglas dissented. Justice Black stated:

> The interest in free association at stake here is not merely the personal interest of the petitioner in being free from burdens that may be imposed upon him for his past beliefs and associations. It is the interest of all the people in having a society in which no one is intimidated with respect to his beliefs or associations. It seems plain to me that the inevitable effect of the majority's decision is to condone a practice that will have a substantial deterrent effect upon the associations entered into by anyone who may want to become a lawyer in California.[50]

In the companion *Anastaplo* case,[51] the Court similarly ruled that a person could be denied bar membership if he refused to talk to the bar officials about membership in the Communist Party. Referring to the *Konigsberg* case, the Court said:

> We have there held it not constitutionally impermissible for a State legislatively, or through court-made regulation as here and in Konigsberg, to adopt a rule that an applicant will not be admitted to the practice of law if, and so long as, by refusing to answer material questions, he obstructs a bar examining committee in its proper functions of interrogating and cross-examining him upon his qualifications.

The Chief Justice, as well as Justices Black, Brennan and Douglas again dissented. These five-to-four decisions must be questioned.

---

49. Konigsberg v. State Bar of Cal., 366 U.S. 36, 81 S. Ct. 997, 6 L. Ed. 2d 105, 117-18 (1961).

50. Konigsberg v. State Bar of Cal., 366 U.S. 36, 81 S. Ct. 997, 6 L. Ed. 2d 105, 129-30 (1961).

51. In re Anastaplo, 366 U.S. 82, 81 S. Ct. 978, 6 L. Ed. 2d 135, 140 (1961).

Earlier the Supreme Court had ruled that membership in a state bar cannot be arbitrarily denied to anyone.[52] Denying membership in the bar for membership many years ago in some subversive organization or even for being an "inactive" member at the moment is, it is suggested, "arbitrary" and unnecessary to protect either the integrity of the courts or the security of the state.

The Supreme Court held in 1971 that a state could not deny membership in the bar to a person solely because he refused to state whether he had ever been a member of the Communist Party or any organization "that advocates the overthrow of the United States Government by force or violence." The Court stated:

> The First Amendment's protection of association prohibits a State from excluding a person from a profession or punishing him solely because he is a member of a particular organization or because he holds certain beliefs. . . . When a State seeks to inquire about an individual's beliefs and associations a heavy burden lies upon it to show that the inquiry is necessary to protect a legitimate state interest . . . whatever justification may be offered, a State cannot inquire about a man's views or associations solely for the purpose of withholding a right or benefit because of what he believes.[53]

The Court the same year also held that membership in a state bar could not be denied because the applicant had refused to provide a list of all the organizations of which he had been a member since the age of 16. The Court further concluded that a state "may not require an applicant for admission to the Bar to state whether he has been or is a member of any organization which advocates the overthrow of the government of the United States by force."[54] That year, too, the Court indicated that a state can inquire of a bar applicant whether the applicant is or was a knowing, active member of an organization aiming to the overthrow of the government by force with the specific intent to further the illegal aims and methods of the organization. Justices Black, Brennan Douglas and Marshall dis-

---

52. Konigsberg v. State Bar of Cal., 353 U.S. 252, 77 S. Ct. 722, 1 L. Ed. 2d 810 (1957); Schware v. Board of Bar Exam. of State of N.M., 353 U.S. 232, 77 S. Ct. 752, 1 L. Ed. 2d 796, 64 A.L.R.2d 288 (1957).

53. Baird v. State Bar of Arizona, 401 U.S. 1, 91 S. Ct. 719, 27 L. Ed. 2d 639 (1971).

54. Application of Stolar, 401 U.S. 23, 91 S. Ct. 713, 27 L. Ed. 2d 657, 57 Ohio Op. 2d 26 (1971).

sented, primarily on the ground that inquires into beliefs and associations were impermissible in this context.[55]

§ 10.36. —private employment

In 1950 the Supreme Court held in a five-to-three decision that the advantages of the National Labor Relations Act need not be made available to unions whose officers fail to file affidavits that they are not members of the Communist Party. However, the Court divided three-to-three on whether Congress can deny such opportunities when an officer refuses to swear that he does not believe in or support any organization favoring the overthrow of the government by violence. The members of the Court willing to deny such opportunities reasoned that Congress can prevent political strikes in interstate commerce and that such controls have a reasonable relation to this end. Said the Court: "The legislative judgment that interstate commerce must be protected from a continuing threat of such strikes is a permissible one in this case."[56] A short time later the Court was equally divided on the belief section of the Act, this time four-to-four.[57] There has never, therefore, been a majority of the Court that has accepted the argument that a man can be denied his post as a union official because of what he believes.

Fifteen years later the Supreme Court invalidated as a bill of attainder a federal statute making it a crime for a member of the Communist Party to serve as an officer or employee of a labor union. The Solicitor General relied upon the *Douds* precedent but the Court said: "This case is not necessarily controlled by Douds. For to prove its assertion that § 9(h) was preventive rather than retributive in purpose the Court in Douds focused on the fact that members of the Communist Party could escape from the class of persons specified by Congress simply by resigning from the Party. . . . Section 504, unlike § 9(h), disqualifies from the holding of union office not only present members of the Communist Party, but also anyone who has within the past five years been a member of the Party. . . . We think that the Court in Douds misread United States v Lovett when it suggested that that case could be distinguished on the

55. Law Students Civil Rights Research Council, Inc. v. Wadmond, 401 U.S. 154, 91 S. Ct. 720, 27 L. Ed. 2d 749 (1971).

56. American Communications Ass'n, C.I.O., v. Douds, 339 U.S. 382, 70 S. Ct. 674, 94 L. Ed. 925 (1950).

57. Osman v. Douds, 339 U.S. 846, 70 S. Ct. 901, 94 L. Ed. 1328 (1950).

ground that the sanction there imposed was levied for purely retributive reasons."[58]

In 1956 the Supreme Court in *Black v. Cutter Laboratories* ruled that the use of state courts to enforce a "just cause" for firing clause in a contract between an employer and a labor union, permitting the discharge of a worker for Communist Party membership, did not violate the Federal Constitution. Chief Justice Warren, as well as Justices Black and Douglas, dissented on the ground that such state action "violates First Amendment guarantees of citizens who are workers in our industrial plants."[59]

§ 10.37. —tax exemptions

The United States Supreme Court has not yet decided whether states and local governments can deny tax exemptions to individuals deemed subversive while giving such exemptions to others. The Court, however, ruled that California could not place upon the citizen the burden of proving that he was not engaged in subversive advocacy as a condition to receiving a prevalent tax exemption. Said the Court: "We hold that when the constitutional right to speak is sought to be deterred by a state's general taxing program, due process demands that the speech be unencumbered until the state comes forward with sufficient proof to justify its inhibition. The state clearly has no such compelling interests at stake as to justify a short-cut procedure which must inevitably result in suppressing protected speech."[60]

§ 10.38. —citizenship

The Nationality Act of 1940 (§ 305) provided that no person was eligible for naturalization who at any time within 10 years preceding his application had been a member of any organization that advocated the overthrow by force or violence of the government of the United States.

Even under previous acts persons had been denaturalized as a result of subversive associations and activities on the theory that such associations and activities proved that they lacked attachment

---

58. U.S. v. Brown, 381 U.S. 437, 85 S. Ct. 1707, 14 L. Ed. 2d 484 (1965).

59. Black v. Cutter Laboratories, 351 U.S. 292, 76 S. Ct. 824, 100 L. Ed. 1188 (1956).

60. Speiser v. Randall, 357 U.S. 513, 78 S. Ct. 1332, 2 L. Ed. 2d 1460 (1958); First Unitarian Church of Los Angeles v. County of Los Angeles, 357 U.S. 545, 78 S. Ct. 1350, 2 L. Ed. 2d 1484 (1958).

to the principles of the Constitution when they swore allegiance to the United States.[61]

In *Polites v. United States*[62] the Supreme Court sustained the denaturalization of a person who had become a naturalized citizen in 1942 because he had been a member of the Communist Party in the period 1931-1938.

Present law expressly denies citizenship to members of the Communist Party[63] and it can be expected the Supreme Court would uphold its constitutionality.

§ 10.39. —passports

In 1964 the United States Supreme Court held unconstitutional a statute making it a crime for a member of a communist organization to apply for or use a passport after the organization had been ordered to register. The Court found particularly objectionable the fact that the statute was not narrowly drawn, banning travel regardless of the reason or the place. Said the Court:

> It is a familiar and basic principle . . . that a governmental purpose to control or prevent activities constitutionally subject to state regulation may not be achieved by means which sweep unnecessarily broadly and thereby invade the area of protected freedoms.[64]

The Court added:

> The Constitution requires that the powers of government must be so exercised as not, in attaining a permissible end, unduly to infringe a constitutionally protected freedom.[65]

§ 10.40. —public housing

In 1955 the Wisconsin Supreme Court ruled that public housing benefits could not be denied to persons because they were thought to be subversive. Such a denial, said the Court, violated due process of law, since any evil was insubstantial, inasmuch as subversive tenants did not ordinarily endanger housing projects, and was far outweighed

---

61. Cf. Knauer v. U.S., 328 U.S. 654, 66 S. Ct. 1304, 90 L. Ed. 1500 (1946).

62. Polites v. U.S., 364 U.S. 426, 81 S. Ct. 202, 5 L. Ed. 2d 173 (1960).

63. 8 U.S.C.A. § 1424(a).

64. Aptheker v. Secretary of State, 378 U.S. 500, 84 S. Ct. 1659, 12 L. Ed. 2d 992, 998 (1964).

65. Aptheker v. Secretary of State, 378 U.S. 500, 84 S. Ct. 1659, 12 L. Ed. 2d 992, 999 (1964).

by freedom of speech and association.[66] The United States Supreme Court denied certiorari[67] and it is suggested the decision will be followed.

§ 10.41. —radio and television licenses

In 1960 the Court of Appeals for the District of Columbia ruled that an individual could be denied a radio operator's license when he refused to tell the FCC whether he was then or ever had been a member of any organization or group which advocated or taught the overthrow of the government by force or violence. When the applicant argued that such denial violated his First Amendment rights, Judge Prettyman for the Court said:

> We cannot agree. His right to be a licensed radio operator is not unlimited, merely because of the First Amendment. Qualifications of character, reliability and judgment apply. The public interest must be served. . . . An unqualified right to pursue any chosen occupation, merely by reason of the First Amendment, is a wholly untenable proposition. As the Court observed in ACA v. Douds (339 US 382), the Amendment "does not require that he be permitted to be the keeper of the arsenal."[68]

Judge Washington dissented.

In 1969 the Supreme Court, in *Red Lion Broadcasting Co. v. Federal Communications Commission,* sustained part of the fairness doctrine providing that when a broadcaster had carried a program containing "an attack . . . upon the honesty, character, integrity or like personal qualities or an identified person or group" in presenting "views on a controversial issue of public importance," it was necessary to notify the person or group attacked and "offer . . . a reasonable opportunity to respond over the licensee's facilities." The Court ruled, first, that "It does not violate the First Amendment to treat licensees given the privilege of using scarce radio frequencies as proxies for the entire community, obligated to give suitable time and attention to matters of great public concern." In balancing interests, the Court ruled that public interest and the interests of victims far outweighed any interests of the broadcasters. The Court stated: "It

---

66. Lawson v. Housing Authority of City of Milwaukee, 270 Wis. 269, 70 N.W.2d 605 (1955) (noted in 69 Harv L Rev 551 (1956)).

67. Housing Authority of City of Milwaukee v. Lawson, 350 U.S. 882, 76 S. Ct. 135, 100 L. Ed. 778 (1955).

68. Borrow v. F. C. C., 109 U.S. App. D.C. 224, 285 F.2d 666, 670 (D.C. Cir. 1960).

is the right of the viewers and listeners, not the right of the broadcasters which is paramount. . . . It is the right of the public to receive suitable access to social, political, aesthetic, moral, and other ideas and experiences which is crucial here." The Court added: "Nor can we say that it is inconsistent with the First Amendment goal of producing an informed public capable of conducting its own affairs to require a broadcaster to permit answers to personal attacks occurring in the course of discussing controversial issues, or to require that the political opponents of those endorsed by the station be given a chance to communicate with the public."[69]

Four years later, the Court ruled, first, that the Columbia Broadcasting System, even as a government licensee, was not engaged in governmental action to bring it within the First Amendment. Then the Court held that CBS was not required by the First Amendment to accept editorial advertisements, stating generally that the Amendment does not require the Federal Communications Commission to mandate a private right of access to the broadcast media. In dissent Justices Brennan and Marshall pointed out that the holding of the Court meant that broadcasters can now refuse absolutely to sell any part of their time to groups or individuals wishing to speak on controversial issues of public importance. They suggested that the majority was balancing the right of the media against "the people's right to engage in and hear vigorous public debate," and they soundly advised that "a proper balancing of the competing First Amendment interests at stake in this controversy must consider not only the interests of broadcasters and of the listening and viewing public, but also the independent First Amendment interest of groups and individual in effective self-expression."[70]

---

69. Red Lion Broadcasting Co. v. F. C. C., 395 U.S. 367, 89 S. Ct. 1794, 23 L. Ed. 2d 371, 389-90 (1969).

70. Columbia Broadcasting System, Inc. v. Democratic Nat. Committee, 412 U.S. 94, 93 S. Ct. 2080, 36 L. Ed. 2d 772, 783, 823 (1973).

CHAPTER ELEVEN

Society's Interest in Safeguarding the Integrity of the Judicial Process

---

§ 11.00. Utterances in the courtroom

Utterances in the courtroom while the court is in session can be punished when they interfere with the effective and impartial administration of justice. Traditionally, courts have been able to summarily place in contempt those who spoke contumaciously or obstreperously in open court, whether they be laymen or lawyers. In the leading case, *Fisher v. Pace,* the United States Supreme Court stated:

> Historically and rationally the inherent power of courts to punish contempts in the face of the court without further proof of facts and without aid of jury is not open to question. This attribute of courts is essential to preserve their authority and to prevent the administration of justice from falling into disrepute. Such summary conviction and punishment accords due process of law.[1]

This was a five-to-four decision with Justices Black, Douglas, Murphy and Rutledge dissenting. It is suggested that the decision and the traditional rule are wrong. The judicial process can be adequately protected by ordering the removal from the courtroom of a person who seems to the judge to be contumacious. Sound constitutional law requires that a trial resulting in deprivation of liberty must be conducted before an impartial judge with full opportunity for the

---

1. Fisher v. Pace, 336 U.S. 155, 69 S. Ct. 425, 427, 93 L. Ed. 569, 572-73 (1949).

accused to cross-examine the judge who initiated the complaint. Furthermore, there must be a decent specification of charges and time for the accused to prepare his defense. Additionally, to the extent the right to a jury trial prevails in federal courts under the Constitution, one faced with imprisonment for contempt of court must be accorded a trial before a jury of his peers.

In 1965, where an alleged contempt occurred in open court before a state trial judge, the Supreme Court reversed the contempt, with Justice Black stating for the Court: "It is settled that due process and the Sixth Amendment guarantee a defendant charged with contempt such as this an opportunity to be heard in his defense—a right to his day in court—and to be represented by counsel." The Court further ruled that a contempt of court ruling violates due process of law when it is not justified by the evidence.[2]

The Supreme Court in 1974 set aside a contempt conviction of a man who, in a prosecution for violating an ordinance, referred to the person who allegedly assaulted him as "chicken shit."[3]

The taking of photographs by members of the press in a courtroom presents another aspect of the clash between freedom of communication and the interest in the fair, impartial, and efficient administration of justice. The courts have customarily sustained bans upon the use of cameras in courtrooms. In so ruling, a federal court has stated:

> When particular conduct is regulated in the interest of public order, and the regulation results in an indirect, conditional, partial abridgement [of freedom of the press] the duty of the courts is to determine which of these two conflicting interests demands the greater protection under the circumstances presented . . . the court order as it relates to the ban on taking photographs within the court room is reasonable and proper and geared to achieve dignity and decorum in the court room and is not an unreasonable impingement upon free speech.[4]

Similarly, in sustaining a ban upon photographers in the courtroom, the Supreme Court of Ohio has stated that the interest in freedom of the press must be weighed with society's interest in the administration of justice. The Court concluded: "A court in enforcing reasonable courtroom decorum is preserving the constitu-

---

2. Holt v. Virginia, 381 U.S. 131, 85 S. Ct. 1375, 1378, 14 L. Ed. 2d 290 (1965).

3. Eaton v. City of Tulsa, 415 U.S. 697, 94 S. Ct. 1228, 39 L. Ed. 2d 693 (1974).

4. Tribune Review Pub. Co. v. Thomas, 254 F.2d 883 (3d Cir. 1958).

tional and unalienable right of a litigant to a fair trial, and in preserving such right, the court does not interfere with the freedom of the press."[5]

At times individuals have distributed literature in a courtroom. In one such case an Illinois appellate court concluded that the clashing interests here were to be resolved by application of the clear and present danger test.[6]

§ 11.01. Opportunity of citizens and press to observe judicial proceedings

In 1979 the Supreme Court, in a five-to-four decision, held that members of the public and the press do not have an independent constitutional right to insist upon access to pre-trial judicial proceedings, where the prosecutor, the accused, and the trial judge have agreed to close the proceedings in an effort to have a fair trial. The Supreme Court stated:

> To safeguard the due process rights of the accused, a trial judge has an affirmative constitutional right to minimize the effects of prejudicial pre-trial publicity. And because of the Constitution's pervasive concern for these due process rights, a trial judge may surely take protective measures even when they are not strictly and inescapably necessary.

Justices Blackmun, Brennan, White and Marshall in their concurring/dissenting opinion emphasized that "there is a societal interest in the public trial," and then remarked: "The important interests of the public and the press [as a part of the public] in open judicial proceedings are [here] rejected and cast aside as of little value or significance."[7]

The following year, in an opinion of Chief Justice Burger, joined only by Justices White and Stevens, the Supreme Court held that the right to attend criminal trials is implicit in the guarantees of the First Amendment and must prevail "absent an overriding interest, articulated in findings." Justice Brennan in a concurring opinion, developed at length why "the conduct of the trial is preeminently a

---

5. State v. Clifford, 162 Ohio St. 370, 55 Ohio Op. 217, 123 N.E.2d 8 (1954).

6. People v. Smith, 329 Ill. App. 442, 69 N.E.2d 27 (1st Dist. 1946) (abstract).

7. Gannett Co., Inc. v. DePasquale, 443 U.S. 368, 99 S. Ct. 2898, 61 L. Ed. 2d 608 (1979).

matter of public interest." The only dissent was by Justice Rehnquist.[8]

In 1984, the Court again recognized the open trial requirement, without clearly stating its basis, but Justice Stevens in his concurring opinion attributed to the First Amendment the requirement of an open trial in its application to the voir dire examination of potential jurors.[9]

The First Amendment right of access to criminal proceedings extends to preliminary hearings as conducted in California, since the Supreme Court saw them as "often the final and most important step in the criminal proceeding." The Court has held that "the proceedings cannot be closed unless specific, on the record, findings are made demonstrating that closure is essential to preserve higher values and is narrowly tailored to serve that interest." A party seeking closure is required to show a substantial probability that the defendant's rights to a fair trial will be denied by publicity that closure would prevent and that reasonable alternatives to closure cannot adequately protect the defendant's rights.[10]

In 1993, in a suit brought by a reporter, the Supreme Court voided the Puerto Rico rule of criminal procedure which provided that the preliminary hearing "shall be held privately" unless the defendant requests otherwise. The Court recognized the legitimate concern that a defendant's fair trial rights may at times be prejudiced by open hearings, but ruled that this concern must be addressed on a case-by-case basis.[11]

§ 11.02. Communicative acts near courthouses

In 1965 the United States Supreme Court indicated that it considered constitutional a Louisiana statute providing for the criminal punishment of anyone whoever, "with the intent of interfering with, obstructing, or impeding the administration of justice, or with the intent of influencing any judge, juror, witness or court officer, in the discharge of his duty pickets or parades in or near a building housing a court of the State of Louisiana." In the *Cox* case, the conviction on this count was set aside only because the chief of

---

8. Richmond Newspapers, Inc. v. Virginia, 448 U.S. 555, 100 S. Ct. 2814, 65 L. Ed. 2d 973 (1980).

9. Press-Enterprise Co. v. Superior Court of California, Riverside County, 464 U.S. 501, 104 S. Ct. 819, 78 L. Ed. 2d 629 (1984).

10. Press-Enterprise Co. v. Superior Court of California for Riverside County, 478 U.S. 1, 106 S. Ct. 2735, 92 L. Ed. 2d 1 (1986).

11. El Vocero de Puerto Rico (Caribbean Intern. News Corp.) v. Puerto Rico, 508 U.S. 147, 113 S. Ct. 2004, 124 L. Ed. 2d 60 (1993).

police had indicated to the paraders that they could legally demonstrate a short distance from the courthouse. Justice Black dissented and would have affirmed the conviction on this count. He stated: "But the history of the past twenty-five years if it shows nothing else show that [minority groups'] constitutional and statutory rights have to be protected by the courts, which must be kept free from intimidation and coercive pressures of any kind. Government under law as ordained by our Constitution is too precious, too sacred, to be jeopardized by subjecting the courts to intimidatory practices that have been fatal to individual liberty and minority rights wherever and whenever such practices have been allowed to poison the streams of justice."[12]

§ 11.03. Speaking and printing out of court about judicial proceedings

On a number of occasions the United States Supreme Court has ruled that editors and others who write outside of court about judicial proceedings cannot be punished without proof that their publications created a clear and present danger to the fair and effective administration of justice.[13] In the *Bridges* case, the Court described the standard as "a working principle that the substantive evil must be extremely serious and the degree of imminence extremely high before utterances can be punished."[14] Again, in *Craig v. Harney,* the Court said that to justify contempt of court or any other sanctions the writing or speech "must constitute an imminent, not merely a likely, threat to the administration of justice. The danger must not be remote or even probable; it must immediately imperil."[15]

In 1962, in *Wood v. Georgia,* the Supreme Court said that "the content of petitioner's statements and the circumstances under which they were published leads us to conclude that they did not present a danger to the administration of justice that should vitiate his freedom to express his opinions in the manner chosen." The Court added:

> Men are entitled to speak as they please on matters vital to them; errors in judgment or unsubstantiated opinions may be

12. Cox v. State of Louisiana, 379 U.S. 536, 85 S. Ct. 466, 13 L. Ed. 2d 487 (1965).

13. Pennekamp v. State of Fla., 328 U.S. 331, 66 S. Ct. 1029, 90 L. Ed. 1295 (1946), and see cases following.

14. Bridges v. State of Cal., 314 U.S. 252, 62 S. Ct. 190, 194, 86 L. Ed. 192, 203-04, 159 A.L.R. 1346 (1941).

15. Craig v. Harney, 331 U.S. 367, 67 S. Ct. 1249, 1255, 91 L. Ed. 1546, 1552 (1947).

exposed, of course, but not through punishment for contempt for the expression. Under our system of government, counter argument and education are the weapons available to expose these matters, not abridgement of the rights of free speech and assembly.[16]

Significantly, in 1966 and again in 1972 the Supreme Court remarked that "the trial court might well have proscribed extrajudicial statements by any lawyer, party, witness, or court official which divulged prejudicial matters."[17]

Four years later the Court held that the First Amendment prohibits a court from enjoining the press in advance of publication from reporting or commenting on information acquired from public court proceedings, public court records, or other sources about pending judicial proceedings, including criminal prosecutions.[18] Comparably, two years later, the Court ruled that a state may not subject persons, including newspapers, to criminal sanctions for divulging information regarding proceedings before a state judicial review commission which is authorized to hear complaints as to judges' disability or misconduct, even though such proceedings are declared confidential by state constitution or statute.[19]

However, in 1984 the Court decided that the First Amendment does not prevent a trial court from issuing a protective order against a newspaper to prevent it using before trial material it secures by discovery in a trial in which it is involved, so long as the protective order furthers a substantial and important societal interest unrelated to suppression of expression and is no greater than necessary to protect that interest.[20]

Observing significantly that "publication of information relating to alleged governmental misconduct [is] speech which has traditionally been recognized as lying at the core of the First Amendment," the Supreme Court in 1990 held violative of the First Amendment a state statute prohibiting a grand jury witness who was a reporter

---

16. Wood v. Georgia, 370 U.S. 375, 82 S. Ct. 1364, 1372, 8 L. Ed. 2d 569 (1962).

17. Sheppard v. Maxwell, 384 U.S. 333, 86 S. Ct. 1507, 16 L. Ed. 2d 600, 6 Ohio Misc. 231, 35 Ohio Op. 2d 431 (1966); Branzburg v. Hayes, 408 U.S. 665, 92 S. Ct. 2646, 33 L. Ed. 2d 626 (1972).

18. Nebraska Press Ass'n v. Stuart, 427 U.S. 539, 96 S. Ct. 2791, 49 L. Ed. 2d 683 (1976).

19. Landmark Communications, Inc. v. Virginia, 435 U.S. 829, 98 S. Ct. 1535, 56 L. Ed. 2d 1 (1978).

20. Seattle Times Co. v. Rhinehart, 467 U.S. 20, 104 S. Ct. 2199, 81 L. Ed. 2d 17 (1984).

from disclosing his own testimony after the term of the grand jury had ended.[21]

§ 11.04. Lawyers' activities and inactivities

At times certain practices attributed to various lawyers, such as "ambulance chasing" and the like, have been deemed serious interferences with society's interest in the fair, efficient and orderly administration of justice.

In 1961 the United States Supreme Court sustained, five-to-four, a disciplinary proceeding by New York against a lawyer who, relying on his state privilege against self-incrimination, refused to answer material questions of a duly authorized investigating authority relating to alleged professional misconduct. Said the Court:

> History and policy combine to establish the presence of a substantial state interest in conducting an investigation of this kind. That interest is nothing less than the exertion of disciplinary powers which English and American courts . . . have for centuries possessed over members of the bar, incident to their broader responsibility for keeping the administration of justice and the standards of professional conduct unsullied.[22]

This case was overruled in 1967, the Court holding that the self-incrimination clause of the Fifth Amendment extends its protection to lawyers, forbidding the imposition of the sanction of disbarment as a penalty for claiming the privilege.[23]

In 1963 the Supreme Court recognized that a state has a legitimate interest in preventing barratry, maintenance, and champerty, but ruled that Virginia could not on the facts punish lawyers for the National Association for the Advancement of Colored People. Said the Court:

> We hold that the activities of the NAACP, its affiliates and legal staff shown on this record are modes of expression and association protected by the First and Fourteenth Amendments which Virginia may not prohibit, under its power to regulate

21. Butterworth v. Smith, 494 U.S. 624, 110 S. Ct. 1376, 108 L. Ed. 2d 572 (1990).

22. Cohen v. Hurley, 366 U.S. 117, 81 S. Ct. 954, 958, 6 L. Ed. 2d 156 (1961) (overruled in part by, Spevack v. Klein, 385 U.S. 511, 87 S. Ct. 625, 17 L. Ed. 2d 574 (1967)).

23. Spevack v. Klein, 385 U.S. 511, 87 S. Ct. 625, 17 L. Ed. 2d 574 (1967).

the legal profession, as improper solicitation of legal business.
. . .[24]

According to the Supreme Court, the Virginia courts had
construed the local statute so that "a person who advises another
that his legal rights have been infringed and refers him to a
particular attorney or group of attorneys . . . for assistance has
committed a crime, as has the attorney who knowingly renders assistance under such circumstances." The Court observed: "There
thus inheres in the statute the gravest danger of smothering all
discussion looking to the eventual institution of litigation on behalf
of the rights of members of an unpopular minority."[25]

In 1964 the Court ruled that lawyers accepting employment under
the plan in use by the Brotherhood of Railroad Trainmen had a
constitutional protection which the state of Virginia could not
abridge. Under the Brotherhood's plan, a secretary of the local
would advise an injured worker or his family to rely upon the
services of a lawyer or firm in the region who had a reputation for
honesty and skill in representing plaintiffs in railroad personal injury
litigation. The Court ruled that the First Amendment rights of free
speech and assembly give members of a labor union or other group
the right "to advice concerning the need for legal assistance—and,
most importantly, what lawyer a member could confidently rely
on." The Court added:

> Virginia undoubtedly has broad powers to regulate the practice
> of law within its borders; but we have had occasion in the past
> to recognize that in regulating the practice of law a State can-
> not ignore the rights of individuals secured by the Constitution.
> . . . A State could not, by invoking the power to regulate the
> professional conduct of attorneys, infringe in any way the right
> of individuals and the public to be fairly represented in lawsuits
> authorized by Congress to effectuate a basic public interest.[26]

The Court held in 1971 that the Brotherhood of Railroad Trainmen could operate a program to protect its members from excessive
fees and incompetent attorneys, by recommending selected attorneys
to its members and their families under contracts limiting attorneys'

---

24. National Ass'n for Advancement of Colored People v. Button, 371 U.S.
415, 83 S. Ct. 328, 335, 9 L. Ed. 2d 405 (1963).

25. National Ass'n for Advancement of Colored People v. Button, 371 U.S.
415, 83 S. Ct. 328, 338, 9 L. Ed. 2d 405 (1963).

26. Brotherhood of R. R. Trainmen v. Virginia ex rel. Va. State Bar, 377 U.S.
1, 84 S. Ct. 1113, 1116-17, 12 L. Ed. 2d 89, 27 Ohio Op. 2d 365, 94 Ohio L. Abs.
33, 11 A.L.R.3d 1196 (1964).

fees to 25%, applicable to suits arising under the Federal Employees Liability Act. The Court ruled that the Union could communicate information about an injured member to the attorney, that the Union could transport an injured member to the attorney's office, and that the Union could protect its members against excessive legal fees.[27]

Seven years later the Court recognized that an attorney working with the American Civil Liberties Union had constitutional rights of association and expression and held that, absent a clear showing that significant state interests were jeopardized, a state may not punish such lawyer for advising a lay person of her legal rights and disclosing later in a letter that free legal assistance is available to her through a non-profit legal organization with which the lawyer is associated.[28] However, the same year, the Court held that a state can punish in-person solicitation by a lawyer, without violating the First Amendment.[29]

The Supreme Court reached the problem of advertising by lawyers in 1982 and decided that the First Amendment prohibits a state bar from banning non-misleading advertising by lawyers showing their specializations and listing the jurisdictions in which they were licensed to practice.[30] Three years later the Court again stated generally that commercial speech that is not false or deceptive and does not concern unlawful activities may be restricted only in the service of a substantial interest, and only through means that directly advance that interest. Finding no substantial interest to limit advertising by lawyers, the Court voided disciplinary action by a state against an attorney who had used newspaper advertising, and found equally wanting a ban upon the use of illustrations in such advertising by lawyers. However, the Court sustained application of a requirement that an attorney advertising his availability on a contingent-fee basis disclose that clients will have to pay costs if their lawsuits are unsuccessful. It is sufficient, said the Court, that "disclosure requirements are reasonably related to the State's interest in preventing deception of consumers."[31]

The Court reaffirmed in 1988 that lawyer advertising is in the category of constitutionally protected commercial speech, and voided

27. United Transp. Union v. State Bar of Mich., 401 U.S. 576, 91 S. Ct. 1076, 28 L. Ed. 2d 339 (1971).

28. In re Primus, 436 U.S. 412, 98 S. Ct. 1893, 56 L. Ed. 2d 417 (1978).

29. Ohralik v. Ohio State Bar Ass'n, 436 U.S. 447, 98 S. Ct. 1912, 56 L. Ed. 2d 444 (1978).

30. In re R. M. J., 455 U.S. 191, 102 S. Ct. 929, 71 L. Ed. 2d 64 (1982).

31. Zauderer v. Office of Disciplinary Counsel of Supreme Court of Ohio, 471 U.S. 626, 105 S. Ct. 2265, 85 L. Ed. 2d 652 (1985).

a state ban upon lawyers soliciting legal business for pecuniary gain by sending truthful and non-deceptive letters to potential clients known to face particular legal problems. The Court stated that such targeted, direct-mail solicitation generally poses much less risk of over-reaching or undue influence than does in-person solicitation. In dissent, Justices O'Connor, Rehnquist and Scalia indicated that they would uphold any control on lawyer advertising that is "potentially or demonstrably misleading."[32]

Two years later the Court held that the First Amendment prevents a state from disciplining an attorney for stating on his letterhead that he is certified as a civil trial specialist by the National Board of Trial Advocacy. So long as such conduct is not misleading, it is held to serve the public interest and is protected. With Justices White, O'Connor, Scalia and Chief Justice Rehnquist dissenting, particular attention should be paid to the concurring opinion of Justices Marshall and Brennan that the state should be able to enact regulations other than total bans to ensure that the public is not misled by this type of communication.[33]

The Supreme Court in 1995 found (1) a substantial public interest, (2) a restriction that directly and materially advanced that interest, and (3) a regulation that was narrowly drawn, and accordingly sustained a Florida Bar rule prohibiting lawyers from direct-mail solicitation to victims of accidents and their relatives for 30 days following an accident or disaster. Noting that members of the bar have many other ways of informing the public of their talents, the Court held that protection of individual's privacy, as well as prevention of outrage and irritation with the state-licensed legal profession, amply justified the rule. Justices Souter, Ginsburg and Stevens dissented, viewing the claimed state's interests as insubstantial and reminding their colleagues that restrictions on communication are not justified on the ground that the message might offend the recipient. They emphasized that injured persons should have an early opportunity to gather information while it is fresh and should be advised not to enter into discussions with investigators for those with likely tort responsibility. The dissenters wrote: "Obscuring the legal profession from public discussion through direct-mail solicitation at the expense

---

32. Shapero v. Kentucky Bar Ass'n, 486 U.S. 466, 108 S. Ct. 1916, 100 L. Ed. 2d 475 (1988).

33. Peel v. Attorney Registration and Disciplinary Com'n of Illinois, 496 U.S. 91, 110 S. Ct. 2281, 110 L. Ed. 2d 83 (1990).

of the least sophisticated members of society is not a laudable constitutional goal."[34]

Compulsory state bar dues can only be used by the bar authorities when "acting essentially as professional advisors to those charged with the regulation of the legal profession. They cannot be used to promote political and ideological causes disfavored by individual members."[35]

---

34. Florida Bar v. Went for It, Inc., 515 U.S. 618, 115 S. Ct. 2371, 132 L. Ed. 2d 541 (1995).

35. Keller v. State Bar of California, 496 U.S. 1, 110 S. Ct. 2228, 110 L. Ed. 2d 1 (1990).

CHAPTER TWELVE

Safeguarding the Electoral Process

---

§ 12.00. Controlling contributions and expenditures seeking to control elections

The United States Supreme Court in 1957 was faced with the question whether Congress could constitutionally prohibit labor organizations, among others, from making a contribution or expenditure in connection with any election for federal office. Justice Frankfurter spoke for the Court as follows:

> What is involved here is the integrity of our electoral process, and not less, the responsibility of the individual citizen for the successful functioning of that process. This case thus raises issues not less than basic to a democratic society.

The Court ruled that it would not pass upon the constitutionality of the statute's application to labor unions at that time, but told the district court that it had erred in dismissing the indictment which charged a union-sponsored political broadcast endorsing the selection of certain candidates for the Congress of the United States. In dissent, Justice Douglas, joined by the Chief Justice and Justice Black, thought the statute was an "assault on the freedom of political expression guaranteed by the First Amendment."[1] In the *UAW* case the Court distinguished the earlier case of *United States v. C.I.O* wherein it had held that under the statute a labor organization was not punishable for distributing only to union members or

---

1. U.S. v. International Union United Auto., Aircraft and Agr. Implement Workers of America (UAW-CIO), 352 U.S. 567, 77 S. Ct. 529, 1 L. Ed. 2d 563, 566 (1957).

purchasers an issue of the "CIO News."[2] The Court made it clear in the *UAW* case that "the evil at which Congress struck [by the statute] is the use of corporate or union dues to influence the public at large to vote for a particular candidate or a particular party."[3]

Although contributions by groups organized by corporations and labor unions were not restricted by a specific statute that was before the Court in 1981, the Court held that Congress could limit the amount an unincorporated association may contribute to a multi-candidate political commission without violating either the First Amendment or the equal protection concept embraced in the Fifth Amendment.[4]

Later the same year the Court held unconstitutional as violative of the First Amendment an ordinance limiting contributions to committees formed to oppose ballot measures to $250. The California Supreme Court had held sufficient the interest to prevent corruption of the initiative process by spending large amounts, but the Court stated: "there is no significant state or public interest in curtailing debate and discussion of a ballot measure" and held that the ordinance "does not advance a legitimate governmental interest significant enough to justify its infringement on First Amendment rights."[5]

The Supreme Court in 1976, in the case of *Buckley v. Valeo,* had sustained a federal statutory limit of $1,000 on individual contributions to any single candidate for an elected federal office. It had also upheld a limit of $5,000 on contributions by political committees (groups registered for six months) to any one candidate, as well as a provision requiring all citizens who contributed over $100 annually to a candidate for federal office or a political committee to report this to a federal agency. The Court additionally accepted the constitutionality of federal funding for candidates in federal elections. In passing upon limitations on contributions, the Court stated that this was "a constitutionally acceptable accommodation of Congress' valid interest in encouraging citizen participation in political campaigns while continuing to guard against the corrupting

---

2. U.S. v. Congress of Indus. Organizations, 335 U.S. 106, 68 S. Ct. 1349, 92 L. Ed. 1849 (1948).

3. U.S. v. International Union United Auto., Aircraft and Agr. Implement Workers of America (UAW-CIO), 352 U.S. 567, 77 S. Ct. 529, 1 L. Ed. 2d 563, 576 (1957).

4. California Med. Ass'n v. Federal Elec. Com'n, 453 U.S. 182, 101 S. Ct. 2712, 69 L. Ed. 2d 567 (1981).

5. Citizens Against Rent Control/Coalition for Fair Housing v. City of Berkeley, Cal., 454 U.S. 290, 102 S. Ct. 434, 70 L. Ed. 2d 492 (1981).

potential of large financial contributions to candidates." So much for the Court's good behavior; now for its bad and sad. The Court branded as unconstitutional under the First Amendment the statutory limitation of $1,000 on independent *expenditures* by an individual or group advocating the election or defeat of a clearly identified candidate for federal office, and further voided limits on expenditures from personal and family resources by such candidates, in the amount of $35,000 for candidates for the Senate and $25,000 for candidates for the House.[6] The five Justices who agreed in the opinion for the Court in effect constitutionalized a right to spend, where previously had been enshrined a right of speech—replacing democratic values with plutocratic concerns. With only the rarest exceptions, candidates for the Senate must be millionaires themselves or be willingly indebted to persons and corporations, and the same is virtually applicable to candidates for the House. Transforming the "speech" right of the First Amendment to a "spending" right is a transmogrification without any precedent in constitutional construction, and it must be rectified. One more word about the Court's behavior in *Buckley v. Valeo*: the Justices who posited Congressional power upon the "general welfare" clause of the Preamble to the Constitution surely should have been aware that no worthy scholar has ever accepted as legitimate the use of the Preamble to expand federal Congressional powers. If Congress has all power to do what it believes is for "the general welfare," the federal government is one of virtually unlimited powers.

Two years later, a five-to-four Supreme Court decision invalidated, in the name of the First Amendment, a state criminal statute forbidding banks and business corporations from spending for the purpose of influencing voting on referendum proposals that did not directly affect their businesses. Justices Brennan, Marshall and White in their dissent stated that the government has a legitimate interest in preventing corporate domination of the electoral process, as well as in protecting minority stockholders from having to finance political causes with which they disagree. Interesting, too, is the fact that Justice Rehnquist also dissented.[7]

In 1985 the Court held unconstitutional as violative of the First Amendment a section of the federal Presidential Election Campaign Act making it a criminal offense for independent political action committees to spend more than $1,000 to further the candidacy of a presidential candidate. The Court repeated that preventing corrup-

---

6. Buckley v. Valeo, 424 U.S. 1, 96 S. Ct. 612, 46 L. Ed. 2d 659 (1976).

7. First Nat. Bank of Boston v. Bellotti, 435 U.S. 765, 98 S. Ct. 1407, 55 L. Ed. 2d 707 (1978).

tion and the appearance of corruption are legitimate and compelling governmental interests identified with the restriction of campaign finances, but the Court believed that any exchange of political favors for such expenditures "remains a hypothetical possibility and nothing more." The Court repeated that its standard of review when the First Amendment is involved is "rigorous."[8]

The next year the Court held that the First Amendment required the invalidation of a federal ban on corporate election expenditures in its application to a non-profit corporation financing such expenditures from its general treasury. Remarking that "the government enjoys greater latitude in limiting contributions than in regulating independent expenditures," the Court ruled that where the corporation was formed for the express purpose of promoting political ideas and cannot engage in business activities, where it had no shareholders or other persons affiliated who might have a claim on its assets or earnings, and where it had the policy of refusing to accept funds from business corporations or labor unions, it could not be subjected to the federal government's regulation of its spending, which was shown to have a practical effect of discouraging expression.[9]

In 1990, however, the Supreme Court held valid a state statute prohibiting corporations, including non-profit ones, from making independent expenditures in connection with state candidate elections. Acknowledging that such statutes stifle corporate "speech," and that they must be justified by a compelling state interest, the Court concluded that a compelling interest exists when "the unique state-conferred corporate structure" allows "corporate wealth [to] unfairly influence elections when it is deployed in the form of independent expenditures." The Court ruled that the statute was precisely tailored, since it did not prevent corporations from making independent political expenditures through separate segregated funds, where persons contributing to such funds know their moneys would be used for a political purpose. The Court emphasized that here, unlike in *FEC v. Massachusetts Citizens for Life,* the protesting chamber of commerce was not formed primarily to express political ideas, its members would be reluctant to withdraw even if they disagreed strongly with the chamber's political spending, and the chamber of commerce could too easily be a conduit for expenditures from for-profit organizations. The Court further held equal protec-

---

8. Federal Election Com'n v. National Conservative Political Action Committee, 470 U.S. 480, 105 S. Ct. 1459, 84 L. Ed. 2d 455 (1985).

9. Federal Election Com'n v. Massachusetts Citizens for Life, Inc., 479 U.S. 238, 107 S. Ct. 616, 93 L. Ed. 2d 539 (1986).

tion was not violated by exempting media corporations from the statute, finding a compelling reason in the press' unique role in disseminating information to the public.

In the same case, the Court further ruled that the statute did not suffer from impermissible underinclusiveness by not imposing a similar ban upon unincorporated labor unions, since the latter may not constitutionally compel employees to support union political activities unrelated to job welfare, and since organizations possessing "the significant state-conferred advantages of the corporate structure" have "unique advantages" in disturbing the sanctity of the electoral process. In a dissenting opinion by Justice Kennedy, joined by Justices O'Connor and Scalia, it was indicated that the state failed to demonstrate a compelling interest to support its speech restriction, and that it could not show that the law was narrowly tailored to the purported statutory end. Nor could they agree with the validity of the media exemption or the majority's finding on underinclusiveness. In a separate dissenting opinion, Justice Scalia saw the majority as "endorsing the principle that too much speech is an evil that the democratic majority can proscribe," and he indicated his belief that any attempt by government to secure a "balanced presentation" of election issues by regulation of political speech "for fairness sake" should always be unconstitutional under the First Amendment.[10]

The Supreme Court has said that "in certain circumstances the balance of interests requires exempting minority political parties from disclosures," and it has held that a state cannot compel a minority party to disclose the names and addresses of campaign contributors and recipients of campaign disbursements where there is a "reasonable probability" this would subject them to "threats, harassment or reprisals."[11]

The Court, in an opinion by Justice Breyer joined by Justices O'Connor and Souter, ruled in 1996 that the First Amendment prohibits application of federal statutes punishing disbursement of funds by political parties for election purposes, when they are only expenditures made by a party "independently" and without "coordination" with any candidate. The facts in the case were that the Colorado Republican Party had spent funds attacking a Democratic candidate for the United States Senate, at a time when no candidate had yet been chosen by the Republican Party for that

---

10. Austin v. Michigan Chamber of Commerce, 494 U.S. 652, 110 S. Ct. 1391, 108 L. Ed. 2d 652 (1990).

11. Brown v. Socialist Workers '74 Campaign Committee (Ohio), 459 U.S. 87, 103 S. Ct. 416, 74 L. Ed. 2d 250 (1982).

office. Such facts, concluded these three Justices, showed no "coordinated" payment for a particular individual that could be construed as a "contribution." On this, there were concurring opinions by Chief Justice Rehnquist, as well as Justices Kennedy, Scalia and Thomas. In a separate opinion by Justice Kennedy, joined by the Chief Justice and Justice Scalia, it was said that "Congress may have authority, consistent with the First Amendment, to restrict undifferentiated political party contributions," but that this type of regulation was not at issue in the instant case. In another concurring opinion by Justice Thomas, joined by the Chief Justice and Justice Scalia, it was stated generally that even "coordinated" contributions by political parties should be constitutionally protected under the First Amendment. In dissent, Justices Stevens and Ginsburg urged that all money spent by a political party to secure the election of a candidate for the United States Senate could be deemed "contributions" and, as such, subject to control by Congress. They explained that "the Government has an important interest in levelling the electoral playing field by constraining the cost of federal campaigns."[12]

Warning that monies could not be spent for "ideological activities" unrelated to collective bargaining, such as political activity, the Supreme Court has sustained a state law authorizing public school teachers who were non-union members, to make payments to the union representing teachers a service fee equal to union dues.[13]

§ 12.01. Ballot provisions

In voiding Ohio election laws making it virtually impossible for third parties to secure a place on ballots, the United States Supreme Court in 1968 told of "the right of individuals to associate for the advancement of political beliefs" as "among our most precious freedoms," and indicated that state controls upon access to the ballot will be invalidated where a state fails "to show any 'compelling interest' which justifies imposing such heavy burdens on the right to vote and associate."[14]

However, three years later, the Court sustained a Georgia ballot position requirement that third-party candidates secure signatures of at least five percent of the voters, finding no denial of the First

---

12. Colorado Republican Federal Campaign Committee v. Federal Election Com'n, 116 S. Ct. 2309, 135 L. Ed. 2d 795 (U.S. 1996).

13. Abood v. Detroit Bd. of Ed., 431 U.S. 209, 97 S. Ct. 1782, 52 L. Ed. 2d 261 (1977).

14. Williams v. Rhodes, 393 U.S. 23, 89 S. Ct. 5, 21 L. Ed. 2d 24, 45 Ohio Op. 2d 236 (1968).

Amendment right of free association, when the record in the case revealed that independents had successfully conformed to the procedure in the past, and that the election laws imposed none of the voided Ohio system's restrictions on the free circulation of nominating petitions, permitting all voters to sign as many as they might wish without being committed to vote for the candidate and without losing the right to participate in their party's primary. Satisfied that, unlike the Ohio situation, "the open quality of the Georgia system is far from theoretical," the Court then found compelling the "state interest in requiring some preliminary showing [to avoid] confusion, deception and even frustration of the democratic process at the general election."[15]

In 1983 the Court recognized that freedom of association is impacted by laws limiting the place of independent parties on the ballot and voided a requirement for filing by March 31 for a place on a November ballot. The Court indicated its awareness that "as a practical matter, there must be a substantial regulation of elections if they are to be fair and honest," adding that "the states' important regulatory interests are generally sufficient to justify reasonable, non-discriminatory restrictions."[16]

Freedom of association being protected by the Fourteenth Amendment against action by the states, the Supreme Court in 1992 held unconstitutional a state statute providing that when a subdivision of a state, such as a county, comprises several large separate districts from which officers are elected, persons seeking to organize political parties to run in the county or other political subdivision must collect 25,000 signatures from each of the districts. The state courts had held that in a county with an urban and a suburban district, that failure to procure enough signatures from the suburban district disqualified candidates from the proposed political party. The Supreme Court repeated that when a state attempts to limit the access of new parties to the ballot, it must be prepared to show an "interest sufficiently weighty to justify the limitation," plus proof that the statute is "narrowly drawn to advance a state interest of compelling importance." The statute at issue, ruled the Court, swept broader than necessary to advance the state interest in electoral order.[17]

In 1997 the Supreme Court held not violative of the First Amendment a state law prohibiting a candidate from appearing on the bal-

15. Jenness v. Fortson, 403 U.S. 431, 91 S. Ct. 1970, 29 L. Ed. 2d 554 (1971).

16. Anderson v. Celebrezze, 460 U.S. 780, 103 S. Ct. 1564, 75 L. Ed. 2d 547 (1983).

17. Norman v. Reed, 502 U.S. 279, 112 S. Ct. 698, 116 L. Ed. 2d 711 (1992).

lot as the candidate of more than one party. The Court readily acknowledged that "the First Amendment protects the right of citizens to associate and to form political parties for the advancement of common political goals and ideas" and it is "also clear States may, and inevitably must, enact *reasonable* regulations for parties, elections and ballots to reduce election- and campaign-related disorder." However, the Court added that "regulations imposing severe burdens on [candidates' and parties'] rights must be narrowly tailored and advance a compelling state interest. Lesser burdens, however, trigger less exacting review." Here, the Court concluded, the burdens on associational rights were "justifiable by 'correspondingly weighty' valid state interests in ballot integrity and political stability."[18]

§ 12.02. Elections

Alabama had by statute forbidden persons "to do any electioneering or to solicit any votes" on the day of election, and the state court had said that the electorate has an interest in being protected from "confusive last-minute charges and counter-charges." The United States Supreme Court, however, reversed the conviction of a newspaper publisher under the statute, stating: "It is difficult to conceive of a more obvious and flagrant abridgment of the constitutionally guaranteed freedom of the press."[19]

There was no violation of the First Amendment, said the Supreme Court in 1981, when the Federal Communications Commission gave candidates for federal office access to the media. Such a decision, said the Court, "properly balances the First Amendment rights of federal candidates, the public and the broadcasters."[20]

In holding unconstitutional under the First Amendment a state statute making it a felony to pay circulators of initiative petitions, the Court in 1988 stated that "the circulation of a petition involves the type of interactive communication concerning political change that is appropriately described as 'core political speech,'" and added that the statute "entrenches upon an area in which the importance of First Amendment protection is at its zenith."[21]

The Court has held that a state cannot prevent a political party

---

18. Timmons v. Twin Cities Area New Party, 117 S. Ct. 1364, 137 L. Ed. 2d 589 (U.S. 1997).

19. Mills v. State of Ala., 384 U.S. 214, 86 S. Ct. 1434, 16 L. Ed. 2d 484 (1966).

20. CBS, Inc. v. F. C. C., 453 U.S. 367, 101 S. Ct. 2813, 69 L. Ed. 2d 706 (1981).

21. Meyer v. Grant, 486 U.S. 414, 108 S. Ct. 1886, 100 L. Ed. 2d 425 (1988).

from permitting independent voters to participate in its primary elections for state and federal offices. The state's asserted interests in preventing raiding, avoiding voter confusion, and protecting the responsibility of party government were held insufficient to support the restraint upon freedom of political association by party members and non-party individuals.[22]

Violative of both freedom of speech and freedom of association was a state election law forbidding the official governing bodies of political parties from endorsing candidates in party primaries. The Supreme Court observed that since "the challenged law burdens the rights of political parties and their members, it can survive constitutional scrutiny only if the State shows it advances a compelling state interest." The Court found no such interest. The Court additionally voided another section of the statute placing restrictions upon the organization and composition of the official governing body of political parties by, inter alia, limiting the term of officers of the state central committee. Because the state could not produce proof that such regulation was necessary to ensure an election that was orderly and fair, that is, to the integrity of the electoral process, the provision was held to constitute an unconstitutional interference with associational rights.[23]

In 1992 the Court held valid a law banning campaign signs and posters, and other campaign materials within 100 feet of the entrance to polling places. Observing that this was one of the rare cases which survived strict scrutiny, the Court recognized a compelling interest in assuring that voters were free from influence, and another "compelling interest in preserving the integrity of the election process," which justified this limitation upon communication.[24]

While acknowledging "the States have a legitimate interest in preserving the integrity of their electoral processes," the Court has emphasized that limitations upon the First Amendment will not be sustained for mere "legitimate" interests. Application of the Kentucky Corrupt Practices Act was held unconstitutional when it had the effect of voiding the election of a candidate because he told the local voters that he would accept less salary than the amount

---

22. Tashjian v. Republican Party of Connecticut, 479 U.S. 208, 107 S. Ct. 544, 93 L. Ed. 2d 514 (1986).

23. Eu v. San Francisco County Democratic Cent. Committee, 489 U.S. 214, 109 S. Ct. 1013, 103 L. Ed. 2d 271 (1989).

24. Burson v. Freeman, 504 U.S. 191, 112 S. Ct. 1846, 119 L. Ed. 2d 5 (1992).

fixed by law (something the Kentucky courts characterized as a "bribe" of the voters).[25]

In 1995 the Court voided an Ohio law prohibiting the writing or distributing of any literature designed to promote the nomination, election, or defeat of any candidate or the adoption or defeat of any issue, or designed to influence voters in any election. "Such category of speech," said the Court, "occupies the core of the protection afforded by the First Amendment." The broadest possible protection under the Amendment is intended for "political expression" such as discussions of governmental affairs and the qualifications of candidates for public office. When a law burdens core political speech, the Court is clear that "no form of speech is entitled to greater political protection" and that "exacting scrutiny" will be applied to attempted controls. Justice Stevens for the Court reminds us that "anonymous pamphleteering is . . . a shield from the tyranny of the majority" intended by the First Amendment "to protect unpopular individuals from retaliation—and their ideas from suppression—at the hands of an intolerant society."[26]

§ 12.03. State controls on political parties

The Supreme Court in 1973 ruled unconstitutional as violative of freedom of association an Illinois rule prohibiting a person from voting in the primary election of a political party, if he had voted in the primary of any other party within the preceding 23 months.[27]

Two years later the Court held that that Illinois courts, in applying Illinois law, could not undo the action of the Democratic National Committee in ordering the seating of certain delegates from that state at the party's 1972 convention, affirming that these delegates were entitled to freedom of association and that it could not be offset except by a compelling interest. Further, the Court ruled that Illinois had no compelling interest in protecting the integrity of the electoral process where a national convention was involved—the convention itself being the forum for resolving such disputes.[28]

In 1979 the Court held valid a state statute requiring each major political party to have a state committee consisting of two persons

25. Brown v. Hartlage, 456 U.S. 45, 102 S. Ct. 1523, 71 L. Ed. 2d 732 (1982).

26. McIntyre v. Ohio Elections Com'n, 514 U.S. 334, 115 S. Ct. 1511, 131 L. Ed. 2d 426 (1995).

27. Kusper v. Pontikes, 414 U.S. 51, 94 S. Ct. 303, 38 L. Ed. 2d 260 (1973).

28. Cousins v. Wigoda, 419 U.S. 477, 95 S. Ct. 541, 42 L. Ed. 2d 595 (1975).

from each county in the state. The statute did not violate the First Amendment, ruled the Court.[29]

Two years later the Court ruled that where a state had demonstrated no compelling interest "to justify its substantial intrusions into the associational freedom of members of the National Party," associational rights under the First Amendment prevailed and the rules of the National Democratic Party controlled how delegates from states to the national convention were to be chosen.[30] Noting that freedom of political association is protected under both the Fifth and Fourteenth Amendments, the Supreme Court in 1992 held violative of the Fourteenth Amendment a state statute providing that when a subdivision of a state, such as a county, comprises large separate districts from which officers are elected, persons seeking to organize political parties to run in a county or other political subdivision must collect 25,000 signatures from each district. The state court had held that, in a county with both urban and suburban districts, failure to gather sufficient signatures in the suburban district disqualified candidates from the political party. The Court reiterated that when a state attempts to limit the access of political parties to the ballot, it must be prepared to demonstrate "an interest sufficiently weighty to justify the limitation," plus proof that the statute is "narrowly drawn to advance a state interest of compelling importance." The Court found that the statute at issue swept more broadly than necessary to advance the state interest in electoral order.[31]

In 1997 the Court held that the states are not constitutionally required under the First Amendment to permit "fusion tickets," as in New York, where parties can nominate an individual who has already been nominated by another or other parties.[32]

---

29. Marchioro v. Chaney, 442 U.S. 191, 99 S. Ct. 2243, 60 L. Ed. 2d 816 (1979).

30. Democratic Party of the U.S. of America v. La Follette, 448 U.S. 909, 100 S. Ct. 3054, 65 L. Ed. 2d 1139 (1980).

31. Norman v. Reed, 502 U.S. 279, 112 S. Ct. 698, 116 L. Ed. 2d 711 (1992).

32. Timmons v. Twin Cities Area New Party, 117 S. Ct. 1364, 137 L. Ed. 2d 589 (U.S. 1997).

CHAPTER THIRTEEN

Interest in the Good Administration of Government

---

§ 13.00. Relations with officers and employees

Millions of federal employees of the executive branch are prevented from expressing themselves fully on partisan political matters because of the Hatch Act, which the United States Supreme Court sustained in 1947 in *United Public Workers v. Mitchell.* "The essential rights of the First Amendment," said the Court, "in some instances are subject to the elemental need for order without which the guarantees of civil rights to others would be a mockery. . . . The government has a legitimate interest in suppressing actively partisan conduct by government employees as a threat to good administration. . . . Congress may regulate the political conduct of Government employees within reasonable limits, even though the regulation trenches to some extent upon unfettered political action."[1] Justices Black and Douglas dissented. Said Justice Black: "Legislation which muzzles several million citizens threatens popular government, not only because it injures the individual muzzled, but also because of its harmful effect on the body politic in depriving it of the political participation and interest of such a large segment of our citizens."[2] Justice Douglas added: "If those rights are to be qualified by the larger requirements of modern democratic government, the restrictions should be narrowly and selectively drawn to define and punish the specific conduct which constitutes a clear and present danger to the operations of government."[3]

Under the Hatch Act, thousands of state officers and employees are likewise barred from partisan politics, since the act applies to

---

1.   United Public Workers of America (C.I.O.) v. Mitchell, 330 U.S. 75, 67 S. Ct. 556, 91 L. Ed. 754, 770, 774 (1947).

2.   United Public Workers of America (C.I.O.) v. Mitchell, 330 U.S. 75, 67 S. Ct. 556, 91 L. Ed. 754, 778 (1947).

3.   United Public Workers of America (C.I.O.) v. Mitchell, 330 U.S. 75, 67 S. Ct. 556, 91 L. Ed. 754, 787 (1947).

state personnel whose principal employment is in connection with an activity financed in whole or in part with federal funds. The United States has upheld the constitutionality of such restraint, relying upon its reasoning in the *Mitchell* case. It added: "While the United States is not concerned and has no power to regulate local political activities as such of state officials, it does have power to fix the terms upon which its money allotments to states shall be disbursed."[4]

In 1973 the Supreme Court upheld, as not suffering from unconstitutional vagueness or overbreadth, a provision of federal law banning employees from taking "an active part in political management or in political campaigns," adding that this refers to "those acts of political management or political campaigning which were prohibited on the part of employees in the competitive service before July 19, 1940, by determination of the Civil Service Commission under the rules prescribed by the President." Justices Brennan, Douglas and Marshall dissented, believing the restraint was both too vague and overbroad.[5] The same year the Court upheld a state ban on a broad range of political activities by merit system personnel, and denied relief on an "overbreadth" attack even though local authorities had interpreted the act to make impermissible the wearing of political buttons or displaying bumper stickers. Justices Brennan, Douglas, Marshall and Stewart dissented, stating that in these cases the Court must apply its ordinary approach in First Amendment situations where, either because of vagueness or overbreadth, legislation would be voided in litigation brought by a citizen whose conduct might well be within range of permissible state controls if the statute were clearly and narrowly drawn.[6]

Three years later the Court held that non-policy, non-confidential government employees cannot be discharged from jobs that they are satisfactorily performing, upon the sole ground that they are members of a political party in opposition to an incumbent sheriff. The Court indicated that, because of the importance of the First Amendment interests involved, "the practice of patronage dismissals" will be unconstitutional in all cases, except as to officers or employees involved in "policy making decisions."[7] In 1980 the Court held the First and Fourteenth Amendments were violated by the

---

4. Oklahoma v. U.S. Civil Service Com'n, 330 U.S. 127, 67 S. Ct. 544, 91 L. Ed. 794, 806 (1947) (noted in 32 Minn L Rev 301).

5. U.S. Civil Service Commission v. National Ass'n of Letter Carriers, AFL-CIO, 413 U.S. 548, 93 S. Ct. 2880, 37 L. Ed. 2d 796 (1973).

6. Broadrick v. Oklahoma, 413 U.S. 601, 93 S. Ct. 2908, 37 L. Ed. 2d 830 (1973).

7. Elrod v. Burns, 427 U.S. 347, 96 S. Ct. 2673, 49 L. Ed. 2d 547 (1976).

discharge of an assistant public defender, satisfactorily performing his work, solely because of his political beliefs. The Court stated that "the ultimate inquiry is not whether the label 'policymaker' or 'confidential' fits a particular position; rather, the question is whether the hiring authority can demonstrate that party affiliation is an appropriate requirement for the effective performance of the public office involved."[8]

Holding that "significant" penalties imposed for the exercise of rights guaranteed by the First Amendment are never valid "unless narrowly tailored to further vital government interests," the Court in 1990 ruled that promotion, transfer, recall, and hiring decisions relating to public employees may not be made solely because they are not supporters of the political party in power. Justice Scalia wrote a dissent, joined by Chief Justice Rehnquist and Justices Kennedy and O'Connor, emphasizing that traditions of American politics should be respected, and that there is a link between patronage and party discipline that is important to the society. Justice O'Connor refused to join part of the dissent, but indicated that the First Amendment should not apply to laws enacted in the government's capacity as employer in the same way as it does to laws regulating private conduct.[9]

Noting "our long-standing recognition that the First Amendment's primary aim is the maximum protection of speech upon issues of public concern," the Court in 1984 indicated that "private speech" uttered by public employees is to be given a lesser protection. The Court then sustained the dismissal of an assistant district attorney for circulating a petition almost entirely on matters of private concern. Speaking of non-tenured employees, the Court announced: "When employee expression cannot be fairly considered as relating to any matter of political, social, or other concern to the community, government officials should enjoy wide latitude in managing their offices, without intrusive oversight by the judiciary in the name of the First Amendment." Justices Brennan, Marshall, Stevens and Blackmun dissented, believing that the majority took too narrow a conception of "public concern" speech, adding that in the instant case the efficient performance of governmental functions had not been jeopardized.[10]

A Supreme Court plurality opinion in 1994 stated that "constitutional review of government employment decisions must rest on dif-

---

8. Branti v. Finkel, 445 U.S. 507, 100 S. Ct. 1287, 63 L. Ed. 2d 574 (1980).

9. Rutan v. Republican Party of Illinois, 497 U.S. 62, 110 S. Ct. 2729, 111 L. Ed. 2d 52 (1990).

10. Connick v. Myers, 461 U.S. 138, 103 S. Ct. 1684, 75 L. Ed. 2d 708 (1983).

ferent principles than review of speech restraints imposed by the government as sovereigns. . . . Government employers should be allowed to use personnel procedures that differ from the evidentiary rules used by courts, without fear that these differences will lead to liability." When a government employee is being dismissed for a speech allegedly critical of the employee's agency or superiors, the employee to void the dismissal under First Amendment principles must show that the utterance was "on a matter of public concern, and the employee's interest in expressing herself on this matter must not be outweighed by any injury the speech could create to the interest of the state, as an employer, in promoting the efficiency of the public service it performs through its employees." The plurality opinion concluded that if employment action against a government employee is based on what the employee supposedly said and a reasonable supervisor would recognize that there was substantial likelihood that what was actually said was protected speech, management must tread with certain amount of care; it need not be the care with which trials and the rules of evidence and procedure are conducted, but it should be a care that a reasonable manager would use before making an employment decision. Justice Souter in concurrence emphasized that the public employer must not only investigate a third-party report of the incident, but must also *believe* it. In dissent, Justices Stevens and Blackmun urged that when the eighteen million Americans who are employees of federal, state, and local governments speak on matters of public concern, the Court should apply its previously stated rule that when a public employer disciplines an employee because of such an utterance, the employee is entitled to a jury determination whether the utterance was unduly disruptive of the operations of the affected agency.[11]

Neither freedom of association nor freedom of speech was denied, ruled the Supreme Court in 1979, upholding per curium an Arkansas rule that the State Highway Commission would refuse to consider or act upon grievances when filed by a union, rather than by the employee directly.[12] Five years later the Court held constitutional as not violative of the First Amendment a statute authorizing state employees to bargain collectively over terms and conditions of employment, and granting professional employees, such as college faculty, the right to "meet and confer" with their employers on matters related to employment that were outside the scope of manda-

---

11. Waters v. Churchill, 511 U.S. 661, 114 S. Ct. 1878, 128 L. Ed. 2d 686 (1994).

12. Smith v. Arkansas State Highway Emp., Local 1315, 441 U.S. 463, 99 S. Ct. 1826, 60 L. Ed. 2d 360 (1979).

tory bargaining, but also providing that, if professional employees forming an appropriate bargaining unit had selected an exclusive representative for mandatory bargaining, their employer could "meet and confer" on nonmandatory subjects only with that representative. The Court held that this restriction on participation in the nonmandatory subject exchange process did not violate the constitutional rights of professional employees within the bargaining unit who were not members of the exclusive representative and who might disagree with its views. Justice Brennan in a dissenting opinion emphasized that such employees had a right to be free from compelled associations and a further right to freely exchange their ideas and proposals. Justice Stevens, in dissent, stated that such statutory limitation denied equal protection of the laws in favoring union members.[13]

Violative of freedom of speech was a Congressional act forbidding federal employees below grade 16, among others, from accepting any compensation for making speeches or writing articles, even when the speech had no connection with the employee's official duties for the federal government. While readily acknowledging that "operational efficiency is undoubtedly a vital governmental interest," the Court found this outweighed by the "significant burden on expressive activity" imposed by the act, as well as by "the public's right to read and hear what the employees would otherwise have written and said."[14]

§ 13.01. Managing federal properties

When the Supreme Court in 1988 held that the Free Exercise Clause of the First Amendment does not forbid the federal government from permitting timber cutting in, or constructing a road through, a portion of a national forest that has traditionally been used for religious purposes by American Indian tribes, it announced that when the federal government is deciding how to use federal lands, it need not show a compelling interest so long as the protestants are not being coerced by the government's action into violating their religious beliefs. Justices Brennan, Marshall and Blackmun in dissent would require the government to come forward with a compelling interest when protestants show that the proposed use "poses a substantial and realistic threat of frustrating their religious practices." They found "without constitutional significance" the

---

13. Minnesota State Bd. for Community Colleges v. Knight, 465 U.S. 271, 104 S. Ct. 1058, 79 L. Ed. 2d 299, 15 Ed. Law Rep. 1050 (1984).

14. U.S. v. National Treasury Employees Union, 513 U.S. 454, 115 S. Ct. 1003, 130 L. Ed. 2d 964 (1995).

majority's distinction between governmental actions that compel affirmative conduct inconsistent with religious belief and governmental
actions that prevent conduct consistent with religious belief.[15]

§ 13.02. Public contractors' criticism of government

The Court in 1996 for the first time recognized that those who
enter into contracts with governmental entities have a First Amendment right to criticize on matters of public concern the entities that
contracted with them. To prevail in defense the government must
show that it did not terminate the contract because of the
contractor's criticisms, but rather would have taken the same action
even in the absence of the protected conduct, or that legitimate
countervailing government interests, in a proper balancing, are
clearly strong enough to outweigh the contractor's First Amendment interests.[16]

---

15. Lyng v. Northwest Indian Cemetery Protective Ass'n, 485 U.S. 439, 108 S.
Ct. 1319, 99 L. Ed. 2d 534 (1988).

16. Board of County Com'rs, Wabaunsee County, Kan. v. Umbehr, 116 S. Ct.
2342, 135 L. Ed. 2d 843 (U.S. 1996).

CHAPTER FOURTEEN

First Amendment Freedoms and Other Opposed Interests

---

§ 14.00. Preserving the integrity of the legislative process

Society has a legitimate interest in controlling the activities of lobbyists who seek to influence our legislatures. This has resulted in the passage of the Federal Regulation of Lobbying Act which, inter alia, requires the reporting of the sources contributing to lobbyists for the passage or defeat of legislation. The Supreme Court in *United States v. Harriss* upheld the Act over claims that it violated freedom of speech and press and the right to petition the government. The Court stated:

> Present-day legislative complexities are such that individual members of Congress cannot be expected to explore the myriad pressures to which they are regularly subjected. Yet full realization of the American ideal of government by elected representatives depends to no small extent on their ability to properly evaluate such pressures. Otherwise the voice of the people may all too easily be drowned out by the voice of special interest groups seeking favored treatment while masquerading as proponents of the public weal. This is the evil which the Lobbying Act was designed to help prevent. . . . Under these circumstances, we believe that Congress, at least within the bounds of the Act as we have construed it, is not constitutionally forbidden to require the disclosure of lobbying activities. To do so would be to deny Congress in large measure the power of self-protection.[1]

Justices Black, Douglas and Jackson dissented, primarily because they deemed the language of the act too vague and too broad, although all three agreed that Congress can regulate lobbyists and require disclosure of their principals.

---

1.   U.S. v. Harriss, 347 U.S. 612, 74 S. Ct. 808, 98 L. Ed. 989, 1000-01 (1954).

Congress is not required by the First Amendment to give tax exemptions to lobbying organizations.[2]

§ 14.01. Enforcing anti-trust laws

Our society has a worthy interest in opposing trusts and monopolies and enforcing the anti-trust laws. On a few occasions publishers have suggested that their freedom of the press would be violated by exposing them to the anti-trust laws. Such claim has never succeeded.

In 1945, in *Associated Press v. United States* the Supreme Court ruled that a monopoly of publishers was not immune from the antitrust laws because of the First Amendment. Said the Court:

> The First Amendment, far from providing an argument against application of the Sherman Act, here provides powerful reasons to the contrary. That Amendment rests on the assumption that the widest possible dissemination of information from diverse and antagonistic sources is essential to the welfare of the public, that a free press is a condition of a free society. Surely a command that the government itself shall not impede the free flow of ideas does not afford nongovernmental combinations a refuge if they impose restraints upon that constitutionally guaranteed freedom. Freedom to publish means freedom for all and not for some. Freedom to publish is guaranteed by the Constitution, but freedom to combine to keep others from publishing is not. Freedom of the press from governmental interference under the First Amendment does not sanction repression of that freedom by private interests. The First Amendment affords not the slightest support for the contention that a combination to restrain trade in news and views has any constitutional immunity.[3]

In 1961 the Court ruled that the federal government could under the anti-trust laws enjoin a newspaper publisher from the practice of refusing to accept advertisements from firms using the local radio station as well. To the suggestion of the publisher that this was an unconstitutional prior restraint violative of freedom of the press, the Court responded: "We find in it no restriction upon any guaranteed freedom of the press. The injunction applies to a publisher what the law applies to others. The publisher may not accept or deny

---

2. Regan v. Taxation With Representation of Washington, 461 U.S. 540, 103 S. Ct. 1997, 76 L. Ed. 2d 129 (1983).

3. Associated Press v. U.S., 326 U.S. 1, 65 S. Ct. 1416, 89 L. Ed. 2013, 2030-31 (1945).

advertisements in an 'attempt to monopolize any part of the trade or commerce among the several States.' Injunctive relief under section four of the Sherman Act is an appropriate a means of enforcing the Act against newspapers as it is against others."[4] Later the Supreme Court reaffirmed that the societal interest in anti-trust law enforcement can in particular instances outweigh claims posited upon the First Amendment.[5]

In 1990 the Court held that application of the Sherman Act to a group of lawyers in the District of Columbia, who refused further to represent indigent defendants in criminal prosecutions without increased compensation, was not violative of the First Amendment, since the expressive component of the boycott was not unique. The Court reaffirmed that application of a neutral regulation that incidentally burdens speech can be valid where the government has compelling interests requiring protection. Justices Brennan and Marshall dissented, asserting that the First Amendment prohibits Federal Trade Commission injunctive action against members participating in an expressive boycott without a showing that the participants possessed market power or that their conduct triggered any anti-competitive effects. Justice Blackmun dissented separately on comparable grounds.[6]

§ 14.02. Government fiscal affairs

The publishers and distributors of newspapers, magazines, and books are entitled to protection of freedom of the press, and, additionally, distributors of religious tracts are entitled to freedom of religion. Both of these interests necessitate at times the invalidation of state and local taxes as applied to such persons or corporations.

In 1936 the United States Supreme Court invalidated a Louisiana tax of two percent upon the gross receipts of all newspapers having circulations over 20,000, which happened to embrace most of the state's opposition newspapers. The Court stated, through Justice Sutherland:

> The tax here involved is bad not because it takes money from the pockets of the appellees. If that were all, a wholly different question would be presented. It is bad because, in the light of its history and of its present setting, it is seen to be a deliberate

4. Lorain Journal Co. v. U.S., 342 U.S. 143, 72 S. Ct. 181, 187-88, 96 L. Ed. 162, 172-74 (1951).

5. California Motor Transport Co. v. Trucking Unlimited, 404 U.S. 508, 92 S. Ct. 609, 30 L. Ed. 2d 642 (1972).

6. F.T.C. v. Superior Court Trial Lawyers Ass'n, 493 U.S. 411, 110 S. Ct. 768, 107 L. Ed. 2d 851 (1990).

and calculated device in the guise of a tax to limit the circulation of information to which the public is entitled in virtue of the constitutional guaranties. A free press stands as one of the greater interpreters between the government and the people. To allow it to be fettered is to fetter ourselves.[7]

In 1943 the Court ruled that an ordinance imposing a flat license tax on distributors of religious materials was an unconstitutional invasion of the freedoms of religion, speech, and press. Justice Jackson for the Court observed: "The power to impose a license tax on the exercise of these freedoms is indeed as potent as the power of censorship which this Court has repeatedly struck down."[8] One can see how readily itinerant evangelists would be impoverished and stifled if subjected to such license taxes by every community in which they preached or distributed religious literature.

The following year the Court invalidated the imposition of another license tax upon a preacher and distributor of religious materials, this time by his own home town. Said Justice Douglas for the Court:

A flat license tax on that constitutional privilege would be as odious as the early "taxes on knowledge" which the framers of the First Amendment sought to outlaw. A preacher has no less a claim to that privilege when he is not an itinerant. . . . The exaction of a tax as a condition to the exercise of the great liberties guaranteed by the First Amendment is as obnoxious as the imposition of a censorship or a previous restraint. For, to repeat, "the power to tax the exercise of a privilege is the power to control or suppress its enjoyment."[9]

Justice Murphy added in the same case: "It is wise to remember that the taxing and licensing power is a dangerous and potent weapon which, in the hands of unscrupulous or bigoted men, could be used to suppress freedoms and destroy religion unless it is kept within appropriate bounds."[10]

Neither newspaper publishers, ministers, nor religionists are free from all burdens to support their government. In the *Murdock* case, Justice Douglas for the majority pointed out clearly that the tax

---

7. Grosjean v. American Press Co., 297 U.S. 233, 56 S. Ct. 444, 80 L. Ed. 660 (1936).

8. Murdock v. Com. of Pennsylvania, 319 U.S. 105, 113, 63 S. Ct. 870, 87 L. Ed. 1292, 1298, 146 A.L.R. 81 (1943).

9. Follett v. Town of McCormick, S.C., 321 U.S. 573, 577, 64 S. Ct. 717, 88 L. Ed. 938, 941, 152 A.L.R. 317 (1944).

10. Follett v. Town of McCormick, S.C., 321 U.S. 573, 579, 64 S. Ct. 717, 88 L. Ed. 938, 942, 152 A.L.R. 317 (1944).

challenged in that case was "something quite different, for example, from a tax on the income of one who engages in religious activities or a tax on property used or employed in connection with those activities. It is one thing to impose a tax on the income or property of a preacher. It is quite another thing to exact a tax from him for the privilege of delivering a sermon."[11] Again, in the *Follett* case, Justice Douglas pointed out that neither "a preacher who preaches or a petitioner who listens . . . is free from all financial burdens of government, including taxes on income or property."[12]

Currently the *Murdock* and *Follett* decisions are seen to stand for the proposition that a flat license tax is a precondition to the free exercise of religious belief and as such is unconstitutional.

In 1983 the Supreme Court held that a state could not, as a substitute for a sales tax, impose a use tax on large newspapers using over a $100,000 worth of ink and newsprint a year. The Court found objectionable singling out "a small group of newspapers" for subjection to the tax. It indicated, however, by way of dictum, that generally applicable sales or use taxes would be constitutional in application to the press.[13]

Six years later, in a plurality opinion by Justices Marshall, Brennan and Stevens, and concurring opinions by Justices White, Blackmun and O'Connor, the Supreme Court through these justices held that the Establishment Clause of the First Amendment was violated by giving religious organizations exemption from state sales taxes when distributing and selling religious materials. Justice Blackmun said: "The Establishment Clause value suggests that a State may not give a tax break to those who spread the gospel, that it does not also give to others who actively might advocate disbelief in religion."[14] The earlier *Walz v. Tax Commission of New York City* case[15] is put in focus and stands for the proposition that property tax exemptions for religious institutions are constitutional only as part of a large exemption statute providing the same to a variety of non-profit organizations, such as hospitals, libraries, etc. Justice Harlan emphasized the "breadth of exemption" as "including groups that

---

11. Murdock v. Com. of Pennsylvania, 319 U.S. 105, 127, 63 S. Ct. 870, 87 L. Ed. 1292, 1306, 146 A.L.R. 81 (1943).

12. Follett v. Town of McCormick, S.C., 321 U.S. 573, 577, 64 S. Ct. 717, 88 L. Ed. 938, 941, 152 A.L.R. 317 (1944).

13. Minneapolis Star and Tribune Co. v. Minnesota Com'r of Revenue, 460 U.S. 575, 103 S. Ct. 1365, 75 L. Ed. 2d 295 (1983).

14. Texas Monthly, Inc. v. Bullock, 489 U.S. 1, 109 S. Ct. 890, 103 L. Ed. 2d 1, 20 (1989).

15. Walz v. Tax Commission of City of New York, 397 U.S. 664, 697, 90 S. Ct. 1409, 25 L. Ed. 2d 697 (1970).

pursue cultural, moral, or spiritual improvement in multifarious ways."

Content-based discrimination in state tax exemptions will violate the First Amendment freedom of the press. Thus, in 1987 the Supreme Court held that freedom of the press was violated by a statute exempting from sales taxes newspapers and sport journals but denying the same to other magazines.[16]

§ 14.03. Relationship to Establishment Clause

It would violate freedom of speech and press for a state university to refuse funds for the printing of a student publication on the basis of its editor's religious viewpoints, held the Court in 1995, the Court noting generally that governmental discrimination on the basis of content is impermissible in First Amendment areas. The Court further held that there was no Establishment Clause violation in the university honoring its constitutional duties under the Freedom of Speech Clause of the First Amendment.[17]

---

16. Arkansas Writers' Project, Inc. v. Ragland, 481 U.S. 221, 107 S. Ct. 1722, 95 L. Ed. 2d 209 (1987).

17. Rosenberger v. Rector and Visitors of University of Virginia, 515 U.S. 819, 115 S. Ct. 2510, 132 L. Ed. 2d 700, 101 Ed. Law Rep. 552 (1995).

PART THREE

RECONCILING THE SOCIETAL INTERESTS IN THE INTEGRITY AND PRIVACY OF THE INDIVIDUAL WITH OTHER IMPORTANT INTERESTS OF SOCIETY

CHAPTER FIFTEEN

Sacrifices in the Names of Health, Morality and Public Safety

---

§ 15.00. Introduction

Our society has a strong interest in protecting the integrity, the dignity and the privacy of human beings. The language of John Stuart Mill in 1848 has eternal lessons for all free and democratic nations. He wrote:

> There is a circle around every individual human being which no government, be it that of one, of a few, or of the many, ought to be permitted to overstep; there is a part of the life of every person who has come to years of discretion, within which the individuality of that person ought to reign uncontrolled either by any other individual or by the public collectively. That there is, or ought to be, some space in human existence thus entrenched around and sacred from authoritative intrusion, no one who professes the smallest regard to human freedom or dignity will call in question.[1]

---

1.   Hill, *Principles of Political Economy* (London 1984) II, 560-1.

Since the formation of the United States of America, this has always been the prime value of our land. Justice Brandeis wrote: "The makers of our Constitution . . . sought to protect Americans in their beliefs, their thoughts, their emotions and their sanctions. They conferred, as against the government, the right to be let alone—the most comprehensive of rights and the right most valued by civilized man."[2]

What is required is, first, constitutional protection of what a distinguished American jurist described as "the inherent right of bodily integrity,"[3] and, secondly, constitutional recognition of, and protection for, the private lives of citizens. The former is discussed in the next and succeeding chapters; the latter has already been examined in the First Amendment materials, but is examined further here. Illustratively, there is a large area of marriage and family life which the Supreme Court protects under both the Due Process and Equal Protection Clauses. When Virginia wanted to prohibit white persons from marrying individuals of another color, the Supreme Court in 1967 voided the legislation, finding it violative of an individual's liberty as well as his right to equal protection of the laws. Freedom to marry is a due process right, ruled the Court, which added that "there can be no doubt that restricting the freedom to marry solely because of racial classifications violates the central meaning of the Equal Protection Clause."[4] Ten years later the Court explained that the Due Process Clause protects the sanctity of both the nuclear and extended families, and voided an ordinance which prohibited a grandmother from residing with her son and two grandchildren. Freedom of personal choice in matters of marriage and family life are important constitutional values, and restrictions thereon must fall absent important opposed public interests that demand protection and which cannot otherwise be safeguarded.[5]

The Supreme Court in 1995 found (1) a substantial public interest, (2) a restriction that directly and materially advanced that interest, and (3) a regulation that was narrowly drawn, and therefore sustained a rule of the Florida bar prohibiting lawyers from direct-mail solicitation to victims of accidents and their relatives for 30 days following an accident or disaster. Observing that members of

---

2. Olmstead v. U.S., 277 U.S. 438, 48 S. Ct. 564, 72 L. Ed. 944, 66 A.L.R. 376 (1928) (dissenting).

3. Smith v. Command, 231 Mich. 409, 204 N.W. 140, 40 A.L.R. 515 (1925) (Wiest J., dissenting).

4. Loving v. Com. of Va., 388 U.S. 1, 87 S. Ct. 1817, 18 L. Ed. 2d 1010 (1967).

5. Moore v. City of East Cleveland, Ohio, 431 U.S. 494, 97 S. Ct. 1932, 52 L. Ed. 2d 531 (1977).

the bar have many other ways of informing the public, the Court ruled that protection of individual privacy and prevention of outrage and irritation with the state-licensed legal profession amply justified such a rule. In dissent, Justice Kennedy, joined by Justices Souter, Ginsburg and Stevens, agreed that following the *Central Hudson* test was proper where commercial speech was involved, but found the state's claimed interests insubstantial and pointed out that restrictions on speech are not justified on the ground that the speech might offend the listener. They noted that it is often imperative that persons injured have an early opportunity to gather information while fresh and be advised not to enter into discussions with investigators for those with likely tort responsibility. The dissenters wrote: "Obscuring the legal profession from public discussion through direct-mail solicitation at the expense of the least sophisticated members of society is not laudable constitutional goal."[6]

§ 15.01. Protecting the public health

One of the most important societal interests is that of safeguarding and protecting the public health, and it can be expected that this interest will prevail over most other interests.

Even though inoculation and vaccination are, of course, intrusions into the sanctity of the individual being, such necessary health measures will generally be sustained. The United States Supreme Court in 1905 ruled that Massachusetts could expose an individual to a smallpox vaccination against his will when epidemic conditions prevailed.[7] The Court noted that it was not then deciding the question of the constitutional application of such a statute to a person who could show "with reasonable certainty that he is not at the time a fit subject of vaccination or that vaccination, by reason of his then-condition, would seriously impair his health or probably cause his death." In 1922, in sustaining a municipal vaccination requirement, the Supreme Court pointed out that the *Jacobson* case "had settled that it is within the police power of a state to provide for compulsory vaccination."[8]

State courts have sustained requirements of compulsory vaccination and immunization though there was no epidemic and, indeed,

---

6. Florida Bar v. Went for It, Inc., 515 U.S. 618, 115 S. Ct. 2371, 132 L. Ed. 2d 541 (1995)

7. Jacobson v. Commonwealth of Massachusetts, 197 U.S. 11, 25 S. Ct. 358, 49 L. Ed. 643 (1905).

8. Zucht v. King, 260 U.S. 174, 43 S. Ct. 24, 67 L. Ed. 194, 198 (1922).

even though there had been no cases of smallpox or diphtheria for as long as forty years.[9]

Fluoridation of the public water supply has been judicially sustained, over objections of individuals who protested the intrusion of this substance into their bodies. In the leading case from the Ohio Supreme Court, the United States Supreme Court dismissed an appeal.[10]

In 1977 the Supreme Court held not violative of individual privacy rights a New York statute requiring doctors to report the names and addresses of all persons who have obtained, pursuant to a doctor's prescription, certain drugs for which there is both a lawful and an unlawful market.[11]

§ 15.02. Protecting the public morality

In 1969, when Georgia desired to reach into a person's private home and control what literature was there read if it should be obscene, the United States Supreme Court set aside a conviction for possessing such material in the privacy of the dwelling. Justice Marshall for the Court emphasized the fundamental nature of "the right to be free, except in very limited circumstances, from unwanted governmental intrusion into one's privacy." Justice Marshall added: "Whatever may be the justifications for other statutes regulating obscenity [these cannot] reach into the privacy of one's home. If the First Amendment means anything, it means that a State has no business telling a man, sitting alone in his own house, what books he may read or what films he may watch."[12]

In voiding a statute prohibiting the distribution of contraceptives to minors under 16, limiting their distribution to pharmacists, and absolutely prohibiting their display or advertisement, the Supreme Court in 1977 ruled that the right of personal privacy in connection with decisions affecting procreation extends to minors as well as to

---

9. Sadlock v. Board of Ed. of Borough of Carlstadt in Bergen County, 137 N.J.L. 85, 58 A.2d 218 (N.J. Sup. Ct. 1948); Board of Ed. of Mountain Lakes v. Maas, 56 N.J. Super. 245, 152 A.2d 394 (App. Div. 1959), judgment aff'd, 31 N.J. 537, 158 A.2d 330 (1960); Stull v. Reber, 215 Pa. 156, 64 A. 419 (1906); State v. Drew, 89 N.H. 54, 192 A. 629 (1937).

10. Kraus v. City of Cleveland, 163 Ohio St. 559, 57 Ohio Op. 1, 127 N.E.2d 609 (1955), appeal dismissed, 351 U.S. 935, 76 S. Ct. 833, 100 L. Ed. 1463 (1956).

11. Whalen v. Roe, 429 U.S. 589, 97 S. Ct. 869, 51 L. Ed. 2d 64 (1977).

12. Stanley v. Georgia, 394 U.S. 557, 89 S. Ct. 1243, 22 L. Ed. 2d 542 (1969).

adults, and held further that the ban on advertising and display was an unconstitutional suppression of expression.[13]

Since the Supreme Court in 1982 made it clear that child pornography, whether obscene or not, is not protected by the First Amendment, and stated that the prevention of sexual exploitation and abuse of children constitutes a governmental objective of "surpassing importance,"[14] individuals receiving child pornography at their dwelling from vendors or mail personnel, will be subject to punishment.[15]

In 1986, the Court, in a five-to-four ruling, held valid a state statute making criminal sodomy committed in private between consenting adults. Justices Blackmun, Brennan, Marshall and Stevens in their dissent wrote that "individual decisions by both married and unmarried persons concerning the intimacies of their physical relationship . . . are a form of 'liberty' protected by the Due Process Clause of the Fourteenth Amendment" and are not to be denied without showing by the state of a legitimate and substantial societal interest.[16]

§ 15.03. Sterilization of mental defectives and certain criminals

In 1927 the Supreme Court held that there is an interest in preventing the propagation of congenital mental defectives, and that the political state is justified in exposing them to compulsory sterilization.[17]

Since the *Buck v. Bell* decision the American community has seen the ravages of the Nazis upon millions of innocent persons because of their religious beliefs or nationality, and has been somewhat more alerted to the perils of asexualization at the hands of the state. Since then, too, the Supreme Court has referred to the right to enter into the marriage relation and procreate children as "fundamental," among "the basic civil rights of man," and truly "a basic liberty."[18]

It is suggested that the Court be encouraged to re-examine its *Buck v. Bell* decision. In areas involving interests less precious than

---

13. Carey v. Population Services, Intern., 431 U.S. 678, 97 S. Ct. 2010, 52 L. Ed. 2d 675 (1977).

14. New York v. Ferber, 458 U.S. 747, 102 S. Ct. 3348, 73 L. Ed. 2d 1113 (1982)

15. Osborne v. Ohio, 495 U.S. 103, 110 S. Ct. 1691, 109 L. Ed. 2d 98 (1990).

16. Bowers v. Hardwick, 478 U.S. 186, 106 S. Ct. 2841, 92 L. Ed. 2d 140 (1986).

17. Buck v. Bell, 274 U.S. 200, 47 S. Ct. 584, 71 L. Ed. 1000 (1927).

18. Skinner v. State of Okl. ex rel. Williamson, 316 U.S. 535, 541, 62 S. Ct. 1110, 86 L. Ed. 1655, 1660 (1942).

the sanctity of the person, the Court has demanded that the state explore reasonable alternatives that will as adequately protect the interest of society without infringing upon the person. Here reasonable alternatives seem to be available to a state concerned with the perpetuation of congenital mental defectives—these unfortunate individuals can be institutionalized and segregated from members of the other sex without prohibitive costs to society. Justice Wiest of the Michigan Supreme Court once wrote:

> The bodies of citizens may not, under legislative mandate, be cut and power of procreation destroyed by litigation or mutilation or carving out of organs.

When pity and mercy and humanitarianism are subordinated to utilitarian considerations and power of the State is employed to destroy the virility of unfortunate human beings rather than their segregation and treatment toward recovery or amelioration, we as a people invite atavism to the state of mind evidenced in Sparta, ancient Rome and the dark ages where individuality counted for naught against the mere animal breeding of human beings for purposes of State or tribe. . . . There is a limit even to the power of the State over the bodies of men and women.[19]

The Supreme Court has invalidated a state sterilization act which authorized the sterilization of those convicted for the third time of larceny but made no similar assault upon the bodies of those for the third time convicted of such crimes as embezzlement. The Court stated:

> When the law lays an unequal hand on those who have committed intrinsically the same quality of offense and sterilizes one and not the other, it has made as invidious a discrimination as if it had selected a particular race or nationality for oppressive treatment.[20]

Under equal protection of the laws, any semblance of unreasonable differentiation in sterilization statutes or their practice will invalidate a statute.

Sterilization cannot be imposed upon persons as punishment for

---

19. Smith v. Command, 231 Mich. 409, 430, 204 N.W. 140, 40 A.L.R. 515 (1925) (Bird and Fellows, JJ. joining in this dissent).

20. Skinner v. State of Okl. ex rel. Williamson, 316 U.S. 535, 62 S. Ct. 1110, 86 L. Ed. 1655 (1942).

crime; courts rather generally agreeing that such is cruel and unusual punishment.[21]

§ 15.04. Detecting crime

Society, of course, has a legitimate interest in suppressing crime and detecting criminals. However, it is established by an abundance of authority that the officers of the state can not degrade the individual in their search for proof of crime and the identity of criminals.

It has long been established that the police cannot use physical force of any kind to compel a suspect to confess.[22] "The rack and torture chamber may not be substituted for the witness stand,"[23] says the Supreme Court. Psychological torture is just as readily outlawed. In the language of the Court, "the use in a state criminal trial of a defendant's confession obtained by coercion—whether physical or mental—is forbidden by the Fourteenth Amendment."[24]

In 1952 the Supreme Court ruled that state authorities could not produce vomiting in a suspect by "stomach pumping" so that he might regurgitate capsules of narcotics he was thought to have swallowed. Said the Court through Justice Frankfurter:

> The proceedings by which this conviction was obtained do more than offend some fastidious squeamishness or private sentimentalism about combating crime too energetically. It is conduct that shocks the conscience. Illegally breaking into the privacy of the petitioner, the struggle to open his mouth and remove what was there, the forcible extraction of his stomach's contents—this course of proceeding by agents of government to obtain evidence is bound to offend even hardened sensibilities. They are methods too close to the rack and the screw to permit of constitutional differentiation. . . . Coerced confessions offend the community's sense of fair play and decency. So here to sanction the brutal conduct which naturally enough was condemned by the court whose judgment is before us, would be to afford brutality the cloak of law. Nothing would be more

---

21. Davis v. Berry, 216 F. 413 (S.D. Iowa 1914), rev'd for mootness, 242 U.S. 468, 37 S. Ct. 208, 61 L. Ed. 441 (1917); Mickle v. Henrichs, 262 F. 687 (D. Nev. 1918).

22. Brown v. State of Mississippi, 297 U.S. 278, 56 S. Ct. 461, 80 L. Ed. 682 (1936).

23. Brown v. State of Mississippi, 297 U.S. 278, 56 S. Ct. 461, 80 L. Ed. 682, 687 (1936).

24. Leyra v. Denno, 347 U.S. 556, 74 S. Ct. 716, 717, 98 L. Ed. 948, 950 (1954).

calculated to discredit law and thereby to brutalize the temper of a society.[25]

In 1957 the Court sustained the practice of state authorities in extracting blood from an unconscious person so as to prove he was under the influence of alcohol and responsible for an automobile collision, so long as the extraction was by a medically trained person. "The blood test procedure has become routine in our everyday life," noted the Court. Due process in these situations is to be measured, according to the Court, "by that whole community sense of 'decency and fairness' that has been woven by common experience into the fabric of acceptable conduct." The Court added:

> As against the right of an individual that his person be held inviolable, even against so light an intrusion as is involved in applying a blood test of the kind to which millions of Americans submit as a matter of course nearly every day, must be set the interests of society in the scientific determination of intoxication, one of the great causes of the mortal hazards of the road.

Chief Justice Warren, as well as Justices Black and Douglas, dissented because they believed the practice violative of the *Rochin* rule. They stated:

> Only personal reaction to the stomach pump and the blood test can distinguish them. To base the restriction which the Due Process Clause imposes on state criminal procedures upon such reactions is to build on shifting sands. . . . If the decencies of a civilized state are the test, it is repulsive to me for the police to insert needles into an unconscious person in order to get the evidence necessary to convict him . . . .[26]

In 1966, over dissents of Chief Justice Warren as well as Justices Black, Douglas and Fortas, the Supreme Court again held that the extraction of blood "in a simple, medically acceptable manner in a hospital environment," by a physician so as to prove alcoholism of a driver involved in an accident was constitutional. This case differs from *Breithaupt* in that here the driver was conscious at the time of

---

25. Rochin v. California, 342 U.S. 165, 72 S. Ct. 205, 96 L. Ed. 183, 25 A.L.R.2d 1396 (1952) (since holding that the Fourth Amendment exclusionary rule applies to the states, the Court has not relied on the *Rochin* "shocks the conscience" standard but has instead applied a Fourth Amendment reasonableness analysis in cases that, like *Rochin*, involved highly intrusive searches or seizures).

26. Breithaupt v. Abram, 352 U.S. 432, 77 S. Ct. 408, 1 L. Ed. 2d 448 (1957) (overruling recognized by, Filmon v. State, 336 So. 2d 586 (Fla. 1976)).

the blood extraction and protested. The Court noted: "The overriding function of the Fourth Amendment is to protect personal privacy and dignity against unwarranted intrusion by the State." It added:

> History and precedent have required that we today reject the claim that the Self-Incrimination Clause of the Fifth Amendment requires the human body in all circumstances to be held inviolate against state expeditions seeking evidence of crime. But if compulsory administration of a blood test does not implicate the Fifth Amendment, it plainly involves the broadly conceived reach of a search and seizure under the Fourth Amendment. That Amendment expressly provides that "the right of the people to be secure in their persons . . . against unreasonable searches and seizures, shall not be violated." . . . Such testing procedures plainly constitute searches of "persons" . . . the Fourth Amendment's proper function is to constrain, not against all intrusions as such, but against intrusions which are not justified in the circumstances, or which are made in an improper manner. In other words, the questions we must decide in this case are whether the police were justified in requiring petitioner to submit to the blood test, and whether the means and procedures employed in taking his blood respected relevant Fourth Amendment standards of reasonableness.

The Court concluded that the search was necessary and performed in a reasonable manner. It thought wise to add this dictum, however: "The integrity of an individual's person is a cherished value of our society. That we today hold that the Constitution does not forbid the States' minor intrusions into an individual's body under stringently limited conditions in no way indicates that it permits more substantial intrusions, or intrusions under other conditions." Said Justice Fortas in dissent: "As prosecutor, the State has no right to commit any kind of violence upon the person, or to utilize the results of such a tort, and the extraction of blood, over protest, is an act of violence."[27]

The Supreme Court in 1971 ruled admissible information overheard by government agents from an electronic device on the person of an informant, placed there with the consent of the informant and used to pick up conversations with the defendant, when the informant was not produced by the government at trial as a witness. The Court stated:

> The law permits the frustration of actual expectations of privacy

---

27. Schmerber v. California, 384 U.S. 757, 86 S. Ct. 1826, 16 L. Ed. 2d 908 (1966).

> by permitting authorities to use the testimony of those associ-
> ates who . . . have determined to turn to the police. . . . If the
> law gives no protection to the wrongdoer whose trusted ac-
> complice is or becomes a police agent, neither should it protect
> him when that same agent has recorded or transmitted the
> conversations which are later offered in evidence to prove the
> State's case.

Justice Harlan warned in his dissenting opinion that if such bugging
becomes prevalent "it might well smother that spontaneity—
reflected in frivolous, impetuous, sacrilegious, and defiant discourse—that liberates our daily life." Justices Douglas and Marshall
also dissented.[28]

In 1985 the Court stated that "a compelled surgical intrusion into
an individual's body for evidence implicates expectations of privacy
and security of such magnitude that the intrusion may be unreasonable even if likely to produce evidence of a crime." The Court then
ruled that a proper balancing of interests required affirmance of a
Court of Appeals order enjoining such operation out of respect for
the command of the Fourth Amendment that the citizen be free
from unreasonable governmental intrusions into any area in which
he has a reasonable expectation of privacy unless there is a "compelling need" for such intrusion to safeguard some very important
societal interest.[29]

§ 15.05. Punishing criminals

Society has a worthy interest in attempting to prevent antisocial
conduct, and it is sometimes thought that physically punishing those
convicted of crime deters them and others from wayward behavior.

The Eighth Amendment in the case of the federal government,
and the Fourteenth in the case of the states, prevents the imposition
of cruel and unusual punishment even upon those convicted of the
most heinous offenses.

In 1910, at a time when the Philippines were possessions of the
United States, the Supreme Court set aside a sentence subjecting a
person to 15 years of *cadena* for having falsified a public record.
Under *cadena*, prisoners at all times carried a chain at the ankle and
hanging from the wrists, and were constantly employed at hard and
painful labor. Said the Court:

> What constitutes a cruel and unusual punishment has not been
> exactly decided. It has been said that ordinarily the terms imply

28. U.S. v. White, 401 U.S. 745, 91 S. Ct. 1122, 28 L. Ed. 2d 453 (1971)
29. Winston v. Lee, 470 U.S. 753, 105 S. Ct. 1611, 84 L. Ed. 2d 662 (1985).

something inhuman and barbarous. . . . It was believed that power might be tempted to cruelty. This was the motive of the clause, and if we are to attribute an intelligent providence to its advocates we cannot think that it was intended to prohibit only practices like the Stuarts, or to prevent only an exact repetition of history. We cannot think that the possibility of a coercive cruelty being exercised through other forms of punishment was overlooked. We say "coercive cruelty" because there was more to be considered than the ordinary criminal laws. Cruelty might become an instrument of tyranny; of zeal for a purpose, either honest or sinister.[30]

Ever since the adoption of the Constitution, it has been understood that persons cannot be punished by burning at the stake, breaking on the wheel, subjection to the pillory, quartering, castration, etc.[31]

Whipping has been upheld at various times by some American courts,[32] although its constitutionality has been questioned from Cooley[33] to the present. The Supreme Court has emphasized that the Eight Amendment is to be given a "progressive" interpretation[34] and, as society matures, this form of punishment undoubtedly will appear to be cruel and unconstitutional.

Taking the life of one convicted of certain crimes is not cruel and unusual punishment at this writing,[35] although a number of justices of the Supreme Court have indicated they may be unwilling to condone its imposition for certain crimes where life was not endangered. Additional materials on this topic will be found in a subsequent chapter concerned with the permissibility of various sentences imposed upon persons convicted of crime.

Quite aside from the question of the kind and amount of punishment that ought to be permitted in a civilized society, there is a growing number of cases holding that the criminal law ought not to be applied at all to certain types of behavior traditionally treated as criminal. For example, even though an individual has violated valid societal interests in being a narcotics addict or in appearing drunk in public, his dignity and the nature of the behavior may prohibit criminal punishment entirely.

---

30. Weems v. U.S., 217 U.S. 349, 30 S. Ct. 544, 54 L. Ed. 793 (1910).

31. Hobbs v. State, 133 Ind. 404, 32 N.E. 1019 (1893); Commonwealth v. Wyatt, 27 Va. 694, 6 Rand. 694 (1828).

32. Foote v. State, 59 Md. 264 (1883) (as a punishment for wife-beating); Commonwealth v. Wyatt, 27 Va. 694, 6 Rand. 694 (1828).

33. Cooley, *Constitutional Limitations* (7th ed, Lane, 1903) p 472.

34. Weems v. U.S., 217 U.S. 349, 30 S. Ct. 544, 54 L. Ed. 793, 803 (1910).

35. Wilkerson v. State of Utah, 99 U.S. 130, 25 L. Ed. 345 (1878).

One way of protecting this value has been the Eighth Amendment's prohibition of cruel and unusual punishment. Thus in *Robinson v. California*[36] it was held that a state may not punish a person for the "status" of being a narcotics addict and being in the state. The Court was careful to point out that the police power is very broad indeed, and that it can be used in a wide variety of ways to protect society without branding narcotics addicts as criminals. Society's strong interest in suppressing the narcotics trade does not extend so far into the sanctity of the individual as to punish a person for being sick. In a most unfortunate 1968 decision, the Supreme Court, divided five-to-four, held that a state could punish a person who was a chronic alcoholic for being drunk in public. Justices Fortas, Douglas, Brennan and Stewart properly dissented, urging that it amounts to cruel and unusual punishment to sentence to jail a chronic alcoholic for being drunk in public. Justice White, whose vote was necessary to constitute the majority, acknowledged that the state cannot punish a person if it can be shown it is impossible for him to resist drunkenness in public places when intoxicated.[37] Worth recalling is the language of the Court six years earlier when it stated: "In the light of contemporary human knowledge, a law which made a criminal offense of such disease [as mental illness, leprosy or venereal disease] would doubtless be universally thought to be an infliction of cruel and unusual punishment in violation of the Eighth and Fourteenth Amendment."[38]

§ 15.06. Military service

The bodies and lives of citizens of the United States can, at the will of Congress, be exposed to injury and death by compulsory service in the national armed forces. The old Civil War veteran, Oliver Wendell Holmes, Jr., said while on the United States Supreme Court: "The public welfare may call upon the best citizens for their lives."[39] Federal draft laws have been sustained by the Supreme Court.[40] It is likely that in wartime the Court would sustain a draft of both men and women for work in essential industries.

---

36. Robinson v. California, 370 U.S. 660, 82 S. Ct. 1417, 8 L. Ed. 2d 758 (1962)

37. Powell v. State of Tex., 392 U.S. 514, 88 S. Ct. 2145, 20 L. Ed. 2d 1254 (1968).

38. Robinson v. California, 370 U.S. 660, 666, 82 S. Ct. 1417, 8 L. Ed. 2d 758 (1962).

39. Buck v. Bell, 274 U.S. 200, 47 S. Ct. 584, 71 L. Ed. 1000 (1927).

40. Estep v. U.S., 327 U.S. 114, 66 S. Ct. 423, 90 L. Ed. 567 (1946).

CHAPTER SIXTEEN

Unreasonable Searches and Seizures of Property

§ 16.00. Introduction

Our society has a strong interest in preventing government personnel from seizing private property. The United States Supreme Court has said: "The Fourth Amendment and the personal rights which it secures, have a long history. At the very core stands the right of a man to retreat into his own home and there be free from unreasonable governmental intrusion."[1] The ban upon unreasonable searches and seizures is directly made applicable to the federal government by the Fourth Amendment, and to the states and their political subdivisions indirectly by the Fourteenth Amendment.[2] The standard of reasonableness has been ruled by the Supreme Court to be "the same under the Fourth and Fourteenth Amendment."[3] Homes and other structures, personal properties such as cars, as well as private correspondence and conversations are all protected from unreasonable searches and seizures by government personnel.[4]

The Supreme Court states that "it is axiomatic that searches conducted outside the judicial process, without prior approval by judge or magistrate, are per se unconstitutional under the Fourth Amendment—subject only to a few specifically established and well delineated exceptions."[5] Administrative searches generally require warrants when there are reasonable expectations of privacy by the individual affected.[6]

The Supreme Court has held that the Fourth Amendment applies in Puerto Rico, and has ruled violative of this Amendment a warrantless search by Puerto Rico government personnel, of persons arriving there by air from the mainland United States[7] However, the Fourth Amendment was held inapplicable where federal agents acting in a foreign country seized property owned by a non-resident alien. "Under these circumstances," said the Court, "the Fourth Amendment has no application." Justices Brennan and Marshall in

---

1.   Silverman v. U.S., 365 U.S. 505, 81 S. Ct. 679, 5 L. Ed. 2d 734, 97 A.L.R.2d 1277 (1961).

2.   Mapp v. Ohio, 367 U.S. 643, 81 S. Ct. 1684, 6 L. Ed. 2d 1081, 16 Ohio Op. 2d 384, 86 Ohio L. Abs. 513, 84 A.L.R.2d 933 (1961).

3.   Ker v. State of Cal., 374 U.S. 23, 83 S. Ct. 1623, 10 L. Ed. 2d 726, 24 Ohio Op. 2d 201 (1963).

4.   U.S. v. Van Leeuwen, 397 U.S. 249, 90 S. Ct. 1029, 25 L. Ed. 2d 282 (1970).

5.   Colorado v. Bannister, 449 U.S. 1, 101 S Ct 42, 66 L. Ed. 2d 1 (1980).

6.   Michigan v. Clifford, 464 U.S. 287, 104 S. Ct. 641, 78 L. Ed. 2d 477 (1984).

7.   Torres v. Com. of Puerto Rico, 442 U.S. 465, 99 S. Ct. 2425, 61 L. Ed. 2d 1 (1979).

dissent remarked: "If we seek respect for law and order, we must observe these principles ourselves. Lawlessness breeds lawlessness."[8]

§ 16.01. A person's home

A person's home, by the general rule, may not be searched by authorities without a search warrant, even though the police have probable cause to suspect that there is within the house some article the possession of which is forbidden by law. The United States Supreme Court states: "Belief, however well founded, that an article sought is concealed in a dwelling house furnishes no justification for a search of that place without a warrant. And such searches are . . . unlawful notwithstanding facts unquestionably showing probable cause."[9] In 1961 the Court voided a search of a house containing a distillery when the authorities had ample time to secure a search warrant and neglected to do so. The Court said: "We think it must be concluded . . . that if the officers in this case were excused from the constitutional duty of presenting their evidence to a magistrate, it is difficult to think of a case in which it should be required."[10]

A tenant is entitled to Fourth Amendment protection in the house he rents.[11]

The Supreme Court has held unconstitutional state statutes that authorize police to enter a private residence without a warrant and with force, if necessary, to make a routine felony arrest. The Court states: "It is a basic principle of Fourth Amendment law that searches and seizures inside a home without a warrant are presumptively unreasonable. . . . In terms that apply equally to seizures of property and to seizures of persons, the Fourth Amendment has drawn a firm line at the entrance to the house. Absent exigent circumstances, that threshold may not reasonably be crossed without a warrant." However, by way of dictum, the Court remarked: "For Fourth Amendment purposes, an arrest warrant founded on probable cause implicitly carries with it the limited

---

8. U.S. v. Verdugo-Urquidez, 494 U.S. 259, 110 S. Ct. 1056, 108 L. Ed. 2d 222 (1990).

9. Agnello v. U.S., 269 U.S. 20, 46 S. Ct. 4, 70 L. Ed. 145, 149, 51 A.L.R. 409 (1925).

10. Chapman v. U.S., 365 U.S. 610, 81 S. Ct. 776, 779, 5 L. Ed. 2d 828 (1961).

11. Chapman v. U.S., 365 U.S. 610, 81 S. Ct. 776, 5 L. Ed. 2d 828 (1961).

authority to enter a dwelling in which the suspect lives when there is reason to believe the suspect is within."[12]

The Court concluded that the expectation of privacy in a motor home was less than in a house, and noted its mobile character; then ruled that police are justified in searching a mobile home without recourse to the authority of a magistrate and a warrant, so long as the standard of probable cause is met. Justices Stevens, Brennan and Marshall in dissent would hold that a warrantless search of living quarters in a motor home is presumptively unreasonable, absent exigent circumstances.[13] On the other hand, a seizure within the meaning of the Fourth Amendment occurred when a deputy sheriff and two employees of a trailer park illegally wrenched sewer and water connections off the side of a trailer home, disconnected the phones, tore off the trailer's canopy and skirting, and hooked up the trailer to a tractor. When two more deputy sheriffs arrived, the trailer home was towed into the street and later moved elsewhere. The Court repeated an earlier statement to the effect that a "'seizure' of property occurs where there is some meaningful interference with an individual's possessive interest in that property," and re-emphasized that "seizures of property are subject to Fourth Amendment scrutiny even though no search within the meaning of the Amendment had taken place." Here, as elsewhere, the reasonableness of the governmental action determines its constitutionality.[14]

The Supreme Court in 1995 readily acknowledged that "the common law of search and seizure leaves no doubt that the reasonableness of a search of a dwelling may depend in part on whether law enforcement officers announced their presence and authority prior to entering" and then held that this principle is an element of the basic reasonableness inquiry in the Fourth Amendment. This, however, does not require an announcement in every case. The Court recognized that the knock-and-announce requirement could give way "under circumstances presenting a threat of physical violence" or "where police officers have reason to believe that evidence would likely be destroyed if advance notice were given." In remanding, the Court indicated that it was for now allowing the lower courts to determine the circumstances under which an unan-

---

12. Payton v. New York, 445 U.S. 573, 100 S. Ct. 1371, 63 L. Ed. 2d 639 (1980).

13. California v. Carney, 471 U.S. 386, 105 S. Ct. 2066, 85 L. Ed. 2d 406 (1985).

14. Soldal v. Cook County, Ill., 506 U.S. 56, 113 S. Ct. 538, 121 L. Ed. 2d 450 (1992).

nounced entry is reasonable under the Fourth Amendment.[15] Four years later the Court explained further that "to justify a 'no knock' entry, the police must have a *reasonable* suspicion that knocking and announcing their presence under the circumstances would be dangerous or futile, or that it would inhibit the effective investigation of the crime by, for example, allowing the destruction of evidence." The task of courts will be to strike an "appropriate balance between the legitimate law enforcement concerns . . . and the individual privacy interests affected by no knock and announcement entries." In the instant case, the Court ruled that entry without knock or announcement was reasonable and valid, since the officers had a reasonable suspicion that the hotel room occupant might destroy evidence if given further opportunity to do so.[16]

§ 16.02. Temporary dwellings

An overnight guest in a house has a Fourth Amendment right to be protected against a warrantless search.[17]

Lawful guests in hotel rooms are protected by the Fourth Amendment.[18] The Supreme Court in 1948 invalidated a search of a hotel room made by officers when they detected a strong odor of burning opium coming from the room. The Court said: "No reason is offered for not obtaining a search warrant except the inconvenience to the officers and some slight delay necessary to prepare papers and present the evidence to a magistrate. These are never very convincing reasons and, in these circumstances, certainly are not enough to bypass the constitutional requirement."[19]

Occupants of boarding houses are constitutionally protected against unreasonable searches and seizures,[20] as are persons lawfully in the apartments or other dwellings of friends.[21]

§ 16.03. Commercial properties

Lawful owners and lessees, as well as persons lawfully on the

---

15. Wilson v. Arkansas, 514 U.S. 927, 115 S. Ct. 1914, 131 L. Ed. 2d 976 (1995).

16. Richards v. Wisconsin, 117 S. Ct. 1416, 137 L. Ed. 2d 615 (U.S. 1997).

17. Minnesota v. Olson, 495 U.S. 91, 110 S. Ct. 1684, 109 L. Ed. 2d 85 (1990).

18. Lustig v. United States, 338 U.S. 74, 69 S. Ct. 1372, 93 L. Ed. 1819 (1949); U.S. v. Jeffers, 342 U.S. 48, 72 S. Ct. 93, 96 L. Ed. 59 (1951); Stoner v. State of Cal., 376 U.S. 483, 84 S. Ct. 889, 11 L. Ed. 2d 856 (1964).

19. Johnson v. U.S., 333 U.S. 10, 68 S. Ct. 367, 92 L. Ed. 436, 441 (1948).

20. McDonald v. U.S., 335 U.S. 451, 69 S. Ct. 191, 93 L. Ed. 153 (1948).

21. Jones v. U.S., 362 U.S. 257, 80 S. Ct. 725, 4 L. Ed. 2d 697, 78 A.L.R.2d 233 (1960) (overruled on other grounds by, U.S. v. Salvucci, 448 U.S. 83, 100 S. Ct. 2547, 65 L. Ed. 2d 619 (1980)).

premises, of offices are entitled to Fourth Amendment protection.[22] Where a union officer shared space in an office where the union records were kept, he had standing to object to an unreasonable search and seizure of the office when the records of the union were offered in evidence against him at a trial on criminal charges.[23]

Business persons are protected in their commercial premises. The Supreme Court has held that a liquor licensee was entitled to suppression and return of liquor seized unlawfully by federal authorities. By way of dictum, the Court suggested that "Congress has broad authority to fashion standards of reasonableness for searches and seizures."[24] Although a warrantless administrative search has been allowed where conducted on business premises, but not within any building,[25] generally such warrantless administrative searches in non-public areas of business buildings are invalid.[26]

In 1974 the Supreme Court held that no Fourth Amendment right of a depositor was violated by Title I of the Bank Secrecy Act of 1970, where the statute required banks to keep records of virtually all commercial transactions, with governmental access to these being governed by existing legal process.[27] Justice Douglas dissented, stating: "Customers have a constitutionally justifiable expectation of privacy in the documentary details of the financial transactions reflected in their bank accounts." Justices Brennan and Marshall also dissented. The same year the Court upheld, over Fourth Amendment objections of the banks, Title II of the same Act, which required banks to make reports of transactions in foreign commerce of over $10,000. The Court concluded that Congress was justified in believing large currency transfers into and out of the country were being used to circumvent United States laws. The reporting requirement for the banks was not deemed an invasion of their Fourth

---

22. Gouled v. U.S., 255 U.S. 298, 41 S. Ct. 261, 65 L. Ed. 647 (1921) (overruled in part on other grounds by, Warden, Md. Penitentiary v. Hayden, 387 U.S. 294, 87 S. Ct. 1642, 18 L. Ed. 2d 782 (1967)); G. M. Leasing Corp. v. U.S., 429 U.S. 338, 97 S. Ct. 619, 50 L. Ed. 2d 530 (1977).

23. Mancusi v. DeForte, 392 U.S. 364, 88 S. Ct. 2120, 20 L. Ed. 2d 1154 (1968).

24. Colonnade Catering Corp. v. U.S., 397 U.S. 72, 90 S. Ct. 774, 25 L. Ed. 2d 60 (1970).

25. Air Pollution Variance Bd. of Colorado v. Western Alfalfa Corp., 416 U.S. 861, 94 S. Ct. 2114, 40 L. Ed. 2d 607 (1974).

26. Air Pollution Variance Bd. of Colorado v. Western Alfalfa Corp., 416 U.S. 861, 94 S. Ct. 2114, 40 L. Ed. 2d 607 (1974).

27. California Bankers Ass'n v. Shultz, 416 U.S. 21, 94 S. Ct. 1494, 39 L. Ed. 2d 812 (1974).

Amendment rights.[28] Two years later the Court ruled that bank records of a depositor were not within a protected zone of privacy, and held that a depositor's Fourth Amendment rights were not violated when the federal government obtained his bank records by a defective subpoena. The Court said that it "has repeatedly held that the Fourth Amendment does not prohibit the obtaining of information revealed to a third party and conveyed by him to government authorities, even if the information is revealed on the assumption that it will be used only for a limited purpose and the confidence placed in the third party will not be betrayed." In dissent, Justices Brennan and Marshall stated that a depositor should have a reasonable expectation of privacy in his bank records.[29]

The Court has recognized that a business, by its special nature and voluntary existence, may open itself to intrusions that would not be permissible in a purely private context. It has upheld a warrantless search of a locked storeroom during business hours, pursuant to the inspection procedure authorized by the Gun Control Act of 1968, 18 U.S.C.A. § 923(g), stating: "When a dealer chooses to engage in this pervasively regulated business and to accept a federal license, he does so with the knowledge that his business records, firearms, and ammunition will be subject to effective inspection."[30]

§ 16.04. The open fields doctrine

Traditionally the protection of the Fourth Amendment does not extend beyond the curtilage to open fields. In 1924, the United States Supreme Court held that officers could seize a jar of spirits from open lands owned by the defendant's father. Justice Holmes said for a unanimous Court: "The special protection accorded by the Fourth Amendment to the people in their 'persons, houses, papers, and effects' is not extended to the open fields. The distinction between the latter and the house is as old as the common law."[31]

The Court in 1974 held within the open fields doctrine, and unprotected by the Fourth Amendment, activities of a public inspector in doing an air pollution test on the property of an industrial

---

28. California Bankers Ass'n v. Shultz, 416 U.S. 21, 94 S. Ct. 1494, 39 L. Ed. 2d 812 (1974).

29. U.S. v. Miller, 425 U.S. 435, 96 S. Ct. 1619, 48 L. Ed. 2d 71 (1976).

30. U.S. v. Biswell, 406 U.S. 311, 92 S. Ct. 1593, 32 L. Ed. 2d 87 (1972).

31. Hester v. U.S., 265 U.S. 57, 59, 44 S. Ct. 445, 68 L. Ed. 898, 890 (1924).

firm without the knowledge or consent of the owner.[32] Ten years later the Court again held that "open fields" are not protected by the Fourth Amendment, nor are the "outdoors . . . except in the area immediately surrounding the home." The Court ruled that an invasion by public servants of private property in open fields is not a "search" under the Fourth Amendment simply because on the facts it was a criminal trespass at common law. In dissent, Justices Brennan, Marshall, and Stevens noted that the police had ignored "no trespassing" signs posted on the properties, and they urged that the Fourth Amendment should generally protect against unreasonable invasions and criminal trespasses on private lands so marked.[33]

In 1988 the Court held that a barn 50 yards from a fence surrounding a ranch house was outside the curtilage of the house and in open fields. The Court indicated that "curtilage questions should be resolved with particular reference to four factors: the proximity of the area claimed to be curtilage to the home; whether the area is included within an enclosure surrounding the home; the nature of the uses to which the area is put, and the steps taken by the resident to protect the area from observation by people passing by." The Court ruled that officers could walk across the "open fields" and look into the barn, so that evidence thereby seen would later support a warrant. It is difficult to disagree with dissenting Justices Brennan and Marshall, who pointed out that both federal and state courts had held that barns on farms and ranches were within the curtilage, and that the owners had a reasonable expectation of privacy in the barnyard that brought the Fourth Amendment into play, so that they were protected from intrusions from officers who had traveled a half mile off a public road over the owner's fenced-in property so that they could shine their flashlight into the barn.[34]

In 1977 the Supreme Court held that federal tax agents could seize automobiles owned by a taxpayer in arrears and kept on public streets, parking lots and other open spaces. The Court analogized this to an earlier sustained seizure of liquor in an open field and found no unconstitutional invasion of personal privacy.[35]

§ 16.05. Scientific and mechanical invasions of privacy

The Supreme Court held in 1961 that the Fourth Amendment

---

32. Air Pollution Variance Bd. of Colorado v. Western Alfalfa Corp., 416 U.S. 861, 94 S. Ct. 2114, 40 L. Ed. 2d 607 (1974).

33. Oliver v. U.S., 466 U.S. 170, 104 S. Ct. 1735, 80 L. Ed. 2d 214 (1984).

34. U.S. v. Dunn, 480 U.S. 294, 107 S. Ct. 1134, 94 L. Ed. 2d 326 (1987).

35. G. M. Leasing Corp. v. U.S., 429 U.S. 338, 97 S. Ct. 619, 50 L. Ed. 2d 530 (1977).

extends to the recording of oral statements overheard without any technical trespass under local property law.[36] Six years later the Court held that the earlier *Olmstead*[37] and *Goldman*[38] decisions, allowing the use of detectaphones placed on the outer wall of a hotel room and the use of microphones to pick up conversations, "can no longer be regarded as controlling."[39] In the *Katz* decision the Court re-emphasized that the reach of the Fourth Amendment does not turn upon the presence or absence of a physical intrusion into any given enclosure. The Court there ruled that the Amendment protects a person making a telephone call from a public booth from governmental use of an electronic listening and recording device affixed to the outside of the booth. The Fourth Amendment protects the individual from intrusion into the areas of his life he desires to keep private from all forms of mechanical and electronic intrusion.

The *Katz* case has added interest because the Court said by way of dictum that a magistrate could have authorized such a search as occurred "with appropriate safeguards."[40] The Court emphasized that before such a search can be made it is necessary to present the estimate of probable cause to a neutral magistrate, there must be precise limits established in advance of the search by specific court order, and after the search is completed the officers must notify the authorizing magistrate in detail of all that was seized.[41]

Two years later the Court held that the rule of the *Katz* case was to be applied only prospectively to cases tried after that decision. The criteria guiding determination of retroactivity of a ruling are these: (a) the purpose to be served by the new standards, (b) the extent of the reliance by law enforcement authorities on the old

---

36. Silverman v. U.S., 365 U.S. 505, 81 S. Ct. 679, 5 L. Ed. 2d 734, 97 A.L.R.2d 1277 (1961).

37. Olmstead v. U.S., 277 U.S. 438, 48 S. Ct. 564, 72 L. Ed. 944, 66 A.L.R. 376 (1928) (overruled in part by, Berger v. State of N. Y., 388 U.S. 41, 87 S. Ct. 1873, 18 L. Ed. 2d 1040 (1967)) and (overruled in part by, Katz v. U.S., 389 U.S. 347, 88 S. Ct. 507, 19 L. Ed. 2d 576 (1967)).

38. Goldman v. U.S., 316 U.S. 129, 62 S. Ct. 993, 86 L. Ed. 1322 (1942) (overruled in part by, Katz v. U.S., 389 U.S. 347, 88 S. Ct. 507, 19 L. Ed. 2d 576 (1967)).

39. Katz v. U.S., 389 U.S. 347, 88 S. Ct. 507, 19 L. Ed. 2d 576, 583 (1967).

40. Katz v. U.S., 389 U.S. 347, 88 S. Ct. 507, 19 L. Ed. 2d 576, 584 (1967).

41. Katz v. U.S., 389 U.S. 347, 88 S. Ct. 507, 19 L. Ed. 2d 576, 585 (1967).

standards, and (c) the effect on the administration of justice of a retroactive application of the new standards.[42]

The Federal Communications Act provides: "No person not being authorized by the sender shall intercept any radio communication and divulge or publish the existence, contents, substance, purport, effect, or meaning of such intercepted communication to any person."[43] The use in federal prosecutions of illegal wire taps by either federal or state officers is barred by the Act.[44] The 1952 *Schwartz v. Texas* case[45] has been repudiated and the Court now holds that the Communications Act prohibits admission in state courts of evidence secured by violations of the federal statute.[46] Under the Act, evidence can be used in federal court if one person to the conversation has consented to the wiretap.[47]

In 1967 the Supreme Court voided a New York practice which allowed electronic eavesdropping. The statute authorized ex parte orders by state judges upon affidavits of local district attorneys or police officers above the rank of sergeant that there was reasonable ground to believe that evidence of crime may be obtained. The order was for two months and could be extended further. The Court found objectionable the lack of particularization in the procedure, since no specific crime had to be named in the warrant, nor did the property sought—the conversations—have to be particularly described. The state, said the Court, cannot give the police "a roving commission to seize any and all conversations." The Court also was critical of the fact that eavesdropping for a two-month period "is the equivalent of a series of intrusions, searches and seizures pursuant to a single showing of probable cause." In addition, the Court found wanting in the statute any provision for termination of the search once the conversation sought was picked up, as well as a provision requiring return on the warrant, thus "leaving full discretion in the officer as to the use of seized conversations of innocent as well as guilty parties." In concluding, the Court noted that it had condoned the use

42. Desist v. United States, 394 U.S. 244, 89 S. Ct. 1048, 22 L. Ed. 2d 248 (1969); Kaiser v. New York, 394 U.S. 280, 89 S. Ct. 1044, 22 L. Ed. 2d 274 (1969).

43. § 605, Federal Communications Act, 47 U.S.C.A. § 605(a).

44. Benanti v. U.S., 355 U.S. 96, 78 S. Ct. 155, 2 L. Ed. 2d 126 (1957).

45. Schwartz v. State of Tex., 344 U.S. 199, 73 S. Ct. 232, 97 L. Ed. 231 (1952) (overruled by, Lee v. State of Fla., 392 U.S. 378, 88 S. Ct. 2096, 20 L. Ed. 2d 1166 (1968)).

46. Lee v. State of Fla., 392 U.S. 378, 88 S. Ct. 2096, 20 L. Ed. 2d 1166 (1968).

47. Rathbun v. U.S., 355 U.S. 107, 78 S. Ct. 161, 2 L. Ed. 2d 134 (1957).

of eavesdropping devices "under specific conditions and circumstances."[48]

In 1971 the Court ruled admissible information overheard by government agents from an electronic device on the person of an informant, placed there with the consent of the informant and used to pick up conversations with the defendant, even though the informant was not produced by the government at trial as a witness. The Court said:

> The law permits the frustration of actual expectations of privacy by permitting authorities to use the testimony of those associates who . . . have determined to turn to the police. If the law gives no protection to the wrongdoer whose trusted accomplice is or becomes a police agent, neither should it protect him when that same agent has recorded or transmitted the conversations which are later offered in evidence to prove the State's case.

Justices Harlan, Douglas and Marshall dissented.[49] However, the following year, the Court held that the federal government cannot conduct electronic surveillance of citizens, without warrants issued by a magistrate, when the Attorney General thinks it necessary to gather information on suspected subversives. The Court indicated it arrived at this result by balancing basic values: protecting against subversion on one hand, and on the other hand the interest in "individual privacy and free expression." Justice Powell, speaking for the Court, said:

> The Fourth Amendment contemplates a prior judicial judgment, not the risk that executive discretion may be reasonably exercised. This judicial role accords with our basic constitutional doctrine that individual freedoms will best be preserved through a separation of powers and division of functions among the different branches and levels of government.[50]

In 1983 the Supreme Court held that use of a beeper placed by government personnel in a container of chloroform, in a defendant's secluded cabin in the woods where he was making amphetamines, did not violate the Fourth Amendment, there being, according to

---

48. Berger v. State of N.Y., 388 U.S. 41, 87 S. Ct. 1873, 1883-85, 18 L. Ed. 2d 1040 (1967).

49. U.S. v. White, 401 U.S. 745, 91 S. Ct. 1122, 28 L. Ed. 2d 453 (1971).

50. U.S. v. U.S. Dist. Court for Eastern Dist. of Mich., Southern Division, 407 U.S. 297, 92 S. Ct. 2125, 32 L. Ed. 2d 752 (1972).

the Court, no invasion of any "legitimate expectations of privacy."[51] The following year, the Court held that the transfer of a container housing a beeper, installed with the consent of the transferor, is not a search or seizure since so long as the beeper remains unmonitored, no information is conveyed, and there is no interference with the transferee's possessory interest.[52] Even though less intrusive than a full-scale search, the monitoring of a beeper in a private residence, a location not open to visual surveillance, violates the Fourth Amendment rights of those who have a justifiable interest in the privacy of the residence.[53]

The Supreme Court, in a 1986 five-to-four decision, ruled that the Fourth Amendment was not violated by aerial observation without a warrant from an altitude of 1,000 feet of a fenced-in backyard within the curtilage of a residence. The majority reasoned "that respondent's expectations that his garden was protected from such observation is unreasonable." Justices Powell, Blackmun, Brennan and Marshall would find violative of the Fourth Amendment police overflight of a residential backyard at low altitudes, solely for the purpose of discovering evidence of a crime, when the police were clearly forbidden to intrude into the area at ground level without a warrant.[54] In a companion case the Court, again divided five-to-four, held permissible aerial photographs of an industrial complex by the Environmental Protection Agency, the majority remarking that the government has "a greater latitude to conduct warrantless inspections of commercial property."[55] And in 1989 a four justice plurality opinion held that there was no impermissible search when police in a helicopter examined the contents of a citizen's backyard. That opinion stated: "As far as this record reveals, no intimate details connected with the use of the home or curtilage were observed, and there was no undue noise, no wind, dust, or threat of injury. In these circumstances, there was no violation of the Fourth Amendment." Justice O'Connor in her concurring opinion would have a citizen bearing the burden of proving that his expectation of privacy in such a matter was a reasonable one, in order to find a "search" within the meaning of the Fourth Amendment. Justice Blackmun in dissent stated that it is for the prosecution to show that the property

---

51. U.S. v. Knotts, 460 U.S. 276, 103 S. Ct. 1081, 75 L. Ed. 2d 55 (1983).

52. U.S. v. Karo, 468 U.S. 705, 104 S. Ct. 3296, 82 L. Ed. 2d 530 (1984).

53. U.S. v. Karo, 468 U.S. 705, 104 S. Ct. 3296, 82 L. Ed. 2d 530 (1984).

54. California v. Ciraolo, 476 U.S. 207, 106 S. Ct. 1809, 90 L. Ed. 2d 210 (1986).

55. Dow Chemical Co. v. U.S., 476 U.S. 227, 106 S. Ct. 1819, 90 L. Ed. 2d 226 (1986).

owner lacked a reasonable expectation of privacy, and that the prosecution had not met the burden. Justices Brennan, Marshall and Stevens also dissented, wondering what visual inspection by police from the air of "intimate activities" the majority would hold violative of the Fourth Amendment.[56]

§ 16.06. Where search warrants are valid

Under the Fourth Amendment, magistrates may not issue a warrant to search private property unless they find probable cause from facts and circumstances presented to them under oath or affirmation.[57] When an affidavit does not provide a sufficient basis for a finding of probable cause by the magistrate, the search warrant is not to be issued.[58]

The term "probable cause" does not mean evidence necessary to convict, and a finding of probable cause may rest upon evidence which is not legally competent at trial.[59] Thus, an affidavit in support of an application for a search warrant may be based on hearsay and need not reflect the direct personal observations of the affiant,[60] so long as there is a substantial basis for crediting the hearsay.[61] However, the magistrate must be informed of some of the underlying circumstances from which the affiant concludes that an informant—whose identity need not be disclosed—is credible or his information is reliable.[62]

A tip from an informant will not be sufficient to provide the basis for a finding of probable cause by a magistrate unless it contains a sufficient statement of the underlying circumstances from which the informant has concluded that the individual to be searched has been engaged in criminal activity. The Supreme Court stated in 1969: "In the absence of a statement detailing the manner in which the information was gathered, it is especially important that the tip describe the accused's criminal activity in sufficient detail so that the magistrate may know that he is relying on something more substantial than a casual rumor circulating in the underworld or an

---

56. Florida v. Riley, 488 U.S. 445, 102 L. Ed. 2d 835, 109 S. Ct. 693 (1989).

57. Nathanson v. U.S., 290 U.S. 41, 54 S. Ct. 11, 78 L. Ed. 159 (1933).

58. Giordenello v. U.S., 357 U.S. 480, 78 S. Ct. 1245, 2 L. Ed. 2d 1503 (1958).

59. Draper v. U.S., 358 U.S. 307, 79 S. Ct. 329, 3 L. Ed. 2d 327 (1959).

60. Jones v. U.S., 362 U.S. 257, 80 S. Ct. 725, 4 L. Ed. 2d 697, 78 A.L.R.2d 233 (1960) (overruled on other grounds by, U.S. v. Salvucci, 448 U.S. 83, 100 S. Ct. 2547, 65 L. Ed. 2d 619 (1980)).

61. Rugendorf v. U.S., 376 U.S. 528, 84 S. Ct. 825, 11 L. Ed. 2d 887 (1964).

62. Aguilar v. State of Tex., 378 U.S. 108, 84 S. Ct. 1509, 12 L. Ed. 2d 723 (1964).

accusation based merely on the individual's general reputation." The Court additionally insisted that it is not enough that a public officer swear that his confidant is reliable; he must provide the magistrate with reasons in support of such a conclusion.[63] Two years later the Court held that a magistrate in determining that an unidentified informant's information to a police agent is truthful, can give consideration to the fact that his statements are against interest and could expose him to criminal punishment, and that a policeman's knowledge of the suspect's reputation is something that a magistrate may properly rely upon in assessing the reliability of an informant. Justices Harlan, Douglas, Brennan and Marshall dissented because they concluded that the affidavit did not provide a sufficient basis for an independent determination by a neutral judicial officer that probable cause existed. Justice Harlan summarized the applicable law as follows:

> Where . . . the affiant states under oath that he has been informed of the existence of certain criminal activity, but has not observed that activity himself, a magistrate in discharging his duty to make an independent assessment of probable cause can properly issue a search warrant only if he concludes that (a) the knowledge attributed to the informant, if true, would be sufficient to establish probable cause, (b) the affiant is likely relating truthfully what the informant said, and (c) it is reasonably likely that the informant's description of criminal behavior accurately reflects reality.

Justice Harlan added that "the affidavit must set forth facts which enable the magistrate to judge for himself both the probable credibility of the informant and the reliability of his information." Justice Harlan concluded:

> A person who has not been shown to possess any of the common attributes of credibility, whose name cannot be disclosed to a magistrate and whose information has not been corroborated, is precisely the sort of informant whose tip should not be the sole basis for the issuance of a warrant.[64]

It is only in this way that the determination of probable cause can be made by an impartial judicial officer. Elsewhere the Supreme Court has emphasized that probable cause cannot "be made out by affidavits which are purely conclusory, stating only the affiant's or an informant's belief that probable cause exists without detailing

---

63. Spinelli v. U.S., 393 U.S. 410, 89 S. Ct. 584, 21 L. Ed. 2d 637 (1969).
64. U.S. v. Harris, 403 U.S. 573, 91 S. Ct. 2075, 29 L. Ed. 2d 723 (1971).

any of the underlying circumstances upon which that belief is based. Recital of some of the underlying circumstances in the affidavit is necessary if the magistrate is to perform his detached function and not serve merely as a rubber stamp for the police."[65]

In 1983 the Court held that whether a magistrate, in issuing a search warrant, has reasonable and probable cause is to be determined by the "totality of the circumstances." The Court nevertheless reaffirmed that conclusory statements before the magistrate are not enough, nor are general statements that the affiants have received reliable information from a credible person and believe something to be true.[66] *Illinois v. Gates* has in effect overruled the earlier two-pronged test which required that the affidavit, first, had to establish the basis of knowledge of the informant, and second, must provide facts establishing either the general veracity of the informant or the specific reliability of the informant's report in the particular case. Now the Fourth Amendment's requirement of probable cause for the issuance of a warrant is to be applied, not according to a fixed and rigid formula, but rather in the light of the totality of the circumstances made known to the magistrate.[67]

Affidavits for search warrants are customarily prepared by persons untrained in the law and they are to be tested and interpreted by magistrates and courts in a common sense and realistic fashion. The Supreme Court has said: "Technical requirements of elaborate specificity once exacted under common law pleadings have no proper place in this area."[68]

Under the Fourth Amendment a defendant in a criminal proceeding has a right, subsequent to an ex parte issuance of a search warrant, to an evidentiary hearing where he can challenge the truthfulness of factual statements made in an affidavit supporting the warrant by making a suitable preliminary proffer to show there were deliberate misstatements or reckless disregard of the truth by the affiant.[69]

The Supreme Court insists that in determining probable cause for a warrant inferences "be drawn by a neutral and detached magistrate," not "by an officer engaged in the often competitive

---

65. U.S. v. Ventresca, 380 U.S. 102, 85 S. Ct. 741, 13 L. Ed. 2d 684 (1965).

66. Illinois v. Gates, 462 U.S. 213, 103 S. Ct. 2317, 76 L. Ed. 2d 527 (1983).

67. Massachusetts v. Upton, 466 U.S. 727, 104 S. Ct. 2085, 80 L. Ed. 2d 721 (1984).

68. U.S. v. Ventresca, 380 U.S. 102, 85 S. Ct. 741, 13 L. Ed. 2d 684, 689 (1965).

69. Franks v. Delaware, 438 U.S. 154, 98 S. Ct. 2674, 57 L. Ed. 2d 667 (1978).

enterprise of ferreting out crime."[70] In invalidating a search warrant issued by a justice of the peace who was also the Attorney General of New Hampshire actively in charge of the accused's investigation and who was later to be the chief prosecutor at trial, the Court cautioned in 1971 that "there could hardly be a more appropriate setting than this for a *per se* rule of disqualification, rather than a case-by-case evaluation of all the circumstances."[71] The Fourth Amendment is also violated when search warrants can be issued by justices of the peace who are paid a statutory sum for issuing warrants but nothing if they decide to deny the warrants.[72] However, the Court has unwisely condoned the issuance of search warrants by federal administrative officers, such as district directors of the Immigration and Naturalization Service.[73]

The Court held in 1978 that neither the Fourth nor the First Amendments were violated when government officers secured a warrant and went into a newspaper's office looking for films of a recent demonstration to identify the persons involved. The Court held that an otherwise valid search warrant is not invalid because it authorizes the search of the property of an admittedly innocent third person. Justices Marshall and Stewart dissented, finding a First Amendment violation and forecasting that with this rule the flow of information to the press will be seriously affected. Justice Stevens also dissented, on Fourth Amendment grounds.[74]

During a lawful search pursuant to a warrant, unanticipated discovery of instrumentalities of crime can result in their seizure.[75] However, "not every item may be seized which is properly inspectable by the government in the course of a legal search; for example, private papers desired by the government merely for use as evidence may not be seized, no matter how lawful the search which discovers them."[76]

The Supreme Court has held that the Fourth Amendment does not require suppression of evidence seized from a private residence pursuant to a valid search warrant, which was issued on information obtained by the police earlier on an illegal entry. The Court did not

---

70. Johnson v. U.S., 333 U.S. 10, 68 S. Ct. 367, 92 L. Ed. 436, 440 (1948).

71. Coolidge v. New Hampshire, 403 U.S. 443, 91 S. Ct. 2022, 29 L. Ed. 2d 564 (1971).

72. Connally v. Georgia, 429 U.S. 245, 97 S. Ct. 546, 50 L. Ed. 2d 444 (1977).

73. Abel v. U.S., 362 U.S. 217, 80 S. Ct. 683, 4 L. Ed. 2d 668 (1960).

74. Zurcher v. Stanford Daily, 436 U.S. 547, 98 S. Ct. 1970, 56 L. Ed. 2d 525 (1978).

75. Abel v. U.S., 362 U.S. 217, 80 S. Ct. 683, 4 L. Ed. 2d 668 (1960).

76. Abel v. U.S., 362 U.S. 217, 80 S. Ct. 683, 4 L. Ed. 2d 668 (1960).

decide whether, following the entry, the internal securing of the premises constituted an impermissible seizure of all the contents of the residence.[77] The "independent source" exception to the exclusionary rule from *Segura v. United States,* above, was held to justify the admission of evidence discovered by police under a valid search warrant, even though the identical police officer had seen the same matter before during an illegal search. So long as the material is "untainted by earlier illegal action," the plurality opinion for the Court would admit it. With Justices Brennan and Kennedy not participating, Justices Marshall, Stevens and O'Connor dissented on the ground that when the same officers illegally search premises, evidence procured by a valid search at a later time should not be admissible.[78]

Search warrants are invalid when they do not with particularity describe the premises to be searched and the things to be seized. The Supreme Court has said:

> General searches have long been deemed to violate fundamental rights. It is plain that the Amendment forbids them. . . . The requirement that warrants shall particularly describe the things to be seized makes general searches under them impossible and prevents the seizure of one thing under a warrant describing another.[79]

Thus, search warrants are unconstitutional when they are too broadly permissive. In 1965, for instance, the Court invalidated a warrant that authorized the seizure of "books, records, pamphlets, cards, receipts, lists, memoranda, pictures, recordings and other written instruments concerning the Communist Party of Texas, and the operations of the Communist Party in Texas." Said the Court: "The indiscriminate sweep of that language is constitutionally intolerable." In effect this was a general warrant, which the Founding Fathers intended to forever outlaw. The Court took the occasion to indicate that when a search warrant authorizes the seizure of books and literature, there are both Fourth Amendment and First Amendment considerations demanding that the warrant be carefully limited. Said the Court: "The constitutional requirement that warrants must particularly describe the things to be seized is to be accorded the most scrupulous exactitude when the 'things' are books, and the basis for their seizure is the ideas which they contain. . . .

---

77. Segura v. U.S., 468 U.S. 796, 104 S. Ct. 3380, 82 L. Ed. 2d 599 (1984).
78. Murray v. U.S., 487 U.S. 533, 108 S. Ct. 2529, 101 L. Ed. 2d 472 (1988).
79. Marron v. U.S., 275 U.S. 192, 195, 48 S. Ct. 74, 72 L. Ed. 231, 236 (1927).

No less a standard could be faithful to First Amendment freedoms."[80]

Also of the Fourth Amendment was an "open-ended" search warrant that did not particularly describe books and films seized.[81] But while readily acknowledging that general warrants are prohibited by the Fourth Amendment, the Supreme Court in 1976 nevertheless sustained a warrant allowing officers to search for "other fruits, instrumentalities and evidence of crime at the [time] unknown." The state court had believed the warrant only authorized search for and seizure of evidence relating to the crime of false pretenses with regard to the sale of a particular lot. The Court held valid the seizure of information regarding other lots as possibly showing the accused's intent with respect to the particular lot in the warrant. Justices Brennan and Marshall dissented, finding such construction of the warrant impermissible as authorizing a general warrant, and emphasizing that the officers who searched and seized took away with them a considerable number of other papers and records, which had been suppressed before trial on constitutional grounds.[82]

§ 16.07. Execution and enforcement of search warrants

The Supreme Court has always said that "the manner in which a warrant is executed is subject to later judicial review as to its reasonableness."[83] A search warrant should preferably be served upon a lawful occupant of the premises to be searched, but if no one is there present, the officers can nevertheless consummate the search.[84] In executing search warrants, officers may break into a house to effectuate the search where they are refused admission after informing the occupants of the search warrant or cannot otherwise make an entry.[85]

The Court found that police officers had acted reasonably when they searched a wrong apartment on the same floor of a building as the one for which they had a valid warrant, and concluded that there was no violation of the Fourth Amendment. Justices Black-

---

80. Stanford v. State of Tex., 379 U.S. 476, 485, 85 S. Ct. 506, 13 L. Ed. 2d 431, 437 (1965).

81. Lo-Ji Sales, Inc. v. New York, 442 U.S. 319, 99 S. Ct. 2319, 60 L. Ed. 2d 920 (1979).

82. Andresen v. Maryland, 427 U.S. 463, 96 S. Ct. 2737, 49 L. Ed. 2d 627 (1976).

83. Dalia v. U.S., 441 U.S. 238, 99 S. Ct. 1682, 60 L. Ed. 2d 177 (1979).

84. U.S. v. Camarota, 278 F. 388 (S.D. Cal. 1922).

85. 18 U.S.C.A. § 3109; Miller v. U.S., 357 U.S. 301, 78 S. Ct. 1190, 2 L. Ed. 2d 1332 (1958).

mun, Marshall and Brennan dissented, noting that the home had always received special protection under the Fourth Amendment, and stated that "the mistakes here, both with respect to obtaining and executing the warrant, are not reasonable and could easily have been avoided."[86] The Court has held that the Fourth Amendment did not prohibit per se a covert entry performed for the purpose of installing otherwise legal electronic bugging equipment. The Court ruled that a court in granting a warrant to install electronic surveillance devices need not set forth precisely the procedures to be followed by the government agents.[87]

A warrant to search for contraband, founded on probable cause, impliedly carries with it the limited authority to detain the occupants of the premises while a proper search is conducted. The Court indicated that it would not decide whether the result would be the same when officers were searching only for evidence.[88] When officers investigating premises with a valid search warrant reasonably and in good faith discover either contraband or articles being used in the commission of a crime, such things can be seized although not named in the search warrant.[89] A federal court has also permitted the officers with a search warrant to seize weapons which could be used to effect an escape.[90]

Officers seizing property pursuant to a search warrant are to give receipts to the occupant of the premises or leave behind such a receipt if no one is in attendance, and then make a return with an inventory of things taken to the judicial officer who authorized the issuance of the warrant.[91]

§ 16.08. Exceptional situations where search warrants are not required

There are a number of fairly well defined situations in which the United States permits searches and seizures without a warrant issued by a magistrate. It was not warrantless searches that were outlawed by the American Founding Fathers but unreasonable ones. The Supreme Court has remarked: "It is unreasonable searches that are prohibited by the Fourth Amendment. . . . It was recognized by

---

86. Maryland v. Garrison, 480 U.S. 79, 107 S. Ct. 1013, 94 L. Ed. 2d 72 (1987).

87. Dalia v. U.S., 441 U.S. 238, 99 S. Ct. 1682, 60 L. Ed. 2d 177 (1979).

88. Michigan v. Summers, 452 U.S. 692, 101 S. Ct. 2587, 69 L. Ed. 2d 340 (1981).

89. Sanders v. United States, 238 F.2d 145 (10th Cir. 1956).

90. Palmer v. U.S., 92 U.S. App. D.C. 103, 203 F.2d 66 (D.C. Cir. 1953).

91. Fed. R. Crim. P. 41(d).

the framers of the Constitution that there were reasonable searches for which no warrant was required."[92]

A situation becomes "exceptional" for Fourth Amendment purposes, first, when the individual claimant had "no reasonable expectation of privacy" in the particular situation,[93] and secondly, where there are exigent circumstances in which police action literally may be "now or never" to preserve the evidence of the crime.[94]

§ 16.09. —consent to search

There is no need to have a warrant to search when the legal owner of the property freely and understandingly consents to the search by government personnel.[95] Consent can be given either in advance, as by contract,[96] or at time of the search.[97]

The United States Supreme Court has been reluctant to find consent from the acquiescence of others. For example, a search of a hotel room without the occupant's consent was not valid simply because a hotel clerk or other employee consented to the search.[98] The Court has stated: "A guest in a hotel room is entitled to constitutional protection against unreasonable searches and seizures. That protection would disappear if it was left to depend upon the unfettered discretion of an employee of the hotel."[99] Nor can a landlord give a valid consent to the search of a tenant's premises. Said the Court: "To uphold such an entry, search and seizure without a warrant would reduce the Fourth Amendment to a nullity and leave tenants' homes secure only in the discretion of landlords."[1]

In 1974 the Court held that "when the prosecution seeks to justify a warrantless search by proof of voluntary consent, it is not limited

---

92. U.S. v. Rabinowitz, 339 U.S. 56, 70 S. Ct. 430, 94 L. Ed. 653, 657 (1950) (overruled in part on other grounds by, Chimel v. California, 395 U.S. 752, 89 S. Ct. 2034, 23 L. Ed. 2d 685 (1969)).

93. Smith v. Maryland, 442 U.S. 735, 99 S. Ct. 2577, 61 L. Ed. 2d 220 (1979).

94. Roaden v. Kentucky, 413 U.S. 496, 93 S. Ct. 2796, 37 L. Ed. 2d 757, 765 (1973).

95. Schneckloth v. Bustamonte, 412 U.S. 218, 93 S. Ct. 2041, 36 L. Ed. 2d 854 (1973).

96. Zap v. U.S., 328 U.S. 624, 66 S. Ct. 1277, 90 L. Ed. 1477 (1946), judgment vacated on reh on other grounds, 330 U.S. 800, 67 S. Ct. 857, 91 L. Ed. 1259 (1947); Davis v. U.S., 328 U.S. 582, 66 S. Ct. 1256, 90 L. Ed. 1453 (1946).

97. U.S. v. Mitchell, 322 U.S. 65, 64 S. Ct. 896, 88 L. Ed. 1140 (1944).

98. Stoner v. State of Cal., 376 U.S. 483, 84 S. Ct. 889, 11 L. Ed. 2d 856 (1964).

99. Chapman v. U.S., 365 U.S. 610, 81 S. Ct. 776, 5 L. Ed. 2d 828 (1961).

1. Amos v. U.S., 255 U.S. 313, 41 S. Ct. 266, 65 L. Ed. 654 (1921); U.S. v. Kelih, 272 F. 484 (S.D. Ill. 1921).

to proof that consent was given by the defendant, but may show that permission to search was obtained from a third party who possessed common authority over or sufficient relationship to the premises or effect sought to be inspected."[2] However, two years later the Court said that "the fact of custody alone has never been enough to demonstrate a . . . consent to search."[3] In 1990 the Court ruled that there is no violation of the Fourth Amendment when police make a warrantless search upon the consent of a third party whom police reasonably believe has authority over the premises, but who in fact does not have such authority. Justices Marshall, Brennan and Stevens dissented, emphasizing that warrantless searches are valid on the consent of a third person only when such person is authorized to give consent.[4]

Consent must be proved by clear and positive testimony, and it must be established that there was no duress or coercion, actual or implied.[5] The government must show a consent that is "unequivocal and specific," and "freely and intelligently given."[6] "Invitations" from a homeowner to enter a dwelling, extended to armed officers of the law who demand entrance, are properly seen as admissions secured by force.[7] A like view has been taken when an officer displays a badge and announces that he has come to make a search,[8] even when the occupant says "all right."[9] There was no consent, ruled the Supreme Court, when an officer without a search warrant told an elderly African-American widow that he had a warrant and she then said "go ahead." The Court stated:

> When a prosecutor seeks to rely upon consent to justify the lawfulness of a search, he has the burden of proving that the consent was, in fact, freely and voluntarily given. This burden cannot be discharged by showing no more than acquiescence to a claim of lawful authority.[10]

A finding of consent in such circumstances has been aptly described

---

2. U.S. v. Matlock, 415 U.S. 164, 94 S. Ct. 988, 39 L. Ed. 2d 242 (1974).

3. U.S. v. Watson, 423 U.S. 411, 96 S. Ct. 820, 46 L. Ed. 2d 598 (1976).

4. Illinois v. Rodriguez, 497 U.S. 177, 110 S. Ct. 2793, 111 L. Ed. 2d 148 (1990).

5. Amos v. U.S., 255 U.S. 313, 41 S. Ct. 266, 65 L. Ed. 654 (1921).

6. Karwicki v. U.S., 55 F.2d 225, 226 (C.C.A. 4th Cir. 1932).

7. Washington v. U.S., 105 U.S. App. D.C. 58, 263 F.2d 742 (D.C. Cir. 1959); U.S. v. Marquette, 271 F. 120 (N.D. Cal. 1920).

8. U.S. v. Slusser, 270 F. 818 (S.D. Ohio 1921).

9. U.S. v. Marra, 40 F.2d 271 (W.D.N.Y. 1930).

10. Bumper v. North Carolina, 391 U.S. 543, 88 S. Ct. 1788, 20 L. Ed. 2d 797, 46 Ohio Op. 2d 382 (1968).

by a Court of Appeals as "unfounded in reason."[11] In 1973 the Supreme Court ruled that the government is not required to prove that a defendant consenting to a search knew that he had the right to withhold his consent, but it also held that knowledge of the right to refuse consent can be taken into account in determining whether a consent was voluntary.[12]

The Supreme Court has ruled that there was no violation of the Fourth Amendment when an individual invited a federal undercover agent into his home for the specific purpose of selling him narcotics, and such narcotics were used at trial. Said the Court: "A government agent, in the same manner as a private person, may accept an invitation to do business and may enter upon the premises for the very purposes contemplated by the occupant." In his concurring opinion Justice Brennan stated:

> The Fourth Amendment protects against governmental intrusions upon "the sanctity of a man's home and the privacies of life." [citing Boyd v. United States (1886) 116 U.S. 616, 630, 29 L. Ed. 746, 6 S. Ct. 524]. However, the occupant can break the seal of sanctity and waive his right of privacy in the premises. Plainly he does this to the extent that he opens his home to the transaction of business and invites anyone willing to enter to come in to trade with him.[13]

Persons using commercial airports in effect consent to reasonable inspections of both their possessions and their persons. While in 1983 the Supreme Court recognized that when, on the basis of reasonable suspicion luggage contains narcotics, law enforcement officers can detain such luggage for "sniffing" by a trained narcotic detection dog, the Court held that detention of baggage for ninety minutes was unreasonable and violative of the Fourth Amendment.[14]

§ 16.10. —search incident to lawful arrest

The validity of arrests is treated at considerable length in the following chapter and, accordingly, here it need only be said generally that arrests are valid when made pursuant to a lawful warrant; when made without a warrant but on probable cause that a crime

---

11. Herter v. U.S., 27 F.2d 521 (C.C.A. 9th Cir. 1928).

12. Schneckloth v. Bustamonte, 412 U.S. 218, 93 S. Ct. 2041, 36 L. Ed. 2d 854 (1973), followed in Florida v. Rodriguez, 469 U.S. 1, 105 S. Ct. 308, 83 L. Ed. 2d 165 (1984).

13. Lewis v. U.S., 385 U.S. 206, 87 S. Ct. 424, 427-28, 17 L. Ed. 2d 312 (1966).

14. U.S. v. Place, 462 U.S. 696, 103 S. Ct. 2637, 77 L. Ed. 2d 110 (1983).

has been committed it and that the arrestee committed it; and in a limited number of exceptional situations which the Supreme Court is inclined to describe an "exigent circumstances."

Materials discovered afterwards can never be used to justify earlier arrests.[15] Otherwise stated, a search is never valid by what it turns up. In law a search is good or bad when it commences and does not change character by reason of its success.[16]

Searches incident to lawful arrests are justified, notwithstanding the absence of a search warrant, by two reasons: (a) the need to seize weapons and other things which might be used to assault the arresting officer and effectuate an escape; and (b) the need to prevent the destruction of evidence of the crime. The Supreme Court has said:

> The rule allowing contemporaneous searches is justified, for example, by the need to seize weapons and other things which might be used to assault an officer or effect an escape, as well as by the need to prevent the destruction of evidence of the crime—things which might easily happen where the evidence or weapon is on the accused's person or under his immediate control.[17]

Even without a search warrant, then, arresting officers after a valid arrest can ordinarily make a search of the person of the arrested individual for weapons or for the fruits of or implements used to commit the crime.[18]

There is good authority for the proposition that officers having an arrest warrant or probable cause and ample opportunity to arrest cannot delay the arrest until the suspect enters a building so as to embark upon a search of the edifice.[19]

Where an administrative arrest warrant is used for a proper administrative function, such as to apprehend a person subject to deportation, the Supreme Court permits an incidental search as broad as one which can be made upon a lawful arrest for crime. Says the Court:

> There can be no doubt that a search for weapons has as much justification here as it has in the case of an arrest for crime, where it has been recognized as proper. . . . Nor is there any

---

15. Henry v. U.S., 361 U.S. 98, 80 S. Ct. 168, 4 L. Ed. 2d 134 (1959).

16. U.S. v. Di Re, 332 U.S. 581, 68 S. Ct. 222, 92 L. Ed. 210 (1948).

17. Preston v. U.S., 376 U.S. 364, 84 S. Ct. 881, 11 L. Ed. 2d 777 (1964).

18. Preston v. U.S., 376 U.S. 364, 84 S. Ct. 881, 11 L. Ed. 2d 777 (1964).

19. McKnight v. U.S., 87 U.S. App. D.C. 151, 183 F.2d 977 (D.C. Cir. 1950).

constitutional reason to limit the search for materials proving the deportability of an alien validly arrested, more severely than we limit the search for materials probative of crime when a valid criminal arrest is made. . . . Government officers who effect a deportation arrest have a right of incidental search analogous to the search permitted criminal law-enforcement officers.[20]

In 1963 four Justices of the Supreme Court took the position that even if officers possessed an arrest warrant or probable cause existed for an arrest of a person within a house, the Fourth Amendment would be violated by the unannounced intrusion of police into a private home, except (a) where the persons within already knew of the officers' authority and purpose, or (b) where the officers were justified in the belief that persons within were in imminent peril of bodily harm, or (c) where those within were made aware of the presence of someone outside (because, for example, by a knock on the door) are then engaged in activity which justifies the officers in the belief that an escape or the destruction of evidence is being attempted.[21] The majority of the Court, however, concluded that the entry was permissible under the law of the state where the arrest occurred and found such practice constitutional.

Scope of search and seizure incident to lawful arrest
A search as incident to a lawful arrest can only be valid if made contemporaneous with the arrest. For example, the Supreme Court has ruled that a search of a garage under a house was not incident to an arrest made in the house two hours later.[22] And the Court has held not contemporaneous a search of a person's hotel room in California on October 27, when the person's arrest occurred in Nevada on October 29.[23]

As the foregoing indicates, searches at totally unrelated locations are not incident to an arrest.[24] The Court has ruled that officers cannot, without a search warrant, sometime after an arrest and at a different place, search the car in which a person was arrested, when the person was in custody.[25]

Since the reasons that justify search as an incident to a lawful ar-

---

20. Abel v. U.S., 362 U.S. 217, 80 S. Ct. 683, 4 L. Ed. 2d 668, 684-85 (1960).

21. Ker v. State of Cal., 374 U.S. 23, 83 S. Ct. 1623, 10 L. Ed. 2d 726, 24 Ohio Op. 2d 201 (1963).

22. Fahy v. State of Conn., 375 U.S. 85, 84 S. Ct. 229, 11 L. Ed. 2d 171 (1963).

23. Stoner v. State of Cal., 376 U.S. 483, 84 S. Ct. 889, 11 L. Ed. 2d 856 (1964).

24. Agnello v. U.S., 269 U.S. 20, 46 S. Ct. 4, 70 L. Ed. 145, 51 A.L.R. 409 (1925).

25. Preston v. U.S., 376 U.S. 364, 84 S. Ct. 881, 11 L. Ed. 2d 777 (1964).

rest as an exception to the general rule forbidding searches without search warrants—protection of the arresting officer and preventing the destruction of evidence—are not present in these circumstances, courts are not to permit searches not contemporaneous in time and place to the arrest. The Supreme Court has well said that "these justifications are absent where a search is remote in time or place from the arrest. Once an accused is under arrest and in custody, then a search made at another place, without a warrant, is simply not incident to the arrest."[26]

Over dissents of Justices Stewart, Douglas, Brennan and Marshall, the Court in 1974 allowed a warrantless search and seizure of an arrested person's clothing the next day, after he had been arrested after 11 p.m. the previous day. The dissenters were surely correct in viewing such a search without a warrant as neither "incident" to the arrest, nor "substantially contemporaneous with the arrest" as required by previous case law for such exceptional situations permitting searches without warrants.[27]

An arresting officer can search a person subjected to lawful arrest, and in 1983 the Court allowed the so-called "inventory search" whereby police searched at the locus of the arrest a shoulder bag possessed by the person arrested.[28] When a person is lawfully arrested, the arresting officers can search the area within his immediate control, which means the area from within which he might gain possession of a weapon or destructible evidence, but the officers cannot search beyond this area without a search warrant.[29] The Supreme Court has stated:

> When an arrest is made, it is reasonable for the arresting officer to search the person arrested in order to remove any weapons that the latter might seek to use in order to resist arrest or effect his escape. Otherwise, the officer's safety might well be endangered, and the arrest itself frustrated. In addition, it is entirely reasonable for the arresting officer to search for and seize any evidence on the arrestee's person in order to prevent its concealment or destruction. And the area into which an arrestee might reach in order to grab a weapon or evidentiary items must, of course, be governed by a like rule.[30]

Earlier the Court had said that an arresting officer can search places

---

26. Preston v. U.S., 376 U.S. 364, 84 S. Ct. 881, 11 L. Ed. 2d 777, 780 (1964).
27. U.S. v. Edwards, 415 U.S. 800, 94 S. Ct. 1234, 39 L. Ed. 2d 771 (1974).
28. Illinois v. Lafayette, 462 U.S. 640, 103 S. Ct. 2605, 77 L. Ed. 2d 65 (1983).
29. Chimel v. California, 395 U.S. 752, 89 S. Ct. 2034, 23 L. Ed. 2d 685 (1969).
30. Chimel v. California, 395 U.S. 752, 89 S. Ct. 2034, 23 L. Ed. 2d 685 (1969).

"within the immediate possession and control" of the person arrested,[31] and that the "immediate public area under the control of the person arrested" could be searched.[32] Broader statements in the *Rabinowitz*[33] and *Harris*[34] cases are now overruled.[35] The Court holds that the doctrine of the *Chimel* case, above, is not to be applied retroactively.[36]

The Supreme Court has ruled that when a person was arrested at a mountain cabin, the entire contents of the cabin could not be seized as incident to the lawful arrest.[37] Similarly, when a person has been lawfully arrested in a building, mass seizures of things throughout the building are unconstitutional.[38] When police arrested a man on the sidewalk near the front steps of his house, the Court ruled the police could not search the house. Said the Court: "If a search of a house is to be upheld as incident to an arrest, that arrest must take place inside the house."[39]

§ 16.11. —the "plain view" doctrine

An exception to the general rule requiring warrants before searches exists when the "plain view" rule is applicable. This allows seizures so long as (a) the police lawfully make the initial intrusion into the premises or motor vehicle (such as by shining a flashlight into a car that has been lawfully stopped), (b) the evidence is discovered inadvertently, and (c) the evidence of a crime or contraband is immediately apparent.[40]

In 1990, when police had a search warrant for stolen coins, which could not be found, and an officer seized weapons used in the crime, in his plain view, the weapons were held admissible, without a warrant and even though their discovery was not inadvertent. Justices

---

31. Marron v. U.S., 275 U.S. 192, 48 S. Ct. 74, 72 L. Ed. 231 (1927).

32. United States v. Rabinowitz, 339 US 56, 70 S. Ct. 430, 94 L Ed 653 (1950).

33. United States v. Rabinowitz, 339 US 56, 70 S. Ct. 430, 94 L Ed 653 (1950).

34. Harris v. U.S., 331 U.S. 145, 67 S. Ct. 1098, 91 L. Ed. 1399 (1947) (overruled in part by, Chimel v. California, 395 U.S. 752, 89 S. Ct. 2034, 23 L. Ed. 2d 685 (1969)).

35. Chimel v. California, 395 U.S. 752, 89 S. Ct. 2034, 23 L. Ed. 2d 685 (1969).

36. Williams v. U.S., 401 U.S. 646, 91 S. Ct. 1148, 28 L. Ed. 2d 388 (1971).

37. Frank v. State of Md., 359 U.S. 360, 79 S. Ct. 804, 3 L. Ed. 2d 877, 890 (1959) (overruled in part on other grounds by, Camara v. Municipal Court of City and County of San Francisco, 387 U.S. 523, 87 S. Ct. 1727, 18 L. Ed. 2d 930 (1967)).

38. Shipley v. California, 395 U.S. 818, 89 S. Ct. 2053, 23 L. Ed. 2d 732 (1969).

39. Vale v. Louisiana, 399 U.S. 30, 90 S. Ct. 1969, 26 L. Ed. 2d 409 (1970).

40. Texas v. Brown, 460 U.S. 730, 103 S. Ct. 1535, 75 L. Ed. 2d 502 (1983); Go-Bart Importing Co. v. U.S., 282 U.S. 344, 51 S. Ct. 153, 75 L. Ed. 374 (1931).

Brennan and Marshall dissented, stating that the plain view exception is properly applicable only where the discovery was inadvertent.[41]

The plain view exception to the Fourth Amendment warrant requirement permits a law enforcement officer to seize what is clearly incriminating evidence or contraband in a place where the officer has a right to be, and the Supreme Court has upheld seizure of contraband drugs seen by a policeman in a dormitory room where he had gone with the occupant who had previously been arrested elsewhere. Justices White, Brennan and Marshall in dissent indicated that there are limits to the plain view exception, and that a policeman, for instance, who looked into a house and saw incriminating evidence therein would not be permitted to enter and seize it without a warrant. They added that an arresting officer has no right to enter the arrested person's home unless it is necessary to protect himself or to prevent an escape.[42]

Where the initial intrusion which brings the police within plain view of such an article is supported by one of the recognized exceptions to the warrant requirement, the seizure is also constitutional. For example, the police may inadvertently happen upon evidence in plain view while in hot pursuit of a fleeting suspect.[43] So, too, when an object comes into plain view during a search incident to an arrest that is appropriately limited in scope, it may be seized without a warrant.[44] And the plain view doctrine has been held applicable where a police officer is not searching for evidence against the accused, but nonetheless inadvertently comes across an incriminating object.[45]

Observing that since "in the vast majority of cases, any evidence seized by the police will be in plain view," the Supreme Court has felt compelled to enunciate two limitations upon the doctrine. First, as a corollary of the principle that no amount of probable cause can justify a warrantless search or seizure absent "exigent circumstances," the Court declared that "plain view alone is never enough to justify the warrantless search of evidence." Secondly, the Court emphasized that "the discovery of evidence in plain view must be

41. Horton v. California, 496 U.S. 128, 110 S. Ct. 2301, 110 L. Ed. 2d 112 (1990).

42. Washington v. Chrisman, 455 U.S. 1, 102 S. Ct. 812, 70 L. Ed. 2d 778, 1 Ed. Law Rep. 1087 (1982).

43. Warden, Md. Penitentiary v. Hayden, 387 U.S. 294, 87 S. Ct. 1642, 18 L. Ed. 2d 782 (1967).

44. Chimel v. California, 395 U.S. 752, 89 S. Ct. 2034, 23 L. Ed. 2d 685 (1969).

45. Harris v. U.S., 390 U.S. 234, 88 S. Ct. 992, 19 L. Ed. 2d 1067 (1968).

inadvertent," lest such seizures turn an initially valid (and therefore limited) search into a "general" one, and explained that "where the discovery is anticipated, where the police know in advance the location of the evidence and intent to secure it . . . the requirement of a warrant to seize imposes no inconvenience whatever, or at least none which is constitutionally cognizable." The Supreme Court explained:

> If the initial intrusion is bottomed upon a warrant which fails to mention a particular object, though the police know its location and intend to seize it, then there is a violation of the express constitutional requirement of warrants . . . particularly describing . . . the things to be seized. The initial intrusion, may, of course be legitimated not by a warrant but by one of the exceptions to the warrant requirement, such as hot pursuit or search incident to lawful arrest. But to extend the scope of such an intrusion to the seizure of objects—not contraband nor stolen, nor dangerous in themselves—which the police know in advance they will find in plain view and intend to seize, would fly in the face of the basic rule that no amount of probable cause can justify a warrantless seizure.[46]

§ 16.12. —motor vehicles on the open road

Exigent circumstances exist which justify police in stopping and searching motor vehicles of all kinds on the open roads when they have reasonable or probable cause to believe that they will find the instrumentality of a crime or evidence pertaining to a crime, before they begin their warrantless search.[47] The Supreme Court has explained: "There are essentially two reasons for the distinction between automobiles and other private property. First, . . . the inherent mobility of automobiles often makes it impracticable to obtain a warrant. In addition, the configuration, use and regulation of automobiles often may dilute the reasonable expectation of privacy that exists with respect to differently situated property."[48] It is orthodoxy that "the physical characteristics of an automobile and its use result in a lessened expectation of privacy therein."[49]

It must, however, be emphasized that the very language of the

---

46. Coolidge v. New Hampshire, 403 U.S. 443, 91 S. Ct. 2022, 29 L. Ed. 2d 564 (1971).

47. Dyke v. Taylor Implement Mfg. Co., 391 U.S. 216, 88 S. Ct. 1472, 20 L. Ed. 2d 538 (1968).

48. Arkansas v. Sanders, 442 U.S. 753, 99 S. Ct. 2586, 61 L. Ed. 2d 235 (1979).

49. Colorado v. Bannister, 449 U.S. 1, 101 S. Ct. 42, 66 L. Ed. 2d 1 (1980); New York v. Class, 475 U.S. 106, 106 S. Ct. 960, 89 L. Ed. 2d 81 (1986).

Fourth Amendment requires all searches and seizures, including those of motor vehicles, to be reasonable. Officers undertaking searches and seizures of motor vehicles must have "reasonable or probable cause to believe that they will find the instrumentality of a crime or evidence pertaining to a crime before they begin their warrantless search."[50] Here, as elsewhere, "exigent circumstances" are necessary to dispense with warrants.[51] Thus, when the police knew of the presence of an automobile parked outside an accused's home and planned all along to seize it, the Supreme Court held that their search was invalid, absent exigent circumstances to justify their failure to obtain a search warrant. The Court stated:

> The warrant requirement has been a valued part of our constitutional law for decades, and it has determined the result in scores and scores of cases in courts all over this country. It is not an inconvenience to be somehow "weighed" against the claims of police efficiency. It is, or should be, an important working part of our machinery of government, operating as a matter of course to check the well-intentioned but mistakenly overzealous executive officers who are a part of any system of law enforcement.[52]

Six years later the Court ruled that a search warrant was required before federal agents could open a locked footlocker which the agents had lawfully seized in a car at the time of arrest of the owner of the footlocker, even though probable cause existed to believe it contained contraband. In holding that warrantless searches are unreasonable under such circumstances, the Court explained:

> A fundamental purpose of the Fourteenth Amendment is to safeguard individuals from unreasonable governmental invasions of legitimate privacy interests, and not simply those interests found inside the four walls of a home. . . . Once law enforcement officers have reduced luggage or other personal property not associated with the person of the arrestee to their exclusive control, and there is no longer any danger that the arrestee might gain access to the property to seize a weapon or

---

50. Dyke v. Taylor Implement Mfg. Co., 391 U.S. 216, 88 S. Ct. 1472, 20 L. Ed. 2d 538 (1968).

51. Torres v. Com. of Puerto Rico, 442 U.S. 465, 99 S. Ct. 2425, 61 L. Ed. 2d 1 (1979).

52. Coolidge v. New Hampshire, 403 U.S. 443, 91 S. Ct. 2022, 29 L. Ed. 2d 564 (1971).

destroy evidence, a search of that property is no longer an incident to the arrest.[53]

Comparably, the Court held in 1981 that a closed opaque container may not be opened without a warrant when found in the course of a lawful search of an automobile.[54] However, ten years later, the Court ruled the warrant requirement should be removed in such situations, so now police may search containers in cars without a warrant so long as the search is supported by probable cause. Probable cause was found to exist where officers knew an individual had just received from Federal Express a package of drugs, then saw him place it in the trunk of his car. The Court indicated, however, that it would not have found probable cause for a warrantless search of other parts of the vehicle.[55]

The Court stated in 1986 that in determining reasonableness under the Fourth Amendment it would in all cases "undertake the necessary balancing of the nature and quality of the intrusion on the individual's Fourth Amendment interests against the importance of the governmental interests alleged to justify the intrusion." The Court then held that the Fourth Amendment had not been violated when a police officer pulled over a speeding car with a cracked windshield, reached into the vehicle to ascertain the vehicle identification number, moved papers obscuring it, and found a gun.[56]

If a vehicle is readily mobile and probable cause exists to believe that it contains contraband, the Fourth Amendment permits police to search the vehicle without more.[57] Police officers who have legitimately stopped an automobile and who have probable cause to believe that contraband is concealed somewhere within it may conduct a warrantless search as thorough as a magistrate could authorize in a warrant particularly describing the place to be searched. Overruling earlier decisions to the contrary, the Supreme Court now allows the warrantless search of packages and containers found in vehicles that have reasonably been stopped.[58]

The Court has held since 1978 that passengers in a car who do

---

53. U.S. v. Chadwick, 433 U.S. 1, 97 S. Ct. 2476, 53 L. Ed. 2d 538 (1977).

54. Robbins v. California, 453 U.S. 420, 101 S. Ct. 2841, 69 L. Ed. 2d 744 (1981).

55. California v. Acevedo, 500 U.S. 565, 111 S. Ct. 1982, 114 L. Ed. 2d 619 (1991).

56. New York v. Class, 475 U.S. 106, 106 S. Ct. 960, 89 L. Ed. 2d 81 (1986).

57. Pennsylvania v. Labron, 116 S. Ct. 2485, 135 L. Ed. 2d 1031 (U.S. 1996).

58. U.S. v. Ross, 456 U.S. 798, 102 S. Ct. 2157, 72 L. Ed. 2d 572 (1982); U.S. v. Johns, 469 U.S. 478, 105 S. Ct. 881, 83 L. Ed. 2d 890 (1985).

not claim ownership of the car or of weapons found in the glove compartment and under the front seat do not have a legitimate expectation of privacy in these areas, and consequently cannot challenge a search of the automobile and a seizure of such items.[59] In 1980 the Court reaffirmed that "a court may not exclude evidence under the Fourth Amendment unless it finds that the unlawful search or seizure violated the defendant's own constitutional rights," adding that "the defendant's Fourth Amendment rights are violated only when the challenged conduct invaded his legitimate expectations of privacy rather than that of a third party."[60] Comparably, the following year the Court ruled that when occupants of an automobile are subject to a lawful custodial search, the search can extend to the passenger compartment of the automobile (a jacket on the backseat containing cocaine).[61]

In 1985 the Court asserted that the expectation of privacy in a motor home was less than in a house, and, noting the mobile character of such a dwelling, it ruled that the police are justified in searching mobile homes without prior recourse to the authority of a magistrate and a warrant, so long as the standard of probable cause is met.[62]

The Court recognizes that a "seizure" occurs when police, seeking to reduce drunk driving, pull a car to a stop at a checkpoint, but it has concluded that the public interest in preventing drunk driving outweighs the degree of intrusion upon the individual motorists who are briefly stopped, and the Court has sustained sobriety tests, when applicable to all drivers and all cars on a particular highway.[63]

Reiterating that a decision to stop a vehicle is generally reasonable where the police have probable cause to believe that a traffic violation has occurred, the Court held in 1966 that the temporary detention of a motorist upon probable cause to believe that the motorist has violated the traffic laws does not violate the Fourth Amendment's prohibition against unreasonable seizures, even if a reasonable officer

---

59. Rakas v. Illinois, 439 U.S. 128, 99 S. Ct. 421, 58 L. Ed. 2d 387 (1978).

60. U.S. v. Payner, 447 U.S. 727, 100 S. Ct. 2439, 65 L. Ed. 2d 468 (1980).

61. New York v. Belton, 453 U.S. 454, 101 S. Ct. 2860, 69 L. Ed. 2d 768 (1981).

62. California v. Carney, 471 U.S. 386, 105 S. Ct. 2066, 85 L. Ed. 2d 406 (1985).

63. Michigan Dept. of State Police v. Sitz, 496 U.S. 444, 110 S. Ct. 2481, 110 L. Ed. 2d 412 (1990).

would not have stopped the motorist absent some additional law enforcement objective.[64]

§ 16.13. —impounded motor vehicles

In a five-to-four decision in 1967 the Supreme Court sustained the search of a car one week after its seizure under a California statute authorizing officers arresting persons for narcotics to impound the vehicle used. "Searches of cars that are constantly movable may make the search of a car without a warrant a reasonable one although the result might be the opposite in a search of a home, a store or other fixed property." After noting that the actual forfeiture did not occur until four months after the impounding, Justice Black said: "It would be unreasonable to hold that the police, having to retain the car in their garage for such a length of time, had no right, even for their own protection to search it."[65]

Three years later the Court allowed police officials with probable cause to seize a car in which individuals had been arrested, and which had then been taken to a police station.[66] Then, in 1976, the Court held that where a car was legally impounded for parking violations, the police could without a search warrant make an inventory of what was in the car, including the contents of the glove compartment, and that marijuana found there could be introduced in a subsequent criminal prosecution of the vehicle's owner.[67]

Where probable cause for a search of a car existed at the time of the driver's arrest, the Court has held that the same probable cause factor still obtained at a police station to which the car was immediately taken.[68] Then, in 1984 the Court held that when a car had been impounded at the time of an arrest, a search made eight hours later and without a warrant was valid.[69] A year later, citing *Meyers* and the *Ross* case,[70] the Court held that that decision authorized a warrantless search of packages several days after they had been

---

64. Whren v. U.S., 116 S. Ct. 1769, 135 L. Ed. 2d 89 (U.S. 1996) (petitioners were convicted of illegal drug-dealing activity after the officers observed bags of crack cocaine in one of the petitioners' hands).

65. Cooper v. State of Cal., 386 U.S. 58, 87 S. Ct. 788, 793, 17 L. Ed. 2d 730 (1967).

66. Cooper v. State of Cal., 386 U.S. 58, 87 S. Ct. 788, 17 L. Ed. 2d 730 (1967).

67. South Dakota v. Opperman, 428 U.S. 364, 96 S. Ct. 3092, 49 L. Ed. 2d 1000 (1976).

68. Texas v. White, 423 U.S. 67, 96 S. Ct. 304, 46 L. Ed. 2d 209 (1975).

69. Florida v. Meyers, 466 U.S. 380, 104 S. Ct. 1852, 80 L. Ed. 2d 381 (1984).

70. See § 16.12, supra.

removed from vehicles the police had probable cause to believe contained contraband.[71]

Repeating in 1990 that inventory searches of cars are an exception to the warrant requirement of the Fourth Amendment, the Supreme Court stated that inventory searches are deemed necessary to protect an owner's property while it is in the custody of the police, to insure against claims of lost, stolen or vandalized property, and to guard the police from danger. It then held reasonable, and hence constitutional, search of a backpack found in a van, so long as it was conducted pursuant to standardized procedures which did not vest undue discretion in the searching officer. Justices Blackmun, Powell and O'Connor concurred, with Justice Marshall and Brennan dissenting, stating that "only the government's interest in protecting the owner's property actually justifies an inventory search of an impounded vehicle." They found such interest lacking on the facts, and further objected to an absence of standardized police procedures in the case.[72]

In 1990 the Court stressed that for inventory searches to be an exception to the general warrant requirement, the state must provide a clear policy limiting discretion of the police and denying them opportunity for a general rummaging in order to discover incriminating evidence. The Court stated: "The individual police officer must not be allowed so much latitude that inventory searches are turned into a purposeful and general means of discovering evidence of crime."[73]

§ 16.14. —border searches

In 1973 the United States Supreme Court ruled that a so-called "border search" of a car made 20 miles into California from Mexico, without a warrant or probable cause, was in violation of the Fourth Amendment,[74] and 2 years later the Court held violative of the Fourth Amendment the practice of federal agents in stopping cars at a checkpoint 62 miles from the Mexican border without a warrant, probable cause, or consent.[75] However, the following year, while acknowledging that checkpoint stops are "seizures" within the meaning of the Fourth Amendment, the Court sustained the

---

71. U.S. v. Johns, 469 U.S. 478, 105 S. Ct. 881, 83 L. Ed. 2d 890 (1985).

72. Michigan Dept. of State Police v. Sitz, 496 U.S. 444, 110 S. Ct. 2481, 110 L. Ed. 2d 412 (1990).

73. Florida v. Wells, 495 U.S. 1, 110 S. Ct. 1632, 109 L. Ed. 2d 1 (1990).

74. Almeida-Sanchez v. U.S., 413 U.S. 266, 93 S. Ct. 2535, 37 L. Ed. 2d 596 (1973).

75. U.S. v. Ortiz, 422 U.S. 891, 95 S. Ct. 2585, 45 L. Ed. 2d 623 (1975).

constitutionality of the use of *permanent* checkpoints at a considerable distance from the border as a necessary means of controlling entry by illegal aliens. Stops and questioning, said the Court, "may be made in the absence of any individualized suspicion at reasonably located checkpoints." Judicial warrants are not necessary, said the Court. Justices Brennan and Marshall in dissent stated: "The Fourth Amendment standard of reasonableness admits of neither intrusion at the discretion of law enforcement personnel, nor abusive or harassing stops, however infrequent. Action based merely on whatever may pique the curiosity of a particular officer is the antithesis of the objective standards requisite to reasonable conduct and to avoiding abuse and harassment."[76]

In 1977 the Court held that border searches are ipso facto reasonable and an exception to the requirement of warrants, and ruled that it was constitutional for federal officials to make a mail search of letters and packages coming into the country when, in the language of the operative statute, they had "reasonable cause to suspect the presence" of contraband. The statute prohibited reading of correspondence, and the Court concluded that there was no First Amendment violation.[77]

Stating that the balance of interests was unusual when searches were conducted at national borders, the Supreme Court ruled in 1985 that detention of a traveler at the border beyond the scope of routine customs searches and inspections is justified at its inception if customs agents, considering all the facts surrounding the traveler and her trip, reasonably suspect that the traveler is smuggling contraband in her alimentary canal. The Court noted that the detention was not unreasonably long. Justices Brennan and Marshall in dissent re-emphasized that the Fourth Amendment required all searches to be reasonable, which means, absent warrants, that they be based upon probable cause, and they found none on the facts.[78]

Acknowledging that border searches must be "reasonable," Courts of Appeal have sustained rectal searches,[79] the use of an emetic to

---

76. U.S. v. Martinez-Fuerte, 428 U.S. 543, 96 S. Ct. 3074, 49 L. Ed. 2d 1116 (1976).

77. U.S. v. Lovasco, 431 U.S. 783, 97 S. Ct. 2044, 52 L. Ed. 2d 752 (1977).

78. U.S. v. Montoya de Hernandez, 473 U.S. 531, 105 S. Ct. 3304, 87 L. Ed. 2d 381 (1985).

79. Murgia v. U.S., 285 F.2d 14 (9th Cir. 1960).

precipitate regurgitation,[80] and the use of a tube passed through the nose into the stomach to occasion regurgitation.[81]

§ 16.15. —certain administrative searches

"Administrative searches" on occasion have been said by the Supreme Court to be generally within the Fourth Amendment. In 1967, the Court reversed the conviction of a property owner who had refused to permit a municipal health inspector to enter without a warrant. By way of dictum, the Court indicated that area inspections upon warrants may well be constitutional if "reasonable legislative or administrative standards for conducting an area inspection are satisfied with respect to a particular dwelling."[82] In a companion case, the Court held that the *Camara* rule applies to similar inspections of commercial structures which are not used as private residences.[83]

In 1984 the Supreme Court indicated that administrative searches and inspections generally require warrants, pointing out that "reasonable privacy expectations may remain in fire-damaged premises." The Court then explained that the constitutionality of warrantless and nonconsensual entries into fire-damaged premises normally turns on several factors, to wit: whether there are legitimate privacy interests in the fire-damaged property that are protected by the Fourth Amendment; whether exigent circumstances justify the governmental intrusion, regardless of any reasonable expectation of privacy; and whether the object of the search is to determine the cause of the fire or to gather evidence of criminal activity. The Court stated: "If reasonable privacy interests remain in the fire-damaged property, the warrant requirement applies and any official entry must be made pursuant to a warrant in the absence of consent or exigent circumstances."[84]

Three years later, Justice O'Connor, writing a plurality opinion for the Court, acknowledged that public employees, like others, have a reasonable expectation of privacy in their place of work. The determination of protected places will depend, said these four Justices, upon "such factors as the intention of the Framers of the Fourth Amendment, the uses to which the individual has put a loca-

---

80. Lane v. U.S., 321 F.2d 573 (5th Cir. 1963).

81. Blefare v. U.S., 362 F.2d 870 (9th Cir. 1966).

82. Camara v. Municipal Court of City and County of San Francisco, 387 U.S. 523, 87 S. Ct. 1727, 18 L. Ed. 2d 930 (1967).

83. See v. City of Seattle, 387 U.S. 541, 87 S. Ct. 1737, 18 L. Ed. 2d 943 (1967).

84. Michigan v. Clifford, 464 U.S. 287, 104 S. Ct. 641, 78 L. Ed. 2d 477 (1984).

tion, and our societal understanding that certain areas deserve the most scrupulous protection from government invasion."[85]

§ 16.16. — —pervasively regulated businesses and activities

The Supreme Court has on a number of occasions ruled that proprietors of pervasively regulated businesses can more readily be subjected to warrantless searches which are seen as reasonable, since the proprietors' expectation of privacy in this area would likely have been minimal—such proprietors should realize that their activities are subject to inspection.

In 1972 the Court sustained a warrantless search during regular business hours of a pawn shop's locked storeroom. Said the Court: "When a dealer chooses to engage in this pervasively regulated business and to accept a federal license, he does so with the knowledge that his business records, firearms, and ammunition will be subjected to effective inspection."[86]

Nine years later the Supreme Court held constitutional a warrantless search of mines, explaining that this field had traditionally been heavily regulated to protect the public safety.[87]

In 1987 the Court sustained a warrantless search of a junkyard where the police found a number of stolen vehicles and parts. In such "closely regulated industries," said the Court, expectations of privacy are "particularly attenuated." Even here, ruled the Court, the privacy claims of entrepreneurs will only be overridden if (a) there is a substantial governmental interest behind the regulatory scheme, (b) a warrantless inspection is necessary to further such scheme, and (c) the state inspection scheme, in terms of certainty and regularity of its application, provides a constitutionally adequate substitute for a warrant. The Court added that the time, place and scope of inspection must be closely limited by the applicable statute.[88]

§ 16.17. —where expectations of privacy are nonexistent or minimal

In 1981, when the Supreme Court sustained warrantless searches of mines, it stated that:

---

85. O'Connor v. Ortega, 480 U.S. 709, 107 S. Ct. 1492, 94 L. Ed. 2d 714 (1987).

86. U.S. v. Biswell, 406 U.S. 311, 92 S. Ct. 1593, 32 L. Ed. 2d 87 (1972).

87. Donovan v. Dewey, 452 U.S. 594, 101 S. Ct. 2534, 69 L. Ed. 2d 262 (1981).

88. New York v. Burger, 482 U.S. 691, 107 S. Ct. 2636, 96 L. Ed. 2d 601 (1987).

legislative schemes authorizing warrantless searches of commercial property do not necessarily violate the Fourth Amendment. The greater latitude to conduct warrantless inspections of commercial property reflects that fact that the expectations of privacy that the owner of commercial property enjoys in such property differs significantly from the sanctity accorded an individual's home, and that the privacy interest may, in certain circumstances, be adequately protected by regulatory schemes authorizing warrantless inspections.[89]

Two years later the Court ruled that a warrant was not required to reopen a container in the possession of an individual, when it had earlier been lawfully opened by customs personnel, at which time drugs had been found. The Court stated: "Absent a substantial likelihood that the contents had been changed, there is no legitimate expectation of privacy in the contents of a container previously opened under lawful authority."[90]

The Court in 1988 held not violative of the Fourth Amendment the action of police in arranging with private collection agencies the examination of trash bags left by householders at the curb, so that products of such searches could be used in support of search warrants to examine contents of the houses. The Court again said that there is no Fourth Amendment protection when owners "could have had no reasonable expectation of privacy in the inculpatory items and that our society would not objectively accept as reasonable the claim of a householder to expectation of privacy in trash left for collection in any area accessible to the public."[91]

The following year the Supreme Court said that "where the privacy interests implicated by a search are minimal, and where an important governmental interest furthered by the intrusion would be placed in jeopardy by a requirement of individualized suspicion, it is not necessary to show some quantum of individualized suspicion, before concluding that the search is reasonable." The Court then upheld urine testing of railroad workers.[92]

At the same term, the Court ruled that customs employees who are directly involved in interdiction of unlawful drugs or who are required to carry firearms in the line of duty have a diminished

---

89. Donovan v. Dewey, 452 U.S. 594, 101 S. Ct. 2534, 69 L. Ed. 2d 262 (1981).

90. Illinois v. Andreas, 463 U.S. 765, 103 S. Ct. 3319, 77 L. Ed. 2d 1003 (1983).

91. California v. Greenwood, 486 U.S. 35, 108 S. Ct. 1625, 100 L. Ed. 2d 30 (1988).

92. Skinner v. Railway Labor Executives' Ass'n, 489 U.S. 602, 109 S. Ct. 1402, 103 L. Ed. 2d 639 (1989).

expectation of privacy, and sustained governmental urinalysis requirement of such workers.[93]

§ 16.18. —"administrative searches" where there were likely expectations of privacy but the contrasting societal interests were very important

In 1987, in a five-to-four decision, the Supreme Court found reasonable a search by administrators of a government hospital of the desk and filing cabinet of a doctor. The plurality opinion of Justice O'Connor, joined by Chief Justice Rehnquist and Justices White and Powell readily acknowledged that public employees have some reasonable expectation of privacy in their place of work, but the opinion indicates that the determination of what is a protected places depend upon "such factors as the intention of the Framers of the Fourth Amendment, the uses to which the individual has put a location, and our societal understanding that certain areas deserve the most scrupulous protection from government invasion." Even though there was no warrant and no probable cause in the case, the Court, balancing a governmental interest in efficient and proper operation of the workplace against the interest in privacy, ruled that the search was reasonable by balancing a governmental interest in efficient and proper operation of the workplace against the interest in privacy.[94]

§ 16.19. —school searches

While readily acknowledging that school children have legitimate expectations of privacy, the Supreme Court in 1985 nevertheless held that the general rule requiring warrants before searches does not apply to searches by officials in public schools, and that the constitutionality of such searches is to depend on the reasonableness, under all the circumstances, of the search. Hopefully, the Court anticipated that "the interests of students will be invaded no more than is necessary to achieve the legitimate end of preserving order in the schools." Justice Stevens indicated his alarm at the language of the majority which stated that searches will be "justified . . . when there are reasonable grounds for suspecting that the search will turn up evidence that the student has violated or is

---

93. National Treasury Employees Union v. Von Raab, 489 U.S. 656, 109 S. Ct. 1384, 103 L. Ed. 2d 685 (1989).

94. O'Connor v. Ortega, 480 U.S. 709, 107 S. Ct. 1492, 94 L. Ed. 2d 714 (1987).

violating either the law or the rules of the school." Justices Brennan and Marshall also dissented.[95]

§ 16.20. —searches and visits by probation officers and social workers

As another "special needs" exception to the warrant requirement, the Supreme Court has held valid, so long as reasonable and even though there was no probable cause, a search of a probationer's home resulting in the finding of a gun. Justices Blackmun, Marshall, Brennan and Stevens agreed that a probation officer should be able to search on "a reduced level of suspicion" and that "reasonable suspicion" that a probationer possessed a gun would suffice, but they stressed that mere speculation by a probation officer that the probationer might have a gun was not enough, and that on these facts a warrant was required.[96]

Noting that "it is unreasonableness which is the Fourth Amendment's standard," the Court has held that it is reasonable, and hence constitutional, for the states to condition aid to dependent children upon subjection to social workers' visits into the homes of recipients, so long as the primary objective is "the welfare, not the prosecution, of the recipient."[97]

§ 16.21. —prisons and jails

The United States Supreme Court ruled in 1984 that a prison inmate has no reasonable expectation of privacy in his prison cell entitling him to the protection of the Fourth Amendment against unreasonable searches and seizures. The Court stated: "The recognition of privacy rights for prisoners in their individual cells simply cannot be reconciled with the concept of incarceration and the needs and objectives of penal institutions."[98]

The same year the Court further held that pre-trial detainees have no constitutional right to be present nearby and observe the irregularly scheduled shake-down searches of their individual cells.[99]

§ 16.22. —emergencies

An exception to the general rule requiring search warrants

---

95. New Jersey v. T.L.O., 469 U.S. 325, 105 S. Ct. 733, 83 L. Ed. 2d 720, 21 Ed. Law Rep. 1122 (1985).

96. Griffin v. Wisconsin, 483 U.S. 868, 107 S. Ct. 3164, 97 L. Ed. 2d 709 (1987).

97. Wyman v. James, 400 U.S. 309, 91 S. Ct. 381, 27 L. Ed. 2d 408 (1971).

98. Hudson v. Palmer, 468 U.S. 517, 104 S. Ct. 3194, 82 L. Ed. 2d 393 (1984).

99. Block v. Rutherford, 468 U.S. 576, 104 S. Ct. 3227, 82 L. Ed. 2d 438 (1984).

properly exists when there is an emergency requiring immediate entry into buildings or vehicles to save lives or property. The United States Supreme Court has said that "a warrantless entry may be legal when there is a compelling need for official action and no time to secure a warrant." Firefighters may remain a reasonable time to seek the cause, but "thereafter additional entries to investigate the cause of the fire must be made pursuant to the warrant procedures governing administrative searches."[1] The Court in 1984 repeated that "reasonable privacy expectations may remain in fire-damaged premises," and stated that the constitutionality of warrantless and nonconsensual entries into fire-damaged premises "normally turns on several factors: whether there are legitimate privacy interests in the fire-damaged property that are protected by the Fourth Amendment; whether exigent circumstances justify the government intrusion regardless of any reasonable expectation of privacy, and whether the object of the search is to determine the cause of the fire or to gather evidence of criminal activity." The Court added: "If reasonable privacy interests remain in the fire-damaged property, the warrant requirement applies and any official entry must be made pursuant to a warrant in the absence of consent or exigent circumstances." After fire department personnel have departed the scene of a fire, any later search requires a warrant or consent, unless there are some exigent circumstances, such as the fire restarting.[2]

An exception to the general rule requiring search warrants properly exists when there is an emergency requiring immediate entry into buildings or vehicles to save lives or property, or to apprehend a fugitive from justice. If, for example, a house is on fire, entry by police or fire personnel is unquestionably in order.

While there is no "murder scene exception" to the requirement of warrants, the Supreme Court indicated in 1984 that it was prepared to hold "that police may make warrantless entries on premises when they reasonably believe that a person within is in need of immediate aid, and that they may make a prompt warrantless search of the area to see if there are other victims or if a killer is still on the premises."[3]

Six years later, a warrantless visual "protective sweep" of premises to ascertain if someone was hiding there was held valid at the arrest of a person pursuant to an arrest warrant, so long as the officer has "a reasonable belief, based on specific and articulable facts which,

---

1. Michigan v. Tyler, 436 U.S. 499, 98 S. Ct. 1942, 56 L. Ed. 2d 486 (1978).

2. Michigan v. Clifford, 464 U.S. 287, 104 S. Ct. 641, 78 L. Ed. 2d 477 (1984).

3. Thompson v. Louisiana, 469 U.S. 17, 105 S. Ct. 409, 83 L. Ed. 2d 246 (1984).

taken together with the rational inferences from those facts, reasonably warrant the officer in believing the area 'swept' harbored a person dangerous to the offices or others." Justices Brennan and Marshall in dissent preferred that probable cause should be required for such a "protective sweep."[4]

§ 16.23. —others

The United States Supreme Court held in 1983 that the Fourth Amendment is not violated when customs officials board a vessel in waters providing ready access to the open sea, to inspect documents, and then find narcotics.[5]

The following year the Court held that federal agents need not have a warrant when called by private parties who had discovered in a damaged package what turned out to be cocaine, and that destruction of a small quantity of the powder during a field test was reasonable under the circumstances.[6]

§ 16.24. The subpoena duces tecum

A subpoena duces tecum that is too broad and in effect a "fishing expedition" is an unreasonable search and seizure, violative of the Fourth Amendment.[7]

A subpoena duces tecum has been held valid when it specifies "with reasonable particularity the subject to which the documents relate." Accordingly, a specification contained in a subpoena duces tecum was held adequate so long as it was "sufficient to enable [the recipients] to know what particular documents were required and to select them accordingly."[8]

The Supreme Court has held that there is no requirement of a judicial warrant as a condition precedent to a valid administrative subpoena duces tecum to look at the records of a business. The Court acknowledges the right of a person subjected to such a subpoena to question the reasonableness of the subpoena, before suf-

---

4. Maryland v. Buie, 494 U.S. 325, 110 S. Ct. 1093, 108 L. Ed. 2d 276 (1990).

5. U.S. v. Villamonte-Marquez, 462 U.S. 579, 103 S. Ct. 2573, 77 L. Ed. 2d 22 (1983).

6. U.S. v. Jacobsen, 466 U.S. 109, 104 S. Ct. 1652, 80 L. Ed. 2d 85 (1984).

7. Oklahoma Press Pub. Co. v. Walling, 327 U.S. 186, 66 S. Ct. 494, 90 L. Ed. 614, 166 A.L.R. 531 (1946).

8. McPhaul v. U.S., 364 U.S. 372, 81 S. Ct. 138, 5 L. Ed. 2d 136 (1960).

fering any penalties for refusing to comply with it, by raising objections in an action in any appropriate district court.[9]

Holding that a "constructive search" is within the Fourth Amendment ban upon unreasonable searches and seizures, the Court stated that "a compulsory production of a man's private papers to establish a criminal charge against him or to forfeit his property is within the scope of the Fourth Amendment, in all cases in which a search and seizure would be, because it is a material ingredient and effects the sole object and purpose of search and seizure." The Court concluded that Congress could not constitutionally provide that statements of the government would be taken as proved if the person refused to produce his papers demanded by the government.[10]

§ 16.25. Remedies available to persons subjected to unreasonable searches and seizures of their properties

A person who has been subjected to an unreasonable search or seizure can prevent the use of the materials as evidence when later prosecuted for the commission of a crime. Since 1914 the Supreme Court has held, as a rule of constitutional law, that such materials cannot be used in a federal court,[11] and in 1961 the Court held that such materials cannot be used in the state courts.[12]

Ever since its inception, the rule excluding evidence seized in violation of the Fourth Amendment has been recognized as a principal mode of discouraging lawless police conduct. Without it, the constitutional guarantee against unreasonable searches and seizures would be a mere form of words.[13]

To qualify as a person aggrieved by an unlawful search or seizure, one must have himself been a victim of such a search or seizure— one against whom a search was directed, as distinguished from one who claims prejudice only thought the use of evidence gathered as a

---

9. Donovan v. Lone Steer, Inc., 464 U.S. 408, 104 S. Ct. 769, 78 L. Ed. 2d 567 (1984).

10. Boyd v. U.S., 116 U.S. 616, 6 S. Ct. 524, 29 L. Ed. 746 (1886).

11. Weeks v. U.S., 232 U.S. 383, 34 S. Ct. 341, 58 L. Ed. 652 (1914) (overruled in part on other grounds by, Elkins v. U.S., 364 U.S. 206, 80 S. Ct. 1437, 4 L. Ed. 2d 1669 (1960)) and (overruled on other grounds by, Mapp v. Ohio, 367 U.S. 643, 81 S. Ct. 1684, 6 L. Ed. 2d 1081, 16 Ohio Op. 2d 384, 86 Ohio L. Abs. 513, 84 A.L.R.2d 933 (1961)); that *Weeks* is a constitutional law ruling, see Mapp v. Ohio, 367 U.S. 643, 81 S. Ct. 1684, 1688, 6 L. Ed. 2d 1081, 16 Ohio Op. 2d 384, 86 Ohio L. Abs. 513, 84 A.L.R.2d 933 (1961).

12. Mapp v. Ohio, 367 U.S. 643, 81 S. Ct. 1684, 6 L. Ed. 2d 1081, 16 Ohio Op. 2d 384, 86 Ohio L. Abs. 513, 84 A.L.R.2d 933 (1961).

13. Terry v. Ohio, 392 U.S. 1, 12, 88 S. Ct. 1868, 20 L. Ed. 2d 889, 44 Ohio Op. 2d 383 (1968).

consequence or a search or seizure of someone else. The Supreme Court has ruled that though evidence is inadmissible against one defendant or conspirator, because tainted by electronic surveillance as to him, it is admissible against other defendants and conspirators. The Court stated: "The established principle is that suppression of the product of a Fourth Amendment violation can be successfully urged only by those whose rights were violated by the search itself, not by those who are aggrieved solely by the introduction of damaging evidence."[14]

In 1993 the Supreme Court re-emphasized that "co-conspirators have no standing to suppress unless they can show that they had a property interest protected by the Fourth Amendment that was interfered with by" government action, "or a reasonable expectation that was invaded by the search."[15]

The Court has said that there will ordinarily be no standing to contest a search and seizure from an edifice where the person challenging the search was not on the premises at the time of the contested search and seizure; had no proprietary or possessory interest in the premises, or was not charged with an offense that includes as an essential element possession of the seized evidence at the time of the contested search and seizure.[16] Where claiming ownership of narcotics or anything else that it is criminal to possess would prove part of the government's case against the claimant, one need not then allege in his motion to suppress that the articles are his.[17] Anyone legitimately on premises where a search occurs may challenge its legality by way of a motion to suppress, when its fruits are proposed to be used against him.[18]

The "fruits of the poisoned tree" doctrine has many applications. Thus, the Supreme Court held in 1963 that verbal evidence by an arrested person which derives immediately from an unlawful entry and an unauthorized arrest is no less the "fruit" of official illegality than the more common tangible fruits for the unwarranted intrusion, remarking that "the danger in relaxing the exclusionary rules in the case of verbal evidence would seem too great to warrant

---

14. Alderman v. U.S., 394 U.S. 165, 89 S. Ct. 961, 22 L. Ed. 2d 176 (1969).

15. U.S. v. Padilla, 508 U.S. 77, 113 S. Ct. 1936, 123 L. Ed. 2d 635 (1993).

16. Brown v. U.S., 411 U.S. 223, 93 S. Ct. 1565, 36 L. Ed. 2d 208 (1973).

17. Jones v. U.S., 362 U.S. 257, 80 S. Ct. 725, 4 L. Ed. 2d 697, 78 A.L.R.2d 233 (1960) (overruled on other grounds by, U.S. v. Salvucci, 448 U.S. 83, 100 S. Ct. 2547, 65 L. Ed. 2d 619 (1980)).

18. Jones v. U.S., 362 U.S. 257, 80 S. Ct. 725, 4 L. Ed. 2d 697, 78 A.L.R.2d 233 (1960) (overruled on other grounds by, U.S. v. Salvucci, 448 U.S. 83, 100 S. Ct. 2547, 65 L. Ed. 2d 619 (1980)).

introducing such a distinction."[19] In a decision by the First Circuit, testimony as to matters observed during an unlawful invasion has been excluded in order to honor the basic constitutional policies.[20] Another Court of Appeals had held that where a person was arrested unlawfully and then fingerprinted, such fingerprints could not be used in evidence at trial.[21]

Remedies available to a person who has been a victim of an unconstitutional search and seizure include suppression of the item at trial, return of the seized property, damages, and appropriate equitable relief.

A person who knows that property has been seized from him must make a timely motion for the suppression and return of his property. In federal practice, the motion is to be made before trial or hearing unless opportunity therefore did not exist or the defendant was not aware of the grounds for the motion, but a court may entertain a motion at the hearing or the trial.[22] The motion is to be made before the district court for the district in which the property was seized.[23] However, where it appears for the first time at trial that illegally seized evidence is to be used against the defendant by the government, it is the duty of the trial court to entertain a motion for the exclusion or suppression of the property.[24] Courts will customarily order return of property illegally seized to the owner, but do not do so when the property is contraband or its possession is contrary to law.[25] In addition, a federal court has refused to return property to an owner when it is subject to a federal lien.[26]

The Supreme Court ruled in 1995 that the exclusionary rule did not require suppression of evidence seized in violation of the Fourth Amendment by an officer who had acted in reliance on a police record indicating the existence of an outstanding arrest warrant, when the record was later determined to be erroneous, so long as the arresting officer was acting reasonably under all the circumstances when he relied upon the police computer record. To sup-

---

19. Wong Sun v. U.S., 371 U.S. 471, 83 S. Ct. 407, 9 L. Ed. 2d 441 (1963); U.S. v. Ceccolini, 435 U.S. 268, 98 S. Ct. 1054, 55 L. Ed. 2d 268 (1978).

20. McGinnis v. U.S., 227 F.2d 598 (1st Cir. 1955).

21. Bynum v. U.S., 104 U.S. App. D.C. 368, 262 F.2d 465 (D.C. Cir. 1958).

22. Fed. R. Crim. P. 41(e).

23. Fed. R. Crim. P. 41(e); United States v. Klapholz, 230 F.2d 494 (2d Cir. 1956).

24. Gouled v. U.S., 255 U.S. 298, 41 S. Ct. 261, 65 L. Ed. 647 (1921) (overruled in part on other grounds by, Warden, Md. Penitentiary v. Hayden, 387 U.S. 294, 87 S. Ct. 1642, 18 L. Ed. 2d 782 (1967)).

25. U.S. v. Jeffers, 342 U.S. 48, 72 S. Ct. 93, 96 L. Ed. 59 (1951).

26. Welsh v. U.S., 95 U.S. App. D.C. 93, 220 F.2d 200 (D.C. Cir. 1955).

press the evidence, said the Court, would not have a significant effect upon court employees who should notify the police that warrants have been quashed. Justices Ginsburg and Stevens in dissent, suggested that applying the exclusionary rule would, as the Arizona Court believed below, be "a powerful incentive" to states to update their computer records.[27]

Persons aggrieved by unlawful searches and seizures may move at trial to exclude evidence when the government seeks to introduce that which was unconstitutionally discovered or the fruits of a poisoned tree.[28] Valid "considerations support the implementation of the exclusionary rule at trial," according to the Supreme Court.[29] Where a citizen was arrested without a warrant and without probable cause, subsequent statements could not be used against him at his trial simply because he had been given a *Miranda* warning before talking. Said the Court: "Miranda warnings by themselves do not purge the taint of an illegal arrest."[30]

The Court has held that neither Fifth Amendment due process nor the Third Article of the Constitution were violated by a provision of the Federal Magistrates Act permitting a district court to refer to a magistrate a motion to suppress evidence and authorizing the court to determine and decide such motion based on the record before the magistrate, including the magistrate's proposed findings of fact and recommendations.[31]

The Court has held that a prosecutor may not use against a defendant in a federal criminal trial any testimony given by that defendant at a pretrial hearing to establish standing to move to suppress evidence.[32]

Federal courts have broad equity power to enjoin the governmental use of products of searches and seizures violative of the Fourth Amendment. The Supreme Court has approved of federal courts enjoining federal officials from testifying even in state courts as to the contents of illegal searches and seizures.[33] However, the Court ruled in 1968 that it would not enjoin state officials from testifying

---

27. Arizona v. Evans, 514 U.S. 1, 115 S. Ct. 1185, 131 L. Ed. 2d 34 (1995).

28. Gouled v. U.S., 255 U.S. 298, 41 S. Ct. 261, 65 L. Ed. 647 (1921) (overruled in part on other grounds by, Warden, Md. Penitentiary v. Hayden, 387 U.S. 294, 87 S. Ct. 1642, 18 L. Ed. 2d 782 (1967)).

29. Stone v. Powell, 428 U.S. 465, 96 S. Ct. 3037, 49 L. Ed. 2d 1067 (1976).

30. Brown v. Illinois, 422 U.S. 590, 95 S. Ct. 2254, 45 L. Ed. 2d 416 (1975).

31. U.S. v. Raddatz, 447 U.S. 667, 100 S. Ct. 2406, 65 L. Ed. 2d 424 (1980).

32. Simmons v. U.S., 390 U.S. 377, 88 S. Ct. 967, 19 L. Ed. 2d 1247 (1968); Brown v. U.S., 411 U.S. 223, 93 S. Ct. 1565, 36 L. Ed. 2d 208 (1973).

33. Rea v. U.S., 350 U.S. 214, 76 S. Ct. 292, 100 L. Ed. 233 (1956).

in state courts as to what was unlawfully seized by federal officers, when there was no proof that the state officials were present at the time of the seizure to avoid federal constitutional requirements. "Such direct intrusion in state processes," said the Court, "does not comport with proper federal-state relationships."[34] The Court has held that the equity power of federal courts to award money damages may properly be invoked to redress the unconstitutional conduct of a federal agent who, acting under color of his authority, violates the Fourth Amendment ban on unreasonable searches and seizures.[35]

Federal civil rights actions under 42 U.S.C.A. § 1983 for both monetary damages and equitable relief are available to persons who have been victims of unreasonable searches and seizures, either of their persons or their properties, by others engaged in state action.[36]

Generally, habeas corpus is available to persons unconstitutionally convicted by the use of illegal evidence from searches and seizures,[37] but the Supreme Court ruled in 1967 that federal habeas corpus is no longer to be available to state prisoners claiming unreasonable searches and seizures when a state has provided them an opportunity for full and fair litigation of any Fourth Amendment claims.[38]

Exceptions to the exclusionary rule have existed since 1954, when the Supreme Court held that the government could use evidence obtained as a result of an illegal search and seizure solely for the purpose of impeaching the direct testimony of a defendant.[39] In 1980 the Court held that evidence suppressed as the fruit of an unlawful search and seizure may nevertheless be used to impeach a defendant's trial testimony, given in response to proper cross-examination, even though the impeaching evidence does not contradict the defendant's testimony on direct examination. Justices Brennan, Marshall, Stew-

---

34. Cleary v. Bolger, 371 U.S. 392, 83 S. Ct. 385, 9 L. Ed. 2d 390 (1963).

35. Bivens v. Six Unknown Named Agents of Federal Bureau of Narcotics, 403 U.S. 388, 91 S. Ct. 1999, 29 L. Ed. 2d 619 (1971).

36. Monroe v. Pape, 365 U.S. 167, 81 S. Ct. 473, 5 L. Ed. 2d 492 (1961) (overruled on other grounds by, Monell v. Department of Social Services of City of New York, 436 U.S. 658, 98 S. Ct. 2018, 56 L. Ed. 2d 611 (1978)).

37. Kaufman v. U.S., 394 U.S. 217, 89 S. Ct. 1068, 22 L. Ed. 2d 227 (1969); Lefkowitz v. Newsome, 420 U.S. 283, 95 S. Ct. 886, 43 L. Ed. 2d 196 (1975); Linkletter v. Walker, 381 U.S. 618, 85 S. Ct. 1731, 14 L. Ed. 2d 601, 5 Ohio Misc. 49, 33 Ohio Op. 2d 118 (1965); Stovall v. Denno, 388 U.S. 293, 87 S. Ct. 1967, 18 L. Ed. 2d 1199 (1967).

38. Stone v. Powell, 428 U.S. 465, 96 S. Ct. 3037, 49 L. Ed. 2d 1067 (1976), followed in Cardwell v. Taylor, 461 U.S. 571, 103 S. Ct. 2015, 76 L. Ed. 2d 333 (1983).

39. Walder v. U.S., 347 U.S. 62, 74 S. Ct. 354, 98 L. Ed. 503 (1954).

art and Stevens here dissented, urging the impropriety of admitting at trial illegally seized evidence to impeach a defendant's testimony deliberately elicited by the government, under the cover of impeaching an accused who takes the stand.[40] While the Court has permitted impeachment of a defendant's own testimony by use of illegally seized evidence, it ruled in 1990 that this exception will not be extended to allow the prosecution to impeach all defense witnesses by the use of illegally obtained evidence. The Court explained that such an extension would deter a defendant from calling all his own witnesses and would significantly weaken the exclusionary rule's deterrent effect on police misconduct. [41]

In 1984 the Court ruled that the Fourth Amendment exclusionary rule does not apply to evidence obtained by police officers who acted in objectively reasonable reliance upon a search warrant issued by a neutral magistrate, when the warrant was ultimately found to be unsupported by probable cause.[42] The same year the Court held that the exclusionary rule does not bar evidence seized pursuant to a warrant subsequently invalidated because of a technical error on the part of the issuing judge, that is, modifying an inappropriate form but failing to describe particularly the items to be seized.[43] In 1987 the Court, in a five-to-four decision, held admissible evidence secured by officers acting in objectively reasonable reliance upon a statute authorizing warrantless administrative searches, where the statute was thereafter declared unconstitutional by the state supreme court. The majority opinion reflected that the prime purpose of the exclusionary rule was to deter unlawful conduct, and concluded that excluding the evidence would deter neither police nor legislative conduct. The majority found no indication that exclusion of evidence seized pursuant to a statute subsequently declared unconstitutional would have a significant deterrent effect on the enactment of similar laws. Justice O'Connor, in a dissent joined by Justices Brennan, Marshall and Stevens pointed out that the Fourth Amendment historically was aimed at legislative bodies intent on too broadly authorizing invasions into personal privacy.[44]

In 1976 the Supreme Court held that evidence obtained by a state criminal law enforcement officer in good-faith reliance on a warrant

40. U.S. v. Havens, 446 U.S. 620, 100 S. Ct. 1912, 64 L. Ed. 2d 559, 6 Fed. R. Evid. Serv. (LCP) 1 (1980).

41. James v. Illinois, 493 U.S. 307, 110 S. Ct. 648, 107 L. Ed. 2d 676 (1990).

42. U.S. v. Leon, 468 U.S. 897, 104 S. Ct. 3405, 82 L. Ed.2d 677 (1984).

43. Massachusetts v. Sheppard, 468 U.S. 981, 104 S. Ct. 3424, 82 L. Ed. 2d 737 (1984).

44. Illinois v. Krull, 480 U.S. 340, 107 S. Ct. 1160, 94 L. Ed. 2d 364 (1987).

that later proved to be defective could be admitted in a federal civil tax proceeding. The Court stated: "The judicially created exclusionary rule should not be extended to forbid the use in the civil proceeding of one sovereign of evidence seized by a criminal law enforcement agent of another sovereign."[45]

While the Court ruled in 1965 that the constitutional exclusionary rule applies to proceedings by state officials for the forfeiture of a car and other "quasi-criminal" proceedings,[46] the Court in 1984 held that the exclusionary rule does not apply in a deportation hearing, since this is a civil proceeding. Accordingly, an admission of unlawful presence in this country, made subsequent to an allegedly unlawful arrest, need not be excluded.[47]

The Court stated in 1978 that "the exclusionary rule should be invoked with much greater reluctance where the claim is based on a causal relationship between a constitutional violation and the discovery of a live witness than when a similar claim is advanced to support suppression of an inanimate object."[48]

---

45. U.S. v. Janis, 428 U.S. 433, 96 S. Ct. 3021, 49 L. Ed. 2d 1046 (1976).

46. One 1958 Plymouth Sedan v. Com. of Pa., 380 U.S. 693, 85 S. Ct. 1246, 14 L. Ed. 2d 170 (1965).

47. I.N.S. v. Lopez-Mendoza, 468 U.S. 1032, 104 S. Ct. 3479, 82 L. Ed. 2d 778 (1984).

48. U.S. v. Ceccolini, 435 U.S. 268, 98 S. Ct. 1054, 55 L. Ed. 2d 268 (1978).

CHAPTER SEVENTEEN

Protection from Unreasonable Searches and Seizures of the Person

---

§ 17.00. Introduction

The Fourth Amendment to the Constitution of the United States safeguards the right of legal persons to be free from unreasonable seizures and searches, and this right has been made binding by the

Supreme Court upon the states and their political subdivisions.[1] Additionally, the term "liberty" in both the Fifth and Fourteenth Amendments, has as its prime purpose protecting the individual from impermissible "seizures" by agents of the state.[2]

The Supreme Court, in construing the language of the Fourth Amendment, has often looked at the intent of the Founding Fathers responsible for the Amendment to discern what they intended to protect.[3] The Court has also looked at the common law antedating our Constitution to ascertain what earlier generations considered "unreasonable" governmental interferences with the privacy and integrity of free peoples.[4] However, in a 1985 case, the Court refused to interpret the Fourth Amendment as limited by the common law when the Amendment was adopted, and found more persuasive and appropriate the practices followed over the years by the American states.[5]

Absent provision otherwise by the Congress, the lawfulness of arrests by federal agents and officers is to be determined by reference to laws of the applicable state so long as not violative of the United States Constitution.[6]

The adjudicatory task here, as elsewhere, is one of identifying, balancing and reconciling the most important societal interests; in this instance, between the societal interests in the sanctity and privacy of the person and society's concern for preventing and punishing crime.

§ 17.01. The "seizure" within the meaning of the Fourth Amendment

Every arrest is a seizure, whether pursuant to warrant or otherwise, whether lawful or unlawful. The problem is present where apprehension and detention, not constituting an arrest, in the formal meaning of that term, is imposed upon the citizenry by agents of the

---

   1. Monroe v. Pape, 365 U.S. 167, 81 S. Ct. 473, 5 L. Ed. 2d 492 (1961) (overruled on other grounds by, Monell v. Department of Social Services of City of New York, 436 U.S. 658, 98 S. Ct. 2018, 56 L. Ed. 2d 611 (1978)).

   2. Meyer v. Nebraska, 262 U.S. 390, 43 S. Ct. 625, 67 L. Ed. 1042, 29 A.L.R. 1446 (1923).

   3. West v. Cabell, 153 U.S. 78, 14 S. Ct. 752, 38 L. Ed. 643, 645 (1894); Wilgus, Arrest Without a Warrant, 22 Mich. L. Rev. 541, 798 (1924).

   4. "The examination of the common law understanding . . . throws light on . . . what the Framers might have thought to be reasonable." Payton v. New York, 445 U.S. 573, 100 S. Ct. 1371, 63 L. Ed. 2d 639, 653-54 (1980).

   5. Tennessee v. Garner, 471 U.S. 1, 105 S. Ct. 1694, 85 L. Ed. 2d 1 (1985).

   6. Ker v. State of Cal., 374 U.S. 23, 83 S. Ct. 1623, 10 L. Ed. 2d 726, 24 Ohio Op. 2d 201 (1963).

government. Then, said the United States Supreme Court in 1985: "it is not always clear what minimal police interferences become a seizure."[7]

We begin by examining the instances in which the Supreme Court held or indicated the event was a "seizure." In the *Garner* case, the Court stated: "Whenever an officer restrains the freedom of a person to walk away, he has seized that person."[8] At that time the Court further made known that apprehension by the use of deadly force will be a seizure within the meaning of the Fourth Amendment.[9]

As early as 1969 the Supreme Court had held that the detention of individuals, even during early investigative stages, is a seizure and generally unconstitutional. Consequently, fingerprints taken from a citizen during an unlawful detention are inadmissible at trial. The Court said:

> To argue that the Fourth Amendment does not apply to the investigatory stage is fundamentally to misconceive the purposes of the Fourth Amendment. Investigatory seizures could subject unlimited numbers of innocent persons to the harassment and ignominy incident to involuntary detention. Nothing is more clear than that the Fourth Amendment was meant to prevent wholesale intrusions upon the personal security of our citizenry, whether these intrusions be termed "arrests" or "investigations."[10]

Six years later the Court ruled that "The Fourth Amendment applies to all seizures of the person, including seizures that involve only a brief detention short of traditional arrest." It then held that individual border patrolmen could not use a roving patrol near the Mexican border to stop and question occupants of a car, when the only ground for suspicion was that they appeared to be of Mexican ancestry.[11]

In 1980 the Court held that a woman arriving at an airport and then physically examined by government agents, who found drugs, had not been "seized" since she had been free to depart, according to two justices in the majority; the other three in the majority took the position there had been a "seizure," but a reasonable one. The

---

7. Tennessee v. Garner, 471 U.S. 1, 105 S. Ct. 1694, 85 L. Ed. 2d 1 (1985).

8. Tennessee v. Garner, 471 U.S. 1, 105 S. Ct. 1694, 85 L. Ed. 2d 1 (1985).

9. Tennessee v. Garner, 471 U.S. 1, 105 S. Ct. 1694, 85 L. Ed. 2d 1 (1985).

10. Davis v. Mississippi, 394 U.S. 721, 89 S. Ct. 1394, 22 L. Ed. 2d 676, 680 (1969).

11. U.S. v. Brignoni-Ponce, 422 U.S. 873, 95 S. Ct. 2574, 45 L. Ed. 2d 607 (1975).

four dissenting justices believed the detention or seizure was impermissible.[12]

Where 15 to 25 Immigration and Naturalization Service agents made a "factory survey" for illegal aliens, with agents stationed at the doors through which no workers departed, and with citizen workers apparently too frightened to assert their constitutional rights to refuse to respond to questioning by the agents, the Supreme Court amazingly described the raid as a "consensual encounter" and ruled the questioning of workers under such circumstances was neither a detention nor a seizure under the Fourth Amendment. Justices Brennan and Marshall in dissent stressed that the test remains whether a citizen is free to disregard questions from public servants and walk away.[13]

Four years later the Court refused to hold that all police chases were "seizures," and indicated that the police can be said to have "seized an individual, only if in view of all the circumstances surrounding the incident, a reasonable person would have believed he or she was not free to leave."[14] The following year, the Court in a five-to-four decision, stated that to find a "seizure" a tribunal must find first that there has been "an intentional acquisition of physical control" by government personnel over citizens. In dissent, Justices Stevens, Brennan, Marshall and Blackmun refused to accept the proposition that every "seizure" had to be intentional.[15]

In 1991 the Court held that there was no seizure in effect at the time an individual, running from the scene of a crime and chased by a police officer, threw away a packet containing crack cocaine. Moments later he was tackled and handcuffed by the officer. In dissent Justices Stevens and Marshall wrote: "Even though momentary, a seizure occurs whenever an objective evaluation of a police officer's show of force conveys the message that the citizen is not entirely free to leave—in other words, that his or her liberty is being restrained in a significant way."[16]

As the Court stated in 1979 that "[w]henever a police officer accosts an individual and restrains his freedom to walk away, he has 'seized' that person . . . ," it recognized the proposition that there

---

12. U.S. v. Mendenhall, 446 U.S. 544, 100 S. Ct. 1870, 64 L. Ed. 2d 497 (1980).

13. I.N.S. v. Delgado, 466 U.S. 210, 104 S. Ct. 1758, 80 L. Ed. 2d 247 (1984).

14. Michigan v. Chesternut, 486 U.S. 567, 108 S. Ct. 1975, 100 L. Ed. 2d 565 (1988).

15. Brower v. County of Inyo, 489 U.S. 593, 109 S. Ct. 1378, 103 L. Ed. 2d 628 (1989).

16. California v. Hodari D., 499 U.S. 621, 111 S. Ct. 1547, 113 L. Ed. 2d 690 (1991).

will be "seizures that are less intrusive than a traditional arrest," that will often be made without probable cause, and which the Court indicated it would be prepared to condone on a "reasonable" balancing of interests.[17]

§ 17.02. The limited area where suspicionless searches of the person may be reasonable and not violative of the Fourth Amendment

Where the privacy interests implicated by a search are minimal, and where an important government interest furthered by the intrusion would be placed in jeopardy by a requirement of individualized suspicion, invasions of personal privacy will be valid, even though they are "searches," so long as they are reasonable on the facts. In this limited area it is not necessary for the government to show that there was probable cause of law violation, nor is it necessary to show some quantum of individualized suspicion, before concluding that the search is reasonable.[18] However, the interests of the government must be substantial.[19] In the *Skinner* case the Court upheld a federal rule requiring urine and blood tests of railworkers involved in accidents, after finding a compelling interest in preventing railway accidents and a minimal expectation of privacy of the workers, noting that they were employed "in an industry that is regulated pervasively to ensure safety."[20]

The same year the Court noted that customs employees who are directly involved in the interdiction of illegal drugs or who are required to carry firearms in the line of duty have a diminished expectation of privacy and that "the Government has a strong interest in detecting drug use" among such employees. It recognized, too, that customs agents had been approached by drug smugglers and that several apparently succumbed. The Court then sustained a governmental requirement that persons seeking transfer or promotion into such positions submit to a urinalysis, stating that "the Government has a compelling interest in ensuring that frontline interdiction personnel are physically fit, and have unimpeachable integrity and judgment." Said the Court: "In certain limited circumstances, the Government's need to discover such latent or hidden conditions, or to prevent their development, is sufficiently compelling" to justify such intrusion into privacy, where the victim

---

17. Brown v. Texas, 443 U.S. 47, 99 S. Ct. 2637, 61 L. Ed. 2d 357 (1979).

18. Skinner v. Railway Labor Executives' Ass'n, 489 U.S. 602, 109 S. Ct. 1402, 103 L. Ed. 2d 639 (1989) (Distinguished by, In re Johnson, 1997 WL 447632 (D.C. 1997).

19. Chandler v. Miller, 117 S. Ct. 1295, 137 L. Ed. 2d 513 (U.S. 1997).

20. Skinner v. Railway Labor Executives' Ass'n, 489 U.S. 602, 109 S. Ct. 1402, 103 L. Ed. 2d 639 (1989) (Distinguished by, In re Johnson, 1997 WL 447632 (D.C. 1997).

has a diminished expectation of privacy from the nature of his work. Justices Scalia, Stevens, Marshall and Brennan dissented, finding no connection between drug use and the "horribles" cited by the majority.[21]

In 1995 the Supreme Court sustained a random drug-testing program for high school students engaged in inter-scholastic athletic competition, indicating that "students within the school environment have a lesser expectation of privacy than members of the population generally. The test remains always . . . whether this search is reasonable."[22]

Two years later the Court held unreasonable and violative of the privacy rights of individuals under the Fourth Amendment, in its application to candidates for Lieutenant-Governor, Commissioner of Agriculture, and membership in the General Assembly, a state statute requiring candidates for designated state offices to certify that they had taken a drug test and that the result was negative. It is settled law that drug tests rank as searches, said the Court, adding that any "need for drug testing must be substantial," that is, "important enough to override the individual's acknowledged privacy interest, sufficiently vital to suppress the Fourth Amendment's normalized requirement of individualized suspicion." The state, said the Court, cannot "diminish personal privacy for a symbol's sake." The Court added by way of dictum that "where the risk to public safety is substantial and real, blanket suspicionless searches calibrated to the risk may rank as 'reasonable,' for example, searches now routine at airports and at entrances to courts and other official buildings."[23]

§ 17.03. Governmental seizures less intrusive than arrests

The United States Supreme Court ruled in 1975 that "the Fourth Amendment applies to all seizures of the person including seizures that involve only a brief detention short of traditional arrest."[24] Consequently, the Amendment invalidates all unreasonable seizures

---

21. National Treasury Employees Union v. Von Raab, 489 U.S. 656, 109 S. Ct. 1384, 103 L. Ed. 2d 685 (1989) and (Distinguished by, In re Johnson, 1997 WL 447632 (D.C. 1997).

22. Vernonia School Dist. 47J v. Acton, 515 U.S. 646, 115 S. Ct. 2386, 132 L. Ed. 2d 564, 101 Ed. Law Rep. 37 (1995).

23. Chandler v. Miller, 117 S. Ct. 1295, 137 L. Ed. 2d 513 (U.S. 1997).

24. U.S. v. Brignoni-Ponce, 422 U.S. 873, 95 S. Ct. 2574, 45 L. Ed. 2d 607 (1975).

even when the police tell a citizen he is not being arrested.[25] The Court has stated:

> The reasonableness of seizures that are less intrusive than a traditional arrest, depends on a balance between the public interest and the individual's right to personal security free from arbitrary interference by law officers. . . . Consideration of the constitutionality of such seizures involves a weighing of the gravity of the public concerns served by the seizure, the degree to which the seizure advances the public interest, and the severity of the interference with individual liberty. . . . A central concern in balancing these competing considerations in a variety of settings has been to assure that an individual's reasonable expectation of privacy is not subject to arbitrary invasions solely at the unfettered discretion of officers in the field. To this end, the Fourth Amendment requires that a seizure must be based on specific, objective facts indicating that society's legitimate interests require the seizure of the particular individual, or that the seizure must be carried out pursuant to a plan embodying explicit, neutral limitations on the conduct of individual officers. . . . We have recognized that in some circumstances an officer may detain a suspect briefly for questioning although he does not have "probable cause" to believe that the suspect is involved in criminal activity, as is required for a traditional arrest. . . . In the absence of any basis for suspecting appellant of misconduct, the balance between the public interest and the appellant's right to personal security and privacy tilts in favor of freedom from police interference.[26]

§ 17.04. Stopping of motor vehicles and questioning occupants

In the *Brignoni-Ponce* case, the Court had held in 1975 that individual border police could not use a roving patrol near the Mexican border to stop cars and question occupants, when the only ground for suspicion was that the occupants appeared to be of Mexican ancestry.[27] Two years later the Court held that there was no impermissible seizure of a person according to the Fourth Amendment, when a driver of a car lawfully stopped by police for a

---

25. Dunaway v. New York, 442 U.S. 200, 99 S. Ct. 2248, 60 L. Ed. 2d 824 (1979).

26. Brown v. Texas, 443 U.S. 47, 99 S. Ct. 2637, 61 L. Ed. 2d 357 (1979).

27. U.S. v. Brignoni-Ponce, 422 U.S. 873, 95 S. Ct. 2574, 45 L. Ed. 2d 607 (1975).

traffic violation was required by the police to step out of the car.[28] Twenty years later the Court held that the rule of the *Mimms* case applied also to passengers in motor vehicles.[29] The Supreme Court had earlier held that police officers can reasonably order passengers out of the cars, which have been lawfully stopped, pending completion of the stop, the interest in ensuring the safety of the officers being more important than the liberty claims of the travelers. Accordingly, when such an occupant dropped cocaine when stepping out, he was ruled lawfully arrested.[30]

In 1979 the Court held that stopping an automobile and detaining the occupants constituted a "seizure" within the meaning of the Fourth and Fourteenth Amendments, even though the purpose of the stop was limited and the resulting detention was quite brief. The Court ruled that stopping a motor vehicle and detaining a driver in order to check his driver's license and the registration of the vehicle was unreasonable under the Fourth Amendment, except in those situations in which there is at least articulable and reasonable suspicion that a motorist is unlicensed, that the automobile is unregistered, or that the vehicle or an occupant is otherwise subject to seizure for violating the law. By way of dictum, the Court indicated that this holding will not prevent a state from developing methods for spot checks that involve less intrusion or that do not involve the unconstrained exercise of discretion evident in the instant case. Throughout this area of restraints less intrusive than arrests the Court has indicated it sees the judicial task as one of balancing "the private interest" against "the governmental interests."[31]

In 1996 the Supreme Court reversed a ruling by an Ohio court which had held that the Fourth Amendment required that citizens stopped for traffic offenses be clearly informed by the detaining officer when they are free to go after a valid detention, before an officer attempts to engage in a consensual interrogation. Emphasizing that the "touchstone of the Fourth Amendment is reasonableness," the Court stated that reasonableness is "to be measured by objective terms by examining the totality of the circumstances," and that the voluntariness of a consent to be searched given by a driver of a car "is a question of fact to be determined from all the circumstances." "It would be unrealistic," said the Court, "to require police officers to always inform detainees that they are free to go before a consent

---

28. Pennsylvania v. Mimms, 434 U.S. 106, 98 S. Ct. 330, 54 L. Ed. 2d 331 (1977).

29. Maryland v. Wilson, 117 S. Ct. 882, 137 L. Ed. 2d 41 (U.S. 1997).

30. Maryland v. Wilson, 117 S. Ct. 882, 137 L. Ed. 2d 41 (U.S. 1997).

31. Delaware v. Prouse, 440 U.S. 648, 99 S. Ct. 1391, 59 L. Ed. 2d 660 (1979).

may be deemed voluntary."[32] When police erected a road block, into which a fleeing suspect drove and was killed, the Supreme Court concluded there had been a "seizure," explaining: "We think it enough for a seizure that a person be stopped by the very instrumentality set in motion or put in place in order to achieve the result."[33] The following year the Court recognized that a "seizure" occurs when police stop a car at a check point, but concluded that the societal interest in preventing drunk driving outweighs the degree of intrusion upon the individual motorists who are briefly stopped, and held constitutional check points on highways to make sobriety tests, when applicable to all drivers and all cars.[34]

§ 17.05. Investigative constraint upon personal liberty

In 1968 the United States Supreme Court initially held that it can be reasonable, and hence constitutional, at times for police officers to stop and frisk a citizen, even though on the facts they would not have had probable cause to arrest the citizen for a crime. The police officer need not be absolutely certain that the individual detained is armed. The test "is whether a reasonably prudent man in the circumstances would be warranted in the belief that his safety or that of others was in danger." If so, the police officer can make a reasonable search for weapons to ensure his protection and the safety of others in the vicinity.[35]

During the same term the Court held that in the case of a self-protective search for weapons by a police officer, he "must be able to point to particular facts from which he reasonably inferred that the individual was armed and dangerous." Furthermore, any search made must be "reasonably limited in scope to the accomplishment of the only goal which might conceivable have justified its inception—the protection of the officer in disarming a potentially dangerous man." Any search beyond such limits will be deemed an unreasonable and unconstitutional intrusion into the sanctity of the person.[36]

Four years later the Court allowed a stop and frisk of a citizen by

---

32. Ohio v. Robinette, 117 S. Ct. 417, 136 L. Ed. 2d 347 (U.S. 1996).

33. Brower v. County of Inyo, 489 U.S. 593, 109 S. Ct. 1378, 103 L. Ed. 2d 628 (1989).

34. Michigan Dept. of State Police v. Sitz, 496 U.S. 444, 110 S. Ct. 2481, 110 L. Ed. 2d 412 (1990).

35. Terry v. Ohio, 392 U.S. 1, 88 S. Ct. 1868, 20 L. Ed. 2d 889, 909, 44 Ohio Op. 2d 383 (1968).

36. Sibron v. New York, 392 U.S. 40, 88 S. Ct. 1889, 20 L. Ed. 2d 917, 44 Ohio Op. 2d 402 (1968).

a police officer on the basis of information received from an informant, so long as the officer's action was "based upon reasonable cause" and was "justifiable" under the circumstances.[37]

Under the *Terry v. Ohio* rule, the Court has held that a police officer could frisk a driver of a car lawfully halted, whom he had ordered out of the car when he saw a bulge looking like a weapon, and that the weapon seized could subsequently be used at trial.[38] Although stopping a car and detaining its occupants constitutes a seizure within the meaning of the Fourth Amendment, the Court in 1985 believed that the societal interest in law enforcement outweighed the interest in citizens being free from detention, when a flyer or bulletin had been issued on the basis of articulable facts supporting a reasonable suspicion that the wanted person had committed an offense, even when the police stop was made 12 days after the crime had been committed. The Court stated generally that "if police have a reasonable suspicion, grounded in specific and articulable facts, that a person they encounter was involved in or is wanted in connection with a complete felony, then a *Terry* stop may be made to investigate that suspicion."[39]

Under the *Terry* investigative protective search exception, the Court has held that, even absent probable cause to arrest, police can stop a person and search the passenger compartment and the trunk of the car that he was driving and may seize narcotics found therein.[40]

When a woman arriving at an airport was questioned and then physically examined by federal officials, who found drugs on her person, two Supreme Court justices believed that she had never been "seized" since she had been free to depart, and three other justices found the federal agents had reasonable suspicion that she was engaged in criminal activity, the five concluding that there had been no Fourth Amendment violation. Justices White, Brennan, Marshall and Stevens believed on the facts the woman had been impermissibly detained and seized.[41] The same year the Court ruled that when an officer at an airport "could not, as a matter of law, have reasonably suspected (an individual) of criminal activity on the basis of reported observed circumstances," search and seizure were

---

37. Adams v. Williams, 407 U.S. 143, 92 S. Ct. 1921, 32 L. Ed. 2d 612 (1972).

38. Pennsylvania v. Mimms, 434 U.S. 106, 98 S. Ct. 330, 54 L. Ed. 2d 331 (1977).

39. U.S. v. Hensley, 469 U.S. 221, 105 S. Ct. 675, 83 L. Ed. 2d 604 (1985).

40. Michigan v. Long, 463 U.S. 1032, 103 S. Ct. 3469, 77 L. Ed. 2d 1201 (1983).

41. U.S. v. Mendenhall, 446 U.S. 544, 100 S. Ct. 1870, 64 L. Ed. 2d 497 (1980).

unconstitutional.[42] Three years later the Court ruled unconstitutional a detention and confinement at an airport which the Justices indicated was tantamount to an arrest. While acknowledging again that "not all seizures of the person must be justified by probable cause to arrest for a crime," and reaffirming that a stop and frisk can be permissible "if there is articulated suspicion that a person has committed or is about to commit a crime," the Court stated that a person approached by law enforcement officials and questioned "need not answer any question put to him; indeed, he may decline to listen to the questions at all and may go on his way. . . . He may not be detained even momentarily without reasonable, objective grounds for doing so; and his refusal to listen or answer does not, without more furnish those grounds." Finding there was no probable cause for either an arrest or a search of the individual, the Court stated: "Where the validity of a search rests on consent, the State has the burden of proving that the necessary consent was freely and voluntarily given, a burden not satisfied by showing a mere submission to claim of lawful authority." Since the confinement of the individual was unlawful, his consent to the search was invalid because tainted by the unlawful confinement.[43]

The following year the Court held that an airport search is to be tested under the lesser *Terry* standard and such a search was upheld "because of the public interest involved in the suppression of illegal transactions in drugs or of any other crime." The general rule henceforth was to be this:

> Certain constraints on personal liberty that constitute "seizures" for purposes of the Fourth Amendment may nonetheless be justified even though there is no showing of "probable cause" if there is articulable suspicion that a person has committed or is about to commit a crime.[44]

In 1985 the Supreme Court rejected a Court of Appeals approach which would have, in effect, ruled a 20-minute detention as per se unjustified. To determine the reasonableness of an investigative stop, made without probable cause for an arrest, the Supreme Court said that it will ask "whether the officer's action was justified at its inception, and whether it was reasonably related to the circumstances which justified the interference in the first place."[45]

Three years later the Supreme Court indicated that for Fourth

---

42. Reid v. Georgia, 448 U.S. 438, 100 S. Ct. 2752, 65 L. Ed. 2d 890 (1980).
43. Florida v. Royer, 460 U.S. 491, 103 S. Ct. 1319, 75 L. Ed. 2d 229 (1983).
44. Florida v. Rodriguez, 469 U.S. 1, 105 S. Ct. 308, 83 L. Ed. 2d 165 (1984).
45. U.S. v. Sharpe, 470 U.S. 675, 105 S. Ct. 1568, 84 L. Ed. 2d 605 (1985).

Amendment analysis, the police can be said to have "seized" an individual only if, in view of all the circumstances surrounding the incident, a reasonable person would have believed that he or she was not free to leave. The Court refused to hold that all police chases are "seizures."[46] The following year the Court stressed that, in determining the validity of a stop, "some minimal level of objective justification," not probable cause, is necessary and that "the totality of the circumstances" must be considered. What thereafter was to be required to support a warrantless stop is, according to the Court, "reasonable suspicion" that an individual is engaged in criminal conduct. As to drug peddlers, the Court seemingly will find such suspicion present when an individual at an airport closely resembles the Drug Enforcement Administration's "profile" of a paradigmatic drug courier.[47] In 1990 the Court held that an anonymous tip, plus other valid corroborative material, could provide the "reasonable suspicion" to justify a *Terry* type investigative stop of a car.[48]

In 1993 the Court held that where police were justified in stopping and frisking a suspect for weapons, but an officer continued exploring the person's pocket after having concluded that it contained no weapon, and then discovered a lump of cocaine, that this sort of evidentiary search was not warranted by the *Terry* doctrine and the seizure of the cocaine was unconstitutional.[49]

As in the case of arrests, investigatory stops and seizures are to be tested by an objective reasonableness standard when claims of unnecessary force are made. Determination of "reasonableness," states the Court, "requires a careful balancing of the nature and quality of the intrusion on the individual's Fourth Amendment interests against the countervailing governmental interests at stake."[50] Reiterating that investigatory stops are permissible if supported by reasonable suspicion and that warrantless searches are valid if based upon probable cause, the Supreme Court ruled in 1996 that questions of reasonable suspicion and probable cause to make warrantless searches must be reviewed de novo by appellate courts.[51]

Rather than employing the more common "stop and frisk" statute

---

46. Michigan v. Chesternut, 486 U.S. 567, 108 S. Ct. 1975, 100 L. Ed. 2d 565 (1988).

47. U.S. v. Sokolow, 490 U.S. 1, 109 S. Ct. 1581, 104 L. Ed. 2d 1 (1989).

48. Alabama v. White, 496 U.S. 325, 110 S. Ct. 2412, 110 L. Ed. 2d 301 (1990).

49. Graham v. Connor, 490 U.S. 386, 109 S. Ct. 1865, 104 L. Ed. 2d 443 (1989).

50. Graham v. Connor, 490 U.S. 386, 109 S. Ct. 1865, 104 L. Ed. 2d 443 (1989).

51. Ornelas v. U.S., 116 S. Ct. 1657, 134 L. Ed. 2d 911 (U.S. 1996).

or ordinance, some local governments have enacted ordinances requiring citizens to answer questions about their identity to the police and to prove their identification, and making it a crime to remain silent. To illustrate, a Detroit ordinance authorized a policeman to stop and question any citizen if he had reasonable cause to believe that the individual's behavior warranted further investigation for criminal activity, and the ordinance was amended to make it unlawful for any person stopped pursuant to the ordinance to refuse to identify himself and produce evidence of his identity. Unfortunately, the Detroit Common Council had forgotten what the United States Supreme Court had ruled in 1969: "While the police have a right to request citizens to answer voluntarily questions concerning unsolved crimes, they have no right to compel them to answer."[52] When the ordinance came to the Michigan Court of Appeals, it held the ordinance unconstitutional and the state Supreme Court refused review. The Court of Appeals explained: "While police may under certain circumstances intrude upon a person's privacy by stopping him and asking questions, there can be no requirement that the person answer."[53]

§ 17.06. Summons and subpoenas to appear before grand juries

The Supreme Court ruled in 1973 that neither a summons nor a subpoena to appear before a grand jury is a "seizure" in the Fourth Amendment sense. The Court held that a directive in the summons to make a voice recording for the grand jury did not infringe any interest protected by the Fourth Amendment, and further held that there was no justification for requiring the grand jury to satisfy the requirement of "reasonableness" applicable to seizures.[54] In a companion case the Court held that the Fourth Amendment was not violated by an order directing a grand jury witness to provide samples of his handwriting and printing.[55] In a dissent in both cases, Justice Marshall said that remand was necessary to allow the government to show that the demands were reasonable. Failing such proof he would hold that the demands were violative of the Fourth

---

52. Davis v. Mississippi, 394 U.S. 721, 89 S. Ct. 1394, 22 L. Ed. 2d 676 (1969).

53. People v. DeFillippo, 80 Mich. App. 197, 262 N.W.2d 921, 924 (1977), cert. granted, 439 U.S. 816, 99 S. Ct. 76, 58 L. Ed. 2d 107 (1978) and judgment rev'd on other grounds, 443 U.S. 31, 99 S. Ct. 2627, 61 L. Ed. 2d 343 (1979).

54. U.S. v. Michigan Nat. Corp., 419 U.S. 1, 95 S. Ct. 10, 42 L. Ed. 2d 1 (1974).

55. U.S. v. Mara, 410 U.S. 19, 93 S. Ct. 774, 35 L. Ed. 2d 99 (1973).

Amendment. Justices Brennan and Douglas were in substantial agreement with this dissent.[56]

The Supreme Court has ruled that a witness summoned to appear and testify before a grand jury may not refuse to answer questions on the ground that they are based on evidence obtained from an unlawful search and seizure.[57]

The enforced production of documents by an invalid grand jury has been held by the Court not an unreasonable search and seizure.[58]

§ 17.07. The arrest warrant—basis for its issuance

The Fourth Amendment to the Constitution is clear that "no warrant shall issue, but upon probable cause supported by oath or affirmation," and the Federal Rules of Criminal Procedure provide that the magistrate or judge can properly issue a warrant for arrest only "if there is probable cause to believe that an offense has been committed and that the defendant has committed it."[59]

When supporting affidavits do not provide a basis for a magistrate properly to find the presence of probable cause, issuance of an arrest warrant is unconstitutional. The Supreme Court states: "Before an arrest warrant can issue [the Fourth Amendment] requires that the judicial officer issuing such a warrant be supplied with sufficient information to support an independent judgment that probable cause exists for the warrant."[60]

Affidavits in support of warrants are deficient when the affiant does not speak from personal knowledge of the matters contained therein or indicate the basis for relying upon the information of others. While by the Federal Rules of Criminal Procedure, "the finding of probable cause may be based upon hearsay evidence in whole or in part,"[61] a police officer, applying for an arrest warrant on the basis of hearsay from an informant, must indicate to the magistrate why the police officer deems the information to be reliable. Insufficient are general statements that the affiants have received reliable information from a credible person and believe it to be true.

---

56. U.S. v. Mara, 410 U.S. 19, 93 S. Ct. 774, 35 L. Ed. 2d 99 (1973).

57. U.S. v. Calandra, 414 U.S. 338, 94 S. Ct. 613, 38 L. Ed. 2d 561, 66 Ohio Op. 2d 320 (1974).

58. U.S. v. Wallace & Tiernan Co., 336 U.S. 793, 69 S. Ct. 824, 93 L. Ed. 1042 (1949).

59. Fed. R. Crim. P. 4(a).

60. Whiteley v. Warden, Wyo. State Penitentiary, 401 U.S. 560, 91 S. Ct. 1031, 28 L. Ed. 2d 306, 311, 58 Ohio Op. 2d 434 (1971).

61. Fed. R. Crim. P. 41(a).

A magistrate cannot accept without question a police officer's mere conclusion that the person whose arrest is sought has committed a crime. The Supreme Court has emphasized that the probable cause necessary for a warrant cannot

> be made out by affidavits which are purely conclusory, stating only the affiant's or an informant's belief that probable cause exists without detailing any of the underlying circumstances upon which that belief is based. Recital of some of the underlying circumstances in the affidavit is essential if the magistrate is to perform his detached function and not serve merely as a rubber stamp for the police.[62]

Informants' tips are not alone sufficient to provide the basis for a magistrate's finding of probable cause. The Supreme Court states:

> In the absence of a statement detailing the manner in which the information was gathered, it is especially important that the tip describe the accused's criminal activity in sufficient detail so that the magistrate may know that he is relying on something more substantial than a casual rumor circulating in the underworld or an accusation based merely upon the individual's general reputation.

The Court added that a police officer swearing that his confident is reliable must provide the magistrate with reasons to support such a conclusion.[63]

The Court held in 1971 that a magistrate, in determining whether an unidentified informant's information to a police agent is truthful, can give consideration to the fact the informant's statements are against interest and could expose him to criminal punishment, and that the policeman's knowledge of the accused's reputation is something that a magistrate can properly rely upon in assessing the reliability of an informant's tip.[64]

The term "probable cause" means less than evidence which would justify conviction at trial, and a finding of "probable cause" may rest upon evidence which is not legally competent in a criminal prosecution. Thus, hearsay may be the basis for the issuance of a warrant so long as there is a substantial basis for crediting the

---

62. U.S. v. Ventresca, 380 U.S. 102, 108, 85 S. Ct. 741, 13 L. Ed. 2d 684 (1965).

63. Spinelli v. U.S., 393 U.S. 410, 89 S. Ct. 584, 21 L. Ed. 2d 637, 644 (1969).

64. U.S. v. Harris, 403 U.S. 573, 91 S. Ct. 2075, 29 L. Ed. 2d 723 (1971).

hearsay.[65] The Supreme Court has said that "an affidavit may be based on hearsay information and need not reflect the direct personal observation of the affiant so long as the magistrate is informed of some of the underlying circumstances supporting the affiant's conclusion and his belief that any informant involved was credible or his information reliable."[66]

§ 17.08. —its contents

The common law requires that a person to be served with an arrest warrant must be named, or described sufficiently to be identified,[67] and the United States Supreme Court has stated that "it is familiar history that indiscriminate searches and seizures under the authority of general warrants were the immediate evil that motivated the framing and adoption of the Fourth Amendment."[68] The Court holds that under the Fourth Amendment arrest warrants must particularly describe the person to be arrested in the warrant.[69] Designation of the person sought as "John Doe" does not satisfy the constitutional requirement.[70] The Court has said:

> The principle of the common law, by which warrants of arrest, in cases criminal or civil, must specifically name or describe the person to be arrested has been affirmed in the American Constitution, and by the great weight of authority in this country, a warrant that does not do so will not justify the officer in making the arrest.[71]

§ 17.09. —its execution

At the common law, the breaking into of a private dwelling to execute an arrest warrant was unlawful where the officer failed first to identify himself and state his authority and purpose for demanding admission. A person, according to the United States Supreme Court, "could not be lawfully arrested in his home by officers break-

---

65. U.S. v. Ventresca, 380 U.S. 102, 85 S. Ct. 741, 13 L. Ed. 2d 684, 688 (1965).

66. U.S. v. Ventresca, 380 U.S. 102, 85 S. Ct. 741, 13 L. Ed. 2d 684, 689 (1965); Aguilar v. State of Tex., 378 U.S. 108, 84 S. Ct. 1509, 12 L. Ed. 2d 723 (1964).

67. Payton v. New York, 445 U.S. 573, 100 S. Ct. 1371, 63 L. Ed. 2d 639, 649 (1980).

68. West v. Cabell, 153 U.S. 78, 14 S. Ct. 752, 38 L. Ed. 643, 644 (1894).

69. West v. Cabell, 153 U.S. 78, 14 S. Ct. 752, 38 L. Ed. 643, 644 (1894).

70. West v. Cabell, 153 U.S. 78, 14 S. Ct. 752, 38 L. Ed. 643, 644 (1894).

71. West v. Cabell, 153 U.S. 78, 14 S. Ct. 752, 38 L. Ed. 643, 645 (1894).

ing in without first giving him notice of their authority and purpose."[72]

The Fourth Amendment is here construed with reference to the common law and to the intent of the generation that enacted the Amendment. The Supreme Court has said of 18 U.S.C.A. § 3109, requiring federal officers to give prior notice of their authority and purpose before forcing entry into a home, that "the statute is designed to incorporate fundamental values and the ongoing development of the common law."[73] Elsewhere the Court adds: "Physical entry of the house is the chief evil against which the wording of the Fourth Amendment is directed."[74]

When customs agents opened the closed but unlocked door of an apartment and entered in order to arrest a citizen, without first announcing their identity, the Supreme Court held that the method of entry vitiated the arrest and made inadmissible at trial evidence seized in the search subsequent to the unlawful arrest.[75]

There are exigent circumstances in which courts have customarily permitted unannounced entries into private homes by officers having arrest warrants. These are: (a) where the person within the dwelling already knows of the officers' authority and purpose, (b) where the officers are justified in the belief that persons within are in imminent peril of bodily harm, and (c) where those within, made aware of the presence of someone outside (because, for instance, there has been a knock at the door), are then engaged in activity which justifies the officers in the belief that an escape or the destruction of evidence is being attempted.[76] The Supreme Court said in 1980: "An arrest warrant founded on probable cause implicitly carries with it the limited authority to enter a dwelling in which the suspect lives, when there is reason to believe the suspect is within."[77] An arrest warrant does not adequately protect the Fourth Amendment interests of persons not named in the warrant, and, except in indigent circumstances, an

---

72. Miller v. U.S., 357 U.S. 301, 78 S. Ct. 1190, 2 L. Ed. 2d 1332 (1958).

73. Sabbath v. U.S., 391 U.S. 585, 88 S. Ct. 1755, 20 L. Ed. 2d 828 (1968).

74. U.S. v. U.S. Dist. Court for Eastern Dist. of Mich., Southern Division, 407 U.S. 297, 92 S. Ct. 2125, 32 L. Ed. 2d 752 (1972).

75. Sabbath v. U.S., 391 U.S. 585, 88 S. Ct. 1755, 20 L. Ed. 2d 828 (1968).

76. Ker v. State of Cal., 374 U.S. 23, 83 S. Ct. 1623, 10 L. Ed. 2d 726, 746, 24 Ohio Op. 2d 201 (1963); Read v. Case, 4 Conn. 166 (1822); People v. Maddox, 46 Cal. 2d 301, 294 P.2d 6 (1956).

77. Payton v. New York, 445 U.S. 573, 100 S. Ct. 1371, 63 L. Ed. 2d 639, 661 (1980).

officer with an arrest warrant must obtain a search warrant to force an entry into the house of a third party.[78]

Before a person can lawfully serve arrest warrants, he must be a peace officer with statutory authority to serve such warrant.[79] Warrants from state magistrates can be executed only in the state in which the warrant was issued, but federal warrants can be served everywhere within the United States.[80] One having legal authority to make an arrest has the right to use whatever amount and kind of force is appropriate and necessary to effectuate the arrest.[81] Deadly force cannot be used in executing an arrest warrant unless it is necessary to prevent the escape of an apparently armed suspected felon and if the officer has probable cause to believe that the suspect poses a significant threat of death or serious physical harm to the officer or others.[82] Arrests are to be tested by an objective reasonableness standard when claims of unnecessary force are made. This requires a careful balancing of the countervailing societal interests at stake.

§ 17.10. —defects in warrant or in execution

When an arrest warrant is defective, a citizen deprived of his liberty has a constitutional right to his immediate freedom, as well as an appropriate statutory right, under the Civil Rights Acts, to damages.[83]

When an arrest warrant is defective and search is conducted incident to such arrest, the person subjected to such an unlawful search and seizure is entitled to the return of any items seized.[84] If evidence produced by such an unlawful arrest and seizure is proffered at trial, it can on motion be suppressed.[85]

§ 17.11. Permissible arrests without warrant—consent as basis for detention by government personnel

It was only a "consensual encounter," said the Supreme Court in

---

78. Steagald v. U.S., 451 U.S. 204, 101 S. Ct. 1642, 68 L. Ed. 2d 38 (1981).

79. State v. Ovens, 4 Ariz. App. 591, 422 P.2d 719 (1967).

80. Anderson v. Dunn, 19 U.S. 204, 5 L. Ed. 242 (1821).

81. Commonwealth v. Bollinger, 198 Ky. 646, 249 S.W. 786 (1923); State v. Smith, 127 Iowa 534, 103 N.W. 944 (1905); Wilgus, Arrest Without a Warrant, 22 Mich. L. Rev. 541, 557 (1922).

82. Sabbath v. U.S., 391 U.S. 585, 88 S. Ct. 1755, 20 L. Ed. 2d 828 (1968)

83. Monroe v. Pape, 365 U.S. 167, 81 S. Ct. 473, 5 L. Ed. 2d 492 (1961) (overruled in part on other grounds by, Monell v. Department of Social Services of City of New York, 436 U.S. 658, 98 S. Ct. 2018, 56 L. Ed. 2d 611 (1978)).

84. Brown v. Illinois, 422 U.S. 590, 95 S. Ct. 2254, 45 L. Ed. 2d 416 (1975).

85. Sabbath v. U.S., 391 U.S. 585, 88 S. Ct. 1755, 20 L. Ed. 2d 828 (1968).

1984 when 15 to 25 Immigration and Naturalization agents undertook a "factory survey" looking for illegal aliens, with agents stationed at the doors through which workers customarily departed, and citizen workers apparently too frightened to assert their constitutional rights to refuse to respond to questioning by the agents. It was not a "seizure," nor even a "detention," ruled the Court.[86] One can imagine the reaction of 1775 workers in a Boston factory if this would have been imposed upon them by British agents.

When police in 1991 requested permission of a passenger on an interstate bus to inspect his baggage, the Supreme Court stated that it must "determine whether the police conduct would have communicated to a reasonable person that the person was not free to decline the officer's request or otherwise terminate the encounter." The Court then ruled that the Fourth Amendment was not violated when the police on the bus, without brandishing their weapons, advised a passenger of his Fourth Amendment rights and then, with consent, searched the baggage, found cocaine, and arrested him.[87]

Finding that a citizen's "consent" at an airport was tainted, the Court has emphasized that where the validity of an arrest depends on claimed consent by the individual, the government has the burden of proving that the necessary consent was freely and voluntarily given, a burden not satisfied by showing a mere submission to claims of lawful authority.[88]

§ 17.12. —commission of crime seen by arresting individual

When a felony is committed in the presence of a police officer he can, without a warrant, arrest the perpetrator.[89] The Supreme Court has held valid a warrantless arrest in a public place made under an Act of Congress authorizing certain postal officers and employees to make arrests "if they have reasonable ground to believe that the person to be arrested has committed or is committing such a felony." Justices Powell and Stewart concurred, indicating that this decision is not to be construed to authorize such arrest in a private home. Justices Brennan and Marshall dissented.[90] At the common law and

---

86. I.N.S. v. Delgado, 466 U.S. 210, 104 S. Ct. 1758, 80 L. Ed. 2d 247 (1984).

87. Florida v. Bostick, 501 U.S. 429, 111 S. Ct. 2382, 115 L. Ed. 2d 389 (1991).

88. Florida v. Royer, 460 U.S. 491, 103 S. Ct. 1319, 75 L. Ed. 2d 229 (1983).

89. Wilgus, Arrest Without a Warrant, 22 Mich. L. Rev. 541, 550 (1924); U.S. v. Rabinowitz, 339 U.S. 56, 70 S. Ct. 430, 94 L. Ed. 653 (1950) (overruled in part on other grounds by, Chimel v. California, 395 U.S. 752, 89 S. Ct. 2034, 23 L. Ed. 2d 685 (1969)).

90. U.S. v. Watson, 423 U.S. 411, 96 S. Ct. 820, 46 L. Ed. 2d 598 (1976).

in most states, a citizen can arrest a person he has seen committing a felony.[91]

Police officers can generally arrest for misdemeanors committed in their presence,[92] although citizens customarily do not have such power, unless a breach of the peace was committed.[93]

§ 17.13. —hot pursuit

When a police officer is in hot pursuit of a person he reasonably suspects as a fleeing criminal, the officer can arrest and hold the suspect without a warrant.[94] Illustratively, when police were informed that a suspected armed robber had fled into a specified house, they were held to be in hot pursuit of him and to have acted reasonably in entering the house without a warrant and in searching for the suspect. The Supreme Court stated: "The Fourth Amendment does not require police officers to delay in the course of an investigation if to do so would gravely endanger their lives or the lives of others."[95]

§ 17.14. —arrest on probable cause

It is generally required that an arrest without a warrant be made on probable cause both that a crime has been committed and that the individual seized has committed the crime. In 1964 the United States Supreme Court stated that the constitutionality of an arrest without a warrant depends upon whether

> at the moment the arrest was made, the officers had probable cause to make it—whether at the moment the facts and circumstances within their knowledge and of which they had reasonably trustworthy information were sufficient to warrant a prudent man in believing that the [arrestee] had committed or was committing an offense. . . . When the constitutional validity of an arrest is challenged, it is the function of the court to determine whether the facts available to the officers at the mo-

---

91. Gaither v. U.S., 134 U.S. App. D.C. 154, 413 F.2d 1061 (D.C. Cir. 1969).

92. Wilgus, Arrest Without a Warrant, 22 Mich. L. Rev. 541 (1924); Johnson v. U.S., 333 U.S. 10, 68 S. Ct. 367, 92 L. Ed. 436 (1948).

93. Gaither v. U.S., 134 U.S. App. D.C. 154, 413 F.2d 1061 (D.C. Cir. 1969).

94. Ker v. State of Cal., 374 U.S. 23, 83 S. Ct. 1623, 10 L. Ed. 2d 726, 24 Ohio Op. 2d 201 (1963); U.S. v. Davis, 461 F.2d 1026 (3d Cir. 1972); U.S. v. Santana, 427 U.S. 38, 96 S. Ct. 2406, 49 L. Ed. 2d 300 (1976).

95. Warden, Md. Penitentiary v. Hayden, 387 U.S. 294, 87 S. Ct. 1642, 18 L. Ed. 2d 782, 787 (1967).

ment of the arrest would warrant a man of reasonable caution in the belief that an offense had been committed.[96]

In 1979 the Court stated it had repeatedly explained:

that "probable cause" to justify an arrest means facts and circumstances within the officer's knowledge that are sufficient to warrant a prudent person, or one of reasonable caution, in believing in the circumstances shown, that the suspect has committed, is committing, or is about to commit an offense.[97]

The Court has properly rejected the argument of a state that probable cause of an arresting officer can be something less than the probable cause sufficient for a magistrate to issue a warrant. "Less stringent standards," explained the Court, "would discourage resort to the procedures for obtaining a warrant."[98]

The validity of a probable cause arrest does not depend on whether the suspect actually committed a crime; the mere fact that the suspect is later acquitted of the offense for which he is arrested is irrelevant to determining the validity of the arrest.[99]

Identification of the suspect by a reliable informant may constitute probable cause for an arrest where the information is sufficiently accurate to lead the officers to the suspect.[1] In the *Draper* case the Court held that information from a reliable informant, corroborated by a government agent's observations as to accuracy of the informant's description of the suspect and his presence at a particular place, were sufficient to establish probable cause.[2] However, a mere tip from an informant does not alone provide probable cause to arrest a person without a warrant.[3] Probable cause

---

96. Beck v. State of Ohio, 379 U.S. 89, 85 S. Ct. 223, 13 L. Ed. 2d 142, 145, 148, 3 Ohio Misc. 71, 31 Ohio Op. 2d 80 (1964).

97. Michigan v. DeFillippo, 443 U.S. 31, 99 S. Ct. 2627, 61 L. Ed. 2d 343, 349-50 (1979).

98. Whiteley v. Warden, Wyo. State Penitentiary, 401 U.S. 560, 91 S. Ct. 1031, 28 L. Ed. 2d 306, 58 Ohio Op. 2d 434 (1971).

99. Whiteley v. Warden, Wyo. State Penitentiary, 401 U.S. 560, 91 S. Ct. 1031, 28 L. Ed. 2d 306, 58 Ohio Op. 2d 434 (1971).

1. Draper v. U.S., 358 U.S. 307, 79 S. Ct. 329, 3 L. Ed. 2d 327, 332 (1959).

2. Draper v. U.S., 358 U.S. 307, 79 S. Ct. 329, 3 L. Ed. 2d 327, 332 (1959).

3. Mallory v. U.S., 354 U.S. 449, 77 S. Ct. 1356, 1 L. Ed. 2d 1479 (1957); Wong Sun v. U.S., 371 U.S. 471, 83 S. Ct. 407, 9 L. Ed. 2d 441, 450 (1963); Recznik v. City of Lorain, 393 U.S. 166, 89 S. Ct. 342, 21 L. Ed. 2d 317, 46 Ohio Op. 2d 397 (1968).

requires a magistrate to be shown both the reliability of an informant and the reliability of the information he made available to the police.[4]

Mere suspicion is never enough for probable cause.[5] Even a "strong reason to suspect" a person is insufficient.[6] Thus, the smell of opium coming from a closed room was held not enough to support an arrest of the occupants without a warrant.[7] Arrests such as these cannot be justified by what resulting searches divulge.[8]

Probable cause does not exist solely because an arresting officer knew that the suspect had a previous record of arrests or even convictions. To accept this as probable cause, explained the Supreme Court, "would be to hold that anyone with a previous criminal record could be arrested at will."[9]

Good faith on the part of arresting officers is not sufficient to show probable cause. The Supreme Court has stated: "If subjective good faith alone were the test, the protections of the Fourth Amendment would evaporate, and the people would be 'secure in their persons, houses, papers and effects' only in the discretion of the police."[10]

To establish "probable cause" the same quantum of evidence required to establish guilt is not necessary.[11]

If an officer acts with probable cause, he is protected even though it turns out that the citizen arrested is innocent.[12]

The Supreme Court ruled in 1990 that when police had probable cause to arrest a suspect, the exclusionary rule did not bar the government from using a statement made by the suspect/accused outside of his home, even though the statement was taken after his *unlawful* arrest in his home. Justices Marshall, Brennan, Blackmun and Stevens dissented, stating that this new rule will be an invitation

4. Warden, Md. Penitentiary v. Hayden, 387 U.S. 294, 87 S. Ct. 1642, 18 L. Ed. 2d 782 (1967).

5. Wong Sun v. U.S., 371 U.S. 471, 83 S. Ct. 407, 9 L. Ed. 2d 441 (1963).

6. Henry v. U.S., 361 U.S. 98, 80 S. Ct. 168, 4 L. Ed. 2d 134, 138 (1959).

7. Johnson v. U.S., 333 U.S. 10, 15, 68 S. Ct. 367, 92 L. Ed. 436, 441 (1948).

8. Johnson v. U.S., 333 U.S. 10, 15, 68 S. Ct. 367, 92 L. Ed. 436, 442 (1948).

9. Beck v. State of Ohio, 379 U.S. 89, 85 S. Ct. 223, 13 L. Ed. 2d 142, 148, 3 Ohio Misc. 71, 31 Ohio Op. 2d 80 (1964).

10. Beck v. State of Ohio, 379 U.S. 89, 85 S. Ct. 223, 13 L. Ed. 2d 142, 148, 3 Ohio Misc. 71, 31 Ohio Op. 2d 80 (1964).

11. Brinegar v. U.S., 338 U.S. 160, 69 S. Ct. 1302, 93 L. Ed. 1879 (1949).

12. Henry v. U.S., 361 U.S. 98, 80 S. Ct. 168, 4 L. Ed. 2d 134 (1959); Wilgus, Search Without a Warrant, 22 Mich. L. Rev. 541, 559 (1924).

to police to break into peoples' homes and drag out the individuals for questioning.[13]

A warrantless search that provides probable cause for an arrest cannot be justified as an incident of that arrest. The Supreme Court states: "It is axiomatic that an incident search may not precede an arrest and serve as part of its justification."[14]

§ 17.15. The need for prompt judicial review of arrests without warrants

Under all the exceptional instances noted, where individuals can lawfully be arrested without a warrant, they must be taken before a neutral magistrate for a probable cause determination as soon as reasonably possible.[15] The Fourth Amendment requires a judicial determination of probable cause as a prerequisite to an extended restraint of liberty following arrest of a person without a warrant.[16] In the *Gerstein* case the Supreme Court held that a citizen arrested under a prosecutor's information is entitled under the Fourth Amendment to a judicial determination of probable cause for the deprivation of his liberty. The Court stated: "When the stakes are this high, the detached judgment of a neutral magistrate is essential if the Fourth Amendment is to furnish a meaningful protection from unfounded interferences with liberty." The Court reversed both lower courts and ruled that the probable cause determination by a magistrate need not be accompanied by such adversary safeguards as counsel, confrontation, cross-examination, and compulsory process for witnesses.

In 1991 the Court clarified the ruling in *Gerstein* and held that a statute requiring the judicial determination of probable cause within 48 hours after seizure of the person will, as a general matter, be sufficient to satisfy demands of the Fourth Amendment. Justices Marshall, Blackmun, Stevens and Scalia strongly dissented, arguing that in cases of warrantless arrests the Constitution demands a probable cause hearing to be held immediately upon completion of the administrative steps incidental to arrest.[17] Three years later, the

---

13. New York v. Harris, 495 U.S. 14, 110 S. Ct. 1640, 109 L. Ed. 2d 13 (1990).

14. Smith v. Ohio, 494 U.S. 541, 110 S. Ct. 1288, 108 L. Ed. 2d 464 (1990).

15. Wilgus, Search Without a Warrant, 22 Mich. L. Rev. 541, 559 (1924); Keefe v. Hart, 213 Mass. 476, 100 N.E. 558 (1913).

16. Gerstein v. Pugh, 420 U.S. 103, 95 S. Ct. 854, 43 L. Ed. 2d 54 (1975).

17. County of Riverside v. McLaughlin, 500 U.S. 44, 111 S. Ct. 1661, 114 L. Ed. 2d 49 (1991).

Court ruled the *McLaughlin* decision was to apply retroactively to all cases not final on the date of that case.[18]

§ 17.16. Legality of search incident to lawful seizure of the person

It is basic that, under limited time and space, an arresting officer can, without a search warrant, examine a parson validly arrested.[19] Such searches are justified by the need to seize weapons and other things which might be used to assault or kill the arresting officer, or to effect an escape, as well as by the need to prevent the destruction of evidence of the crime.[20]

Such permissible warrantless searches must be incident to the arrest and substantially contemporaneous with the arrest.[21] Impossible to defend is a five-to-four Supreme Court ruling under this general test allowing search of a person the next day after he had been arrested.[22]

To be incident to an arrest, a search must be not only contemporaneous, but it must be somewhere near the locus of the arrest. The Court has used varying language, and varying rulings, in defining proximity to the place of arrest. In 1927 the Court announced that an arresting officer can lawfully search places "within the immediate possession and control" of the person arrested.[23] After some alternative or deviating language over the years, the Court in 1969 resumed its original approach and held that when a person is lawfully arrested, the arresting officers can search the area within his immediate control—which means the area from within which he might gain possession of a weapon or destructible evidence. The officers can no longer search beyond this area without a search warrant. The Court explained:

> When an arrest is made, it is reasonable for the arresting officer to search the person arrested in order to remove any weapons that the latter might seek to use in order to resist arrest or effect his escape. Otherwise, the officer's safety might well be endangered, and the arrest itself frustrated. In addition, it is entirely reasonable for the arresting officer to search for and

18. Powell v. Nevada, 511 U.S. 79, 114 S. Ct. 1280, 128 L. Ed. 2d 1 (1994).

19. Preston v. U.S., 376 U.S. 364, 84 S. Ct. 881, 11 L. Ed. 2d 777 (1964).

20. Preston v. U.S., 376 U.S. 364, 84 S. Ct. 881, 11 L. Ed. 2d 77; (1964).

21. Preston v. U.S., 376 U.S. 364, 84 S. Ct. 881, 11 L. Ed. 2d 777, 780 (1964).

22. U.S. v. Edwards, 415 U.S. 800, 94 S. Ct. 1234, 39 L. Ed. 2d 771 (1974); Preston v. U.S., 376 U.S. 364, 84 S. Ct. 881, 11 L. Ed. 2d 777 (1964).

23. Marron v. U.S., 275 U.S. 192, 48 S. Ct. 74, 72 L. Ed. 231 (1927).

seize any evidence on the arrestee's person in order to prevent its concealment or destruction. And the area into which an arrestee might reach in order to grab a weapon or evidentiary items must, of course, be governed by a like rule.[24]

Searches at totally unrelated locations are not incident to an arrest.[25] The Supreme Court has stated: "Once an accused is under arrest and in custody, then a search made at another place, without a search warrant, is simply not incident to the arrest."[26] Not incident to an arrest made in Nevada was a search of the person's hotel room in California.[27] A search of a garage under a house was not incident to an arrest made in the house above.[28]

When a person is arrested outside his house, the police are not constitutionally authorized to search within the house.[29] Correlatively, when a person has been lawfully arrested in a house, there is no constitutional authority for a search outside the house and some distance away.[30] So, too, when a person is arrested in a building, mass seizures of things throughout the building are unconstitutional.[31] When a person was arrested and then taken to a police station, the Supreme Court permitted a so-called "inventory search" of a shoulder bag belonging to the arrestee.[32]

§ 17.17. Remedies available to persons subjected to unreasonable seizures and searches

A person unconstitutionally arrested or "seized" can secure

---

24. Chimel v. California, 395 U.S. 752, 89 S. Ct. 2034, 23 L. Ed. 2d 685 (1969).

25. Agnello v. U.S., 269 U.S. 20, 46 S. Ct. 4, 70 L. Ed. 145, 51 A.L.R. 409 (1925).

26. Preston v. U.S., 376 U.S. 364, 84 S. Ct. 881, 11 L. Ed. 2d 777 (1964).

27. Stoner v. State of Cal., 376 U.S. 483, 84 S. Ct. 889, 11 L. Ed. 2d 856 (1964).

28. Fahy v. State of Conn., 375 U.S. 85, 84 S. Ct. 229, 11 L. Ed. 2d 171 (1963).

29. Shipley v. California, 395 U.S. 818, 89 S. Ct. 2053, 23 L. Ed. 2d 732 (1969); Vale v. Louisiana, 399 U.S. 30, 90 S. Ct. 1969, 26 L. Ed. 2d 409 (1970).

30. Coolidge v. New Hampshire, 403 U.S. 443, 91 S. Ct. 2022, 29 L. Ed. 2d 564 (1971).

31. Von Cleef v. New Jersey, 395 U.S. 814, 89 S. Ct. 2051, 23 L. Ed. 2d 728 (1969).

32. Illinois v. Lafayette, 462 U.S. 640, 103 S. Ct. 2605, 77 L. Ed. 2d 65 (1983).

monetary damages for false imprisonment,[33] as well as relief under the federal civil rights acts.[34]

Where evidence is seized from a person following an unlawful arrest or "seizure," the person can bring locally appropriate action for the return of his goods that are not illegal or contraband.[35] Before trial he can move for the suppression of all goods and materials seized, as well as all "fruits of the poisoned tree"—goods and properties discovered as a result of leads from material seized at the arrest. Speaking of the Fourth Amendment, the Supreme Court stated in *Wong Sun v. United States* that "the exclusionary prohibition extends as well to the indirect as the direct products of such invasions [as illegal seizures and searches]. . . . The exclusionary sanction applies to any 'fruits' of a constitutional violation—whether such evidence be tangible, physical material actually seized, items observed, etc."[36] Verbal evidence deriving from an unlawful seizure and search cannot be used under the fruit of the poisoned tree doctrine.[37]

If there has been no unreasonable delay in contesting the evidence flowing from an unlawful arrest, a timely motion at trial can secure the suppression of such material.[38] In 1975 the Supreme Court held that where a citizen was arrested without a warrant and without probable cause, subsequent statements could not be used against him at his trial simply because he had been given a *Miranda* warning before talking. *Miranda* warnings, said the Court, do not alone and per se make the act of confession a product of free will to break, for Fourth Amendment purposes, the causal connection between the illegal arrest and the confession.[39] Eight years later the Court said that statements made during a period of illegal detention are inadmissible although voluntarily given, if they are the product of the illegal detention and not the result of an independent act of free will. The Court held on the facts that the "bounds of an investiga-

33. Sindle v. New York City Transit Authority, 33 N.Y.2d 293, 352 N.Y.S.2d 183, 307 N.E.2d 245 (1973).

34. Monroe v. Pape, 365 U.S. 167, 81 S. Ct. 473, 5 L. Ed. 2d 492 (1961) (overruled in part on other grounds by, Monell v. Department of Social Services of City of New York, 436 U.S. 658, 98 S. Ct. 2018, 56 L. Ed. 2d 611 (1978)); Pritchard v. Perry, 508 F.2d 423 (4th Cir. 1975).

35. Brown v. Illinois, 422 U.S. 590, 95 S. Ct. 2254, 45 L. Ed. 2d 416 (1975).

36. Wong Sun v. U.S., 371 U.S. 471, 484, 83 S. Ct. 407, 9 L. Ed. 2d 441 (1963).

37. Florida v. Royer, 460 U.S. 491, 103 S. Ct. 1319, 75 L. Ed. 2d 229 (1983).

38. Elkins v. U.S., 364 U.S. 206, 80 S. Ct. 1437, 4 L. Ed. 2d 1669 (1960).

39. Brown v. Illinois, 422 U.S. 590, 95 S. Ct. 2254, 45 L. Ed. 2d 416 (1975).

tive stop had been exceeded" by detention of a person at an airport, and hence his consent was tainted.[40]

Even though an arrest was unlawful and subsequent identification proceedings had to be suppressed, the Supreme Court held in 1980 that an in-court identification of the defendant could be used to convict without violating the Fourth Amendment, where such in-court identification rested on an independent recollection of the witness' initial encounter with the defendant, uninfluenced by the pretrial identification.[41]

The Court now holds that federal habeas corpus cannot be available to state prisoners claiming unlawful seizures, provided the state has given them an opportunity for a full and fair litigation of all Fourth Amendment claims.[42]

---

40. Florida v. Royer, 460 U.S. 491, 103 S. Ct. 1319, 75 L. Ed. 2d 229 (1983).

41. U.S. v. Crews, 445 U.S. 463, 100 S. Ct. 1244, 63 L. Ed. 2d 537 (1980).

42. Stone v. Powell, 428 U.S. 465, 96 S. Ct. 3037, 49 L. Ed. 2d 1067 (1976).

CHAPTER EIGHTEEN

The Privilege Against Self-Incrimination

---

§ 18.00. Introduction

The Fifth Amendment provides that "[no] person . . . shall be compelled in any Criminal Case to be a witness against himself." This guarantee against testimonial compulsion, in the language of the Supreme Court, "was added to the original Constitution in the conviction that too high a price may be paid even for the unhampered enforcement of the criminal law and that, in its attainment, other social objects of a free society should not be sacrificed."[1] On another

---

1. Feldman v. United States, 322 U.S. 487, 489, 64 S. Ct. 1082, 88 L. Ed. 1408, 1412, 154 A.L.R. 982 (1944) (overruled in part on other grounds by, Murphy v. Waterfront Commission of New York Harbor, 378 U.S. 52, 84 S. Ct. 1594, 12 L. Ed. 2d 678 (1964)).

occasion the Court has noted: "The immediate and potential evils of compulsory self-disclosure transcend any difficulties that the exercise of the privilege may impose on society in the detection and prosecution of crime."[2]

On a number of occasions the Supreme Court has indicated that "This provision of the Amendment must be accorded liberal construction in favor of the right it was intended to secure."[3] In 1956 Justice Frankfurter, speaking for the Court, said: "This constitutional protection must not be interpreted in a hostile or niggardly spirit. Too many, even those who should be better advised, view this privilege as a shelter for wrongdoers. They too readily assume that those who invoke it are either guilty of crime or commit perjury in claiming the privilege. Such a view does scant honor to the patriots who sponsored the Bill of Rights as a condition to acceptance of the Constitution by the ratifying States."[4]

Justices Black and Douglas have written: "The guarantee against self-incrimination contained in the Fifth Amendment is not only a protection against conviction and prosecution but a safeguard of conscience and human dignity and freedom of expression as well."[5]

The Supreme Court has also stated:

> The privilege against self-incrimination "registers an important advance in the development of our liberty-one of the great landmarks in man's struggle to make himself civilized." It reflects many of our fundamental values and most noble aspirations: our unwillingness to subject those suspected of crime to the cruel trilemma of self-accusation, perjury or contempt; our preference for an accusatorial rather than an inquisitorial system of criminal justice; our fear that self-incriminating statements will be elicited by inhumane treatment and abuses; our sense of fair play which dictates "a fair state-individual balance by requiring the government to leave the individual alone until good cause is shown for disturbing him and by requiring the government in its contest with the individual to shoulder the

---

2. U.S. v. White, 322 U.S. 694, 698, 64 S. Ct. 1248, 88 L. Ed. 1542, 1545, 152 A.L.R. 1202 (1944).

3. Counselman v. Hitchcock, 142 U.S. 547, 562, 12 S. Ct. 195, 35 L. Ed. 1110, 1113 (1892) (overruled in part on other grounds by, Kastigar v. U.S., 406 U.S. 441, 92 S. Ct. 1653, 32 L. Ed. 2d 212 (1972)); Arndstein v. McCarthy, 254 U.S. 71-73, 41 S. Ct. 26, 65 L. Ed. 138-42 (1920); Hoffman v. U.S., 341 U.S. 479, 71 S. Ct. 814, 818, 95 L. Ed. 1118, 1123-24 (1951).

4. Ullmann v. U.S., 350 U.S. 422, 76 S. Ct. 497, 500, 100 L. Ed. 511, 518, 53 A.L.R.2d 1008 (1956).

5. Ullmann v. U.S., 350 U.S. 422, 76 S. Ct. 497, 510, 100 L. Ed. 511, 527, 53 A.L.R.2d 1008 (1956).

entire load;" our respect for the inviolability of the human personality and of the right of each individual "to a private enclave where he may lead a private life" our distrust of self-deprecatory statements; and our realization that the privilege while sometimes "a shelter to the guilty" is often "a protection to the innocent."[6]

The Court has indicated that it:

must condemn the practice of imputing a sinister meaning to the exercise of a person's constitutional right under the Fifth Amendment. The right of an accused person to refuse to testify . . . has been recognized as "one of the most valuable prerogatives of the citizen. In *Ullman v. United States* we scored the assumption that those who claim this privilege are either criminals or perjurers. The privilege against self-incrimination would be reduced to a hollow mockery if its exercise could be taken as equivalent either to a confession of guilt or a conclusive presumption of perjury. As we pointed out in *Ullman*, a witness may have a reasonable fear of prosecution and yet be innocent of any wrongdoing. The privilege serves to protect the innocent who otherwise might be ensnared by ambiguous circumstances."[7]

Even though the privilege against self-incrimination would justify a citizen in not answering a query from a government official, the Supreme Court points out that the citizen "cannot with impunity knowingly and willfully answer with a falsehood."[8]

§ 18.01. Who is entitled to the privilege

Only natural persons can claim the privilege against self-incrimination. The United States Supreme Court since 1967 has ruled that "the constitutional privilege against self-incrimination is applicable in the case of juveniles as it is with respect to adults."[9] In 1957 the Court stated:

It is settled that a corporation is not protected by the constitutional privilege against self-incrimination. A corporate

---

6. Murphy v. Waterfront Commission of New York Harbor, 378 U.S. 52, 84 S. Ct. 1594, 12 L. Ed. 2d 678, 681-82 (1964).

7. Slochower v. Board of Higher Ed. of City of New York, 350 U.S. 551, 76 S. Ct. 637, 640-41 100 L. Ed. 692, 698-700 (1956).

8. Bryson v. U.S., 396 U.S. 64, 90 S. Ct. 355, 24 L. Ed. 2d 264 (1969).

9. Application of Gault, 387 U.S. 1, 87 S. Ct. 1428, 1458, 18 L. Ed. 2d 527, 40 Ohio Op. 2d 378 (1967).

officer may not withhold testimony or documents on the ground that his corporation would be incriminated . . . the books and records of corporations cannot be insulated from reasonable demands of governmental authorities by a claim of personal privilege on the part of their custodian.[10]

In 1968 the Court held that a corporation could not attack as violative of the privilege against self-incrimination a statute providing that no firm was to be given a public contract for five years when any officer, director, or member of the firm refused to testify before a grand jury or to waive his immunity. The Court explained:

> The privilege against self-incrimination is essentially a personal one, applying only to natural individuals. It cannot be utilized by or on behalf of any organization, such as a corporation. . . . If a corporation cannot avail itself of the privilege against self-incrimination, it cannot take advantage of the claimed invalidity of a penalty imposed for refusal of an individual, its president, to waive the privilege.[11]

The papers and effects which the privilege protects must be the private property of the person claiming the privilege, or at least in his possession in a purely personal capacity. The privilege against self-incrimination does not enable an individual to plead the fact that some third person might be incriminated by his testimony, even if he is the agent of such person.[12] Official records and documents of an organization that are held by individuals in a representative or official capacity, rather than in a personal capacity, cannot be the subject of the personal privilege against self-incrimination, even though production of the papers might tend to incriminate the persons individually.[13] In 1963 the Supreme Court noted: "Our Court has uniformly held that one who is a mere custodian of

---

10. Curcio v. United States, 354 U.S. 118, 77 S. Ct. 1145, 1148, 1 L. Ed. 2d 1225, 1228 (1957).

11. George Campbell Painting Corp. v. Reid, 392 U.S. 286, 88 S. Ct. 1978, 20 L. Ed. 2d 1094 (1968).

12. Hale v. Henkel, 201 U.S. 43, 69, 26 S. Ct. 370, 50 L. Ed. 652 (1906) (overruled in part on other grounds by, Murphy v. Waterfront Commission of New York Harbor, 378 U.S. 52, 84 S. Ct. 1594, 12 L. Ed. 2d 678 (1964)).

13. Hale v. Henkel, 201 U.S. 43, 26 S. Ct. 370, 50 L. Ed. 652 (1906) (overruled in part on other grounds by, Murphy v. Waterfront Commission of New York Harbor, 378 U.S. 52, 84 S. Ct. 1594, 12 L. Ed. 2d 678 (1964)); U.S. v. White, 322 U.S. 694, 64 S. Ct. 1248, 88 L. Ed. 1542, 152 A.L.R. 1202 (1944); McPhaul v. U.S., 364 U.S. 372, 81 S. Ct. 138, 5 L. Ed. 2d 136, 142-43 (1960).

records cannot invoke the Fourth or Fifth Amendments to resist an order to produce such records."[14]

The Supreme Court has held that a partner in a small law firm may not invoke his personal privilege against self-incrimination to justify his refusal to comply with a subpoena requiring production of the partnership's financial records, noting that a long line of cases has established "that an individual cannot rely upon the privilege to avoid producing the records of a collective entity which are in his possession in a representative capacity, even if these records might incriminate him personally."[15] Similarly, the custodian of corporate books can not withhold them on the ground that he personally might be incriminated by their production.[16] Even where a custodian of corporate records was the sole shareholder in the company, the Supreme Court ruled that he could not resist a subpoena for the corporate records on the ground that production would incriminate him in violation of the Fifth Amendment. Justices Kennedy, Brennan, Marshall and Scalia dissented, urging that such a corporate agent fearing incrimination should not be forced to perform a "testimonial act" that would incriminate him personally.[17] Even after the dissolution of a corporation and the transfer of its books to individual stockholders, the transferees may not invoke their privilege with respect to the former corporate records.[18]

Even though officers of labor unions cannot avail themselves of the privilege as to union books, the Supreme Court has held that such an officer cannot be forced to testify orally as to the whereabouts of non-produced records of the union. The Court looked upon this as compulsion to convict himself out of his own mouth which is "contrary to the spirit and letter of the Fifth Amendment."[19]

The Supreme Court has ruled that a lawyer cannot be held in contempt by a trial judge for having advised his client in good faith

---

14. Owen v. Kennedy, 84 S. Ct. 12, 11 L. Ed. 2d 18-19 (U.S. 1963).

15. Bellis v. U.S., 417 U.S. 85, 94 S. Ct. 2179, 40 L. Ed. 2d 678 (1974).

16. Wilson v. U.S., 221 U.S. 361, 31 S. Ct. 538, 55 L. Ed. 771 (1911); Essgee Co. of China v. U.S., 262 U.S. 151, 43 S. Ct. 514, 67 L. Ed. 917 (1923).

17. Braswell v. U.S., 487 U.S. 99, 108 S. Ct. 2284, 101 L. Ed. 2d 98, 25 Fed. R. Evid. Serv. (LCP) 609, 632 (1988).

18. Grant v. U.S., 227 U.S. 74, 33 S. Ct. 190, 57 L. Ed. 423 (1913); Wheeler v. U.S., 226 U.S. 478, 33 S. Ct. 158, 57 L. Ed. 309 (1913).

19. Curcio v. United States, 354 U.S. 118, 128, 77 S. Ct. 1145, 1152, 1 L. Ed. 2d 1225, 1233 (1957).

to resist a court order to produce materials which would likely incriminate him.[20]

§ 18.02. Where the privilege can be claimed

The privilege against self-incrimination protected by the United States Constitution can be claimed in both federal and state proceedings.[21] In spite of the literal language of the Fifth Amendment, "No person . . . shall be compelled in any criminal case to be a witness against himself," it is by now firmly established that the privilege is available not only in criminal cases, by both the accused and witnesses alike, but also in civil litigation,[22] before grand juries,[23] before legislative committees,[24] and before administrative agencies.[25] Indeed, it is available to a person when queried by any officer of government.

However, while they have the right to refuse to answer particular questions in the aforementioned circumstances, defendants in civil actions have no general constitutional right to refuse to testify. The privilege against self-incrimination was held not available in a "sexually dangerous person" proceeding the Court deemed "civil in nature." Justices Stevens, Brennan, Marshall and Blackmun dissented stating that the proceeding was in essence "a criminal case."[26]

When a state employs a bifurcated procedure in capital cases, it violates the defendant's privilege against self-incrimination and his right to counsel to allow the state in seeking the death penalty to use statements made by the defendant before trial to a psychiatrist who was determining the accused's eligibility to stand trial, at a time when no warning was given the defendant that he had a right to remain silent and that any statement he made could be used against him at a sentencing proceeding. The Supreme Court announced that "a criminal defendant, who neither initiates a psychiatric evaluation nor attempts to introduce any psychiatric evidence, may not be compelled to respond to a psychiatrist if his

20. Maness v. Meyers, 419 U.S. 449, 95 S. Ct. 584, 42 L. Ed. 2d 574 (1975).

21. Malloy v. Hogan, 378 U.S. 1, 84 S. Ct. 1489, 12 L. Ed. 2d 653 (1964).

22. U.S. ex rel. Vajtauer v. Commissioner of Immigration at Port of New York, 273 U.S. 103, 71, 47 S. Ct. 302, L. Ed. 560 (1927); Graham v. U.S., 99 F.2d 746 (C.C.A. 9th Cir. 1938).

23. Blau v. U.S., 340 U.S. 159, 71 S. Ct. 223, 95 L. Ed. 170 (1950).

24. Emspak v. U.S., 349 U.S. 190, 75 S. Ct. 687, 99 L. Ed. 997 (1955).

25. U.S. ex rel. Vajtauer v. Commissioner of Immigration at Port of New York, 273 U.S. 103, 47 S. Ct. 302, 71 L. Ed. 560 (1927).

26. Allen v. Illinois, 478 U.S. 364, 106 S. Ct. 2988, 92 L. Ed. 2d 296 (1986).

statements can be used against him at a capital sentencing proceeding." The Court added: "If, upon being adequately warned, respondent had indicated that he would not answer the psychiatrist's questions, the validly ordered competency examination nevertheless could have proceeded upon the condition that the results would be applied solely for that purpose."[27]

§ 18.03. A defendant's freedom from self-incrimination in a criminal prosecution

Under the privilege against self-incrimination, a person on trial in a criminal prosecution need not take the stand to testify.[28] Moreover, when a defendant in a criminal prosecution chooses not to testify, the constitutional privilege against self-incrimination "forbids either comment by the prosecution on the accused's silence or instructions by the court that such silence is evidence of guilt."[29]

In two 1968 cases the Supreme Court held that improper comments by a prosecutor, and in one case by the trial judge, were not "harmless error." The Court stated that "[c]omment on a defendant's failure to testify cannot be labeled harmless error in a case where such comment is extensive, where an inference of guilt from silence is stressed to the jury as a basis of conviction, and where there is evidence that could have supported acquittal."[30] Ten years later the Court held not violative of the privilege against self-incrimination the giving of an instruction by a trial judge to the jury not to draw any adverse inference from the defendant's decision not to testify, over the objections of the defendant who wanted no such instruction to the jury.[31] However, when *requested* by a defendant, a trial judge must instruct the jury not to draw adverse inferences from the defendant's decision not to take the stand.[32]

When defense counsel had several times told a jury that the government had unfairly denied the defendant the opportunity to explain his actions, the Supreme Court held that the defendant's privilege against self-incrimination was not violated when the trial court remarked on summation to the jury that the defendant "could

---

27. Estelle v. Smith, 451 U.S. 454, 101 S. Ct. 1866, 68 L. Ed. 2d 359 (1981).

28. Griffin v. California, 380 U.S. 609, 85 S. Ct. 1229, 14 L. Ed. 2d 106, 110, 5 Ohio Misc. 127, 32 Ohio Op. 2d 437 (1965).

29. Chapman v. California, 386 U.S. 18, 87 S. Ct. 824, 17 L. Ed. 2d 705, 24 A.L.R.3d 1065 (1967).

30. Anderson v. Nelson, 390 U.S. 523, 88 S. Ct. 1133, 20 L. Ed. 2d 81 (1968); Fontaine v. California, 390 U.S. 593, 88 S. Ct. 1229, 20 L. Ed. 2d 154 (1968).

31. Lakeside v. Oregon, 435 U.S. 333, 98 S. Ct. 1091, 55 L. Ed. 2d 319 (1978).

32. Carter v. Kentucky, 450 U.S. 288, 101 S. Ct. 1112, 67 L. Ed. 2d 241 (1981).

have taken the stand and explained it to you."[33] The Court has held due process was not violated by an improper question about the post-arrest silence of the defendant, when it had been cured by instructions of the trial court.[34]

Both due process of law and the privilege against self-incrimination were violated by a state statute compelling an accused to be heard before all other defense witnesses if he desires to testify.[35]

When an accused voluntarily takes the stand and testifies, he waives his privilege against self-incrimination as to all matters within the proper scope of cross-examination.[36]

The Supreme Court has ruled that a defendant's privilege against self-incrimination was not violated in a criminal prosecution when the court ordered an investigator's report turned over to the prosecution, and the defense counsel proposed to call the investigator to impeach prosecution witnesses. The Court observed generally that the privilege against self-incrimination is personal to the defendant and does not extend to statements of third parties.[37]

In 1966 the Court attributed to the Fifth Amendment protection against compelled self-incrimination the right to counsel at custodial interrogations.[38] Eight years earlier the Court had concluded that the Constitution is not violated by the government using the prearrest silence of an accused to impeach the defendant's credibility. Justice Stevens in his concurring opinion stated that the privilege against compulsory self-incrimination "is simply irrelevant to a citizen's decision to remain silent when he is under no official compulsion to speak." Justices Brennan and Marshall found Justice Stevens' view as "incomprehensible," stating that "permitting the jury to draw an adverse inference from his silence is to place an impermissible burden on his exercise of the privilege."[39]

A government's introduction into evidence of a defendant's refusal to submit to a blood alcohol test when exiting his motor vehicle does not violate the accused's privilege against self-incrimination.[40]

---

33. U.S. v. Robinson, 485 U.S. 25, 108 S. Ct. 864, 99 L. Ed. 2d 23 (1988).

34. Greer v. Miller, 483 U.S. 756, 107 S. Ct. 3102, 97 L. Ed. 2d 618 (1987).

35. Brooks v. Tennessee, 406 U.S. 605, 92 S. Ct. 1891, 32 L. Ed. 2d 358 (1972).

36. Brown v. U.S., 356 U.S. 148, 78 S. Ct. 622, 626, 2 L. Ed. 2d 589, 72 A.L.R.2d 818 (1958).

37. U.S. v. Nobles, 422 U.S. 225, 95 S. Ct. 2160, 45 L. Ed. 2d 141 (1975).

38. Michigan v. Jackson, 475 U.S. 625, 106 S. Ct. 1404, 89 L. Ed. 2d 631 (1986).

39. Jenkins v. Anderson, 447 U.S. 231, 100 S. Ct. 2124, 65 L. Ed. 2d 86 (1980).

40. South Dakota v. Neville, 459 U.S. 553, 103 S. Ct. 916, 74 L. Ed. 2d 748 (1983).

§ 18.04. Right of persons other that the accused in criminal prosecutions

Witnesses who are not defendants in criminal prosecutions do not have a blanket right to refuse to testify, but must claim the privilege a question at a time in response to particular queries.[41] The privilege is deemed waived unless invoked.[42]

The United States Supreme Court has held that if in prison disciplinary proceedings inmates are compelled "to furnish testimonial evidence that might incriminate them in later criminal proceedings, they must be offered whatever immunity is required to supplant their privilege against self-incrimination and may not be required to waive such immunity."[43]

When the Supreme Court labeled a proceeding to remove from society an individual suspected of being a sexually dangerous person "civil in nature" the five-to-four majority condoned the denial to the citizen of his privilege against self-incrimination. Justices Stevens, Brennan, Marshall and Blackmun properly decried such escapism of labels and stated that removing from society an individual because of his vices was in essence "a criminal case."[44]

§ 18.05. Availability of the privilege in other contexts

The privilege against self-incrimination is most clearly available when an individual is asked if he is guilty of a crime. It is also available when he is asked if he has committed one of the essential elements of a particular crime, e.g., "Did you shoot Jones?" Additionally, the privilege is available when a person is asked to give evidence which could be used by the prosecution to convict, e.g., "Where did you bury the gun?" Furthermore, the privilege is available to refuse answering questions whose answers could "furnish a link in the chain of evidence needed in a prosecution" of the party queried. To illustrate, when a woman suspected of being a communist was asked questions concerning her employment by the Communist Party, the United States Supreme Court ruled she need not answer after claiming the privilege. Provisions of the Smith Act, said the Court, "made future prosecution of petitioner far more than a mere imaginary possibility; she reasonably could fear that criminal charges might be

---

41. Emspak v. U.S., 349 U.S. 190, 75 S. Ct. 687, 99 L. Ed. 997 (1955).

42. U.S. v. Murdock, 284 U.S. 141, 52 S. Ct. 63, 76 L. Ed. 210, 82 A.L.R. 1376 (1931) (overruled in part on other grounds by, Murphy v. Waterfront Commission of New York Harbor, 378 U.S. 52, 84 S. Ct. 1594, 12 L. Ed. 2d 678 (1964)).

43. Baxter v. Palmigiano, 425 U.S. 308, 96 S. Ct. 1551, 47 L. Ed. 2d 810 (1976).

44. Allen v. Illinois, 478 U.S. 364, 106 S. Ct. 2988, 92 L. Ed. 2d 296 (1986).

brought against her if she admitted employment by the Communist Party or intimate knowledge of its workings." The Court added:

> Whether such admissions by themselves would support a conviction under a criminal statute is immaterial. Answers to the questions asked by the grand jury would have furnished a link in the chain of evidence needed in a prosecution of petitioner for violation of (or conspiracy to violate) the Smith Act. Prior decisions of this Court have clearly established that under such circumstances, the Constitution gives a witness the privilege of remaining silent.[45]

A witness is not exonerated from answering questions merely because he declares that in so doing he would incriminate himself—his say-so does not of itself establish the hazard of incrimination. It is for a court to determine whether a person's claim of the privilege is justified,[46] and to require him to answer if it clearly appears to the court that the witness is mistaken.[47] A witness in interposing his claim, however, is not required to prove the hazard in the sense in which a claim is usually required to be established in court, for he would thus often be compelled to surrender the very protection which the privilege is designed to guarantee. To sustain the privilege, it need only be evident from the implications of the question, in the setting in which it is asked, that a responsive answer to the question or an explanation of why it cannot be answered might be dangerous because injurious disclosure could result.[48]

The same standards determine whether a person's silence in either a federal or state proceeding is justified. Says the Supreme Court: "It would be incongruous to have different standards determine the validity of a claim of privilege based on the same feared prosecution, depending on whether the claim was asserted in the state or federal court."[49]

A witness in a state proceeding is protected when his response might incriminate under federal, as well as state, law.[50] The Supreme Court has stated "the constitutional rule to be that a state witness may not be compelled to give testimony which may be incriminating under federal law unless the compelled testimony and its fruits can-

---

45. Blau v. U.S., 340 U.S. 159, 71 S. Ct. 223, 224, 95 L. Ed. 170-71 (1950).

46. Rogers v. U.S., 340 U.S. 367, 71 S. Ct. 438, 95 L. Ed. 344, 19 A.L.R.2d 378 (1951).

47. Temple v. Commonwealth, 75 Va. 892, 899 (1881).

48. Hoffman v. U.S., 341 U.S. 479, 71 S. Ct. 814, 95 L. Ed. 1118 (1951).

49. Malloy v. Hogan, 378 U.S. 1, 84 S. Ct. 1489, 1495, 12 L. Ed. 2d 653 (1964).

50. Malloy v. Hogan, 378 U.S. 1, 84 S. Ct. 1489, 1495, 12 L. Ed. 2d 653 (1964).

not be used in any manner by federal officials in connection with a criminal prosecution against him."[51] Correlatively, a witness in a federal proceeding can now invoke the privilege when a response would incriminate him under either state or federal law.[52]

A person cannot successfully claim the privilege against self-incrimination because an answer would expose him to civil liability. The Supreme Court holds that the possibility of "civil penalties" is insufficient to give rise to privilege against self-incrimination claims when persons are required to file reports. The Court remarked that it "has often stated that the question whether a particular statutorily defined penalty is civil or criminal is a matter of statutory construction," and added that it will inquire "whether the statutory scheme was so punitive either in purpose or effect as to negate" a possible legislative intention to make the penalty "civil."[53]

The Court has held that the Fifth Amendment privilege against self-incrimination was not infringed by California's "hit and run" statute which requires the driver of a motor vehicle involved in an accident to stop at the scene and give his name and address. The Court reasoned that "disclosure of name and address is an essentially neutral act" and that "it identifies but does not by itself implicate anyone in criminal conduct." Justice Harlan concurred because he was unwilling to extend the privilege against self-incrimination "to regulatory schemes of the character involved in this case."[54]

A person cannot successfully claim the privilege as to testimony regarding an offense which can no longer be prosecuted because of the statute of limitations.[55] The same is true as to offenses for which the accused has already been tried or pardoned.[56]

A refusal to answer cannot be justified by a desire to protect others from punishment or from interrogation by a grand jury.[57] Remarking that "it is settled that a person inculpated by materials sought by a subpoena issued to a third party cannot seek shelter in the Self-incrimination Clause of the Fifth Amendment," the Supreme

---

51. Murphy v. Waterfront Commission of New York Harbor, 378 U.S. 52, 84 S. Ct. 1594, 1609, 12 L. Ed. 2d 678 (1964).

52. Murphy v. Waterfront Commission of New York Harbor, 378 U.S. 52, 84 S. Ct. 1594, 1609, 12 L. Ed. 2d 678 (1964).

53. U.S. v. Ward, 448 U.S. 242, 100 S. Ct. 2636, 65 L. Ed. 2d 742 (1980).

54. California v. Byers, 402 U.S. 424, 91 S. Ct. 1535, 29 L. Ed. 2d 9 (1971).

55. Brown v. Walker, 161 U.S. 591, 598, 16 S. Ct. 644, 40 L. Ed. 819, 821 (1896).

56. Brown v. Walker, 161 U.S. 591, 599, 16 S. Ct. 644, 40 L. Ed. 819, 821 (1896).

57. Rogers v. U.S., 340 U.S. 367, 71 S. Ct. 438, 95 L. Ed. 344, 19 A.L.R.2d 378 (1951).

Court ruled that the Constitution does not require the government to notify the target of an investigation when it issues a subpoena to a third party. The Court further stated that "neither the Due Process Clause of the Fifth Amendment nor the Confrontation Clause of the Sixth Amendment is offended when a federal administrative agency, without notifying a person under investigation, uses its subpoena power to gather evidence adverse to him."[58]

§ 18.06. Registration and reporting forms—compelled disclosures

The United States Supreme Court held in 1968 that a person claiming his privilege against self-incrimination under the Fifth Amendment cannot be punished for failing to abide by the provisions of the federal wagering legislation requiring registration and divulgence of those in the business of accepting wager. The Court emphasized that it was not holding the wagering tax provisions constitutionally impermissible, but "only that those who properly assert the constitutional privilege as to those provisions may not be criminally punished for failure to comply with their requirements." For the first time, the Court announced that the privilege against self-incrimination embraces not only previous and present actions, but extends also to prospective activity whenever there is a substantial risk of incrimination.[59] The next year the Court held that even though a person could not be compelled to file a wagering form that would incriminate him, if he actually filled out such a form and included false information, he could be prosecuted for making false statements on the wagering registration form.[60]

In 1969, when the federal Marijuana Tax Act required dealers to register and also required the filling out of order forms showing that the transferee was unregistered when marijuana was being transferred, which order forms were available to both state and local officials charged with the enforcement of marijuana controls, and another section of the act made it a crime to transport or conceal marijuana acquired without paying the transfer tax, the Supreme Court ruled that the conviction of the petitioner for failing to comply with the transfer tax provisions of the action violated his privilege against self-incrimination. The Court explained that "petitioner had

---

58. S.E.C. v. Jerry T. O'Brien, Inc., 467 U.S. 735, 104 S. Ct. 2720, 81 L. Ed. 2d 615 (1984).

59. Marchetti v. U.S., 390 U.S. 39, 88 S. Ct. 697, 19 L. Ed. 2d 889, 43 Ohio Op. 2d 215 (1968) (overruling United States v. Kahriger, 345 U.S. 22, 73 S. Ct. 510, 97 L. Ed. 754 (1953)).

60. U.S. v. Knox, 396 U.S. 77, 90 S. Ct. 363, 24 L. Ed. 2d 275 (1969).

ample reason to fear that transmittal to such officials of the fact that he was a recent, unregistered transferee of marijuana would surely provide a significant 'link in a chain' of evidence tending to establish his guilt under the state marijuana laws in effect."[61]

After the *Leary* decision, the Court ruled in 1969 that the privilege against self-incrimination was not violated by a federal law forbidding sellers of narcotics and marijuana to make sales except to persons who produced official order forms that listed the names of the seller. Pointing out that sellers will seldom be confronted with unregistered persons willing and able to secure the order form, the Court concluded that there were "only imaginary and insubstantial hazards of incrimination, rather than the 'real and appreciable' risks needed to support a Fifth Amendment claim."[62]

Two years later the Court held not violative of the privilege against self-incrimination the provisions of the amended National Firearms Act which ordained that only possessors who lawfully made, manufactured, or imported firearms could and must register them; that the transferee did not and could not register; that it was unlawful for any person "to receive or possess a firearm which is not registered to him in the National Firearms Registration and Transfer Record;" and that no information or evidence provided in compliance with the registration or transfer provisions of the Act could be used, directly or indirectly, as evidence against the registrant or applicant "in a criminal proceeding with respect to a violation of law occurring prior to or concurrently with the filing of the application or registration, or the compiling of the records containing the information or evidence." The Court found that the defendants were not confronted by "substantial and real" but merely "trifling or imaginary hazards of incrimination"—first by reason of the statutory barrier against use in a prosecution for prior or concurrent offenses, and second by reason of the unavailability of the registration data, as a matter of administration, to local, state, and other federal agencies. Since the state and other federal agencies would never see the information, the defendants were left in the same position as if they had not given it but had claimed their privilege in the absence of a grant of immunity. This, combined with the protection against use to prove prior or concurrent offenses, satisfied the Fifth Amendment requirements respecting self-incrimination.[63]

That year, too, all the Justices on the Court agreed that if information is compelled over a claim of privilege against self-incrimination,

---

61. Leary v. U.S., 395 U.S. 6, 89 S. Ct. 1532, 23 L. Ed. 2d 57 (1969).
62. Minor v. U.S., 396 U.S. 87, 90 S. Ct. 284, 24 L. Ed. 2d 283 (1969).
63. U.S. v. Freed, 401 U.S. 601, 91 S. Ct. 1112, 28 L. Ed. 2d 356 (1971).

application of the *Marchetti* case requires that the individual be protected against the use of that information in state prosecutions under the statutes making criminal the taxed activity, and to complete immunity from prosecutions under federal statutes of like kind. The majority of the Court held that registration and excise tax returns filed by a gambler in response to the requirements of a federal statute "were compelled statements within the meaning of the Fifth Amendment and accordingly were inadmissible as part of the prosecution's case-in-chief" when the gambler was being prosecuted for preparing false and fraudulent tax returns. Justices Brennan and Marshall, in their concurring opinion, stated that the Fifth Amendment should not prevent the use of the gambling tax returns to show a likely source of unreported income in a criminal prosecution for false and fraudulent income tax returns, remarking that the federal government "may surround a taxing or regulatory scheme with reporting requirements designed to insure compliance with the scheme," and that here "the privilege may not be claimed if the danger of incrimination is only that the information required may show a violation of the taxing or regulatory scheme."[64]

When depositors in banks claimed their privilege against self-incrimination was violated by regulations of the Secretary of the Treasury requiring them to report transfers of sums in and out of the country, the Court refused to entertain the claim, since there were no allegations that the information required would incriminate them, the Court stating: "It will be time enough for us to determine what, if any relief, from the reporting requirement they may obtain in a judicial proceeding when they have properly and specifically raised a claim of privilege with respect to particular items of information required by the Secretary, and the Secretary has over-ruled their claim of privilege."[65]

A requirement that a college student applying for federal financial assistance file with the institution a statement attesting to his compliance with the draft registration law and regulations was held not to compel him to incriminate himself.[66]

§ 18.07. Unavailability of the privilege—public and quasi-public records

In a five-to-four decision, the Supreme Court in 1948 ruled that

---

64. Mackey v. U.S., 401 U.S. 667, 91 S. Ct. 1160, 28 L. Ed. 2d 404 (1971).

65. California Bankers Ass'n v. Shultz, 416 U.S. 21, 94 S. Ct. 1494, 39 L. Ed. 2d 812 (1974).

66. Selective Service System v. Minnesota Public Interest Research Group, 468 U.S. 841, 104 S. Ct. 3348, 82 L. Ed. 2d 632, 18 Ed. Law Rep. 115 (1984).

the privilege against self-incrimination which exists as to private papers "cannot be maintained in relation to records required by law to be kept in order that there may be suitable information of transactions which are the appropriate subjects of governmental regulation and the enforcement of regulations validly established." There is great merit in the words of one of the dissenters, Justice Jackson, who said:

> The protection against compulsory self-incrimination, guaranteed by the Fifth Amendment, is nullified to whatever extent this Court holds that Congress may require a citizen to keep an account of his deeds and misdeeds and turn over or exhibit the record on demand of government inspectors, who then can use it to convict him.[67]

In holding that a compelled execution of a consent form directing disclosure of foreign banks' record did not violate the Fifth Amendment, the Court ruled that contents of such bank records sought by the government were not privileged; that the Fifth Amendment does not proscribe immunity statutes eliciting information; and that "the privilege may be asserted only to resist compelled explicit or implicit disclaimers of immune information." Justice Stevens in dissent stressed that the consent form would lead to immune information.[68]

The Court has ruled that, since only compulsion is banned, where the preparation of business records is voluntary the records are not protected by the Fifth Amendment. However, in a particular case where the trial court was justified in finding that production would involve testimonial self-incrimination, the act of producing the business records by order of a subpoena was protected under the Fifth Amendment, and could not be compelled without a statutory grant of use immunity.[69]

§ 18.08. "Real evidence"; non-testimonial behavior and utterances

The United States Supreme Court has held a number of times that

---

67. Shapiro v. United States, 335 U.S. 1, 68 S. Ct. 1375, 92 L. Ed. 1787 (1948).

68. Doe v. U.S., 487 U.S. 201, 108 S. Ct. 2341, 101 L. Ed. 2d 184, 25 Fed. R. Evid. Serv. (LCP) 632 (1988).

69. U.S. v. Doe, 465 U.S. 605, 104 S. Ct. 1237, 79 L. Ed. 2d 552, 15 Fed. R. Evid. Serv. (LCP) 1 (1984)

"the Fifth Amendment's protection applies only when the accused is compelled to make a testimonial communication."[70]

The Court has allowed the government to compel suspects and defendants to perform various acts on the theory that such forced behavior does not violate the privilege against self-incrimination. In 1910 the Court permitted a witness to testify at trial that the defendant put on a blouse allegedly worn at the crime and that it fit him.[71]

In 1966 the Court in a five-to-four decision held that the privilege against self-incrimination was not violated when blood was taken from a drunk-driving suspect over his objections. The majority said a distinction is to be drawn under the privilege against self-incrimination between an accused's "communications" in whatever form, vocal or physical, and "compulsion which makes a suspect or accused the source of 'real or physical evidence.'" The dissenters were firmly of the belief that the self-incrimination clause was designed to bar the government from forcing any person to supply proof of his own crime, precisely what the suspect was forced to do when he was forced to supply his blood.[72]

In 1967 the Court allowed a federal official to force a suspect into a lineup where he had to have strips of tape on his face and state "put the money in the bag," words supposedly uttered by the robber. Said the Court:

> Neither the lineup itself nor anything shown by this record that Wade was required to do in the lineup violated his privilege against self-incrimination. We have only recently reaffirmed that the privilege protects an accused only from being compelled to testify against himself, or otherwise provide the State with evidence of a testimonial or communicative nature. . . . We have no doubt that compelling the accused merely to exhibit his person for observation by a prosecution witness prior to trial involves no compulsion of the accused to give evidence having testimonial significance. . . . Similarly, compelling Wade to speak within hearing distance of the witnesses, even to utter words purportedly uttered by the robber, was not compulsion to utter statements of a "testimonial" nature; he was required to use his voice as an identifying physical characteristic, not to speak his guilt.

---

70. Baltimore City Dept. of Social Services v. Bouknight, 488 U.S. 1301, 109 S. Ct. 571, 102 L. Ed. 2d 682 (1988).

71. Holt v. U.S., 218 U.S. 245, 31 S. Ct. 2, 54 L. Ed. 1021 (1910).

72. Schmerber v. California, 384 U.S. 757, 86 S. Ct. 1826, 16 L. Ed. 2d 908 (1966).

The Court further volunteered the dictum that it is constitutional to use "compulsion to submit to fingerprinting, photography, or measurements, to write or speak for identification, to appear in court, to stand, to assume a stance, to walk, or to make a particular gesture." "None of these activities become testimonial within the scope of the privilege because required of the accused in a pretrial lineup." The Court, however, reversed the conviction, since the post-indictment lineup was deemed a critical stage of the prosecution at which counsel must be present. Seven Justices dissented in part. Justice Black, asserted that the compulsory lineup violates the privilege against self-incrimination. The Chief Justice, as well as Justices Douglas and Fortas found the lineup constitutional, but deemed unconstitutional compelling a person in a lineup to say anything.[73]

On the same day in 1967 the Supreme Court ruled that the taking of handwriting samples by a state does not violate the privilege against self-incrimination. Said the Court:

> One's voice and handwriting are, of course, means of communication. It by no means follows, however, that every compulsion of an accused to use his voice or write compels a communication within the cover of the privilege. A mere handwriting exemplar, in contrast to the content of what is written, like the voice or body itself, is an identifying physical characteristic outside its protection.

Justices Black, Douglas and Fortas in dissent, indicated their belief that taking handwriting exemplars violates the privilege against self-incrimination.[74]

The Court has held that compelling production of voice exemplars from a person called before a grand jury did not violate his privilege against self-incrimination,[75] and on the same date in 1973 comparably ruled that requiring a person called before a grand jury to provide samples of his handwriting and printing did not violate the privilege.[76]

Three years later the Court held that the Fifth Amendment was not violated when the federal government compelled an attorney to turn over a taxpayer's accountant's working papers, since he was

---

73. U.S. v. Wade, 388 U.S. 218, 87 S. Ct. 1926, 1929-30, 18 L. Ed. 2d 1149 (1967).

74. Gilbert v. California, 388 U.S. 263, 87 S. Ct. 1951, 18 L. Ed. 2d 1178 (1967).

75. U.S. v. Dionisio, 410 U.S. 1, 93 S. Ct. 764, 35 L. Ed. 2d 67 (1973).

76. U.S. v. Mara, 410 U.S. 19, 93 S. Ct. 774, 35 L. Ed. 2d 99 (1973).

not thereby being a witness against himself. The Court stated more generally that the Amendment does not proscribe compelling anyone to produce documents, "but applies only when the accused is compelled to make a testimonial communication that is incriminating."[77]

In 1990 the Court decided that a mother may not use the privilege against self-incrimination to resist producing her child, as ordered by a juvenile court. The Court advised that "the ability to invoke the privilege may be greatly diminished when invocation would interfere with the effective operation of a generally applicable civil regulatory requirement." In dissent Justices Marshall and Brennan indicated their preference for an approach which "would target the [citizen's] particular claim of privilege, the precise nature of the testimony sought, and the likelihood of self-incrimination caused by this [citizen's] compliance."[78] And the Court held in 1983 that admission into evidence of a defendant's refusal to submit to a blood alcohol test when leaving his car did not violate his privilege against self-incrimination.[79]

§ 18.09. Claiming the privilege

No particular phrase is necessary to invoke the privilege against self-incrimination. It is sufficient if the language of the witness is such that the court, the grand jurors, the legislators, or any public official can "reasonably be expected to understand as an attempt to invoke the privilege."[80]

The Supreme Court has ruled that a lawyer cannot be put in contempt by a trial judge for advising his client in good faith to resist a court order to produce materials which would likely incriminate him.[81]

§ 18.10. Waiver of the privilege

A person entitled to the privilege against self-incrimination can knowingly and voluntarily waive the privilege in advance of

77. Fisher v. U.S., 425 U.S. 391, 96 S. Ct. 1569, 48 L. Ed. 2d 39 (1976).

78. Baltimore City Dept. of Social Services v. Bouknight, 488 U.S. 1301, 109 S. Ct. 571, 102 L. Ed. 2d 682 (1988).

79. South Dakota v. Neville, 459 U.S. 553, 103 S. Ct. 916, 74 L. Ed. 2d 748 (1983).

80. Emspak v. U.S., 349 U.S. 190, 75 S. Ct. 687, 99 L. Ed. 997 (1955).

81. Maness v. Meyers, 419 U.S. 449, 95 S. Ct. 584, 42 L. Ed. 2d 574 (1975).

questioning—for example, by a valid contractual consent.[82] In addition, the privilege can be waived in a criminal prosecution by the accused testifying.[83]

The Supreme Court held in 1970 that where a person queried by federal officials in a *civil* proceeding by the Food and Drug Administration failed to claim his privilege against self-incrimination and answered interrogatories, these answers could be used against him in a *criminal* prosecution for violating the Food, Drug and Cosmetic Act.[84] Six years later, the Court ruled there was no violation of a citizen's privilege against self-incrimination when the government used against him in a non-tax criminal prosecution information supplied by him on his income tax returns. The Court remarked that he could have invoked the privilege against self-incrimination when called upon to file his tax return in lieu of supplying information now used against him, and remarked generally: "In the ordinary case, if a witness under compulsion to testify makes disclosures instead of claiming the privilege, the government has not 'compelled' him to incriminate himself."[85]

In 1978 the Court held that a defendant who was given a *Miranda* warning and then voluntarily waived his Fifth Amendment privilege could then be questioned on crimes *other* than the one for which he was arrested. Justices Marshall and Brennan, in dissent, emphasized that the government's burden of proving that a suspect's waiver was voluntary, knowing, and intelligent is a "heavy" one, and would have sustained the decision of the Colorado court that the suspect had not so waived his privilege against self-incrimination.[86]

Whenever a witness voluntarily reveals incriminating facts, he cannot then invoke the privilege to avoid disclosure of the details. Disclosure of a fact waives the privilege as to details, according to the Supreme Court.[87] The Court has stated that, once incriminating testimony has been given, the witness "cannot invoke the privilege

82. Zap v. U.S., 328 U.S. 624, 66 S. Ct. 1277, 90 L. Ed. 1477 (1946), judgment vacated on reh on other grounds, 330 U.S. 800, 67 S. Ct. 857, 91 L. Ed. 1259 (1947).

83. Brown v. U.S., 356 U.S. 148, 78 S. Ct. 622, 2 L. Ed. 2d 589, 72 A.L.R.2d 818 (1958).

84. U.S. v. Kordel, 397 U.S. 1, 90 S. Ct. 763, 25 L. Ed. 2d 1 (1970).

85. Garner v. U.S., 424 U.S. 648, 96 S. Ct. 1178, 47 L. Ed. 2d 370 (1976).

86. Colorado v. Spring, 479 U.S. 564, 107 S. Ct. 851, 93 L. Ed. 2d 954 (1987).

87. Rogers v. U.S., 340 U.S. 367, 71 S. Ct. 438, 95 L. Ed. 344, 349, 19 A.L.R.2d 378 (1951).

where response to the specific question in issue would not further incriminate."[88]

Oral testimony of a witness constitutes a waiver of the privilege as to all matters within the proper scope of cross-examination.[89]

The Supreme Court ruled in 1963 that the Fifth Amendment privilege against self-incrimination did not bar the use at trial by the government of material disclosed "fraudulently" by the taxpayer under the government's then-existing "voluntary disclosure policy." The Court stressed that the case was "not merely one of volunteers but also one in which the facts disclosed were deliberately misrepresented."[90]

The Court has ruled that a citizen may not invoke her Fifth Amendment privilege against compulsory self-incrimination to prevent the production of her business and tax records in the possession of her accountant.[91] The explanation of the Court that there had been a "divulgence" or waiver when the citizen turned her papers over to an accountant to help in preparing income tax reports is extremely farfetched, and the other explanation of the court—that the taxpayer was not compelled to do anything when the summons was addressed to her accountant—is utterly without merit. A citizen should have the opportunity to utilize an accountant to prepare forms demanded by the government with some assurance that possibly incriminating records would not be subject to production compulsion by the government any more than if they remained in her hands at all times.

The Court has held there was no waiver of the privilege against self-incrimination by a police officer when he testified after being informed that if he refused to answer he would be subject to removal from office. Whether on the facts there has been a valid waiver remains a question for the Supreme Court.[92]

Although Justices Stevens, Marshall, Blackmun and Brennan in 1986 urged in a death sentence case that it was unconstitutionally violative of the Fifth Amendment right against compelled self-incrimination for a court to allow a psychiatrist to testify as to what

---

88. Rogers v. U.S., 340 U.S. 367, 71 S. Ct. 438, 95 L. Ed. 344, 349, 19 A.L.R.2d 378 (1951).

89. Brown v. U.S., 356 U.S. 148, 78 S. Ct. 622, 2 L. Ed. 2d 589, 72 A.L.R.2d 818 (1958).

90. Shotwell Mfg. Co. v. U.S., 371 U.S. 341, 83 S. Ct. 448, 9 L. Ed. 2d 357, 365 (1963).

91. Couch v. U.S., 409 U.S. 322, 93 S. Ct. 611, 34 L. Ed. 2d 548 (1973).

92. Garrity v. State of N. J., 385 U.S. 493, 87 S. Ct. 616, 17 L. Ed. 2d 562 (1967).

the defendant had told him, the majority ruled habeas corpus should be denied in such instances where there had been a deliberate tactical decision by defendant's counsel not to object to the psychiatrist's testimony in the state court.[93]

§ 18.11. The "immunity bath"

The United States Supreme Court held in 1972 that the Fifth Amendment privilege against self-incrimination permits a government to compel a person to testify, so long as the individual has been given an immunity grant, even though it does not contain full transactional immunity, so long at it protects the citizen from the later use of the compelled testimony. The Court thought that the grant of such immunity "is coextensive with the privilege and suffices to supplant it." The Court re-emphasized that in a subsequent prosecution, the burden of proof is upon the government to show that its evidence is not tainted and that it had an independent, legitimate source for the disputed evidence.[94]

When the Court made the Fifth Amendment privilege against self-incrimination binding upon the states, the Court indicated:

> In order to implement this constitutional rule and accommodate the interests of the State and Federal Governments in investigating and prosecuting crime, the Federal Government must be prohibited from making any [use of evidence compelled in state courts] and its fruits.[95]

Congress will often have power to grant immunity from state prosecutions.[96] The Supreme Court has said:

> Congress may legislate immunity restricting the exercise of state power to the extent necessary and proper for the more effective exercise of a granted power, and distinctions based upon the particular granted power concerned have no support in the Constitution.[97]

A deponent's civil deposition testimony, repeating or closely tracking his prior testimony immunized under a congressional statute

---

93. Smith v. Murray, 477 U.S. 527, 106 S. Ct. 2661, 91 L. Ed. 2d 434 (1986).

94. Piccirillo v. New York, 400 U.S. 548, 91 S. Ct. 520, 27 L. Ed. 2d 596 (1971).

95. Murphy v. Waterfront Commission of New York Harbor, 3/8 U.S. 52, 84 S. Ct. 1594, 12 L. Ed. 2d 678, 695 (1964)

96. Ullmann v. U.S., 350 U.S. 422, 76 S. Ct. 497, 100 L. Ed. 511, 520, 53 A.L.R.2d 1008 (1956).

97. Reina v. U.S., 364 U.S. 507, 81 S. Ct. 260, 5 L. Ed. 2d 249 (1960).

providing that no testimony after immunity may be used against the witness in any criminal case, is privileged under the Fifth Amendment. By way of dictum the Supreme Court observed that a trial court "cannot compel [a person] to answer deposition questions, over a valid assertion of the Fifth Amendment right, absent a duly authorized assurance of immunity at the time."[98]

The Fifth Amendment privilege against compulsory self-incrimination is not violated by allowing prosecutions for perjury in answering questions following grants of immunity, when the trial court permits the government to introduce portions of the immunized testimony, other than the alleged perjuries, to prove its case.[99]

An "immunity bath" need not protect a citizen from public opprobrium, ostracism, loss of job, or civil disabilities. The Supreme Court has said: "The immunity need only remove those sanctions which generate the fear justifying invocation of the privilege."[1]

§ 18.12. The need for public officials to warn persons of the privilege

While the *Miranda* rule is frequently perceived as an aspect of the right to counsel, and is discussed as such in a subsequent chapter of this work, it is arguably more important to be understood as a court-made implementation of the Fifth Amendment privilege against self-incrimination. In deciding that case, the United States Supreme Court ordained that when there is a custodial interrogation, statements of a suspect cannot later be used in his prosecution for crime, unless he was first warned that he has a constitutional right to remain silent and informed that any statement he makes may be used in evidence against him. The Court added that a person may waive these rights, provided his waiver is made voluntarily, knowingly, and intelligently.[2]

The Court held in 1981 that when an accused has invoked his right to have counsel present during custodial interrogation, he is not subject to further interrogation by the authorities until counsel has been made available to him, and waiver of the right to counsel will not be found "unless the accused himself initiates further com-

---

98. Pillsbury Co. v. Conboy, 459 U.S. 248, 103 S. Ct. 608, 74 L. Ed. 2d 430, 12 Fed. R. Evid. Serv. (LCP) 1 (1983).

99. U.S. v. Apfelbaum, 445 U.S. 115, 100 S. Ct. 948, 63 L. Ed. 2d 250 (1980).

1. Ullmann v. U.S., 350 U.S. 422, 76 S. Ct. 497, 100 L. Ed. 511, 520, 53 A.L.R.2d 1008 (1956).

2. Miranda v. Arizona, 384 U.S. 436, 86 S. Ct. 1602, 16 L. Ed. 2d 694, 10 Ohio Misc. 9, 36 Ohio Op. 2d 237, 39 Ohio Op. 2d 63, 10 A.L.R.3d 974 (1966).

munication, exchanges or conversation with the police."[3] In 1994, however, the Supreme Court held that when a suspect makes reference to counsel that is insufficiently clear to invoke the *Edwards v. Arizona* rule prohibiting further questioning, then "after a knowing and voluntary waiver of Miranda rights, law enforcement officers may continue questioning until and unless the suspect clearly requests an attorney."[4]

State court "in custody" determinations under the *Miranda* doctrine involve mixed questions of fact and law, and are subject to review by a federal court in habeas corpus proceedings. The federal court is not compelled to honor a federal statutory provision creating a presumption of correctness to earlier rulings in the case on questions of fact. The federal court is to ascertain, in such "custody" cases, how a reasonable person in the citizen's position when questioned would have understood his or her position.[5]

In 1968 the Court held that when a federal Internal Revenue agent questioned a citizen in jail—before a criminal investigation had commenced—without warning him that any evidence could be used against him and that he had the right to remain silent, statements made by the defendant and documents obtained from him could not be used at trial when the defendant was charged with knowingly filing false claims for income tax refunds. The Court readily rejected "the contention that tax investigations are immune from the Miranda requirements for warnings to be given a person in custody."[6]

Over dissents of Justices Brennan, Blackmun, Douglas and Marshall, a majority of the Court improvidently ruled in 1971 that even though a statement is inadmissible to prove the prosecution's case because of government failure to give a proper *Miranda* warning, it could still be used purely for impeachment purposes if the defendant took the stand.[7] Three years later, when questioning of a suspect had occurred before the *Miranda* ruling, but the trial occurred thereafter, the Supreme Court ruled that *Miranda* was applicable, but nevertheless held constitutional such questioning, whereat the state had learned the identity of a witness who then helped convict the accused. While the Court said it was significant to its decision

---

3. *Edwards v. Arizona*, 451 U.S. 477, 101 S. Ct. 1880, 68 L. Ed. 2d 378 (1981).

4. *Davis v. U.S.*, 512 U.S. 452, 114 S. Ct. 2350, 129 L. Ed. 2d 362 (1994) (Distinguished by, State v. Bohn, 950 S.W.2d 277 (Mo. Ct. App. E.D. 1997).

5. *Thompson v. Keohane*, 116 S. Ct. 457, 133 L. Ed. 2d 383 (U.S. 1995).

6. *Mathis v. U.S.*, 391 U.S. 1, 88 S. Ct. 1503, 20 L. Ed. 2d 381 (1968).

7. *Harris v. New York*, 401 U.S. 222, 91 S. Ct. 643, 28 L. Ed. 2d 1 (1971).

that the questioning had occurred prior to *Miranda*, Justice Douglas emphasized that when *Miranda* warnings are not provided in custodial interrogations, both testimony elicited as well as the fruits thereof must be suppressed.[8] The following year the Court held that when a suspect who is in the custody of a police officer has been given warnings adequate under the *Miranda* rule, subsequently states that he would like to telephone a lawyer, but is informed he cannot until the police station is reached, and the suspect then provides inculpatory information, that information can be used solely for impeachment purposes after the suspect testifies contrarily to the inculpatory information. Justices Brennan and Marshall in dissent forecast that "after today's decision, if an individual states that he wants an attorney, police interrogation will doubtless now be vigorously pressed to obtain statements before the attorney arrives."[9]

Volunteered statements of any kind are not barred by the Fifth Amendment and *Miranda* warnings are necessary only when there is "interrogation." The Court has stated that "interrogation" extends only to words or actions on the part of police officers that they should have known were reasonably likely to elicit an incriminating response.[10] Thus, a defendant who takes the stand in a criminal prosecution can be cross-examined about prior inconsistent statements voluntarily made after *Miranda* warnings.[11] The Court held in 1982 that by requesting a polygraph examination a defendant voluntarily "initiated interrogation" and waived his rights by making a "knowing and intelligent relinquishment or abandonment of his rights."[12]

In a 1987 five-to-four decision, the Supreme Court held that the *Miranda* rule was not violated when a trial court allowed in a criminal prosecution the playing of a tape between the defendant in custody and his wife, made by a police officer with the knowledge of the defendant during a visit of his wife to the police station, concluding that this was not "interrogation." Justices Stevens, Brennan, Marshall and Blackmun dissented, stating that the term "interrogation" embraces all situations where the police intend to use a

---

8. Michigan v. Tucker, 417 U.S. 433, 94 S. Ct. 2357, 41 L. Ed. 2d 182 (1974).

9. Oregon v. Hass, 420 U.S. 714, 95 S. Ct. 1215, 43 L. Ed. 2d 570 (1975).

10. Rhode Island v. Innis, 446 U.S. 291, 100 S. Ct. 1682, 64 L. Ed. 2d 297 (1980) (finding on the facts an absence of interrogation).

11. Anderson v. Charles, 447 U.S. 404, 100 S. Ct. 2180, 65 L. Ed. 2d 222 (1980).

12. Wyrick v. Fields, 459 U.S. 42, 103 S. Ct. 394, 74 L. Ed. 2d 214 (1982).

defendant's utterances against him.[13] Three years later, when an undercover agent was placed in an accused's cell posing as a fellow inmate, and the accused talked about the crime, the Court held the statements admissible, indicating generally that *Miranda* warnings are not necessary when a suspect is unaware he is speaking to a law enforcement officer and he then makes incriminating statements.[14]

§ 18.13. Possible consequences of claiming the privilege

No implication of guilt can be drawn by a trial court from the fact that the accused invoked the privilege against self-incrimination before the grand jury, nor is this a proper subject of crosshypen;examination of a defendant who takes the stand. In so ruling, the United States Supreme Court has added:

> Recent reexamination of the history and meaning of the Fifth Amendment has emphasized anew that one of the basic functions of the privilege is to protect innocent men. Too many, even those who should be better advised, view this privilege as a shelter for wrongdoers. They too readily assume that those who invoke it are either guilty of crime or commit perjury in claiming the privilege. The privilege serves to protect the innocent who might otherwise be ensnared by ambiguous circumstances.[15]

If an accused in a criminal prosecution refuses to testify, neither the judge nor the prosecutor can comment upon his failure to take the stand.[16]

By contrast, the failure of a party in a civil action to testify may be freely commented on by his adversary and the trier of fact may draw such inferences from the abstention as he sees fit on the issues in the case.[17] The Supreme Court has stated that the "Fifth Amendment does not forbid adverse inferences against parties to civil actions when they refuse to testify in response to probative evidence against them." So stating, the Court in 1976 ruled that an adverse inference could be drawn from an inmate's refusal to testify to

---

13. Arizona v. Mauro, 481 U.S. 520, 107 S. Ct. 1931, 95 L. Ed. 2d 458 (1987).

14. Illinois v. Perkins, 496 U.S. 292, 110 S. Ct. 2394, 110 L. Ed. 2d 243 (1990).

15. Grunewald v. U.S., 353 U.S. 391, 77 S. Ct. 963, 982, 1 L. Ed. 2d 931, 952, 62 A.L.R.2d 1344 (1957).

16. Griffin v. California, 380 U.S. 609, 85 S. Ct. 1229, 14 L. Ed. 2d 106, 5 Ohio Misc. 127, 32 Ohio Op. 2d 437 (1965).

17. U.S. ex rel. Bilokumsky v. Tod, 263 U.S. 149, 153, 154, 44 S. Ct. 54, 68 L. Ed. 221, 223 (1923); Brown v. U.S., 356 U.S. 148, 78 S. Ct. 622, 629, 2 L. Ed. 2d 589 72 A.L.R.2d 818 (1958).

relevant facts in a state prison disciplinary proceeding. In dissent, Justices Brennan and Marshall would hold that "compulsion violating the privilege is present in any proceeding, criminal or civil, where a government official puts questions to an individual with the knowledge that the answers might tend to incriminate him."[18]

The Court ruled in 1956 that a municipal employee could not be summarily dismissed because he invoked the privilege against self-incrimination before federal authorities.[19] However, when public employees claimed their privilege before various investigatory bodies, the Court, in five-to-four decisions, allowed local governments to dismiss the employees on theories of "insubordination," "doubtful trust and reliability," and "incompetence."[20] In 1960 the Court divided four-to-four on this question.[21] Seven years later the Supreme Court in effect held that policemen could not be fired for claiming the privilege against self-incrimination. The Court stated:

> The choice given appellants was whether to forfeit their jobs or to incriminate themselves. The options to lose their means of livelihood or to pay the penalty of self-incrimination is the antithesis of free choice to speak out or remain silent. . . . There are rights of a constitutional stature whose exercise a State may not condition by the exaction of a price.[22]

The following year the Court ruled violative of the privilege against self-incrimination a local charter provision that a municipal employee would lose his job if he refused to waive his privilege against self-incrimination and sign a waiver of immunity from prosecution in an inquiry related to his job. The Court stated: "The mandate of the great privilege against self-incrimination does not tolerate the attempt, regardless of its ultimate effectiveness, to coerce a waiver of the immunity it confers on penalty of the loss of employment." The Court added significantly by way of dictum that

If appellant, a policeman, had refused to answer questions

---

18. Baxter v. Palmigiano, 425 U.S. 308, 96 S. Ct. 1551, 47 L. Ed. 2d 810 (1976).

19. Slochower v. Board of Higher Ed. of City of New York, 350 U.S. 551, 76 S. Ct. 637, 100 L. Ed. 692 (1956).

20. Lerner v. Casey, 357 U.S. 468, 78 S. Ct. 1311, 2 L. Ed. 2d 1423 (1958); Beilan v. Board of Public Ed., School Dist. of Philadelphia, 357 U.S. 399, 78 S. Ct. 1317, 2 L. Ed. 2d 1414 (1958).

21. Nelson v. Los Angeles County, 362 U.S. 1, 80 S. Ct. 527, 4 L. Ed. 2d 494 (1960).

22. Garrity v. State of N. J., 385 U.S. 493, 87 S. Ct. 616, 618-20, 17 L. Ed. 2d 562 (1967).

specifically, directly, and narrowly relating to the performance of his official duties, without being required to waive his immunity with respect to the use of his answers or the fruits thereof in a criminal prosecution of himself . . . the privilege against self-incrimination would not have been a bar to his dismissal.

This dictum prompted Justice Harlan in his concurring opinion to observe: "I find in these opinions a procedural formula whereby, for example, public officials may now be discharged . . . for refusing to divulge to appropriate authority information pertinent to the faithful performance of their office."[23]

The same year the Court held unconstitutional a municipal charter provision authorizing the firing of employees who refused to testify regarding their jobs on the ground the answer would tend to incriminate them, as well as the dismissal of employees who refused to waive their immunity from prosecution on account of any such matter. Such dismissals, said the Court, were impermissible penalties for invoking and refusing to waive the constitutional rights against self-incrimination. The Court repeated its dictum from the preceding case that public employees subject themselves to dismissal if they refuse to account for their performance of their public trust, after proper proceedings which do not involve an attempt to coerce them to relinquish their constitutional rights.[24]

Nine years later the Court voided a state statute providing that political party bosses subpoenaed by a grand jury must testify and waive immunity or else face loss of their public offices. Stating that the touchstone of the Fifth Amendment is compulsion, the Court ruled that the state could not constitutionally require a person to forfeit one constitutional right, that of freedom of association in political matters, in order to exercise another, the Fifth Amendment privilege against self-incrimination.[25]

Whenever a governmental entity compels testimony by threatening to inflict potent sanctions unless the privilege against self-incrimination is surrendered, that testimony is obtained in violation of the Fifth Amendment and cannot be used against the declarant in a subsequent criminal proceeding. The Supreme Court has held unconstitutional a state statute providing that if a contractor refused

23. Gardner v. Broderick, 392 U.S. 273, 88 S. Ct. 1913, 20 L. Ed. 2d 1082 (1968).

24. Uniformed Sanitation Men Ass'n v. Commissioner of Sanitation of City of New York, 392 U.S. 280, 88 S. Ct. 1917, 20 L. Ed. 2d 1089 (1968).

25. Lefkowitz v. Cunningham, 431 U.S. 801, 97 S. Ct. 2132, 53 L. Ed. 2d 1 (1977).

to waive immunity or to answer questions when called to testify concerning his contracts with the state or with any political subdivision of the state, his existing contracts could be canceled and he would be disqualified from further transactions with the state for five years. The Court explained its earlier government employee cases as follows: "Employees of the state do not forfeit their constitutional privilege and . . . they may be compelled to respond to questions about the performance of their duties but only if their answers cannot be used against them in subsequent criminal prosecutions." The state cannot compel from either public employees or contractors testimony that has not been immunized, ruled the Court.[26]

While the Court had initially sustained the action of New York in disbarring an attorney who claimed the privilege against self-incrimination when questioned about "ambulance chasing" activities,[27] this decision was overruled six years later when the Court ruled that the privilege against self-incrimination "should not be watered down by imposing the dishonor of disbarment and the deprivation of a livelihood as a price for asserting it."[28]

---

26. Lefkowitz v. Turley, 414 U.S. 70, 94 S. Ct. 316, 38 L. Ed. 2d 274 (1973).
27. Cohen v. Hurley, 366 U.S. 117, 81 S. Ct. 954, 6 L. Ed. 2d 156 (1961).
28. Spevack v. Klein, 385 U.S. 511, 87 S. Ct. 625, 627, 17 L. Ed. 2d 574 (1967).

CHAPTER NINETEEN

Privacy Rights Protected by The First, Third, and Ninth Amendments, and Other Constitutional Provisions

---

§ 19.00. First Amendment protection

It became apparent in 1957 that the First Amendment would embrace not only freedom of speech but also a freedom to remain silent. In *Sweezy v. New Hampshire*, the Supreme Court ruled that the state could not compel a citizen to discuss what he had taught at a lecture given to a class at the University of New Hampshire, nor could it force him to divulge the extent of his activities on behalf of the Progressive Party. The Court ruled that "there unquestionably was an invasion of petitioner's liberties in the areas of academic freedom and political expression—areas in which government should be extremely reticent to tread."[1]

Since then the Court has indicated that there is no absolute right not to speak under the First Amendment. Consequently, the First Amendment gives the citizen no right to remain silent where the interest of society in individual privacy is outweighed by some other interest of society. On three occasions, the Court ruled that society's interest in seeing that the national legislature is informed on the Communist peril outweighed the interest in personal privacy, at least where the Congressional investigators had strong previous assurance that the party questioned was an active member of the

---

1. Sweezy v. State of N.H. by Wyman, 354 U.S. 234, 77 S. Ct. 1203, 1 L. Ed. 2d 1311, 1324 (1957).

Communist apparatus.[2] Where is no such proof, the interest in personal privacy will almost surely outweigh the interest in providing legislative bodies with information.

In 1966 the Court ruled that the freedom to remain silent under the First Amendment enabled a citizen to refuse to tell the New Hampshire attorney general about his involvement in Communist activities in that State prior to 1957.[3] The Court stated that whatever justification may have supported exposure of the citizen in *Uphaus v. Wyman*[4] was absent here. It noted: "The staleness of both the basis for the investigation and its subject matter makes indefensible such exposure of one's associational and political past—exposure which is objectionable and damaging in the extreme to one whose associations and political views do not command majority approval."[5] The Court added that:

> investigation is a part of lawmaking and the First Amendment, as well as the Fifth, stands as a barrier to state intrusion of its privacy. . . . There is no showing of "overriding and compelling state interest" that would warrant intrusion into the realm of political and associational privacy protected by the First Amendment. . . . [T]he First Amendment prevents [the Government from using] the power to investigate enforced by the contempt power to probe at will and without relation to existing need. The present record is devoid of any evidence that there is any Communist movement in New Hampshire. . . . There is no showing whatsoever of present danger of sedition against the State, the only area to which the authority of the State extends. . . . New Hampshire's interest on this record is too remote and conjectural to override the guarantee of the First Amendment that a person can speak or not, as he chooses, free of all governmental compulsion.[6]

Elsewhere, too, the Court has emphasized there is a privacy of as-

---

2. Barenblatt v. U.S., 360 U.S. 109, 79 S. Ct. 1081, 3 L. Ed. 2d 1115 (1959); Wilkinson v. U.S., 365 U.S. 399, 81 S. Ct. 567, 5 L. Ed. 2d 633 (1961); Braden v. U.S., 365 U.S. 431, 81 S. Ct. 584, 5 L. Ed. 2d 653 (1961).

3. DeGregory v. Attorney General of State of N. H., 383 U.S. 825, 86 S. Ct. 1148, 16 L. Ed. 2d 292 (1966).

4. Uphaus v. Wyman, 360 U.S. 72, 79 S. Ct. 1040, 3 L. Ed. 2d 1090 (1959).

5. DeGregory v. Attorney General of State of N. H., 383 U.S. 825, 86 S. Ct. 1148, 1151, 16 L. Ed. 2d 292 (1966).

6. DeGregory v. Attorney General of State of N. H., 383 U.S. 825, 86 S. Ct. 1148, 1151-52, 16 L. Ed. 2d 292 (1966).

sociation that is protectable against government interferences.[7] The Court emphasized in 1960 that "inviolability of privacy in group association may in many circumstances be indispensable to preservation of freedom of association, particularly where a group espouses dissident beliefs."[8]

When in 1990 the University of Pennsylvania sought to resist a subpoena from the Equal Employment Opportunities Commission seeking file documents on a woman professor complaining about sexual harassment and sexual discrimination by the faculty, and on five male colleagues, the Supreme Court refused in the name of the First Amendment to "create a new privilege against the disclosure of peer review materials." The Court noted that the burden imposed by the EEOC was neither content-based nor direct, that the claimed injury to the University's academic freedom was only speculative, and that "the substantial relation between the Commission's request and the overriding and compelling interest in eradicating invidious discrimination."[9]

§ 19.01. Third Amendment protection

The Third Amendment to the Constitution provides: "No soldier shall, in time of peace, be quartered in any house, without the consent of the Owner, nor in time of war, but in a manner to be prescribed by law," and in 1965 the United States Supreme Court reported that "The Third Amendment in its prohibition against the quartering of soldiers in any house in time of peace without the consent of the owner is another facet of that privacy,"[10] and this was repeated in substantially the same language two years later.[11]

§ 19.02. The Ninth Amendment as a source of protection for individual privacy

The Ninth Amendment to the Constitution provides: "The

---

7. Gibson v. Florida Legislative Investigation Committee, 372 U.S. 539, 83 S. Ct. 889, 9 L. Ed. 2d 929 (1963); National Ass'n for Advancement of Colored People v. State of Ala., ex rel. Patterson, 357 U.S. 449, 78 S. Ct. 1163, 2 L. Ed. 2d 1488, 1499 (1958).

8. Bates v. City of Little Rock, 361 U.S. 516, 80 S. Ct. 412, 4 L. Ed. 2d 480, 485 (1960).

9. University of Pennsylvania v. E.E.O.C., 493 U.S. 182, 110 S. Ct. 577, 107 L. Ed. 2d 571, 590, 57 Ed. Law Rep. 666, 28 Fed. R. Evid. Serv. (LCP) 1169, 15 Fed. R. Serv. 3d (LCP) 369 (1990).

10. Griswold v. Connecticut, 381 U.S. 479, 85 S. Ct. 1678, 14 L. Ed. 2d 510, 515 (1965).

11. Katz v. U.S., 389 U.S. 347, 88 S. Ct. 507, 19 L. Ed. 2d 576, 581 (1967) ("Third Amendment's prohibition against the unconsented practice of quartering soldiers protects another aspect of privacy from governmental intrusion").

enumeration in the Constitution, of certain rights, shall not be construed to deny or disparage others retained by the people." When in 1965 the United States Supreme Court established as constitutionally protected the right of privacy, the result was reached largely by the reasoning of Chief Justice Warren, Justices Brennan and Goldberg, in the concurring opinion by Justice Goldberg, who saw the basis for the right in the Ninth Amendment. They believed, and correctly, that this language was added to the Bill of Rights to make it clear that other "natural" rights, not previously specified, were also to be protected by the Constitution.[12] Were there natural rights known to the Founding Fathers that they deemed worthy of constitutional protection? Of course there were, such as freedom of association, freedom of enterprise, and the right of personal privacy, rights recognized then, as now, as "fundamental" and basic to a society of free individuals. The opinion for the Court in *Griswold* was written by Justice Douglas, who posited the constitutional recognition of the privacy right as based upon the fact "that specific guarantees in the Bill or Rights have penumbras, formed by emanations from those guarantees that help give them life and substance."[13]

§ 19.03. The penumbras of rights in the United States Constitution

In *Griswold v. Connecticut*, Justice Douglas, who wrote the opinion for the United States Supreme Court, explained "that specific guarantees in the Bill of Rights have penumbras, formed by emanations from those guarantees that help give them life and substance," and that from the totality of such penumbras, the Court deduced the right of privacy. In dissent, Justices Black and Stewart said that "I get nowhere in this case by talk about a constitutional 'right of privacy' as an emanation from one or more constitutional provision."[14]

The Court of Appeals for the Fifth Circuit in 1990 held that a secretary for a public school system could not be punished for exercising her private right of sending a daughter to a private school.

---

12. Griswold v. Connecticut, 381 U.S. 479, 85 S. Ct. 1678, 14 L. Ed. 2d 510 (1965).

13. Prof. Gerald Watson, The Ninth Amendment: Source of a Substantive Right of Privacy, 19 John Marshall L. Rev. 959 (1986), explores some of the future potentials for protecting privacy by means of the Ninth Amendment.

14. Griswold v. Connecticut, 381 U.S. 479, 85 S. Ct. 1678, 14 L. Ed. 2d 510 (1965).

The Court there posited the privacy right upon the First Amendment and "the penumbra of familial privacy rights."[15]

§ 19.04. Privacy as a natural right, protectable under both natural law and state constitutions

In a memorable 1905 decision, the Georgia Supreme Court announced that the constitutional right of privacy is "derived from natural law." As such, this "liberty" said the Court, is to be protected not only against the state, but also against invasion by individuals.[16]

A New Jersey Court stated in 1945 that "it is now well settled that the right of privacy, having its origin in natural law, is immutable and absolute, and transcends the power of any authority to change or abolish it. . . . It is one of the 'natural and unalienable rights' recognized in the New Jersey Constitution."[17]

A number of other state constitutions identify privacy as an inalienable right. Illustratively, the California Constitution states that "All people . . . have inalienable rights. Among these is privacy."[18] The California Supreme Court is clear that privacy is, as an inalienable right, to be accorded constitutional protection.[19]

Additionally, privacy as a constitutional right has been spelled out in modern constitutions, such as in Alaska,[20] Arizona,[21] Illinois,[22] Louisiana,[23] Montana,[24] South Carolina[25] and Washington.[26] Hawaii's Constitution provides: that "The right of the people to privacy is recognized and shall not be infringed without the showing of a compelling state interest."[27]

State constitutions are being afforded broader interpretations than

---

15. Fyfe v. Curlee, 902 F.2d 401, 60 Ed. Law Rep. 398 (5th Cir. 1990).

16. Pavesich v. New England Life Ins. Co., 122 Ga. 190, 50 S.E. 68 (1905).

17. McGovern v. Van Riper, 137 N.J. Eq. 24, 43 A.2d 514, 519 (Ch. 1945), aff'd in part, 137 N.J. Eq. 548, 45 A.2d 842 (Ct. Err. & App. 1946).

18. California Constitution, Article I, § 1.

19. Vinson v. Superior Court (Peralta Community College Dist.), 43 Cal. 3d 833, 239 Cal. Rptr. 292, 740 P.2d 404, 41 Ed. Law Rep. 330 (1987).

20. Alaska Constitution, Article I, § 22.

21. Arizona Constitution, Article II, § 8.

22. Illinois Constitution, Article I, § 6.

23. Louisiana Constitution, Article I, § 5.

24. Montana Constitution, Article II, § 10.

25. South Carolina Constitution, Article I, § 10.

26. Washington Constitution, Article I, § 7.

27. Hawaii Constitution, Article I, § 6, as amended in 1978.

the Supreme Court has yet accorded to the privacy right.[28] Furthermore, state constitutions frequently provide for a constitutional right to pursue happiness, which has been held to included the privacy right. A California appellate court states:

> The right to pursue and obtain happiness is guaranteed to all by the fundamental law of our State. This right by its very nature includes the right to live free from the unwarranted attack of others upon one's liberty, property and reputation. Any person living a life of rectitude has the right to happiness which includes a freedom from unnecessary attacks on his character, social standing, or repartition.[29]

All states provide constitutional protection for "liberty," defined customarily by fundamental values and capable of a construction protective of individual privacy.[30]

---

28. City of Tukwila v. Nalder, 53 Wash. App. 746, 770 P.2d 670 (1989); Timothy Stallcup, The Arizona "Right of Privacy" and the Invasion of Privacy Tort, 24 Az St L J 687 (1992).

29. Melvin v. Reid, 112 Cal. App. 285, 297 P. 91, 93 (4th Dist. 1931).

30. Pavesich v. New England Life Ins. Co., 122 Ga. 190, 50 S.E. 68 (1905).

PART FOUR

THE SOCIETAL INTERESTS IN PRIVATE PROPERTY, FREEDOM OF ENTERPRISE, AND FREEDOM OF CONTRACT

CHAPTER TWENTY

The Societal Interest In Private Property

---

§ 20.00. Introduction

The American Founding Fathers customarily believed in the doctrine of natural rights, and ordinarily included the right to property in their listing of such rights. To some the right to own and possess property was not a "prime" natural right but rather a secondary right that society must honor and protect in order to ensure more effectively the basic natural rights to life and liberty.

The United States Constitution and practically all state constitutions provide that a person shall not be deprived of his "property, without due process of law; nor shall private property be taken for public use, without just compensation."[1] In a number of instances the state constitutions have been amended specifically to require just compensation when private property is either "taken" or "damaged."

§ 20.01. Interference with the use of private property generally

The federal government, under the Fifth Amendment, and the states, under the Fourteenth, can regulate the use of private property whenever such regulation is reasonable and reasonably related to the public health, safety, morality, or general welfare.[2] It is only unreasonable, arbitrary or capricious interference with the use of private property that is unconstitutional.[3]

Many times the Supreme Court has held, in effect, that statutes and ordinances enacted to protect valid societal interests, but affecting property interests, come to the courts with a presumption of reasonableness, validity, and constitutionality.[4]

Since the generous language of the Court in the 1954 *Berman v. Parker* case, admittedly not a police power case, courts now generally recognize that communities have a legitimate interest in protecting aesthetic values which permits reasonable regulation of uses of property.[5]

In 1972 the Court held that a lower court decision acknowledging the right of a group protesting the Vietnam War to distribute literature in a privately owned shopping center violated the private property rights protected by the federal Constitution. The Court explained: "It would be an unwarranted infringement of property rights to require them to yield to the exercise of First Amendment rights under circumstances where adequate alternative avenues of

---

1. U.S. Constitution Fifth Amendment.

2. Goldblatt v. Town of Hempstead, N.Y., 369 U.S. 590, 82 S. Ct. 987, 8 L. Ed. 2d 130 (1962).

3. Nectow v. City of Cambridge, 277 U.S. 183, 48 S. Ct. 447, 72 L. Ed. 842 (1928).

4. E.g., Goldblatt v. Town of Hempstead, N.Y., 369 U.S. 590, 82 S. Ct. 987, 8 L. Ed. 2d 130 (1962).

5. E.g., People v. Stover, 12 N.Y. 2d 462, 191 N.E.2d 272, 240 N.Y.S. 2d 734 (1963).

communication exist."[6] However, eight years later the Court concluded there was no unconstitutional interference with property rights when state constitutional provisions permitted individuals to exercise freedom of speech and petition on the property of a privately owned shopping center to which the public had been invited. The opinion was by Justice Rehnquist and there was no dissent.[7]

The constitutionality of government controls affecting private property interests should properly require examination by courts of such matters as: (a) the legality of a "property" claim under applicable law, (b) the extent to which an owner has dedicated the property to public use, (c) paramountcy of other interests requiring protection, such as First Amendment freedoms and public health, (d) the existence of alternative measures available to the government that would adequately protect the opposed interests; (e) our history of deciding whether society should pay the individual, as when it is necessary to destroy his property to save dozens of other properties, and (f) the adjustments utilized by other free societies in like circumstances. However, the Supreme Court, over the sound advice of Justice Brandeis, has trapped itself into a jurisprudence of "takings," and, accordingly, we look at the occasions when it has found permissible and impermissible "takings."

§ 20.02. Imposition of controls upon private property by actions of individuals, pursuant to local laws

When any governmental entity authorizes restrictions upon the use of private property to be set by other private individuals, to whom part of the police power has been delegated, due process of law is violated. Illustratively, the United States Supreme Court voided a Richmond, Virginia ordinance which required public authorities to establish a set-back line where requested by the immediate neighbors.[8]

The Supreme Court and some state courts have sustained local legislative enactments which ban certain structures or uses in specified areas, and then provide for the lifting of such restrictions if the owner can secure consent of a designated number or percent of

6. Lloyd Corp., Limited v. Tanner, 407 U.S. 551, 92 S. Ct. 2219, 33 L. Ed. 2d 131 (1972).

7. PruneYard Shopping Center v. Robins, 447 U.S. 74, 100 S. Ct. 2035, 64 L. Ed. 2d 741 (1980).

8. Eubank v. City of Richmond, 226 U.S. 137, 33 S. Ct. 76, 57 L. Ed. 156 (1912).

neighbors within a defined area of proximity.[9] Such ordinances can become unreasonable on their particular facts, either in attempting to exclude from the area something that is not there dangerous to the public health, safety, morality, or general welfare, or because the provision for securing consents is impossible or grossly unfair.[10] The majority of state courts hold all consent provisions unconstitutional.[11]

§ 20.03. Governmental taking of private property by intentional condemnation

Both federal and state governments have power to take private property by intentional condemnation, as perquisites of traditional sovereignty. The United States Supreme Court states:

> It has not been seriously contended during the argument that the United States government is without power to appropriate lands or other property within the States for its own use, and to enable it to perform its proper functions. Such an authority is essential to its independent existence and perpetuity. . . . The right is the offspring of political necessity; and it is inseparable from sovereignty, unless denied to it by the fundamental law.[12]

There has traditionally, often by the very language of state constitutions, been a requirement that private property be taken by eminent domain only for "public uses," but the Supreme Court has for a long time deferred to the judgment of federal and state legislative bodies that a particular taking satisfies this concept. Illustratively, the condemnation of private land was held by the Court to be for a public use, notwithstanding it was to be redeveloped by private firms, the Court indicating that the role of that tribunal in determining whether the eminent domain power "is being exercised for a public purpose is an extremely narrow one."[13]

Since 1984 the Court has held that the "public use" requirement is only "coterminous with the scope of a sovereign's police powers," and has ruled that a state can with just compensation take property from one owner/lessor and transfer it to the lessees, in order to

9. Thomas Cusack Co. v. City of Chicago, 242 U.S. 526, 37 S. Ct. 190, 61 L. Ed. 472 (1917).

10. State of Washington ex rel. Seattle Title Trust Co. v. Roberge, 278 U.S. 116, 49 S. Ct. 50, 73 L. Ed. 210, 86 A.L.R. 654 (1928).

11. Concordia Collegiate Institute v. Miller, 301 N.Y. 189, 93 N.E.2d 632, 21 A.L.R.2d 544 (1950).

12. Kohl v. U.S., 91 U.S. 367, 372, 23 L. Ed. 449, 451 (1875).

13. Berman v. Parker, 348 U.S. 26, 75 S. Ct. 98, 99 L. Ed. 27, 37 (1954).

reduce what had been a concentration of fee simple ownership in a relatively few hands. The Court has indicated that it will not reverse the determination of any sate legislature, so long as the "legislature's purpose is legitimate and its means are not irrational."[14]

§ 20.04. Just compensation

Due process of law, in both the Fifth and Fourteenth Amendments, requires that just compensation be made by a government to the owner of private property which is taken by that government.[15]

It is the owner's loss, not the government's gain, that is the measure of the value of the property taken in compensable situations.

Market value fairly determined is the normal measure of the recovery, when a fee is taken by a government.[16] In a five-to-four decision, the Supreme Court held that the government need not include in just compensation value accruing to a citizen's land from his permit to use adjoining federal lands which could be revoked by the government at any time.[17]

When a leasehold interest is taken, recovery is measured by the market rental value of the interest taken.[18] In the case of a leasehold, the Court has ruled that compensation may include the value of improvements made by the lessee, if he has a reasonable expectancy that the lessor will renew the lease and that a willing buyer would pay for the improvements as part of the purchase price of the lease.[19]

Market value is ordinarily what a willing buyer who does not have to purchase is agreeable to pay a willing seller who does not have to sell.[20] The market value is to be ascertained as of the date of taking

---

14. Hawaii Housing Authority v. Midkiff, 467 U.S. 229, 104 S. Ct. 2321, 81 L. Ed. 2d 186 (1984).

15. Chicago, B. & Q.R. Co. v. City of Chicago, 166 U.S. 226, 17 S. Ct. 581, 41 L. Ed. 979 (1897).

16. U.S. ex rel. and for Use of Tennessee Valley Authority v. Powelson, 319 U.S. 266, 63 S. Ct. 1047, 87 L. Ed. 1390, 1397 (1943); U.S. v. Miller, 317 U.S. 369, 63 S. Ct. 276, 87 L. Ed. 336, 147 A.L.R. 55 (1943).

17. U.S. v. Fuller, 409 U.S. 488, 93 S. Ct. 801, 35 L. Ed. 2d 16 (1973).

18. U.S. v. General Motors Corporation, 323 U.S. 373, 65 S. Ct. 357, 89 L. Ed. 311, 156 A.L.R. 390 (1945).

19. Almota Farmers Elevator & Warehouse Co. v. U.S., 409 U.S. 470, 93 S. Ct. 791, 35 L. Ed. 2d 1 (1973).

20. U.S. v. Miller, 317 U.S. 369, 63 S. Ct. 276, 87 L. Ed. 336, 147 A.L.R. 55 (1943).

by a government.[21] However, the Supreme Court has held that in condemnation cases there must be a procedure for modifying condemnation awards when there is a substantial delay between the date of valuation and the date the judgment is paid, during which time the value of the land has materially changed.[22]

The general rule of market value is, however, not to be applicable where such price is difficult to ascertain, or when its application would result in manifest injustice to the owner or the public.[23] In cases where the government has imposed artificial price ceilings upon properties previous to their condemnation, the Supreme Court has ruled that such prices were not to be deemed fair market value.[24] Where the market value of land used as a sanitary landfill by a local government and condemned by the United States was readily ascertainable, the Court held that the federal government, under the just compensation requirement, was not obligated to provide the cost of acquiring a replacement facility which the local government was required to install under applicable state law. The Court indicated that there must be respect for "the principle that just compensation must be measured by an objective standard that disregards subjective values which are only of significance to an individual owner."[25]

Where a taking is compensable the Court has indicated that in determining loss caused to the owner by the appropriation, the courts can consider the extent to which the remaining parts of the owner's property are specially and directly increased in value by the improvement.[26] Noting that when a distinct tract is condemned, in whole or in part, other lands in the neighborhood frequently increase in market value due to the proximity of the public improvement on the land taken, the Court has ruled that if the government at a later date determines to take these properties, it must pay their market value as enhanced by this factor of proximity. If, however, the public project from the beginning included taking certain tracts, but only one was taken in the first instance, the owner of the other

21. U.S. v. Clarke, 445 U.S. 253, 100 S. Ct. 1127, 63 L. Ed. 2d 373 (1980).

22. Kirby Forest Industries, Inc. v. U.S., 467 U.S. 1, 104 S. Ct. 2187, 81 L. Ed. 2d 1, 39 Fed. R. Serv. 2d (LCP) 929 (1984).

23. U.S. v. 564.54 Acres of Land, More or Less, Situated in Monroe and Pike Counties, Pa., 441 U.S. 506, 99 S. Ct. 1854, 60 L. Ed. 2d 435 (1979); U.S. v. 50 Acres of Land, 469 U.S. 24, 105 S. Ct. 451, 83 L. Ed. 2d 376 (1984).

24. U.S. v. Commodities Trading Corp., 339 U.S. 121, 70 S. Ct. 547, 94 L. Ed. 707 (Ct. Cl. 1950).

25. U.S. v. 50 Acres of Land, 469 U.S. 24, 105 S. Ct. 451, 83 L. Ed. 2d 376 (1984).

26. Bauman v. Ross, 167 U.S. 548, 17 S. Ct. 966, 42 L. Ed. 270 (1897).

tracts, according to the Court, should not be allowed an increased value for his lands when later taken, any more than the owner of the tract first condemned is entitled to be allowed an increased market value because adjacent lands not immediately taken increased in value due to the projected improvement.[27]

Indirect costs to the property owner caused by the taking of his land are generally not part of the just compensation to which an owner is entitled when the government condemns his lands. The Court has held that the government need not compensate an owner for his expenses in securing appraisals of the land.[28]

When the federal government takes lands from Indian tribes, it is held to a requirement that it make a good faith effort to pay the Indians the full value of their lands, and this test is not satisfied by the government's simple assertion that it acted in good faith.[29]

§ 20.05. Government interferences with private properties held not to be "takings"—generally

There have been many instances in which governments have regulated private properties and the Supreme Court has found no "taking" and denied compensation to the owners. Illustratively, during World War II, the federal government ordered owners of gold mines to cease operations. When they sued, the Supreme Court in 1958 held that the regulation did not constitute a "taking" for which compensation would be required. The Court stated:

> Traditionally, we have treated the issue as to whether a particular governmental restriction amounted to a constitutional taking as being a question properly turning upon the particular circumstances of each case. In doing so, we have recognized that action in the form of regulation can so diminish the value of property as to constitute a taking. However, the mere fact that the regulation deprives the property owner of the most profitable use of his property is not necessarily enough to establish the owner's right to compensation. In the context of war, we have been reluctant to find that degree of regulation which so requires compensation to be paid for resulting losses of income. . . . [W]artime economic restrictions, temporary in

27. U.S. v. Miller, 317 U.S. 369, 63 S. Ct. 276, 87 L. Ed. 336, 147 A.L.R. 55 (1943), followed in U.S. v. Reynolds, 397 U.S. 14, 90 S. Ct. 803, 25 L. Ed. 2d 12 (1970) (holding that the determination of whether the lands later taken were part of the original project was for the court, not for the jury).

28. U.S. v. Bodcaw Co., 440 U.S. 202, 99 S. Ct. 1066, 59 L. Ed. 2d 257 (1979).

29. U.S. v. Sioux Nation of Indians, 448 U.S. 371, 100 S. Ct. 2716, 65 L. Ed. 2d 844 (Ct. Cl. 1980).

character, are insignificant when compared to the wide-spread uncompensated loss of life and freedom of action which war traditionally demands.[30]

Even earlier, when in the years 1927 and 1928 cedar rust was about to ruin the economically profitable apple growing economy of Virginia, that state was upheld by the United States Supreme Court in ordering the destruction of many privately owned cedar trees. Justice Stone, speaking for the Court wrote: "When forced to such a choice the state does not exceed its constitutional powers by deciding upon the destruction of one class of property to save another which, in the judgment of the legislature, is of greatest value to the public." There was no dissent.[31] In 1952 the Court held that destruction by the military of oil depots in the Philippines during World War II was not compensable.[32] And in 1969, the Court held that "the temporary, unplanned occupation of an owner's buildings in the course of battle does not constitute direct and substantive enough government involvement to warrant compensation under the Fifth Amendment." This will be the result generally, forecasts the Court, in all "unusual circumstances in which governmental occupation does not deprive the private owner of any use of his property," such as when firemen occupy a burning building. Justice Harlan indicated that just compensation should be required only "when the military had reason to believe that its action placed the property in question in greater peril than if no form of protection had been provided at all." Justices Black and Douglas stated that "Whenever the government determines that one person's property—whatever it may be—is essential to the war effort and appropriates it for the common good, the public purse rather than the individual should bear the loss."[33]

When, in 1946, the Supreme Court sustained legislation requiring the installation of sprinkler systems in buildings of non-fire-proof construction used as lodging houses, the Court remarked: "Little need be said on the due process question. We are not concerned with the wisdom of this legislation or the need for it."[34]

The Court ruled in 1984 that intentional destruction of a prisoner's property by the random and unauthorized conduct of prison officials

---

30. United States v. Central Eureka Mining Company, 357 U.S. 155, 78 S. Ct. 1097, 2 L. Ed. 2d 1228, 1236-37 (1958).

31. Miller v. Schoene, 276 U.S. 272, 48 S. Ct. 246, 72 L. Ed. 568, 571 (1928).

32. United States v. Caltex, 344 U.S. 149, 73 S. Ct. 200, 97 L. Ed. 157 (1952).

33. National Bd. of Young Men's Christian Ass'ns v. U.S., 395 U.S. 85, 89 S. Ct. 1511, 23 L. Ed. 2d 117 (Ct. Cl. 1969).

34. Queenside Hills Realty Co. v. Saxl, 328 U.S. 80, 66 S. Ct. 850, 90 L. Ed. 1096 (1946).

was not an unconstitutional deprivation of private property without due process of law, so long as the state provided a meaningful post-deprivation remedy.[35]

The Court indicated in 1987 that it will find there is no "taking" of utilities' properties by just and reasonable regulation of rates. The Court has stated: "So long as the rates set are not confiscatory, the Fifth Amendment [Due Process Clause in the case of federal controls] does not bar their imposition."[36] Two years later, in sustaining Pennsylvania's utility rates based predominantly, but not entirely, on historical cost, the Court emphasized that there is no single theory of valuation as a constitutional requirement.[37]

In 1987 the Court ruled that there was no "taking" as a result of reasonable government regulation of coal mining companies intended to prevent subsidence, where public buildings, noncommercial buildings generally used by the public, dwellings used for human habitation, and cemeteries were being protected. Recognizing that an important public interest is served by controlling subsidence in such circumstances, the Court indicated that it now takes an essentially ad hoc approach to "taking" claims in regulatory cases, considering "the economic impact of the regulation, its interference with reasonable investment-backed expectations, and the character of the government action," and found the mining interests had not come close to satisfying their burden of proving that they had been denied the economically viable use of their property.[38]

The Court held that there was no compensable taking by the federal government of sand and gravel from the bed of a river over which an Indian tribe had a general sovereignty, when damage thereto was necessarily occasioned by the government's construction designed to improve navigation of the river, under its plenary power flowing from the Commerce Clause, which the Court saw in effect as "a dominant servitude."[39] In 1992 the Supreme Court sustained a mobile home control ordinance which set back rents to 1986 levels, prohibited rent increases without consent of the city council, and required owners to accept new purchasers of space to replace former

---

35. Hudson v. Palmer, 468 U.S. 517, 104 S. Ct. 3194, 82 L. Ed. 2d 393 (1984)

36. F.C.C. v. Florida Power Corp., 480 U.S. 245, 107 S. Ct. 1107, 94 L. Ed. 2d 282 (1987).

37. Duquesne Light Co. v. Barasch, 488 U.S. 299, 109 S. Ct. 609, 102 L. Ed. 2d 646 (1989)

38. Keystone Bituminous Coal Ass'n v. DeBenedictis, 480 U.S. 470, 107 S. Ct. 1232, 94 L. Ed. 2d 472 (1987).

39. U.S. v. Cherokee Nation of Oklahoma, 480 U.S. 700, 107 S. Ct. 1487, 94 L. Ed. 2d 704 (1987).

occupants so long as they were able to pay the charges. The Court stated:

> Where the government merely regulates the use of property, compensation is required only if considerations such as the purpose of the regulation or the extent to which it deprives the owner of the economic use of the property suggest that the regulation has unfairly singled out the property owner to bear a burden, that should be borne by the public as a whole.[40]

§ 20.06. Government regulations held to be "takings"—generally

In the 1920's, when a coal company in Pennsylvania desired to mine coal in an area which was underneath a dwelling and owners of the house brought suit to prevent the mining, which probably would result in subsidence of both their land and house, relying upon an act of the Pennsylvania Legislature forbidding mining under such circumstances, the Supreme Court voided the statute. Justice Holmes, writing for the Court, stated: "The general rule at least is, that while property may be regulated to a certain extent, if regulation goes too far it will be recognized as a taking." Justice Brandeis wrote an extensive dissent, pointing out that "every restriction upon the use of property imposed in the exercise of the police power deprives the owner of some right theretofore enjoyed, and, is, in that sense, an abridgment by the State of rights in property without making compensation. But restriction imposed to protect the public health, safety or morals from dangers threatened is not a taking." He added: "A prohibition of mining which causes subsidence of such structures and facilities is obviously enacted for a public purpose."[41]

Recovery from a governmental entity can be posited upon the Just Compensation Clause of the Fifth Amendment or the Due Process Clause of the Fourteenth Amendment, and the "going too far" rule is applicable alike to both.[42]

The *Pennsylvania Coal* case left future Justices the unenviable task of deciding when comparable regulation affecting private properties goes "too far," and the companion determination of the extent of

---

40. Yee v. City of Escondido, Cal., 503 U.S. 519, 112 S. Ct. 1522, 118 L. Ed. 2d 153 (1992)

41. Pennsylvania Coal Co. v. Mahon, 260 U.S. 393, 43 S. Ct. 158, 67 L. Ed. 322, 28 A.L.R. 1321 (1922).

42. PruneYard Shopping Center v. Robins, 447 U.S. 74, 100 S. Ct. 2035, 64 L. Ed. 2d 741 (1980); Suitum v. Tahoe Regional Planning Agency, 117 S. Ct. 1659, 137 L. Ed. 2d 980 (U.S. 1997)

judicial respect that is to be accorded, if in different degrees, to Congress, to state legislatures, and to municipal councils when their regulations impact upon owners of private property, in peace and in war. Most commonly it is said that regulation constitutes a "taking" when it deprives a lawful owner of land of "all reasonable and economically viable use of his property."[43]

A minor but permanent occupation of an owner's property, authorized by governmental action, has been held to constitute a "taking" of property for which just compensation must be paid. The Court held that a statute requiring a landlord to permit a cable television company to install its facilities on his property results in a compensable taking. While an administrative regulation had provided for a one-time payment of one dollar to each landlord, the Court offered no opinion on the amount of compensation due.[44]

"Takings" by governments can exist even when there was no desire to condemn the property, and no attempt to regulate its use. Illustratively, when a county operating an airport permitted planes to fly low over neighbors' lands to the annoyance, detriment, and loss of such citizens, the Supreme Court ruled that there had been a "taking" of an air easement which required the county to make just compensation.[45] When the federal government temporarily "took over" a coal mine to avert a strike, the Court found a "taking" which required just compensation to the owners for the losses sustained.[46]

When the federal government has participated in attempting to control floods, on some occasions the Supreme Court has held that the government's action amounted to a "taking" as a result of the lessened use of the private land.[47] When the federal government directly subjected private lands to flooding, it had to make compensation.[48] However, in another case, the Court held that the mere location by the government of a flood overflow outlet near a citizen's property was not a compensable "taking," even though in a

43. Williamson County Regional Planning Com'n v. Hamilton Bank of Johnson City, 473 U.S. 172, 105 S. Ct. 3108, 87 L. Ed. 2d 126 (1985); Suitum v. Tahoe Regional Planning Agency, 117 S. Ct. 1659, 137 L. Ed. 2d 980 (U.S. 1997)

44. Loretto v. Teleprompter Manhattan CATV Corp., 458 U.S. 419, 102 S. Ct. 3164, 73 L. Ed. 2d 868 (1982).

45. Griggs v. Allegheny County, Pa., 369 U.S. 84, 82 S. Ct. 531, 7 L. Ed. 2d 585 (1962).

46. U.S. v. Pewee Coal Co., 341 U.S. 114, 71 S. Ct. 670, 95 L. Ed. 809 (Ct. Cl. 1951).

47. U.S. v. Kansas City Life Ins. Co., 339 U.S. 799, 70 S. Ct. 885, 94 L. Ed. 1277 (Ct. Cl. 1950).

48. Jacobs v. U.S., 290 U.S. 13, 54 S. Ct. 26, 78 L. Ed. 142, 96 A.L.R. 1 (1933).

severe flood it might be inundated.[49] When the federal government attempted to create a public right of access to a privately owned pool, the Supreme Court stated that the right of an owner to exclude others is an integral aspect of property ownership and held that if the government wanted to create such access by others it must first condemn the property and pay just compensation.[50]

The Court recognizes that state law may acknowledge a property interest in data submitted by business concerns to the federal government and, if it does, the data is protectable under the Fifth Amendment. While the Court held that some data was unprotectable because the business firm could not have had a "reasonable expectation" that the Environmental Protection Agency would not disclose the data, as to other data the Court found a taking when the statute in effect at the time contained an explicit assurance of confidentiality or exclusive use by the federal administrative agency. The Court ruled the taking was for a public use, since the disclosure by the agency was to the general public.[51]

Imposing punitive damages that are "grossly excessive" is, in effect, taking the property of a litigant without due process of law, held the Supreme Court in 1996 in a five-to-four decision. In dissent, Justice Ginsburg, speaking also for Chief Justice Rehnquist, thought the test unrealistic, referring to it as "a raised eyebrow" norm of what is constitutional.[52]

If a state provides an adequate procedure for seeking just compensation for property that has been "taken," a property owner cannot claim violation of the Just Compensation Clause of the federal Constitution until it has used the indicated proceedings and been denied just compensation.[53]

§ 20.07. Land use controls—zoning

In 1924 the United States Supreme Court announced that zoning ordinances, restricting some desired uses of private property, can be constitutional under due process of law under both the Fifth and Fourteenth Amendments. The Court noted that earlier it had held

---

49. U.S. v. Sponenbarger, 308 U.S. 256, 60 S. Ct. 225, 84 L. Ed. 230 (1939).

50. Kaiser Aetna v. U.S., 444 U.S. 164, 100 S. Ct. 383, 62 L. Ed. 2d 332 (1979)

51. Ruckelshaus v. Monsanto Co., 467 U.S. 986, 104 S. Ct. 2862, 81 L. Ed. 2d 815 (1984)

52. BMW of North America, Inc. v. Gore, 116 S. Ct. 1589, 134 L. Ed. 2d 809 (U.S. 1996).

53. Suitum v. Tahoe Regional Planning Agency, 117 S. Ct. 1659, 137 L. Ed. 2d 980 (U.S. 1997)

constitutional laws and regulations fixing the height of buildings within reasonable limits, minimizing the danger of fire or collapse, and excluding from residential areas offensive trades, industries, and structures likely to create nuisances, and the Court concluded that zoning ordinances will be constitutional unless a court is convinced that such provisions are clearly arbitrary and unreasonable, having no substantial relation to the public health, safety, morals, or general welfare.[54]

The Court in 1976 sustained a city charter provision requiring proposed zoning changes to be approved by 55% of the voters, as not violative of due process rights of landowners seeking changes in the zoning of their properties.[55] Four years later the Court upheld a local government in zoning a five-acre plot to "Residential Planned Development and Open Space Zone," limiting building to five houses, with open space. The Court saw a legitimate municipal interest "to protect the residents from the ill effects of urbanization," and ruled there was no unconstitutional "taking" of private property under this zoning ordinance.[56] But where the effect of a zoning ordinance is to deprive the owner of real property of "all reasonable and economically viable use" of the property, it will constitute an impermissible taking in violation of the Fifth Amendment and, in such action by state and local governments, violative of the Fourteenth Amendment Due Process Clause.[57]

While most of the state court decisions have held that due process of law was violated by governmental attempts to zone out nonconforming uses of property which were existing and valid when the zoning controls were imposed, some cases have concluded that under particular circumstances retroactive zoning can be reasonable and hence constitutional.[58] Comparably, a number of courts are now ruling that amortization ordinances, giving existing non-conforming uses and structures a reasonable time to wind down, can be reasonable and constitutional under due process of law clauses.[59]

---

54. Village of Euclid, Ohio v. Ambler Realty Co., 272 U.S. 365, 47 S. Ct. 114, 71 L. Ed. 303, 4 Ohio L. Abs. 816, 54 A.L.R. 1016 (1926).

55. City of Eastlake v. Forest City Enterprises, Inc., 426 U.S. 668, 96 S. Ct. 2358, 49 L. Ed. 2d 132 (1976).

56. Agins v. City of Tiburon, 447 U.S. 255, 100 S. Ct. 2138, 65 L. Ed. 2d 106 (1980).

57. Suitum v. Tahoe Regional Planning Agency, 117 S. Ct. 1659, 137 L. Ed. 2d 980 (U.S. 1997)

58. Standard Oil Co. v. City of Tallahassee, 183 F.2d 410 (5th Cir. 1950).

59. Harbison v. Buffalo, 4 N.Y. 2d 553, 152 N.E.2d 42, 176 N.Y.S. 2d 598 (1958).

§ 20.08. —other than zoning

The United States Supreme Court in 1917 had held valid under due process of law a municipal ordinance banning billboards in city blocks wherein half of the lots on both sides of the street were used for residences.[60] Ten years later the Court ruled constitutional an ordinance requiring owners of lots desiring to build thereon to honor a set-back area to be kept free from permanent structures.[61]

Holding in 1978 that there was no "taking" of land for which compensation was required when New York City refused to allow changes in Grand Central Terminal so that an office building fifty stories in height could be built above the terminal, the Supreme Court acknowledged there was no set formula to determine when a compensable taking occurs. After noting that the city gave the terminal company development rights transferable to eight parcels of land in the vicinity of the terminal, the Court concluded: "The restrictions imposed are substantially related to the promotion of the general welfare and not only permit reasonable beneficial use of the landmark site but afford appellants opportunities further to enhance not only the terminal site proper but also other properties."[62] In 1980 the Supreme Court ruled there was no unconstitutional deprivation of property when a state constitutional provision permitted individuals to exercise free speech and petition rights on the property of a privately owned shopping center to which the public generally had been invited. Students were there seeking to secure support for a proposal desired by them. The Court said:

> The determination whether a state law unlawfully infringed a landowner's property in violation of the Taking Clause requires an examination of whether the restriction on private property forces some people alone to bear public burdens which, in all fairness and justice, should be borne by the public as a whole. This examination entails inquiry into such factors as the character of the governmental action, its economic impact and its interference with reasonable investment-back expectations.[63]

In a five-to-four ruling in 1982 the Court held that due process of

---

60. Thomas Cusack Co. v. City of Chicago, 242 U.S. 526, 37 S. Ct. 190, 61 L. Ed. 472 (1917).

61. Gorieb v. Fox, 274 U.S. 603, 47 S. Ct. 675, 71 L. Ed. 1228, 53 A.L.R. 1210 (1927).

62. Penn Cent. Transp. Co. v. City of New York, 438 U.S. 104, 98 S. Ct. 2646, 57 L. Ed. 2d 631 (1978).

63. PruneYard Shopping Center v. Robins, 447 U.S. 74, 100 S. Ct. 2035, 64 L. Ed. 2d 741 (1980)

law was not violated by a statute extinguishing severed interests in minerals that were not being developed after twenty years, unless the owner filed a statement of claim. In dissent, Justices Brennan, White, Marshall and Powell stated: "The Due Process Clause of the Fourteenth Amendment was designed to guard owners of property from the wholly arbitrary actions of state governments."[64]

Five years later the Court stated that a permit condition upon building must serve the same governmental purpose as a ban on development, and held that a government could not condition grant of a permit to rebuild a house upon transfer from the owner to the public of an easement across its beachfront property, believing that this was not rationally related to the regulatory purposes involved. The Court concluded that if the government desired such an easement it would have to condemn a property interest in an easement and pay for it. Justices Brennan, Marshall, Blackmun and Stevens in dissent, claimed there was no compensable "taking" on the facts—in these cases it should be sufficient that there is a reasonable relationship between a permit condition and the specific type of burden on public access created by an owner's proposed development.[65]

When in 1992, the Supreme Court was faced with a state statute effectively prohibiting use of two residential lots along a beach front, for which the owner had paid $975,000, it stated that in the past it had only found an impermissible "taking" by regulatory statutes when (a) there was a physical invasion of the property by the government, or (b) the statute denied all economic benefits that were legal when purchased. In remanding the case to allow the state to identify both common law and statutory prohibition of nuisances and property laws that allegedly banned some uses of the property at the time it was acquired by the present owner, the Court stated that in such cases a state "may resist compensation only if the logically antecedent inquiry into the nature of the owner's estate shows that the proscribed area interests were not part of his title to begin with." In dissent, Justice Stevens described the new rule as "unsupported by precedent, arbitrary and unsound in practice, and theoretically unjustified."[66]

Five years earlier, when a local government placed church-owned land in a temporary flood plain category and forbade building

---

64. Texaco, Inc. v. Short, 454 U.S. 516, 102 S. Ct. 781, 70 L. Ed. 2d 738 (1982).

65. Nollan v. California Coastal Com'n, 483 U.S. 825, 107 S. Ct. 3141, 97 L. Ed. 2d 677 (1987).

66. Lucas v. South Carolina Coastal Council, 505 U.S. 1003, 112 S. Ct. 2886, 120 L. Ed. 2d 798 (1992).

thereon, the Court concluded that on the facts the church had been denied "all use of the property for a considerable number of years," and held that when a government imposes even temporary regulations, the Just Compensation Clause of the Constitution requires it to pay for their impact upon private property "where the burden amounts to a taking." Justices Stevens, Blackmun and O'Connor in dissent noted that this was the first time the Court had held that temporary regulation of land uses could activate compensation requirements. They forecast that the ruling would prevent enactment by governments of "much important legislation."[67]

While acknowledging the constitutionality of some required dedications of property as conditions for securing building permits, the Court in 1994 in a five-to-four decision held on the facts that a city had not made a sufficient case to justify conditioning a building permit on a requirement of land dedication to help cope with flooding and traffic problems in the area, in the form of a greenway comprising the portion of the property owner's lot falling within a flood plain and a pedestrian/bicycle pathway taking up an additional 15-foot strip adjacent to the flood plain. The Court indicated that in such cases a tribunal must first determine whether an "essential nexus" exists between the "legitimate state interest" and the permit condition exacted by the city, then it must decide "whether the degree of exaction demanded by the city's permit conditions bears the required relationship to the projected impact of petitioner's proposed development." While acknowledging that the state courts only require municipalities to show a reasonable relationship between the required dedication and the impact of the proposed development, the Court rejected this and held that "a city must make some sort of individualized determination that the required dedication is related both in nature and extent to the impact of the proposed development." The Court concluded that the findings in the case "do not show the required reasonable relationship between the flood plain easement [desired by the city] and the petitioner's proposed new building." While the Court deprecates the city's decision as "adjudicative," there is some suggestion in the opinion that greater deference might be appropriate when there has been a legislative determination. The opinion of the Court would place upon the city the "burden of demonstrating that the additional burden of vehicle and bicycle trips generated by the petitioner's development

---

67. First English Evangelical Lutheran Church of Glendale v. Los Angeles County, Cal., 482 U.S. 304, 107 S. Ct. 2378, 96 L. Ed. 2d 250 (1987).

reasonably relates to the city's requirement for dedication" of the easement desired.[68]

Justices Stevens, Souter, Ginsburg and Blackmun dissented. Justice Souter was convinced the majority erred in placing the burden of producing evidence of a close relationship between the required dedication and the impact of the proposed development upon the city. Justices Stevens, Blackmun and Ginsburg agreed that the majority made a serious error by abandoning the traditional presumption of constitutionality and imposing a novel burden of proof on a city. They believed that it should be enough if a local government "shows conditions in a land-use permit are rational, impartial and conducive to fulfilling the aims of a land-use plan," and that "a strong presumption of validity should attach to their conditions."[69]

§ 20.09. Forfeiture of private property

As sovereigns, the United States and the 50 states can, without compensation, seize articles put to illicit use in violation of law. Furthermore, a long line of Supreme Court cases have established the principle that statutory forfeiture authorizations are not rendered unconstitutional because of their application to property interests of innocent owners.[70] In 1974, the Court held it proper for the government to seize a yacht which had been used, not by the owner but by his lessee, for the transportation of marijuana, without the knowledge or consent of the owner. The Court explained:

> Forfeiture of conveyances that have been used in violation of the narcotics laws fosters the purposes served by the underlying criminal statutes, both by preventing further illicit use of the conveyance and by imposing an economic penalty, thereby rendering illegal behavior unprofitable.[71]

In 1996 the Supreme Court recognized "a long and unbroken line of cases holding that an owner's interest in property may be forfeited by reason of the use to which the property is put even though the

---

68. Dolan v. City of Tigard, 512 U.S. 374, 114 S. Ct. 2309, 129 L. Ed. 2d 304 (1994).

69. Dolan v. City of Tigard, 512 U.S. 374, 114 S. Ct. 2309, 129 L. Ed. 2d 304 (1994).

70. Van Oster v. State of Kansas, 272 U.S. 465, 47 S. Ct. 133, 71 L. Ed. 354, 47 A.L.R. 1044 (1926); J. W. Goldsmith, Jr., Grant Co. v. U.S., 254 U.S. 505, 41 S. Ct. 189, 65 L. Ed. 376 (1921).

71. Calero-Toledo v. Pearson Yacht Leasing Co., 416 U.S. 663, 94 S. Ct. 2080, 40 L. Ed. 2d 452, 470 (1974).

owner did not know that it was to be put to such use," and held that due process did not prevent forfeiture of a car used in the commission of a crime, even over claims of one joint owner (a wife) who knew nothing of the crime committed by the other joint owner (her husband.)[72] The same year the Court held that allowing punishment for a criminal conviction and subsequent civil forfeiture of property as proceeds of the criminal activity does not constitute double jeopardy. Despite the underlying tie between the civil and criminal proceedings, they remain separate, and civil forfeiture is distinguishable from imposition of a criminal penalty.[73]

The Court holds that in "limited" and "extraordinary" instances, seizures of private property, without an opportunity for a prior hearing, are constitutionally permissible, as when a seizure is directly necessary to secure an important public interest and there is a special need for very prompt action.[74] This was true in the seizure of the yacht,[75] and a prior hearing was also not required when immediate seizure was necessary to protect the public from contaminated foods[76] or from misbranded rugs being marketed,[77] or because of a bank failure,[78] as well as when it was required in aid of the war effort.[79]

§ 20.10. Escheat of property

When a person dies without heirs under local law, the state can escheat real property owned by him and located within the state.[80] It can similarly escheat tangible chattels that are owned by the decedent and physically located within the state.[81] The state where an intangible has situs can escheat such intangible.[82]

---

72. Bennis v. Michigan, 116 S. Ct. 994, 134 L. Ed. 2d 68 (U.S. 1996).

73. U.S. v. Ursery, 116 S. Ct. 2135, 135 L. Ed. 2d 549 (U.S. 1996)

74. Fuentes v. Shevin, 407 U.S. 67, 92 S. Ct. 1983, 32 L. Ed. 2d 556, 10 U.C.C. Rep. Serv. (CBC) 913 (1972).

75. Calero-Toledo v. Pearson Yacht Leasing Co., 416 U.S. 663, 94 S. Ct. 2080, 40 L. Ed. 2d 452 (1974).

76. North American Cold Storage Co. v. City of Chicago, 211 U.S. 306, 29 S. Ct. 101, 53 L. Ed. 195 (1908).

77. Ewing v. Mytinger & Casselberry, 339 U.S. 594, 70 S. Ct. 870, 94 L. Ed. 1088 (1950).

78. Coffin Bros. & Co. v. Bennett, 277 U.S. 29, 48 S. Ct. 422, 72 L. Ed. 768 (1928).

79. U.S. v. Pfitsch, 256 U.S. 547, 41 S. Ct. 569, 65 L. Ed. 1084 (1921).

80. People v. Folsom, 5 Cal. 373 (1855).

81. State v. Reeder, 5 Neb. 203 (1876).

82. In re Rapoport's Estate, 317 Mich. 291, 26 N.W.2d 777 (1947).

When land is abandoned, the state of situs can escheat it.[83] The same can be said to be true as to abandoned chattels and documents representing intangible interests. "It is clear," says the United States Supreme Court, "that a state, subject to constitutional limitations, may use its legislative power to dispose of property within its reach, belonging to unknown persons."[84] So stating, the Court upheld a New Jersey statute escheating unpaid dividends and undelivered stock certificates held by New Jersey corporations for owners they could not find.

Writing in 1944, the Supreme Court said: "It is no longer open to doubt that a state, by a procedure satisfying constitutional requirements, may compel surrender to it of deposit balances, when there is substantial ground for belief that they have been abandoned or forgotten."[85]

In 1948 the Court observed: "We think that the state has the same power to seize abandoned life insurance moneys as abandoned bank deposits . . . ."[86] The Court then sustained the power of the state of New York to seize unclaimed moneys due its residents on policies, issued for delivery in the state, by life insurance corporations chartered outside the state.

The Court ruled in 1961 that Pennsylvania could not escheat moneys held there by Western Union for payees who had left the moneys unclaimed for more than seven years, since Pennsylvania could not protect Western Union from claimants in other states who sent the funds.[87] The Court suggested an original suit in the Supreme Court between the states claiming such funds. In 1965 the Court resolved such a suit between Texas, New Jersey, Pennsylvania, and Florida in which all claimed the power to escheat funds held for many years by the Sun Oil Company, a New Jersey corporation doing its principal business in Pennsylvania but keeping in Texas the books which showed funds owing to unclaimed creditors. There were a number of persons whose last known address was in Florida, and the Court held that ordinarily only the state of last known address could escheat. It ruled additionally, however, that where there was no record of any address, or where the state of last known ad-

---

83. Holliman's Heirs v. Peebles, 1 Tex. 673 (1847).

84. Standard Oil Co. v. State of N.J., by Parsons, 341 U.S. 428, 71 S. Ct. 822, 95 L. Ed. 1078, 1086-87 (1951).

85. Anderson Nat. Bank v. Luckett, 321 U.S. 233, 64 S. Ct. 599, 88 L. Ed. 692, 701, 151 A.L.R. 824 (1944).

86. Connecticut Mut. Life Ins. Co. v. Moore, 333 U.S. 541, 68 S. Ct. 682, 92 L. Ed. 863, 869 (1948).

87. W. U. Tel. Co. v. Com. of Pa., by Gottlieb, 368 U.S. 71, 82 S. Ct. 199, 7 L. Ed. 2d 139 (1961).

dress did not provide for escheat, then the state of corporate domicile could escheat the unclaimed funds.[88]

The Court ruled in 1980 that it is unconstitutional for a county to take interest accruing on an interpleader fund held by a county court, such earnings on a fund being private property just as the fund itself is private property and, consequently, the county had no right to appropriate for itself the use of the fund for the period in which it was held. Justice Blackmun, speaking for the Court, wrote:

> A State, by ipse dixit, may not transform private property into public property without compensation, even for the limited duration of the deposit in court. This is the very kind of thing that the Taking Clause of the Fifth Amendment was meant to prevent. That Clause stands as a shield against the arbitrary use of government power.[89]

The states and, where appropriate, the Congress have broad power to adjust the rules governing the descent and devise of property without implicating the guarantees of the Just Compensation Clause.[90] However, in 1987 the Supreme Court ruled unconstitutional as a taking without just compensation a provision of a federal statute to the effect that certain undivided fractional interests in land within an Indian reservation, owned by individual members of the tribe, could not be passed by these individuals either by intestacy or devise but would in effect be escheated to the tribe.[91] The *Irving* decision was followed ten years later by a Supreme Court holding that amendment of the statute involved in the earlier case was not sufficient to make it constitutional. Amendment "of an ever-so-slight class of individuals to receive fractional interests by devise," said the Court, does not rehabilitate the measure, since "allowing a decedent to leave an interest only to a current owner in the same parcel shrinks drastically the universe of possible successors." The amended version remained unconstitutional, said the Court, because it still "continues to restrict devise even in circumstances when the governmental purpose sought to be advanced, consolidation of ownership of Indian lands, did not conflict with the descent of the property," in as much as the will did not bequeath any single

---

88. State of Tex. v. State of N. J., 379 U.S. 674, 85 S. Ct. 626, 13 L. Ed. 2d 596 (1965), opinion supplemented, 380 U.S. 518, 85 S. Ct. 1136, 14 L. Ed. 2d 49 (1965).

89. Webb's Fabulous Pharmacies, Inc. v. Beckwith, 449 U.S. 155, 101 S. Ct. 446, 66 L. Ed. 2d 358 (1980).

90. Irving Trust Co. v. Day, 314 U.S. 556, 62 S. Ct. 398, 86 L. Ed. 452, 137 A.L.R. 1093 (1942).

91. Hodel v. Irving, 481 U.S. 704, 107 S. Ct. 2076, 95 L. Ed. 2d 668 (1987).

factional interest to multiple devisees, each individual plot being devised to a single member of the enrolled tribe.[92]

§ 20.11. Taxing private property—due process of law

Under due process of law as required by the Fifth and Fourteenth Amendments, taxes upon property are only unconstitutional when there is no jurisdictional base for the government levying the imposition, or where by amount or otherwise the levy is "palpably unreasonable."[93] Where the amount of a property tax is being questioned, the United States Supreme Court has stated: "So far as due process is concerned, the only question is whether the tax in practical operation has relation to opportunities, benefits, or protection conferred or afforded by the taxing State."[94]

While the Court held in 1925 that a state which was the domicile of a person could not impose an inheritance tax upon the passage at death of property which had acquired a situs elsewhere, and was subject to taxation there,[95] and this leaves the impression with some that due process still forbids double taxation of tangibles,[96] it is clear that there is no due process ban upon double taxation where interests in intangibles is at issue. The Court has said: "There is no constitutional rule of immunity from taxation of intangibles by more than one state."[97] When in 1974 the Supreme Court sustained a 20 percent tax on gross receipts of private parking lots in Pittsburgh, even when the private lots were in competition with a public parking authority which received tax exemptions and other advantages enabling it to charge rates lower than those which private operators could charge to operate profitably, the Court reported that it has consistently held that it will not undertake to pass on the reasonableness of taxes within state power "or to hold that a tax is unconstitutional because it renders a business unprofitable." Justice Powell, concurring, suggested that there may be "some combination of

---

92. Babbitt v. Youpee, 117 S. Ct. 727, 136 L. Ed. 2d 696 (U.S. 1997)

93. Railway Exp. Agency, Inc. v. Com. of Va., 358 U.S. 434, 79 S. Ct. 411, 3 L. Ed. 2d 450 (1959).

94. Ott v. Mississippi Val. Barge Line Co., 336 U.S. 169, 69 S. Ct. 432, 93 L. Ed. 585, 589 (1949).

95. Frick v. Com. of Pennsylvania, 268 U.S. 473, 45 S. Ct. 603, 69 L. Ed. 1058, 42 A.L.R. 316 (1925).

96. Treichler v. State of Wis., 338 U.S. 251, 70 S. Ct. 1, 94 L. Ed. 37 (1949).

97. State Tax Commission of Utah v. Aldrich, 316 U.S. 174, 62 S. Ct. 1008, 86 L. Ed. 1358, 1370, 139 A.L.R. 1436 (1942).

unreasonably burdensome taxation and direct competition" from a government agency that will violate due process of law.[98]

Fifteen years later the Court ruled that there was no unconstitutional taking when the federal government deducted a "user fee" of two percent from an award received by a United States corporation from an international tribunal, to which the government had assigned all such claims. It is enough, explained the Court, that a user fee levied upon citizens and corporations "be a fair approximation of the cost of benefits supplied."[99]

§ 20.12. Jurisdiction to tax realty and private property

Any state wherein land is situated has jurisdiction to tax it. Furthermore, where tangible personal property is located permanently in a state, the state has jurisdiction to impose property taxes on it, regardless of the domicile of the owner.[1] Illustratively, the United States Supreme Court has sustained Pennsylvania in taxing portraits located there, where the New York owner had placed them there and such location "was not merely transient, transitory or temporary, but it was fixed in an established abiding place in which they remained for a long time" and where the owner lacked "a definite intention" to return them to New York.[2] Habitual use within a non-domiciliary can establish situs in a non-domiciliary state.[3] On the other hand, temporary use of tangible property in a non-domiciliary state does not give that state jurisdiction to tax that property.[4]

Where personal properties have acquired a permanent situs away from the domicile of the owner they are no longer subject to property taxes at the domicile of the owner. The Supreme Court said in the leading case: "As respects tangible personal property having an actual situs in a particular state, the power to subject it to state taxation rests exclusively in that State, regardless of the domicile of the owner."

---

98. City of Pittsburgh v. Alco Parking Corp., 417 U.S. 369, 94 S. Ct. 2291, 41 L. Ed. 2d 132 (1974)

99. U.S. v. Sperry Corp., 493 U.S. 52, 110 S. Ct. 387, 107 L. Ed. 2d 290 (1989).

1. Old Dominion S.S. Co. v. Commonwealth of Virginia, 198 U.S. 299, 25 S. Ct. 686, 49 L. Ed. 1059 (1905).

2. City Bank Farmers' Trust Co. v. Schnader, 293 U.S. 112, 55 S. Ct. 29, 79 L. Ed. 228, 232 (1934).

3. Braniff Airways v. Nebraska State Bd. of Equalization and Assessment, 347 U.S. 590, 74 S. Ct. 757, 98 L. Ed. 967 (1954).

4. Curry v. McCanless, 307 U.S. 357, 59 S. Ct. 900, 83 L. Ed. 1339, 123 A.L.R. 162 (1939).

Tangible property which is physically present in a non-domiciliary state for the sole purpose of transit through the state is not subject to property taxes there.[5] However, where property has been moving in interstate commerce and there is a discernible break in movement, with the property coming to rest, it can then be taxed in that state.[6] If the purpose of the break in transit is only incidental to movement of the property, it is not taxable by the state where it has paused.[7]

Where property owned by a nonresident is within a state for only a fraction of the year, an attempt to impose upon its owners a tax not apportioned to the period of time actually there will be held unconstitutional.[8] However, where the state or local tax is properly apportioned, a state can impose a property tax upon such property used there for a part of the year, even though the property is owned by a nonresident and used within the taxing state exclusively in interstate commerce.[9]

Tangible chattels can acquire a tax situs away from the domicile of the owner and they will be taxable where situated rather than by the state of domicile of the owner. Said the Supreme Court in the leading case: "As respects tangible personal property having an actual situs in a particular state, the power to subject it to state taxation rests exclusively in that State, regardless of the domicile of the owner."[10] The reason for the rule is that "property which is wholly and exclusively within the jurisdiction of another State, receives none of the protection for which the tax is supposed to be the compensation."[11]

In 1952 the Court held that a domiciliary state can tax only on an apportioned basis where some of the property of the carrier is subject to taxation in a non-domiciliary state in which the carrier also operates. The Court stated:

5. Kelley v. Rhoads, 188 U.S. 1, 23 S. Ct. 259, 47 L. Ed. 359 (1903).

6. State of Minnesota v. Blasius, 290 U.S. 1, 54 S. Ct. 34, 78 L. Ed. 131 (1933).

7. Champlain Realty Co. v. Town of Brattleboro, 260 U.S. 366, 43 S. Ct. 146, 67 L. Ed. 309, 25 A.L.R. 1195 (1922).

8. Hays v. Pacific Mail S. S. Co., 58 U.S. 596, 17 How. 596, 15 L. Ed. 254 (1854); Morgan v. Parham, 83 U.S. 471, 21 L. Ed. 303 (1872).

9. Ott v. Mississippi Val. Barge Line Co., 336 U.S. 169, 69 S. Ct. 432, 93 L. Ed. 585 (1949); Braniff Airways v. Nebraska State Bd. of Equalization and Assessment, 347 U.S. 590, 74 S. Ct. 757, 98 L. Ed. 967 (1954).

10. Frick v. Com. of Pennsylvania, 268 U.S. 473, 489, 45 S. Ct. 603, 69 L. Ed. 1058, 1062, 42 A.L.R. 316 (1925).

11. Union Refrigerator Transit Co. v. Commonwealth of Kentucky, 199 U.S. 194, 204, 26 S. Ct. 36, 50 L. Ed. 150, 153 (1905).

> The rule which permits taxation by two or more states on an
> apportionment basis precludes taxation of all of the property by
> the state of the domicile. . . . Otherwise there would be
> multiple taxation of interstate operation and the tax would have
> no relation to the opportunities, benefits, or protection which
> the taxing state gives these operations.[12]

However, 10 years later the Court held that it is possible for the
domiciliary state to tax all the equipment used by one of its interstate
carriers so long as the carrier does not introduce proof that
particular items are subject to the taxing jurisdiction of another
state.[13]

§ 20.13. Jurisdiction to tax intangibles

Following the maxim, "mobilia sequuntur personam," the United
States Supreme Court has permitted states of domicile to tax the
intangibles owned by domiciliaries.[14] Thus, the Court states:

> Generally speaking, intangible property in the nature of a debt
> may be regarded, for the purpose of taxation, as situated at the
> domicile of the creditor and within the jurisdiction of the State
> where he has such domicile. It is property within that State.[15]

Additionally, intangible interests can be taxed by states other than
the domicile of the owner where the owners have sufficient contacts
with the jurisdiction to make it fair and reasonable that the tax be
paid. To illustrate, bank deposits can be taxed by the state where the
money is kept, even though the depositor be a nonresident.[16] Again,
a state providing legal protection to a document of title into which
all right and interest has been fused by the proper law can tax the
document in its presence, even though the owner resides elsewhere.[17]

Where intangibles, such as funds, have over a period of time
become an integral part of a local business, and have acquired a

---

12. Standard Oil Co. v. Peck, 342 U.S. 382, 72 S. Ct. 309, 96 L. Ed. 427, 430,
47 Ohio Op. 81, 63 Ohio L. Abs. 559, 26 A.L.R.2d 1371 (1952).

13. Central R. Co. of Pa. v. Com. of Pa., 370 U.S. 607, 82 S. Ct. 1297, 8 L. Ed.
2d 720 (1962).

14. Hawley v. City of Malden, 232 U.S. 1, 34 S. Ct. 201, 58 L. Ed. 477 (1914).

15. Buck v. Beach, 206 U.S. 392, 401, 27 S. Ct. 712, 51 L. Ed. 1106, 1111
(1907).

16. Fidelity & Columbia Trust Co. v. City of Louisville, 245 U.S. 54, 38 S. Ct.
40, 62 L. Ed. 145 (1917).

17. Scottish Union & National Ins. Co. v. Bowland, 196 U.S. 611, 25 S. Ct.
345, 49 L. Ed. 619 (1905).

"business situs," the Supreme Court allows the state where the business is located to tax the intangibles, even though owned by non-residents or foreign corporations.[18] Additionally, the Court has attributed to some corporations a "commercial domicile" apart from their legal domicile so as to enable the state which is the commercial domicile to get at the intangibles owned by the company. To deny such a state of principal business activities the power to tax intangibles "upon the ground that it violates due process to treat the credits as within its jurisdiction, is to make a legal fiction dominate realities," according to the Court.[19] There is also authority for the proposition that a beneficial interest in a trust of intangibles is taxable at the domicile of the beneficiary, regardless of where the trustee resides.[20]

§ 20.14. The public purpose doctrine as a limitation on taxing property

In 1875 the United States Supreme Court ruled that states and their political subdivisions could not tax except for a public purpose. The Court observed:

> To lay with one hand the power of the government on the property of the citizen, and with the other to bestow it upon favored individuals to aid private fortunes, is none the less robbery because it is done under the forms of law and is called taxation.

The Court did not clearly attribute the source of this principle to the Due Process of Law Clause in the Fourteenth Amendment; rather it appeared to be posited upon one of the vague emanations from the Constitution that the Court occasionally finds.[21] Later cases have treated the rule as an aspect of due process of law.

Once a tax has been authorized by the Congress or a state legislature and then approved by the highest court of the jurisdiction, there is presently little likelihood that the Supreme Court will invalidate the tax as being for something other than for a public purpose. According to the Court, "the judgment of the highest

---

18. Metropolitan Life Ins. Co. v. City of New Orleans, 205 U.S. 395, 27 S. Ct. 499, 51 L. Ed. 853 (1907).

19. Wheeling Steel Corp. v. Fox, 298 U.S. 193, 211, 56 S. Ct. 773, 80 L. Ed. 1143, 1148 (1936).

20. Com. v. Stewart, 338 Pa. 9, 12 A.2d 444 (1940), judgment aff'd, 312 U.S. 649, 61 S. Ct. 445, 85 L. Ed. 1101 (1941).

21. Citizens' Savings & Loan Ass'n v. City of Topeka, 87 U.S. 655, 22 L. Ed. 455, 461 (1874).

court of the State upon what should be deemed a public use in a particular State is entitled to the highest respect."[22] If a state sees fit to engage in commercial or even manufacturing activities, the Court has said: "[w]e are not prepared to say that it is within the authority of this Court . . . to set aside such action by judicial decision."[23]

§ 20.15. Equal protection of the laws in taxing property

Owners of property have a constitutional right to equal protection of the laws, which means that their property cannot be exposed to invidious discrimination in taxation. Both persons and corporations within the jurisdiction are protected by the Equal Protection Clause of the Fourteenth Amendment against arbitrary inequalities by the states, and both are entitled to equality of treatment from the federal government under the Fifth Amendment Due Process Clause.

For example, where a state had authorized a foreign corporation to conduct therein a local business, it could not thereafter unreasonably discriminate against such taxpayer in regard to property taxes because it was a foreign corporation. The Supreme Court said: "After a state has chosen to domesticate foreign corporations, the adopted corporations are entitled to equal protection with the state's own corporate progeny, at least to the extent that their property is entitled to an equally favorable ad valorem tax basis."[24]

Equal protection does not prevent the states from classifying property for the purpose of taxation so long as the classification is reasonable. "The equal protection clause does not forbid discrimination with respect to things that are different," says the Supreme Court.[25] On another occasion, the Court added:

> If the selection or classification is neither capricious nor arbitrary, and rests upon some reasonable consideration of difference or policy, there is no denial of the equal protection of the law.

That a statute may discriminate in favor of a certain class does not

---

22. Jones v. City of Portland, 245 U.S. 217, 222, 38 S. Ct. 112, 62 L. Ed. 252 (1917).

23. Green v. Frazier, 253 U.S. 233, 243, 40 S. Ct. 499, 64 L. Ed. 878 (1920).

24. Wheeling Steel Corp. v. Glander, 337 U.S. 562, 571-72, 69 S. Ct. 1291, 93 L. Ed. 1544, 1550-51, 40 Ohio Op. 101, 55 Ohio L. Abs. 305 (1949).

25. Puget Sound Power & Light Co. v. City of Seattle, Wash., 291 U.S. 619, 624, 54 S. Ct. 542, 78 L. Ed. 1025, 1029 (1934).

render it arbitrary if the discrimination is founded upon a reasonable distinction, or difference in state policy.[26]

The power of the state and federal governments to classify for the purpose of taxation is very broad. Equal protection only requires that classification rest on real and not feigned differences, that the distinction have some relevance to the purpose for which the classification is made, and that the different treatments be not so disparate, relative to the difference in classification, as to be wholly arbitrary.[27] It has long been settled, said the Supreme Court in 1959, "that a classification, though discriminatory, is not arbitrary nor violative of the Equal Protection Clause of the Fourteenth Amendment if any state of facts reasonably can be conceived that would sustain it."[28] "To hold otherwise," explains the Court, "would be to subject the essential taxing power of the State to an intolerable supervision, hostile to the basic principles of our government and wholly beyond the protection which the general clause of the Fourteenth Amendment was intended to assure."[29]

A state tax statute is not automatically violative of equal protection because the state has left untaxed some other kinds of property. In sustaining a Pennsylvania tax that treated corporate securities somewhat differently than others, the Supreme Court stated:

> The provision in the Fourteenth Amendment, that no State shall deny to any person within its jurisdiction the equal protection of the law, was not intended to prevent a State from adjusting its system of taxation in all proper and reasonable ways. It may, if it chooses, exempt certain classes of property from any taxation at all, such as churches, libraries, and the property of charitable institutions. It may . . . tax real estate and personal property in a different manner; it may tax visible property and not tax securities for payment of money; it may allow deductions for indebtedness, or not allow them . . . the Fourteenth

---

26. Allied Stores of Ohio, Inc. v. Bowers, 358 U.S. 522, 79 S. Ct. 437, 3 L. Ed. 2d 480, 9 Ohio Op. 2d 321, 82 Ohio L. Abs. 312 (1959).

27. Walters v. City of St. Louis, Mo., 347 U.S. 231, 74 S. Ct. 505, 509, 98 L. Ed. 660, 665 (1954).

28. Allied Stores of Ohio, Inc. v. Bowers, 358 U.S. 522, 79 S. Ct. 437, 441, 3 L. Ed. 2d 480, 9 Ohio Op. 2d 321, 82 Ohio L. Abs. 312 (1959).

29. Ohio Oil Co. v. Conway, 281 U.S. 146, 159, 50 S. Ct. 310, 74 L. Ed. 775, 781 (1930).

Amendment was not intended to compel the States to adopt an iron rule of equal taxation.[30]

"The States have a very wide discretion in the laying of their taxes," according to the Court.[31] Similarly, the Court has referred to as "familiar doctrine" the rule that states have a wide discretion in allowing exemptions and deductions from their taxes.[32]

However, where a classification or discrimination in a tax statute or ordinance is arbitrary, has no rational basis, or bears no reasonable relation to the purpose for which the categorization is made, equal protection is denied.[33] In the language of the Supreme Court, "The State must proceed upon a rational basis and may not resort to a classification that is palpably arbitrary."[34] "Classification," says the Court, "must rest upon some ground of difference having a fair and substantial relation to the object of the legislation."[35]

The Court generally accords to classifications in tax statutes a presumption that the categorization is reasonable and constitutional.[36] A classification in a tax statute must be "palpably arbitrary" before it violates equal protection, according to the Court.[37]

---

30. Bell's Gap R. Co. v. Com. of Pennsylvania, 134 U.S. 232, 237, 10 S. Ct. 533, 33 L. Ed. 892, 895 (1890).

31. Allied Stores of Ohio, Inc. v. Bowers, 358 U.S. 522, 79 S. Ct. 437, 441, 3 L. Ed. 2d 480, 9 Ohio Op. 2d 321, 82 Ohio L. Abs. 312 (1959).

32. Aero Mayflower Transit Co. v. Georgia Public Serv. Com'n, 295 U.S. 285, 55 S. Ct. 709, 79 L. Ed. 1439 (1935).

33. Connolly v. Union Sewer Pipe Co., 184 U.S. 540, 560, 22 S. Ct. 431, 46 L. Ed. 679, 690 (1902) (overruled in part on other grounds by, Tigner v. Texas, 310 U.S. 141, 60 S. Ct. 879, 84 L. Ed. 1124, 130 A.L.R. 1321 (1940)); Quaker City Cab Co. v. Commonwealth of Pennsylvania, 277 U.S. 389, 400, 48 S. Ct. 553, 72 L. Ed. 927, 929 (1928).

34. Allied Stores of Ohio, Inc. v. Bowers, 358 U.S. 522, 79 S. Ct. 437, 441, 3 L. Ed. 2d 480, 9 Ohio Op. 2d 321, 82 Ohio L. Abs. 312 (1959).

35. F.S. Royster Guano Co. v. Commonwealth of Virginia, 253 U.S. 412, 415, 40 S. Ct. 560, 64 L. Ed. 989, 990 (1920).

36. Madden v. Commonwealth of Kentucky, 309 U.S. 83, 60 S. Ct. 406, 84 L. Ed. 590, 593, 125 A.L.R. 1383 (1940).

37. Metropolis Theater Co. v. City of Chicago, 228 U.S. 61, 69, 33 S. Ct. 441, 57 L. Ed. 730, 733 (1913).

CHAPTER TWENTY-ONE

Freedom of Enterprise

---

§ 21.00. Freedom to develop one's talents

The American Founding Fathers in enshrining in our early constitutions "liberty" and "the pursuit of happiness" intended to recognize jurally the right of all men to develop their talents as they saw fit, subject only to reasonable controls necessitated by the common weal. The United States Supreme Court has recognized such a constitutional right. Thus, in 1959, the Court stated: "The right to hold specific private employment and to follow a chosen profession free from unreasonable governmental interference comes within the 'liberty' and 'property' concepts of the Fifth Amendment."[1]

Two years previously the Court had held for the first time that no person can be arbitrarily denied the opportunity to practice law.[2] In the *Schware* case the Supreme Court stated: "A State cannot exclude a person from the practice of law or from any other occupation in a manner or for reasons that contravene the Due Process or Equal Protection Clauses of the Fourteenth Amendment." The Court added:

> Any qualification must have a rational connection with the applicant's fitness or capacity to practice law. . . . Even in applying permissible standards, officers of a State cannot exclude an applicant when there is no basis for their finding that he fails to

---

1. Greene v. McElroy, 360 U.S. 474, 79 S. Ct. 1400, 3 L. Ed. 2d 1377, 1358 (1959).

2. Konigsberg v. State Bar of Cal., 353 U.S. 252, 77 S. Ct. 722, 1 L. Ed. 2d 810 (1957).

meet these standards, or when their action is invidiously discriminatory.[3]

Equal protection of the laws is violated when individuals seeking to develop their talents are exposed to unreasonable discriminations. For example, no person has a constitutional right to be appointed to a governmental post, but a person does have a constitutional right not to be arbitrarily denied the opportunity to qualify for such employment—as well as the right not to be exposed to invidious discrimination in such application.[4] Similarly, once a person has a public post, he has the constitutional right to be free from arbitrary discharge.[5] However, the Supreme Court has ruled that neither due process nor equal protection were violated when a school board terminated employment of a teacher because she refused to continue her education, conduct which the board had previously punished only by withholding salary increases.[6]

Once a person has qualified to practice a profession or a calling and has been licensed, due process voids governmental attempts to suspend or revoke such license arbitrarily,[7] but such action that is reasonable and not arbitrary is permissible.[8]

While acknowledging the federal courts can review deprivation of both liberty and property rights by public educational institutions, the Supreme Court held in 1985 that the judgment of university authorities in dismissing students may not be overridden by federal courts unless it is such a substantial departure from accepted academic norms as to demonstrate that the person or committee responsible did not actually exercise professional judgment. The Court added that "considerations of profound importance counsel restrained judicial review of the substance of academic decisions."[9]

3. Schware v. Board of Bar Exam. of State of N.M., 353 U.S. 232, 77 S. Ct. 752, 1 L. Ed. 2d 796, 801-02, 64 A.L.R.2d 288 (1957).

4. Beasley v. Cunningham, 171 Tenn. 334, 103 S.W.2d 18, 110 A.L.R. 306 (1937); Wilson v. City of Los Angeles, 54 Cal. 2d 61, 4 Cal. Rptr. 489, 351 P.2d 761 (1960).

5. Wieman v. Updegraff, 344 U.S. 183, 73 S. Ct. 215, 97 L. Ed. 216 (1952).

6. Harrah Independent School Dist. v. Martin, 440 U.S. 194, 99 S. Ct. 1062, 59 L. Ed. 2d 248 (1979).

7. Czarra v. Board of Medical Sup'rs of District of Columbia, 25 App. D.C. 443 (App.D.C D.C. Cir. 1905).

8. Semler v. Oregon State Bd. of Dental Examiners, 294 U.S. 608, 55 S. Ct. 570, 79 L. Ed. 1086 (1935); Barsky v. Board of Regents of University, 347 U.S. 442, 74 S. Ct. 650, 98 L. Ed. 829 (1954).

9. Regents of University of Michigan v. Ewing, 474 U.S. 214, 106 S. Ct. 507, 88 L. Ed. 2d 523, 28 Ed. Law Rep. 720 (1985).

§ 21.01. Freedom of commercial enterprise—regulation under due process

Freedom of commercial enterprise is one of the basic, fundamental rights protected within the "liberty" concept of both the Fifth and Fourteenth Amendments.[10] Nonetheless, freedom of economic enterprise can be subjected to governmental regulation by both the federal and state governments so long as the regulation is reasonable and has a reasonable tendency to protect the public health, safety, morality, or general welfare. In the landmark case of *Nebbia v. New York*, the Supreme Court stated:

> The guaranty of due process . . . demands only that the law shall not be unreasonable, arbitrary or capricious, and that the means selected shall have a real and substantial relation to the object sought to be attained.

The Court continued:

> So far as the requirement of due process is concerned . . . a state is free to adopt whatever economic policy may reasonably be deemed to promote public welfare, and to enforce that policy by legislation adapted to its purpose. The courts are without authority either to declare such policy, or, when it is declared by the legislature, to override it. If the laws passed are seen to have a reasonable relation to a proper legislative purpose, and are neither arbitrary nor discriminatory, the requirements of due process are satisfied.[11]

Long before 1934 the better Justices on the Supreme Court had endorsed what was to become the Nebbia Rule as proper constitutional doctrine. For instance, when the majority of the Court in 1905, in a five-to-four decision, invalidated a New York statute forbidding bakers to work over 10 hours a day and over 60 hours a week, Justices Harlan, Holmes, White and Day dissented. Justice Holmes wrote:

> My agreement or disagreement has nothing to do with the right of the majority to embody their opinions into law. The Fourteenth Amendment does not enact Mr. Herbert Spencer's Social Statics. This case is decided upon an economic theory

---

10. Allgeyer v. State of La., 165 U.S. 578, 17 S. Ct. 427, 41 L. Ed. 832 (1897); Coppage v. State of Kansas, 236 U.S. 1, 35 S. Ct. 240, 59 L. Ed. 441 (1915) (overruled in part on other grounds by, Phelps Dodge Corp. v. N.L.R.B., 313 U.S. 177, 61 S. Ct. 845, 85 L. Ed. 1271, 133 A.L.R. 1217 (1941)).

11. Nebbia v. People of New York, 291 U.S. 502, 54 S. Ct. 505, 78 L. Ed. 940, 89 A.L.R. 1469 (1934).

which a large part of the country does not entertain. If it were a question whether I agreed with that theory, I should desire to study it further and long before making up my mind. But I do not conceive that to be my duty. . . . [A] Constitution is not intended to embody a particular economic theory, whether of paternalism and the organic relation of the citizen to the state, or of laissez faire. It is made for people of fundamentally differing views, and the accident of our finding certain opinions natural and familiar, or novel, and even shocking, ought not to conclude our judgment upon the question whether statutes embodying them conflict with the Constitution of the United States.[12]

In 1908 the Court, speaking through Justice Harlan, said: "The right of liberty and property guaranteed by the Constitution against deprivation without due process of law is subject to such restraints as the common good or the general welfare may require."[13] Again, in 1921 when the Court's majority showed a willingness to invalidate economic controls they could not appreciate, Justice Holmes said in dissent:

There is nothing that I more deprecate than the use of the Fourteenth Amendment beyond the absolute compulsion of its words to prevent the making of social experiments that an important part of the community desires, in the insulated chambers afforded by the several states, even though the experiment may seem futile or even noxious to me and to those whose judgment I most respect.[14]

In 1936 when the Court's majority struck down the New York minimum wage law, Justice Stone wrote in dissent:

It is difficult to imagine any grounds, other than our own personal economic predilections, for saying that the contract of employment is any the less an appropriate subject of legislation than are scores of others, in dealing with which this Court has held that legislatures may curtail individual freedom in the public interest. . . . [T]he Fourteenth Amendment has no more embodied in the Constitution our preference for some particular

---

12. Lochner v. People of State of New York, 198 U.S. 45, 25 S. Ct. 539, 49 L. Ed. 937 (1905).

13. Adair v. U.S., 208 U.S. 161, 174, 28 S. Ct. 277, 52 L. Ed. 436, 442 (1908) (overruled in part by, Phelps Dodge Corp. v. N.L.R.B., 313 U.S. 177, 61 S. Ct. 845, 85 L. Ed. 1271, 133 A.L.R. 1217 (1941)).

14. Truax v. Corrigan, 257 U.S. 312, 344, 42 S. Ct. 124, 66 L. Ed. 254, 268, 27 A.L.R. 375 (1921).

set of economic beliefs than it has adopted, in the name of liberty, the system of theology which we happen to approve.[15]

Shortly thereafter the views of Holmes, Stone, Brandeis and Cardozo permanently prevailed. In 1955, when the Court upheld Oklahoma's control of the business of selling eyeglasses, Justice Douglas could aptly say for the Court: "The day is gone when this Court uses the Due Process Clause of the Fourteenth Amendment to strike down state laws, regulatory of business and industrial conditions, because they may be unwise, improvident, or out of harmony with a particular school of thought."[16] The Court has pointed out that when Congress is regulating the economy, its statutes "are beyond attack without a clear and convincing showing that there is no rational basis for the legislation; that it is an arbitrary fiat."[17]

Congress and the states have many times been sustained in controlling prices. In 1940 the Supreme Court stated: "Price control is one of the means available to the States and to the Congress for the protection and promotion of the welfare of the economy."[18] Comparably, the rates of utilities and carriers can be set so long as the action is not unjust or unreasonable.[19] The Court reminds us that "[a]ll that is protected against, in a constitutional sense is that the rates fixed by the [Federal Energy Regulatory] Commission be higher than a confiscatory level."[20]

Government can fix the maximum hours of employees and determine minimum wages. In 1941 Justice Stone said for a unanimous Court that:

> it is no longer open to question that the fixing of a minimum wage is within the legislative power and that the bare fact of its exercise is not a denial of due process under the Fifth more

---

15. Morehead v. People of State of New York ex rel. Tipaldo, 298 U.S. 587, 56 S. Ct. 918, 80 L. Ed. 1347, 103 A.L.R. 1445 (1936) (overruled in part by, Olsen v. State of Nebraska ex rel. Western Reference & Bond Ass'n, 313 U.S. 236, 61 S. Ct. 862, 85 L. Ed. 1305, 133 A.L.R. 1500 (1941)).

16. Williamson v. Lee Optical of Okl., 348 U.S. 483, 75 S. Ct. 461, 464, 99 L. Ed. 563, 571 (1955).

17. Carolene Products Co. v. U.S., 323 U.S. 18, 65 S. Ct. 1, 89 L. Ed. 15, 155 A.L.R. 1371 (1944).

18. Sunshine Anthracite Coal Co. v. Adkins, 310 U.S. 381, 60 S. Ct. 907, 84 L. Ed. 1263 (1940).

19. Federal Power Commission v. Hope Natural Gas Co., 320 U.S. 591, 64 S. Ct. 281, 88 L. Ed. 333 (1944).

20. Federal Energy Regulatory Commission v. Pennzoil Producing Co., 439 U.S. 508, 99 S. Ct. 765, 58 L. Ed. 2d 773, 783 (1979).

than under the Fourteenth Amendment. Nor is it any longer open to question that it is within the legislative power to fix maximum hours.[21]

Reminding us in 1992 that "as a general matter, the Court has always been reluctant to expand the concept of substantive due process because guide-posts for responsible decision-making are scarce and open-ended," the Supreme Court stated that "the doctrine of judicial self-restraint requires us to exercise the utmost care whenever we are asked to break new ground in this field." Accordingly, the Court held that the widow of a municipal employee who died of asphyxia working in a clogged sewer line did not state a constitutional cause of action in her 42 U.S.C.A. § 1983 suit against the city, since the Federal Constitution under the Fourteenth Amendment Due Process Clause does not demand that a city provide its employees with a safe working environment. The Court added that it could not characterize as "arbitrary or conscience-shocking in a constitutional sense" the failure of the city to train its employees, or to warn them about known risks of harm. The Court noted its general unreceptivity to claims as federal duties, those obligations "traditionally imposed by state tort law."[22]

Noting that generally there will be a "limited judicial review accorded economic legislation under the Fifth Amendment Due Process Clause," the Supreme Court now allows retroactive application of a federal statute, "provided that the retroactive application of a statute is supported by a legitimate purpose furthered by rational means." The Court added that "judgments about the wisdom of such legislation remain within the exclusive province of the legislative and executive branches." It then held constitutional provisions of the Multi-Employer Pension Plan Amendment Act of 1980, which required an employer withdrawing from a covered pension plan to pay a fixed and certain debt to the pension plan, with a clause making the new provisions take effect five months before the enactment of the statute.[23]

One of the contemporary rare cases of the Supreme Court voiding state legislation in the area occurred in 1994 when the Due Process Clause of the Fourteenth Amendment was held violated by an

---

21. U.S. v. Darby, 312 U.S. 100, 61 S. Ct. 451, 85 L. Ed. 609, 132 A.L.R. 1430 (1941); U.S. v. Darby, 312 U.S. 657, 61 S. Ct. 451, 85 L. Ed. 609, 132 A.L.R. 1430 (1941).

22. Collins v. City of Harker Heights, Tex., 503 U.S. 115, 112 S. Ct. 1061, 117 L. Ed. 2d 261 (1992).

23. Pension Ben. Guar. Corp. v. R.A. Gray & Co., 467 U.S. 717, 104 S. Ct. 2709, 81 L. Ed. 2d 601 (1984).

Oregon constitutional amendment prohibiting judicial review of the amount of punitive damages awarded by a trial court, "unless the court can affirmatively say there is no evidence to support the verdict." The Court believed that "punitive damages present an acute danger of arbitrary deprivation of property," and gave weight to the fact that the common law authorized judicial review of the sum, as did the practice in the federal courts and in all state courts except Oregon. Commenting that "traditional practice provides a touchstone for constitutional analysis," the Court held that "Oregon's abrogation of a well-established common law protection against deprivation of property raises a presumption that its procedures violate the Due Process Clause." Chief Justice Rehnquist and Justice Ginsburg dissented because the state had carefully enacted a body of standards confining punitive damages in products liability cases.[24]

Punitive damages may properly be imposed by state courts to further a state's legitimate interests in punishing unlawful conduct and deterring its repetition, but when such damages become "grossly excessive" the Court has ruled that they violate the Due Process Clause of the Fourteenth Amendment. The Court also held that a state may not impose economic sanctions violative of its laws to change a tortfeasor's lawful conduct in other states.[25]

In a case where a chief of police had power to recommend against issuance to an applicant of an amusement license if he finds the applicant has any "connection with criminal elements," the Supreme Court found no violation of the traditional ban upon vague and indefinite language in restrictions upon basic freedoms.[26]

§ 21.02. Regulation under equal protection of the laws

Equal protection of the laws will not allow government in regulating private business to expose entrepreneurs to unreasonable or invidious discriminations. The United States Supreme Court has said: "There is a point beyond which the State cannot go without violating the Equal Protection Clause. The State must proceed upon

---

24. Honda Motor Co., Ltd. v. Oberg, 512 U.S. 415, 114 S. Ct. 2331, 129 L. Ed. 2d 336 (1994).

25. BMW of North America, Inc. v. Gore, 116 S. Ct. 1589, 134 L. Ed. 2d 809 (U.S. 1996).

26. City of Mesquite v. Aladdin's Castle, Inc., 455 U.S. 283, 102 S. Ct. 1070, 71 L. Ed. 2d 152 (1982).

a rational basis and may not resort to a classification that is palpably arbitrary."[27]

Statutory distinctions cannot be justified if the discrimination has no reasonable relation to the differences between businesses. Classifications, to be constitutional, must be based upon some factor having proper relation to the purpose of the control.

Governmental regulations of entrepreneurs on the basis of color, race, or national ancestry will almost always be invalidated as unreasonable. Thus, the Supreme Court has ruled that California could not deny economic opportunity to individuals solely because they were of Japanese ancestry, and at that time ineligible for citizenship. It did not follow, ruled the Court, that because the federal government classified aliens for eligibility for citizenship that "a state can adopt one or more of the same classifications to prevent lawfully admitted aliens within it borders from earning a living in the same way that other state inhabitants earn their living."[28]

Some distinctions based upon alienage may be reasonable. It would thus almost certainly be constitutional to deny the practice of law to aliens. The Supreme Court once ruled that a city could exclude aliens from the operation of pool and billiard halls.[29] It is hard, however, to accept such classification as reasonable, and the decision must be questioned.

A law which affects the activities of some groups differently from the way in which it affects the activities of other groups is not necessarily violative of the Equal Protection Clause. The Supreme Court explains:

> Otherwise, effective regulation in the public interest could not be provided, however essential that regulation might be. For it is axiomatic that the consequences of regulation by setting apart a classified group is that those in it will be subject to some restrictions or receive certain advantages that do not apply to other groups or to all the public.[30]

The Equal Protection Clause does not prevent a governmental entity from classifying businesses for purposes of regulation so long

---

27. Allied Stores of Ohio, Inc. v. Bowers, 358 U.S. 522, 79 S. Ct. 437, 441, 3 L. Ed. 2d 480, 9 Ohio Op. 2d 321, 82 Ohio L. Abs. 312 (1959).

28. Torao Takahashi v. Fish and Game Commission, 334 U.S. 410, 68 S. Ct. 1138, 92 L. Ed. 1478 (1948).

29. State of Ohio ex rel. Clarke v. Deckebach, 274 U.S. 392, 47 S. Ct. 630, 71 L. Ed. 1115 (1927).

30. Kotch v. Board of River Port Pilot Com'rs for Port of New Orleans, 330 U.S. 552, 67 S. Ct. 910, 91 L. Ed. 1093, 1096-97 (1947).

as there is a reasonable basis for the differentiated treatment. Thus, the Supreme Court states:

> If the selection or classification is neither capricious nor arbitrary, and rests upon some reasonable consideration of difference or policy, there is no denial of equal protection of the laws.[31]

In sustaining some remarkable classifications in Sunday laws, the Court observed in 1961:

> Although no precise formula has been developed, the Court has held that the Fourteenth Amendment permits the States a wide scope of discretion in enacting laws which affect some groups of citizens differently than others. The constitutional safeguard is offended only if the classification rests on grounds wholly irrelevant to the achievement of the State's objective. State legislatures are presumed to have acted within their constitutional power despite the fact that, in practice, their laws result in some inequality. A statutory discrimination will not be set aside if any state of facts reasonably may be conceived to justify it.[32]

In denying women who were neither wives nor daughters of tavern owners the opportunity to work as barmaids, the Michigan legislature did not, according to the Supreme Court, draw the line "without a basis in reason," adding that this is all that is required. "The Constitution does not require situations which are different in fact or opinion to be treated in law as though they were the same," said the Court.[33] Similarly, ruled the Court, Kansas could limit the business of debt adjustment to lawyers. Said the Court:

> Statutes create many classifications which do not deny equal protection; it is only "invidious discrimination" which offends the Constitution. . . . If the State of Kansas wants to limit debt adjusting to lawyers, the Equal Protection Clause does not forbid it.[34]

A classification having some reasonable basis does not offend

---

31. Brown-Forman Co. v. Commonwealth of Kentucky, 217 U.S. 563, 573, 30 S. Ct. 578, 54 L. Ed. 883, 887 (1910).

32. McGowan v. Maryland, 366 U.S. 420, 81 S. Ct. 1101, 6 L. Ed. 2d 393, 399, 17 Ohio Op. 2d 151 (1961).

33. Goesaert v. Cleary, 335 U.S. 464, 69 S. Ct. 198, 93 L. Ed. 163, 165-66 (1948).

34. Ferguson v. Skrupa, 372 U.S. 726, 83 S. Ct. 1028, 10 L. Ed. 2d 93, 95, 95 A.L.R.2d 1347 (1963).

against the Equal Protection Clause merely because it is not made with mathematical nicety or because in practice it results in some inequality.[35] In sustaining a statute regulating restaurants and eating places in hotels, while exempting eating houses operated in connection with railroads, the Supreme Court through Justice Holmes stated in 1919:

> The 14th Amendment is not a pedagogical requirement of the impracticable. The equal protection of the laws does not mean that all occupations that are called by the same name must be treated in the same way. The power of the state may be determined by degrees of evil, or exercised in cases where detriment is specially experienced. It may do what it can to prevent what is deemed an evil, and stop short of those cases in which the harm to the few concerned is thought less important than the harm to the public that would ensue if the rule laid down were made mathematically exact.[36]

The Court has referred to as "a truism" the proposition "that the Equal Protection Clause does not require that every state regulatory statute apply to all in the same business."[37] Where size is an index of the evil at which the law is directed, discrimination between large and small entrepreneurs is permissible.[38] "Distinctions in the treatment of business entitles engaged in the same business activity," says the Court, "may be justified by genuinely different characteristics of the business involved. This is so even where the discrimination is by name."[39]

The concept of equal protection permits a government to initiate regulation by controlling some aspect of an industry without reaching all. Many times the Supreme Court has acknowledged that

---

35. Gallagher v. Crown Kosher Super Market of Mass., Inc., 366 U.S. 617, 81 S. Ct. 1122, 6 L. Ed. 2d 536, 81, 17 Ohio Op. 2d 195 (1961); Lindsley v. Natural Carbonic Gas Co., 220 U.S. 61, 31 S. Ct. 337, 55 L. Ed. 369, 377 (1911).

36. Dominion Hotel v. State of Arizona, 249 U.S. 265, 39 S. Ct. 273, 63 L. Ed. 597 (1919).

37. Morey v. Doud, 354 U.S. 457, 77 S. Ct. 1344, 1 L. Ed. 2d 1485, 1491 (1957) (overruled on other grounds by, City of New Orleans v. Dukes, 427 U.S. 297, 96 S. Ct. 2513, 49 L. Ed. 2d 511 (1976)).

38. Engel v. O'Malley, 219 U.S. 128, 138, 31 S. Ct. 190, 55 L. Ed. 128, 136 (1911); Morey v. Doud, 354 U.S. 457, 77 S. Ct. 1344, 1 L. Ed. 2d 1485, 1491 (1957) (overruled on other grounds by, City of New Orleans v. Dukes, 427 U.S. 297, 96 S. Ct. 2513, 49 L. Ed. 2d 511 (1976)) (citing cases).

39. Morey v. Doud, 354 U.S. 457, 77 S. Ct. 1344, 1 L. Ed. 2d 1485, 1492 (1957) (overruled on other grounds by, City of New Orleans v. Dukes, 427 U.S. 297, 96 S. Ct. 2513, 49 L. Ed. 2d 511 (1976)).

"reform may take one step at a time, addressing itself to the phase of the problem which seems most acute to the legislative mind."[40]

By way of exemplifying the foregoing rules, the Court has upheld regulations of business which: denied bartender licenses to women unless they were the wife or daughter of the male owner;[41] in effect denied pilot licenses at the Port of Orleans to all but relatives of previously licensed pilots;[42] applied to restaurants and dining places in hotels but did not apply to dining houses operated by railroads.[43] required in 1976 a license for all those purveying food from pushcarts on the streets, but exempting all who were engaged in this business on January 1, 1972.[44]

On the other hand, the Court has voided regulations of business which: required licenses of firms issuing money orders, but exempted the American Express Company;[45] required motor common carriers to furnish bonds or insurance policies for the protection of the public against injuries, but excepted vehicles carrying specified products;[46] denied stock insurance companies the right to act through salaried resident employees, but permitted mutual insurance companies to so act;[47] in effect denied a person the right to engage in an occupation solely because he was Chinese.[48]

Even though a statute or ordinance is fair on its face, there will be a denial of equal protection from its application in an arbitrarily discriminatory manner. Thus, in the leading case of *Yick Wo v. Hopkins*, the Supreme Court stated:

> Though the law itself be fair on its face and impartial in appearance, yet, if it is applied and administered by public author-

---

40. Williamson v. Lee Optical of Okl., 348 U.S. 483, 489, 75 S. Ct. 461, 99 L. Ed. 563, 573 (1955); Morey v. Doud, 354 U.S. 457, 77 S. Ct. 1344, 1 L. Ed. 2d 1485, 1491 (1957) (overruled on other grounds by, City of New Orleans v. Dukes, 427 U.S. 297, 96 S. Ct. 2513, 49 L. Ed. 2d 511 (1976)).

41. Goesaert v. Cleary, 335 U.S. 464, 69 S. Ct. 198, 93 L. Ed. 163 (1948).

42. Kotch v. Board of River Port Pilot Com'rs for Port of New Orleans, 330 U.S. 552, 67 S. Ct. 910, 91 L. Ed. 1093 (1947).

43. Dominion Hotel v. State of Arizona, 249 U.S. 265, 39 S. Ct. 273, 63 L. Ed. 597 (1919).

44. City of New Orleans v. Dukes, 427 U.S. 297, 96 S. Ct. 2513, 49 L. Ed. 2d 511 (1976).

45. Morey v. Doud, 354 U.S. 457, 77 S. Ct. 1344, 1 L. Ed. 2d 1485 (1957) (overruled on other grounds by, City of New Orleans v. Dukes, 427 U.S. 297, 96 S. Ct. 2513, 49 L. Ed. 2d 511 (1976)).

46. Smith v. Cahoon, 283 U.S. 553, 51 S. Ct. 582, 75 L. Ed. 1264 (1931).

47. Hartford Steam Boiler Inspection & Ins. Co. v. Harrison, 301 U.S. 459, 57 S. Ct. 838, 81 L. Ed. 1223 (1937).

48. Yick Wo v. Hopkins, 118 U.S. 356, 6 S. Ct. 1064, 30 L. Ed. 220 (1886).

ity with an evil eye and an unequal hand, so as practically to make unjust and illegal discriminations between persons in similar circumstances, material to their rights, the denial of equal justice is still within the prohibition of the Constitution.[49]

§ 21.03. Taxation of private enterprise—due process limitations

Due process of law permits the taxation of private enterprise when there is "a sufficient nexus between such a tax and transactions within a state for which the tax is an exaction."[50] It is constitutional to tax when the taxpayer is "sufficiently involved in local events to forge some definite link, some minimum connection sufficient to satisfy due process requirements."[51]

Conversely, due process of law is violated in the imposition of state excise taxes upon entrepreneurs when the taxpayers' contacts with the taxing jurisdiction are so limited that it would be unfair that the firm pay the tax. The United States Supreme Court treats as "firmly established the doctrine that when a tax is imposed on an out-of-state vendor, 'nexus' between the taxing State and the taxpayer is the outstanding prerequisite on state power to tax. Consistent with this requirement, there must be some 'definite link, some minimum connection, between a state and the person, property or transaction it seeks to tax.'"[52]

Under this general rule, state and local taxes upon activities will be valid so long as the tax bears some reasonable fiscal relationship to the protection, opportunities, and benefits given by the taxing entity—otherwise stated, when the governmental entity has provided the taxpayer with something for which in fairness it can ask such a return. For example, in sustaining a Wisconsin tax on foreign corporations permitted to do local business in that state, measured by dividends attributable to Wisconsin business, the Supreme Court stated:

> A state is free to pursue its own fiscal policies, unembarrassed by the Constitution, if by the practical operation of a tax a state has exerted its power in relation to opportunities which it has given, to protection which it has afforded, to benefits which it

49. Yick Wo v. Hopkins, 118 U.S. 356, 373, 6 S. Ct. 1064, 30 L. Ed. 220, 227-28 (1886).

50. State of Wisconsin v. J.C. Penney Co., 311 U.S. 435, 445, 61 S. Ct. 246, 85 L. Ed. 267, 271, 130 A.L.R. 1229 (1940).

51. Northwestern States Portland Cement Co. v. State of Minn., 358 U.S. 450, 79 S. Ct. 357, 3 L. Ed. 2d 421, 481, 67 A.L.R.2d 1292 (1959).

52. American Oil Co. v. Neill, 380 U.S. 451, 85 S. Ct. 1130, 14 L. Ed. 2d 1, 5-6 (1965).

has conferred. . . . The simple but controlling question is whether the state has given anything for which it can ask a return.[53]

Due process of law permits a state to impose both net income and gross receipts taxes upon nonresidents and foreign corporations, so long as the taxes are reasonably apportioned to the income or receipts from the local business.[54] The Supreme Court states generally that:

> the Due Process Clause places two restrictions on a State's power to tax income generated by the activities of an interstate business. First, no tax may be imposed, unless there is some minimal connection between those actions and the taxing state. . . . Second, the income attributed to the State for tax purposes must be rationally related to values connected with the taxing state.[55]

The Commerce Clause, too, permits such taxation.[56]

Where the interstate business being taxed is a unitary enterprise, a state can with a properly apportioned net income tax include in the tax base dividends received by the taxpayer from foreign sources.[57] The Supreme Court has refrained from attempting to define any single appropriate method of apportionment, but has sought to ensure that the methods used display a modicum of reasonable relation to business activities within the taxing state. The Court has approved formulae based on the geographical distribution of corporate property and those based on the standard three-factor formula of plant, payroll, and sales. Says the Court: "The standard three-factor formula can be justified as a rough, practical approximation of the distribution of either a corporation's sources of income or the social

---

53. State of Wisconsin v. J.C. Penney Co., 311 U.S. 435, 445, 61 S. Ct. 246, 85 L. Ed. 267, 271, 130 A.L.R. 1229 (1940).

54. Northwestern States Portland Cement Co. v. State of Minn., 358 U.S. 450, 79 S. Ct. 357, 3 L. Ed. 2d 421, 67 A.L.R.2d 1292 (1959); General Motors Corp. v. Washington, 377 U.S. 436, 84 S. Ct. 1564, 12 L. Ed. 2d 430 (1964) (overruled on other grounds by, Tyler Pipe Industries, Inc. v. Washington State Dept. of Revenue, 483 U.S. 232, 107 S. Ct. 2810, 97 L. Ed. 2d 199 (1987)).

55. Moorman Mfg. Co. v. Bair, 437 U.S. 267, 98 S. Ct. 2340, 57 L. Ed. 2d 197 (1978).

56. Exxon Corp. v. Wisconsin Dept. of Revenue, 447 U.S. 207, 100 S. Ct. 2109, 65 L. Ed. 2d 66 (1980).

57. Mobil Oil Corp. v. Commissioner of Taxes of Vermont, 445 U.S. 425, 100 S. Ct. 1223, 63 L. Ed. 2d 510 (1980) (subsidiaries and affiliates operating outside the United States).

costs which it generates."[58] There is a hint in the *District of Columbia* case that an apportionment on the basis of the sales factor alone may be invalid.

Due process of law allows a state to tax the income of a resident earned in another state, including income from land in another state. "It would be pressing the protection which the due process clause throws around the taxpayer too far," says the Court, "to say that because a state is prohibited from taxing land which it neither protects nor controls, it is likewise prohibited from taxing the receipt and command of income from the land by its resident, who is subject to its control and enjoys the benefits of its laws."[59]

Consistent with due process of law, many activities involving intangibles can be taxed by states not the domicile of the owner. Thus, where all right, title, and interest has been fused by the proper law into a stock certificate, its transfer can be taxed by the state of transfer, though it is issued by a foreign corporation and owned by a nonresident.[60] So, too, the transfer of a stock certificate at death can be taxed by the state of transfer, though the owner and certificate are both outside the state.[61] The exercise within a state of a power of appointment over tangibles can be taxed there.[62] Acting within a state as trustee of intangibles created by a nonresident for nonresident beneficiaries can also be taxed.[63]

A state where land or tangible chattels have situs can tax the inheritance of the chattels. A state, however, cannot tax the inheritance of land located outside the state, nor can a state under due process tax the inheritance of tangible personal property owned by a domiciliary where the property has acquired a situs outside the state.[64] Any state providing protection to intangible interests can tax

---

58. General Motors Corp. v. District of Columbia, 380 U.S. 553, 85 S. Ct. 1156, 14 L. Ed. 2d 68, 73 (1965).

59. People of State of New York ex rel. Cohn v. Graves, 300 U.S. 308, 314, 57 S. Ct. 466, 81 L. Ed. 666, 671, 108 A.L.R. 721 (1937).

60. People of State of New York ex rel. Hatch v. Reardon, 204 U.S. 152, 27 S. Ct. 188, 51 L. Ed. 415 (1907).

61. State Tax Commission of Utah v. Aldrich, 316 U.S. 174, 62 S. Ct. 1008, 86 L. Ed. 1358, 139 A.L.R. 1436 (1942).

62. Graves v. Schmidlapp, 315 U.S. 657, 62 S. Ct. 870, 86 L. Ed. 1097, 141 A.L.R. 948 (1942); Curry v. McCanless, 307 U.S. 357, 59 S. Ct. 900, 83 L. Ed. 1339, 123 A.L.R. 162 (1939).

63. Greenough v. Tax Assessors of City of Newport, 331 U.S. 486, 67 S. Ct. 1400, 91 L. Ed. 1621, 172 A.L.R. 329 (1947).

64. Frick v. Com. of Pennsylvania, 268 U.S. 473, 45 S. Ct. 603, 69 L. Ed. 1058, 42 A.L.R. 316 (1925); Treichler v. State of Wis., 338 U.S. 251, 70 S. Ct. 1, 94 L. Ed. 37 (1949).

their succession.[65] For example, the Supreme Court has said: "We perceive no better reason for denying the right of New York to impose a succession tax on debts owned by its citizens than upon tangible chattels found within the State at the time of the death."[66]

At times the Court has allowed governmental entities to use the tax power to destroy what had been previously considered a lawful endeavor. For example, in 1934 the Court affirmed a Washington tax of fifteen cents per pound on the sale of all butter substitutes. The protesting company had made an annual profit of over twenty thousand dollars from selling "Nucoa," an oleomargarine, but the profit disappeared completely under the tax. Among other things, the Court said:

> Except in rare and special instances, the Due Process Of Law Clause contained in the Fifth Amendment is not a limitation upon the taxing power conferred upon Congress by the Constitution. And no reason exists for applying a different rule against a state in the case of the Fourteenth Amendment. That clause is applicable to a taxing statute such as the one here assailed only if the act be so arbitrary as to compel the conclusion that it does not involve exertion of the taxing power, but constitutes, in substance and effect, the direct exertion of a different and forbidden power, as, for example, the confiscation of property.

The Court continued:

> Collateral purposes or motives of a legislature in levying a tax of a kind within the reach of its lawful power are matters beyond the scope of judicial inquiry. Nor may a tax within the lawful power of a state be judicially stricken down under the Due Process Clause simply because its enforcement may or will result in restricting or even destroying particular occupations or business . . . unless indeed, . . . its necessary interpretation and effect be such as plainly to demonstrate that the form of taxation was adopted as a mere disguise, under which there was exercised, in reality, another and different power denied by the federal Constitution to the State. The present case does not furnish such a demonstration.

---

65. State Tax Commission of Utah v. Aldrich, 316 U.S. 174, 62 S. Ct. 1008, 86 L. Ed. 1358, 139 A.L.R. 1436 (1942).

66. Blackstone v. Miller, 188 U.S. 189, 206, 23 S. Ct. 277, 47 L. Ed. 439, 445 (1903) (overruled in part on other grounds by, Farmers' Loan & Trust Co. v. State of Minnesota, 280 U.S. 204, 50 S. Ct. 98, 74 L. Ed. 371, 65 A.L.R. 1000 (1930)).

The Court concluded:

> The point may be conceded that the tax is so excessive that it
> may or will result in destroying the intrastate business of appel-
> lant; but . . . the power to tax may be exercised oppressively
> upon persons, but the responsibility of the legislature is not to
> the courts, but to the people by whom its members are elected.
> . . . From the beginning of our government, the courts have
> sustained taxes imposed with the collateral intent of effecting
> ulterior ends which, considered apart, were beyond the
> constitutional power of the lawmakers to realize by legislation
> directly addressed to their accomplishment.[67]

It is suggested the Court was wrong. An average efficient entrepre-
neur in an activity not harmful to the public should be no more
subject to being driven out of business by oppressive taxation than
by executive or legislative fiat. There is no conceivable reason why
the state should be permitted to destroy lawful businesses by the
indirect means of the tax power when it could not do so directly
under the police power.

In 1981 the Supreme Court ruled not violative of due process of
law was a 1976 amendment to the Internal Revenue Code when
made applicable to transactions prior to the enactment of the amendment, but that same year.[68]

§ 21.04. —equal protection limitations

Equal protection of the laws will not permit a government to tax
businesses, activities or events with invidious or arbitrary discrimination.[69] "The State," says the United States Supreme Court, "must
proceed upon a rational basis and must not resort to a classification
that is palpably arbitrary."[70] On another occasion the Court stated:
"Arbitrary selection can never be justified by calling it classification.
. . . The mere fact of classification is not sufficient to relieve a
statute from the reach of the Equality Clause of the Fourteenth
Amendment . . . it must appear . . . that it is one based upon some

---

67. A. Magnano Co. v. Hamilton, 292 U.S. 40, 44, 54 S. Ct. 599, 78 L. Ed.
1109, 1114 (1934).

68. U.S. v. Darusmont, 449 U.S. 292, 101 S. Ct. 549, 66 L. Ed. 2d 513 (1981)

69. Connolly v. Union Sewer Pipe Co., 184 U.S. 540, 22 S. Ct. 431, 46 L. Ed.
679 (1902) (overruled in part on other grounds by, Tigner v. Texas. 310 U.S. 141,
60 S. Ct. 879, 84 L. Ed. 1124, 130 A.L.R. 1321 (1940)); Quaker City Cab Co. v.
Commonwealth of Pennsylvania, 277 U.S. 389, 48 S. Ct. 553, 72 L. Ed. 927
(1928).

70. Allied Stores of Ohio, Inc. v. Bowers, 358 U.S. 522, 79 S. Ct. 437, 3 L. Ed.
2d 480, 484-85, 9 Ohio Op. 2d 321, 82 Ohio L. Abs. 312 (1959).

reasonable ground.''[71] Equal protection, the Court has elsewhere emphasized, ''does require that the classification be not arbitrary but based on a real and substantial difference having a reasonable relation to the subject of the particular legislation.''[72]

Equal protection does not prevent governmental entities from classifying business and activities for the purpose of taxation, so long as the classification is reasonable. The power of a State to classify for purpose of taxation is very broad. ''The States have a very wide discretion in the laying of their taxes,'' says the Supreme Court.[73] In 1973 the Court sustained a state law taxing corporations' personal property, but not personal property owned by individuals, the Court stating: ''Where taxation is concerned and no specific federal right, apart from equal protection, is imperiled, the states have large leeway in making classifications and drawing lines which in their judgment produces reasonable systems of taxation.''[74]

Equal protection only requires that classifications rest on real and not feigned differences, that the distinctions have some relevance to the purpose for which the classification is made, and that the different treatments be not so disparate, relative to the difference in classification, as to be wholly arbitrary.[75] According to the Court, the Equal Protection Clause ''imposes no iron rule of equality, prohibiting the flexibility and variety that are appropriate to reasonable schemes of state taxation. A state may impose different specific taxes upon different trades and professions and may vary the rate of excise upon various products. It is not required to resort to close distinctions or to maintain a precise, scientific uniformity with reference to composition, use or value.''[76]

A tax is not automatically invalid because the state has left untaxed some businesses, occupations or activities. The Supreme Court has said:

> A tax may be imposed only upon certain callings and trades,

---

71. Connolly v. Union Sewer Pipe Co., 184 U.S. 540, 560, 22 S. Ct. 431, 46 L. Ed. 679, 690 (1902) (overruled in part on other grounds by, Tigner v. Texas, 310 U.S. 141, 60 S. Ct. 879, 84 L. Ed. 1124, 130 A.L.R. 1321 (1940)).

72. Quaker City Cab Co. v. Commonwealth of Pennsylvania, 277 U.S. 389, 400, 48 S. Ct. 553, 72 L. Ed. 927, 929 (1928).

73. Allied Stores of Ohio, Inc. v. Bowers, 358 U.S. 522, 79 S. Ct. 437, 3 L. Ed. 2d 480, 484-85, 9 Ohio Op. 2d 321, 82 Ohio L. Abs. 312 (1959).

74. Lehnhausen v. Lake Shore Auto Parts Co., 410 U.S. 356, 93 S. Ct. 1001, 35 L. Ed. 2d 351 (1973).

75. Walters v. City of St. Louis, Mo., 347 U.S. 231, 74 S. Ct. 505, 509, 98 L. Ed. 660, 665 (1954).

76. Allied Stores of Ohio, Inc. v. Bowers, 358 U.S. 522, 79 S. Ct. 437, 441, 3 L. Ed. 2d 480, 9 Ohio Op. 2d 321, 82 Ohio L. Abs. 312 (1959).

for when the State exerts its power to tax, it is not bound to tax all pursuits or all property that may be legitimately taxed for governmental purposes. It would be an intolerable burden if a State could not tax any property or calling unless, at the same time, it taxed all property or all callings. Its discretion in such matters is very great.[77]

On another occasion the Court asserted that a state "may even tax wholesalers of specified articles on account of their occupation without exacting a similar tax on the occupations of wholesale dealers in other articles."[78] Comparably, the Court has spoken of as "familiar doctrine" the rule that governments have a "wide discretion" in allowing exemptions and deductions from their taxes.[79]

The Court has generally found no denial of equal protection in tax statutes adjusting the amount of the tax to the business done.[80] The Court has sustained "chain store tax statutes" whereby, for example, the owner of one store was taxed $3 while the owner of over 20 stores was taxed $25 per store.[81]

On the other hand, the Court stated in 1981 that, whatever the extent of a state's authority to exclude foreign corporations from doing local business within its boundaries, "that authority does not justify imposition of more onerous taxes or other burdens on foreign corporations than imposed on domestic corporations, unless the discrimination between foreign and domestic corporations bears a rational relation to a legitimate purpose." On the facts of the particular case, the Court held that a retaliatory state tax upon foreign insurance corporations doing business there did not violate equal protection of the laws, since it was at least debatable that the statute advanced a legitimate end of the state.[82]

---

77. Connolly v. Union Sewer Pipe Co., 184 U.S. 540, 562, 22 S. Ct. 431, 46 L. Ed. 679, 690 (1902) (overruled in part on other grounds by, Tigner v. Texas, 310 U.S. 141, 60 S. Ct. 879, 84 L. Ed. 1124, 130 A.L.R. 1321 (1940)).

78. Walters v. City of St. Louis, Mo., 347 U.S. 231, 74 S. Ct. 505, 509-10, 98 L. Ed. 660, 665-66 (1954).

79. Aero Mayflower Transit Co. v. Georgia Public Serv. Com'n, 295 U.S. 285, 55 S. Ct. 709, 79 L. Ed. 1439 (1935).

80. Clark v. City of Titusville, 184 U.S. 329, 22 S. Ct. 382, 46 L. Ed. 569 (1902).

81. State Board of Tax Com'rs of Ind. v. Jackson, 283 U.S. 527, 51 S. Ct. 540, 75 L. Ed. 1248, 73 A.L.R. 1464, 75 A.L.R. 1536 (1931); Great Atlantic & Pacific Tea Co. v. Grosjean, 301 U.S. 412, 57 S. Ct. 772, 81 L. Ed. 1193, 112 A.L.R. 293 (1937).

82. Western and Southern Life Ins. Co. v. State Bd. of Equalization of California, 451 U.S. 648, 101 S. Ct. 2070, 68 L. Ed. 2d 514 (1981).

CHAPTER TWENTY-TWO

Freedom of Contract

---

§ 22.00. Fifth and Fourteenth Amendment protection—generally

Freedom of contract is a basic right, protected under the liberty concept of both the Fifth and Fourteenth Amendment Due Process Clauses.[1] The United States Supreme Court long ago indicated that it is "not disposed to question" that "freedom in the making of contracts . . . is an elementary part of the rights of personal liberty and private property, not to be struck down directly, or arbitrarily interfered with, consistently with the due process of law guaranteed by the Fourteenth Amendment."[2]

The Due Process Clauses allow governmental regulation of freedom of contract so long as the control is not arbitrary. Otherwise stated, this freedom "is subject to such restraints as the State in the

---

1. Prudential Ins. Co. of America v. Cheek, 259 U.S. 530, 536, 42 S. Ct. 516, 66 L. Ed. 1044, 1051, 27 A.L.R. 27 (1922).

2. Adair v. U.S., 208 U.S. 161, 174, 28 S. Ct. 277, 52 L. Ed. 436, 442 (1908) (overruled in part on other grounds by, Phelps Dodge Corp. v. N.L.R.B., 313 U.S. 177, 61 S. Ct. 845, 85 L. Ed. 1271, 133 A.L.R. 1217 (1941)).

exertion of its police power reasonably may put upon it."[3] The applicable law has been stated thus by the Supreme Court:

> Freedom of contract is a qualified and not an absolute right. There is no absolute freedom to do as one wills or to contract as one chooses. The guaranty of liberty does not withdraw from legislative supervision that wide department of activity which consists of the making of contracts, or deny to government the power to provide restrictive safeguards. Liberty implies the absence of arbitrary restraints, not immunity from reasonable regulations and prohibitions imposed in the interests of the community.[4]

Governmental regulations of freedom of contract currently are accorded a presumption of reasonableness and constitutionality by the Supreme Court.[5]

§ 22.01. Contracts with the United States Government

Rights arising out of contracts with the United States are protected against action by the government under the Due Process Clause of the Fifth Amendment. Thus, in 1934 the Supreme Court through Justice Brandeis stated:

> The Fifth Amendment commands that property be not taken without making just compensation. Valid contracts are property, whether the obligor be a private individual, a municipality, a State or the United States. Rights against the United States arising out of a contract with it are protected by the Fifth Amendment.[6]

Congress is completely without power to abrogate contractual obligations of the United States. In 1879 the Supreme Court stated:

> The United States are as much bound by their contracts as are individuals. If they repudiate their obligations, it is as much repudiation, with all the wrong and reproach that term implies,

---

3. Advance-Rumely Thresher Co. v. Jackson, 287 U.S. 283, 53 S. Ct. 133, 77 L. Ed. 306, 309, 87 A.L.R. 285 (1932).

4. Chicago, B. & Q.R. Co. v. McGuire, 219 U.S. 549, 567, 31 S. Ct. 259, 55 L. Ed. 328, 338 (1911); Note also: Prudential Ins. Co. of America v. Cheek, 259 U.S. 530, 536, 42 S. Ct. 516, 66 L. Ed. 1044, 1051, 27 A.L.R. 27 (1922).

5. O'Gorman & Young, Inc. v. Hartford Fire Ins. Co., 282 U.S. 251, 51 S. Ct. 130, 75 L. Ed. 324, 72 A.L.R. 1163 (1931).

6. Lynch v. U.S., 292 U.S. 571, 54 S. Ct. 840, 78 L. Ed. 1434, 1440 (1934).

as it would be if the repudiator had been a State or a municipality or a citizen.[7]

In the leading case, *Perry v. United States*, the Court in 1935 held that a Congressional joint resolution repudiating the Government's earlier obligation to pay gold on certain certificates "went beyond the congressional power."[8] In 1969 the Court again acknowledged that the Fifth Amendment protects rights arising out of contracts with the federal government. The Court ruled, however, that the Department of Housing and Urban Development could, because of its "wholly independent rule-making power," impose new obligations upon a local housing authority not contained in the original contract, in the form of a new circular requiring housing authorities financed by federal funds to give reasons to tenants before their evictions. The Court added: "The obligations of each of these contracts, however, can be impaired only by a law which renders them invalid, or releases or extinguishes them [or by a law] which without destroying [the] contracts, derogates from substantial contractual rights. The HUD circular does neither."[9]

Even though the federal Social Security Act, when California entered the system, permitted states to withdraw, Congress had reserved the power to amend the Act and, accordingly, California was held not to have a "property" subject to Fifth Amendment due process protection violated by a subsequent Congressional act prohibiting states and local governments from withdrawing from the Social Security System.[10]

§ 22.02. Forbidden contracts

Notwithstanding a general liberty of contract, it has been accepted since the adoption of the Constitution that certain contracts can be forbidden when it is reasonably necessary to do so to protect the public health, safety, morality, or general welfare. Thus, a state can make void such contracts as those to commit a crime,[11] to interfere

---

7. Sinking-Fund Cases, 99 U.S. 700, 25 L. Ed. 496, 504 (Ct. Cl. 1878).

8. Perry v. U.S., 294 U.S. 330, 55 S. Ct. 432, 79 L. Ed. 912, 919, 95 A.L.R. 1335 (Ct. Cl. 1935).

9. Thorpe v. Housing Authority of City of Durham, 393 U.S. 268, 89 S. Ct. 518, 21 L. Ed. 2d 474, 49 Ohio Op. 2d 374 (1969).

10. Bowen v. Public Agencies Opposed To Social Sec. Entrapment, 477 U.S. 41, 106 S. Ct. 2390, 91 L. Ed. 2d 35 (1986).

11. Hoggard v. Dickerson, 180 Mo. App. 70, 165 S.W. 1135 (1914).

improperly with judicial, legislative or administrative action,[12] or to restrain trade unreasonably.[13]

§ 22.03. Reading into, and requiring certain clauses in, contracts

Parties contracting can be subjected to many legislative controls—which in effect become parts of the contract—so long as the regulation is reasonable. In 1906, for example, the Supreme Court sustained a Missouri statute cutting off any defense by a life insurance company based upon false and fraudulent statements in the application, unless the matter misrepresented actually contributed to the death of the insured.[14]

On another occasion the Court upheld a North Dakota statute providing in effect that hail insurance companies would be deemed to have accepted applications at the end of 24 hours from the time they were given to agents, unless they notified the applicant to the contrary within that period.[15] And the Court held in 1932 that North Dakota could provide that a buyer in a sales contract could not waive the warranty of fitness.[16]

In 1934 the Court ruled further that a state can impose an attorney's fee upon an insurance company which wrongfully refused to honor its obligations under the insurance contract.[17]

§ 22.04. Contract clause protection—generally

The Contract Clause of the United States Constitution provides: "No State shall . . . pass any . . . law impairing the obligation of contracts."[18] State constitutions often contain comparable clauses prohibiting legislatures from impairing the obligation of contracts.[19] These should, of course, be locally consulted. As is evident from the wording of the Clause, the federal government is not restricted by the language of the Contract Clause.

---

12. Ewing v. National Airport Corporation, 115 F.2d 859 (C.C.A. 4th Cir. 1940).

13. Tawney v. Mutual System of Md., 186 Md. 508, 47 A.2d 372 (1946).

14. Northwestern Nat. Life Ins. Co. v. Riggs, 203 U.S. 243, 27 S. Ct. 126, 51 L. Ed. 168 (1906).

15. National Union Fire Ins. Co. v. Wanberg, 260 U.S. 71, 43 S. Ct. 32, 67 L. Ed. 136 (1922).

16. Advance-Rumely Thresher Co. v. Jackson, 287 U.S. 283, 53 S. Ct. 133, 77 L. Ed. 306, 87 A.L.R. 285 (1932).

17. Life & Cas. Ins. Co. of Tenn. v. McCray, 291 U.S. 566, 54 S. Ct. 482, 78 L. Ed. 987 (1934).

18. United States Constitution, Article 1 § 10.

19. See e.g., Colorado Constitution, Article 2 § 11 (1876).

Where state legislative action does not impair the rights of third parties, state controls over its own units of local government will not violate the Contract Clause. To illustrate, even though a municipality has a valid franchise with a utility indicating rates, the state public service commissions can, so far as the Contract Clause is concerned, increase the rate upon application of the utility.[20]

§ 22.05. —governmental action proscribed

Only one form of governmental action is outlawed by the Contract Clause—namely, the passing of laws or legislative action. Judicial retroactivity affecting contracts is not banned by this Clause. The United States Supreme Court has stated:

> In order to come within the provision of the Constitution of the United States, which declares that no state shall pass any law impairing the obligation of contracts, not only must the obligation of contract be impaired, but it must have been impaired by some act of the legislative power of the state and not by a decision of the judicial department only.[21]

Behavior of the executive or administrative departments of government will not ordinarily be deemed violative of the Contract Clause for the same reason.[22] Thus, a governmental decision to breach a contract, though actionable, is not a violation of the Contract Clause.[23]

Legislative action forbidden by the Contract Clause can take the form of state statutes,[24] state constitutional clauses,[25] and municipal ordinances.[26]

§ 22.06. —private contracts

Private contracts that are valid and enforceable under the ap-

---

20. Railroad Commission of California v. Los Angeles Ry. Corp., 280 U.S. 145, 50 S. Ct. 71, 74 L. Ed. 234 (1929).

21. Central Land Co. of West Virginia v. Laidley, 159 U.S. 103, 16 S. Ct. 80, 82, 40 L. Ed. 91, 94 (1895).

22. New Orleans Waterworks Co. v. Louisiana Sugar-Refining Co., 125 U.S. 18, 8 S. Ct. 741, 31 L. Ed. 607 (1888).

23. Hays v. Port of Seattle, 251 U.S. 233, 40 S. Ct. 125, 64 L. Ed. 243 (1920).

24. U.S. ex rel. Hoffman v. City of Quincy, 71 U.S. 535, 18 L. Ed. 403 (1866).

25. Ohio & M.R. Co. v. McClure, 77 U.S. 511, 19 L. Ed. 997 (1870); Coombes v. Getz, 285 U.S. 434, 52 S. Ct. 435, 76 L. Ed. 866 (1932).

26. John P. King Mfg. Co. v. City Council of Augusta, 277 U.S. 100, 48 S. Ct. 489, 72 L. Ed. 801 (1928).

plicable law are protectable under the Contract Clause.[27] A private contract, for this purpose, is an agreement to which all parties are private persons or corporations.

Most states follow the rule of substantive law to the effect that the present statutory and common law of contracts is part of every contract, and that later valid changes in the law will likewise be part of the undertaking. Indeed, the United States Supreme Court treats this as constitutional doctrine. "The reservation of essential attributes of sovereign power," says the Court, "is also read into contracts as a postulate of the legal order."[28]

§ 22.07. —public contracts

Public contracts, as well as private agreements, are protected by the Contract Clause.[29] A public contract, for this purpose, is a contract to which at least one of the parties is a governmental body.

Bond contracts of the states and their local governments are illustrative of the type of public contracts protectable.[30] The United States Supreme Court held in 1977 that when New Jersey and New York wrote into bond contracts of their Port of New York Authority in 1962 a provision that funds produced by the Authority could not be diverted to railroad purposes not specified in the statute, the Contract Clause of the Federal Constitution was violated when the states in 1974 attempted to repeal this covenant. While observing that "a technical impairment" does not alone violate the Contract Clause, the Court added: "The Contract Clause is not an absolute bar to subsequent modification of a State's own financial obligations. As with laws impairing the obligation of private contracts, an impairment may be constitutional if it is reasonable and necessary to serve an important public purpose," noting however, that "complete deference to a legislative assessment of reasonableness and necessity is not appropriate because the State's self-interest is at stake."[31]

Various grants by states and their political subdivisions, once accepted by a private party, have been deemed contracts within the

---

27. Home Bldg. & Loan Ass'n v. Blaisdell, 290 U.S. 398, 54 S. Ct. 231, 78 L. Ed. 413, 88 A.L.R. 1481 (1934); Taylor v. Thomas, 89 U.S. 479, 22 L. Ed. 789 (1874).

28. Home Bldg. & Loan Ass'n v. Blaisdell, 290 U.S. 398, 437, 54 S. Ct. 231, 78 L. Ed. 413, 428, 88 A.L.R. 1481 (1934).

29. U.S. Trust Co. of New York v. New Jersey, 431 U.S. 1, 97 S. Ct. 1505, 52 L. Ed. 2d 92 (1977).

30. U.S. ex rel. Hoffman v. City of Quincy, 71 U.S. 535, 18 L. Ed. 403 (1866).

31. U.S. Trust Co. of New York v. New Jersey, 431 U.S. 1, 97 S. Ct. 1505, 52 L. Ed. 2d 92 (1977).

meaning of the Contract Clause. Protectable, accordingly, are franchises given to utilities and others,[32] land grants,[33] charters given to private corporations,[34] and tax exemptions.[35]

Charters granted by states to their municipal corporations are not deemed to be contracts within the meaning of this Clause.[36]

The Contract Clause affords no protection to public contracts that are invalid under local law. Most states and their political subdivisions under local law have no power to bargain away either the police power or the power of eminent domain, and, accordingly, contracts of this sort, being invalid, are not protectable under the federal constitution's Contract Clause.[37] "The legislature cannot bargain away the public health or the public morals," observes the Supreme Court.[38]

In many states, under the governing local law, municipal corporations can by contract agree not to exercise their rate-making powers over various utilities and where valid such agreements are protected under the Contract Clause. The Supreme Court has indicated:

> It is possible for a state to authorize a municipal corporation by agreement to establish public service rates and thereby to suspend for a term of years not grossly excessive the exertion of governmental power by legislative action to fix just compensation to be paid for service furnished by public utilities.[39]

§ 22.08. —permissible changes in remedies

It has been traditional constitutional law that, notwithstanding the Contract Clause, states could change the remedies available to parties having protected contracts without violating the Clause. The

---

32. New Orleans Gas-light Co. v. Louisiana Light & Heat Producing & Manufacturing Co., 115 U.S. 650, 6 S. Ct. 252, 29 L. Ed. 516 (1885).

33. Fletcher v. Peck, 10 U.S. 87, 3 L. Ed. 162 (1810).

34. Trustees of Dartmouth College v. Woodward, 17 U.S. 518, 4 L. Ed. 629 (1819).

35. Atlantic Coast Line R. Co. v. Phillips, 332 U.S. 168, 67 S. Ct. 1584, 91 L. Ed. 1977, 173 A.L.R. 1 (1947).

36. City of Trenton v. State of New Jersey, 262 U.S. 182, 43 S. Ct. 534, 67 L. Ed. 937, 29 A.L.R. 1471 (1923).

37. Contributors to Pennsylvania Hospital v. City of Philadelphia, 245 U.S. 20, 38 S. Ct. 35, 62 L. Ed. 124 (1917).

38. Home Bldg. & Loan Ass'n v. Blaisdell, 290 U.S. 398, 437, 54 S. Ct. 231, 78 L. Ed. 413, 428, 88 A.L.R. 1481 (1934).

39. Railroad Commission of California v. Los Angeles Ry. Corp., 280 U.S. 145, 151-52, 50 S. Ct. 71, 74 L. Ed. 234, 299-308 (1929); City of Detroit v. Detroit Citizens' St. Ry. Co., 184 U.S. 368, 22 S. Ct. 410, 46 L. Ed. 592 (1902).

distinction was first drawn by Chief Justice Marshall in 1819. He then stated for the Supreme Court:

> The distinction between the obligation of a contract, and the remedy given by the legislature to enforce that obligation, has been taken at the bar, and exists in the nature of things. Without impairing the obligation of the contract, the remedy may certainly be modified as the wisdom of the nation shall direct.[40]

As later generations have learned about the disappearing line between substance and procedure, so, too, the distinction between obligation and remedy may be less than Marshall suspected. It can safely be conjectured that a legislative attempt to strip a contracting party of all remedies would impress the Supreme Court as violative of the Contract Clause. That tribunal, indeed, has indicated that the Clause is violated when a state so changes "the existing remedy that there is no effective and enforceable one left, or the remedy is so impaired that the party desirous of enforcing the contract is left practically without any efficient means of doing so."[41] On another occasion the Court has stated:

> The legislature may modify, limit, or alter the remedy for enforcement of a contract without impairing its obligation but, in so doing, it may not deny all remedy or so circumscribe the existing remedy with conditions and restrictions as seriously to impair the value of the right. The particular remedy existing at the date of the contract may be altogether abrogated if another equally effective for the enforcement of the obligation remains or is substituted for the one taken away.[42]

The Court admits that it has made no successful attempt "to fix definitely the line between the alterations of the remedy, which are to be deemed legitimate, and those which under the form of modifying the remedy impair substantial rights." It could only indicate: "Every case must be determined upon its own circumstances."[43]

Notwithstanding the Marshallian auspices, it is suggested that the duality between obligation and remedy be discarded; that changes in either be permitted under the Contract Clause when reasonably necessary to safeguard the common weal. For the time being, the

---

40. Sturges v. Crowninshield, 17 U.S. 122, 4 L. Ed. 529, 549 (1819).

41. Waggoner v. Flack, 188 U.S. 595, 23 S. Ct. 345, 348, 47 L. Ed. 609 (1903).

42. Richmond Mortgage & Loan Corporation v. Wachovia Bank & Trust Co., 300 U.S. 124, 128, 57 S. Ct. 338, 81 L. Ed. 552, 555, 108 A.L.R. 886 (1937).

43. U.S. ex rel. Hoffman v. City of Quincy, 71 U.S. 535, 18 L. Ed. 403, 409 (1866).

Court suggests that it is constitutional if a remedy "is left or provided which is fairly sufficient."[44]

§ 22.09. —permissible changes in obligations

At an earlier date, while a seeming distinction separated obligation from remedy, changes in the former were often suggested to be as impermissible as changes in the latter were allowable. This was never sound and clearly in error since at least 1878, as a previous section has indicated.

Today the Supreme Court is clear that changes in the obligation, like changes in remedy, can be constitutional. A statute imposing a "minimal burden on contractual obligations is not violative of the Contract Clause," according to the Court in 1982.[45] However, where the contractual obligation being changed by legislative action is the state's own, the Supreme Court under the Contract Clause should scrupulously hold the states to their obligations unless a change is imperatively demanded to protect the people of the state in one of their most compelling interests. In 1965 the Court stated: "It is not every modification of a contractual promise that impairs the obligation of contract under federal law." In that year the Court, in sustaining a Texas statute limiting to five years previously unlimited rights to reinstate contracts of purchase of public lands by paying missed installments of principal and interest, remarked:

> Laws which restrict a party to those gains reasonably to be expected from the contract are not subject to attack under the Contract Clause, notwithstanding that they technically alter an obligation of a contract.

In concluding that the five-year limitation allowed defaulting purchasers was a reasonable time to reinstate, the Court observed that the state "need not allow defaulting purchasers with a speculative interest in the discovery of minerals to remain in endless default while retaining a cloud on title." Justice Black dissented. He stated:

> A State may not pass a law repudiating contractual obligations without compensating the injured parties. Especially should this be true when, as in the case before us, the contractual obligation repudiated is the State's own. . . . It is not the happiest of days for me when one of our wealthiest States is permit-

---

44. Waggoner v. Flack, 188 U.S. 595, 23 S. Ct. 345, 348, 47 L. Ed. 609, 612 (1903).

45. Texaco, Inc. v. Short, 454 U.S. 516, 102 S. Ct. 781, 70 L. Ed. 2d 738 (1982).

ted to enforce a law that breaks faith with those who contracted with it.[46]

Without accepting any absolutist interpretation of the Contract Clause, one must agree that the states are to be held to contractual integrity by the Contract Clause. Changes in the contract in the case above cannot be justified as imperatively or even reasonably necessary to protect the public health, safety, morality, or general welfare. Legislation may well be presumed unreasonable and unconstitutional when it denies to private parties who relied upon the word of the state preexisting contract rights.

In 1987 the Supreme Court remarked that "it is well-settled that the prohibition against impairing the obligations of contracts is not to be read literally," and held valid a state regulation of coal mine subsidence, even though the owners of the coal had secured waivers of damages from some of the surface owners. The Court stated that in such government regulation of private contractual arrangements, "a court must satisfy itself that the legislature's adjustment of the rights and responsibilities of contracting parties is based upon reasonable conditions and is of a character appropriate to the public purpose justifying the legislature's adoption." It added that "unless the State is itself a contracting party, courts should properly defer to legislative judgment as to the necessity and reasonableness of a particular measure."[47]

However, even today, if states by legislative action substantially impair contractual obligations between private parties, without necessity to meet an important general social problem, the Supreme Court occasionally indicates its willingness to use the Contract Clause to void state legislation. Thus, when an employer had a retirement contract with its employees, the Contract Clause was in 1978 held violated when Minnesota enacted legislation imposing "pension fund charges" of $185,000 upon the employer to provide for the purchase of deferred annuities for the employees, when the company closed its Minnesota operations. There was, said the Court, a "substantial impairment of a contractual relationship . . . a completely unexpected liability in potentially disabling amounts," with "no showing in the record before us that this severe disruption

---

46. City of El Paso v. Simmons, 379 U.S. 497, 85 S. Ct. 577, 13 L. Ed. 2d 446, 465-66, 470 (1965).

47. Keystone Bituminous Coal Ass'n v. DeBenedictis, 480 U.S. 470, 107 S. Ct. 1232, 94 L. Ed. 2d 472 (1987).

of contractual expectations was necessary to meet an important general social problem."[48]

§ 22.10. Implied reservation of the police power

When a state permits within its jurisdiction certain contracts, or enters into contracts itself with private parties, it always reserves the right as a sovereign to make whatever changes are necessary to protect the public health, safety, morality, or general welfare.

As early as 1878 the United States Supreme Court ruled that, even though a corporate charter was a contract, a state could impose necessary police power controls upon the recipient to protect the public health.[49] Two years later the Court also ruled that controls deemed necessary to protect the public morality could be imposed, thus terminating a lottery by legislative act even though the grant of authority to operate a lottery was admittedly a contract within the meaning of the Clause.[50]

By 1914 the Court could say that it was "settled" that "neither the 'contract' clause nor the 'due process' clause has the effect of overriding the power of the State to establish all regulations that are reasonably necessary to secure the health, safety, good order, comfort, or general welfare of the community."[51] Embraced within the concept of general welfare are legitimate attempts to legislate for the economic health of the community. Accordingly, in the language of the Court, "[t]he economic interests of the State may justify the exercise of its continuing and dominant protective power notwithstanding interference with contracts."[52]

In holding that Kansas could protect consumers from the escalation of natural gas prices following deregulation, in spite of contractual terms between producers and users, the Supreme Court in 1983 remarked that the [Kansas] statute "rests on and is prompted by significant and legitimate state interests." The Court continued:

> Although the language of the Contract Clause is facially

---

48. Allied Structural Steel Co. v. Spannaus, 438 U.S. 234, 98 S. Ct. 2716, 57 L. Ed. 2d 727 (1978).

49. Northwestern Fertilizing Co. v. Village of Hyde Park, 97 U.S. 659, 24 L. Ed. 1036 (1878).

50. Stone v. State of Mississippi, 101 U.S. 814, 1 Ky. L. Rptr. 146, 25 L. Ed. 1079 (1879).

51. Atlantic Coast Line R. Co. v. City of Goldsboro, 232 U.S. 548, 34 S. Ct. 364, 368, 58 L. Ed. 721, 726 (1914).

52. Home Bldg. & Loan Ass'n v. Blaisdell, 290 U.S. 398, 437, 54 S. Ct. 231, 78 L. Ed. 413, 428, 88 A.L.R. 1481 (1934).

absolute, its prohibition must be accommodated to the inherent police power of the State to safeguard the vital interests of its people. . . . If the state regulation constitutes a substantial impairment, the State in justification must have a significant and legitimate public purpose behind the regulation, such as the remedying of a broad and general social and economic problem.[53]

---

53. Energy Reserves Group, Inc. v. Kansas Power and Light Co., 459 U.S. 400, 103 S. Ct. 697, 74 L. Ed. 2d 569 (1983).

PART FIVE

THE REMAINING LIBERTIES AND FREEDOMS

CHAPTER TWENTY-THREE

The Liberties

---

§ 23.00. Liberty generally

Justice Frankfurter wrote in 1949 that "liberty is a broad and majestic term, purposely left to gather meaning from experience."[1] Twenty-three years later the Supreme Court emphasized that "in a Constitution for a free people, there can be no doubt that the meaning of 'liberty' must be broad indeed."[2]

In the 1920's the Court expanded the content of the term in significant ways. In 1923 the Court voided as violative of the Liberty Clause in the Fourteenth Amendment a Nebraska statute making it

---

1.   National Mut. Ins. Co. of Dist. of Col. v. Tidewater Transfer Co., 337 U.S. 582, 69 S. Ct. 1173, 93 L. Ed. 1556 (1949).

2.   Board of Regents of State Colleges v. Roth, 408 U.S. 564, 92 S. Ct. 2701, 33 L. Ed. 2d 548 (1972).

a misdemeanor to teach German or any other foreign language before high school. Said the Court:

> While this Court has not attempted to define with exactness the liberty thus guaranteed, the term has received much consideration and some of the included things have been definitely stated. Without doubt, it denotes not merely freedom from bodily restraint but also the right of the individual to contract, to marry, establish a home and bring up children, to worship God according to the dictates of his own conscience and generally to enjoy those privileges long recognized at common law as essential to the orderly pursuit of happiness by free men. . . . The established doctrine is that this liberty may not be interfered with, under guise of protecting the public interest, by legislative action which is arbitrary or without reasonable relation to some purpose within the competency of the State to effect.[3]

Two years later the Court held unconstitutional an Oregon statute requiring all children between 8 and 16 to be sent to public schools. The Court explained:

> The fundamental theory of liberty upon which all governments in this union repose excludes any general power of the State to standardize its children by forcing them to accept instruction from public teachers only. The child is not the mere creature of the State.[4] Into the early 70's the Supreme Court was continuing to illustrate the breadth of the term "liberty" in the Fourteenth Amendment. In 1971 it embraced within the term "the right to purchase or obtain liquor in common with the rest of the community" and honored the propriety of an action against a state when a woman was effectively excluded from exercising this "liberty" because a local police chief, without notifying the woman, sent a bulletin to all distributors of liquor in the community not to make the beverage available to the plaintiff.[5]

Notwithstanding the expansive construction of a half century, a majority of the Court surfaced in 1976 with a more narrow view, apparently bothered by the number of cases flooding the federal

---

3. Meyer v. Nebraska, 262 U.S. 390, 43 S. Ct. 625, 67 L. Ed. 1042, 29 A.L.R. 1446 (1923).

4. Pierce v. Society of the Sisters of the Holy Names of Jesus and Mary, 268 U.S. 510, 45 S. Ct. 571, 69 L. Ed. 1070, 39 A.L.R. 468 (1925).

5. Wisconsin v. Constantineau, 400 U.S. 433, 91 S. Ct. 507, 27 L. Ed. 2d 515 (1971).

courts which were essentially tort actions under either the common law or the applicable statutory laws of the states and in which substantial justice could be done by the award of money judgments in the courts of the state wherein the conduct occurred. That year, in an opinion by (then) Justice Rehnquist, the Court was unable to find a Fourteenth Amendment "liberty" interest, actionable in federal courts under the federal constitution, when a local police chief had negligently circulated a notice depicting the plaintiff as an active shoplifter. State remedies were sufficient, believed the Court, and relief was there readily available to the injured party.[6]

The following year, while the Court readily acknowledged that students who had been harshly paddled by school personnel had a "liberty" interest invaded, it refused federal constitutional relief, when it was apparent that both common-law tort recovery and criminal sanctions against the perpetrators were available under state law.[7]

Four years later, the Court found no "liberty" deprivation under the Fourteenth Amendment Due Process Clause when property belonging to a prisoner had been lost, inasmuch as state remedies were adequate to reimburse the prisoner for his loss.[8]

In a 1986 case the Court ruled that no Fourteenth Amendment Due Process "liberty" right was invaded when a prisoner slipped on a pillow negligently left by a deputy sheriff on a stairway in a jail. The Due Process Clause, said the Court, is "simply not implicated by a negligent act of an official" causing "unintended loss of liberty."[9] In a companion case, the Court found no due process "liberty" right violated sufficient to justify a federal action, when prison officials failed to prevent an assault on a prisoner. No compensation is required under the federal Constitution, said the Court, when government personnel are "merely negligent in causing the injury."[10]

However, in a 1990 case the Supreme Court held a due process "liberty" right of a patient was violated, and a federal constitutional action existed, where a state failed to provide adequate safeguards when the plaintiff applied for "voluntary" admission to a state

---

6. Paul v. Davis, 424 U.S. 693, 96 S. Ct. 1155, 47 L. Ed. 2d 405 (1976).

7. Ingraham v. Wright, 430 U.S. 651, 97 S. Ct. 1401, 51 L. Ed. 2d 711 (1977).

8. Parratt v. Taylor, 451 U.S. 527, 101 S. Ct. 1908, 68 L. Ed. 2d 420 (1981) (overruled in part on other grounds by, Daniels v. Williams, 474 U.S. 327, 106 S. Ct. 662, 88 L. Ed. 2d 662 (1986)) and (overruled in part on other grounds by, Davidson v. Cannon, 474 U.S. 344, 106 S. Ct. 668, 88 L. Ed. 2d 677 (1986)).

9. Daniels v. Williams, 474 US 327, 106 S Ct 662, 88 L Ed 2d 662 (1986).

10. Davidson v. Cannon, 474 U.S. 344, 106 S. Ct. 668, 88 L. Ed. 2d 677 (1986).

mental hospital. Since institutional officials knew or should have known the person involved was incapable of informed consent on their admissions form, and should have realized he would also be incompetent to exercise his statutory right to be discharged, the patient was thus unconstitutionally deprived of a "liberty" interest under due process of law.[11]

The task of determining which claims of right are to be embraced within the "liberty" concept and made binding upon federal and state governments under the due process clauses is one not easily or readily undertaken by the present Justices. The Court is seemingly willing to consider the works of historians and even, on occasion, those of political philosophers, in its determination of the "fundamentality" that identifies a constitutional "liberty." However, in a 1997 decision in the area—the "assisted suicide" case—the Court unfortunately misused history in seeming to define the rights of contemporary Americans in a free, democratic society through a comparison with the rights of twelfth century persons in England, beings who were virtually owned by the Crown.[12]

In the *Glucksberg* case the Court seemingly indicates it is going to give great weight in determining "fundamentality" to how majorities in the states will act on issues concerning suicide and the role of doctors when people ask for help in "crossing over." In the past Supreme Courts tied to the majoritarian influences of the moment have sustained such now outmoded practices as slavery and the infliction of torture upon persons in detention.

One wonders if the Court understands the relevance of ethical and religious values held in our society to determinations of "fundamentality" as a determinant of constitutional "liberties" to be protected although not specifically named in the organic law. Could the Justices possibly fear some critics would see an "establishment of religion" were they to request friend-of-the-court briefs from leading Jewish, Muslim, Christian, and other denominational leaders and theologians? Surely, such persons' concept of "fundamentalities" will be more relevant than notions of twelfth century English monarchs.

The Supreme Court has readily acknowledged that freedom from physical restraint "has always been at the core of the liberty protected by the Due Process Clause from arbitrary governmental

---

11. Zinermon v. Burch, 494 U.S. 113, 110 S. Ct. 975, 108 L. Ed. 2d 100 (1990).

12. Washington v. Glucksberg, 117 S. Ct. 2258, 138 L. Ed. 2d 772 (U.S. 1997), discussed further in § 23.11, infra.

action,"[13] but there has long been an understanding that such liberty can be limited when absolutely necessary for the common good.

The Court said in 1905:

> The liberty secured by the Constitution of the United States to every person within its jurisdiction does not import an absolute right in each person to be, at all times and in all circumstances, wholly free from restraint. There are manifold restraints to which every person is necessarily subject for the common good. On any other basis organized society could not exist with safety to its member.[14]

In 1997 the Court reminded us that "the liberty interest is not absolute." Restraint under civil statutes is as permissible as under a criminal statute, according to the Court. In holding that "criminal" proceedings and involuntary confinement pursuant to the Kansas Sexually Violent Predator Act were not punitive, thus precluding a finding of any double jeopardy or ex post facto violation, the Court noted that states have in certain narrow circumstances provided for the forcible civil detainment of people who are unable to control their behavior and who thereby pose a danger to the public. The Court stated: "It thus cannot be said that the involuntary civil commitment of a limited subclass of dangerous persons is contrary to the understanding of ordered liberty."[15]

§ 23.01. Liberty of the citizens to be where they will

Liberty of the individual, under both the Fifth and Fourteenth Amendment Due Process Clauses, embraces the people's constitutional right to be, not only in their own dwellings, but also everywhere in public places long recognized as dedicated to use by the citizenry. In 1965, the United States Supreme Court voided as unconstitutional the arrest of an individual under a Birmingham, Alabama, ordinance making it unlawful "for any person to stand or loiter upon any street or sidewalk" in the city, after having been requested by a police officer to move on. There is a strong suggestion in the case that, under a properly drawn ordinance, reasonable

---

13. Foucha v. Louisiana, 504 U.S. 71, 112 S. Ct. 1780, 118 L. Ed. 2d 437 (1992).

14. Jacobson v. Commonwealth of Massachusetts, 197 U.S. 11, 25 S. Ct. 358, 49 L. Ed. 643 (1905).

15. Kansas v. Hendricks, 117 S. Ct. 2072, 138 L. Ed. 2d 501 (U.S. 1997), discussed further in § 23.10, infra.

orders clearly necessitated to protect other pedestrians and citizens would be valid.[16]

Six years later, when a city attempted to enforce an ordinance providing for the punishment of "any person who wanders about the streets or other public ways or who is found abroad at late or unusual hours in the night without any visible or lawful business and who does not give satisfactory account of himself," the Supreme Court voided a conviction under the ordinance, ruling it unconstitutional for vagueness.[17]

Lower courts have shown a somewhat greater willingness to enforce loitering ordinances so long as they are narrowly drawn and limited in their application to particular areas or situations which are closely related to conduct that must be controlled to safeguard the public safety and good order.[18]

The Supreme Court has held a person who desired to observe closely the arrest of a friend and discuss the matter with the arresting officer "was not, without more, protected by the First Amendment," and that his arrest, as authorized by statute, for refusing "to comply with a lawful order of the police to disperse," was constitutional. Justice Douglas in dissent suggested it would be far better to acknowledge the constitutional right of a citizen to observe the acts of the police in arresting a friend, and protesting politely the same.[19]

§ 23.02. Liberty to travel—generally

Some of the American Founding Fathers who reflected upon the matter concluded that freedom of movement was one of man's natural rights. It was in this tradition that the Court of Appeals for the District of Columbia said in 1955: "The right to travel, to go from place to place, as the means of transportation permit, is a natural right, subject to the rights of others and to reasonable regulation under law."[20]

The United States Supreme Court states: "Freedom of movement is basic in our scheme of values," adding, "The right to travel is a

---

16. Shuttlesworth v. City of Birmingham, 382 U.S. 87, 86 S. Ct. 211, 15 L. Ed. 2d 176 (1965).

17. Palmer v. City of Euclid, Ohio, 402 U.S. 544, 91 S. Ct. 1563, 29 L. Ed. 2d 98, 58 Ohio Op. 2d 231 (1971).

18. People v. Merolla, 9 N.Y.2d 62, 211 N.Y.S.2d 155, 172 N.E.2d 541 (1961); Middlebrooks v. City of Birmingham, 42 Ala. App. 525, 170 So. 2d 424 (1964); State ex rel. De Concini v. Gatewood, 10 Ariz. App. 274, 458 P.2d 368 (1969).

19. Colten v. Kentucky, 407 U.S. 104, 92 S. Ct. 1953, 32 L. Ed. 2d 584 (1972).

20. Shachtman v. Dulles, 225 F.2d 938, 941 (D.C. Cir. 1955).

part of the 'liberty' of which the citizen cannot be deprived without due process of law under the Fifth Amendment."[21]

The now acknowledged freedom of association under the First Amendment should be interpreted to include a right to associate with persons not only throughout the country, but also throughout the world. The relevance of this Amendment to the right to travel is most direct where reporters seek to travel so that eventually American readers will be better informed as to events around the world. The Court of Appeals for the District of Columbia has aptly ruled that "a newspaperman's right to travel is a part of the freedom of the press."[22] Even so, the right to travel is not apt to be treated as beyond control. Thus, in 1965 the Supreme Court concluded that there was no denial of First Amendment rights from the refusal of passports to Cuba, even though, in the words of the Court, such refusal "renders less than wholly free the flow of information concerning that country." The Court added: "The right to speak and publish does not carry with it the unrestrained right to gather information."[23] Two years later the Court ruled that, under a statute which at the time made it a criminal offense for United States citizens to depart from the United States without a valid passport, it was not then a crime to recruit and arrange for travel to Cuba of a number of American citizens whose passports, otherwise valid, were not validated for that country.[24]

§ 23.03. —traveling inside the United States

In 1868 the United States Supreme Court invalidated a Nevada tax of one dollar imposed upon all vehicular passengers leaving the state. The Court stated that every citizen of the United States

> has the right to come to the seat of government to assert any claim he may have upon that government, or to transact any business he may have with it. To seek its protection, to share its offices, to engage in administering its functions. He has a right of free access to its sea-ports, through which all the operations of foreign trade and commerce are conducted, to the sub-treasuries, the land offices, the revenue offices, and the courts of justice in the several States, and this right is in its nature

21. Kent v. Dulles, 357 U.S. 116, 78 S. Ct. 1113, 2 L. Ed. 2d 1204, 1210 (1958), followed U.S. v. Laub, 385 U.S. 475, 87 S. Ct. 574, 17 L. Ed. 2d 526 (1967).

22. Worthy v. Herter, 270 F.2d 905, 908 (D.C. Cir. 1959).

23. Zemel v. Rusk, 381 U.S. 1, 85 S. Ct. 1271, 14 L. Ed. 2d 179, 190 (1965).

24. U.S. v. Laub, 385 U.S. 475, 87 S. Ct. 574, 17 L. Ed. 2d 526 (1967).

independent of the will of any State over whose soil he must pass in the exercise of it.[25]

Originally, in the Slaughter-House Cases of 1873, the Supreme Court saw the right to travel around the United States as one of the privileges and immunities of all citizens of the United States,[26] but in 1969, while the Court readily acknowledged the right to travel interstate as a fundamental right, it refused to ascribe the source of this right to a particular constitutional provision, noting that at times it had been grounded on the Privileges and Immunities Clause of the Fourth Article, on the Privileges and Immunities Clause of the Fourteenth Amendment, and on the Commerce Clause. Justice Harlan in dissent saw the proper source of the right as the Due Process Clause of the Fifth Amendment. After this prelude, the Court said that it "long ago recognized that the nature of our Federal Union and our constitutional concepts of personal liberty unite to require that all citizens be free to travel throughout the length and breadth of our land uninhibited by statutes, rules, or regulations which unreasonably burden or restrict this movement." The Court held that "the purpose of inhibiting migration by needy persons into the State is constitutionally impermissible," and further held that classifications denying the right to travel into a state cannot be sustained on the rational basis test, but will be invalid "unless shown to be necessary to promote a compelling governmental interest."[27]

Five years later the Court held violative of the right to travel an Arizona statute denying non-emergency medical care to indigents who had not been residents of a particular county for a year. The Court applied the compelling interest test and found that the state had no such interest to support an invidious classification impinging on the right to travel interstate.[28] In 1986 the Court again emphasized that the right to travel can be penalized only when there is "a compelling interest," and where no such interest appeared the Court voided a state provision affording a preference in civil service opportunities to resident veterans who had lived in the state at the time they entered into military service but denying the preference to

---

25. Crandall v. State of Nevada, 73 U.S. 35, 18 L. Ed. 745, 747 (1867).

26. Slaughter-House Cases, 83 U.S. 36, 21 L. Ed. 394 (1872).

27. Shapiro v. Thompson, 394 U.S. 618, 89 S. Ct. 1322, 22 L. Ed. 2d 600, 614 (1969) (overruled in part on other grounds by, Edelman v. Jordan, 415 U.S. 651, 94 S. Ct. 1347, 39 L. Ed. 2d 662 (1974)).

28. Memorial Hospital v. Maricopa County, 415 U.S. 250, 94 S. Ct. 1076, 39 L. Ed. 2d 306 (1974).

present resident veterans who had moved into the state after entering service.[29]

In 1975 the Supreme Court sustained a one-year residence requirement as a prerequisite for a divorce in the state of Iowa, although Justices Brennan and Marshall in dissent would find no compelling public interest to justify such a restraint upon the right to travel interstate.[30] The following year the Court sustained, as not violative of the constitutional right of travel, a municipality's requirement that firemen reside within the municipality.[31] Two years later the Court held that the right to travel does not require the invalidation of a Congressional welfare statute cutting off benefits paid by a person's former state when the person moved to Puerto Rico. In a footnote, the Court observed: "For purposes of this opinion we may assume that there is a virtually unqualified constitutional right to travel between Puerto Rico and any of the fifty states of the Union."[32] Three years later the Court held not violative of the constitutional right to travel a state statute punishing more severely parents who abandoned children and left the state than those who abandoned their children but remained in the state.[33]

Persons traveling within the United States are also entitled to the protection of the Equal Protection Clause of the Fourteenth Amendment, which will invalidate state and local attempts to discriminate or segregate because of race or color.[34]

At times the Supreme Court has utilized the Commerce Clause to invalidate attempts by the states to prevent the entry into their borders of the unemployed or impoverished. No single state, said the Court, can "isolate from difficulties common to all of them by restraining the transportation of persons and property across its borders."[35]

It is clear that Congress has power to protect against individual

---

29. Attorney General of New York v. Soto-Lopez, 476 U.S. 898, 106 S. Ct. 2317, 90 L. Ed. 2d 899 (1986).

30. Sosna v. Iowa, 419 U.S. 393, 95 S. Ct. 553, 42 L. Ed. 2d 532 (1975).

31. McCarthy v. Philadelphia Civil Service Commission, 424 U.S. 645, 96 S. Ct. 1154, 47 L. Ed. 2d 366 (1976).

32. Califano v. Gautier Torres, 435 U.S. 1, 98 S. Ct. 906, 55 L. Ed. 2d 65 (1978).

33. Jones v. Helms, 452 U.S. 412, 101 S. Ct. 2434, 69 L. Ed. 2d 118 (1981).

34. Flemming v. South Carolina Elec. & Gas Co., 224 F.2d 752 (4th Cir. 1955), appeal dismissed, 351 U.S. 901, 76 S. Ct. 692, 100 L. Ed. 1439 (1956).

35. Edwards v. People of State of California, 314 U.S. 160, 176, 62 S. Ct. 164, 86 L. Ed. 119, 126 (1941).

action a citizen in his federal constitutional right of interstate travel.[36]

§ 23.04. —traveling abroad

The right to travel abroad is a basic freedom protected by the Fifth Amendment. In 1958 the United States Supreme Court said:

> The right to travel is a part of the "liberty" of which the citizen cannot be deprived without the due process of law of the Fifth Amendment. . . . Freedom of movement across frontiers in either direction, and inside frontiers as well, was a part of our heritage. Travel abroad, like travel within the country, may be necessary for a livelihood. It may be as close to the heart of the individual as the choice of what he eats, or wears, or reads. Freedom of movement is basic in our scheme of values. . . . Freedom to travel is, indeed, an important aspect of the citizen's "liberty."[37]

That there is a constitutional right to travel abroad does not mean it is beyond control by the federal government. "The fact that a liberty cannot be inhibited without due process of law," says the Supreme Court, "does not mean that it can under no circumstances be inhibited." The Court thereupon sustained a ban upon travel to Cuba.[38] In 1978 the Court stated that there is a "crucial difference between the freedom to travel internationally and the right of interstate travel," and suggested that a rational justification suffices for Congress to limit international travel. It held valid a federal law denying social security benefits to individuals who remain outside the country more than thirty days.[39]

In 1964 the Court held unconstitutional a federal law making it a crime for a member of a Communist organization, ordered to register as subversive, to make application for or to use a passport. The Court ruled that the act "too broadly and indiscriminately restricts the right to travel and thereby abridges the liberty guaranteed by the Fifth Amendment," noting that the statute banned travel by innocent as well as knowing members and regardless of the purpose or the destination. The Court added:

---

36. Griffin v. Breckenridge, 403 U.S. 88, 91 S. Ct. 1790, 29 L. Ed. 2d 338 (1971).

37. Kent v. Dulles, 357 U.S. 116, 78 S. Ct. 1113, 1118-19, 2 L. Ed. 2d 1204 (1958).

38. Zemel v. Rusk, 381 U.S. 1, 85 S. Ct. 1271, 14 L. Ed. 2d 179, 189 (1965).

39. Califano v. Aznavorian, 439 U.S. 170, 99 S. Ct. 471, 58 L. Ed. 2d 435 (1978).

Since freedom of association is itself guaranteed in the First Amendment, restrictions imposed upon the right to travel cannot be dismissed by asserting that the right to travel could be fully exercised if the individual would first yield up his membership in a given association.[40]

There is additional authority from the Court of Appeals for the District of Columbia to the effect that the government cannot arbitrarily deny passports. That Court concluded that it was arbitrary and unreasonable for the Secretary of State to deny an applicant a passport because he was a member of an organization listed by the Attorney General as subversive, which list had been primarily a guide to fitness for federal employment.[41]

The Supreme Court has indicated that it will not give expansive interpretation to Congressional delegations of authority to the Secretary of State to withhold passports. Where rights to travel and passports are denied by the Secretary, the Court has announced that it "will construe narrowly all delegated powers that curtail or dilute" these rights.[42] Furthermore, the Court will insist that "the standards must be adequate to pass scrutiny by the accepted tests."[43]

Not violative of the freedom to travel protected by the Fifth Amendment, according to a 1984 five-to-four Supreme Court decision, is a Treasury regulation in effect banning travel to Cuba by forbidding the diversion of hard currency to that country. Implementing foreign policy objectives was thought by the majority adequate to limit the constitutional right of travel.[44]

In denying or revoking passports, the federal government must afford the citizen a fair hearing.[45] This includes not only the right of the applicant to testify and present evidence but also the right to know that the decision will be reached upon evidence of which he is aware and has an opportunity to refute. In effect this means that evidence considered by passport officials must appear on the record so that the applicant has the chance to refute it and courts the op-

---

40. Aptheker v. Secretary of State, 378 U.S. 500, 84 S. Ct. 1659, 12 L. Ed. 2d 992, 998 (1964).

41. Shachtman v. Dulles, 225 F.2d 938 (D.C. Cir. 1955).

42. Kent v. Dulles, 357 U.S. 116, 78 S. Ct. 1113, 1120, 2 L. Ed. 2d 1204 (1958); Dayton v. Dulles, 357 U.S. 144, 78 S. Ct. 1127, 2 L. Ed. 2d 1221 (1958).

43. Kent v. Dulles, 357 U.S. 116, 78 S. Ct. 1113, 2 L. Ed. 2d 1204, 1212 (1958).

44. Regan v. Wald, 468 U.S. 222, 104 S. Ct. 3026, 82 L. Ed. 2d 171 (1984).

45. Bauer v. Acheson, 106 F. Supp. 445 (D.D.C. 1952); Nathan v. Dulles, 129 F. Supp. 951 (D.D.C. 1955).

portunity to review it.[46] The better view would seem to be that one tentatively denied a passport should be entitled to a full disclosure type hearing with the right of confrontation, although there has been a suggestion that this right can be denied when confrontation would likely reveal governmental intelligence detrimental to the national security.[47]

Observing that freedom to travel is "subject to reasonable governmental regulation," the Supreme Court in 1981 held that the President, under Congressional authorization, can revoke the passport of a citizen on the ground that his activities in foreign countries are likely to cause trouble for the United States. The Court additionally held that procedural due process does not demand a pre-revocation hearing in cases such as this, where there is a substantial likelihood of serious damage to the national security.[48]

Lower federal courts have sustained a Congressional requirement that narcotic addicts and users crossing our borders register.[49]

§ 23.05. The liberty of persons to control their own appearance

While the United States Supreme Court assumed without deciding that "the citizenry at large has some sort of 'liberty' interest within the Fourteenth Amendment in matters of personal appearance," the Court held that local authorities can regulate the length and style of hair, beards, goatees, and mustaches of policemen. The Court said such regulations will be voided as unconstitutional infringements of individual liberty only if there is "no rational connection between the regulation . . . and the promotion of safety of persons and property." Justice Powell, explained more appropriately that "when the State has an interest in regulating one's appearance . . . there must be a weighing of the degree of infringement of the individual's liberty against the needs for the regulation."[50] Justices Brennan and Marshall in dissent indicated there was no connection between the regulations and the offered rationales.[51] Two years later, the Court of Appeals for the Seventh Circuit held that "choice of appearance

---

46. Boudin v. Dulles, 136 F. Supp. 218 (D.D.C. 1955).

47. Freedom to Travel, Report of the Committee to Study Passport Procedures of the Assn. of the bar of the City of New York (Dodd, Mead & Co. NY, 1958).

48. Haig v. Agee, 453 U.S. 280, 101 S. Ct. 2766, 69 L. Ed. 2d 640 (1981).

49. Palma v. U.S., 261 F.2d 93 (5th Cir. 1958); Reyes v. U.S., 258 F.2d 774 (9th Cir. 1958); U.S. v. Eramdjian, 155 F. Supp. 914 (S.D. Cal. 1957).

50. Kelley v. Johnson, 425 U.S. 238, 96 S. Ct. 1440, 47 L. Ed. 2d 708 (1976), concurring.

51. Kelley v. Johnson, 425 U.S. 238, 96 S. Ct. 1440, 47 L. Ed. 2d 708 (1976).

is an element of liberty," and voided dismissal of a school bus driver who had dared to grow a mustache.[52]

Part of one's personal liberty is the right of males and females of all ages to determine the hair style they like best. Judge Wyzanski of the District of Massachusetts has, in honoring the right of a student to wear his hair as he pleases, noted that "fundamental liberties" are here involved, adding:

> The right claimed by plaintiff might be described as one of the aspects of personal liberty, that is liberty of appearance, including the right to wear one's hair as he pleases or, alternatively, as one of the aspects of freedom of expression, that is the right symbolically to indicate his association with some of the younger generation in expressing their independent aesthetic and social outlook and their determination to reject many of the customs and values of some of the older generation.[53]

Another distinguished federal judge, Frank Johnson of the United States District Court for the Middle District of Alabama, in voiding school controls of hair styles, has stated:

> There can be little doubt that the Constitution protects the freedoms to determine one's own hair style and otherwise to govern one's personal appearance. Indeed, the exercise of these freedoms is highly important in preserving the vitality of our traditional concepts of personality and individuality . . . the freedom here protected is the right to some breathing space for the individual into which the government may not intrude without carrying a substantial burden of justification. . . . Until one's appearance carries with it a substantial risk of harm to others, it should be dictated by one's own taste or lack of it.

Judge Johnson emphasized that this liberty right of the individual is not to be taken away because others who preferred their own hair styles were threatening violence. He aptly stated that "the exercise of a constitutional right cannot be curtailed because of an undifferentiated fear that the exercise of that right will produce a violent reaction on the part of those who would deprive one of the exercise of that constitutional right."[54] Many cases are in accord,[55] although there are contra rulings, as well.[56]

---

52. Pence v. Rosenquist, 573 F.2d 395 (7th Cir. 1978).

53. Richards v. Thurston, 304 F. Supp. 449 (D. Mass. 1969), judgment aff'd, 424 F.2d 1281 (1st Cir. 1970).

54. Griffin v. Tatum, 300 F. Supp. 60 (M.D. Ala. 1969), judgment aff'd in part, rev'd in part on other grounds, 425 F.2d 201 (5th Cir. 1970).

55. E.g., Breen v. Kahl, 296 F. Supp. 702 (W.D. Wis. 1969), judgment aff'd, 419 F.2d 1034 (7th Cir. 1969).

56. E.g., Jackson v. Dorrier, 424 F.2d 213 (6th Cir. 1970).

An aspect of personal liberty is the right to determine one's own wardrobe for use in public and, absent outfits that clearly demoralize the community or occasion traffic accidents and pile-ups, individuals should be able to wear the clothing most appealing to themselves. In the case of school children attending public schools, "liberty" is to embrace attire chosen by the parents as appropriate and affordable, at least so long as neat and clean.[57] Without proof that the wearing of dungarees seriously inhibits the educational process, bans upon them are unconstitutional infringements upon personal "liberty" in violation of the Fourteenth Amendment.[58]

When Chicago enacted an ordinance prohibiting a person from wearing in public clothing of the opposite sex with the intent to conceal his or her sex, the Illinois Supreme Court voided convictions of two men thereunder who were beginning to wear women's attire as part of psychiatric therapy preparatory to sex change operations.[59]

The same court has held unconstitutional legislation requiring motorcycle riders to wear helmets. Said the Court: "it serves no function of safeguarding the motoring public."[60] There are contra decisions.[61]

§ 23.06. Liberty in family matters

When in 1967, the United States Supreme Court invalidated a state anti-miscegenation statute, it stated that "the freedom to marry has long been recognized as one of the vital personal rights essential to the orderly pursuit of happiness by free men." The Court added: "Marriage is one of the 'basic civil rights of man,' fundamental to our very existence and survival. To deny this fundamental freedom" by racial classifications "is surely to deprive all the State's citizens of liberty without due process of law."[62] The Supreme Court wrote in 1974 that it "has long been recognized that freedom of personal choice in matters of marriage and family life is one of the liberties protected by the Due Process Clause of the Fourteenth Amend-

---

57. Richards v. Thurston, 424 F.2d 1281 (1st Cir. 1970).

58. Bannister v. Paradis, 316 F. Supp. 185 (D.N.H. 1970).

59. City of Chicago v. Wilson, 75 Ill. 2d 525, 27 Ill. Dec. 458, 389 N.E.2d 522, 12 A.L.R.4th 1242 (1978).

60. People v. Fries, 42 Ill. 2d 466, 250 N.E.2d 149 (1969).

61. E.g., Com. v. Howie, 354 Mass. 769, 238 N.E.2d 373 (1968).

62. Loving v. Com. of Va., 388 U.S. 1, 87 S. Ct. 1817, 18 L. Ed. 2d 1010 (1967).

ment. . . . [T]here is a right to be free from unwarranted governmental intrusion into matters so fundamentally affecting a person as the decision whether to bear or beget a child." Then it invalidated overly restrictive maternity leave regulations applicable to teachers, stating that "the Due Process Clause of the Fourteenth Amendment requires that such rules must not needlessly, arbitrarily, or capriciously impinge upon this vital area of a teacher's constitutional liberty."[63]

Justice Brennan spoke for the Court in 1977 when he remarked: "The individual's freedom to marry and reproduce is 'older than the Bill of Rights.'"[64]

Whether married couples desire to regulate the birth of their offspring is surely their constitutional right.[65] Justice Powell, speaking for the Supreme Court in 1987, reported that "The Court has recognized that the freedom to enter into and carry on certain intimate and private relationships is a fundament of liberty protected by the Bill of Rights."[66]

When parents desire to provide a private or a religious education for their children, rather than use the public schools, this is their constitutional right,[67] and the Supreme Court has acknowledged that the relationship between parents and children is constitutionally protected.[68] In the *Quilloin* case the Court added that this liberty right is qualified by the "best interests of the child" which, on the facts, allowed a state to grant an adoption without consent of the father, who at the time was not married to the mother, even though the state's statute gave both divorced parents a right to veto an adoption.

In holding that state procedures governing the removal of children from foster homes were in accord with due process of law, Justice Brennan, speaking for the Court, observed: "It is, of course, true that freedom of choice in matters of . . . family life is one of the liberties protected by the Due Process Clause of the Fourteenth

---

63. Cleveland Bd. of Educ. v. LaFleur, 414 U.S. 632, 94 S. Ct. 791, 39 L. Ed. 2d 52, 67 Ohio Op. 2d 126 (1974)

64. Smith v. Organization of Foster Families For Equality and Reform, 431 U.S. 816, 97 S. Ct. 2094, 53 L. Ed. 2d 14, 35 (1977), inner quote from *Griswold v. Connecticut*.

65. Griswold v. Connecticut, 381 U.S. 479, 85 S. Ct. 1678, 14 L. Ed. 2d 510 (1965).

66. Board of Directors of Rotary Intern. v. Rotary Club of Duarte, 481 U.S. 537, 107 S. Ct. 1940, 95 L. Ed. 2d 474, 484 (1987).

67. Pierce v. Society of the Sisters of the Holy Names of Jesus and Mary, 268 U.S. 510, 45 S. Ct. 571, 69 L. Ed. 1070, 39 A.L.R. 468 (1925).

68. Quilloin v. Walcott, 434 U.S. 246, 98 S. Ct. 549, 54 L. Ed. 2d 511 (1978).

Amendment. . . . There does exist a private realm of family life which the state may not enter."[69] The Supreme Court has held unconstitutional a city ordinance which was interpreted to prohibit a grandmother from residing with her son and two grandchildren. The Court concluded that the ordinance was violative of freedom of personal choice in matters of family life, without justification in any important government interest. Justice Stevens in his concurring opinion indicated that the ordinance was not substantially related to the health, safety or general welfare of the city, while impinging upon fundamental rights normally associated with home ownership in violation of due process of law.[70]

§ 23.07. A woman's liberty to have an abortion

The United States Supreme Court in 1973 held that the right of personal privacy includes the right of a woman to decide whether she will have an abortion, but it also held that this new right is not unqualified and must be considered in light of important governmental interests in regulation. While holding that the word "person" did not include the unborn, and that abortions can be accomplished until the end of the first trimester without interference by the state, the Court also ruled that for the period immediately after the first trimester, the state, in promoting its interest in the health of the mother, may, if it chooses, regulate abortion procedures in ways that are reasonably related to maternal health; and for the stage subsequent to viability, the state in promoting its interest in the potentiality of human life may, if it chooses, regulate, and even proscribe, abortions, except where it is necessary, in appropriate medical judgment, for the preservation of the life or health of the mother. Viability occurs when the fetus has the capability of meaningful life outside the mother's womb.[71] At the same term, the Court ruled that a woman's right to an abortion was violated by provisions in Georgia law (1) limiting the operation to hospitals approved by the Joint Commission on Accreditation of Hospitals, (2) requiring the medical decision to be confirmed by two additional doctors, and (3) denying abortions within the state to nonresidents.[72]

Three years later the Supreme Court, while sustaining a part of a Missouri statute requiring the written consent of a woman to an

---

69. Smith v. Organization of Foster Families For Equality and Reform, 431 U.S. 816, 97 S. Ct. 2094, 53 L. Ed. 2d 14, 33 (1977).

70. Moore v. City of East Cleveland, Ohio, 431 U.S. 494, 97 S. Ct. 1932, 52 L. Ed. 2d 531 (1977).

71. Roe v. Wade, 410 U.S. 113, 93 S. Ct. 705, 35 L. Ed. 2d 147 (1973).

72. Doe v. Bolton, 410 U.S. 179, 93 S. Ct. 739, 35 L. Ed. 2d 201 (1973).

abortion, held that a state may not constitutionally require the consent of the husband to an abortion during the first 12 weeks of pregnancy; and further ruled that a state may not require the consent of a parent or person *in loco parentis* as a condition to an abortion of an unmarried minor during the first 12 weeks of her pregnancy. The Court additionally voided as unreasonable a provision of the statute prohibiting, after the first week of pregnancy, abortion by withdrawing of amniotic fluid and its replacement in the amniotic sac of saline or other fluid. Language imposing a standard of care upon physicians was voided because of its overbreadth.[73]

In 1979 the Court emphasized that the determination of whether a fetus is viable is for the judgment of a physician and voided for vagueness a statute exposing physicians to criminal punishment under language that was ambiguous and uncertain as to viability and the proper standard of care.[74]

The Court in 1979 held unconstitutional a state statute requiring for girls under eighteen (1) parental notification or consultation in every case before being allowed to have an abortion, and (2) parental consent to the abortion, with provision that if one or both of the parents refuse consent, consent may be obtained from a judge. Noting that "a child, merely on account of his [or her] minority, is not beyond the protection of the Constitution," the Supreme Court ruled:

> Every minor must have the opportunity—if she so desires—to go directly to a court without first consulting or notifying her parents. If she satisfies the court that she is mature and well-informed enough to make intelligently the abortion decision on her own, the court must authorize her to act without parental consultation or consent. If she fails to satisfy the court that she is competent to make this decision independently, she must be permitted to show that an abortion nevertheless would be in her best interests. If the court is persuaded that it is, the court must authorize the abortion.[75]

In 1983 the Court affirmed the conviction of a medical doctor for performing a second trimester abortion outside a hospital, in violation of a state statute which embraced within the term "hospitals"

---

73. Planned Parenthood of Central Missouri v. Danforth, 428 U.S. 52, 96 S. Ct. 2831, 49 L. Ed. 2d 788 (1976).

74. Colautti v. Franklin, 439 U.S. 379, 99 S. Ct. 675, 58 L. Ed. 2d 596 (1979).

75. Bellotti v. Baird, 443 U.S. 622, 99 S. Ct. 3035, 61 L. Ed. 2d 797 (1979).

more than full-service hospitals.[76] That year, too, the Court sustained a statute requiring the presence of a second doctor at a third-trimester abortion when the fetus was viable. The statute, said the Court, "furthers the State's compelling interest in protecting the lives of viable fetuses."[77]

Also in 1983, the Supreme Court held unconstitutional provisions of a municipal ordinance requiring (1) all abortions after the first trimester to be performed in a hospital; (2) notification and consent of parents when the woman was an unmarried minor; (3) the medical doctor to recite a lengthy litany of data to the woman seeking abortion; (4) a 24-hour waiting period; and (5) the fetus to be disposed of in a "humane and sanitary manner." The Court ruled that "restrictive state regulation of the right to choose abortion . . . must be supported by a compelling state interest," adding that such an interest is "only the beginning of the inquiry. The State's regulation may be upheld only if it is designed to further that interest." Addressing the parental consent requirement, the Court stated: "The State must provide an alternative procedure whereby a pregnant minor may demonstrate that she is sufficiently mature to make the abortion decision herself or that, despite her immaturity, an abortion would be in her best interests." By way of dictum, the Court indicated that "regulations that have no significant impact on the woman's exercise of her right may be permissible where justified by important state health objectives," and indicated that a narrow "informed consent requirement" would be sustained.[78]

Since "the Constitution embodies a promise that a certain sphere of individual liberty will be kept largely beyond the reach of government," the Supreme Court in 1986 voided a provision of state law detailing the method of securing informed consent for abortions and requiring a physician's report that would be generally available to the public. The Court remarked that states cannot "intimidate women into continuing pregnancies."[79]

In 1989, the Chief Justice, writing the opinion for the Court, joined only by Justices White and Kennedy, stated "We do not see

---

76. Simopoulos v. Virginia, 462 U.S. 506, 103 S. Ct. 2532, 76 L. Ed. 2d 755 (1983).

77. Planned Parenthood Ass'n of Kansas City, Mo., Inc. v. Ashcroft, 462 U.S. 476, 103 S. Ct. 2517, 76 L. Ed. 2d 733 (1983).

78. City of Akron v. Akron Center for Reproductive Health, Inc., 462 U.S. 416, 103 S. Ct. 2481, 76 L. Ed. 2d 687 (1983) (overruled on other grounds by, Planned Parenthood of Southeastern Pennsylvania v. Casey, 505 U.S. 833, 112 S. Ct. 2791, 120 L. Ed. 2d 674 (1992)).

79. Thornburgh v. American College of Obstetricians and Gynecologists, 476 U.S. 747, 106 S. Ct. 2169, 90 L. Ed. 2d 779 (1986) (overruled in part on other why the state's interest in protecting human life should come into existence only at the point of viability." The decision sustained a state law requiring a medical doctor, before performing an abortion after 20 weeks, to determine if the fetus was viable. The decision of the Court also sustained a ban on the use of public facilities or employees for performing abortions. Justice O'Connor, while concurring, indicated she would bar such a statute "if it unduly burdens the right to seek an abortion." Justice Scalia thought the Court should have repudiated *Roe v. Wade*. Justice Blackmun wrote a dissenting opinion, joined by Justices Brennan and Marshall, indicating there was no medical proof to support allowing the state to interfere throughout pregnancy, and these Justices being seemingly prepared to hold invalid regulatory controls by the state during the first and second trimesters. Justice Stevens characterized as a theological opinion violative of the Establishment Clause the state's language in the preamble of the statute that life begins at conception.[80]

In 1990 the Supreme Court held valid a state prohibition on abortions to unmarried, unemancipated minors, absent either notice given 24 hours before by the physician to one parent, or judicial approval. Justice Kennedy, writing for the Court, indicated that any bypass provision to be valid must (1) allow a minor to show that she has maturity and information to make her decision, in consultation with a medical doctor, without parental notice; (2) allow a minor to show that, even if she cannot make the abortion decision herself, an abortion would be in her best interests, (3) must assure the minor anonymity, In addition, the Court's opinion required that courts conduct a bypass procedure with expedition, to allow the minor an effective opportunity to obtain an abortion. The Court sustained a provision of the statute requiring the minor to bear the burden of proof on the issues of maturity and her best interests, or to show one of the parents has engaged in a pattern of physical, sexual or emotional abuse.[81]

While, the same year, ruling invalid a requirement that *both* parents be notified 48 hours before a woman under 18 has an abortion, the Court held the statute as a whole valid because it provided for a judicial bypass of the notice requirements if a judge was convinced the minor was "mature and capable of giving informed consent to the proposed abortion," or that an abortion without

grounds by, Planned Parenthood of Southeastern Pennsylvania v. Casey, 505 U.S. 833, 112 S. Ct. 2791, 120 L. Ed. 2d 674 (1992)).

80. Webster v. Reproductive Health Services, 492 U.S. 490, 109 S. Ct. 3040, 106 L. Ed. 2d 410 (1989).

81. Ohio v. Akron Center for Reproductive Health, 497 U.S. 502, 110 S. Ct. 2972, 111 L. Ed. 2d 405 (1990).

notice to both parents would be in her best interests. Justice Stevens
emphasized that "a woman's decision to beget or to bear a child is a
component of her liberty that is protected by the Due Process of
Law Clause of the Fourteenth Amendment," and that requiring
notice to both parents did not serve any legitimate state interests. In
joining the majority, Justice O'Connor indicated that a regulation of
abortion will be valid when "the regulation rationally relates to a
legitimate state purpose."[82]

In 1991, the Court, while acknowledging a constitutional right of
a woman to procure an abortion, upheld a federal funding program
forbidding participants from counseling abortions and from referring pregnant women to abortion counselors. The Court said:
"Government has no constitutional duty to subsidize an activity
merely because this activity is constitutionally protected."[83]

The Court in 1992 reaffirmed that the privacy right is a protected
"liberty" under the Constitution and that it embraces the right of a
woman to determine if she desires an abortion. However, the Court
then stated that it "rejects the rigid trimester framework of Roe v.
Wade," and announced that henceforth "only where a State regulation imposes an undue burden on a woman's ability to make this
decision does the power of the State reach into the heart of the
liberty protected by the Due Process Clause." This ruling allows
regulation even during the first trimester. The opinion of the Court,
written by Justice O'Connor and signed also by Justices Kennedy
and Souter, warns that "substantial obstacles" to exercising the
woman's right will be invalidated, at least during the first trimester.
The decision invalidated as an "undue burden" a part of the statute
before the Court that required report to state authorities about various personal matters such as the "number of the woman's prior
pregnancies and abortions." Another "undue burden" was the statutory provision that a woman must notify her spouse before undergo-
ing an abortion. However, observing that a state can ensure that a
woman's choice "is thoughtful and informed," the Court held valid
a provision of the statute requiring that, at least 24 hours before
performing an abortion, a medical doctor must inform the woman
of the nature of the procedure, the health risks of an abortion, and
the probable gestational age of the unborn child. This, said the
opinion for the Court, was not an "undue burden." Similarly held
valid was a statutory provision requiring consent of one parent or
guardian, so long as there was an adequate bypass provision allow-

82. Hodgson v. Minnesota, 497 U.S. 417, 110 S. Ct. 2926, 111 L. Ed. 2d 344
(1990).

83. Rust v. Sullivan, 500 U.S. 173, 111 S. Ct. 1759, 114 L. Ed. 2d 233 (1991).

ing judicial consent. Justice Souter, agreeing to the "undue burden" test here announced, would have found the waiting period unconstitutional as well as the provision requiring a medical person to provide the woman with a range of materials intended to persuade a woman not to have an abortion. Justice Blackmun, joining the result of the Court's ruling, indicated that he would have gone further and found unconstitutional the 24-hour delay requirement, the parental consent provision, and the content-based counseling requirement.

The Chief Justice, Justices White, Scalia and Thomas dissented, generally being critical of the new "undue burden" test, willing to allow the states to regulate abortions at any time of pregnancy "in ways rationally related to a legitimate State interest," and considering all provisions of the statute to be constitutional.[84]

§ 23.08. Liberty to bear arms

The Second Amendment to the Constitution of the United States provides that "a well-regulated Militia, being necessary to the security of a free State, the right of the people to keep and bear Arms, shall not be infringed."

The United States Supreme Court held in 1886 that this constitutional provision was applicable only to the federal government and not to the States or their political subdivisions.[85] In 1939 the Court upheld the National Firearms Act, regulating and taxing the transfer of sawed-off shotguns, stating that the "obvious purpose" of the Second Amendment was "to assure the continuation and render possible the effectiveness of" the state militia. It then added:

> In the absence of any evidence tending to show that possession of a "shotgun having a barrel of less than eighteen inches in length" at this time has some reasonable relationship to the preservation or efficiency of a well-regulated militia, we cannot say that the Second Amendment guarantees the right to keep and bear such an instrument.[86]

Since the Second Amendment is not directly binding upon the States, it does not prevent them from having an effective organized militia, nor is it a limitation upon the powers of the states to enact

---

84. Planned Parenthood of Southeastern Pennsylvania v. Casey, 510 U.S. 1309, 114 S. Ct. 909, 127 L. Ed. 2d 352 (1994).

85. Presser v. People of State of Ill., 116 U.S. 252, 6 S. Ct. 580, 29 L. Ed. 615 (1886).

86. U.S. v. Miller, 307 U.S. 174, 59 S. Ct. 816, 83 L. Ed. 1206 (1939).

appropriate regulatory laws. It is not, added an Ohio court, "a grant of individual privileges or rights to keep arms."[87]

By the weight of authority, reasonable regulations by the states and their political subdivisions are constitutional.[88]

§ 23.09. The "liberty" interests of prisoners

The right of access to the courts in civil litigation has long been accepted as a constitutional "liberty" interest protectable under the Fifth and Fourteenth Amendments,[89] and in 1977 the Supreme Court held that prisoners, like other persons, have a constitutional right of "adequate, effective and meaningful" access to the courts. The Court stated: "Persons in prison, like other individuals, have the right to petition the Government for redress of grievances which, of course, includes access of prisoners to the courts for the purpose of presenting their complaints."[90] The Court added: "The right of access to the courts . . . is founded on the Due Process Clause and assures that no person will be denied the opportunity to present to the judiciary allegations concerning violations of fundamental constitutional rights."[91]

Three years later the Supreme Court said that certain changes in prison conditions may be so severe or so different from ordinary conditions of confinement that, whether or not state law gives state authorities broad discretionary power to impose them, the state authorities may not do so "without complying with minimum requirements of due process."[92] Again, the following year the Court

---

87. Photos v. City of Toledo, 19 Ohio Misc. 147, 48 Ohio Op. 2d 274, 344, 250 N.E.2d 916 (C.P. 1969).

88. Brown v. City of Chicago, 42 Ill. 2d 501, 250 N.E.2d 129 (1969); Jackson v. State, 37 Ala. App. 335, 68 So. 2d 850 (1953); Watson v. Stone, 148 Fla. 516, 4 So. 2d 700 (1941); Moore v. Gallup, 267 A.D. 64, 45 N.Y.S.2d 63 (3d Dep't 1943), order aff'd, 293 N.Y. 846, 59 N.E.2d 439 (1944); State v. Krantz, 24 Wash 2d 350, 164 P2d 453 (1945); Photos v. City of Toledo, 19 Ohio Misc. 147, 48 Ohio Op. 2d 274, 344, 250 N.E.2d 916 (C.P. 1969).

89. Cotting v. Godard, 183 U.S. 79, 22 S. Ct. 30, 46 L. Ed. 92 (1901).

90. Bounds v. Smith, 430 U.S. 817, 97 S. Ct. 1491, 52 L. Ed. 2d 72 (1977) (overruled in part on other grounds by, Lewis v. Casey, 116 S. Ct. 2174, 135 L. Ed. 2d 606).

91. Bounds v. Smith, 430 U.S. 817, 97 S. Ct. 1491, 52 L. Ed. 2d 72, 83 (1977) (overruled in part on other grounds by, Lewis v. Casey, 116 S. Ct. 2174, 135 L. Ed. 2d 606).

92. Vitek v. Jones, 445 U.S. 480, 100 S. Ct. 1254, 63 L. Ed. 2d 552 (1980).

acknowledged that the "liberty" interest of prisoners triggers procedural due process rights in various instances.[93]

However, in 1983 the Court in a six-to-three decision could find no violation of a "liberty" interest under the Fourteenth Amendment Due Process Clause when Hawaiian law permitted transfer of a prisoner from a prison there to one on the mainland. In dissent, Justices Brennan, Marshall and Stevens said that in such a case the "question is whether the change constitutes a sufficiently 'grievous loss' to trigger the protection of due process."[94]

In 1990 a Court majority was willing to recognize that a prisoner "possesses a significant liberty interest in avoiding the unwanted administration of antipsychotic drugs," but held that such administration is to be judged under a test of whether it is "reasonably related to legitimate penological interests."[95]

The Court in 1995 stated, in a five-to-four ruling, that, while the states and federal government may "under certain circumstances" create liberty interests applicable to prisoners which will be protected by the Due Process Clause, this is to be narrowly limited to governmental actions that impose "atypical and significant hardships on the inmate in relation to the ordinary incidents of prison life."[96]

When a prisoner charged with disciplinary infractions was denied a request to present witnesses at his hearing and was then sentenced to 30 days' segregation, the federal district court granted summary judgment for the prison officials, but the Court of Appeals for the Ninth Circuit reversed, concluding that the state prisoner had a liberty interest in remaining free from disciplinary segregation. The Court of Appeals relied upon *Wolff v. McDonnell*,[97] a 1974 decision where the Supreme Court had held there was a state-created liberty interest and a Fourteenth Amendment interest entitling a prisoner subjected to a prison disciplinary proceeding to present his witnesses to the board.[98]

However, two years later the Supreme Court held that transfer-

---

93. Connecticut Bd. of Pardons v. Dumschat, 452 U.S. 458, 101 S. Ct. 2460, 69 L. Ed. 2d 158 (1981).

94. Olim v. Wakinekona, 461 U.S. 238, 103 S. Ct. 1741, 75 L. Ed. 2d 813 (1983).

95. Washington v. Harper, 494 U.S. 210, 110 S. Ct. 1028, 108 L. Ed. 2d 178 (1990).

96. Sandin v. Conner, 515 U.S. 472, 115 S. Ct. 2293, 132 L. Ed. 2d 418 (1995).

97. Wolff v. McDonnell, 418 U.S. 539, 94 S. Ct. 2963, 41 L. Ed. 2d 935, 71 Ohio Op. 2d 336 (1974).

98. McFarland v. Cassady, 779 F.2d 1426 (9th Cir. 1986).

ring state prison inmates to a prison where living conditions were "substantially more burdensome" than at the previous prison did not *ipso facto* constitute a deprivation of liberty requiring procedural Due Process. Central to the holding was the absence of any state-created right of the prisoner grounded in either law or practice.[99]

In *Sandin v. Connor*, a 1995 case, the Supreme Court recognized "that States may under certain circumstances create liberty interests which are protected by the Due Process Clause," but then added that these interests will be generally limited to a freedom from restraint which "imposes atypical and significant hardship on the inmate in relation to the ordinary incidents of prison life." Connor, who had been convicted of numerous state crimes, including murder, kidnapping, robbery, and burglary, and was serving an indeterminate sentence of thirty years to life, was only subjected, said the Chief Justice speaking for the five majority justices, to a proceeding which "was within the range of confinement to be normally expected for one serving an indeterminate term of thirty years to life." Seemingly, the Court reaffirms that the "liberty" of prisoners protected by the Fourteenth Amendment Due Process Clause includes interests that state law may create. Justices Breyer and Souter, in dissent, indicated that even accepting the "atypical and significant hardship" doctrine, an interest protectable by the Fourteenth Amendment was present. Also in dissent, Justices Ginsburg and Stevens took the position that subjecting a prisoner to "disciplinary confinement" impacted upon his "liberty" interest under the Amendment.[1]

§ 23.10. Permissible civil restraints upon sexually violent predators

In 1997, the Supreme Court sustained a Kansas civil commitment procedure for confinement of any "sexually violent predator," the term being defined as "any person who has been convicted of or charged with a sexually violent offense and who suffers from a mental abnormality or personality disorder which makes the person likely to engage in the predatory acts of sexual violence." Commitment under the act was limited in time to so long as the person suffers from a mental abnormality rendering him unable to control his dangerousness.

The Court stated that it has "never held that the Constitution prevents a State from civilly detaining those for whom no treatment is available, but who nevertheless pose a danger to others."

---

99. Meachum v. Fano, 427 U.S. 215, 96 S. Ct. 2532, 49 L. Ed. 2d 451 (1976).

1. Sandin v. Conner, 515 U.S. 472, 115 S. Ct. 2293, 132 L. Ed. 2d 418 (1995).

Involuntary confinement under such circumstances, said the Court, "is not punitive."

Justice Kennedy, in his concurring opinion, warned, however, that "if civil confinement were to become a mechanism for retribution or general deterrence, or if it be shown that mental abnormality is too imprecise a category to offer a solid basis for concluding that civil detention is justified, our precedents would not suffice to validate it."[2]

§ 23.11.   Liberty of individuals to choose to end their existence, with a liberty of requesting others to help

The Supreme Court in 1997 held constitutional Washington's statute making "promoting a suicide attempt" a crime and providing that "a person is guilty of promoting a suicide attempt when he knowingly causes or aids another person to attempt suicide." The attack upon the statute had been brought by medical doctors who indicated they would assist patients in terminating their lives, but for the statute.

Relying heavily upon English common-law authorities from the Middle Ages, when men and their bodies were "possessions" of the Crown, which enacted laws making suicide a crime, as well as seventeenth century laws applicable to settlers in what is now the United States, the Court could not see an historical basis for a "liberty" right to be honored under due process. From the fact that the majority of states have laws prohibiting assisted suicide, the Court could find no contemporary overwhelming support for it.

While acknowledging what it had said only seven years ago, that "the principle that a competent person has a constitutionally protected liberty interest in refusing unwanted medical treatment may be inferred from our prior decisions,"[3] the Court explained that this was "entirely consistent with this Nation's history and constitutional traditions" while the same could not be said about the practice of assisting suicide. A right to the latter, said the Court, was outweighed by society's "unqualified interest in the preservation of human life," by the belief that "the State has a real interest in preserving the lives of those who will contribute to society and enjoy life," plus "an interest in protecting the integrity and ethics of the medical profession," as well as "interests in protecting various groups from abuse, neglect, and mistakes, plus a fear that permitting suicide will start down the path to voluntary and perhaps even

---

2.   Kansas v. Hendricks, 117 S. Ct. 2072, 138 L. Ed. 2d 501 (U.S. 1997).

3.   Cruzan by Cruzan v. Director, Missouri Dept. of Health, 497 U.S. 261, 110 S. Ct. 2841, 111 L. Ed. 2d 224 (1990).

involuntary euthanasia." The Court welcomed "earnest and profound debate" about the "morality, legality, and practicality of physician-assisted suicide" throughout this country.[4]

In a case decided the same day as *Washington v. Glucksberg*, the Supreme Court ruled that equal protection was not violated by a state statute which permitted competent persons to refuse life-sustaining medical treatment, while denying what the respondents saw as "the same thing"—physician-assisted suicide. The Court ruled that the distinction was supported by a rational relation to legitimate ends and hence in accord with equal protection. The Court stated: "We think the distinction between assisting suicide and withdrawing life-sustaining treatment, a distinction widely recognized and endorsed in the medical profession and in our legal traditions, is both important and logical; it is certainly rational."

Interesting and for the time being important is the observation of the Court that its assumption in *Cruzan* of a right to refuse unwanted medical treatment was *not* grounded "on the proposition that patients have a general and abstract 'right to hasten death.'" Rather the Court now explains it was founded on "well-established traditional rights to bodily integrity and freedom from unwanted touching."

Justice Stevens' concurring opinion carefully notes that the Washington statute was only held not invalid "on its face," which "does not foreclose the possibility that some applications of the statute might well be invalid." We "must acknowledge that there are situations in which an interest in hastening death is legitimate. Indeed, not only is that interest sometimes legitimate. I am also convinced that there are times when it is entitled to constitutional protection. . . . Some individuals who no longer have the option of deciding whether to live or to die because they are already on the threshold of death have a constitutionally protected interests that may outweigh the State's interest in preserving life at all costs."[5]

---

4. Kansas v. Hendricks, 117 S. Ct. 2072, 138 L. Ed. 2d 501 (U.S. 1997).
5. Vacco v. Quill, 117 S. Ct. 2293, 138 L. Ed. 2d 834 (U.S. 1997).

CHAPTER TWENTY-FOUR

Freedom From an Establishment of Religion

I. In General

I. In General

§ 24.00. Generally

The First Amendment to the Constitution of the United States provides, inter alia, that "Congress shall make no law representing an establishment of religion." The language is clear; it was intended only to restrict the *federal* government, only *Congress* in the enacting of laws, and those representing an *establishment* of religion. At the time of ratification of the Amendment, the people of many states favored the Christian religion and furthermore it was Protestantism that was advantaged. Different versions of Protestantism were favored in the north from in the south. Ultimately, without any noticeable respect for history, the United States Supreme Court was to hold that the Establishment Ban applied to the states through the Due Process Clause of the Fourteenth Amendment,[1] a proposition that would have been shocking to the people of the states that ratified the Amendment.

The establishment ban was never intended to outlaw all relations between government and religion. Chief Justice Warren Burger, speaking for the Supreme Court, stated in 1971: "Our prior holdings do not call for total separation between church and state; total separation is not possible in an absolute sense. Some relationship between government and religious organizations is inevitable."[2]

How then to separate the permissible relations from the impermissible? In the *Lemon* case, the Supreme Court indicated the relationship was permissible when (a) there was a secular legislative purpose, (b) the principal or primary effect was one that does not advantage religion, and (c) the legislation did not foster "an excessive entanglement with religion."[3] Application of the test has not, the Court admits, been easy. The Court indicates that it has looked for guidance to what the Americans responsible for the Establishment Clause intended. Its "interpretation of the Establishment Clause," said the Court in 1984, "has comported with what history reveals was the

---

1. Everson v. Board of Ed. of Ewing Tp., 330 U.S. 1, 67 S. Ct. 504, 91 L. Ed. 711, 168 A.L.R. 1392 (1947).

2. Lemon v. Kurtzman, 403 U.S. 602, 91 S. Ct. 2105, 29 L. Ed. 2d 745, 756 (1971).

3. Lemon v. Kurtzman, 403 U.S. 602, 91 S. Ct. 2105, 29 L. Ed. 2d 745, 756 (1971).

contemporaneous understanding of its guarantees."[4] Comparably, the Court has sought guidance in the history of the United States since the Amendment was adopted. The "unbroken practice" of centuries was the principal justification when the Court in 1983 sustained the practice of state legislatures in opening their sessions with prayers offered by chaplains paid with public funds.[5] The Supreme Court states: "A proper respect for both the Free Exercise and the Establishment Clauses compels the State to pursue a course of 'neutrality' toward religion, favoring neither one religion over others nor religious adherents over nonadherents."[6] It is clear that the Establishment Clause is not violated, under the "excessive entanglement with religion test," by the governmental imposition of relatively small burdens upon religions. In 1990 the Supreme Court ruled the test was not violated by a governmental imposition of sales and use taxes upon a religious organization, since "the evidence of administrative entanglement is thin." Here, said the Court, "such administrative and record-keeping burdens do not rise to a constitutionally significant level" where there was no State inquiry "into the religious content of the items sold or the religious motive for selling or purchasing the items, because the materials are subject to the tax regardless of content or motive."[7] In 1985 the Court noted that the Establishment Clause does not exempt religious institutions from a variety of governmental regulations, such as fire protections, building and zoning regulations, etc., and ruled a provision of the Fair Labor Standards Act requiring recordkeeping not violative of the Establishment Clause in its application to a foundation of a religious nature. This was no "excessive entanglement," said the Court.[8]

There is no violation of the establishment ban "where government acts with the proper purpose of lifting a regulation that burdens the exercise of religion." So saying, the Court held constitutional a provision of the federal civil rights acts giving an exemption even to some secular activities of religious institutions, here operation of a

---

4. Lynch v. Donnelly, 465 U.S. 668, 104 S. Ct. 1355, 79 L. Ed. 2d 604 (1984).

5. Marsh v. Chambers, 463 U.S. 783, 103 S. Ct. 3330, 77 L. Ed. 2d 1019 (1983).

6. Board of Educ. of Kiryas Joel Village School Dist. v. Grumet, 512 U.S. 687, 114 S. Ct. 2481, 129 L. Ed. 2d 546, 91 Ed. Law Rep. 810 (1994).

7. Jimmy Swaggart Ministries v. Board of Equalization of California, 493 U.S. 378, 110 S. Ct. 688, 107 L. Ed. 2d 796 (1990).

8. Simopoulos v. Virginia, 462 U.S. 506, 103 S. Ct. 2532, 76 L. Ed. 2d 755 (1983).

gymnasium.[9] *Incidental* benefits to religious individuals and to churches, from laws principally valid as secular controls, do not make them violative of the Establishment Clause.[10]

Provisions of federal or state statutes are not violative of the Establishment Clause simply because they are in accord with a particular religion or religions. "It does not follow," stated the Supreme Court in 1980, "that a statute violates the Establishment Clause because it happens to coincide or harmonized with the tenets of some or all religions."[11] The Court repeated in 1984 that the Constitution does not "require complete separation of church and state. . . . It affirmatively mandates accommodation, not merely tolerance of all religions, and forbids hostility toward any."[12]

In 1995, the Court held there was no violation of the Establishment Clause when it felt compelled to rule a state university had to honor First Amendment Speech and Press obligations, by providing funds to a student paper for printing costs, which the university officials had discriminatorily refused because of displeasure with a distinct Christian commitment of the editors.[13]

Discrimination by federal or state governments advantaging or disadvantaging particular religious bodies, beliefs, or practices are unconstitutional. Thus, the Supreme Court held in 1982 that a statute granting older religious denominations preferences was not justified by any compelling societal interest, was not closely fitted to the furtherance of such an interest and, accordingly, was violative of the Establishment Clause. The statute had imposed registration and reporting requirements upon religious organizations (such as the Unification Church) soliciting more than 50% of their funds from nonmembers.[14]

Three years later, the Court determined that the primary effect of legislation before it was to advance a particular religious practice impermissibly and thus held violative of the Establishment Clause a state statute conferring upon certain employees an absolute right not

---

9. Corporation of Presiding Bishop of Church of Jesus Christ of Latter-day Saints v. Amos, 483 U.S. 327, 107 S. Ct. 2862, 97 L. Ed. 2d 273 (1987).

10. Meek v. Pittenger, 421 U.S. 349, 95 S. Ct. 1753, 44 L. Ed. 2d 217, 228 (1975); Hunt v. McNair, 413 U.S. 734, 93 S. Ct. 2868, 37 L. Ed. 2d 923 (1973).

11. Harris v. McRae, 448 U.S. 297, 100 S. Ct. 2671, 65 L. Ed. 2d 784, 806 (1980).

12. Lynch v. Donnelly, 465 U.S. 668, 104 S. Ct. 1355, 79 L. Ed. 2d 604, 610 (1984).

13. Rosenberger v. Rector and Visitors of University of Virginia, 515 U.S. 819, 115 S. Ct. 2510, 132 L. Ed. 2d 700, 101 Ed. Law Rep. 552 (1995).

14. Larson v. Valente, 456 U.S. 228, 102 S. Ct. 1673, 72 L. Ed. 2d 33 (1982).

to work on their chosen Sabbath.[15] The Supreme Court in 1982 voided a state statute giving religious bodies veto power over individuals applying for liquor licenses in the immediate area. By delegating "important, discretionary powers" to religious bodies, the statute impermissibly entangled government and religion. Thus, the law had a "primary and principal effect of advancing religion" and violated the Establishment Clause.[16]

II. Aid to Churches

§ 24.01. Use of government property by religious organizations

Where government properties are rented to the public generally, rental to churches should present no constitutional problem so long as the customary rent is paid, especially if the use is temporary. The Supreme Court of New Jersey has held that neither federal nor state constitutions are violated when religious groups, which fully reimburse school boards for related out-of-pocket expenses, use school facilities on a temporary basis for religious purposes as well as education classes.[17] In 1993 the United States Supreme Court ruled that when school premises are available generally to groups after school hours, the Establishment Clause does not require denial of the school premises to a church for exhibition of a film, open to the public, dealing with family and child-rearing issues faced by today's parents. The Court added that freedom of speech is violated by such a denial.[18]

Where government properties, such as parks, are customarily made available to groups of citizens, use by religious groups on customary terms has been accepted as valid.[19] In 1973 the Court of Appeals for the Tenth Circuit held not violative of the Establishment Clause the erection of a three-by-five foot granite monolith on courthouse grounds in Salt Lake City, the monolith having inscribed upon it the Ten Commandments and certain other symbols representing the All-Seeing Eye of God, the Star of David, the Order of Eagles, letters of the Hebraic alphabet, and Christ or peace. The Court deemed the monolith primarily secular, rather than

---

15. Estate of Thornton v. Caldor, Inc., 472 U.S. 703, 105 S. Ct. 2914, 86 L. Ed. 2d 557 (1985).

16. Larkin v. Grendel's Den, Inc., 459 U.S. 116, 103 S. Ct. 505, 74 L. Ed. 2d 297 (1982).

17. Resnick v. East Brunswick Tp. Bd. of Ed., 77 N.J. 88, 389 A.2d 944 (1978).

18. Lamb's Chapel v. Center Moriches Union Free School Dist., 508 U.S. 384, 113 S. Ct. 2141, 124 L. Ed. 2d 352, 83 Ed. Law Rep. 30 (1993).

19. E.g., Koerner v. Borck, 100 So. 2d 398 (Fla. 1958).

religious.[20] Eleven years later the United States Supreme Court held that the placing of a nativity scene in a public park at the Christmas season did not violate the establishment ban. The Court, with a five-to-four majority, stated that the Constitution does not "require complete separation of church and state; it affirmatively mandates accommodation, not merely tolerance of all religions, and forbids hostility toward any." The Court indicated that its "interpretation of the Establishment Clause has comported with what history reveals was the contemporaneous understanding of its guarantees." The Court found a secular purpose in the crèche as a celebration of a holiday and as a means of attracting persons downtown to promote retail sales and engendering a spirit of good will and neighborliness commonly associated with the Christmas season. In dissent, Justices Brennan, Marshall, Blackmun and Stevens found no historical support for the practice, and concluded that the primary effect was to place the imprimatur of government on a particular religious belief, with discrimination against those holding other religious beliefs.[21]

Five years later, the Court voided as violative of the Establishment Clause a crèche display set up at Christmas time on the grand staircase of the Allegheny County, Pa. court house, while sustaining an exhibit in front of a city-county building consisting of a Christmas tree, a menorah, and a sign saluting liberty. Justice Blackmun, for the Court, wrote "The government's use of religious symbolism is unconstitutional if it has the effect of endorsing religious beliefs, and the effect of the government's use of religious symbolism depends upon the context." The Court said that the crèche "has the effect of endorsing a patently Christian passage: Glory to God for the Birth of Jesus Christ." On the other hand, the Court saw in the menorah exhibit no endorsement or disapproval of any religious belief. Justice O'Connor, concurring, indicated that the establishment ban is violated by a governmental practice "if it endorses or disapproves of religion." Justices Brennan, Marshall, and Stevens would have held both practices violative of the Establishment Clause. In an opinion by Justice Kennedy, joined by the Chief Justice, Justices White and Scalia, it was indicated that both practices should be deemed constitutional. Rejecting the "endorsement test," they stated that communities should be able to make reasonable judgments respecting the accommodation or acknowledgment of holidays with both cultural and religious aspects. They suggested as the proper test: "Non-coercive government action within the realm of flexible accommodation or passive acknowledgment of existing symbols does

20. Anderson v. Salt Lake City Corp., 475 F.2d 29 (10th Cir. 1973).

21. Lynch v. Donnelly, 465 U.S. 668, 104 S. Ct. 1355, 79 L. Ed. 2d 604 (1984).

not violate the Establishment Clause unless it benefits religion in a way more direct and more substantial than practices that are accepted in our national heritage."[22]

A state does not violate the Establishment Clause when it permits a private individual or organization (such as the Ku Klux Klan) to display an unattended religious symbol, such as a cross, in a park that has become a traditional public forum. By dictum the Supreme Court noted that "giving sectarian religious speech preferential access to a forum close to the seat of government (or anywhere else) would violate the Establishment Clause." Justices Souter, O'Connor and Breyer indicated in dissent that the Establishment Clause would be violated if a reasonable observer of such action would find endorsement of religion by the state.[23]

§ 24.02. Impermissible delegation of governmental power to churches

The United States Supreme Court has held that the Establishment Clause of the First Amendment is violated when a state statute allows the governing bodies of churches to ban liquor licenses from establishments within a 500-foot radius of the church. "The churches' power under the statute is standardless," said the Court, adding that the Act "substitutes the unilateral and absolute power of a church for the reasoned decision-making of a public legislative body acting on evidence and guided by standards."[24]

§ 24.03. Payment of rent to church authorities for use of facilities

Mere rental of facilities from church bodies by the government, such as for use of schools, should be seen as not violative of constitutional establishment bans.[25] However, two federal district courts have held unconstitutional arrangements whereby public school districts rented or leased classrooms in parochial school buildings and sent over public school teachers who taught secular

22. County of Allegheny v. American Civil Liberties Union Greater Pittsburgh Chapter, 492 U.S. 573, 109 S. Ct. 3086, 106 L. Ed. 2d 472 (1989).

23. Capitol Square Review and Advisory Bd. v. Pinette, 515 U.S. 753, 115 S. Ct. 2440, 132 L. Ed. 2d 650 (1995).

24. Larkin v. Grendel's Den, Inc., 459 U.S. 116, 103 S. Ct. 505, 74 L. Ed. 2d 297 (1982).

25. Crain v. Walker, 222 Ky. 828, 839-40, 2 S.W.2d 654, 659 (1928); Scripture v. Burns, 59 Iowa 70, 12 N.W. 760 (1882).

subjects there to the children, who generally were there in regular attendance at the parochial schools.[26]

Where the rental by public school authorities of parochial school facilities is accompanied by a continuation of significant sectarian influences upon the public school children, the arrangement has been deemed unconstitutional.[27]

III. Aid to Charitable Organizations Operated by Churches

§ 24.04. Hospitals

The United States Supreme Court has upheld a contract whereby the federal government agreed to erect a building for, and pay for poor patients at, Providence Hospital in the District of Columbia, an institution operated by the Catholic Sisters of Charity. The Court stated:

> Assuming that the hospital is a private eleemosynary corporation, the fact that its members . . . are members of a monastic order or sisterhood of the Roman Catholic Church, and the further fact that the hospital is conducted under the auspices of said church is wholly immaterial. . . . There is no allegation that its hospital work is confined to members of that church or that in its management the hospital has been conducted so as to violate its character in the smallest degree. It is simply the case of a secular corporation being managed by people who hold to the doctrines of the Roman Catholic Church. . . .[28]

The Tennessee Supreme Court has held constitutional a statute authorizing a state board to issue bonds, acquire land and existing buildings of church-related hospitals, and then execute leases of the hospitals back to the earlier owners, with rentals sufficient to provide for the liquidation of principal and interest on the bonds when due.[29]

Under a number of state constitutions, the courts have sustained

26. Americans United for Separation of Church and State v. Paire, 359 F. Supp. 505 (D.N.H. 1973); Americans United for Separation of Church and State v. Board of Ed. of Beechwood Independent School Dist., 369 F. Supp. 1059 (E.D. Ky. 1974).

27. Dorner v. School District No. 5, 137 Wis. 147, 118 N.W. 353 (1908); Knowlton v. Baumhover, 182 Iowa 691, 166 N.W. 202, 5 A.L.R. 841 (1918); Zellers v. Huff, 55 N.M. 501, 236 P.2d 949 (1951).

28. Bradfield v. Roberts, 175 U.S. 291, 20 S. Ct. 121, 44 L. Ed. 168 (1899).

29. Fort Sanders Presbyterian Hospital v. Health and Educational Facilities Bd. of Knox County, 224 Tenn. 240, 453 S.W.2d 771 (1970).

the grant of public funds to hospitals operated by religious groups, so long as the hospitals served all regardless of creed and there was no effort made to advance a particular religion.[30]

Some state constitutions are worded so as to ban public aid to all sectarian or denominational institutions, and courts in these jurisdictions have invalidated public aid to hospitals operated by religious groups.[31]

§ 24.05. Custodial institutions

A number of state court cases have sustained the constitutionality of public payments to institutions operated by religious groups for the custody of orphans, children committed by juvenile courts, etc.[32] Many of the courts have theorized that these were not gifts but payments for services rendered.

There is some authority to the contrary, at least where some of the children were given religious training in the faith of the sponsoring institution.[33]

§ 24.06. Welfare organizations

There is very little judicial authority on whether public funds can be given to welfare institutions operated by religious groups.

A Georgia court has ruled unconstitutional a contract between a municipal corporation and the Salvation Army, whereby the latter would assume responsibility for charitable work in the city.[34] And a Nebraska court has refused to allow a public body to contribute to

---

30. Craig v. Mercy Hospital-Street Memorial, 209 Miss. 490, 47 So. 2d 867 (1950); Opinion of the Justices, 99 N.H. 519, 113 A.2d 114 (1955); Kentucky Bldg. Com'n v. Effron, 310 Ky. 355, 220 S.W.2d 836 (1949).

31. Collins v. Kephart, 271 Pa. 428, 117 A. 440 (1921); Parker v. Bates, 216 S.C. 52, 56 S.E.2d 723, 728 (1949) (dictum); Board of Managers of James Walker Memorial Hospital of Wilmington v. City of Wilmington, 237 N.C. 179, 74 S.E.2d 749 (1953).

32. Shepherd's Fold of Protestant Church v. City of New York, 96 N.Y. 137 (1884); Sargent v. Board of Education of City of Rochester, 177 N.Y. 317, 69 N.E. 722 (1904) (but note provision of New York Constitution); Schade v. Allegheny County Institution Dist., 386 Pa. 507, 126 A.2d 911 (1956); Dunn v. Chicago Industrial School for Girls, 280 Ill. 613, 117 N.E. 735 (1917); Dunn v. Addison Manual Training School for Boys, 281 Ill. 352, 117 N.E. 993 (1917); St. Mary's Indus. School for Boys v. Brown, 45 Md. 310 (1876); Murrow Indian Orphans Home v. Childers, 197 Okla. 249, 171 P.2d 600 (1946).

33. State v. Hallock, 16 Nev. 373 (1882).

34. Bennett v. City of La Grange, 153 Ga. 428, 112 S.E. 482, 22 A.L.R. 1312 (1922).

the local Community Chest, where this charity passed on some of the funds to religious organizations doing charitable work.[35]

Louisiana's constitution is interpreted to ban aid by the state, but to permit aid by local governments, to charitable and benevolent institutions.[36] A Utah court once sustained a public appropriation to the Daughters of Utah Pioneers for a display largely dedicated to the Mormon Church. This, noted the court, was "a coincidence of history rather than a deliberate attempt to further that faith."[37]

IV. Aid to Church-Related Educational Institutions

§ 24.07. Provision of funds or property for church-related primary and secondary schools

In 1973 the Supreme Court held unconstitutional an appropriation by New York State to reimburse church-related schools which had incurred expenses to satisfy a testing program mandated by state law. Somehow, the jurists imagined that the tests would be designed to infect students with the religious precepts of the sponsoring religion.[38] In 1977 after the New York Legislature appropriated authorized payments to those church-related schools which had incurred expenses before the *Levitt* ruling, in reliance upon the earlier statute, the Court decided that even this later statute was violative of the Establishment Clause. The reason given is hard to believe and defend. Such efforts by a state to reimburse for expenses it had mandated "will of necessity either have the primary effect of aiding religion, or will result in excessive state involvement in religious affairs," opined the tribunal.[39]

In 1973, the Supreme Court held violative of the Establishment Clause a state program providing for maintenance and repair grants to church-related schools. The Court noted that nothing in the program prevented a school from paying out state funds for the salary of employees who would maintain chapels and classrooms where religion would be taught, and the Court concluded that the program

---

35. United Community Services v. Omaha Nat. Bank, 162 Neb. 786, 77 N.W.2d 576 (1956).

36. State ex rel. Orr v. City of New Orleans, 50 La. Ann. 880, 24 So. 666 (1898).

37. Thomas v. Daughters of Utah Pioneers, 114 Utah 108, 197 P.2d 477 (1948), appeal dismissed, 336 U.S. 930, 69 S. Ct. 739, 93 L. Ed. 1090 (1949).

38. Levitt v. Committee for Public Ed. and Religious Liberty, 413 U.S. 472, 93 S. Ct. 2814, 37 L. Ed. 2d 736 (1973)

39. New York v. Cathedral Academy, 434 U.S. 125, 98 S. Ct. 340, 54 L. Ed. 2d 346 (1977)

"has a primary effect that advances religion in that it subsidizes directly the religious activities of sectarian elementary and secondary schools."[40] Two years later the Court held unconstitutional the loan of instructional material and equipment to church-related schools. In both cases, said the Court, the primary effect was advancing religion because of the religious character of the schools.[41]

Fortunately, dawn arrived in 1980 when the Court sustained a statute providing for payments to non-public (including church-related) schools for the actual costs incurred by them in compliance with state-mandated requirements of testing and pupil attendance reporting. Here, the Court recognized, there was a primary purpose that was secular, a primary effect that neither advanced nor inhibited religion, and no evidence that excessive entanglement of government with religion would ensue.[42]

§ 24.08. Provisions of funds or property to church-related universities and colleges

The Supreme Court has been generally receptive to programs to state aid to church-related universities and colleges. In 1971 the Court sustained a federal statute providing for construction grants to such church-related institutions, limited to structures that would be utilized for "secular" purposes. The majority of the Court seemingly was convinced that the dangers of impermissible entanglement are not very great from such one-time, single purpose construction grants. Invalid, however, was a provision allowing use of the property for sectarian purposes after 20 years.[43] Two years later, the Court held not violative of the Establishment Clause a South Carolina statute providing that a Baptist college would convey land to a state authority; that the authority would then issue revenue bonds to be paid back from fees to be charged by the college; that the authority would erect a facility on the property, which facility would be leased to the college; and that at the time the bonds were fully paid off the property would be conveyed to the college. The legislation provided that the property was not to be used for sectarian instruction or worship or for the college's department of divinity. The Court held that the primary purpose was secular, that the plan did not either advance or inhibit religion, and that possible

---

40. Committee For Public Ed. and Religious Liberty v. Nyquist, 413 U.S. 756, 93 S. Ct. 2955, 37 L. Ed. 2d 948 (1973).

41. Meek v. Pittenger, 421 U.S. 349, 95 S. Ct. 1753, 44 L. Ed. 2d 217 (1975).

42. Committee for Public Ed. and Religious Liberty v. Regan, 444 U.S. 646, 100 S. Ct. 840, 63 L. Ed. 2d 94 (1980).

43. Tilton v. Richardson, 403 U.S. 672, 91 S. Ct. 2091, 29 L. Ed. 2d 790 (1971).

entanglements were not of a constitutional dimension, even though the state had reserved the right to inspect the building's uses.[44]

Then in 1976 the Court, in an opinion by Justice Blackmun, joined by Chief Justice Burger and Justice Powell, held as not violative of the establishment ban a Maryland program providing an annual subsidy to private colleges, including church-related institutions. These Justices saw (a) a secular legislative purpose, (b) a primary effect that neither advanced nor inhibits religion, and (c) an absence of excessive entanglement between the government and churches. Justices White and Rehnquist concurred, although not happy with the "excessive entanglement test." Justices Brennan and Stevens dissented because of the interdependence between church and state promoted by the statute.[45]

§ 24.09. Payment of teachers' salaries

The United States Supreme Court in 1971 held unconstitutional a state statute under which payments were made by the state as supplements to the salaries of teachers of secular subjects in religiously operated schools, and similarly ruled unconstitutional a statute in another state providing for reimbursement to church-related schools of payments for teachers' salaries, books, and instructional materials in "secular" subjects. There was, said the Court, an impermissible entanglement from the surveillance necessary by the state to see that religion was not fostered under the programs. The Establishment Clause prohibits statutes fostering an excessive governmental entanglement with religion.[46] Two years later the Court added that a state could reimburse non-public schools for services provided under contract before its decision in the *Lemon* case.[47]

In 1985 the Court applied its customary three-pronged test of purpose, effect, and entanglement and found two school district programs void because, in spite of their admitted secular purpose, they promoted religion. The first invalid program was one of shared time, wherein public school teachers taught classes in mathematics, reading, physical education, art, and music in classrooms located in

---

44. Hunt v. McNair, 413 U.S. 734, 93 S. Ct. 2868, 37 L. Ed. 2d 923 (1973).

45. Roemer v. Board of Public Works of Maryland, 426 U.S. 736, 96 S. Ct. 2337, 49 L. Ed. 2d 179 (1976).

46. Lemon v. Kurtzman, 403 U.S. 602, 91 S. Ct. 2105, 29 L. Ed. 2d 745 (1971).

47. Lemon v. Kurtzman, 411 U.S. 192, 93 S. Ct. 1463, 36 L. Ed. 2d 151 (1973).

private schools and leased by the school district. Forty of the forty-one participating private schools were sectarian.[48]

The second program violative of the Establishment Clause was one of community education offering home economics, Spanish, drama, arts and crafts, gym, humanities, and nature appreciation at various sites, including private and public schools, after the end of the school day. The courses were taught by part-time school district employees, who were generally teachers in the non-public schools where the courses were offered. The Supreme Court concluded that religion was impermissibly promoted by the two programs in three ways: (1) the teachers could subtly indoctrinate the students in the particular religious tenets at public expense; (2) the symbiotic union threatened to convey a message of state support of a religious group by paying part of its instructional expenses, and (3) the programs in effect subsidized the religious functions of the parochial schools by taking over a substantial portion of their responsibility for teaching secular subjects. Even where the purpose was admittedly secular, government programs will be invalid where the primary effect will be to advance religion.[49]

The same year the Supreme Court held violative of the ban on establishment of religion a New York City program providing for the payment of salaries of public employees for teaching remedial reading, skills, remedial mathematics, and English as a second language in private schools, 84% of which were Catholic and 8% of which were Hebrew. Under the program public supervisors visited the classes once a month to ensure the public employees were not involved in any religious activity. Finding a "pervasive monitoring by public authorities in the sectarian schools," and noting that "ongoing inspection is required to ensure the absence of a religious message," the Court ruled the practice unconstitutional "owing to the nature of the interaction of Church and State in the administra-

---

48. School Dist. of City of Grand Rapids v. Ball, 473 U.S. 373, 105 S. Ct. 3216, 87 L. Ed. 2d 267, 25 Ed. Law Rep. 1006 (1985) (overruled by, Agostini v. Felton, 117 S. Ct. 1997, 138 L. Ed. 2d 391, 119 Ed. Law Rep. 29, 37 Fed. R. Serv. 3d (LCP) 1051 (U.S. 1997)).

49. School Dist. of City of Grand Rapids v. Ball, 473 U.S. 373, 105 S. Ct. 3216, 87 L. Ed. 2d 267, 25 Ed. Law Rep. 1006 (1985) (overruled by, Agostini v. Felton, 117 S. Ct. 1997, 138 L. Ed. 2d 391, 119 Ed. Law Rep. 29, 37 Fed. R. Serv. 3d (LCP) 1051 (U.S. 1997)).

tion of that aid." Chief Justice Burger, as well as Justices White, Rehnquist and O'Connor dissented.[50]

§ 24.10. Reimbursements and tax credits to parents sending children to church-related schools

In 1973 the Supreme Court voided a provision of a New York statute providing for a tuition reimbursement plan to parents of children attending private schools if their annual taxable income was less than five thousand dollars, when the children were sent to church-related schools. The Court concluded that the primary effect was to aid religion and produced an objectionable "potentially divisive political effect." In dissent, Chief Justice Burger and Justices Rehnquist and White indicated their greater willingness to sustain payments to such parents than to the schools, so long as a secular purpose was served.[51] Void also was another provision of the statute allowing parents of children attending church-related schools credit against state income taxes for tuition paid to such schools, up to fixed limits depending upon gross income. Such payments, said the Court, "have the impermissible effect of advancing the sectarian activities of religious schools." The Chief Justice and Justices White and Rehnquist dissented as to this, too.[52]

However, 10 years later the Court ruled that there was no violation of the Establishment Clause by a state statute allowing all taxpaying parents to deduct from the state income tax expenditures incurred in providing tuition (subject to a $700 limit), textbooks for non-religious courses, and transportation for children attending private, including church-related, schools. The Court by then concluded that the prime purpose of the legislation was education, clearly a secular concern, that the program did not have the primary effect of advancing the sectarian aims of non-public schools, and that there was no excessive entanglement. Justices Marshall, Brennan, Blackmun and Stevens dissented, believing that both the purpose and effect of the statute was to aid religious schools.[53]

---

50. Aguilar v. Felton, 473 U.S. 402, 105 S. Ct. 3232, 87 L. Ed. 2d 290, 25 Ed. Law Rep. 1022 (1985) (overruled by, Agostini v. Felton, 117 S. Ct. 1997, 138 L. Ed. 2d 391, 119 Ed. Law Rep. 29, 37 Fed. R. Serv. 3d (LCP) 1051 (U.S. 1997)).

51. Committee For Public Ed. and Religious Liberty v. Nyquist, 413 U.S. 756, 93 S. Ct. 2955, 37 L. Ed. 2d 948 (1973); Sloan v. Lemon, 413 U.S. 825, 93 S. Ct. 2982, 37 L. Ed. 2d 939 (1973).

52. Committee For Public Ed. and Religious Liberty v. Nyquist, 413 U.S. 756, 93 S. Ct. 2955, 37 L. Ed. 2d 948 (1973).

53. Mueller v. Allen, 463 U.S. 388, 103 S. Ct. 3062, 77 L. Ed. 2d 721, 11 Ed. Law Rep. 763 (1983).

§ 24.11. Transportation for children

The United States Supreme Court ruled in 1947 that nothing in the federal constitution required the invalidation of state programs providing transportation for children to all schools, including church-related institutions.[54]

§ 24.12. Textbooks for children

In 1930 the United States Supreme Court found nothing in the federal constitution requiring the invalidation of state programs providing secular textbooks to children in attendance at church-related schools.[55] And the Court in 1968 held constitutional a state statute requiring local school authorities to lend free of charge textbooks to children in parochial schools. Proceeding "on the assumption that books loaned to students are books that are not unsuitable for use in the public schools because of religious content," the Court added: "Perhaps free books make it more likely that some children choose to attend a sectarian school, but that was true of the state-paid bus fares in Everson and does not alone demonstrate an unconstitutional degree of support for a religious institution."[56] The constitutionality of state and local governments lending to children attending church-related schools secular textbooks approved by public school authorities was reaffirmed by the Court seven years later.[57]

The Court in 1977 upheld state financial assistance in the form of secular textbook loans, diagnostic and therapeutic aid, and testing assistance in secular subjects to students attending church-related schools. The diagnostic services were recognized as directly contributing to the welfare of the children, and sufficiently removed from the educational goals and influence of the institution to be constitutional. Since they were offered in a truly religiously neutral setting, the therapeutic services were also valid. However, expenditures for instructional equipment were voided, since they inescapably had the effect of directly aiding sectarian enterprise. Field trip subsidies were also invalidated as requiring an impermissible amount

---

54. Everson v. Board of Ed. of Ewing Tp., 330 U.S. 1, 67 S. Ct. 504, 91 L. Ed. 711, 168 A.L.R. 1392 (1947)

55. Cochran v. Louisiana State Board of Education, 281 U.S. 370, 50 S. Ct. 335, 74 L. Ed. 913 (1930).

56. Board of Ed. of Central School Dist. No. 1 v. Allen, 392 U.S. 236, 88 S. Ct. 1923, 20 L. Ed. 2d 1060 (1968).

57. Meek v. Pittenger, 421 U.S. 349, 95 S. Ct. 1753, 44 L. Ed. 2d 217 (1975).

of supervision from the public school personnel to insure the secular use of the funds.[58]

§ 24.13. Auxiliary services and help for disadvantaged children

The Supreme Court in 1975 held unconstitutional the provision by public school systems to children in attendance at church-related schools of certain auxiliary services, namely remedial instruction, counseling, testing, and speech and hearing services, the Court believing that the primary effect was the advancement of religion.[59] The year before the Court had intimated that federal funds can be used to help educationally deprived children attending church-related schools,[60] and in 1986 the Court held valid a state statute extending vocational rehabilitation assistance to a blind person at a Christian college who hoped to become a minister. The Court ruled that the primary purpose was clearly secular, and that the primary effect was not to advance religion, since there was little likelihood that any significant portion of the funds under the program would accrue to religious education.[61]

Seven years later the Court ruled that the Establishment Clause was not violated when, under a federal act, a public school district provided a sign language interpreter to a student from the district attending a Catholic high school. The Court stated generally that "government programs that neutrally provide benefits to a broad class of citizens defined without reference to religion are not readily subject to Establishment Clause challenge just because sectarian institutions may also receive an attenuated financial benefit." The Court also indicated that "the Establishment Clause lays down no absolute bar to the placing of a public employee in a sectarian school."[62]

§ 24.14. Payment of government funds to veterans for use at church-related educational institutions

It has always been accepted that the "G.I. Bill," enacted at the end of World War II and providing for veterans to use the funds at any institution of higher learning, including ones operated by vari-

---

58. Wolman v. Walter, 433 U.S. 229, 97 S. Ct. 2593, 53 L. Ed. 2d 714, 5 Ohio Op. 3d 197 (1977).

59. Meek v. Pittenger, 421 U.S. 349, 95 S. Ct. 1753, 44 L. Ed. 2d 217 (1975).

60. Wheeler v. Barrera, 417 U.S. 402, 94 S. Ct. 2274, 41 L. Ed. 2d 159 (1974).

61. Witters v. Washington Dept. of Services for the Blind, 474 U.S. 481, 106 S. Ct. 748, 88 L. Ed. 2d 846, 29 Ed. Law Rep. 496 (1986).

62. Zobrest v. Catalina Foothills School Dist., 509 U.S. 1, 113 S. Ct. 2462, 125 L. Ed. 2d 1, 2 A.D.D. 176, 83 Ed. Law Rep. 930 (1993).

ous church groups, was constitutional. The Supreme Court has not passed upon it.

At the end of World War I, the Wisconsin Supreme Court dismissed a challenge to state legislation giving veterans $30 per month while attending schools and colleges of their choice within the state.[63] However, in a 1955 case the Virginia Supreme Court held that payments for children of dead or disabled veterans could not be used at sectarian schools.[64]

§ 24.15. Sale of public property to church-related schools

There is little authority on point, but Missouri[65] and New York courts have sustained the sale of public property to church-related educational institutions at a fair price, as part of redevelopment projects, even though such fair resale price was below the government's cost of condemning and clearing. The New York court stated: "Since this sale is an exchange of considerations and not a gift or subsidy, no 'aid to religion' is involved and a religious corporation cannot be excluded from bidding."[66]

§ 24.16. Governmental provision of services to children at church-related schools

What sparse authority there is has accepted the provision of public health services to children in church-related schools,[67] as well as services for children with speech defects, those who are hard of hearing, and those physically disabled,[68] as well as other programs of child welfare,[69] so long as excessive entanglement is avoided. Two federal district courts have held unconstitutional arrangements whereby public school districts rented or leased classrooms in parochial school buildings and sent over public school teachers who

---

63. State ex rel. Atwood v. Johnson, 170 Wis. 251, 176 N.W. 224 (1920).

64. Almond v. Day, 197 Va. 419, 89 S.E.2d 851 (1955).

65. Kintzele v. City of St. Louis, 347 S.W.2d 695 (Mo. 1961).

66. 64th St. Residences, Inc. v. City of New York, 4 N.Y.2d 268, 174 N.Y.S.2d 1, 150 N.E.2d 396 (1958).

67. Scales v. Board of Ed. of Union Free School Dist. No. 12, Town of Hempstead, 41 Misc. 2d 391, 245 N.Y.S.2d 449, 455 (Sup. Ct. 1963).

68. Scales v. Board of Ed. of Union Free School Dist. No. 12, Town of Hempstead, 41 Misc. 2d 391, 245 N.Y.S.2d 449, 455 (Sup. Ct. 1963).

69. Scales v. Board of Ed. of Union Free School Dist. No. 12, Town of Hempstead, 41 Misc. 2d 391, 245 N.Y.S.2d 449, 455 (Sup. Ct. 1963).

taught secular subjects there to the children, who generally were there in regular attendance at the parochial schools.[70]

In 1997, the Supreme Court ruled consistent with the Establishment Clause a federal statute seeking to provide "full, educational opportunity to every child regardless of economic environment" through allocation of funds to "local educational agencies," as in New York City, where the teaching was done in private school facilities, by employees chosen by, and only responsible to, the school board; the instruction was only on remedial and enrichment topics; only instructional materials provided by the board were used; the teachers could not introduce any religious matter into their teaching or become involved in any way with religious teachings in the private schools; and lastly, all religious symbols had to be removed from any classroom used by the public teachers. The opinion of the five-to-four Court repeats basic principles customarily used by the tribunal, e.g., "whether the government acted with the purpose of advancing or inhibiting religion," whether the law had "a basic secular purpose," and "whether aid to religion has the 'effect' of advancing or inhibiting religion." What has been changed in the opinion is the unwillingness of these five Justices in the majority to accept faulty assumptions and presumptions mistakenly utilized by Court members in earlier cases. Here and now, said Justice O'Connor in the opinion for the Court, "we have abandoned the presumption . . . that the placement of public employees on parochial school grounds inevitably results in the impermissible effect of state-sponsored indoctrination or constitutes a symbolic union between government and religion." Utterly unjustified, said the Court, will be a presumption utilized in some previous cases, that "solely because of her presence on private school property, a public employee will be presumed to inculcate religion in the students." Repudiated, too, is the rule used on occasion that "all government aid that directly aids the educational function of religious schools is invalid." The Court concluded by stating thus the three primary criteria it is using in Establishment cases: (1) does the law have "the effect of advancing religion?" (2) does the law "define its recipients by reference to religion?" and (3) does the law "create an excessive entanglement?"

In dissent, Justice Souter, joined by three others, argued *inter alia* that "sharing the teaching responsibilities within a school having religious objectives is far more likely to telegraph approval of the

---

70. Americans United for Separation of Church and State v. Paire, 359 F. Supp. 505 (D.N.H. 1973); Americans United for Separation of Church and State v. Board of Ed. of Beechwood Independent School Dist., 369 F. Supp. 1059 (E.D. Ky. 1974).

school's mission than keeping the State's distance would do," seemingly the very kind of unfounded assumption the Court's majority seeks to abandon.[71]

§ 24.17. Graduation exercises

The United States Supreme Court in 1992 held that the use of a member of the clergy to give the invocation at a graduation ceremony for middle school and high school students was violative of the Establishment Clause. The Court saw this occasion as one at which attendance, in theory "voluntary," was in effect forcing a child to attend and participate in a religious exercise, and that she could feel she was being forced by the state to pray in a way in which she could not believe. "In a fair and real sense" attendance was obligatory, said the Court. A dissent by Justice Scalia was joined by Chief Justice Rehnquist and Justices White and Thomas.[72]

In a case three years earlier from California, a state court found impermissible a graduation ceremony that contained an invocation by a Lutheran minister, with references to the Christian religion, the court concluding that the ceremony constituted a governmental seal of approval upon that religion. The government cannot, said the court, "say to some parents and students, we do not recognize your religious beliefs. Our beliefs are superior to yours."[73] This opinion was ultimately upheld by the California Supreme Court, which held that religious invocations and benedictions at public high school graduation ceremonies violate the Federal Constitution.[74]

V. Cooperative Arrangements

§ 24.18. Release of public school children for attendance at religious services

In 1952 the United States Supreme Court upheld the released time program used by the New York City schools. The program released students from public school for attendance at religious instruction the last hour of the day on one day each week. There was no comment by teachers or principals on attendance or nonattendance of

---

71. Agostini v. Felton, 117 S. Ct. 1997, 138 L. Ed. 2d 391, 119 Ed. Law Rep. 29, 37 Fed. R. Serv. 3d (LCP) 1051 (U.S. 1997).

72. Lee v. Weisman, 505 U.S. 577, 112 S. Ct. 2649, 120 L. Ed. 2d 467, 75 Ed. Law Rep. 43 (1992).

73. Sands v. Morongo Unified School Dist., 214 Cal. App. 3d 45, 225 Cal. App. 3d 1385, 262 Cal. Rptr. 452, 55 Ed. Law Rep. 1027 (4th Dist. 1989).

74. Sands v. Morongo Unified School Dist., 53 Cal.3d 863, 809 P.2d 809, 281 Cal.Rptr. 34 (1991).

the children at such instruction. There was neither supervision nor approval of religious teachers and there was no solicitation of pupils or distribution of cards, and no announcement of any kind in the public schools relative to the program.[75]

State courts have rather generally agreed that released time programs can be valid under the state constitutions.[76] However, courts have found objectionable certain related practices, such as allowing religious representatives to make announcements in the classrooms, distribution of application cards in classes, and provision of such cards at public expense.[77]

§ 24.19. Use of school facilities for religious activities during non-instructional time

The United States Supreme Court in 1990 held constitutional the federal Equal Access Act, 20 U.S.C.A. §§4071-4074, which prohibits public secondary schools that receive federal assistance and that maintain a "limited open forum" from denying "equal access" to students who wish to meet within the forum on the basis of the "religious, political, philosophical, or other content" of the speech petitioner, and held that the Act was violated where officials denied the request of a student for permission to form a Christian club that would have the same privileges and meet on the same terms and conditions as other student groups at the school, except that it would have no faculty sponsor. Construing the Act as mandating equal access for religious as well as secular gatherings, the Court held the Act to be valid, finding no excessive entanglement, no school support of religion, and a need for neutrality, stating that "if a state refused to let religious groups use the facilities open to others, then it would demonstrate not neutrality, but hostility toward religion." The plurality opinion stated: "To the extent a school makes clear that its recognition of respondents' proposed club is not an endorsement of the ideas of the club's participants," the program could be constitutional. In their concurring opinion, Justices Brennan and Marshall agreed that when a school opens its facilities as "a

---

75. Zorach v. Clauson, 343 U.S. 306, 72 S. Ct. 679, 96 L. Ed. 954 (1952).

76. Gordon v. Board of Ed. of City of Los Angeles, 78 Cal. App. 2d 464, 178 P.2d 488 (2d Dist. 1947); People ex rel. Latimer v. Board of Ed. of City of Chicago, 394 Ill. 228, 68 N.E.2d 305, 167 A.L.R. 1467 (1946); People ex rel. Lewis v. Graves, 219 A.D. 233, 219 N.Y.S. 189 (3d Dep't 1927), aff'd, 245 N.Y. 195, 156 N.E. 663 (1927); Zorach v. Clauson, 303 N.Y. 161, 100 N.E.2d 463 (1951), judgment aff'd, 343 U.S. 306, 72 S. Ct. 679, 96 L. Ed. 954 (1952); Perry v. School Dist. No. 81, Spokane, 54 Wash. 2d 886, 344 P.2d 1036 (1959).

77. Stein v. Brown, 125 Misc. 692, 211 N.Y.S. 822 (Sup. Ct. 1925); Perry v. School Dist. No. 81, Spokane, 54 Wash. 2d 886, 344 P.2d 1036 (1959).

forum generally open to student groups [it] is therefore constitutionally prohibited from enforcing a content based exclusion of other
students' speech." They emphasized somewhat more than the plurality opinion that a school "must fully disassociate itself from the
Christian Club's religious speech and avoid appearing to sponsor or
endorse the Club's goals."[78]

Where a school board had created an open forum using its
auditorium, the Third Circuit held that the school board had been
under no obligation to open up its facilities to outsiders for expressive acts, but that when it did, it could not deny the forum to a
group called the Campus Crusade for Christ solely because of the
religious content of the group's message, and that such use was not
violative of the First Amendment.[79]

§ 24.20. Shared time

As early as 1913 the Pennsylvania Supreme Court ruled that
children in non-public schools could attend part of the day at public
school classes.[80] There has been some later support for the
constitutionality of shared time—wherein children spend part of
their school day in a church-related institution and part of a public
school.[81] There is, however, some Iowa authority suggesting that
there, at least, shared time may be unconstitutional.[82]

§ 24.21. Public school credit for bible courses

In some states public school credit can be given for courses in the
Bible, which instruction is provided away from the public school. In
the single reported case in point, a Washington Court voided a
program under which high school students could be given one credit
(out of 30-32 required for graduation) for Bible study away from
school. Said this court: "To give a credit in the public school for
such instruction, is to give a credit for sectarian teaching and influence which is the very thing outlawed by the Constitution."[83]

---

78. Board of Educ. of Westside Community Schools v. Mergens By and
Through Mergens, 496 U.S. 226, 110 S. Ct. 2356, 110 L. Ed. 2d 191, 60 Ed. Law
Rep. 320 (1990).

79. Gregoire v. Centennial School Dist., 907 F.2d 1366, 61 Ed. Law Rep. 845
(3d Cir. 1990).

80. Commonwealth ex rel Wehrle v. School Dist. of Altoona, 241 Pa. 224, 88
A. 481 (1913).

81. Utah Ops Atty Gen Oct 30, 1963.

82. Iowa Ops Atty Gen May 17, 1939; and cf. Knowlton v. Baumhover, 182
Iowa 691, 166 N.W. 202, 5 A.L.R. 841 (1918).

83. State v. Frazier, 102 Wash. 369, 379, 380, 173 P. 35 (1918).

§ 24.22. Research

The Supreme Court in 1988 held not violative of the Establishment Clause on its face a federal statute providing for participation of religious organizations in a program of "service and research in the area of adolescent sexual relations and pregnancy," including "educational services." The Court ruled that religious institutions are not disabled from participating in publicly sponsored social welfare programs and that there is no impermissible "advancement of religion" because some religious group receives federal funding to carry out Congressional non-religious aims. Nor is there "excessive government entanglement with religion" from federal monitoring of the program alone. There is dictum, however, that such legislation could have the primary effect of advancing religion if the aid flows to institutions that are "pervasively sectarian." In dissent, Justices Blackmun, Brennan, Marshall and Stevens took the position that the statute should be voided in the absence of a specific provision that federal funds were not to be used for any religious purpose.[84]

§ 24.23. Creating special school districts for religious groups

Separation of church and state was held violated by the United States Supreme Court in 1994 when a state created a school district exclusively for members of a particular religious sect. The Court indicated that the Establishment Clause is violated when a governmental entity "singles out a particular religious sect for special treatment," such as when it gives a particular sect "exclusive control of a political subdivision." The Court added that "a State may not delegate its civic authority to a group chosen according to a religious criterion." Justices Stevens, Blackmun and Ginsburg in concurrence, found objectionable "state provision of official support to cement the attachment of young adherents to a particular faith." Chief Justice Rehnquist and Justices Scalia and Thomas in dissent would have held that the establishment ban prohibits a state church "and nothing more." They asserted that the state should generally accommodate religious differences, and they saw no obstacle to a school district for a religious group, just as one was valid for "Indians, gypsies, etc."[85]

---

84. Bowen v. Kendrick, 487 U.S. 589, 108 S. Ct. 2562, 101 L. Ed. 2d 520 (1988).

85. Board of Educ. of Kiryas Joel Village School Dist. v. Grumet, 512 U.S. 687, 114 S. Ct. 2481, 129 L. Ed. 2d 546, 91 Ed. Law Rep. 810 (1994).

VI. Religion in the Public Schools

§ 24.24. Prayers

The United States Supreme Court has held that public schools cannot conduct programs of Bible reading or prayers during the regular school day, even when children who choose not to participate are excused.[86] Said the Court: "To withstand the strictures of the Establishment Clause there must be a secular legislative purpose and a primary effect that neither advances nor inhibits religion." "The concept of neutrality," says the Court, "does not permit a State to require a religious exercise even with the consent of the majority of those affected. . . . "

Because there was no secular purpose, and the evidence showed clearly that the statute was enacted to encourage religious activities, the Supreme Court in 1985 voided under the establishment ban a statute authorizing a one-minute period in all public schools "for meditation or voluntary prayer." From the legislative debates, the Court found a clear intent to return religion to the public schools, and emphasized that, where as here, there is no secular purpose, a court need not consider the other parts of the *Lemon* test. Chief Justice Burger, Justices White and Rehnquist in dissent suggested that it would be desirable to undertake a basic reconciliation of the Establishment Clause precedents.[87]

§ 24.25. Recitations and hymns

In 1967 the Court of Appeals for the Seventh Circuit ruled it unconstitutional for a kindergarten teacher to require the children to recite before their morning snack: "We thank you for the flowers so sweet, we thank you for the food we eat; we thank you for the birds that sing; we thank you for everything." The Court of Appeals saw the primary purpose of the practice as teaching the religious act of praising the deity, with the avowed secular purpose of teaching gratitude and good manners as only secondary. The United States Supreme Court denied certiorari.[88]

Singing religious hymns as a devotional exercise is likely unconstitutional since the *Schempp* decision, discussed in § 24.24,

---

86. School Dist. of Abington Tp., Pa. v. Schempp, 374 U.S. 203, 83 S. Ct. 1560, 10 L. Ed. 2d 844 (1963); Engel v. Vitale, 370 U.S. 421, 82 S. Ct. 1261, 8 L. Ed. 2d 601, 20 Ohio Op. 2d 328, 86 A.L.R.2d 1285 (1962).

87. Wallace v. Jaffree, 472 U.S. 38, 105 S. Ct. 2479, 86 L. Ed. 2d 29, 25 Ed. Law Rep. 39 (1985).

88. DeSpain v. DeKalb County Community School Dist. 428, 384 F.2d 836, 30 A.L.R.3d 1342 (7th Cir. 1967).

supra. However, as part of a musical lesson or concert they would seem to be permissible.

As early as 1902 a Nebraska court had ruled that religious hymns could not be sung in public school classrooms.[89] Eight years later an Illinois court ruled that Catholic children attending the public schools could not be forced to sing Protestant hymns.[90] The Iowa Supreme Court in an early case held that the singing of religious songs in public schools was not unconstitutional.[91]

§ 24.26. Bible readings in public schools

There are decisions that, so long as the Bible is used solely for secular educational purposes, as for its historical and literary values, without any advocacy of religion, this kind of use in public schools is not violative of the Establishment Clause.[92]

§ 24.27. Distribution of bibles within public schools

A Bible can be part of libraries in public schools without violating the Establishment Clause,[93] and there are cases approving the distribution of Bibles in the public schools,[94] although on this issue there are rulings to the contrary as well.[95]

§ 24.28. Religious officials as teachers in public schools

The weight of authority finds nothing unconstitutional about

89. State v. Scheve, 65 Neb. 853, 91 N.W. 846 (1902), aff'd, 64 Neb. 853, 93 N.W. 169 (1903).

90. People ex rel. Ring v. Board of Education of Dist. 24, 245 Ill. 334, 92 N.E. 251 (1910).

91. Moore v. Monroe, 64 Iowa 367, 20 N.W. 475 (1884).

92. Hall v. Board of School Com'rs of Conecuh County, 656 F.2d 999 (5th Cir. 1981); Berger by Berger v. Rensselaer Cent. School Corp., 766 F. Supp. 696, 68 Ed. Law Rep. 626, 111 A.L.R. Fed. 735 (N.D. Ind. 1991), decision rev'd, 982 F.2d 1160, 80 Ed. Law Rep. 68 (7th Cir. 1993) (Seventh Circuit held, in reversing, that distribution of Gideon Bibles to fifth grade students violated Establishment Clause).

93. Evans v. Selma Union High School Dist. of Fresno County, 193 Cal. 54, 222 P. 801, 31 A.L.R. 1121 (1924).

94. Gregoire v. Centennial School Dist., 907 F.2d 1366, 61 Ed. Law Rep. 845 (3d Cir. 1990); Berger by Berger v. Rensselaer Cent. School Corp., 766 F. Supp. 696, 68 Ed. Law Rep. 626, 111 A.L.R. Fed. 735 (N.D. Ind. 1991), decision rev'd, 982 F.2d 1160, 80 Ed. Law Rep. 68 (7th Cir. 1993) (Seventh Circuit held, in reversing, that distribution of Gideon Bibles to fifth grade students violated Establishment Clause).

95. Lubbock Civil Liberties Union v. Lubbock Independent School Dist., 669 F.2d 1038, 2 Ed. Law Rep. 961 (5th Cir. 1982); Tudor v. Board of Ed. of Borough of Rutherford, 14 N.J. 31, 100 A.2d 857, 45 A.L.R.2d 729 (1953).

ministers, nuns and other religious officials teaching in the public schools.[96] Additionally, it is frequently suggested that a rule denying such persons the opportunity to serve as teachers in the public schools would be unconstitutional.[97] Contra to the foregoing authority, a Missouri court has ruled that "because of the character of their obligations . . . nuns are disqualified from teaching in any public school in the State."[98]

§ 24.29. Wearing of religious garb by public school teachers

The authority is divided on whether it is permissible for teachers in the public schools to wear distinctive religious garb. New Mexico, New York and Pennsylvania Courts have sustained statutes banning the wearing of religious garb by teachers in the public schools.[99] On the other hand, the wearing of such attire was upheld by Indiana, Kentucky and North Dakota Courts,[1] although the North Dakota electorate thereafter passed a law banning such attire in the public schools.

§ 24.30. Holy day services

A Florida court has enjoined the religious observance in the public schools of Christmas, Easter, and Hanukkah holy days.[2] On the other hand, a New York court has refused to enjoin local school authorities from erecting a crèche on school grounds at Christmas, where it was agreed the display would not be installed until after

---

96. State ex rel. Johnson v. Boyd, 217 Ind. 348, 28 N.E.2d 256 (1940); O'Connor v. Hendrick, 184 N.Y. 421, 77 N.E. 612 (1906); Zellers v. Huff, 55 N.M. 501, 236 P.2d 949 (1951); Knowlton v. Baumhover, 182 Iowa 691, 166 N.W. 202, 5 A.L.R. 841 (1918).

97. State ex rel. Johnson v. Boyd, 217 Ind. 348, 28 N.E.2d 256 (1940); Gerhardt v. Heid, 66 N.D. 444 (1936).

98. Berghorn v. Reorganized School Dist. No. 8, Franklin County, 364 Mo. 121, 260 S.W.2d 573 (1953).

99. Zellers v. Huff, 55 N.M. 501, 236 P.2d 949 (1951); O'Connor v. Hendrick, 184 N.Y. 421, 77 N.E. 612 (1906); Commonwealth v. Herr, 229 Pa. 132, 78 A. 68 (1910).

1. State ex rel. Johnson v. Boyd, 217 Ind. 348, 28 N.E.2d 256 (1940); Rawlings v. Butler, 290 S.W.2d 801, 60 A.L.R.2d 285 (Ky. 1956); Gerhardt v. Heid, 66 N.D. 444 (1936).

2. Chamberlin v. Dade County Bd. of Public Instruction, 143 So. 2d 21 (Fla. 1962), vacated on other grounds, 374 U.S. 487, 83 S. Ct. 1864, 10 L. Ed. 2d 1043 (1963).

school was recessed for the vacation and would be removed before the return of students.[3]

Where devotional, holy day exercises are probably unconstitutional. However, where days such as Christmas, Thanksgiving and Easter are celebrated as part of our secular cultural heritage, celebration of these occasions may be quite valid.[4]

§ 24.31.   Bans upon teaching evolution; requirements that "creation science" be taught in the public schools

The United States Supreme Court in 1968 held unconstitutional as violative of the ban upon the establishment of religion an Arkansas statute forbidding the teaching of the Darwinian theory of evolution in the public schools. The Court observed that "no suggestion has been made that Arkansas' law may be justified by considerations of state policy other than the religious views of some of its citizens," and ruled that "the First Amendment does not permit the State to require that teaching and learning must be tailored to the principles or prohibitions of any religious sect or dogma." The Court again emphasized its neutrality requirement, remarking:

> Government in our democracy, state and national, must be neutral in matters of religious theory, doctrine, and practice. It may not be hostile to any religion or to the advocacy of non-religion; and it may not aid, foster, or promote one religion or religious theory against the militant opposite. The First Amendment mandates governmental neutrality between religion and religion and between religion and non-religion. [The First Amendment] forbids alike the preference of a religious doctrine or the prohibition of theory which is deemed antagonistic to a particular dogma.[5]

In 1987 the Court held unconstitutional as violative of the First Amendment Louisiana's "Balanced Treatment for Creation-Science and Evolution-Science in Public Schools Act," which prevented the teaching of evolution in the public schools act unless "creation science" was also taught, the Court finding that a primary purpose of the legislation was to advance a religious viewpoint. However, the Court advised that "the teaching of a variety of scientific theories about the origin of humankind to school children might be validly

---

3.   Baer v. Kolmorgen, 14 Misc. 2d 1015, 181 N.Y.S.2d 230 (Sup. Ct. 1958). See also Lawrence v. Buchmueller, 40 Misc. 2d 300, 243 N.Y.S.2d 87 (Sup. Ct. 1963).

4.   Mass Ops Atty Gen Aug. 20, 1963.

5.   Epperson v. State of Ark., 393 U.S. 97, 89 S. Ct. 266, 21 L. Ed. 2d 228 (1968).

done with the clear secular intent of enhancing the effectiveness of science instruction." Justice Scalia, in a dissent joined by Chief Justice Rehnquist, recommended abandoning the *Lemon* "purpose" test, remarking:

> We have held that intentional governmental advancement of religion is sometimes required by the Free Exercise Clause. . . . We have also held that in some circumstances government may act to accommodate religion, even if that action is not required by the First Amendment. . . . We have implied that voluntary governmental accommodation of religion is not only permissible but desirable.[6]

VII. Tax Exemptions

§ 24.32. Churches and religious organizations

The grant of tax exemptions by state and local governments to churches can be compatible with the Establishment Clause of the First Amendment and thus constitutional.[7]

When a federal district court held constitutional the policy of Dade County, Florida, in granting tax exemption to a church property rented for commercial parking on weekdays,[8] the United States Supreme Court vacated the judgment and remanded the case to the lower court, since the Florida Legislature had repealed the full tax exemption law in effect when the district court judgment was entered, and had enacted new legislation providing that church property was exempt from taxation only if the property was used predominantly for religious purposes.[9]

In 1989 the Supreme Court held violative of the Establishment Clause a state provision granting a tax exemption from sales taxes to publications advancing the tenets of a religious faith, while denying a like exemption for other publications. Justice Brennan, writing for the Court, indicated that the exemption would be valid if it extended to "all groups that contributed to the community's cultural, intellectual and moral betterment." Justices Blackmun and O'Connor in

---

6. Edwards v. Aguillard, 482 U.S. 578, 107 S. Ct. 2573, 96 L. Ed. 2d 510, 39 Ed. Law Rep. 958 (1987).

7. Walz v. Tax Commission of City of New York, 397 U.S. 664, 90 S. Ct. 1409, 25 L. Ed. 2d 697 (1970).

8. Diffenderfer v. Central Baptist Church of Miami, Fla., Inc., 316 F. Supp. 1116 (S.D. Fla. 1970), judgment vacated, 404 U.S. 412, 92 S. Ct. 574, 30 L. Ed. 2d 567 (1972).

9. Diffenderfer v. Central Baptist Church of Miami, Fla., Inc., 404 U.S. 412, 92 S. Ct. 574, 30 L. Ed. 2d 567 (1972).

a concurring opinion stated their belief that "the Free Exercise Clause suggests that a special exemption for [the sale of] religious books is required," while agreeing with the opinion for the Court that an exemption limited to the sale of religious literature by religious organizations violated the Establishment Clause. Justice Scalia's opinion, joined by Chief Justice Rehnquist and Justice Kennedy, suggests that a tax exemption for sales of religious literature comes close to being a constitutionally required accommodation, stating that when "it is constitutionally compelled in order to avoid interference with the dissemination of religious ideas," it is permissible, notwithstanding the Establishment Clause.[10]

The following year the Court held that the excessive entanglement prong of the test for violation of the Establishment Clause was not violated by the imposition of sales and use taxes upon a religious organization. The Court noted that (1) that the evidence of administrative entanglement was thin; (2) such administrative and recordkeeping burdens did not rise to a constitutionally significant level, and (3) there was no state inquiry into the religious content of the items sold or the religious motivation for selling or purchasing the items, because the materials were subject to the tax regardless of content or motive. There was no dissent.[11]

§ 24.33. Church-related schools

The great weight of authority sustains the constitutionality of tax exemptions to church-related educational institutions.[12]

§ 24.34. Church-controlled hospitals, nursing homes and other charitable institutions

States frequently exempt from property taxes hospitals,[13] nursing

---

10. Texas Monthly, Inc. v. Bullock, 489 U.S. 1, 109 S. Ct. 890, 103 L. Ed. 2d 1 (1989).

11. Jimmy Swaggart Ministries v. Board of Equalization of California, 493 U.S. 378, 110 S. Ct. 688, 107 L. Ed. 2d 796 (1990).

12. Garrett Biblical Institute v. Elmhurst State Bank, 331 Ill. 308, 163 N.E. 1 (1928). Additional case law, as well as the state constitutional clauses authorizing or requiring such exemptions, can be found in Antieau, Carroll and Burke, *Religion under the State Constitutions* (Central Law Book Co., Brooklyn, N.Y., 1965).

13. Baptist Hospital v. City of Nashville, 156 Tenn. 589, 3 S.W.2d 1059 (1928).

homes[14] and all charitable organizations, and this is accepted as not violative of the Establishment Clause.[15]

Comparably, properties of the Young Men's Christian Association[16] and the Salvation Army[17] are customarily held exempt from taxation under state statutes and constitutions.

VIII. Religion in Civil Courts

§ 24.35. Resolution of church controversies in the civil courts

The United States Supreme Court has held that state courts are not barred by the First and Fourteenth Amendments from adjudicating purely property controversies between different groups within a church, where the resolution of the dispute involves no inquiry into religious doctrine,[18] although the First Amendment does not permit federal or state courts to determine property controversies between two or more factions of a church on the ground that one or more deviated from the tenets of the faith. The Supreme Court states: "First Amendment values are plainly jeopardized when church property litigation is made to turn on the resolution by civil courts of controversies over a religious doctrine and practice. . . . The Amendment therefore commands civil courts to decide property disputes without resolving underlying controversies over religious doctrine."[19]

Under the First and Fourteenth Amendments, when a church establishes tribunals to adjudicate matters of internal discipline and government, civil courts cannot reverse the ecclesiastical tribunals.[20]

In 1979 the Supreme Court reaffirmed that courts can apply "neutral principles of law" and adjudicate property matters between groups within a church. Justice Blackmun, for the Court, summarized the applicable rules in this area as follows:

---

14. Evangelical Lutheran Good Samaritan Soc. v. Board of Review of Fayette County, 267 N.W.2d 413 (Iowa Ct. App. 1978).

15. Burd Orphan Asylum v. Upper Darby School Dist., 90 Pa. 21 (1879). Additional authority is available in Antieau, Carroll and Burke, *Religion under the State Constitutions* (Central Law Book Co., Brooklyn, N.Y., 1965).

16. Appeal of Young Men's Christian Ass'n of Pittsburgh, 383 Pa. 176, 117 A.2d 743 (1955).

17. Salvation Army v. Hoehn, 354 Mo. 107, 188 S.W.2d 826 (1945).

18. Maryland and Virginia Eldership of Churches of God v. Church of God at Sharpsburg, Inc., 396 U.S. 367, 90 S. Ct. 499, 24 L. Ed. 2d 582 (1970).

19. Presbyterian Church in U.S. v. Mary Elizabeth Blue Hull Memorial Presbyterian Church, 393 U.S. 440, 89 S. Ct. 601, 21 L. Ed. 2d 658 (1969).

20. Serbian Eastern Orthodox Diocese for U.S. of America and Canada v. Milivojevich, 426 U.S. 696, 96 S. Ct. 2372, 49 L. Ed. 2d 151 (1976).

The First Amendment prohibits civil courts from resolving church property disputes on the basis of religious doctrine and practice. As a corollary to this commandment, the Amendment requires that civil courts defer to the resolution of issues of religious doctrine or polity by the highest court of a hierarchical church organization. Subject to these limits, however, the First Amendment does not dictate that a State must follow a particular method of resolving church property disputes. Indeed, a State may adopt any one of various approaches for settling church property disputes so long as it involves no consideration of doctrinal matters, whether the ritual and liturgy of worship or the tenets of faith.

Four Justices in dissent indicated their understanding that civil courts must accept decisions reached within the polity chosen by the church members themselves.[21]

IX. Additional Rulings

§ 24.36. Additional judicial rulings construing the Establishment Clause

The Court of Appeals for the District of Columbia held that the Establishment Clause was violated by the regulations of the various service academies requiring Sunday attendance at church or chapel services by cadets. The Supreme Court denied certiorari.[22]

The Court of Appeals for the Ninth Circuit has ruled constitutional the use of the inscription "In God We Trust" on United States coins and currency, as well as the use of the national motto "In God We Trust."[23]

The second Justice John Harlan wrote in 1970 that if Congress chooses to grant exemptions from the military draft "it cannot draw the line between theistic and non-theistic religious beliefs on the one hand and secular beliefs on the other. Any such distinctions are not, in my view, compatible with the Establishment Clause of the First Amendment." The Supreme Court's opinion avoided this constitutional issue, limiting itself to statutory interpretation.[24]

---

21. Jones v. Wolf, 443 U.S. 595, 99 S. Ct. 3020, 61 L. Ed. 2d 775 (1979).
22. Anderson v. Laird, 466 F.2d 283 (D.C. Cir. 1972).
23. Aronow v. U.S., 432 F.2d 242 (9th Cir. 1970).
24. Welsh v. U.S., 398 U.S. 333, 90 S. Ct. 1792, 26 L. Ed. 2d 308 (1970).